Dear Valued Customer,

We realize you're a busy professional with deadlines to hit. Whether your goal is to learn a new technology or solve a critical problem, we want to be there to lend you a hand. Our primary objective is to provide you with the insight and knowledge you need to stay atop the highly competitive and ever-changing technology industry.

Wiley Publishing, Inc., offers books on a wide variety of technical categories, including security, data warehousing, software development tools, and networking — everything you need to reach your peak. Regardless of your level of expertise, the Wiley family of books has you covered.

- For Dummies – The *fun* and *easy* way to learn
- The Weekend Crash Course –The *fastest* way to learn a new tool or technology
- Visual – For those who prefer to learn a new topic *visually*
- The Bible – The *100% comprehensive* tutorial and reference
- The Wiley Professional list – *Practical* and *reliable* resources for IT professionals

The book you hold now, *Macromedia Studio MX Bible*, is the expert guide to Macromedia's most popular product ever. If you are a Web-development newbie, or even if you are an expert, this book has everything you need to master the power of Studio MX and to quickly and easily build rich Web applications and Web services. Written by the crème de la crème of the Macromedia development community, this book guides you through the development of a complete Web application using all of the tools included in Studio MX: Dreamweaver MX, Flash MX, Fireworks MX, ColdFusion MX, and FreeHand MX.

Our commitment to you does not end at the last page of this book. We'd want to open a dialog with you to see what other solutions we can provide. Please be sure to visit us at www.wiley.com/compbooks to review our complete title list and explore the other resources we offer. If you have a comment, suggestion, or any other inquiry, please locate the "contact us" link at www.wiley.com.

Finally, we encourage you to review the following page for a list of Wiley titles on related topics. Thank you for your support and we look forward to hearing from you and serving your needs again in the future.

Sincerely,

Richard K. Swadley
Vice President & Executive Group Publisher
Wiley Technology Publishing

15 HOUR WEEKEND CRASH COURSE

Visual

Bible

DUMMIES FOR

WILEY

Wiley Publishing, Inc.

**more information
on related titles**

Authoritative Books on Studio MX
Available from Wiley Publishing

0-7645-3656-7

Take your projects to the next level with tips from over 30 Flash experts

0-7645-4931-6

The authoritative reference to Dreamweaver MX

0-7645-3614-1

Master advanced scripting techniques

0-7645-3662-1

Create traffic-stopping Web graphics and animations

0-7645-4622-8

Comprehensive coverage of ColdFusion MX

WILEY

Wiley Publishing, Inc.

Available at your favorite bookseller or visit
www.wiley.com/compbooks

Macromedia® Studio MX Bible

Macromedia® Studio MX Bible

Joyce J. Evans

with Donna Casey, Ron Rockwell, and Charles Mohnike

Wiley Publishing, Inc.

Macromedia® Studio MX Bible

Published by
Wiley Publishing, Inc.
10475 Crosspoint Boulevard
Indianapolis, IN 46256
www.wiley.com

Copyright © 2003 by Wiley Publishing, Inc., Indianapolis, Indiana

Published by Wiley Publishing, Inc., Indianapolis, Indiana

Published simultaneously in Canada

Library of Congress Control Number: 200214836

ISBN: 0-7645-2523-9

Manufactured in the United States of America

10 9 8 7 6 5 4 3 2 1

1B/RS/QS/QT/IN

For general information on our other products and services or to obtain technical support, please contact our Customer Care Department within the U.S. at (800) 762-2974, outside the U.S. at (317) 572-3993 or fax (317) 572-4002.

Wiley also publishes its books in a variety of electronic formats. Some content that appears in print may not be available in electronic books.

About the Authors

Joyce J. Evans developed the scope and focus of this book as well as wrote the Fireworks and Flash sections. Joyce is a training veteran with over 10 years of experience in educational teaching, tutorial development, and Web design. She has received Editors Choice Awards for her book *Fireworks 4 F/X and Design* and has authored several computer books including *Dreamweaver MX Complete Course* and *Fireworks MX: Zero to Hero*. Joyce is a Team Macromedia Volunteer. Her work can also be found in the Macromedia Design/Developer center. She can be reached at Joyce@JoyceJEvans.com. Her Web site is www.JoyceJEvans.com.

Donna Casey wrote the Dreamweaver section of this book. Donna is a designer, developer, and instructor with over eight years of experience working on Web and CD-ROM based projects for corporations such as AirTouch Cellular, Macromedia, Palm Computing, Verizon Wireless, and Aeris.net. She is a painter/sculptor with a Fine Arts degree and brings real-world design and production expertise to teaching Web design and development. Her website (www.n8vision.com) was featured the *Fireworks 3 Bible*. She has been a featured designer on Macromedia's Web site as well as a speaker at Macromedia's EUCON (Paris) and WebBoston and CNETBuilder (New Orleans.). As an experienced instructor, she has also authored the Intermediate Dreamweaver 4 and Fireworks 4 Training CDs for Lynda.com and contributed to the books *Fireworks F/X and Design* book aand *Dreamweaver MX Magic*.

Ron Rockwell wrote the FreeHand section of this book. Ron has been employed as a graphic designer for a manufacturing company in Nevada for several years, but he is a compulsive worker and has many freelance accounts reaching from California to Massachusetts (and very little free time). He is a member of the National Association of Photoshop Professionals and the Graphic Artists Guild. In 1999, he won the People_s Choice Award for Infographics at Macromedia_s UCON _99 in San Francisco. In 2001, Ron wrote *FreeHand 10 f/x & Design,* and in 2002 he co-authored the *Digital Photography Bible* with Ken Milburn.

Charles Mohnike wrote the ColdFusion portion of this book. Ron has been involved with the Internet since the days of text links and gray backgrounds. He built his first Web application for Moon Travel Handbooks in 1994, a then-ambitious interactive map site that gained national attention, and launched his career as a developer of note. He rode the dot-com boom as a freelance consultant in Northern California, building sound, robust Web applications. Charles develops in Perl and ColdFusion, as well as several database platforms. With a background in print publishing, he currently runs a small development shop specializing in porting print publications to the Web. He writes on Internet technical and cultural topics for publications such as *Wired Webmonkey, Microsoft Bookshelf, Smart TV*, and *Videomaker*. He is the author of several instructional titles.

Guest Experts

Doug Sahlin
Japi Honoo
Kim Cavanaugh
Steven Grosvenor
David C. Nicholls
Charles E. Brown
Brad Halstead
Murray R. Summers
Samuel Neff

For a list of guest expert tutorials by title, refer to Tutorials at a Glance.

For a list of contact and background information of Authors, refer to Appendix B.

Credits

Executive Editor
Chris Webb

Project Editor
Neil Romanosky

Technical Editors
Mary Rich
Samuel Neff

Copy Editor
Sydney Jones

Development Editor
Marcia Ellet

Editorial Manager
Mary Beth Wakefield

Vice President & Executive Group Publisher
Richard Swadley

Vice President and Executive Publisher
Bob Ipsen

Executive Editorial Director
Mary Bednarek

Project Coordinators
Jennifer Bingham
Regina Snyder

Graphics and Production Specialists
Amanda Carter
Carrie Foster
Joyce Haughey
Kristin McMullan
Jeremey Unger

Quality Control Technicians
John Tyler Connoley
David Faust
John Greenough
Andy Hollandbeck
Carl Pierce

Senior Permissions Editor
Carmen Krikorian

Media Development Specialist
Angela Denny

Proofreading and Indexing
TECHBOOKS Production Services

To my loving family

Preface

I recall the days prior to Dreamweaver 1 when I hand-coded or used inferior tools that wrote horrible code. I rejoiced when I started using Dreamweaver. Prior to using Fireworks, I was using Photoshop. I approached Fireworks with a, "Why doesn't this work like Photoshop?" attitude. As Fireworks has matured into Fireworks MX, I now ask, "Why can't Photoshop do this?" Because Dreamweaver, Fireworks, and Flash were all developed specifically for the Web, they are powerful and innovative tools. FreeHand has been used primarily for print design but has been adding Web functions as of version 10. FreeHand MX has added even more Web features while maintaining its strong hold in the field of print design.

The Macromedia Studio MX bundle of Web development tools has matured into a powerful suite of tools that covers the gamut of what developers need to or want to develop. Flash MX is the best version yet, giving designer/developers almost unlimited possibilities including communication with ColdFusion and other Web-server technologies.

The Macromedia Studio MX bundle includes Flash MX, Dreamweaver MX, Fireworks MX, ColdFusion MX Developer Edition, and FreeHand 10 (or MX). Each of these topics can or does fill an entire bible of its own. (Flash MX has two bibles: one for Flash MX and one for Flash MX ActionScripting!) As you get a feel in this book for which application you want to explore or learn more about, pick up one of the bibles specific to the application in which you are interested.

The *Macromedia Studio MX Bible* author team offers you the benefit of a lot of inside information and first-hand experience. The authors' combined expertise encompasses being Macromedia beta testers, volunteers, and on the advisory board. You'll reap the benefits of this experience by having each author share experience from his or her respective areas of specialization. The team worked together on all portions of the book to develop the Habitat Alert Web site.

Who Is This Book For?

Macromedia Studio MX Bible is the most comprehensive reference for using all the Macromedia Web development applications together. This book will get the beginner or new user of any of the applications started and help him or her move quickly to intermediate and advanced topics. This book is also a reference for a more experienced user: you can pick it up and investigate a specific topic or application.

People who will benefit from this book are:

+ Beginners using any of the Macromedia design/development tools

+ Intermediate users who want to learn how to leverage the power of the entire suite of tools

+ Advanced users who may be advanced in one application but not in others

✦ All design/developers who may be experienced in one application but not in others

✦ Anyone who has a desire to tap into the power of the Macromedia Studio MX design/developer tools working together

How This Book Is Organized

Because each of the Macromedia Studio MX applications can fill an entire Bible of its own, this book was quite a challenge. We decided the best thing we could do was to focus on the core features of each application and concentrate on using the suite together to demonstrate the fantastic integration features of the suite.

Each of the applications has a section of the book devoted to it. But interwoven into each section are assets and functions of the other applications.

Because some of the authors wanted to give you more material than the book could allow, we have special Bonus Tutorial and Movies folders on the CD-ROM where you'll find additional tutorials and movies. Since there are two Bibles devoted to Flash alone, you can imagine how difficult it was to try and cover it in one section. We give you the basics and many of the new features in the book. There are several projects on the CD-ROM for you to practice the techniques discussed in print. The sections of the book are

Part I: Introduction to Macromedia Studio MX

In this section, you see a brief outline of each of the Macromedia Studio MX applications' strengths and abilities. Then you see a preview of the hottest new features of each application. In Chapter 3, you see how the *Macromedia Studio MX Bible* author team worked together to develop the Habitat Alert Web site.

Part II: Finessing Macromedia FreeHand

In the FreeHand section, you quickly learn how to use the powerful vector tools in FreeHand. You make logos, business cards, brochures, and even movies! Along the way, you see some of the cool special effects you can achieve. The section wraps up with a chapter on the new features of FreeHand MX.

Part III: Mastering the Power of Macromedia Fireworks MX

The Fireworks section teaches you how to prepare graphics for use on the Web. You learn how to make vector graphics as well as manipulate, edit, and enhance bitmaps. You learn ways to make navigation elements quickly and easily. You learn to optimize your images for smaller file sizes and slice and export them as a fully functioning Web page or for use in Dreamweaver. Because you have more control over a Dreamweaver layout, that method is used for the book's project sample.

Part IV: Unleashing the Power of Macromedia Flash MX

In the Flash section, you discover how its vector tools differ from those in FreeHand and Fireworks, plus how to use its interface and how to get around. You see how to work with the State, the Timeline, make buttons, Movie Clips, and use the new Flash components to add sound. Basic ActionScripting is discussed as well as using the Actions panel. Flash remoting is used in conjunction with ColdFusion, but the text for this is in the ColdFusion section, where it's easier to comprehend.

Part V: Developing in Macromedia Dreamweaver MX

The Dreamweaver section takes you from a blank page to a fantastic layout. You learn the ins and outs of using tables or adding CSS style sheets, adding forms, using the new pop-up menu behavior, and using third-party extensions. You even learn how to set up a database connection and provide dynamic content from a database. There are topics such as using scripts, snippets, DHTML, and all kinds of special tips and tricks.

Part VI: Creating Dynamic Content with Macromedia ColdFusion MX

The chapters in this section are designed to take you beyond the basics — to help you understand what goes on in a ColdFusion application, how it works with other Macromedia tools, and how you can use it to add functionality to the Web sites you build. Some of the examples are shown in the context of the Dreamweaver interface, but most are displayed as plain text to help you understand how ColdFusion's programming language works behind the scenes in your application.

Conventions Used in This Book

Several conventions used in this book help you understand the instructions:

+ **Menu and keyboard commands** — When you need to press a keyboard command, you'll see the PC command followed by the Mac command, such as Control (Command) +F3. Control is the control key on the PC and Command is the Command key on the Mac. Both use the F3 key.

+ **Application menu** — When you access one of the application menus, such as File, View, Window, and so on, you are told to choose File⇨Check Page⇨Check Links. The menu and the command are separated by an arrow. If there are submenus, you'll see another arrow and so on. Menus in panels are referred to by name. If there is a contextual menu, you will commonly see instructions to right/Control+click to access the menu.

+ **Bold text** is used for words that you need to type.

+ Code font is used for code and file names.

+ You can jump around anywhere in the book. Of course, if you are just learning, it will do you more good to start at the beginning of a section or, at the very least, the beginning of a chapter. Because this is a reference book as well as a training book, we have provided files for the book's project site for every chapter that uses the Habit Alert Web site files. We can't assume you are doing any of the exercises in any order. Because of this, when you save or export from Fireworks, read the save and/or export directions carefully. You'll need to have a Dreamweaver site defined (refer to Chapter 32) to have the roundtrip editing work its magic. In the Dreamweaver section, you'll be told when you need to define a new site for a specific chapter's exercise files. By setting it up this way, you can work in any chapter and have the resources needed to complete any of the project exercises.

Icons

The following icons are used to highlight important points throughout the book.

 Tips offer you extra information that further explains a given topic or technique, often suggesting alternatives or workarounds to a listed procedure.

 Notes provide supplementary information to the text, shedding light on background processes or miscellaneous options that are critical to the basic understanding of the material.

 When you see the Caution icon, take special note; it tells you something important to watch out for.

 If you want to find related information to a given topic in another chapter, look for the Cross-Reference icons.

 This icon indicates that the CD-ROM contains a related file and points you to the folder location.

 This icon indicates a new important feature to the specific application.

 The Heron icon is used to alert you that an exercise or project was used for the Habitat Alert site.

Dreamweaver, Fireworks, FreeHand, Flash, ColdFusion

 These icons are used to show you important integration features among the applications. When an asset or technique is used from one of the other applications you'll frequently see the specific icon of the application used.

Expert tutorials

A group of experts wrote tutorials that give additional insight into many areas of the Macromedia Studio MX suite of applications. As this book got larger and larger, it was necessary to move some of these tutorials onto the CD-ROM. These tutorials provide additional practice and insight into some of the functions of Fireworks and Flash.

The Habitat Alert Project

In addition to being a book for learning the specific applications and reference material, this Bible includes a unique feature: a Web site built throughout the book that uses all the applications within the Macromedia Studio MX bundle of software to demonstrate how they work together.

Since we develop a working site, which resides at `www.habitat-alert.org`, what you see online may vary from what is provided here. Web sites have a tendency to change frequently. Some of the functionality such as the shopping cart was not taught in this book, so it's not included in the source files. There is also a separate folder for the site-administration pages that will make a great model to use for an intranet. You have permission to use any of the files for your learning purposes only.

Companion Web Sites and CD-ROM

There are two supporting Web sites available to you. Wiley has a site at `www.wiley.com/compbooks/evans`, and the author has her site at `www.JoyceJEvans.com/MXbible/MXbible.htm`.

On the CD-ROM, you'll find all the files and images needed for the Habitat Alert site project. Each chapter that has files you'll need has a folder on the CD. You'll also find bonus tutorials and movies.

Acknowledgments

I'd like to first and foremost give gratitude to my God, who empowers my family and me and supports my efforts. A book of this magnitude took the dedication and talent of many people. I'd like to thank the members of the main author team of Donna Casey, Ron Rockwell, and Charles Mohnike for their great work and dedication to the project. I'd also like to thank the expert guests. You provided tutorials that added another level of expertise to various subjects.

I'd like to thank everyone at Wiley who supported us as we made changes and asked a lot of questions. Special thanks to Chris Webb, whose excitement for the book was encouraging. I'd also like to thank Neil Romanosky, our project editor; Mary Rich and Samuel Neff, the tech editors; and all the folks behind the scenes who were involved in the layout and made special icons for us.

Special thanks go to David Morris (Macromedia), who referred me to Jennefer Tchejeyan (Macromedia), who referred me to Carol Sheehan (Wiley), who referred me to Chris Webb, my acquisitions editor. What a great group of people! Heather Hollaender from Macromedia was a great help in getting me in contact with the people I needed to speak with.

Thanks go to my agent Margot Maley Hutchisen of Waterside Productions who put so much work into all the gory details and negotiations of a book.

Tutorials at a Glance

Chapter Tutorials

Bonus Tutorials (on the CD-ROM)

Contents at a Glance

Contents

PART I: Introduction to Macromedia Studio MX   1

PART II: Finessing Macromedia FreeHand   21

PART III: Mastering the Power of Macromedia Fireworks MX   213

Chapter 15: Getting Around in Fireworks 215

PART IV: Unleashing the Power of Macromedia Flash MX 413

Chapter 24: Navigating through Flash MX 415

PART V: Developing in Macromedia Dreamweaver MX   507

Introduction to Macromedia Studio MX

What Is Macromedia Studio MX?

Macromedia Studio MX is an integrated suite of development
tools for building professional Web sites and rich Internet
applications. The suite also supports emerging standards and Web
technologies. The applications included in the Macromedia Studio
MX suite are FreeHand 10 (or MX), Fireworks MX, Flash MX,
Dreamweaver MX, and ColdFusion MX Developer Edition. All the
applications have a common interface, cutting the learning curve
considerably.

FreeHand 10

FreeHand was developed as a vector drawing program and has grown
to be arguably the best program on the market for the production of
pure vector art. Over the last 15 years of continual change and
improvement, FreeHand has become an extremely versatile program
for anyone in the graphic arts community. FreeHand was the first
drawing program to be built from the ground up with Mac OS X compatibility. That created a few minor problems on the Mac side of the
aisle. Apple engineers were hard at work introducing an entirely new
operating system, and Macromedia engineers were working on
FreeHand 10 with daily changes from Apple. As a problem was fixed
at one company, the solution would break something in the other
company's software. Both companies had deadlines to meet, and
both products were delivered with problems.

The version of FreeHand that is installed as part of Studio MX is a
slightly modified version of the original FreeHand 10. The changes
that were made to the program are minimal: Tabs in panels have a
new way of operating due to a lawsuit with Adobe, and the program
plays better with OS X and Windows XP. Other than that, the version
won't get the full upgrade to an MX label until the engineering and
marketing departments can get a handle on what is necessary to satisfy customers and the operability of the program — both in terms of
the cost to accomplish it and its profitability. For now, FreeHand
10.0.1 is a great program, but it lacks some of the bells and whistles
of the MX user interface.

Nearly anyone will tell you that the grass is greener on the other side
of the fence, and the same is true of FreeHand's and Adobe Illustrator's
yards. Both programs contain similar tools and features, and both have

tools and features the other program lacks. A comparison of the programs' common functions is located at the end of this section of the book. If you are an experienced Illustrator user and need only a jump-start, that comparison may be a good place for you to start.

FreeHand MX

Some of you may have purchased Studio more recently or may have upgraded and have FreeHand MX instead of version 10. The first thing you'll notice when you start FreeHand MX is the location of panels, which used to be known as palettes, along the right side of the screen. They snap in and out of your workspace as you need them, and you can remove or float individual panels on the desktop. The Toolbox has also been modified. Tools of a feather are nested together, and you have to click and hold the cursor down on one tool to bring up the available group of tools. Most of the Xtras are grouped in the Toolbox as well. You'll also see a few new tools: Output Area, Extrude, Action, and Connector, to name a few. Beyond the abilities these new tools give you, the main thrust of the upgrade is the way you can apply multiple strokes, fills, and effects to a single object. Draw an object once, and add squiggly lines, drop shadows, Gaussian blurs, and glows. Then do it again. Each attribute is added to an object "tree" that you can edit by moving branches up and down in the tree, or removing them altogether.

Gradient fills got a big boost, too. You can apply one of three new modifiers to any gradient fill. The modifiers reflect, duplicate, or fit the object precisely. The gradient is editable directly within the document with a new set of control handles. Rounded corners are definitely easier to create with the tricks you can perform on rectangles using the Subselect tool, and ellipses can have precise sections of their arcs removed. Polygons are now extremely editable. You can make changes in stars or straight-sided polygons live on the object, or through options in the Object panel.

You can import a SWF (Flash) file and make it part of your FreeHand page and then export the page with the SWF embedded in it. During all that, you can click a button to open Flash, where you can modify the SWF file. It's automatically updated in the FreeHand document.

Fireworks MX

Fireworks MX is an integral part of the Macromedia Studio MX Web development workflow. Fireworks, while playing nicely with the other programs in the Studio, helps you design, optimize, slice, and export all the images you'll need for any project. In Fireworks, you can design spectacular text effects as editable vectors, or you utilize its powerful bitmap functions; this new version has powerful new bitmap tools, such as Dodge, Burn, Smudge, Sharpen, and Blur. Design your text on the screen complete with kerning, leading, paragraph leads, and more. If you used Fireworks before, you'll really appreciate the improvements made to the pop-up menu editor.

Cross-Reference   For a full list of new features, see Chapter 2.

It's now much easier to move between vector and bitmap modes. When you select a vector or bitmap tool, Fireworks is smart enough to know which mode you need to be in and automatically makes the switch.

Working with bitmaps and vectors together is a huge advantage in Macromedia Fireworks. You can create vector shapes filled with bitmap images, or you can place vectors over a bitmap and integrate them.

Flash MX

Flash is one of the fastest growing technologies on the Web today. Flash is used to make Web movies but now with this latest version it is also able to communicate back and forth with a database. To play a Flash movie, the user needs to have the Flash plug-in, but that's no problem these days because it ships with most browsers and operating systems. You can find Flash graphics and movies all over the Web. Customers today are demanding more engaging interfaces with great graphics and sound. Using Flash, you can provide a rich user experience with small file sizes.

One of the great advantages of using Flash is that fact that you can provide engaging content with a minimal wait time. You can reduce file sizes by using reusable content, such as symbols. Most multimedia formats can be integrated into Flash. You can use vector formats, such as EPS, and files from FreeHand and Illustrator. You can even use bitmaps, such as GIF, TIF, JPEG, and PNG. PNG files even maintain their alpha transparency in Flash. You can use sound formats, such as WAV, AIF, and MP3, and AVI and MOV movie formats.

An exciting addition to the Flash capabilities enables you to communicate with a database to display text and movies images. You can send information from a database to the movie and vice versa. You can also save Flash MX files as Flash 4 or 5 files to make it backward compatible.

Dreamweaver MX

Dreamweaver MX is a feature-rich, professional Web design and development program. Its tightly integrated environment enables you to design, build, and manage Web sites and Internet applications with easy-to-use visual design tools and a customizable coding environment that supports current and next-generation technologies for static Web sites or server-based Web applications. Dreamweaver's features and tools are supported by panels that you can group and dock. Design and Code view options enable you to work in a comfortable environment. A single-click option enables you to change views at any time. Contextual menus and panel options provide convenient access to tools and are often supported with custom keyboard shortcuts. Program preferences enable you to select specific settings for your workflow, from opening new documents, to previewing work in progress. Dreamweaver is also extensible, which means you can add new objects, behaviors, and commands to include new tools, features, and functions in your application.

ColdFusion MX

When Macromedia merged with the Allaire Corporation in 2001, it added this extremely powerful tool to its arsenal of design applications. ColdFusion gives Flash developers and Dreamweaver designers the ability to create technically sophisticated Web and Intranet applications, and the inclusion of ColdFusion MX makes it easier and more intuitive for nonprogrammers to do so.

The relationship between ColdFusion MX and other Macromedia Studio products is now so closely integrated that it's possible you have already been using ColdFusion features in your

Flash movies or Dreamweaver sites without realizing it. Dreamweaver, in particular, makes it easy to create basic ColdFusion applications without knowing much about ColdFusion Markup Language (CFML) or how ColdFusion Server works.

The ColdFusion chapters in this section are designed to take you beyond the basics to help you understand what goes on in a ColdFusion application. You learn how it works with other Macromedia tools, and how you can use it to add functionality to the Web sites you build. Some of the examples will be shown in the context of the Dreamweaver interface, but most will be displayed as plain text and code to help you understand how ColdFusion's programming language works behind the scenes in your application. Based on the restrictions of this books size we won't go into a lot of detail on using Dreamweaver intuitive tools (refer to the help menu for that) but we will be taking a programming approach to work with fairly advanced concepts like complex variables and functions by the end of the section. It will build to the point that you work with some Flash Remoting in the last chapter. If you came to ColdFusion from a design background, don't worry. Although ColdFusion is a different tool than Dreamweaver, Flash, or Fireworks, it was designed with simplicity and ease of use in mind.

Summary

In this chapter you saw an overview of each of the applications in the Macromedia Studio MX bundle. The new interface helps cut the learning curve of each application, once you learn the basics of one you'll pick up the nuances of the others very quickly. You'll soon discover how powerful it is to have all the Web development tools you need at your fingertips.

✦   ✦   ✦

What's New in Macromedia Studio MX

✦ ✦ ✦ ✦

In This Chapter

Learning new features
of the Studio MX
products

✦ ✦ ✦ ✦

A new streamlined, easy-to-use interface is common to each of
the applications in Studio MX. A Property inspector is now in
Fireworks and Flash as well as in FreeHand MX (released after Studio
MX shipped). Windows users will see an integrated workspace, but
for Macs the panels will still float on the side of the Document window. Dreamweaver users can choose to use the new MX workspace
or they can continue to use a Dreamweaver 4 workspace.

What's New in FreeHand 10

FreeHand 10 includes many changes to increase your productivity.
The major changes are listed here. Refer to Chapter 14 for an in-depth
look at the FreeHand MX changes.

Brush strokes

You can now convert any stroke into a custom brush stroke. What's a
brush stroke? Basically, it's a graphic that follows a path. You can distort it to stretch the entire length of the stroke, or iterate it along the
path, according to your needs. The graphic element you use to make
the brush can be made from strokes and fills, text, geometric
shapes — anything you can make in FreeHand.

Contour gradient fill

There's now a new way to make a gradient fill in FreeHand. Whereas a
linear fill changes color in a straight line, and a radial fill has its color
change in a bull's-eye shape, the new contour fill follows the outer
shape of the object it fills. Think of a bull's-eye series of rings applied
to an irregular shape, with each ring changing slightly in color. The
center point of the contour fill can be moved by use of a control
knob, and the taper can be set to increase or decrease the abrupt-
ness of the color shift.

Navigation panel

Prior to the introduction of the Studio MX, Macromedia added the Navigation panel to FreeHand 10. This added integration with other Studio MX programs is even more evident now. The Navigation panel not only allows you to link a URL to graphics on a page, but it provides the framework for some basic actions so you can make a basic page—or site—to test your design. The resulting FreeHand artwork can be used in Dreamweaver or Flash for further work.

Library panel

Prior to FreeHand 10, there was no library, but a Symbols panel acted as a repository for symbols. Macromedia has augmented this panel, and the new Library holds master pages, symbols, and custom brushes. You can export any of the Library's contents so they may be imported into another FreeHand document, and it's all handled through the library and its Options menu. The use of symbols in the library allows recurring files such as logos or key elements to be shared among other members of a team, or as a quick and easy filing system.

Master pages

Master pages will be a boon to anyone working on multipage documents, or repetitive production projects. If you've been working with Adobe Illustrator, this concept may seem strange in a drawing program, since Illustrator only allows single-page documents. The master page can be as simple as a blank page with guidelines, or as complicated as a navigation panel for a Web site. Key elements and layouts can be developed one time and used again and again without the need to build anything from scratch—and the master pages can be shared among computers and across operating system platforms.

Pen Tool features

The Pen tool underwent several modifications between FreeHand 9 and 10. There's a QuickTime movie on the CD-ROM (PenToolTheMovie.mov) that shows how the Pen tool's Smart Cursors work and what to expect from the tool. If you enable Smart Cursors in FreeHand's Preferences, small icons will appear near the tool tip of the Pen and Bezigon tools that tell you what the next click of the mouse will do—add a point, delete a point, close a path, and so on. The tool's attributes are explained fully in Chapter 6.

Enhanced tools panel

The Tools panel now includes a Subselect tool that you use to select objects within a group, modify paths between points, and other specialized effects explained in Chapter 6. The Hand, or Grabber, tool was also added so you can move the pasteboard around the monitor without scrolling. New graphic icons for Freeform, Zoom, and Line match the same icons in Fireworks, but the tools work exactly as they did in prior versions.

Color boxes

In prior versions of FreeHand, you went to the Swatches panel to choose colors that have been added to your document. Now there is a second location at the bottom of the Tools panel. The top color box indicates stroke colors; the bottom color box controls fill colors. At first I felt that this box was pure eye candy, but I've grown to rely on it, and use it more than I use the Swatches panel after I get a drawing or layout underway.

Editing symbols

Symbols can be made from any object in a FreeHand document. The symbol is saved in the Library and can be placed in any document while retaining every attribute of the original. You will read more on symbols in Chapter 8, but in short, FreeHand 10 makes symbol editing easy and efficient. Just click and drag the symbol's icon from the Library preview window onto the desktop, and use the symbol as if you had just made it. Changes made to a symbol will be reflected throughout all the instances of that symbol in the document, which is a real time-saver in complicated layouts.

File Info dialog box

While this feature may not be of use to many users, it's a nice one to have if you're involved in the newspaper industry. This feature is described as the industry-standard file information for cataloging files destined for news media. Just go to Xtras ⇨ Other ⇨ File Info, and fill out the form. The information contains name, copyright information, captions, titles, dates, and more that are used by the International Press Telecommunications Council Protocol (IPTC) to keep track of information about graphics and photos used in the publishing industry.

Flash integration

The vector artwork done in FreeHand can be utilized directly in Flash. You can draw and test simple animations in FreeHand, but Flash is a much more powerful animation tool. Doing all the groundwork in FreeHand can save you a lot of time and provide superior results, due to the larger drawing and graphic toolset. After building an animation, it's a simple matter to export the file in SWF (ShockWave Flash) format that can be utilized in Flash. A Flash Anti-alias preview is one of the optional ways to view your artwork in FreeHand and gives you a hint of what your work will look like in Flash.

Print Area feature

Select a single print area from the entire pasteboard with the new Print Area feature. Use the Page tool to align multiple pages together in reader's spreads, and then print them on the same sheet of paper.

Unsaved Document indicator

When you've made a change to a document, or printed it, the Save icon in the Main toolbar is grayed out. In version 10 of FreeHand, there's now also an asterisk (*) after the file's name in the document's title bar. When you save the document, the asterisk goes away.

Working conditions in OS X and Windows XP

FreeHand 10 works a little faster under OS X than OS 9x, and it's more fun to work with the program on OS X, but basically you won't notice anything different about the program. And that's the way it should be.

What's New in FreeHand MX

FreeHand MX became available after Macromedia Studio MX shipped. For this reason the majority of users getting this book will be using FreeHand 10, but for those who want to upgrade Chapter 14 covers the 47 new FreeHand MX features. Pen tool improvements, new panel arrangements, vector effects, raster effects, and round-trip editing between FreeHand and Fireworks and Flash are just the tip of the FreeHand MX iceberg.

What's New in Fireworks MX

The interface change is a welcome addition to Fireworks but there are other features listed here that have made Fireworks even better and easier to use than ever.

Modeless vector and bitmap editing

Fireworks is capable of producing vector images (mathematical formula that calculates the curve of a path between two anchor points) and bitmap images (pixel based). In previous versions of Fireworks you'd frequently have to change from vector to bitmap mode. With Fireworks MX, you no longer have to be conscious of which mode you are working in. When you select a vector tool the mode changes and vice versa for bitmap.

Pop-up menu enhancements

Pop-up menus were first introduced to Fireworks 4. As great as they are, they also had problems, one of the biggest being the absolute positioning of the menus. In other words, when you designed the menu, it would stay in the position it was designed, regardless of the position of the button. If you put the navigation into a Dreamweaver fluid layout, the menus did not change position with the buttons. This has been resolved in Fireworks MX. There are other enhancements such as the ability to change border colors and bevels right from the Pop-Up menu editor, without having to edit the JavaScript.

Property inspector

The Property inspector is a welcome addition to Fireworks MX. If you've used Dreamweaver then this tool isn't new to you. It is open by default at the bottom of your document window. The Property inspector is context sensitive depending on the tool or object selected. It has replaced panels such as the Effects panel, Stroke panel, and Objects panel. You can now edit strokes, fills, and effects all from within the easy-to-use Property inspector.

Quick Export button

A new icon has been added to the top-right corner of the document window, which has shortcuts to export to different applications and file types. You can export for use in Dreamweaver (HTML) and you can even export as Update HTML for Dreamweaver. This way if you change a file that you've inserted into Dreamweaver it will update (if you've exported to the root folder). You can also export to Flash as SWF, or to FreeHand and Director.

Data-Driven Graphics Wizard

Now that Fireworks is extensible, a new command called the Data-Driven Graphics Wizard has been added. You can connect graphics files with XML files to automatically generate graphics.

Extensible

In Fireworks MX you can make custom commands as you could in previous versions, but now you can develop them using an SWF interface. There is also a growing list of commands/extensions available from the Macromedia Exchange. The Align menu, the Data-Driven Graphics Wizard, the Add Arrowheads, Twist and Fade, and Fade Image commands were all made using the extensibility features. You can find more at www.macromedia.com/support/fireworks/extensibility.html.

Photoshop compatibility

In Fireworks MX you can open and edit Photoshop native PSD file and maintain layers, masks, and text properties. Many of the effects such as drop shadows and bevels are maintained as long as they are supported in Fireworks. You can also export to PSD from Fireworks.

Button symbols with text

You can now add text to a button symbol and change the text in the Property inspector without producing an entirely new symbol. This is a fantastic time-saver. In previous versions, each text change would produce a new symbol (unless you did a workaround method).

What's New in Flash MX

There have been a multitude of improvements made to Flash MX. We'll look at some of the changes made to the Flash workflow.

Timeline

The Timeline can be collapsed without removing it from the Stage. A new option, Insert Layer Folder icon, has been added, and you'll see that there are icons for Insert Layer and Insert Motion Guide as well. A new preference (Edit ➪ Preferences) has been added where you can change the default frame selection to span-based selection for the Timeline, which selects an entire frame sequence.

Toolbox

The Toolbox is divided into several categories with the drawing tools on top. There are two new tools called the Fill Transform tool and the Free Transform tool. The Free Transform tool includes an envelope option to warp a non-grouped shape. Some of the tools, when selected, have additional modifiers you can see in the Options area of the Toolbox and/or in the Property inspector. The Toolbox works in tandem with the Property inspector.

Property inspector

The Property inspector is new to Flash MX and is very similar in function to the one found in Dreamweaver. As a tool or object on the Stage is selected, the Property inspector changes to reflect that items properties. The Property inspector has replaced nine panels, which are Stroke, Fill, Character, Paragraph, Text Options, Instance, Effect, Frame, and Sound.

Actions panel

There are two modes to work with actions in Flash, Normal and Expert. In Flash MX there have been changes made to both modes. In Expert mode some of the notable changes include a keyboard shortcut of F2 to launch the Output dialog box, the ability to navigate to other scripts (symbols and frames containing ActionScript), insert a target path (Relative or Absolute), check syntax, autoformat, which applies formatting rules to your ActionScript. The Actions panel also offers a built-in context-sensitive ActionScript dictionary and gives you access to debug options (with breakpoints) and lets you view line numbers.

Components

The Smart Clips of Flash 5 have evolved into even smarter components in Flash MX. Components are complex reusable movie clips. These components can be dragged directly into your movie. You can also change the appearance of the components. Some of the UI components that ship with Flash MX are CheckBox, ComboBox, ScrollBar, and more. There are more available at the Flash Exchange.

Distribute to layers

You can now distribute multiple objects into a different layer if you'd like by choosing Modify ⇨ Distribute to layers. This comes in handy if you break text apart that you want to animate.

Other features include:

✦ Bookmarking and Back. By using named anchors a user can now use the browser Back button and bookmark a Flash page.

✦ Accessible. There is now a new panel accessed by choosing Window ⇨ Accessibility, which allows you to make your movie accessible.

✦ New modifiers for the Transform tool such as distort and envelope.

✦ Unicode and UTF8 and vertical text.

✦ True embedded video codec in the Flash player.

✦ Standard size templates for things such as banners, ads, and mobile devices.

What's New in Dreamweaver MX

Macromedia Dreamweaver MX incorporates many new features and functionality that help users of all levels build static and dynamic sites that meet today's tough standards for accessibility, functionality, and fast-paced content management. Through its functional new workspace with integrated, all-in-one layout to new and reinvented panel groups, Dreamweaver MX brings a wide range of new features for site accessibility, efficient workflow, CSS development, and, most importantly, the tools and functions you'll need to build data-driven sites without ever hand-writing complex server-side logic.

Document Gallery

New and experienced users will appreciate the new Document Gallery — a gallery of prebuilt pages of all sorts, such as ASP, ASP.NET, JSP, and more. There are even style sheet and framed site templates to start with.

Site-Definition Wizard

The Site-Definition Wizard provides an easier method of defining a site for new users that features user-friendly questions that elicit the right info every time.

Code hints

For die-hard coders, Dreamweaver practically reads your mind, offering a complete menu of appropriate tag attributes as you type in Code view.

Snippets panel

You can now write your own code and store it for later reuse. Dreamweaver even ships with some snippets for you to use such as a meta snippet called, "Do Not Cache," accessibility code, header, navigation, and many more categories of code snippets are provided.

File Explorer

Integrated into the Site panel, the File Explorer enables you to browse for assets and files on the desktop and network volumes without having to leave Dreamweaver.

Answers panel

The Answers panel is a quick way to get current support answers. It connects directly with online resources from the Macromedia Support Center. You can retrieve new content at will from updates to the latest tips and tricks.

Server code libraries

You can now easily use all the leading server-side technologies, including ColdFusion, ASP, ASP.NET, JSP, and PHP, with most backend data sources. Dreamweaver supports coders who use Homesite as well as the visual designer, writing much of the code for you.

Insert bar

The Object panel from previous versions is now called the Insert bar and is by default docked above the Document window. The categories such as Tables, Templates, Forms, Layout, Text, and many more are all accessed by tabs. There are new objects in some of the categories as well. For instance, the Template category now has Optional or Repeating regions.

Enhanced CSS support

You can add new style sheets, embed style sheets and edit styles all in the CSS Styles panel. You can see all the CSS elements in your document, including redefined tags and CSS selectors. Classes can be applied via a drop-down menu or by right- (Control) clicking on a specific tag. Setting up CSS Style Sheets couldn't be easier.

Accessibility

Accessibility options are a great addition to Dreamweaver MX. You can choose which options to turn on. For instance, you can set up the preferences to open a dialog box for alternative text every time you insert an image (or tables or forms).

Added template functionality

You can now define one template based on another using template inheritance. You can also nest templates inside each other. New features, such as repeating regions, optional regions, and editable tag attributes, allow the user to edit the parameters of the tag while the tag itself is locked. The user can then do things such as change an image without affecting the locked tag.

Cloaking

A new feature of the Site panel is the ability to cloak file types or even folders when using put, get, or synchronization features. By cloaking certain files, they will not be uploaded or included in any synchronization actions you take. For instance, you may have Fireworks source files or templates within your root that you don't want to automatically upload to the server. You can cloak these files to prevent it.

Flash MX integration

You can launch and edit Flash files from within Dreamweaver, and edit the file in Flash. When you save and close it, a new SWF is generated and you are returned to Dreamweaver.

Fireworks MX integration

Along with the roundtrip editing of Fireworks MX from within Dreamweaver MX you can now add an image placeholder. This placeholder can be edited by clicking a Create button, which opens Fireworks with a document the size of the placeholder. There is also improved support for editing Fireworks HTML and updating it in Dreamweaver. You can also now edit Fireworks Pop-up menus in Dreamweaver.

Pop-up menus

Pop-up menus are new to Dreamweaver MX. The pop-up menus first appeared in Fireworks 4. The ones in Dreamweaver MX are similar to Fireworks MX except you don't have the option of using images for buttons, just HTML text.

Tag Chooser, editor, and library

The Tag Chooser opens the tag editor, enabling you to set general properties, browser attributes, and style sheet information for that tag. The tag library editor enables you to set the code formatting and syntax coloring for every tag.

XHTML code writing and validation

You can convert any HTML page into XHTML. The DocType will be added and nonpaired tags will be closed properly.

Dynamic data

All the database functions of UltraDev are now included in Dreamweaver. There is also improved support of ColdFusion and JSP as well as ASP.NET and PHP support. The Insert bar includes application objects categories and context-specific categories for JSP, ColdFusion, and more.

What's New in ColdFusion MX

Macromedia Studio MX marks the first time ColdFusion has been bundled with Dreamweaver, Fireworks, and Flash and as you might expect from this union, compatibility and interactivity between the applications has markedly improved. Dreamweaver in particular has gained some new features allowing ColdFusion MX developers to create and troubleshoot their code. Dreamweaver also serves as the replacement for ColdFusion Studio, the development interface many ColdFusion developers used with previous versions of the software.

The ColdFusion MX server product has also undergone a complete revamp. While previous versions of ColdFusion were written in C, ColdFusion MX is written in Java, which brings the program into the J2EE fold and allows Macromedia to offer a version of the program that is directly compatible with J2EE application servers such as IBM's WebSphere and BEA's WebLogic.

Other additions and modifications found in the MX version of ColdFusion are as follows.

Java integration

ColdFusion Server now comes in two varieties: the standard ColdFusion MX Server and ColdFusion MX Server for J2EE Application Servers. The latter enables Java developers to integrate the Java platform seamlessly with ColdFusion's ease of use. Both server versions also allow Java Server Pages (JSPs) to be used.

Macromedia Flash remoting

ColdFusion MX and Flash MX can now seamlessly exchange data, enabling ColdFusion developers to take advantage of Flash's advanced interface capabilities, and Flash developers to use ColdFusion's powerful programming tools.

ColdFusion components

ColdFusion components, or CFCs, expand on ColdFusion custom tags by enabling developers to create powerful, reusable components that may be called from ColdFusion templates, Macromedia Flash, clients, or as Web services.

XML support

ColdFusion MX enables developers to read, parse, and write XML documents using standard ColdFusion tags. When XML documents are read into ColdFusion MX, they become native ColdFusion objects, which can be treated like any other standard ColdFusion variable.

Improved integration with Dreamweaver MX

ColdFusion developers who use Dreamweaver MX as an interface will find a host of new features including a redesigned code editor and improved debugging tools.

Character-based language support

ColdFusion MX now enables you to build applications that support character-based languages, such as Chinese, Japanese, and Korean.

Graphing and Charting

ColdFusion MX has vastly improved the performance and features of its graphing and charting functions, allowing developers to quickly and easily create several types of charts, build configurable "drill down" data presentations, and integrate graphing and charting functions with Flash MX.

Summary

In this chapter you saw a condensed list of some of the major new features and enhancements to the Macromedia Studio MX applications.

✦   ✦   ✦

Developing the Habitat Alert Web Site

The author team of *Macromedia Studio MX Bible* decided to take an approach a bit different from other books. They decided to do a real site for a nonprofit organization. They wanted to teach how to work in a real work environment by having you work in one. The authors encountered obstacles and problems that you won't get to experience, such as saving in multiple folders instead of just one root folder because of the non-linear fashion of the book. But then they did encounter things that all designers/developers will encounter — client changes. For example, the name of the domain was changed two times. This wasn't a problem because the authors had a good working relationship with the hosting server, but it did make the writing process a challenge.

This book shows you how easy it is to maintain a site using Dreamweaver and how easy even a name change can be when you've set up your site with site management in mind from the beginning. A well-planned site saves you from numerous headaches and problems down the line.

The Planning

The first step was to get with the client (phone and e-mail) and determine what his vision for the site was and what kind of services he wanted to provide. One of the first things that needed to be defined was the purpose of the site and what the client wanted to accomplish. The main purpose is to educate the public about the preservation of migratory species, sensitive breeding habitats, and endangered ecosystems. Habitat Alert provides a way to educate the public including children. It also accepts donations and sells a few items to raise money.

The author team then began to collaborate. After the authors had a feel for what was needed, they kicked around ideas about how to give the client what he needed and made other suggestions. In the end, the main site features included the following components:

✦ A mission statement.

✦ An information area to inform users about the current and past fight to save the herons.

✦ A children's section to inform, entertain, and teach children how to participate in the endeavor. Some of the features included a quiz to test their knowledge, puzzles of the herons, and information about how to petition and participate in the cause.

✦ An online petition that can be signed.

✦ E-cards that visitors can send to friends as an awareness feature.

✦ Shopping carts to sell small items to raise funds.

✦ A section for accepting donations.

You will develop many of these sections throughout this book. There are some areas such as a shopping cart that go beyond the focus of this book. But check the links page on the CD for recommendations.

Site Mockup

Mockups can be done in FreeHand or in Fireworks. FreeHand is great for multiple-page mock-ups and is a great tool for animation storyboards. Because Ron Rockwell (author of the FreeHand chapters) had enough to do with the graphic development, the mockup was done in Fireworks. Plus the majority of the graphics were bitmaps and best suited to be worked on in Fireworks. The client was then presented with two different color schemes. Donna Casey (author of the Dreamweaver chapters) met with the client in person and already knew the design style the client liked (she had samples from her portfolio) so it was simply a matter of color choices.

A list of categories was developed based on the client's needs and a flowchart was drawn out. Since the mockup was already basically done in Fireworks and already laid out in Dreamweaver the authors created a flowchart using the Site panel. Flowcharts can be made in Dreamweaver, FreeHand, and Fireworks.

Division of Labor

The next step was to decide who would do what. One of the first priorities was getting the graphics done. First the illustrations in FreeHand needed to be done, because most of the site relies on these. The authors decided that the logo and vectors for the e-cards would be done in FreeHand, not only because FreeHand has the most robust vector capabilities but because Ron Rockwell is a fantastic illustrator. He also did the layout for the business cards, brochures, and a few cartoon-type movies.

Joyce Evans was responsible for making the e-cards, adding sound, and preparing the Flash assets for the site. For the most part, she used the vectors that Ron had drawn instead of making new drawings in Flash, not because Flash is inferior but because she's not an artist. Doug Sahlin then incorporated the e-cards into a Flash interface, which connects to ColdFusion (Charles Mohnike wrote the ColdFusion section). Charles Mohnike did the ColdFusion coding of the e-cards and Doug did the Flash remoting.

Joyce was responsible for preparing all additional graphics in Fireworks (supplied by the client and Donna), optimizing, slicing, and exporting. The files also had to be exported into the proper folders for use in Dreamweaver to facilitate round-trip editing. Because of the book the authors did, at times, do things several different ways. For instance, the rollovers were created in Dreamweaver, but the authors show you how to do them in Fireworks as well as how to insert that code directly in a Dreamweaver layout.

Donna did the layout in Dreamweaver. She had direct contact with the client and she did the actual mockups of the site. Charles recommended using only one server technology, which of course was ColdFusion. But the authors also wanted to show you how you could connect to a database by using ASP. So as an alternative Donna shows you how to build an administrator section using ASP and an Access database to manage a contacts list. A newsletter was also developed and would be deployed using ColdFusion.

Charles was responsible for connecting all the dynamic data using ColdFusion. The newsletter, e-cards, petition, and shopping cart are all powered by ColdFusion. Only the e-cards are covered in this book.

Testing and Deploying

The site was tested in Dreamweaver, checking for broken links and running various site reports and validations. After this was done, it was tested on the local server. After everything checked out locally the authors were ready to upload to their hosting server. They found Nexpoint (`www.nexpoint.com`) to be very reasonably priced for their client, and it supported ColdFusion MX. Actually they were still using ColdFusion 5 on their main servers but agreed to host Habitat Alert on a private server, which is running ColdFusion MX. Don't be afraid to ask your potential host for what you need.

Our Workflow Overview

Listed here is a brief overview of how the team's workflow was organized.

✦ Vector illustrations for the Web site and print media were prepared in FreeHand.

✦ All Web site images were prepared in Fireworks, laid out, sliced, optimized, and exported to a folder in the sites root folder.

✦ The Flash assets were developed, such as the e-cards, banners, and puzzles.

✦ Everything was then brought into Dreamweaver and laid out.

✦ The dynamic portion of the site was then connected to ColdFusion.

✦ The completed site was tested on the local server.

✦ The site was then uploaded to the live hosting server and tested again.

Summary

In this chapter you saw a bit of how a team worked together to build a Web site. We took you through the planning process, the purpose of the site, the division of responsibilities, and a list of the workflow processes that were done.

✦   ✦   ✦

Finessing Macromedia FreeHand

Getting to Know FreeHand

FreeHand is a very powerful drawing program. If you can learn its basics, you can do just about anything in the graphic arts field. In this chapter you'll get a feel for its power and capabilities, from simple drawing through Web page design and animations.

What to Expect from FreeHand

FreeHand was the first drawing program to be built from the ground-up with Mac OS X compatibility. That created a few minor problems on the Mac side of the aisle. Apple engineers were hard at work with the introduction of an entirely new operating system, and Macromedia engineers were working on FreeHand 10 with daily changes from Apple. As a problem was fixed at one company, the solution would break something in the other company's software. Both companies had deadlines to meet, and both products were delivered with problems of one kind or another.

Why don't I have FreeHand MX?

The version of FreeHand that is installed as part of the MX Studio is a slightly modified version of the original FreeHand 10. The only changes that have been made to the program are minimal: Tabs in panels have a new way of operating, due to a lawsuit with Adobe, and the program plays better with OS X and Windows XP. Other than that, the version doesn't get the full upgrade to an MX label until the engineering and marketing departments can get a handle on what is necessary to satisfy customers and the operability of the program — both in terms of the cost to accomplish it and its profitability. For now, FreeHand 10.0.1 is a great program, but it lacks some of the bells and whistles of the MX user interface — I can work with that, easily.

FreeHand was developed as a vector drawing program and has grown to be arguably the best program on the market for the production of pure vector art. Over the last 15 years or so of continual change and improvement, FreeHand has become an extremely versatile program for anyone in the graphic arts community. Nearly anyone will tell you that the grass is always greener on the other side of the fence, and the same is true of FreeHand's and Adobe Illustrator's yards. Both programs contain similar tools and features, and both have tools and features the other program lacks. If you are an experienced Illustrator user and just need a jump-start to functionality, that chapter may be a good place for you to start.

Comparisons aside, this book is about Macromedia products, and this chapter is devoted to FreeHand, so let's dig in!

Page layout

FreeHand stands alone among drawing programs in the regard that it supports multiple-page documents. The FreeHand desktop is 22-feet square, and you can fill that desktop with as many pages of different sizes as you want. The only restriction is the amount of disk space and RAM you have on your machine. Master pages enable you to have common design elements on specific pages to make your layout less time-consuming. Certainly, programs such as Adobe InDesign, PageMaker, and QuarkXPress are more suited to long-document production, but I've personally done many multipage documents solely in FreeHand.

The advantage to working on multipage documents in FreeHand lies in the amount of artwork that's necessary for the project. If you have a lot of drawings, spot illustrations, logos, or icons in the publication, FreeHand is a natural program to choose for the entire undertaking. Because the entire project is in a vector-based program, there's no need to import EPS files. All the drawings can be live vector illustrations. That means a smaller file size.

Single projects, such as catalogs or instruction manuals, are easy to create in FreeHand, but you can also place all of a company's stationery in a single document. The letterhead, envelopes, second sheets, and business cards can all be in the same document. You can have the logo on one page, and use special Lens effects to place live copies of the logo on the other elements. Then you can make a change to the logo and the changes ripple throughout the whole set of documents.

Of course, you can also use symbols to get the same results. That's one of the beauties of FreeHand. Another beauty is the text-handling capabilities within the program. FreeHand *is* a drawing program, not a page-layout program, but there's not much in the way of manipulating text that can't be done in FreeHand. Chapter 9 goes into FreeHand's text features in detail.

Package design

FreeHand makes it easy for you to design packaging. Most box manufacturers require you to draw the lines for the die cuts that form the box after it has been printed. It's an easy task to draw the die lines and then simply duplicate the page. You leave one page as-is for the die-cutting process, and use the other page to place design elements — photos, blocks of color, and text. Use a separate layer for the die lines on the "art" page so you can place all the elements in their correct location. Hide that layer before printing. Because both pages (die and art) are the same size, the printer registers the die to the printed sheet. With other illustration programs, you would have to contend with two separate documents, and minor changes and adjustments become major stumbling blocks. Through a judicious use of some of the tools available in FreeHand, such as master pages and custom pages, you can go a long way in label design.

Technical illustration

I call myself a technical illustrator, and FreeHand has been my tool of choice since its first release. Technical illustrations vary in style and complexity, from the line drawings that show you how to set your VCR's clock to colorful exploded or cutaway views of mechanical devices such as a car or airplane. The FreeHand toolset is well-defined and easy to use and master. Symbols can be developed for items that must be drawn multiple times. Styles are easy to set up so you can change a single path or an entire drawing with a single mouse-click. Most graphic programs have layers, and learning to use them should be one of your first priorities. Through layers, you can show or hide various parts of a drawing to make construction of other parts easier.

Maps

Many cartographers around the world use FreeHand in the execution of their jobs. FreeHand's layers, styles, and custom brushes are a mainstay of map creation. It's not uncommon to have dozens and dozens of layers in a map, and strict organizational skills are a must.

Web graphics

By definition, everything you see on a Web page is graphic, and all those graphics have to start somewhere. There's no better place to start than right here! You can design buttons, page layouts, and construct all the elements you need while you're working in FreeHand. This is a really good place to start a Web site's development by making a storyboard layout for the pages.

Basic animation

Simple animations are very easy to do, and you'll catch on to the system very quickly. It's a matter of creating a blend between two objects and assigning the steps of the blend to an animated sequence. You'll learn all about the finer points in Chapter 11. The resulting file can be exported in .SWF format and imported into Flash for further work.

New FreeHand Features

The new features available in Studio MX were touched on in Chapter 2, but we'll look at them in closer detail here. Many people think that the future of print is doomed, and that it won't be long until everything is accomplished through an electronic media of some kind. For now, that seems to be the Internet. Macromedia Studio MX contains everything you could possibly need to build and maintain an efficient, graphically pleasing, useful, and entertaining Web site — or a jillion of them. This release of FreeHand brings both Web and print features to artists.

Brush stroke

In this newest release of FreeHand, any stroke can be converted into a custom brush stroke. A brush stroke is a graphic that follows a path. It can be distorted to stretch the entire length of the stroke, or it can be iterated along the path, according to your needs. The graphic element you use to make the brush can be made from strokes and fills, text, geometric shapes — anything you can make in FreeHand.

To apply a brush stroke to a path, use the Pointer tool to select a path, and open Windows ⇨ Inspectors ⇨ Stroke. Then select Brush from the drop-down menu. The path takes on the attributes of the brush stroke that happens to be currently selected. That stroke will probably be the Default Paint stroke, which is a sort of a fat, wet Number 12 sable watercolor brush. You can change the brush from a long continual stroke to a series of paint dabs by changing the menu to Default Spray. The percent box to the right of the brush name changes the height of the brush. If the brush is too fat, change the field to 50 percent; conversely, you can make the brush thicker by putting a large number, such as 350 percent, in the field. This adjustment works the same for the Paint or Spray brushes.

As an illustrator, I got tired of these two selections pretty quickly, and I imagine you will too. So, why not add a few novel brushes?

1. Click the Stroke Options triangle in the top-right corner of the Stroke panel to access the pop-up menu.

2. Drag down to the Import listing to a dialog box that opens the English ➪ Brushes folder.

3. You have two choices: Default Brushes.FH10, and More Brushes.FH10. FreeHand installed the Default Brushes, select More Brushes.FH10 and click the Choose button. This opens another window with thumbnail versions of several interesting brushes. The examples that are provided also give you a good idea of how much work and creativity you can put into this new feature.

To actually import the brushes, you must select them individually. You can click the brush in the top-left corner, scroll to the bottom of the list and Shift+click the last brush to select all the brushes. If you only want to import two or three brushes, press the Control (Command) key to select noncontiguous brushes. When you've made your selection, click the Import button. All the brushes you selected will be available to you every time you open FreeHand.

But what if you really feel like designing a super brush that's all your own? The good news is that it's not that much more difficult than importing a brush. For example, follow these steps to make a brush that will be a row of black dots:

1. First, draw a small circle (about 0.25-inches in diameter) by holding down the Alt (Option) key while dragging the Ellipse tool (all tools are fully detailed in Chapter 6). Give the circle a stroke of None, and a fill black.

2. With the circle still selected, choose Modify ➪ Brush ➪ Create Brush to open a dialog box asking you whether you want to make the brush by copying the selected element or by converting the selected element. If you select Copy, your original element will be live and well on your page when you're done making the brush. Choosing Convert turns the selected element into a symbol. I usually go with Copy, just in case I want to make some changes later.

   After you've made your decision, you'll get the Edit Brush dialog box you see in Figure 4-1.

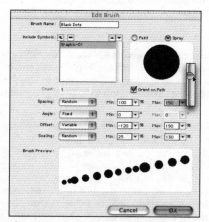

Figure 4-1: The Edit Brush dialog box

3. You should start by naming the brush in the Brush Name field. Be descriptive so you can choose the brush from the menu when you're in a hurry later. In this example, we want a row of dots, not one really big long dot, so click the Spray button above the thumbnail of the dot.

4. Now adjust the various attributes of your brush stroke. Start with the Spacing fields. This determines how much or little space you want between the elements you've chosen for a brush. If you put a number smaller than 100 percent, the elements overlap. As you can see, a pop-up slider appears if you click the triangles, but you can easily enter numbers directly in the text fields.

   The Align to Path box check box can give you a little problem if you're not paying attention. If you place a check mark in this box, the brush follows the path as you would expect — think of a school of fish following each other, head to tail. Unchecking this box (when the brush is a Spray) aligns all the brush strokes in the same direction. When the brush is a Paint style (not a Spray), the path will go from beginning to end points of the path in a straight line. Figure 4-2 has examples of the differences.

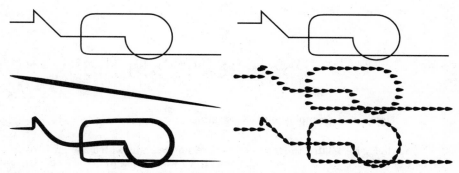

Figure 4-2: From top to bottom: original strokes, Paint strokes, Spray strokes. The left column is a Paint brush, and the right column is a Spray brush.

   Each of the attributes has a menu that enables you to choose random, fixed, or variable iterations. The angle of a circle's rotation won't matter much, so it's been left at Fixed: 0-percent. Offset refers to how far off the original stroke an element will stray. Scaling relegates the amount of change in element size as it is placed along the path. A Brush Preview appears at the bottom of the window to show you what you're building. Click OK when you're through adjusting your brush.

5. You can use anything in your current library as a component of a brush. Just click the plus sign near the Include Symbols callout in the Edit Brush dialog box to have the symbols available in the Brush Edit menu.

   The element you choose for a brush stroke does not have to be very large. For example, look at Figure 4-3. The brush element is made up of a 12-point stroke that's only 6 points wide. On top of that is a clone of the path, set to a 3-point stroke. The actual brush element is shown in the small circle; it is enlarged for a better view in the large circle.

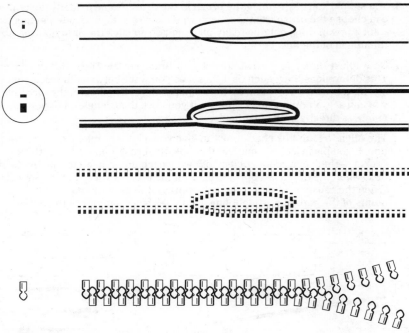

Figure 4-3: Examples of the Brush stroke

Notice in Figure 4-3 that the top two lines are simple paths with a 2-point stroke. The second pair of lines uses the brush set as a Paint stroke with Orient to Path selected. It's important that you see how the looped line has been deformed. The horizontal runs in the path curve upward from the left, and amble downward on the right. The third set of paths are clones of the first two, but the brush has been made to Spray, and is not set to Orient On Path. This arrangement follows the path closely. The last example is how you can use a brush in real life. The zipper tooth was drawn and converted to a brush. The spacing is set to 200% Fixed, and Orient to Path is checked. A path was drawn and cloned. The clone was flopped vertically with the Reflect tool. Both paths were given the Zipper brush stroke. The bottom path was then selected and Reverse Direction was applied, which turned the zipper elements upside-down. Then the path was adjusted so the zipper teeth meshed properly.

Contour Gradient

Adobe Illustrator users have been able to brag about their Gradient Mesh tool for a couple years now. Until this latest version, FreeHand users could only smile and remind the Illustrator artists that they may have a fancy gradient tool, but it isn't vector art. To the casual user who works with these drawing programs occasionally, or for fun, that's no big deal. But for professional artists who regularly output their work to print, it's a major factor. The Gradient Mesh art must be rasterized before it can be printed. That means it is going to turn into a bitmap, and *that's* a big deal when it comes to reproducing your artwork. A detailed discussion of bitmap and vector art can be found in Chapter 6. Vector art can be scaled up or down without suffering jaggies. Rastered art is designed to be reproduced at a specific size. Reduce it or enlarge it, and you've changed the integrity of the artwork.

You might ask, "Who cares?" Why not just do the art the size you want it, and raster it to fit the printed page and forget it. That's fine until the new guy at the agency decides to use your file at a different size or document. Then you can expect a phone call or a botched job. Thanks, I'll stick with strict vector illustrations, and do them in FreeHand. If someone wants to enlarge my EPS file, they can do it in a jiffy, and I don't have to worry about a job heading south. When I need bitmapped artwork (which is quite often), I'll continue using a bitmap-editing program, such as Adobe Photoshop. I'd rather not work in a hybrid drawing situation.

So what does the Contour Gradient do, you ask? Well, you would get the same results if you made a clone of the closed path and reduced it or used the Inset Path Xtra to make it smaller, and changed the color. The Contour Gradient has the advantage of moving the color break and center of the gradient. See Figure 4-4 for a comparison between the Contour Gradient and a run-of-the-mill blend.

Figure 4-4: A Contour Gradient on the left, and a standard blend on the right

Navigation panel

There's no better way to put something on the Web than to use the Studio MX, and that starts with FreeHand. This program is primarily a drawing program, but it does offer several aids to Web productivity, including HTML page and SWF (ShockWave Flash files used for animation) exporting. The new Navigation panel (see Figure 4-5) not only enables you to link a URL to graphics on a page, it provides the framework for some basic actions so you can make a basic page or site to test your design.

Access the Navigation panel by going to Windows ⇨ Panels ⇨ Navigation. After you name your object in the Name field (up to 26 characters), you can find the object by choosing Edit ⇨ Find and Replace, clicking the Select tab, and searching by Object Name. The field is case-sensitive, so try to be consistent in your naming practices.

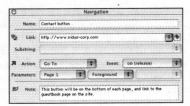

Figure 4-5: The Navigation panel leads the way to the Web.

Immediately beneath the Name field is the Link field. Type a URL here, or select a page within the current document from the drop-down menu on the right of the Link field. This menu lists every page in your document, and all the URLs you have entered for other objects. The binocular icon at the far right is a Link Search button. If you enter a URL in the Link field and click the icon, all objects in the document that have that link will be selected. This is a super aid in fine-tuning a Web site design, as you can readily check to see that all the buttons are linked properly.

When you want to link to a line of text, select the text, and open the Navigation panel. The selected text will appear in the Substring field. You can link to this text just as you would a graphic object.

Just below the Substring field lie the Action and Event menus. Action contains several Flash ActionScripts, including GoTo, Play, Stop, Full Screen, Start/Stop Drag, and Print. If you want the user to print a portion of an HTML page or Flash movie, the Print button will do the trick for you. The Event menu lists normal mouse/cursor actions, and a Frame Event. The Actions you choose provide various parameters in a separate menu.

At the bottom of the panel you'll find the Note field where you can enter up to 256 characters about the purpose of the object/link, or let the next person working on the job better understand what you're up to.

Library panel

Prior to FreeHand 10, there was no library, but a Symbols panel that acted as a repository for symbols. Macromedia augmented this panel considerably, and the new Library holds master pages, symbols, and custom brushes. You can export any of the Library's contents so they may be imported into another FreeHand document, and it's all handled through the Library and its Option menu.

The Library lists the number of times an element is used in the document, and on which date it was placed. If you or anyone else has edited a symbol, the date can be a real clue as to the correctness of the symbol on the pasteboard. Knowing how many instances exist in the document is big news too, because you may have forgotten about one or two symbols that could impact your decision to make changes.

Master pages

Master pages will be a boon to anyone working on multipage documents or repetitive production projects. The master page can be as simple as a blank page with guidelines, or as complicated as a navigation panel for a Web site. When it comes to Web pages utilizing links, however, you must remember that a child page will contain the links but the links are inoperable. You may be thinking, "Huh? Are you nuts?" Well, yes and no. You can place objects with links attached to them on a master page. When a child page is made from that page, the links do not work, and cannot be searched out. But, release the child page and the links are just fine. Master pages are explained more in Chapter 5.

I use a library full of master pages that are representative of my major workload. It makes sense to drag a child page onto the desktop, release the child, ungroup everything, and make the appropriate changes for the new project. After all, why invent the wheel three or four times a week?

Pen tool features

The Pen tool underwent several modifications between FreeHand 9 and 10. People new to FreeHand or coming in from Illustrator or Flash didn't have a problem with the changes, but long-time FreeHand users have had a tough time getting used to them. There's a QuickTime movie on the CD (PenTooltheMovie.mov) that shows how the Pen tool's Smart Cursor works and what to expect from the tool. The tool's attributes are explained fully in Chapter 6.

Enhanced Tools panel

The Tools panel has been blessed with a Subselect tool that you use to select objects within a group, modify paths between points, and other specialized effects explained in Chapter 6. The Hand, or Grabber, tool was also added so you can move the pasteboard around the monitor without scrolling. New graphic icons for Freeform, Zoom, and Line match the same icons in Fireworks, but the tools work exactly as they did in prior versions.

Color boxes

At first I felt that this box was pure eye candy, but I've grown to rely on it, and use it more than the Swatches panel once I get a drawing or layout under way. The color wells represent the Stroke and Fill colors, and both boxes work in the same manner: click the well and a box of color appears. You can have a selection of Web-safe colors, or only the colors that are in the Swatches panel, by choosing one or the other from a pop-up menu within the color box. I work on two monitors, and my Swatches panel is far enough away that I would rather make the short jump to the bottom of the Tools panel than mouse over to the second monitor to select a color.

Editing symbols

I discuss symbols in depth in Chapter 8, but in short, FreeHand 10 makes symbol editing easy and efficient. Just double-click the icon in the Library preview window, its name in the Library list, or select the symbol's instance on the page and select Edit from the Library Options pop-up menu. An Auto-update option shows changes in the document as you make them. Deselecting this option holds the changes until you close the edit window or change FreeHand documents. The changes are ultimately made, but the effects aren't as dynamic as watching them occur as you do the edits.

File Info dialog box (International Press Telecommunications Council Protocol)

If you're involved in the newspaper industry this is a nice feature to have. As shown in Figure 4-6, the panel allows artists to apply pertinent data to their artwork. This feature is reached by selecting Xtras ➪ Other ➪ File Info, and is described as the industry-standard file information for cataloging files destined for news media. The document's name appears in the text field if you click the Filename button at the top of the page.

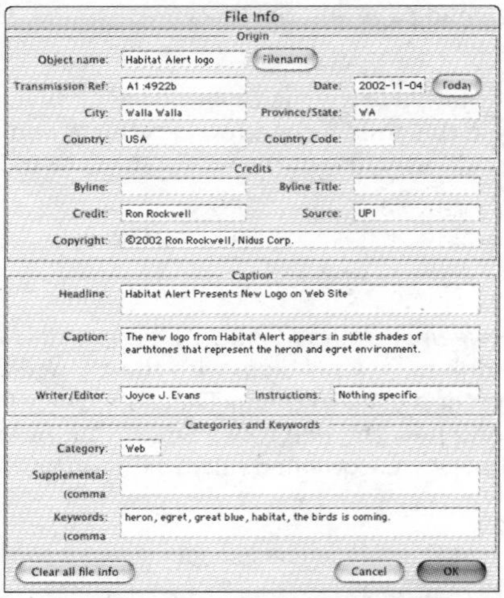

Figure 4-6: Information used by the IPTC is placed in the File Info Xtra dialog box.

Flash integration

The vector artwork done in FreeHand can be utilized directly from Flash. Simple animations can be drawn and tested in FreeHand, but I wouldn't call it an animation tool. But all the groundwork can be done here, and that saves time and provides superior results. I like to use FreeHand to make a quick animation for client approval before cranking Flash into action. The Controller panel is identical to the one in Flash (in function if not cosmetically). We can all see the effect of the animation without getting tangled up in timelines, Keyframes, and so on. The client sees the message instead of the medium.

Print Area

Select a single print area from the entire pasteboard with the new Print Area feature. Use the Page tool to align multiple pages together in reader's spreads, and print them on the same sheet of paper. If your printer doesn't output large enough pages, you can choose Fit On Paper to have FreeHand reduce the pages to fit your paper size automatically. You can also use Print Area to encompass a selection covering all the pages in your document for use as a storyboard. If you want to print only a particular section of a page, this tool isolates that part of the page for you.

Unsaved Document indicator

When you've made a change to a document, or printed it, the Save icon in the Main toolbar is grayed out. In FreeHand 10, there's now also an asterisk (*) after the file's name in the document's title bar. When you save the document, the asterisk goes away.

Working Conditions in OS X and Windows XP

As you can imagine, changing an operating system is a nightmare for engineers. They have to write code that doesn't break the older operating systems, and still take advantage of the newer, classier, and hopefully more stable systems. In some areas everything works well, and in other spots it's less than exciting. FreeHand 10 works a little faster under OS X than OS 9x, and it's more fun to work with the program on OS X, but basically you won't notice anything different about the *program*. And that's the way it should be.

Installation is simple. Just install FreeHand while OS X is the startup system. If you restart the computer using OS 9x, FreeHand 10 opens and works just fine.

FreeHand's Relationship to Other MX Programs

As you've read before, and will read again, FreeHand is a drawing program, but it does simple double-duty for Dreamweaver and Flash, while creating basic files for Fireworks. However, in relationship to these programs, FreeHand should be considered a support program. We discuss actual projects related to these three programs in Chapters 10, 11, and 12.

Dreamweaver MX

Exporting to Dreamweaver MX

When it comes to ease of use *and* power, Dreamweaver comes to mind. FreeHand can be of great assistance in preliminary and design work, and as a basis for Web pages. If you want to stick within a predesigned format, you can choose Web from the Document Inspector page sizes. That provides you with a 550-pixel by 400-pixel page ready to fill with your ideas. Work out your visual ideas here, and make the graphics that you want to use. Then add links to various buttons or text strings by using the Navigation panel. Finally, you can export the entire document of one or several pages to HTML by choosing Publish as HTML from the File menu. The HTML Output panel (shown in Figure 4-7) appears with basic choices. The Setup button brings the HTML Setup panel into view, allowing further specifics to be chosen.

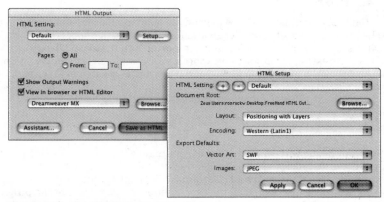

Figure 4-7: The HTML Output panel

If you have problems that will hamper the page's operation, an Output Warning box appears if you have selected the Show Output Warnings button. You should leave this selected as it shows you simple problems that will have major effects on your final output.

When you choose Dreamweaver as your editor, and click the Save as HTML button, the completed page opens in Dreamweaver, and you can do your "real work."

Exporting to Fireworks

Fireworks MX

When you design graphic elements for Web use, you can save them directly out of FreeHand in JPEG, GIF, PNG, or SWF formats, but you won't necessarily have the control over the image that you will get in Fireworks. You should choose the format you want to use based on the type of graphic you have designed. Fireworks will not open a SWF, so count that out unless you're moving into Flash, but the other formats are all viable.

If you have a graphic that is basically continuous tone — that is, it involves gradients of color, or is relatively photo-realistic, then you will probably be best off with a JPEG export. If the design has solid blocks of color, and little gradation effects, a GIF file is your best choice. Use PNG if you want the same quality of a JPEG, but a transparent background at the same time. PNG files are usually larger than JPEGs or GIFs. Different tools are better for certain operations, and Fireworks happens to give you more control when you need artwork converted to JPEG or GIF files. Remember that the JPEG format deletes some detail as the file is compressed, and you don't want to work on a file that has already been degraded to a certain degree. You're best off exporting in PNG format when you're going to be working with the file in Fireworks.

The file you export from FreeHand can be modified graphically and as to file type in Fireworks. Again, think of FreeHand as your jumping-off point for Web graphics. Do the heavy lifting there, and polish and fine-tune the work for the Web after you have the design in Fireworks. Naturally, you can create the rollover graphics in FreeHand, but you won't be able to test the results as a "mouseover" effect. However, you can check the visual effect by placing each state of the button on a different layer. Then just turn the various layers on or off in the Layers panel to mimic the effect of a mouseover.

Exporting to Flash

Flash MX

FreeHand can be the basis for a simple shape tween-type animation, or it can be used to make a multipage Flash-type animated site complete with mouse actions, hot spots, and links. You can make a graphic and export it as an object to be imported into the Flash Library as a symbol, or you can make the entire animation and export it as a complete Flash movie. In Chapter 11, you make an animation of a bird in flight. All the artwork is created in FreeHand, but tweaked in Flash.

Summary

This chapter filled your heads with what you can expect to do with FreeHand 10.0.1 (because as of this writing there is no FreeHand MX). You learned that this is an excellent drawing program that does double-duty as a page-layout program, a Web page layout program, and an animation program. Then you discovered all the new features in this release of the program, including master pages, the new Pen tool functionality, and other enhancements. Finally, this chapter touched upon the interactivity of FreeHand with the other Studio MX programs: Dreamweaver, Fireworks, and Flash.

✦   ✦   ✦

Setting Up a FreeHand Document

This chapter teaches you how to set up different types of FreeHand pages that will simplify your workflow and help you work more efficiently.

The Anatomy of a FreeHand Page

You will see several panels and toolbars scattered across your monitor when you start FreeHand the first time. If you're on a Windows system, a Wizard will prompt you to choose whether you want to open a new document, an existing document, and other options. Macintosh users will see the menus and panels appear. This can be a little disorienting, so go to File ⇨ New to open a blank untitled document. Now you can rearrange panels around the document window as you see fit. You move the panels by clicking on the top bar and dragging the panel to a new location. To collapse the panel double-click the top bar or click the collapse box in the right corner. You can adjust the various toolbars to a vertical or horizontal orientation by clicking and dragging the lower-right corner of the toolbox. To gain the most real estate from the program, most illustrators place the main tools in the horizontal Main toolbar at the top of the screen. You can nest several tool sets in the toolbar space.

When you have the tools and panels adjusted, look at the document window. The default letter-sized page is centered in the window, and it is surrounded by white space. This white space is called the *paste-board*, and this area can be used to store elements as you are drawing. Anything that is not on the document page itself will not print. The pasteboard is 18.5-feet square and contains all the pages in the document. (In case you're interested, that can be up to 520 letter-sized pages, or a single 18-foot square sign.)

The bottom of the window (shown in Figure 5-1) contains several informational and navigational aids. You'll find the current magnification percentage or custom view name in the field on the far left. Next to that is a pair of page selector buttons. If you have multiple pages in the document, clicking these buttons takes you to the previous or next page. The next field shows the current page number, and a drop-down menu that lets you select a particular page in the document. Selecting any page brings that page to fit completely in the document window. The drawing mode is shown in the next field. You can change the way your document looks as you are working by changing the mode in this field. Most drawing is done in the *Preview* or *Keyline* modes:

✦ Preview shows you the correct line weights, and all the colors as they are applied in the document.

✦ Keyline reduces everything to thin lines — all paths are the same width — and no color is visible. Any photographs or imported graphics are shown as an outlined box with an "x" in it. You cannot print the Keyline view. If you print the document while in this view, you get the actual color and line treatment that you have chosen.

Finally, the Units menu fills out the information bar. Change the units of measurement for the document by clicking on this menu and making a selection. To make adjustments or simplify your drawing efforts, you can change these units as many times as you like while working.

Figure 5-1: Valuable information is found at the bottom of the FreeHand window.

FreeHand Panels and Inspectors

Much of the work done in Macromedia FreeHand is controlled with information found or entered in the program's panels. You'll notice how intuitive the engineers have made the program as you come to work more and more with Macromedia FreeHand. The inspectors or panels contain everything you need to adjust, alter, or specify every part of your document. The differences between Windows and Macintosh panels are mostly cosmetic. If you are comfortable working on either platform, you won't be surprised by the way these panels or inspectors look or feel. All the screenshots in this section were done on Macintosh OS X 10.2 Jaguar.

All the panels float over the workspace, and you can move them at any time. Panels can consist of one or many tabbed panels that can be customized to fit your particular work style. For instance, the main inspector contains tabs for Objects, Stroke, Fill, Text, and the Document, but you could easily remove the Text panel and have it floating on the desktop at all times.

You can dock and undock panels and group together or set apart various tabs. To dock panels together, hold down the Control key on a Mac or PC, as you drag a panel directly beneath another panel. A thin gray bar appears between the docked panels, showing the link between them. If you move one panel, the other tags along. To undock the panels, double-click the linking bar. To group an individual tab with another set of tabs within a panel, click the pop-up triangle in the top-right corner of the panel and select the grouping you want. At the bottom of that menu, you can choose New Panel Group, which removes the currently live panel from a group and makes a panel of its own.

If you have panels docked together, and you click the Maximize or Minimize bar, all the panels in the dock are affected. Clicking the Close box on any of the panels closes the entire dock of panels; conversely, choosing to open a panel that is part of a dock (from the Windows menu or through a keyboard shortcut) makes the entire dock appear, not just the one you selected.

Object inspector

The Object inspector changes according to the tool or object that you select. If a stroke is selected, the inspector relates the following information:

✦ The position of the currently selected point

✦ The type of point selected

✦ The flatness of the path

✦ Whether the path is open or closed

✦ Buttons that allow the retraction of control handles (these terms are covered later in this section)

When you select a regular geometric shape, such as a rectangle or ellipse, the Object inspector supplies the dimensions of the object's bounding box, and the location of the XY coordinates of the bottom-left corner of the object's bounding box (Figure 5-2).

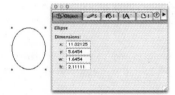

Figure 5-2: The Object inspector with an ellipse selected

If you select text, the inspector tells you the dimensions of the text block and the block's top-left corner XY coordinates. If the text is to be inset in the text block, the inset value can be input in this inspector.

The Object inspector tells you the XY coordinates of the bottom-left corner of an imported bitmap, as well as its dimensions. The inspector also lets you know what the file type is (TIFF, JPEG, EPS) and its color mode (CMYK, RGB). A Link button enables you to replace the file with another graphic, or get additional information from the Links panel. A pair of scale windows shows the amount of reduction or enlargement, and changing these numbers changes the physical size of the graphic on the page, although the file *size* remains the same.

Stroke inspector

Virtually all the work done in FreeHand involves a stroke in one way or another. Certainly this is true in the case of pure drawing. The Stroke inspector (Figure 5-3) provides a drop-down menu with information about the type of stroke. The following stroke choices are available:

✦ **None** — No stroke prints, but a perimeter exists.

✦ **Basic** — You can choose this fixed-width stroke from another drop-down menu, or through an input field.

✦ **Brush** — Choose from default brushes or develop your own. A separate drop-down menu enables you to choose these brushes from a library.

✦ **Custom** — Nearly two dozen strokes are available to choose from, including hearts, teeth, snowflakes, and arrows.

✦ **Pattern** — Basic bitmap patterns, such as mezzotint, weave, and fish scale, are found here, but are not meant for printing on high-resolution devices.

✦ **PostScript**—Roll your own PostScript code for strokes, or find them on the Web. A PostScript printer is necessary to print these correctly, and the strokes aren't visible on the monitor. Instead it shows a pattern of Cs.

Figure 5-3: The Stroke inspector

The most common stroke style is Basic, and this panel enables you to determine the cap and join of strokes, as well as the stroke width and any dashes you may want. A drop-down menu contains a selection of arrowheads. Arrowheads can be placed at either or both ends of an open path.

Fill inspector

The Fill inspector panel (Figure 5-4) controls the color inside an object. A drop-down menu enables you to choose different types of fills:

✦ **None**—The object has no color. Basically you could call the object transparent, but that's a different type of fill. Think of None as an empty fill.

✦ **Basic**—A Basic fill is a solid color. The color can be RGB, HLS, Hexadecimal, or CMYK. Choose the color from the drop-down menu, or by selecting a color from the Swatches inspector. An option to have the color overprint is available. Overprinting occurs when you want one color to print on top of another. This concept is dealt with more in detail in Chapter 13.

✦ **Custom**—This fill does not appear onscreen, but it prints fine from a PostScript printer. Custom fills include bricks, noise, grass, and tiger teeth. After you select a custom fill, you can then select the color of the fill and the color of the background. You can also use this panel to adjust the angle and density of the fill.

✦ **Gradient**—FreeHand 10 supplies three types of gradients: Linear, Radial, and Contour. Colors are placed in a color "ramp," and you can adjust the angle or center point of the gradient by entering numbers in a field, or by moving a joystick adjuster within the panel.

✦ **Lens**—A Lens fill converts spot colors to process colors for output, and an EPS file that is viewed under a Lens fill isn't affected by the Lens when it is printed. There are six Lens types: Transparency, Magnify, Invert, Lighten, Darken, and Monochrome. Each has special attributes that are described in Chapter 7.

✦ **Pattern**—The same array of patterns utilized in the Strokes panel are available for fill. Again, these patterns are not meant to be output to a high-resolution printing device.

✦ **PostScript**—Just as with the Strokes inspector, you can write your own PostScript code or find it on the Web. A PostScript printer is necessary for output, and the effects are not visible on the monitor. Instead, a pattern of PS fills the object.

✦ **Textured** — You can fill an object with sand or gravel, wrap it in burlap or denim, or give the object a mezzotint appearance.

✦ **Tiled** — Draw or import a graphic. Copy it to the Clipboard, and paste it into the Tiled fill window. Then you can adjust the rotation, scale, and location of the pasted-in graphic, using text input fields and an angle wheel. Any object can now be filled with this tiled fill.

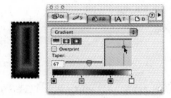

Figure 5-4: The Fill inspector, showing a contour gradient

Text inspector

The Text inspector (Figure 5-5) contains many subpanels that enable you to specify character and paragraph attributes, as well as spacing, column styles, and font choice. Text handling is covered in detail in Chapter 9.

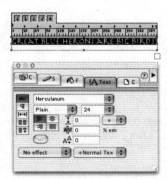

Figure 5-5: The Text inspector

Document inspector

You navigate your entire document from the Document inspector (Figure 5-6), and you can add or delete pages, duplicate pages, and move pages on the pasteboard. In the figure, you can see that I've moved my default page to the top-left corner of the pasteboard to make the addition of pages in the document a more logical arrangement. This is explained fully in the next chapter, but basically, just click the page thumbnail and drag it to the new location. You can also change the size of individual pages and adjust the printer resolution and amount of bleed for each page. Master pages can be selected here, and Child pages can be emancipated (set free from their Master page). A thumbnail shows the location of all the pages in the document. Three different view sizes are available with simple button clicks. New pages can be selected at several standard sizes, such as letter, tabloid, legal, A3, A4, A5, B4, B5, Web (550 × 400 pixels), or Custom.

Figure 5-6: The Document inspector. Note the customized location of the default page.

If you select Custom, you must enter width and height numbers in text entry fields. The units of measurement set at the bottom of the document window are utilized in the Custom page size fields. If you are looking at pixels and want decimal inches, change the units of measurement at the bottom of the document window. The fields convert the measurements automatically. You can also enter numbers such as "1.0 in" (for inches) or "2p6" (picas).

Layers panel

One of the busier panels in FreeHand is the Layers panel (Figure 5-7). That's because an efficient illustrator builds the drawing on several layers to make selection of particular objects or groups in the drawing an easier process. The Layers panel lists all layers in the document and has four icons preceding the name of each layer. The first icon is a check mark that indicates that a layer is visible. Clicking the check mark makes the check disappear, and the layer becomes hidden. The next icon is a small dark circle. Clicking it makes the circle hollow with a dot in the center, indicating that the layer is in Keyline view. Next is a padlock that enables you to select and draw on a layer if the lock is open. When you close or lock the layer, the layer cannot be moved or modified in any way.

You cannot select objects on a locked layer. If you copy everything on a page (to paste it elsewhere), locked layers aren't copied. The last icon is a colored square. Use this square to indicate which level a selected object is on. Drag a color from the Mixer or Swatches panel onto the layer's color square. Anything on that layer reflects the color you've chosen. This step makes it easy to navigate through a multilayered drawing.

Figure 5-7: The Layers panel

There is a horizontal bar midway down the Layers panel. This bar demarks the foreground from the background of a document. Everything above the bar prints, and nothing below the bar prints. But, if you are developing an animation, everything below the bar appears in every frame of your movie. The layers below the bar appear grayed-out on the monitor.

Swatches panel

In the Swatches panel (Figure 5-8) you can build a library of colors to use throughout a document. You can make colors in the Mixer or Tints panels, or choose colors from libraries in the Options pop-up menu, which you find by clicking the triangle in the upper-right corner of the panel. You can import color libraries from other sources, or export your own swatch library for use in other FreeHand documents or even to other computers.

Figure 5-8: The Swatches panel contains colors that you want to use in the document.

The Swatches panel enables you to apply color in a couple different ways. At the top of the panel there are three selectors and an arrow. The arrow is used to add color to the Swatches panel. Simply drag a color onto the arrow and let go. The color is added to the list. The three selectors are, from left to right, the Fill color, the Stroke color, and both Stroke and Fill color. Choose any one of the three selectors by clicking it. Then click a color swatch *name* in the list. If you select the Fill selector, the object's fill becomes the color you clicked. If you choose the Stroke color, only the stroke changes to the new color. When you click the Both selector, the Fill and Stroke choices gain the color you selected. If the fill and stroke are different colors, there is a horizontal dash in the middle of an outlined box.

You can apply color swatches to objects in the document in a variety of ways. It's an easy task to drag a color swatch into the middle of an unselected object to change its color. Dropping the color swatch on the path surrounding the object changes just the path's color. If you're working with a very small object, you can use modifier keys to be sure that color changes where you want it to change. Hold down the Shift key as you drop the color (release the mouse), to affect only the fill. The cursor is an open arrow attached to a square of the color you selected. Hold down Control + Shift (Command+Shift) to change the stroke color. This cursor differs from the fill cursor in that a hollow square appears in its center. Alt (Option) turns the cursor into the open arrow with a circle of the selected color, and when released, the object has a radial gradient fill. The Control (Command) key provides a diamond cursor under the arrow and results in a linear gradient fill. Finally, the Alt+Control (Option +Command) Control keys make a contour gradient fill with a notched-square cursor.

Changing the color of a selected object provides more methods of working. With an object selected, you can drag a color to the object as previously described, or you can drag the color swatch onto the appropriate selector at the top of the Swatches panel. Depending on which selector is active, double-clicking on the color's name effects a color change.

It makes no difference which tool you are in when it comes to applying colors through the Swatches panel. All tools convert to an open arrow tool when they pass onto the panel.

Mixer panel

You use the Mixer panel (Figure 5-9) to mix colors through various color modes and methods. There are three primary mixing methods:

✦ **CMYK** — Cyan, Magenta, Yellow, and Black inks are used in commercial printing processes to achieve an approximation of full color on paper.

✦ **RGB** — Red, green, and blue light combine to form the colors you see on your monitor. This color model is useful for Web-based projects.

✦ **HSL** — Hue, Saturation, and Lightness in various combinations give a fairly broad color gamut for colors to be viewed on the monitor.

And, depending on your computer platform, you have these additional options:

✦ **System Color Picker** — This is the Windows basic 48-color set; other colors can be added.

✦ **Apple Color Picker** — Macintosh users are treated to a larger scale version of CMYK, HSL, and RGB color mixers, plus HSV (Hue, Saturation, Value), HTML, and an array of crayon colors.

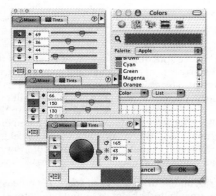

Figure 5-9: The Mixer panel. From top-left down: CMYK, RGB, HSL, and the Apple Colors panel on the right side.

After you move the sliders, circles, and other devices, or input values in text input fields, you can add your color to the Swatches panel by clicking the Add To Swatches button at the bottom-left of the panel. This action opens a dialog box that has the color breakdown in its respective color mode (such as 35r, 126g, 16b, or 82c, 18m, 97y, 3k), but you can type in any name you want the color to have.

There are two wells at the bottom of the Mixer panel. The well on the left is the last mixed color, and the right well is the currently mixed color. Dragging a color onto either of the wells by using the eyedropper tool changes both wells to that color. Any adjustments you make in the Mixer panel are shown in the right well. You can click in the color well and drag a block of the color onto the Swatches panel and release the mouse. The color is added to the panel using its default color-breakdown name. Double-click either side of the color well to open the Tints panel.

Tints panel

This panel literally pales in comparison to the Mixer panel. The right side of the color well is the color you have just mixed at 100 percent intensity. A drop-down menu enables you to choose any color from the Swatches panel. Or, you can use the Eyedropper tool to drag a color from the document — or simply drag a color from the Swatches panel — into the color well. No matter which method you use to get the color into the well, you can choose from nine tints — from 10 percent to 90 percent — of the color (Figure 5-10). You can also enter a specific percentage of color, or drag the slider until you see the tint you want to use. The same Add To Swatches button appears in this panel. Tints are treated as if they were any other kind of color and can be applied to strokes, solid fills, or gradient fills.

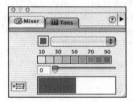

Figure 5-10: Make light of your colors in the Tints panel.

Styles panel

A super way to save time and energy is to learn to use Styles. All you need to do is get any object or section of text looking the way you want it. Open the Styles panel. Click New in the pop-up Options menu from the triangle in the upper-right corner of the panel, and double-click the new style to give it a unique name. If you save the style as part of a default FreeHand document, or a FreeHand template, the style is available for you to use any time. I have a set of line weight (stroke width) styles, and a group of common fill types in my Styles panel, along with several common typography treatments. It really saves time because it shortcuts trips to other panels and menus. A graphic style is indicated by a square with four boxes in its corners; a text style has a capital "A" in front of it in the Styles menu (Figure 5-11).

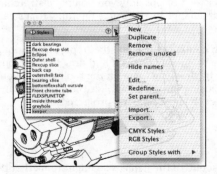

Figure 5-11: The Styles panel can save you hours of needless work. Notice the cursor has opened the Options pop-up menu.

After you develop a style, you can change all iterations of objects containing that style by clicking Edit in the pop-up menu. You can also draw or set type attributes and use them to redefine a style, thereby changing every object you have used with that style attached.

There's also a library of CMYK and RGB styles that you can choose from. Some, such as Chrome, can be useful to build upon in a drawing. Others, like Diamonds or Confetti, are more akin to a custom-tiled fill and have more limited use.

Custom Keyboard Shortcuts

FreeHand is a very adaptable program that makes it easy for you to learn and use efficiently. If you have various artists using the same computer, each one can have a personal keyboard shortcut set up, so everyone can be comfortable while working. (This has to be just about my favorite feature of the program.) Go to Edit ⇨ Keyboard Shortcuts (Figure 5-12). The panel provides access to nearly every tool, so you can place any keyboard shortcut you want on it. Keyboard Shortcuts Setting menu contains a list of 10 (Windows) or 14 (Macintosh) programs that enable you to choose keyboard shortcuts from other programs. So, for instance, if you are experienced in Illustrator or CorelDRAW, you can choose those keyboard shortcut settings and be right at home. I type on a DVORAK keyboard layout, so my keys are in a different arrangement from that on the QWERTY keyboard. Macromedia FreeHand's custom shortcuts let me put my odd fingerings into use, so I can work quickly and easily. I save the settings with a unique name by clicking the plus sign to the left of the shortcut name text box and move them from computer to computer as I switch platforms and machines.

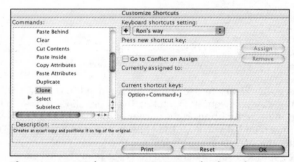

Figure 5-12: Make your own custom keyboard shortcuts in this panel.

If you use one particular tool more than any other tool, or possibly you don't like stretching for a Control+U (Command+U) keyboard shortcut, change it! Make up something that's easy for you to remember, and use it.

The same panel contains the Toolbars tab, which contains the icons that represent various tools and functions. All you need to do is find the tool/icon you want and drag the icon onto the toolbar. You can remove icons you don't use by dragging them off the toolbar, and you can rearrange icons to suit your working style. Closing this panel applies the shortcuts and menu items immediately, and they remain in effect the next time the program is started.

Master Pages

Master pages are new in FreeHand 10. From the sound of the name, you might think that this feature is similar to a master page in InDesign, PageMaker, or QuarkXPress, but you'd be missing some very important differences.

First of all, the similarities are that you can use a master page to have consistency between layout pages within a multiple-page document. Simple graphic elements, such as running header lines, recurring graphics, or chapter heads, are examples of such a use. In this manner, every child page of the master page has the exact same elements as the master page. To modify elements on the child page, you must release it from the master page. At that point, all the elements from the master page are applied to the new, orphaned page, and any relationship to the master page is lost.

An example of the use of a master page would be to place a running head, such as "Chapter 1," in a font, such as Poppl-Laudatio Bold, and give it a nice rich red color. You might decide that you want this text at the top of each page, and create a master page by getting the page to look the way you want it, and selecting Convert to Master Page from the pop-up menu in the Document panel. You can then go about your business and build the chapter.

At some point, you might decide it's time to work on Chapter 2, so you would release a child page from the master page (in that same pop-up menu), and change the number in the heading. To finish Chapter 2, you'd need to create a new master page with the changes you just applied. The rest of your project would proceed in the same way.

If you decide to change the color of the text to blue, you'd have to modify the master page you built for each chapter. To get around this extra work, you could apply a style to the text. After that it's a simple matter to modify the style, which would ripple through the entire document.

But a more unexpected use of the master page feature is to build pages that you produce frequently, for instance a series of labels for different-sized cans or small boxes. Build the label with all the correct elements in their respective places on an accurate page — in other words, the job that was just approved and printed last week. Make it a master page. Import another final job, and make it a master page, and yet another job and master page. Save the document as a FreeHand Template; then when you need to make a new label, open the template and choose the appropriate master page. Modify colors, text, and other elements that must be changed, and you'll find the job is complete in less than half the time it would usually take. Each label you produce is consistent with others you create. Best of all, the file size is no larger than the original label all by itself — the master pages take up no file space because the master pages themselves are stored in the program folder.

To further understand the master page filing system, you must realize that a master page is just a complicated symbol. Well, it's as complicated as you want to make it, anyway. To get the most out of master pages, export them when they are completed to your satisfaction. Go to the Library Options menu and be sure that Show Master Pages is checked. Your master pages then appear in the Library list. Select a page and choose Export in the Library Options menu. The file should be saved in the Macromedia FreeHand 10 ⇨ English ⇨ Symbols folder, which should open as a default when you export any symbols. If you have several master pages in one document, you can export them all at one time, with one filename. At some future time, choose Import from the Library Options menu, and select the master page file that you made in the Symbols folder. A dialog box opens with thumbnails of all the master pages in that file. Shift-click to select contiguous pages, or use Control-click (Command-click) to select noncontiguous items. Click Import, and the master page moves to your Library, ready for use.

Developing a master page

You can make a master page from an existing page by clicking the pop-up Options menu in the top-right corner of the Document Inspector panel, and selecting Convert to Master Page. Or, you can get a page laid out the way you want it, and select Convert to Master Page from the Library pop-up Options menu.

To build your own brand new master page, go to the Document Options menu and select Make New Master page. If you do that, a new window opens with the currently selected page size in it. You can draw, set type, and do everything in this window that you can do in the regular Macromedia FreeHand window. When you have everything the way you like it, close the window, and the master page is complete. It appears listed in the Document panel and in the Library (providing you have Show Master Pages checked). You can rename the master page by double-clicking its generic name in the Library list.

To apply a master page to an existing page, select the page with the Page tool and go to the Document inspector panel. Click the Master Page drop-down menu there to choose the master page you want to use. Another method is to be sure that Show Master Pages is selected in the Library pop-up menu. Then just drag a master page icon onto a page in your document (Figure 5-13). All the elements in the master page go to the lowest layer in the document.

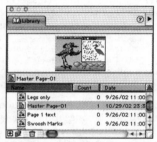

Figure 5-13: The Library contains your master pages.

To start a child page based on an existing master page, choose Add Pages from the Document inspector's Options menu. When that dialog box opens, you can choose a master page from the Make Child of Master Page drop-down menu.

Releasing a child page

If you made a child page and discover that you need to make changes to the elements that are on the master page, then you have to release the child page. You accomplish this by selecting the child page with the Page tool. Go to the Document inspector's Option menu, and select Release Child Page. The page is no longer connected in any way to the master page. Each layer you built in the master page is transformed into a group consisting of the objects on a given layer. It takes a bit of getting used to, but after you understand how the master page/child page relationship works, you won't have any trouble at all.

Child page caveats

When you work with a child page, you cannot alter any of the elements that are part of the master page. It is as if those elements were on a locked layer. The upshot of this is that you can't edit text or change the arrangement of elements in the child page. If various elements have been given a style formatting, you can modify colors, fonts, and strokes within the child page by editing the styles.

Child pages have no running page numbers, a shortcoming that will be addressed in the next release of Macromedia FreeHand. There are two workarounds for the problem, however. Both are available at www.FreeHandsource.com; one is an Xtra, and the other is an AppleScript (only useable on a Mac). FreeHandSource.com is a great site for short tutorials on many common FreeHand drawing situations. Ian Kelleigh has built up quite a stock of program news, tutorials, hints, tricks, and a history of the program. It's a site worth checking out if you will be spending any time at all in FreeHand.

Default Pages

A good default page saves you more time than you can imagine. It's also very easy to set up, and I recommend that you make new ones as your drawing style or project types change. Start by using the Document inspector to make a page that is representative of your usual work. For some people it may be a horizontal tabloid page; for most of us it will be a vertical letter-sized page. Set the bleed area if you usually have bleeds, and the resolution you like. In the Text panel, choose the font that you use the most, and set all the attributes — size, leading, paragraph style. and so on. Without selecting a drawing tool, go to the Stroke panel and select the stroke weight and color that you use most often. Make any other attribute selections you want, such as caps, joins, dashes, and so on. Then go to the Swatches panel. If you have company-wide colors, import them from the Swatches Option menu, or build them in the Mixer/Tint panels. Name them appropriately in the Swatches panel, and arrange them in an order that looks right to you.

If you want all your shapes to be filled with a particular color, you can choose that color (and fill type) in the Fills panel. I suggest that you leave the Fill at None to keep from going nuts, however. It's much easier to add color as you need than to delete color from most of the objects you draw.

Now for a really important trick, go back to the Document inspector. Notice the thumbnail arrangement of the pages in the document — click the "small" icon to see the whole pasteboard. You'll notice that the default location for a Macromedia FreeHand page is at the lower-left corner of the pasteboard. As you add pages to the document, the new pages are usually added from left to right (until they meet the right edge of the pasteboard). Then a new row is started beneath the first row of pages. After a few pages, the bottom of the pasteboard fills, and new pages are added starting at the top-left corner of the pasteboard.

To get around this little bugaboo, I drag the page in the Document inspector thumbnail window to the top-left corner. This lets all the pages flow from left to right, top to bottom, in a natural order.

Tip   Here's the trick though: Be sure to double-click the page in the thumbnail, or somehow navigate to the page before proceeding. If you don't, you'll be greeted with a blank pasteboard every time you start Macromedia FreeHand.

If you work primarily as an illustrator, create stroke and fill styles and add them to the Styles panel. Place logos and common text elements in the Symbols library. Think of this page as a Swiss Army Knife — you want everything you may possibly need on this page.

Now arrange all your panels on the monitor (or monitors) so you can work comfortably. Go to File ➪ Save As, and navigate to the Macromedia FreeHand 10 folder. Then open the English folder. On a Mac, give the file a name, and choose Macromedia FreeHand Template from the Format pop-up menu. On the Windows platform, name the file (FT10 is added as an extension to the filename) and choose Macromedia FreeHand Template format from the Save As Type pop-up menu. Click Save, and go to Edit ➪ Preferences. Select the Document tab, and choose your new default page from the New Document Template drop-down menu.

Quit Macromedia FreeHand, and start it up again. You should see your customized page in all its glory. After you work with it for a while, you'll find other elements or attributes that you'd like to have handy. Make those modifications, add a few master pages and other symbols, and repeat the saving process. This process chops (not shaves) hours from your schedule.

Templates

A template is built exactly the way a default page, covered in the previous paragraphs, is. The only difference is that you don't save these pages in the English folder, and, unless you want to, you don't choose them as a new document page. Instead, save templates in job folders for easy access in starting jobs. You should think of the file as a type of master page, only you don't have to go through the Library to reach it. Just double-click the template file in its folder, and your entire page is ready to go, with text blocks, logos, fold lines, die cut patterns — anything the job requires — already in place and ready to manipulate. Objects are grouped or ungrouped as you see fit, and they're on layers you have chosen. You don't have to release the page from a master page, and it's an efficient way to work.

The file is titled, "Untitled," until you save it the first time. That's one of the beauties of working with templates; you never make changes to the original document. You change only a copy of the original. If a global change must be made, you have to make a new template. On the other hand, if you have been working on a number of jobs with common elements, a master page arrangement could allow you to make global changes by changing the master page. All the child pages would reflect the change. Template pages can contain master pages as well, so there's a lot of flexibility to work with here.

Summary

In this chapter, you learned the makeup of a Macromedia FreeHand document, including a brief discussion of the panels that control the attributes of elements in the document. You found out how useful custom keyboard shortcuts can be. You also learned how to make and work with master pages, and templates, and how to set up a customized default page that contains nearly everything you need in your most common projects.

✦   ✦   ✦

Vector Art in an Eggshell

This chapter shows you how to use the multitude of tools and Xtras in FreeHand, and what you can do with them in the fine art of vector art.

What's Vector Art?

"Computer artwork" consists of two main groups of images: vectors and bitmaps. Macromedia FreeHand and Adobe Illustrator are examples of vector drawing programs. Macromedia Fireworks and Adobe Photoshop are both bitmap or raster imaging programs.

A vector is the product of a mathematical formula that calculates the curve of a path between two anchor points. This formula uses the x and y coordinates and the angle and length of the control handles of each point to determine the amount or degree of the curve. A vector path is resolution-independent, meaning that no matter how much a path is enlarged or reduced, the visual sharpness of the curve remains constant; the file size also remains the same. A one-inch square drawing has the same file size (20k) when printed at that size, or enlarged to a three-foot square.

A raster images consists of a grid of cells called *pixels*. Each pixel has a specific color and location, and if you are editing a raster image, you are actually editing individual pixels by changing their color. Raster images are resolution-dependent, meaning that they have a finite number of pixels that create the image. If the image is enlarged, the image gets larger by definition, but so do the pixels, and the image becomes blocky or "gets the jaggies." (See Figure 6-1.) The small graphic on the left is the original drawing. It was exported to Photoshop and printed at the same size to the right of the vector drawing. Then the drawings were enlarged to show what happens to pixels when an image is expanded. The black line is easily five times wider than the white line, but when you reduce it to a finite number of pixels per inch, the bitmap uses barely twice as many pixels to portray the black line as it does the white line.

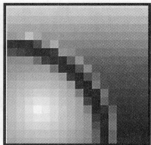

Figure 6-1: Notice the differences between vector and bitmapped artwork at various enlargements.

In contrast to a vector image, a 300 dpi (dots per inch resolution), one-inch square RGB drawing is 264k, and the same drawing at three feet would be a whopping 333.7MB! If you simply enlarge the one-inch square to three feet, each pixel would be approximately an eighth of an inch square, creating a pretty blocky image.

This is not to say that vectors are good and bitmaps are bad. They are used side by side in many projects. Vectors are often used in preliminary work for a project that will be finalized in a bitmap program, and the opposite is also true. To complicate matters a little, Adobe has added raster effects to Illustrator so it's possible to make a vector-based drawing, add subtle shading and color mixing, and rasterize the final drawing. That drawing is a resolution-dependent bitmap, however, not a vector drawing. If you wish, you may convert your vector graphics to bitmaps using the Rasterize command. When you do the image becomes an embedded TIFF file that will reside in the FreeHand document. You will lose the resolution-independency.

What Can FreeHand Do for You?

This section describes a few of the types of projects for which FreeHand is extremely well suited.

Basic FreeHand Tools panel

You use several tools to draw with in FreeHand. No single tool is more valuable than another tool; instead, each tool does a specific type of work. The Pen or Bezigon tools can make straight lines, but if all you're going to do is draw straight lines, the Line tool is a better choice for the job. When you work on a drawing or layout in FreeHand, you will use many tools, and the more you learn about each tool, the easier your work will be. The default Tools panel is broken into two main groups, with the first group having four sections. You can change the orientation of the Tools panel to a single or double horizontal or vertical row of tools and place anywhere on your monitor. It rides above the entire document, but beneath the top menu bar. Some tools have a mark in the top-right corner of their icon. Double-click these tools to bring up a dialog box to modify settings for that particular tool.

Note   You can customize the tool bar and menu bar by going to Windows ➪ Toolbars ➪ Customize. When this window is active, you can drag tools onto or off of any of the bars, or relocate them to suit your preferences.

Sound Advice

Before learning about the various tools, I suggest that you enable sounds in FreeHand if you work on a Mac (sounds are unavailable on Windows computers), unless you're working in an environment where the clicking and ticking from the program might annoy others. In the Edit ⇨ Preferences panel, you can enable sounds for Snap To Grid, Snap To Point, Snap To (horizontal or vertical) Guide, and Snap To Path-Guide. This makes it really easy to know exactly where a point is going to be placed, or that you've gotten an object right where you want it to be. At times it will sound like you've got a high level of radiation coming out of your computer, but I find the sounds invaluable.

Selection tools

Selection is the name of the game. Arrow selection tools select any object or block of text that is not locked or on a locked layer. By using specific points on an object or bounding box, you can change the size or shape of most objects with these tools. The Text tool is the oddball in this section of tools, as it only works on text, but the other tools work on everything in a FreeHand document. Keyboard shortcuts are in parentheses after the tool's name. If there is no shortcut, you can usually add one in the Edit ⇨ Keyboard Shortcut menu.

The Pointer tool (V or 0 [zero])

The most often-used selection tool is the solid or black arrow, called the Pointer. If an object is filled, you can select the object by clicking anywhere within its boundaries. If it is not filled, you must click the Pointer directly on the stroke to select it. You can change the Pick Distance in the Edit ⇨ Preferences panel. The smaller the number (in pixels) you input in the field, the closer you must be to the object before you can select it. The default is three pixels, and is usually an ample amount.

If you need to select an odd-shaped object or many objects at once, click and drag a marquee (use the pointer to drag a selection) around the objects or points. Virtually everything enclosed within the marquee will be selected. Dragging the Pointer over a grouped object doesn't select the group or parts of it unless the Alt (Option) key is pressed. To select an entire group, object, or block of text by marquee-selecting, you must completely encompass the object.

You can change any tool into the Pointer tool when necessary by holding down the Control (Command) key. Release the modifier key to revert to the original tool. Clicking the Pointer tool anywhere on the page or pasteboard (not on an object) deselects anything that is selected.

Note

Double-click the Pointer tool in the toolbox to open the Contact Sensitive window, which is turned off by default. If you turn it on, you don't have to surround an entire object to select it. Just dragging the cursor over a section of an object select that objects — without the extra effort of clicking (I know all that clicking sure tires me out). The Contact Sensitive window is available for the Subselect and Lasso tools, as well. Just drag the cursor over part of any object or group of objects to select them. If you happen to surround any points, they become actively selected; just crossing into a text block selects the block itself.

On the CD-ROM

On the CD in the Movies folder is a movie named Contact Sensitive.mov.

The Subselect tool (A or 1)

This is the open or hollow arrow tool, and is new to FreeHand 10. Use this tool to select objects that are in back of other objects, either on the same or different layers. (If you have the Pointer tool selected, you can achieve the same effect by holding down the Alt (Option) key.) The Subselect tool can also be used to modify the shape of a path by selecting a segment of the path between two points and dragging the path. The control handles of the points on each side of the segment move toward or away from the center of the segment as you drag the cursor.

The Page tool (no keyboard shortcut)

This tool selects an entire page with a single mouse-click. The page can then be moved around the pasteboard to align with other pages. If you click Delete, the page is deleted; you receive a warning that there are elements on the page, and you must decide to delete the objects or cancel. When you have Snap To Grid enabled (in the View menu), you can align multiple pages. You can quickly duplicate a page or range of pages by selecting them with the Page tool, holding down the Alt (Option) key, and dragging the duplicate pages to a new location. The engineering staff didn't want to take a chance that you would delete several pages of work in a single mouse-click, so you can only delete one page at a time with this tool.

The Lasso tool (L)

Use the Lasso to select individual points in an ungrouped object or objects. This tool is useful for selecting points that are very close together — a high zoom level helps, too.

The Eyedropper tool (no keyboard shortcut available)

In its basic sense, the Eyedropper is used to color objects. Click the Eyedropper in the color well, the Swatches panel, the Mixer or Tints panels, and drag the little box onto whatever you want colored. However, that's just as easily done with the Pointer tool. A better use of the Eyedropper is to select color from other objects on the page, and drag the color onto an object you want to have the same color. The Eyedropper tool can perform different functions when modifier keys are used. (These modifiers do not work with blocks of live text.) Table 6-1 lists the modifiers and their corresponding functions.

Table 6-1: Eyedropper Modifiers

Modifier	Function
Control (Command)	Changes color of stroke only.
Shift	Changes color of fill only.
Alt (Option)	Radial fill centered on location of pointer at mouse release.
Alt+Control (Option+Command)	Contour gradient fill.
Command+Control (Mac)	Linear gradient, experiment for angle and direction of gradient. Gradient tends to start nearest the vertical or horizontal edge or a corner of the object, creating a vertical, horizontal, or diagonal gradient.

The Eyedropper can also be used to choose a color within a gradient. This is extremely useful if you're trying to make another object blend seamlessly into a gradient.

The Text tool (T)

As previously mentioned, the Text tool works only with text. Conversely, the Pointer tool becomes the Text tool on occasion. That occasion occurs when you double-click a block of text with the Pointer tool. Actually, triple-clicking a block of text usually turns the Pointer into the Text tool. But at times, all that clicking will add the Transform handles to the block of text, and the third click may move or rotate the block of text — it's a scary thought, but it happens now and then. You're better off selecting the block of text and then double-clicking directly on a line of text.

You can just click the Text tool in the Tools panel. No matter how you get there, you're ready to set type. You can start typing in a couple different ways. The way you choose to proceed depends on what you want to do. If you want to set a quick line of text to print out and hand to your boss, such as, "I QUIT!" you can simply click the Text tool in the middle of the page and start typing. On the other hand, if you want to write a formal resignation, you can drag a text block of a specific size and shape, just as you would if you were drawing a rectangle. As you begin to type, your words fill the text block, depending on the various attributes and preferences you have set for the program.

Cross-Reference

For further information on setting attributes and preferences, see Chapter 9, where type is covered in detail.

When you choose the Pointer tool and you click a text block, the text block is treated as an object. If you choose the Text tool click in a text block, and select or double-click the text, the selection is treated as text, and not as an object. This can be a tough concept to get through to people who are new to the program. For example, if you select a block of 72-point text with the Pointer tool and choose an 8-point red stroke and a black fill, your block of text becomes a black rectangle surrounded by a thick red stroke. Conversely, select the text itself by dragging the Text tool over it and highlighting it. Then choose the same stroke and fill. Your letters will be black and be surrounded by a red stroke.

Note

The red stroke described in the preceding paragraph is divided in half: four points of the stroke will be inside the letterform, and four points of the stroke's width will lie outside the letterform. To preserve the shape of the letters, you need to create a clone of the letters — without a stroke to them — and place it in front of the stroked text.

The Text tool changes to the Pointer tool when the cursor is moved outside the text block. This is a wonderful, but sometimes confusing, process, and it does give cause for irritation if you want to begin typing a new text block. To continue typing, you must select the Text tool again.

Drawing tools

The four basic drawing tools in FreeHand are the Pen, Bezigon, Pencil, and Line. The first two create paths by the placement of individual points; Line and Pencil work differently. Again, default keyboard shortcuts are in parentheses, but you can change them.

The Pen tool (P)

This is the most used tool when I'm at work. Until FreeHand version 9, the Pen tool worked predictably, but there seems to be some confusion as to what happened when FreeHand 10 was released — the Pen tool changed. Long-time users went crazy because what they expected to happen didn't, and the unexpected happened constantly.

That said, the new and improved Pen tool works — it just works differently. Smart Cursors are tiny additions to the tool icon that tell you what the Pen or Bezigon tool is up to at a particular time. In no particular order, here's a list of what the new tool does. The Bezigon tool's icons employ the same attributes, but the tool has its own way of placing points.

✦ Pen tool with no "smart cursor" icons, just the Pen icon — The next mouse click begins a path.

✦ Pen tool with open circle — This pen point indicates that you will close a path with the next mouse click.

✦ Pen tool with carat — Present point retracts the handle that would control the curve of the next path segment with the next mouse click. Note that a double-click doesn't remove the handle extending back to the previous point. The Carat icon over an existing point within a path retracts both control handles with the next mouse click.

✦ Pen tool with plus sign — The next mouse click places a point between existing points on a path. It also shows up when you are about to place a point very close to the currently selected path. To keep either from happening, hold down the Shift key as you click. This may (or may not) conflict with your attempt to use the Shift key to constrain point placement to 45-degree alignment — proceed with caution! If this happens, the workaround is to place the new point as near as you can to where you want it, then move the point to its preferred location.

✦ Pen tool with minus sign — The next mouse click withdraws both control handles of a point in the middle of a path if the point is a Curve or Connector point. It deletes the point under your cursor if the point is a Corner point. The path's curve will be determined by existing points on either side of the deleted point.

✦ Pen tool with slash — The next mouse click makes the end point (the last point that has been placed) of an existing path live. Your subsequent click continues the path.

✦ Pen tool with "X" — This cursor appears when you have an existing path selected, but the end point is not live. You begin a new path with this cursor, but if you move the cursor over other points in the selected path, the cursor changes to match the attributes of the existing point.

✦ Pen tool with button-hole (circle with horizontal lines to the side) — Your next mouse click connects to an end path — the current path's, or another unselected path. Long-time FreeHand users, be wary!

In the Preferences panel, you can change the appearance of points in your documents. The FreeHand default point is a three-pixel solid square, and a selected point is a five-pixel open square. If you select the Show Solid Points option, points on a selected path are shown as three-pixel open squares, and the selected point is a solid five-pixel square. The points act exactly the same; they just appear differently. Try drawing with each of the preferences to see which works best for you.

As you place points, you can control the curvature of the preceding section of the path *and* the next section's curves at the same time. Visualizing what is happening helps if you think of the path as a flexible steel strap, similar to a long metal ruler. Each point controls the previous and next sections of the path — including the first point you place. A single mouse click with the Pen tool places a Corner point on the page. If you simply click the mouse elsewhere on the page, you get a straight path between the points. However, if you make that first click a click-and-drag movement, you apply a curve to the path that becomes apparent when you make the next mouse click. Depending on the location of the second point, you get something between a straight line and a severe curve.

The only way to get a handle on the way these drawing tools work is to use them. After a short learning curve, you'll discover that you know just how much to click and drag to achieve the curve you're after. Believe me, it's well worth the time to master the Pen and/or Bezigon tools by drawing intricate objects.

If you want your path to complete a circuit and become what is called a Closed Path, you have a few alternatives to choose from. The easiest way is to make your last click on the first point you placed in the path. The cursor changes to have the little circle next to it, indicating that the path is closed. Another way to close a path is to go to the Object inspector and check the Closed box; the beginning and end points connect, with the path section reflecting any curves you applied on those points. Your last option is to install the Closed Path Xtra button on your toolbar or menu bar. Clicking that button closes the path.

In the Movies folder on the CD is a movie named pen_bezigon_movie.mov.

The Bezigon tool (B, 8)

 For years, I ignored the Bezigon tool because it just seemed strange — but I've learned that it has a time and place, and now I use it frequently.

What makes the Bezigon different than the Pen tool? It's the placement of the points as you draw. When you click the Pen tool on the page you get a Corner point. Click the Bezigon tool on the page and you also get a Corner point. However, say you're used to using click-and-drag to place a Curve point with the Pen tool. Using the Bezigon tool, a click-and-drag operation moves the point around the page. That's good and bad, depending on what you're trying to accomplish. If you want the point to stay put as you make a Curve point, you must hold down Alt (Option) as you click — forget about the dragging part for now. The Bezigon tool places a point with two Curve point control handles installed. Click the Bezigon on the page again and a curved path appears between the points. If you hold the Alt (Option) key down as you place that second path, you'll see that the new Curve point also has control handles on it. If you misplace the point (that is, put it in the wrong spot), keep the mouse down and move the point until it reaches the location you want.

I use the Bezigon tool to trace a curvy object or an ellipse that's at an odd angle. An ellipse that is horizontally or vertically oriented is easy enough to approximate with the Ellipse tool, but if the ellipse is at an angle, it's easier to draw with the Bezigon tool. Just place Curve points at the four points on the ellipse where the minor and major axes intersect the ellipse. The Bezigon tool usually does a great job of drawing the ellipse with only minor adjustments needed.

The Pencil tool (Y)

   If you're good with a mouse or trackball, you can draw directly on your FreeHand page with the Pencil tool. I consider myself pretty dexterous, but mastery of the Pencil tool with my trackball eludes me.

When you draw with any of the Pencil tools, you trace a path on the page, and as you reach places in the path that mark a significant change in direction, the program places a Beziér point as you continue drawing your path. To speed up the drawing/redraw process on the monitor, you can have the program draw a dashed line as the temporary path. When you release the mouse, the path gains the visual effect you've chosen, according to the stroke type and its options.

Another option that you can use to your benefit is the amount of precision. Use the slider to choose a low number for loose, flowing lines with few points, or move to a higher number for a more precise rendering of the path you've drawn. The higher the number you choose, the more points FreeHand places on the path—sometimes it goes so far as to make printing difficult, so use your own judgment on a case-by-case basis.

The Pencil tool has variants that make using the tool interesting, fun, and invaluable. You find them by double-clicking the Pencil tool icon on the Tools panel. First, there's the Freehand version. With this option selected, you get a constant-weight stroke as you draw.

Then, there's the Variable Stroke, which is a natural for digital tablet users, and only slightly more complicated for mouse/trackball artists. To make a line thinner, press the left keyboard arrow; to make the line fatter, press the right keyboard arrow. The Pencil dialog box enables you to set a limit on the minimum and maximum line weights. Pressure sensitivity on a digital tablet makes this kind of drawing fun. There's another option in the dialog box that deals with overlapping strokes. If you select Auto Remove Overlap, the program converts the finished stroke into a compound path. This takes a bit of time for the computer to process, and also leaves you with compound path editing considerations. Compound paths are dealt with in the projects later in this book.

The other Pencil tool variation is the Calligraphic Pen. It's just like writing with a SpeedBall pen without the ink on your fingers. You have the option of setting minimum and maximum stroke width, and the angle of the pen. You can also choose to have a constant-width pen stroke.

The Line tool (N)

Who says you can't draw a straight line without a ruler? The line tool only does one thing, but it does it very well. It places a starting point and an end point, with a straight path between the points. The line can be at any angle or length you choose, but it doesn't curve unless you go back with another tool (Pen or Bezigon) and change the starting or ending points. You can constrain the angle of the stroke to 45-degree increments by holding down the Shift key. You can also change the constraint angle to any angle you want by going to Modify ➪ Constrain, and entering an angle in the field. This is useful for drawing ellipses and moving elements at precise angles, as well as making straight lines.

To get more out of a straight line, just switch to the Pen, Bezigon, or Pencil tool. Then select the end point you want to extend, and continue drawing. The Line tool only places the beginning and end points, so it's tough to make a closed path unless you use the Join command.

Geometric drawing tools

Sometimes you want to draw simple things, like circles and squares. That's where this group of tools fits in. There really aren't many bells and whistles to them, but they're functional and elementary tools of the trade.

The Rectangle tool

Use the Rectangle tool to draw four-sided boxes. Hold down the Shift key to constrain the rectangle to a square. Double-click the Rectangle tool icon to round the corners of the rectangle. Whichever unit of measure the document is currently set to will be the unit you use to mark the radius of the corners. If you're not conversant in points or picas but know inches really well, change the units setting at the bottom of the window before opening this dialog box—you can't change the units after this box is open.

Click the mouse on the page and drag in any direction — the rectangle is drawn from wherever you clicked the mouse on the page. Press the Alt (Option) key to draw the rectangle from the center out. Press the Alt (Option) key and the Shift key draws a square from its center point out.

The Polygon tool

Whereas the Rectangle tool builds rigid four-sided objects, the Polygon tool creates objects with any number of sides. The objects can be straight-sided polygons, such as an octagonal stop sign shape, or star-shaped. Double-click the tool's icon to bring up the Polygon dialog box. At the top of the box is a field and slider for adjusting the number of sides to the polygon. The slider itself has a maximum of 20 sides, but you can enter any number in the field. However, I won't guarantee that your computer won't crash if you get into the hundreds. A thumbnail box shows the shape you are developing as you modify the settings.

The Shape choices are located beneath the information about the number of sides. You can have a polygon or a star. The Polygon choice has straight sides, and the more sides you add, the closer to a circle the polygon appears. The Star choice has interior and exterior points that are modifiable, as explained in the next section.

Star Points provides you with two adjustments: Automatic and Manual. An Automatic selection provides you with "badge shapes" for sheriffs and other police officers, until you reach 10 sides. After that, the polygon more or less turns into a circle with small points. By using the Manual option, however, you can make anything from a pointy starburst to a flat-edged polygon by moving the slider from Acute to Obtuse. The closer the slider is to Acute, the closer the inner star points come to the center of the polygon.

When you finish making adjustments to the polygon, click the OK button. The cursor changes to a crosshair. When you click the mouse and drag, the polygon is drawn from its center point. Modifier keys do not affect this tool, but you can manipulate the angle and dimensions of the polygon with any of the transformation tools.

The Ellipse tool

Ellipses run the gamut from circles to thin "ovals," and anything in between. The Ellipse tool draws an ellipse from wherever you first touch the mouse to wherever you stop. To draw from the center out, hold down the Alt (Option) key, and to make a perfect circle, hold down the Shift key as you drag the mouse. Speaking of mice, you can draw Mickey Mouse with just a few click-and-drags of the Ellipse tool — if you're so inclined.

The Spiral tool

This tool is not as useful as the other tools that have been discussed, unless you need a spiral. Then it's invaluable. Double-click the Spiral tool icon to bring up its dialog box. You can choose between two types of spirals. The regular spiral (left icon button) provides an input field so that you can employ the exact number of lines or rings in the spiral. The proportional spiral (right icon button) enables you to determine the amount of growth between lines or rings in the spiral. Both types of spirals allow you to draw the spiral from the Center, the Edge, or the Corner of its bounding box. You can also choose from clockwise or counter-clockwise spirals. See Figure 6-2 for a comparison of the two spiral types and their results.

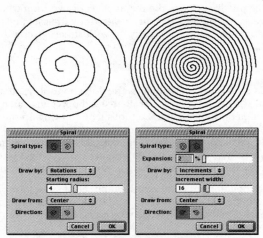

Figure 6-2: Spiral dialog boxes differ according to the type of spiral that you select.

In Figure 6-3, you can see an effect that would be tough to accomplish without the different spiral types. Using the specifications shown in Figure 6-2, two spirals were drawn from the same center point. Start with a horizontal and vertical set of guidelines; drag the first spiral (settings as shown in the left half of Figure 6-2) from the center line out to the right, while holding down the Shift key. Then bring up the Spiral dialog box again and change the specs to match the right side of Figure 6-2. Click the insertion point at the guideline intersection again (note that when the spiral is drawn, the first point is *not* at that intersection), and press Shift and drag the spiral to the right until the end points meet.

Select both spirals, and choose Modify ⇨ Join. In the Object inspector, be sure that the path is closed. Then give the spiral a black fill and a stroke of None. You won't often need spirals, but a little experimentation can lead you to something more exciting than canned effects.

Transformation tools

The first thing to commit to memory about FreeHand transformations is that if you double-click an object while using the Pointer tool, you see a dotted-line box with eight black boxes in corners and in the centers of each side. These are called transformation handles. When the transform handles are in view, you can click and drag on any of the black boxes to scale, skew, or rotate your selection. The selection can be a single object, a grouped object, several objects or groups, or text blocks. Everything that is selected within the transformation handles is affected by your adjustments.

You can also open the Transform panel at this juncture, and select the various means of transformations. In this panel, you can enter specific increments of relocation, rotation, scale, skew, or reflection. You can also enter the center point of transformation in two ways: Enter the x/y coordinates if you know them, or click on the document. The mouse click causes the coordinates to be entered in their proper fields.

Figure 6-3: The development of a spiral

The Perspective tool

This is probably the scariest tool in the FreeHand toolset, but it doesn't have to be. It's only scary because all the tools react just a bit differently, and some things don't work at all. Let's start with what does work, and why.

Making the grid work

Draw an object or set some text that you want to see in perspective. Go to the View menu, and choose Perspective Grid ➪ Show. This places a one-point perspective grid on your document. Select the Perspective tool, and play a bit: Look at the cursor as you move it near a grid line. It turns into a vertical or horizontal triangle with a line. The triangle points to the grid that you are approaching. You can change the amount of perspective by clicking (when you have the triangle/line cursor) and dragging the mouse to move the vanishing point. All the lines that make up the grid are active, so it takes a bit of patience if you have a two- or three-point perspective and you happen to be zoomed in to a spot on the drawing that has multiple grids overlapping. The key is to watch the cursor, and look for the direction the triangle is pointing.

Attaching objects to the perspective grid

How do you put things in perspective? Keep the Perspective tool active, and select the object you want to have in perspective. For practice, put the object on the vertical face of the grid — lightly tap the left keyboard arrow and let go of the mouse. The object should appear in place on the grid. (If you only have one-point perspective active, press the right or left keyboard arrows to place the object on the active vertical face.) To place the object on the floor of the page, click the object again, tap the down keyboard arrow and release the mouse. If you select the object, you can move it around the grid and watch its perspective change.

Removing objects from the perspective grid

When you have the drawing the way you want it, select the objects that you're happy with and click View ➪ Perspective Grid ➪ Release With Perspective. Now the object is the same as any other FreeHand object and is not controlled by the Perspective Grid. In fact, if you select it with the Perspective tool and reapply the object to the grid, the distortion will be extremely dramatic — and basically senseless.

To remove an object from the grid so you can reapply it after making modifications, choose Remove Perspective. This places the object back on the pasteboard as a regular FreeHand object. Make your changes and reapply the object to the grid.

Adding more vanishing points

To get a second grid, in other words, two-point perspective, click View ➪ Perspective Grid ➪ Define Grids. In the dialog box, you can add the number of grids you want and change their colors. Adding grids has absolutely no effect on objects you already placed on a grid. If you want to have a second *set* of grids, open the Define Grids dialog box again, and select New. This lets you set up another grid that you can manipulate separately from the first grid. I advise you to set up a completely different color scheme and make a unique name for each grid you have just to keep your head in perspective. You can only see the grids one at a time; click View ➪ Perspective Grid, and at the very bottom of the pop-up menu you'll see a list of the grids you've made.

Changing object dimensions

Taking an object off the grid and putting it back on again is easy enough, but what if you just want to make it a tad larger or smaller? The solution is a bit of a mind-bender because of all the keys involved, but here is how it works. The changes work *one pixel at a time*. Select the object with the Perspective tool. Press the 2 key to enlarge height and width equally; for width alone, press the 4 key; for height only, use the 6 key. Notice that you use even-numbered keys for enlargement. To reduce an object's size, use the 1 key to reduce height and width by one pixel; use the 3 key for width alone, and the 5 key for height only.

Moving things around on the perspective grid

To move an object around the grid — up, down, left, right — use the Perspective tool. If you haven't moved the object with any other means, you'll get the effect you're after. If you want to constrain movement parallel to the grid, hold down the Shift key as you drag. To move an object *and the grid* that it's on, select the object, and move the cursor to a grid line (look for the triangle/line cursor). Hold down the Shift key and drag. To duplicate the grid — for instance, to make a ceiling out of the horizontal grid — hold down the Alt (Option) key as you drag the grid. If you have an object on a grid and you want to duplicate both the object and the grid, hold down Shift+ Alt (Shift+Option) as you drag, and a copy of the object will follow the grid in perspective.

Mirroring objects on the perspective grid

To make type (or an object) look as if it were applied to a glass store window that you are viewing from inside the store, select the object and press the Space Bar. Conversely, you can select the object; hold down the Shift key as you drag the grid from one extreme to another. The object mirrors itself as it passes through the vertical or horizontal plane, as seen in Figure 6-4.

Figure 6-4: This illustration uses two sets of Perspective Grids; only one is visible.

Common situations with the Perspective Grid

Table 6-2 lists situations that commonly occur with the Perspective Grid and their solutions.

Table 6-2: Common Perspective Grid Situations and Solutions

Situation	Solution
You can't distort a bitmap by placing it on the Perspective Grid.	Import the bitmap, and outline it using an appropriate drawing tool (that is, if the bitmap has an irregular edge, use the Pen or Bezigon tool to make the outline). Apply the outline (not the bitmap) to the Perspective Grid. Then release the object from the grid and save it as a Photoshop or Illustrator EPS file. Open the bitmap file, and import the EPS file. Distort the bitmap to fit the EPS outline, and save the distortion, discarding the EPS outline. Back in FreeHand, import the distorted bitmap, but don't place it on the Perspective Grid, just place it as you would any other bitmap.
Text is impossible to edit on the Perspective Grid.	Just a misconception. Hold down the Opt (Command) or Alt (Control) keys as you double-click the text with the Pointer tool. The Text Editor box appears, and you can make any text changes there. Click Apply or OK, and the changes are effective and in perspective. Keep in mind, however, that once you release the text from the grid (Release With Perspective), you *can't* edit that text again. It is now a group of compound paths and can only be treated as such.

Continued

Table 6-2: *(continued)*

Situation	Solution
The perspective is too severe.	Move the vanishing points off the page. You have the entire pasteboard to work with. Note: If you have multiple pages, the vanishing points may not be usable if they happen to fall on an existing page — that page becomes active with its own set of perspective grids.
As things are moved around the Perspective Grid, they don't change perspective.	It's a matter of what you've done to the object since you placed it on the grid. If you place the object and then move it with any tool other than the Perspective tool (including keyboard arrow keys), you release the object from the grid. To move anything on the Perspective Grid, you must be in the Perspective tool. If you've goofed and moved something, don't be alarmed. Just select the Perspective tool again, and tap the appropriate arrow key to reattach the object to the grid. Then move it to the proper location.
The Perspective Grid doesn't work. Nothing you do makes stuff stick on the grid.	To apply an object to the grid, you must, first, select the Perspective Tool, and second, *TAP* the arrow key that applies to the correct grid. I repeat: TAP the key. If you hold the key down, nothing happens. Just hit it lightly and let it go and your object sticks to the grid as it should. Then you can move it around all you want.
Fill and stroke adjustments don't change color or size the way you'd expect.	With text, use the Opt (Command) or Alt (Control) keys while you double-click the text. Change attributes in the Text Editor. You can select objects with the Perspective or Pointer tools, and change their colors by selecting the Fill, Stroke, or Both boxes in the Swatches panel.
You can't seem to get the horizon to be at an angle.	It's a matter of perception. You can get it to an angle, but that angle is always perfectly flat — horizontal — and perpendicular to the vertical vanishing point. If it's necessary to have the horizon at an angle, you have to improvise by drawing within the grid, and then releasing the object(s) from the grid with perspective and rotating them.
The grid lies on top of your artwork, making it difficult to see what you're doing.	Turn off the grid's visibility. The Perspective Grid is active as long as you have the Perspective tool selected.

Note   The perspective of a stroke isn't affected when placed on the Perspective Grid; a box with a 12-point stroke turns into a trapezoid with a 12-point stroke if the box is applied to the Perspective Grid. To make the stroke have visible perspective, you must outline the path. In this case, you would use Xtras ➪ Path Operations ➪ Expand Stroke and type 12 in the Width field. When the object is attached to the Perspective Grid, the "stroke" (which is now a filled path or compound path) has the correct perspective.

The Freeform tool

  Personally, I prefer to draw paths or manipulate paths one point and Beziér curve at a time. But, when you need to make organic shapes, such as a tree, seaweed, or a bowl of warm soup, you absolutely can't miss with the Freeform tool. It works with two different operational methods: Push/Pull, and Reshape Area. Both methods add or subtract points to the path as you use the tool on a path.

You must double-click the Freeform tool to activate the dialog box that lets you to choose the tool type and various options. Figure 6-5 shows the dialog boxes for the two different Freeform tools. The cursor changes depending on which type of distortion you choose and the location of the cursor in relationship to the path itself. Use the Pressure settings if you have a digital tablet.

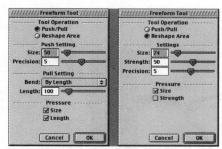

Figure 6-5: The type of Freeform tool settings are different for Push/Pull and Reshape Area.

Push/Pull

When you move the cursor around a path, notice how it changes. A small "o" next to the arrow means you are in the Push mode. The Push mode works by moving the shape of the path away from the cursor according to the size and precision values you enter. You enter the Size value in pixels from 1 to 1,000. A low number in the Precision setting adds fewer points to the changed path. A large circular cursor appears, showing the area you are distorting. To increase the size of the push pointer, press the right arrow key or right bracket (]) key; to decrease the pointer, press the left arrow key or left bracket ([) key.

If the cursor has a small "s" next to it, you're going to pull the path. The Pull setting enables you to choose a Bend option: By Length, or Between Points. By Length enables you to set the length of the segment (in pixels) that is affected. Between Points bends the path from the spot where the cursor touches the path and affects the control handles of the point on either side of the path segment if they're within the length setting.

You can constrain the pointer movement by holding down the Shift key. If you want to switch between the By Length and Between Points methods as you draw, hold down the Alt (Option) key *then* drag the mouse. If you start dragging and then hold down the Alt (Option) key, you clone the path.

Reshape Area

I use the Reshape Area tool when I need to draw little pointy things, which doesn't happen all that often, but this tool is a real time-saver when I use it. Just as with the Push/Pull option, you can set the size of the pointer from 1 to 1,000 pixels, and set the precision from 1 to 10 — with

10 being the highest precision and adding many points to the path. The Reshape Area tool also has a Strength setting. The higher the number you enter, the greater the distortion you make in the path.

Use the same keys to increase or decrease the size of the pointer as indicated for the Push/Pull tool. Use the up arrow key to increase the strength of the distortion, and the down arrow key to decrease distortion. The changes you make with the keys show up immediately in the size of the cursor.

Figure 6-6 shows the different types of drawings you can make with the Freeform tool. Both drawings started out as a vertical rectangle. The left side of the drawing was done completely with the Push/Pull tool (as set in Figure 6-5). The tree form on the right side of the figure was done entirely with the Reshape Area tool (with settings in Figure 6-5).

Figure 6-6: The Freeform tool has two different ways of working.

The Scale tool

You'll use this tool often enough to warrant creating your own keyboard shortcut. When the tool is selected, the cursor turns into a star cluster. Wherever you click, the cursor (and hold or begin drawing) is the center point around which the scaling occurs. With that in mind, you can select an object and click anywhere on the page or pasteboard to enlarge or reduce the size of the object. Drag the cursor to the left or down to shrink an object; move the cursor right or up to enlarge it. To keep the change in size proportional, hold down the Shift key as you drag.

Certain attributes are affected when you use the Scale tool. Those attributes are found in the Transform panel. Double-click the Scale tool to open it. The three check boxes marked Contents, Fills, and Strokes usually cause the most confusion. Any of the three that are checked will be scaled along with the size of the object itself. A 12-point stroke is reduced to a 6-point stroke if the object is reduced about 50 percent, and it will be enlarged to about 18 points wide if the object is enlarged by about 50 percent. Uncheck this box, and the stroke remains 12 points wide at either size. With Contents checked, anything you have pasted inside an object is enlarged or reduced along with the object. Deselecting Contents leaves the pasted-inside content at its original size while the object gets bigger or smaller. The Fills box relates to tiled fills. Checking the box scales the tile; unchecking it leaves the tiled fill at the original size.

A neat option to the Scale transformation panel is the Copies box. If you enter a number in the Scale box, such as 150 percent, then type 4 in the Copies box and click Apply, the object you selected is cloned and enlarged 150 percent, then cloned and enlarged 150 percent, and again until the fourth iteration is complete. They will be nested concentrically—providing sort of a tunnel vision look. It's akin to the effect you get by making a blend between two different-sized objects, only with this method, the space between the shapes can be varied instead of regular.

The Scale tool isn't just for sizing—you can draw with it, too. Look at Figure 6-7. First I drew an eight-point star. Then I selected only the center points of the star, and clicked the Scale tool at about the ten o'clock position inside the center grouping. I dragged the mouse downward while I pressed Shift to make the points "smaller"—but in fact, it brought them closer together, creating a pretty neat bug splat. Then I selected the outer points and planted the Scale tool far to the right of the star and dragged to the right to "enlarge" the star. I didn't hold down the Shift key for this action, and all the points moved to the right of center, making this a powerful graphic that demands a "POW!" or "BLAM!" (You can create the same effect by making the star shape very acute in the Polygon panel. Then select only the inner points of the star and drag them to a new location. In FreeHand, there's always another way to do something.)

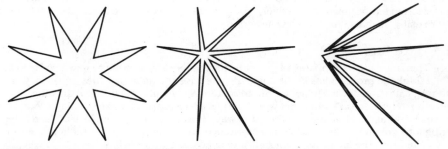

Figure 6-7: You can draw with the Polygon and Scale tools.

The Rotate tool

The Rotate tool's options are few, but it does the job required. Select an object, choose the Rotate tool, and determine where you want the center of rotation to be. Click the mouse in that spot and drag. The center of the rotation is always wherever you click the mouse when you're using this tool. Double-click the tool's icon to bring up the Transform panel and Rotation attributes. You can enter a specific angle and x-y coordinates for the center of the rotation. Just as with the Scale transform panel, you can enter a number of copies in this panel and create some really quick artwork.

The Mirror tool

With some projects, this little gem can cut your drawing time in half, literally. If you are drawing a symmetrical object, just draw one half of it. Then make a clone of it and use the Mirror tool to flop the clone to the other side. (Conversely, you can double-click the

Mirror tool, and enter 1 in the Copies field. Clicking the Mirror tool throws a clone of the original across the page for you.) Adjust the halves so their midpoints touch, and join the paths.

The Mirror tool can appear a little squirrelly with objects flying all around your page. Most mirroring is done from left to right or top to bottom. Holding the Shift key down as you drag the mouse constrains the mirrored image to 45-degree increments and calms down the screen activity.

The Skew tool

When you want to put a different slant on things, this is the tool you need. Select an object and choose the Skew tool. Click the cursor somewhere near the object so you can have a better feel for what the tool is doing. Also, skewing is not restricted to simple parallel shifting of an object's sides. You can skew an object all over the drawing board. (It's similar to the 3-D Rotation Xtra in that respect.) If you just click and drag, the results are pretty haphazard, so hold down the Shift key to constrain the distortion to horizontal and vertical. When you drag the mouse up or down, skewing depends on the side of the object the mouse is clicked. Click the left side and drag up to make the right side of the object skew up. If you click the right side and drag up, the left side goes down. The side you drag from will remain in place. You get the same results, but have to think differently as you do it. The same concept works for left/right skewing.

On the CD in the Movies folder is a movie named skew tool.mov.

Double-clicking the Skew tool icon brings up the Transform panel, where you can enter positive numbers in the Y and V text boxes to skew the object right or up; negative entries skew the selection left or down, respectively. You can enter copies to create clones of the object if you're using the panel for the skewing action.

The Trace tool

The Trace tool is probably responsible for the most frustration to new FreeHand users. I think the problem lies in the name: People have the hope that they can click this tool and magically transform a full-color photo of Aunt Marge into a really cool drawing. Unfortunately, it doesn't work that way. The Trace tool looks a lot like the Magic Wand in Photoshop — and works in much the same way. However, whereas the Magic Wand selects contiguous colors within a particular color range, the Trace tool can select contiguous color and it can break the image into blocks of a defined color range — 2, 4, 8, 16, 24, 32, 64, 128, and 256 colors — and outlines each contiguous color section. The left drawing in Figure 6-8 is an example of what the Trace tool does using 16 colors, and very high sensitivity settings. The art in the center is the same trace as in the grayscale rendering, except that the closed paths have no fills. More than likely, though, you'll be looking for the drawing on the right, which is pure vector drawing.

To utilize the Trace tool, start by double-clicking the tool in the Tools panel. This brings up the Trace Dialog box seen in Figure 6-9. Color settings are determined in the various fields: the number of colors; Grays or Colors; RGB (Red, Green, Blue) or CMYK (Cyan, Magenta, Yellow, Black); Low, Medium, or High Resolution; and Trace Foreground, Background, or All layers. The Path Conversion enables you to choose where to draw the path: Outline, Centerline, Centerline/Outline, or Outer Edge. Outline traces the outside edge of objects or colors and makes a closed, filled path. Choose Tight or Loose for the Path Overlap to determine how precise the tracing will be. If you choose Centerline, the Trace tool splits the middle of graphic strokes. Then you can apply Uniform (1-point) strokes to the line, or deselect

Uniform to make a variable line weight. Figure 6-9 shows the difference between Uniform being selected or not. When you choose Centerline/Outline, the trace takes on the attributes of both Outline and Centerline, and you have the option of determining how wide a path must be before it is ignored. Any paths under the number of pixels you select (from 2 to 10 pixels) are left open. The last Path Conversion choice is Outer Edge. This selection creates a very tight clipping path to the graphic that has been traced. I use this frequently to make an object that I can fill with solid white (or a light gradient) and send to the back so the line work stands out on colored backgrounds.

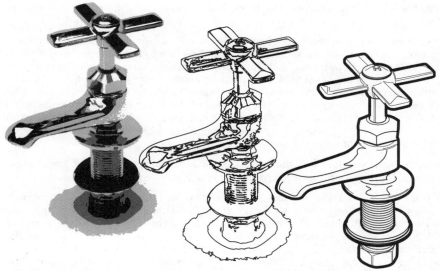

Figure 6-8: The faucet on the left is a 16-color trace to grayscale; the center drawing is the same trace without fills; and the right drawing was done with the Pen tool.

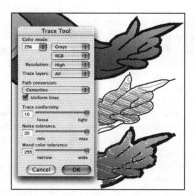

Figure 6-9: Trace tool options include the Uniform option. The original image is at the top, Uniform is selected in the middle, and at the bottom Uniform has been deselected.

Trace Conformity deals with just how tight you want the tracing to be to the original. Higher numbers make a tighter conformity to the object, and also place more points on the path. This also makes a larger file. Noise Tolerance is used as a means to get rid of stray pixels (noise) in a low-quality image. The higher the number you input here, the less noise you'll trace. Finally, the Wand Color Tolerance slider determines the sensitivity when selecting contiguous color ranges. A small number (0) selects a smaller number of colors; select wider ranges by using a higher number — up to 255.

All these settings are made in preparation for you to click and drag a selection box around the entire graphic, or a part of it. As with most drawing tools, holding down the Shift key constrains the selection to a square. The Trace tool works on type, bitmaps (color or grayscale), and vector graphics.

On the other hand, if you want to select particular colors in an image, such as the eyes, nostrils, and lips of a model for a special effect, use the Trace tool in a Magic Wand manner. Click an area that you want to trace. The Wand Color Tolerance comes into play here. If you end up with too much data in your selection, lower the tolerance until you get what you want. When you click the graphic, the program takes a second or two to make its selection, and then you'll see a row of marching red ants. If you want to add other areas of the image, Shift+click them. Use the same Shift-click to delete areas from a selection. When you're satisfied with your selection (this may take two or three attempts), click the wand on a selected area to open the Wand Options dialog box.

Choose to Trace Selection with the selections you set up in the Trace Dialog box, or Convert Selection Edge to trace the outer perimeter of your selection.

The Trace tool is often used to turn a bitmap into vector art for export to Flash or Fireworks. Be careful — depending on your settings, you can make a tracing that is many times larger than the original bitmap. You can also use the Trace tool operation to replace a graphic, which is very useful if you have a bitmap that you want to distort — for example by placing it on the Perspective Grid. The bitmap won't distort on the Perspective Grid, but if you do a nominal tracing of the bitmap, it will go onto the grid with no problems. For more information, see Table 6-2 above. Depending on its size (and importance), most viewers won't even notice that the image was posterized.

The Knife tool (K, 7)

You can use the Knife tool to cut paths in a couple different ways. Double-click the Knife tool icon to open its dialog box, which presents you with two choices: Freehand and Straight. The Freehand knife works just like the Pencil tool: it draws a freeform cutting line wherever you drag the mouse. If you draw it across a *selected* path, the path is cut where the knife intersected it. Because all open paths must have an anchor point at each end, two points are created at the intersection. If you want to remove a section of the path, make another cut and deselect the path. Then select the section you want to remove, and cut or delete it. You have the option of creating a cut of a definite width, which is like using a paintbrush to wipe out a section of a path. All you have to do is adjust the slider in the dialog box to determine the cut's width. Another option is to leave the path cut, or Close Cut Paths. If you choose to close the paths, the path is where you want it, but an additional point (or points) is placed to one side of the path. When you have chosen a specific width to the cut, closing the cut path makes the path look as if you've taken a bite out of it. The tool places a point on each side of the width of the cut and continues pushing the path away from the cut, but in the shape of the cursor (which is a circle the diameter of the cut you selected). The last option you have is to have a Tight Fit to the cut. This option tries to maintain the location of the cut points on the path. Remember that you are cutting a Beziér curve, and that curve might not fall exactly where a point can be placed according to the program's math. So when you cut the path, the two end points may move slightly. If you're after precision, select both points and use the Align panel to center the points on each other vertically and horizontally.

On the CD in the Movies folder is a movie named Knife tool.mov.

Finally, there's the Straight knife action. Instead of drawing a wiggly line around your page, this selection lets you make a perfectly straight line, which facilitates placing the cut exactly where you want it. By its nature the Straight knife goes only from one side of an object to another, but if the object's path winds around (think of a dollar sign), the knife cuts the path every time it crosses the object. The Freehand knife can cut a path many times, even if you backtrack on the path. Holding down the Shift key while using the Straight knife constrains the direction of the cutting path to 45-degree increments, but the Shift key does absolutely nothing for the Freehand knife.

Viewing tools

In discussing Viewing tools, I mean the tools you use to navigate around the FreeHand document. The Hand or Grabber tool, and the Zoom tool both lie near the bottom of the Tools panel.

The Hand/Grabber tool (Spacebar)

FreeHand old-timers worked without this tool as a concept in a Tools panel until FreeHand 10. This latest version of the program places the Hand in the Tools panel. Select it and click somewhere in the FreeHand window. As you drag the mouse, you move the pasteboard in the window. Long-time users can still press the Spacebar to bring this tool up temporarily, instead of selecting the tool in the toolbox. No matter how you select the tool, you can cover a lot of screen real estate in a click/drag or two.

The Zoom tool

Zoom in or zoom out on the page with this tool (Spacebar+ Control (Command) or Spacebar+Control+Alt Spacebar+CommandOpt). The Zoom tool has been in the toolbox forever, but I find it much quicker to hold down the keyboard shortcuts: Spacebar+ Control (Control) to Zoom in, and add the Alt (Opt) key to Zoom out. Any trick that can save me a trip to a Tools panel or menu is something I like to learn and use. The point at which you click the cursor on the page becomes the center of the window when the view changes.

Color tools

Although these two items are just boxes, and not really "tools," they are located in the toolbox. They function much as the Swatches panel, but if you have two monitors, these two boxes are probably closer to your page than the Swatches panel is.

The Stroke and Fill color boxes

Both of these boxes work exactly the same way. One box applies to an object's stroke, and the other box determines the object's fill. The same explanation of their workings suffices for both. If the box has a color in it, any object you make (excepting text) has that color. The box with a red slash in it indicates a color of None for the stroke or fill. The color attributes of any object you select are indicated in these two boxes as well.

To change the color in the box—and therefore in present or future elements—you can drag a swatch of color from the Swatches panel, the Mixer panel, or the Tints panel. You can also use the Eyedropper tool to drag a color onto the color box. A more efficient method can be to click the box itself. A pop-up menu appears (see Figure 6-10) displaying either colors in the Swatches menu, or a grid of Web-safe color cubes. As you place the cursor over a color in the menu, the color's name and RGB or CMYK breakdown appears in a text field.

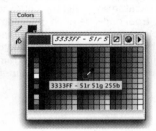

Figure 6-10: Flyout Stroke and Fill color menu

Next to the text field, a box with a red slash in it appears. Click this to give the element a color of None. To the right of that is a color wheel icon. When clicked, you get the Color Picker for further color choices. A PC shows a window with 56 color choices. A Mac has menus for CMYK, Crayons, HSV, Web Safe Colors, or RGB from which to choose. The color menu also has a pop-up Options menu that you activate by clicking the triangle in the top-right corner. When that menu is open, you can choose between Swatches and Color Cubes.

Description of Tools in the Main Toolbar

The Main toolbar runs across the top of the screen by default. If you have a penchant for floating panels, you can easily pull the toolbar into the window while you have Windows ➪ Toolbars ➪ Customize selected. This toolbar has within it all the controls you need for basic FreeHand functions. There are 16 controls in the default program setup, but you can remove or add as many controls as you want to. Those default controls or commands are listed in Table 6-3.

Table 6-3: FreeHand Default Controls and Commands

Control	Command
🗋	Create a new document
📂	Open an existing document
💾	Save the active file
📲	Import a graphic object or file
🖨	Print the document

Control	Command
	Print a section of the document
	Open the Align panel
	Lock selected objects
	Unlock selected objects
	Open Find and Replace
	Open Object inspector
	Open Transform panel
	Open Swatches panel
	Open Color Mixer panel
	Open Layers panel
	Open Library panel

Xtras or Necessities?

FreeHand has many main-line tools for you to work with that are a core part of the program. Other features are added to the program in the form of Xtras. FreeHand comes out of the box with about a dozen and a half Xtras that make your life easier. Third-party Xtras can also be found on the Web (start at www.macromedia.com). Xtras will look to you like any other tool, but they aren't hard-wired into the program. Instead, they work within the program.

The great news is that they work. You can place their icons in the Main toolbar, or in the Tools panel. My default setup has a Main toolbar filled with three full rows of mainstream tools and Xtras that I use all the time. If you're short on window space, you can always access Xtras through the Xtras menu in the FreeHand menu. Here's a short description of the default Xtras in alphabetical order.

Tip

The top item in the Xtras menu is Repeat (specific Xtra tool listed here) Xtra. This can be a real time-saver when you're doing repetitive tasks.

✦ **Animate: Release to Layers** — Takes objects in a blend and places them on new, separate layers for animation or export to SWF (learn all about ShockWave Flash format in Chapters 11 and 12).

✦ **Chart** — Create objects that can be used as the "bars" in charts. This Xtra makes a pictograph for that purpose.

✦ **Cleanup** — Includes the following four controls:

• Correct Direction — Used for odd-even fills in compound paths

• Remove Overlap — Creates compound path from object crossing itself (as in making an "x")

• Reverse Direction — Switches beginning and end points of path

• Simplify — Reduces number of points in a path using user input; attempts to maintain path integrity

✦ **Color Control** — Sliders allow change in color makeup in CMYK, RGB, or HSL modes.

✦ **Convert to Grayscale** — Changes all colors in selected objects to grayscale. Color data is lost.

✦ **Create** — Includes the following three controls:

• Blend — Blends compound paths just as Modify blends normal paths.

• Emboss — Makes crude embossing effect by cloning, offsetting, and modifying colors of an object.

• Trap — Used when light and dark colors abut each other in a print job. The press can go out of register minutely, causing the paper to show between the abutting colors. Trapping eliminates any show-through due to press misregistration.

✦ **Darken Colors** — Decreases brightness of colors in 10 percent increments.

✦ **Delete** — Includes the following two controls:

• Delete Empty Text Blocks — Discards text blocks in document that contain no data

• Delete Unused Named Colors — Discards colors that have been dragged into the Swatches panel without being named

✦ **Desaturate Colors** — Incrementally reduces intensity of color, ultimately becoming gray.

✦ **Distort** — Includes the following two choices:

• Add Points — Places a point between every two points on a path

• Fractalize — Makes abstract, geometric patterns

✦ **Import RGB Color Table** — A color table contains all the colors in a bitmap. Use this to import those colors to FreeHand for use in modifying an existing drawing or making a new one using the same color scheme.

✦ **IPTC** — Found under Other: File Info. Used by newspapers and magazines to keep track of copyright, author/artist, date, and other information.

✦ **Lighten Colors** — Increases brightness of colors in 10 percent increments.

✦ **Name All Colors** — Click this Xtra to move colors that have been dragged into the Swatches panel without being named in one step.

✦ **Path Operations** — Includes eight of my favorite tools, each requiring one object on top of another:

- Crop — Top object removes anything belonging to the lower object that lies outside the top object's borders
- Divide — Makes separate elements obtained by overlaps
- Expand Stroke — Makes a closed and filled path of constant width centered on original path
- Inset Path — Makes a concentric path inside (positive numbers) or outside (negative numbers) a selected path
- Intersect — Retains only areas that overlap; discards other areas
- Punch — Takes a "bite" out of lower object
- Transparency — Gives appearance of transparency by making a mix of top and bottom object colors
- Union — Combines both objects into one single object with a single outline

✦ **Randomize Named Colors** — Say you want to know what a drawing would look like if you suddenly experienced one of the acid flashbacks from the sixties your weird uncle tells you about — this Xtra changes colors for no apparent reason. For example, you draw a handful of six flowers. Each flower has a different (named) color. Clone the bouquet, and use this Xtra to get a group of flowers that may be more abstract or random than you could have created on your own. Every time you click it, the colors go off in another direction.

✦ **Saturate** — Increase the intensity of colors — move away from gray.

✦ **Sort Color List By Name** — Alphabetical colors, why not? Doesn't make much sense if the name is 30r 24g 65b, though — name the colors first.

Summary

This chapter covered the tools that make FreeHand work. It started with a definition of vector art and went on to explain each of the tools in the Tools panel and Main toolbar. Finally, the chapter covered the specifics of using FreeHand Xtras.

✦   ✦   ✦

Getting Around in a FreeHand Document

This chapter explains how to work with FreeHand's key tools and features. Understanding these tasks and processes will help you work efficiently and with less stress.

Modifying Objects

Remember how Clark Kent used to step inside a phone booth to change into his Superman outfit? FreeHand uses transformation handles for the same purpose. First you must have Double-click enables transform handles selected in the General tab of FreeHand's preferences. Then, use the Pointer tool to double-click an object, and eight transformation handles connected by a dotted line appear around your selection (see Figure 7-1). A double circle marks the center point of the selection. You can select as many objects as you want — the handles adjust to fit the array you choose.

Transforming with the Pointer tool

Some artists never use the transform handles. Instead, they prefer to choose individual tools to rotate, skew, or whatever. However, I like one-stop shopping, and one-tool transforming. With just the Pointer tool, I can scale, rotate, skew, and move everything that's selected within the transform handles. I'm able to perform several operations without changing tools. I only have to move the cursor to a different spot around the handles.

When using the Pointer tool, all transformations are relative to the opposite side or corner handle that you've chosen. If you select a top-right corner point, the bottom-left corner point will be anchored. However, if you have the transformation handles showing, and you decide to use the Transform panel (so you can enter specific amounts of change, or add a certain number of copies as the changes are made), changes are relative to the center point of the transformation handle's group.

Figure 7-1: The transformation handles allow you to scale, skew, and rotate everything within the selection.

Scaling an object

To scale an object proportionately, click and drag on a corner handle while holding down the Shift key. To change the vertical dimension without modifying the width, select a handle in the middle of the horizontal transformation border; for a horizontal change, use the middle handles on either vertical side.

Rotating an object

To rotate the selection, move the Pointer tool near a corner transformation handle, and the cursor will turn into an arc with arrowheads on either end. Click and drag to rotate the selection around the center point. If you want the object to revolve around a different point, move the center point to that location. Moving the center point is a matter of clicking the mouse on the double circle icon and moving it to its new location — which can be anywhere on the page or Pasteboard.

Skewing an object

To skew a selection, place the Pointer tool along the dotted lines connecting the transformation handles to convert the cursor to a double-arrow cursor. Click and drag to skew the artwork. To constrain the skewing to horizontal, vertical, or 45-degree increments, hold down the Shift key.

Moving objects with the transformation handles is more useful than you'd think. If you dragged a selection marquee around several objects, depending on whether those objects are grouped or not, and how inclusive your selection was, you may have selected several points on a path but neglected one or two. When you apply a transformation — even as simple as moving the selection — that lonely point or two will remain fixed on the layout. Instead, make your selection and double-click any of the selected objects. That brings up the transformation handles with the bonus of selecting all parts of every object (making a temporary group of everything), so everything will transform as a unit. If you hold down the Control (Command) key, you can select a new object, deselecting the original object in the process. The Control (Command) or Alt (Option) key will deselect other objects and select only the object you've clicked. The benefit — or trap — of using these keys is that the center point remains in the same location as when you originally invoked the transformation handles. Holding down the Shift key with either of those other keys enables you to add an object — and leave the center point where it was in the first place. If you hold down the Alt (Option) key after you begin scaling, rotating, or skewing, you perform that modification on a copy of the original selection. To further confuse the issue, you can have several objects selected with the Transformation Handles, and hold down Shift+ Alt (Shift+Option) to deselect an object within the grouping. If you use the Option/Alt key by itself on a non-grouped object within the Transformation Handles, you will select the section of path instead of the entire object.

Bend tool

The Bend tool sits on my Main menu bar or in the Xtras panel and rarely gets used, but when it's needed, there's absolutely no replacement tool. The transformation the Bend tool performs is pretty simple and straightforward: it bends the path between any two points. I use the tool to make a splash or an explosion in seconds. In the example in Figure 7-2, I drew several ellipses with different fill colors around a central ellipse. I selected the ellipses, choose Add Points from the Xtras menu, and clicked the Bend tool in the center of the mass and dragged it down, creating the center image in this figure. The points of each object stay in place, but the path between points is bowed out from the mouse-click. After the paths were removed, the bottom half of the object was selected and modified with the 3D Rotation tool to complete the splash effect. In shades of green, you could make some pretty good bushes or trees.

Figure 7-2: The Bend tool can be effective for making a splash.

I really like the Bend tool when I need an explosive look that needs to appear random. In this type of bending, drag the mouse up or to the left. The left example in Figure 7-3 shows how to make a circle of thorns — it wouldn't take too much to put radial gradients in them to make them look three-dimensional. I modified the second example by using Add Points several times, and the Bend tool multiple times. Finally, on the right, I ran Add Points again, and gave all the shapes the same fill color.

Figure 7-3: The Bend tool also makes some pretty good points and explosions.

Lens Fills

Lenses don't get used often enough. FreeHand has had them since version 8, and it introduced artists to transparency in vector art. A lens fill can only be applied to open or closed paths. To clarify that statement, if you elect to use Show Fill for New Open Paths in the Preferences menu, a fill appears as soon as you draw the third point in a path. I keep this option turned off so I can see what I'm drawing, but if you have it turned on, you can have any type of fill you want, including another lens fill.

At any rate, the lens fill is capable of doing many things, and an object can be covered with Lens fill effects up to eight deep. The ninth lens fill negates the bottom fill in the drawing stack. These fills are usually placed above other objects in your drawing or layout because they affect anything beneath themselves. All lens fills convert spot colors to CMYK values for printing. This isn't a concern if you're working for the Web, but it's a good thing to remember if you're printing a map or brochure. Keep in mind that this is a very memory-intensive operation, and you can choke the best printer if you have too many effects going at the same time. You're better off thinking the project out a little and being efficient in your drawing. A lens fill can create any and all of the following effects:

✦ **Transparency** — Using this fill gives the appearance of taking a sheet of colored cellophane or plastic and placing it over the other objects in your layout. You can choose any color you want, and adjust the amount of transparency — zero shows no effect at all, 100 percent is opaque color.

✦ **Magnify** — This lens is great for enlarging areas of a drawing or map for clarity. You magnify objects under the lens by entering a number from 1 to 100 in the text field, or moving the slider. The results of a high enlargement will amaze you (see Figure 7-4).

✦ **Invert** — If you ever need to invert the colors of part of your drawing, choose this type of lens fill. It turns blue into yellow, red into green — simply changes colors to their complementary colors on the color wheel. Remember, this will be CMYK.

✦ **Lighten** — You can use this lens as a device to create depth, brightness from an external light source, or in text that has been converted to paths and placed over elements in an illustration. A setting of zero creates no change; 100 percent creates a totally white overlay.

✦ **Darken** — This lens adds black to colors (including the background color or white), darkening everything beneath the lens by the percentage you choose.

✦ **Monochrome** — The monochrome lens fill changes everything under the lens to varying shades of the color you've chosen. A multicolored drawing will appear as if it were done in black and white and printed in your chosen color.

Figure 7-4: The text above the heron's head on the right was 1.5-point before converting to paths. Notice how well it enlarges (700 percent) with the Magnify Lens fill.

A lens fill cannot be applied to everything. You cannot get a lens fill effect on an EPS file, or on a clipping path. You won't see any difference if you apply a lens fill to live text. However, if you convert the text to paths, its fill can be a lens fill. Remember to keep a live version of the text somewhere safe on another page or on the Pasteboard in case you need to make changes or adjustments in fonts later.

In the Lens Fill panel, you have the following three options to check:

✦ **Centerpoint** is a fairly easy concept to follow. When you choose a lens fill, you can decide to have the fill apply to objects immediately beneath the fill, or you can select an object elsewhere on the document as the subject of the fill. The first fill method uses the fill just as you would any other fill, but the second method requires the Centerpoint. Click this check box, and a small diamond cluster (identical to the Paste Inside centerpoint) appears in the middle of the object that is being filled. Use the Pointer tool to move the centerpoint over another area of the document, and that area appears in your lens-filled object—with the adjustments dictated by the type of lens you've chosen. You can see where the various centerpoints were placed on each of the eight lenses in Figure 7-5. After you apply a lens fill to an object using Centerpoint, you can move the object anywhere in the document and the centerpoint remains fixed; the image in the lens fill continues showing the image around the centerpoint.

Figure 7-5: A screenshot of eight lens fills and their respective centerpoints

✦ **Snapshot** is a neat feature, but requires caution because changes to the original elements affected by the lens will not change in the lens fill—that's why it's called a snapshot. For example, consider that you are designing three boxes of wine, and the company wants to use vector art instead of photography. You could draw the first comprehensive layout (comp) with Chablis in the dynamically tilted wineglass, and place a lens fill on another page that will be printed for the client to discuss. Using the Centerpoint option to align the graphics and Snapshot, the wine in the lens fill remains Chablis as you make changes for the Rosé and Burgundy versions. Consequently, you could make changes in the name and color in the original comp, and have all three boxes (as snapshots) lined up for review. If you made a change in the comp—such as the client's new Blue Blush wine that will replace Rosé—just clicking the Snapshot option off, to deselect it, turns the lens back into a live lens.

✦ **Objects Only** is a little tougher to explain, but easy to see. When this option is selected, only objects within the lens outline are affected—empty areas are transparent. A solid-colored background is considered an object; the document background is not. When it is deselected, the lens effect fills the entire lens area without regard to elements beneath the lens, as demonstrated in Figure 7-6. The birds at the top of the figure are printed at 85 percent black, and the text (converted to paths) is solid black. The rectangle at the bottom of the figure contains several elements. At the bottom of everything is a rectangle with a 20 percent black tone. The rounded-corner rectangle was drawn and divided into eight separate sections, with each section receiving a different lens fill combination. All have Centerpoint turned on to place the images correctly within the lens.

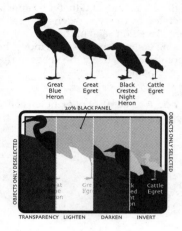

Figure 7-6: The effects of lens fill options

The top lenses are set with Objects Only selected, and you can plainly see the 20 percent tone in the background. This shows that only the objects in the area under the centerpoint have been used in the lens. The page's background appears transparent. The bottom lenses were built with Objects Only deselected. Here, you can see that the background area, as well as the objects, has been treated with the lens effect.

No gradient lens fills

As much as FreeHand artists would like to see it, a lens fill doesn't provide a way to get a gradient of any kind. Workarounds exist, but they stand a good chance of choking the printer, and aren't generally recommended. You can find workaround details at the FreeHand Source (www.freehandsource.com), where Ian Kelleigh has compiled a large mass of FreeHand tricks.

I use the Lighten Lens to cover a photograph that I'm tracing. (I place it on a layer between the photo and my drawing and lock both the photo and Lens fill layers.) The reduced contrast makes it easier to see the paths that I'm drawing.

My friend uses Lens fills with Snapshot selected so she can make a dynamic master page layout of business cards. This would also work for disk labels or any other printing situation that requires duplicate multiple images.

1. Make a 2-inch by 3.5-inch page and lay out one business card with the information that is common to all the cards. Be sure to convert all text to paths, and keep a copy of the live text somewhere safe in the document in case you need to make changes later. You can also put guidelines where they're appropriate.

2. Add a letter-sized page, and place a vertical guideline at the center.

3. Draw a rectangular selection the same size as the business card, and give it the Magnify (set to 1), Lighten or Darken (set to zero), or Transparency (also set to zero) Lens fill.

4. Turn on Snapshot and Centerpoint.

Cloudy lens outlook?

You do stand the chance of ending up with an orphaned lens fill. That's when you have a document containing a lens fill, but the elements that make up the lens are not to be found. You can't ungroup it or split it, and a Cut Contents command does absolutely nothing. You can tell that there's a Paste Inside going on by the Centerpoint icon, but nothing seems to work. At that point, check the Fill panel and hope for a lens fill. Keep in mind that FreeHand enables you to export documents in older versions of FreeHand — even versions that didn't have lens fills.

Just export the orphaned lens as an older FreeHand file. Don't try to change the type of fill it is, or attempt to remove it — just choose File ➪ Export ➪ FreeHand 7. Because there were no lens fills at that time, the document works with what it has, which happens to end up being a simple clipping path. Open the new FreeHand 7 file in FreeHand 10, select the lens, and choose Edit ➪ Cut Contents. You get more than you bargained for — any element that was under the lens appears in this new document, and it is in its full, uncropped state. If the Magnify lens was used, the elements are enlarged to the extent the lens was set.

Composite Paths

A composite path is simply the combining of two or more paths into one single path. A longer definition would include an explanation about using the Join, Split, Union, Divide, Intersect, Punch, Crop, and Transparency commands, and the conversion of text to paths. A few preferences can also affect the outcome of a composite path.

Using Join/Split

Paths have a set direction. Rectangle, Polygon, and Ellipse tools all draw in a clockwise direction. The direction in which you draw or place points sets the direction of the path when you use the Line, Pen, and Bezigon tools. This concept must be foremost in your mind when you make composite paths, but it's most important when making composite paths from multiple closed paths. The best way to provide for a possible compound path is to draw in a clockwise direction on the outside of objects, and counterclockwise on the "holes." As a rule, type fonts are built this way to create a "natural" compound path if the type is converted to paths.

Note

To be confident that everything will work as you've planned, you can use one of two tools found in three locations. The Correct Direction Xtra is found in the Xtras ➪ Cleanup menu, or on your Main menu bar if you've put it there. It's also found in the Modify ➪ Alter Path menu. These tools will change the direction of paths if it is necessary in order to make a compound path.

You have two ways to combine two or more open paths into a single path. You can continue drawing one path, and place a point on an existing end point on another path. You can also connect the two paths by choosing Modify ➪ Join. This command does one of two things, depending on the physical relationship of the paths to each other: It connects the two end points that are nearest each other; or, if the four end points are equidistant, it connects the end points (not the beginning points) of both lines. In the latter instance, changing the direction of a line changes the connecting points, because the end points on the path are reversed. In real life, if you want two specific points to connect, you'll save a lot of time by continuing one path and connecting to the other path.

Working with closed paths expands the possibilities even more. Figure 7-7 begins on the left with a grouping of herons and egrets of different colors and fills. In the Objects inspector, an option named Even/Odd Fill utilizes the direction of the paths as explained previously. The center illustration shows what happens when the four objects are selected and Modify ➪ Join is used with Even/Odd Fill turned on (default). Notice how overlapping objects change color to transparent and the bottom object's color (black here). If you rearrange the colors of the objects, the final result will have a different color, as well. On the left side of the figure, the Great Blue Heron at the rear has been given a light gray tone, and the Cattle Egret (smallest bird here) was given a black fill. The group was joined and Even/Odd Fill was turned off.

Figure 7-7: The effect of Join with Even/Odd Fill turned on (middle) and off (right)

The opposite of Join is Split. If you select a single point on a path and choose Modify ➪ Split, the point turns into two disconnected points, and the path becomes two paths. If you have a compound path, such as the birds in Figure 7-6, each shape becomes a separate entity, and all the shapes gain the same fill and stroke attributes of the bottom object — in this example everything turns black. The overall effect is the same as choosing the Union command, except there are the four original shapes with the same fill. The Union command presents one single shape.

The Combine commands

I use Union, Divide, Intersect, and Punch so often that I've installed buttons for them on my Main toolbar so I don't have to travel through the Modify ➪ Combine menu. They work only on closed paths. Figure 7-8 gives an example of each command. Here's how they work. The

Path Operations Consume Original Paths option in Preferences enables you to either delete the original paths or keep them. Holding down the Shift key as you select the various commands achieves the same effect without the trip to the Preferences menu, and only affects the present operation.

Union

Union combines all selected overlapping objects into one single element, as shown in the top-left corner of Figure 7-8. If the objects do not overlap, a compound path is created that enables you to apply gradient fills to the various objects as a whole (this concept is explained later in the chapter). The new object contains the fill and stroke of the bottom object. If you hold down the Shift key as you select the command from the Modify ➪ Alter Path menu or the button in the menu, you'll think you've been tricked, because the unionized object appears. Move the new object, and you'll find the original group of objects lying below it. I use this feature at times when I want to apply a solid fill — usually white — to the objects so the drawing appears to have a clipping path when it's placed on other backgrounds. I just select the whole drawing, click Union (while holding down the Shift key held), and send the new shape to the back. Then I give it the stroke and fill I want.

Divide

An example of Divide is shown in the top right of Figure 7-8 (shapes in the example have been moved for clarity). This command makes a new object wherever objects overlap. Two long rectangles at right angles to each other in a cross formation would result in five separate objects. Each of the objects retains its fill and stroke. The new objects can be removed or moved around as you see fit. This command is the basis for the Transparency command, and if you experiment with it a bit, you'll find all kinds of uses for it.

Punch

The Punch tool is the topmost element in your group. It takes a bite out of the element immediately beneath it. Sadly, it doesn't go all the way through a grouping. To accomplish that, you must continue clicking the Punch button. In Figure 7-8, the middle left example used Punch for the top two birds, and the bottom two birds were selected and punched again. You can get some very striking effects in your artwork with this tool.

Intersect

The same group of birds was attacked with the Intersect command, and it left what you see in Figure 7-8 (middle right). This command is really only useful on objects that overlap. If all of the objects do not overlap in one place or another, the entire mass disappears (unless Path Operations Consume Original Paths has been deselected). In this example, only a portion of the smallest bird happens to overlap all the other birds. The result of Intersect has the stroke and fill of the bottom object.

Crop

Crop is the opposite of Punch in that anything under it will be captured inside the topmost shape. The top shape loses its fill and stroke, but the other objects retain theirs. The bottom left image in Figure 7-8 is an example of Crop at work.

Figure 7-8: Six examples of compound path construction

Transparency

This command (Figure 7-8 bottom right) changes the opacity of various objects. Transparency is similar to Punch in that it only goes one level deep at a time. In this example, Transparency was applied to the bottom two birds, followed by the top two birds. When you invoke this command, a dialog box opens to enable you to change the level of transparency. Here, the levels were set at 25 percent both times. If you tear the final results apart, you'll find that the original birds are intact, but a new object inside the topmost object appears to be transparent. In reality, it's a combination of the bottom element impacted by a percentage of the top element.

Text Composite paths

The counters in letterforms — the holes in letters and numbers, such as a, o, e, g, 8, and so on — become a special problem when you convert text to paths. Simple letterforms such as an L or J are converted to simple closed paths. Letters with counters must be converted to compound paths, however, and they are created with counter-directional paths for that purpose.

You can't have a gradient fill in text. Instead, you must convert the text to paths. At that point, you can do pretty much what you want with the text (except edit it). It has become a graphic element in the form of a compound path.

This brings up some interesting situations. Fonts are built within invisible guidelines; the top of the letter won't go above the ascent, and the bottom won't drop below the descent. This rule seems to be broken on many fonts, where ascenders, such as the vertical paths on an h, b, or l rise above the height of a capital letter. However, that only serves to move the ascent to the height of the lowercase letters' ascender. Descenders on p, g; swash f, and so on go to various depths according to the font's design. All this causes a confusing mix of tones if you want to place a gradient fill inside the letters, as shown at the top of Figure 7-9. The bold gray line shows the midpoint of the gradient, and the text has been given a stroke for clarity. Notice how much the midpoint of the gradient varies up and down from one letter to another. It's obvious that all letters aren't of equal size. It also creates a cacophony of color in the text.

Figure 7-9: The effects of gradient fills in text that has been converted to compound paths

To get around the seemingly haphazard gradient balance, use Modify ➪ Join to make all the letters in the text group into a compound path. (Yes, the counters are now compound-compound paths.) In this way, the gradient goes from the absolute bottom of the group to the absolute top, and the tonal effect is even. The letters at the bottom of Figure 7-9 have been joined, but the gradient fill is exactly the same fill as the example above it. The text now has a homogenous appearance.

Fills and gradients in compound paths

The same logic holds true with "normal" compound paths, as shown in Figure 7-10. The flock on the left side is individual shapes with equally individual gradient fills, but the right flock has been joined, making a compound path that employs a single gradient. Sometimes you want the effect shown on the left, and at other times you want the effect shown on the right; it all depends on the job, your mood, and creativity.

Figure 7-10: Normal compound paths

Working with Paths

If you're going to make FreeHand work for you, you must learn to control paths. I'll assume that you're capable of placing and modifying points on a path. This section explains how those paths can be manipulated to suit your purpose.

Pressure Pen on OS X

Unfortunately, the Variable Stroke pen does not work with a pressure sensitive pen (Wacom tablet) if your machine is running FreeHand 10 on OS X. The pen itself works; you just can't obtain a variable stroke through the pressure sensitivity of the pen. It does work fine on all other Mac and PC operating systems, however, and has been fixed in FreeHand MX.

Adjusting path between points

I'm fairly methodical, so I like to place a point and control the path as I draw an object. Some of you like to place multiple points in a hurry, and go back and modify each to fit. For you, there's the Subselect tool. Just click the tool between points on a path and you can bend the path. The bending is accompanied by the extension of control handles (that can be further extended or withdrawn). This will not work on a path made with the Rectangle or Ellipse tool — unless you first ungroup the path (see Figure 7-11).

Figure 7-11: An ungrouped ellipse turned into a teardrop with a single click and drag

You also use this same tool or Pen/Bezigon tool plus the Alt (Option) key to adjust individual control handles. If you have the Subselect tool active and hold down the Alt (Option) key, you duplicate the object. If you click the Subselect tool on a segment and begin to move the mouse, you move only the object.

Add points

When you need more points on a path, simply choose Xtras ⇨ Distort ⇨ Add Points. FreeHand places a point between every two points in the path. These points are placed equidistantly between existing points, and you can add as many as you want. This Xtra works on envelopes, as well.

For more information on envelopes, refer to Chapter 11.

Roughen/Smooth

These two Xtras distort paths by changing the path's texture. Activate the Xtra by clicking its icon to open the Roughen dialog box. You'll see a slider and two buttons. The slider determines how much of a change you want to make to the path — the smaller the number, the less the distortion. However, the actual degree of distortion is determined by how far you click and drag the mouse. The two buttons are Roughen and Smooth. Both add points to the line, with Roughen adding corner points and Smooth adding curve points. The number of points added to the path is based on the slider's position, but the number in the field doesn't really correspond to the actual number of points. In Figure 7-12, two identical circles were distorted with a setting of 9, and both circles ended up with a total of 32 points. The left circle has been smoothed, and you can see curve points and control handles on the selected half. The center circle was roughened the same degree, and you can see that no control handles are on the points. The square on the far right was smoothed with a value of 3 (creating 8 curve points), and roughened on the other edges with a value of 35, resulting in 128 corner points.

Figure 7-12: Both Roughen and Smooth add points and distort the path.

Expand Stroke

This is another Xtra that is good to get to know. It's useful in quite a few instances for both boilerplate drawing and line/style techniques. Choose a unit of measurement that you're comfortable with in choosing a stroke width before you open this Xtra, because you can't make a change after the dialog box is open. My inch-to-point mental conversion abilities are severely hampered, so I change the units of measurement to points or picas. That way I'm converting apples to apples (or Windows to Windows).

Tip

There is an easy workaround to the units-of-measurement situation in virtually any of FreeHand's value-input text fields. Just type the desired units, such as 0p4 or 4pt to get a 4-point line. If you want a quarter-inch measurement and the units are set to millimeters, type .25in; if you want metric measurements, use mm or cm as a suffix to the number.

Select a path and double-click the Expand Stroke icon to open the dialog box shown in Figure 7-13. The stroke width of your selected path will be in the dialog box. If you want to, you can leave this value, or you can move the slider or enter a new number in the text field. Choose the type of cap and join, and enter a miter limit before clicking the OK button.

Figure 7-13: The Expand Stroke dialog box converts a path into a compound path.

The result of your Expand Stroke depends on the condition of the stroke and fill attributes you have previously set. That is, if you happen to have a red fill and a 4-point green stroke set as your default, the new compound path also has those attributes. That may be exactly what you had in mind. If not, just make the appropriate changes. I like to use Expand Stroke to make wires or other objects by using the expanded stroke as a clipping path and placing objects inside the clipping path with Paste Inside.

Inset path

This is a dual-purpose tool; even though it's called Inset Path, you can also "outset" a path. By default, this Xtra is designed to move the path inwards on itself by the distance you enter in the text field or determine by using the slider, as shown in Figure 7-14. Note that the path itself is going to change — if you want to see the original path and the results of your Inset Path activity, you must first clone the original path.

Figure 7-14: The Inset Path dialog box

The Steps field in the dialog box determines the number of iterations of the object that will be inset. Six steps were used for the example in Figure 7-15. The left group of boxes was set for a Uniform inset, the middle group is Farther, and the right group is Nearer.

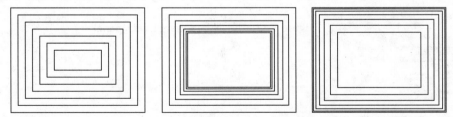

Figure 7-15: Inset Paths, left to right: Uniform, Farther, and Nearer

To outset an object, put a minus sign (–) in front of the number in the Inset field. In this manner, you can put round corners on a square box or triangle, as shown in Figure 7-16. The gray objects in the centers of these examples were modified with a negative amount in the Inset Path dialog box. I set the square to a multiple of 2 and Farther and rounded the joins; the star has a multiple of 3, is set to Nearer, and has rounded joins; the triangle has a beveled join. The result of an Inset Path operation is a compound path, giving you many options pertaining to fills, strokes, and transformations.

Figure 7-16: Inset Paths was applied to each of the gray objects (the objects were turned gray after Inset Paths was applied).

FreeHand Layers

You can imagine the layers concept as a drawing done on several sheets of clear acetate. Each layer is transparent and can contain any number and kind of elements. An extremely complicated layout or illustration can be accomplished on a single layer, but placing groups of related objects on their own layer is usually more efficient.

The Layers panel

You can accomplish many things in your illustration through the Layers panel (shown in Figure 7-17). By default, new documents contain a Guides, a Foreground, and a Background layer. To create a new layer, go to the Layers Option pop-up menu triangle in the top-right corner of the panel and choose New Layer. A new layer appears at the top of the layers list, and is named Layer-1, Layer-2, and so on. Double-click the name and type a distinctive name for your new layer. To select a layer, click it to highlight it, as the Logo/drwgs layer is in the figure. When you select anything in the document, that object's layer is automatically highlighted.

Figure 7-17: The all-important Layers panel

You'll notice four icons to the left of the name. A single mouse click on any of the icons switches the function off or on. The check mark indicates visibility (the Lines layer has been turned off, and any elements on it are not visible). The circle tells you whether a layer is shown in Preview or Keyline views (the Middle layer's objects are in Keyline view). The padlock icon indicates whether a layer is locked. When the padlock icon is open, objects can be placed on that layer and modified. If the padlock is closed, as the Top layer is here, nothing on that layer can be selected or moved, and items cannot be placed on that layer. Drag a color to the square icon, and elements use that color as the bounding box and other selection indicators for that layer. This is a great aid if you're trying to select something that's in a mass of layers; Alt (Option) clicking the mouse takes you down a layer at a time, and you can watch the colors change to find the layer you want. The last element in the Layers panel is the separator bar between the Background layer and the rest. Any layer below the separator bar doesn't print and is grayed-out onscreen. You can either move the separator bar above layers, or move a layer below the separator bar, the result is the same.

Assigning objects to layers

Refer to Figure 7-17. If you draw another object that you want to place on the Lines layer, keep the new object selected and click the Lines layer. The object disappears so you have to click the blank spot to bring back the check mark and the new object's visibility. Then you realize that the lines are being blocked by something in the Top layer. Correct this by clicking and holding the mouse on the layer's name and dragging it to the new location. Locked layers can be moved up and down in the list, even though you can't modify elements on them.

Selecting objects on layers

When you need to select an object, it's a matter of clicking it with the Pointer tool. But what if you want to select all the elements on a layer (for instance, if you want to change the stroke width, or font style)? Just hold down the Alt (Option) key as you click the layer's name in the Layers panel, and all the elements on the layer are selected at the same time.

Summary

This chapter gave you information on working with drawing elements in FreeHand. You learned the ins and outs of Lens fills. Creation and modification of composite paths were explained, including the Union, Divide, Crop, Transparency, Punch, and Intersect commands. Then you discovered several features that make new objects out of old objects, such as the Inset Path and Expand Stroke Xtras. Finally, you found out how easy it is to organize a project by efficient use of layers.

✦　　✦　　✦

Using FreeHand Symbols and Styles

This chapter shows you how to streamline your work processes through the use of symbols and styles. You also get a handle on the Graphic Hose tool to make some truly creative drawings.

The Difference Between Symbols and Styles

Symbols are graphic objects, text items, and master pages that are placed in a Library for convenient retrieval at any time. For example, you might create a symbol for a company logo. Another purpose for a symbol would be an address line or "text slug" that you use frequently, such as on brochures, flyers, or Web pages. The basic need for a symbol is anything that will be used more than once in a document or in several documents.

Styles, on the other hand, are divided into two types: graphic and text. If you do a lot of drawings with a 1-point green stroke and a magenta fill, you can make a style for that setup. Next time you need that combination, make the drawing in any tool you choose, and simply click the appropriate style to give the selected graphic the style's attributes. Text styles are great if you are making a brochure, manual, or Web page and have items such as headlines, subheads, body copy, indented text, or other formatting situations. Just make a style, insert the Text tool cursor into a block of text, and click the style.

Symbol Management

You may be used to importing files, such as logos, when you need them. That's worked for years, but it takes a couple steps — first you have to save (just in case the computer picks this time to crash on you); then you go to the File menu and select Import or Open, or you click a button in your Main toolbar. Then you have the fun of trying to remember where you've filed the document you need. If you decided to open the document instead of importing it, you have to select everything and copy it. Finally, you place the graphic on your page.

Clicking a symbol in the Library and dragging it to the document is much quicker.

A distinct advantage to working with a symbol is that you can make global changes in a document quickly by editing the symbol. In that way, you can change every instance of an outdated logo in one edit. If a company phone number changes and you have the phone number as part of a symbol, change the number in the symbol, and all the instances of the number are corrected.

It's all in a name

When an element is in the Library, it's called a symbol. Drag the symbol onto the page and it becomes an instance. Choose Modify ⇨ Symbol ⇨ Remove Instance, and the element is a grouped object. Once you've used Remove Instance on a symbol, it will not be affected by any changes you make to the symbol from which it came. The original symbol will not be affected by this command. Ungroup the object and you are back to the original element — providing you haven't changed the symbol.

Getting symbolic

Making a symbol is really pretty simple, and you have a couple ways to accomplish the task. To do it by the book, select whatever it is you want to symbolize, and go to the Modify ⇨ Symbol menu. Choose to make the symbol by copying or converting the object. As previously mentioned, if you choose to use Copy to Symbol, the original remains editable on the page. This is good if you might want to make slight modifications — such as in the beginning stages of a project — or if you know you want different variations of this object to use as other symbols. Conversely, if you know you're not going to be changing the object in the foreseeable future, choose Convert to Symbol. That leaves the object in place on the page, and there's no original to move or throw away.

Either method places a thumbnail image of the new symbol in the Library. It is also listed with a generic name: Graphic-01, Graphic-02, and so on — even if the graphic is a block of text. Double-click the generic name to retype a new name for the symbol.

You can also create a symbol by dragging the object into the Library list window. This alternative uses the Convert to Symbol method to make the symbol. Or, you can select the object and click the plus sign in the lower-left corner of the Library panel to convert the object into a symbol.

Symbols are stored in the Library in alphanumeric order, so sometimes I add leading numbers to the symbol's name to push it up or down the list. You can store symbols in groups of your own choosing. Groups are also sorted alphanumerically within the Library, but you have the option of opening or collapsing groups to conserve room in the Library. I use groups for particular companies, and subgroups within those for text and graphic symbols. I also have groups of "boilerplate" items used in various standard drawings, such as bolt heads, threaded rods, electronic schematic symbols, and so on.

One of the greatest attributes of a symbol — or a style or master page, for that matter — is that it can be exported. Symbols and master pages end up in the Symbols folder in the FreeHand ⇨ English folder, and styles appear in the Styles folder inside the English folder. After exporting a symbol, you can import that same symbol into a new FreeHand document for use.

Using a symbol

Now that you've got a Library full of useful symbols (see Figure 8-1), how do you use them? Just click through the symbol name list in the Library. Each time you select a symbol, its thumbnail appears in the preview window. When you find the one you want, drag the thumbnail or the symbol name onto your document. When you release the mouse, the symbol is selected, and you can start modifying its location and size, as needed.

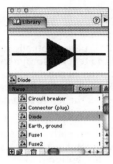

Figure 8-1: This library is filled with electronic schematic symbols.

Editing symbols

Double-click a symbol name or its thumbnail, or click the Library Options pop-up menu triangle in the top-right corner of the panel and select Edit from the menu to open a new window with the symbol in it. You are free to do any modification, including deleting the object and replacing it with something else. When your modifications are complete, just close the window — there's no Save or OK button to worry about in this process. You return to the document window, and all instances of the symbol have the changes you just made to the original. If you used Remove Instance on any symbols, those objects are affected.

Remember that if you decide to edit a symbol, the changes occur only in that particular document. For instance, consider that you created a symbol, and dragged an instance of it onto another document. In the original document, you double-click the symbol to enter the Edit Symbol window, and you make changes to the symbol. Auto-update is selected by default, and will cause the symbol to be updated as soon as you close the Edit Symbol window. But, the symbol in the second document will remain in its original unedited state. If you choose to edit a symbol from its location in the English ➪ Symbols folder, the changes are reflected in any future instances, but do not affect existing instances. Any instances remain in place in their original state.

Style Management

My personal work is eased considerably by my consistent use of styles. I set up styles for particular types of jobs. Each company, package type, or product line has distinct fonts, colors, and other graphic attributes that I make into styles and import as needed. These styles are also part of my templates or master pages, so they're constantly available.

Think about setting up a package line that involves four or five different-sized packages, but has the same look as far as fonts, graphic elements, and instructional drawings. By making a separate style for the product's name, descriptive subhead, bullet point text, and body copy for the first project, you have one-click attribute settings for the next three packages. By using a style, you cut down on the chances of making a mistake by setting the wrong leading, or using the wrong color fill. Styles mean consistency.

You can go to the Stroke panel and select a new stroke weight, or install the Xtras that increase or decrease stroke weights. However, I find it much quicker to have a series of strokes and strokes with fills set as styles so I can quickly click them from the Styles menu that can be placed anywhere on my screen.

Making it with style

Creating a text style is simple. Set any text attributes, including leading, paragraph alignment, color, baseline shift, and so on, the way you want them to be. Leave the text cursor active in the text, and click the Styles Options pop-up menu in the top-right corner of the Styles panel. The first item in the pop-up menu is New. Select New to add the style to the bottom of the Styles panel list with the name Style-01, Style-02, and so on. Double-click the name to rename it something meaningful. Text styles are preceded with an "A" icon.

Stroke and fill styles are just as easy. Draw an object with a closed or open path. Then set up the various attributes, such as stroke weight and color, fill type and color, arrowheads, dashes, and anything else that is necessary. Choose New from the Styles Option pop-up menu. Stroke and fill styles have the same numerical listing as the text styles, but a square icon appears in front of the name. Again, double-click the name to change it to your liking.

You can apply a style before you start working on something, or do the work (set text, draw an object) and then click the appropriate style from the list in the Styles menu, as shown in Figure 8-2. You can also select several objects and apply a style to them all at the same time. You can even apply a graphic style to a text object. Actually, it applies the style to the text block, not the text itself. So you can place text in a stroked box with a solid fill. If you make the text style with the appropriate leading or baseline shift, and have the proper insets or paragraph attributes, you can easily mix text and graphic styles for decorative effects in layouts.

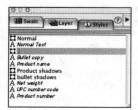

Figure 8-2: The Styles panel can save time and prevent errors.

Editing styles

Inevitably, as soon as you get everything to work, someone will make a change that louses up everything. For a text style edit, select the appropriate style, and choose Edit in the Styles Options pop-up menu. The Edit Style menu appears, as shown in Figure 8-3. In this window, you can do just about anything required of a text selection, including changing the following:

✦ Font

✦ Size

✦ Leading

✦ Spacing

✦ Alignment

✦ Tabs

✦ Paragraph rules

Make your changes and click OK to change all instances of the style immediately. This is a huge time-saver.

Figure 8-3: The Edit Styles dialog box for text styles

To edit a graphic style, select a style and choose Edit from the Styles Options pop-up menu. As shown in Figure 8-4, the dialog box covers everything to do with strokes and fills, including halftone information. If you begin to rely on styles in your drawings, you can make rapid and powerful changes to a job just by changing the styles. This approach gives you the opportunity to show different approaches to your client, and lets you test various ideas.

Figure 8-4: The Edit Styles dialog box for strokes and fills

Graphic Hose Tool

A further use of symbols lies in the Graphic Hose tool (seen at the left). With this feature, you can place multiple instances of a graphic element on the page, make each instance a different size, rotate each a little or a lot, and adjust the spacing from tight overlapping to wide gaps. Or, the instances can be scattered along the path just as a custom brush would do—it's all up to you.

Working with the Graphic Hose involves two different phases of its dialog box. Open the dialog box by double-clicking the Graphic Hose icon in the Xtras toolbar. Hose is the first window you should work in, as shown in Figure 8-5. If it's not open, click the Hose button in the dialog box.

Figure 8-5: Choose groups to spray, or place graphics in the Hose window.

To make a new Graphic Hose group, do the following:

1. Select a graphic element in the document and copy it to the Clipboard.

2. Double-click the Graphic Hose Xtra button in the Main toolbar. Then select New from the menu at the top of the Hose dialog box.

3. In the next panel, name the group and click Save. The preview window will be empty.

4. Click the Paste In button. Your graphic appears in the preview window and a new item named Object 1 is added to the Contents menu at the bottom of the dialog box.

5. Select and copy other elements and use the Paste In button to get them into your Graphic Hose. (If you decide at any time that you want to remove an object from the hose, find it in the Contents menu and click Delete. If you want to use an object, but you don't want it to be associated with the Graphic Hose, simply choose it and use the Copy Out button. Then paste the item on your page.)

Now you have to decide how the Graphic Hose will spray objects on the page. Click the Options button to open that dialog box. Refer to Figure 8-6 to see the available options.

✦ **Order** — Dictates the order in which the objects are sprayed; the variables are Loop, Random, and Back and Forth.

✦ **Spacing** — Modifies the spacing of the objects. Choose from Grid, Random, and Variable. Use the slider or enter a number to program the distance between objects.

✦ **Scale** — Adjusts the size of sprayed objects from Uniform to Random. Again, use the slider to input the amount of change you desire. Regardless of the settings here, you can use the up/down or left/right arrow keys on your keyboard to enlarge or reduce the size of the objects as you're spraying them on the page.

✦ **Rotate** — Change the orientation of the objects. Zero places objects in the same attitude as they were placed in the hose, but you can enter a number or use the wheel to set the angle of rotation within Uniform, Random, and Incremental variables.

You should test and experiment with the Graphic Hose. Each type of graphic you place in the hose necessitates a different group of Options settings, according to what you're trying to accomplish.

After you've filled the hose with objects and set the options, it's time to put the hose to work. Check to see that you're still in the Graphic Hose tool — it's an arrowhead without a shaft. Then click and drag. Depending on how fast you move the cursor, and the direction you drag, you'll get different results. Overlapping is permitted — you can drag the tool across an area as many times as you need. Figure 8-7 shows the grass hose I made using seven freeform grass shapes. You could do this by drawing each of the elements individually, but without a graphics tablet, each stroke must be carefully placed, and the random effect is lost completely. I'm pretty rigid and grid-like in my work, so when I need a truly random effect, the Graphic Hose is the tool I use, without question.

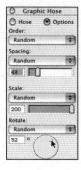

Figure 8-6: The Options dialog box enables you to change many attributes of sprayed objects.

Figure 8-7: The effects of a simple Graphic Hose swamp as used in the Habitat Alert logo.

If you make a spray pattern and decide that it's close but needs a little work, choose the Pointer tool (or hold down the Control (Command) key to temporarily invoke the Pointer tool) to move or delete individual objects. The object that has been sprayed is a simple grouped object, so you can change colors, stroke widths, and fills just as you would with any other regular object.

FreeHand enables you to have as many as 10 objects in any single hose. You can export your hoses and import hoses from other artists or your other computers. All you need to do is copy the hose into the FreeHand 10 ➪ English ➪ Xtras ➪ Graphic Hose folder. Any hoses that you no longer need can be deleted by dragging the file to the Trash.

Summary

This short chapter taught you the powerful uses of symbols and styles and explained how their utilization can save you time and increase your efficiency. You also learned how to easily make random graphic effects by working with the Graphic Hose Xtra.

✦   ✦   ✦

Understanding
FreeHand
Typography

One of FreeHand's strongest selling points is its type handling capabilities. With just a few preparations, you can work through the most text-heavy jobs in no time at all. Beyond general typesetting, FreeHand offers numerous effective graphic possibilities.

Import Text or Set It in FreeHand?

As you know, workflow can take many directions. What's logical to one artist isn't to another, but both can get the job done. That said, my philosophy on setting body text was shaped in the days of hot type, cold type, photo type, and press type. I really don't miss those days all that much. Today you have two basic choices: use a word processor, or type directly in your page layout or drawing program. With a headline or a couple lines of text, there's no question — just type it in FreeHand, but what if there's more text than that?

Word-processing programs

For large bodies of text, you are best off setting the text in a word-processing program. When I bought my first computer, I purchased Microsoft Word at the same time. I've been using it ever since, but many programs, such as WordPerfect, do the job just as well. A word-processing program is equipped to take text as fast as you can input it, and some have interactive spell checking and grammar checking, too.

You must remember to save the files as Rich Text Format (RTF) or ASCII (plain text), however, or you won't be able to import them into FreeHand. Remember also that while inputting text any tabs you set will be ignored as far as its locations go. The tabs will be in place, but measurements fly out the window. Other than placing a tab in Word, there's no reason to worry about the tab's placement, because that information will be lost when the file gets to FreeHand.

Word processing in FreeHand

If the text is less than five or six paragraphs, setting it in FreeHand is simple enough. Just click the Text tool (type a T if you're in any other tool) and the cursor turns into a text input icon. You can click anywhere on the page and begin typing, or you can drag a text block of a specific size. Letting go of the mouse places the insertion point of the text appropriately to the paragraph alignment setting that is currently in use (in other words, if paragraphs are set to be centered, the cursor blinks in the center of the first line of the text block). Conversely, you can click the text icon on the page, or click/drag a box, and adjust the width and height of the box, as well as its location on the page in the Text inspector. Any of the above situations enable you to begin setting the text.

The default font on a Mac is 24-point Times. However, I most often use 12-point Helvetica Condensed in my work. I chose that font as part of my custom default page, so it's my default font. If you type a few characters and decide that you want a different font, you must select the entire block of copy before you change the font. If no text is selected and you change a font (and its attributes), text *from that point on* is in the new font, but previous text remains unchanged. Alternatively, if you select a text block with the Pointer tool, you can change attributes to *all* of the text in the block through the Text inspector or Text toolbar.

Refer to Chapter 5 for a discussion on custom pages.

The Text Editor

Where you type in FreeHand depends on how you like to work and the amount of text you will be inputting. If it's not a lot of text, you can type directly on the page, but if you want to see just the text without waiting for the page to redraw, go to Text ➪ Editor Shift+Control+E (Shift+Command +E). (You can also hold down the Alt (Option) key and double-click the text block.) In Windows, you can also right-click a text block with the Text tool and choose Editor from the menu. A small window appears that contains only the text in the currently selected text block. You have the option of viewing the text as it appears in the document (see Figure 9-1), or click the button to see everything in 12-point black text. When you click the Show Invisibles button, spaces, tabs, paragraphs, discretionary hyphens, and line breaks appear as gray marks to aid you in typesetting. You can apply any text attributes you want through the means discussed above while in the Text Editor. When you're done typing, just click the OK button; if you want to see the effects of your typing without closing the Text Editor window, click the Apply button.

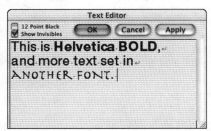

Figure 9-1: The Text Editor box, showing such invisibles as spaces and end of line marks

Checking your spelling

FreeHand is just like a word-processing program when it comes to performing a spelling check. Just place the Text cursor in a text block and choose Text ➪ Spelling. You can click the

Setup button in the Spelling dialog box () to open the FreeHand Preferences window and turn on or off several conditions. When the Spelling Checker finds a word that is not in the dictionary, you can add it to your custom dictionary by clicking Add, and the Exactly as Typed, or All Lowercase buttons.

Text hyphenation

In just about every block of justified text, you'll end up having to break a word to create a line break and avoid unsightly gaps in the text. Too many hyphenated words in a row also look pretty bad, and sometimes you just don't want any hyphens at all—whether it's in a particular word, or an entire paragraph. All of these hyphenation situations are controlled from the Paragraph tab of the Text inspector. Click the Hyphenate option, to allow hyphenation in the selected text, and click the ellipsis (...) button to open the Edit Hyphenation window. Here you can select the dictionary to use from the dictionaries that are installed with FreeHand (the English version allows a choice of English or British). You can also set limits on consecutive hyphens, and choose to Skip Capitalized Words and/or Inhibit Hyphens In Selection.

Discretionary hyphens

At times, you must break a word that doesn't fall in a location that FreeHand hyphenates automatically, or FreeHand might not place the hyphen where you want it. In those instances, you can insert a discretionary hyphen. If you simply place a hyphen where you want it and press Return, you get the break you want, but if the text reflows for any reason, the hyphen and paragraph break remain intact, and louse up your typography. Placement of a discretionary hyphen (Text ➪ Special Characters ➪ Discretionary Hyphen), or Control+hyphen (Command+ hyphen) puts the hyphen where *you* want it—not where the program figures it should go. As an added benefit, when text reflows, causing the word to be placed in the middle of a line where a hyphen is not needed, the discretionary hyphen disappears, leaving the word unbroken in the text.

Smart quotes

Smart quotes change the vertical quote marks found in general word processing to "curly quotes" found in professional typesetting. In Preferences, you can select the style of quote marks you want to use. Choices include the standard American style of quotes, plus several European language styles. When you need to use straight quote marks (for feet, inches, minutes, and so on), hold down the Control key as you type a single quote or press Shift+Control to get straight double-quotation marks.

Searching for text

It happens. You type "warm fuzzy feeling" throughout the instruction manual because "fuzzy worm feeling" just doesn't sound right to you. Then you find out that you're making a package for a stuffed worm... now what? Just select Edit ➪ Find & Replace ➪ Text. When the dialog box opens, you can type in words you are searching for, and words to replace them. You can also find and replace several text features, as shown in Figure 9-2. You can choose to replace all instances at once by clicking Change All, or find and replace individual instances by using the Find Next and Change buttons. To make the search more specific, options are available for Whole Word, Match Case, or Show Selection. (You can click any or all of those buttons.) When you want to select (or select and change) all text that happens to be a particular font, use the Find Graphics button in the Main menu, and choose Font from the drop-down menu.

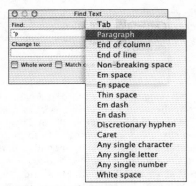

Figure 9-2: This Find Text dialog box looks for paragraph marks in the selected text.

Applying Text Attributes

Keep the tool you're using in mind as you work. For instance, say you have chosen the Pointer tool and selected a block of text. You decide to make the color of the text green, and click a green swatch in the Swatches panel. Instead of the text changing color, the background of the text block is filled with green. The same holds true with strokes. To affect the text, you must be in the Text tool, and the text must be selected.

If you have a text block on the page and you are currently using the Pointer tool, double-click the cursor inside the text block and the cursor turns into the Text tool. Set any text or make any necessary changes. When you move the cursor outside the text block, the cursor becomes the Pointer tool. Move it over the text block again, and it reverts to the Text tool. The only shortcoming to this feature is that if you want to make another text block, you must either press the T key, or select the Text tool from the toolbar again to draw the text block.

If you use the Pointer tool to select multiple text blocks, you can change some text attributes, such as font, size, leading, and whether it is roman, italics, or bold. Don't attempt to change fill color or stroke, though, or you'll be surprised as explained earlier. You can only select contiguous text in a single text block at any given time. If you linked text blocks, you technically have multiple text blocks, but FreeHand sees them as a single block of text and enables you to select contiguous text from one block to another.

Text Block Anatomy

When you select a text block with the Pointer tool or move the Text cursor outside the text block, you can do several things to the block itself. Notice that the text's bounding box has eight control handles. If you use the Pointer on any of the corner points, you can change the dimensions of the text block. Use the middle side and bottom control handles with extreme caution. If you drag one of those handles, the text inside is modified vertically or horizontally, depending on which handle you choose to drag and which direction you moved the cursor. In essence, you add or remove leading (the spacing between lines of text), or you modify the letter spacing (space between letters and words). Unless you have a great text design in mind, these handles are better left "undragged."

Note You can get different letter spacing or leading by changing the appropriate setting in the Text inspector.

However, those same handles are extremely valuable in other instances. When you double-click a bottom handle, you can then stretch the text block to stretch vertically to fit the text you input. Add 16 lines of text and the block fits. Delete eight of the lines and the block becomes half the size vertically. Double-click the side handles to make the text block auto-expanding. If you're working on a document and can't seem to get the text block to resize to a different shape, chances are good that the block has been set to auto-expanding. Double-click the side or bottom control handles to convert the text block to fixed-size.

Text Flow and Linked Text Blocks

By default, a single click of the Text tool starts a fixed-size text block, and enables you to type a line of text as wide as you want to go — until you click Return. If you've drawn a text block, you can type to the boundaries of the block, and text automatically flows to the next line. When the copy gets to the end of the text block, you won't see the new copy that you input, and a square with a circle inside appears at the bottom-right corner of the text block. That icon indicates a text overflow. To see your new text, resize the text block by dragging one of the corner control handles on the text block. On the other hand, maybe you want to continue the text somewhere else in the document. In FreeHand, you can link text from one text block to another, to be set inside any object, or you can attach it to a path. To link text blocks, click and drag a new text block. Click the overflow icon, and drag the cursor over the new text block. You know it's working correctly if you see a pigtail path from the overflow icon to the cursor. When you release the mouse over the new text block, the copy automatically flows into the new area (see Figure 9-3). Treat this new text block as you would any other, and if you shrink or stretch the first block in the text chain (or change the size or leading of the text), the text in the second block grows or shrinks to fit.

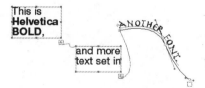

Figure 9-3: Linked text blocks display a double-arrow icon and connecting path to the next block.

The overflow situation is good and bad. It's great for creating simple newsletters, brochures, or manuals, and not bad for larger, multipage books. I hesitate to use this feature over many pages (8–10) because performance can suffer, and a greater chance of problems exists with the file. You're better off cutting the thread along the way and starting a new thread. Another reason to cut the thread is to convert the text into paths. You might want to convert text to paths for many reasons. For example, you may want to export the file into Illustrator, or Adobe Acrobat, or just make the file easier to transfer to someone. By converting text to paths, you have no fonts to worry about, and people on the other end of your production chain cannot edit the text either (another good/bad situation, depending on circumstances). You cannot convert linked text blocks into paths.

To unlink text blocks (or cut the thread), you must basically break the large body of copy into smaller chunks.

1. Decide where you want to break the link.

2. Select all the text *after* that link and cut it to the Pasteboard.

3. Click the overflow icon at the bottom-right of the previous text block, and drag the cursor to an empty spot on the document. This kills the link.

4. Double-click the Pointer tool inside the first text block of your new section (to return to the Text tool and place an insertion point) and paste the text. The copy automatically flows forward to any other linked text blocks, objects, or paths.

Setting Text in Columns

Making columns and rows of text in FreeHand is easy. You can turn on the grid and drag text blocks to fit the layout, or you can place guidelines and place the text blocks between them. However, if you have a lot of text, or want true equity in the columnar layout, it's time to head to the bottom two buttons in the Text inspector: Columns and Rows, and Adjust Columns.

The Columns and Rows dialog box (shown in Figure 9-4) has arranged a body of text in three columns of equal width and two rows deep. The rows are of equal height, but due to the amount of text, the last column is completely empty, and the next-to-last column is not completely full. You can see that the entire array of text is a single text block. This makes moving the block of text around the layout a breeze. Only one adjustment is required instead of moving several text blocks or grouping them. Notice that you can input the spacing between columns and rows and the height and width of the columns and rows. You can add paragraph rules in this panel, and you can change the flow of the text from up and down to left and right.

Figure 9-4: The Columns and Rows panel arranges text in a tight grid.

Balance text columns

In FreeHand, to balance text columns, click the bottom button to access the Adjust Columns panel, as shown in Figure 9-5. This figure shows the same text, but the Balance button has been clicked and the columns have been balanced. Notice that the first five columns are equal in the number of lines of text and their leading. However, the last column came up short on lines, and the leading is adjusted to fill the column as much as possible. I accomplished it by clicking the Modify Leading button. I'm obsessive-compulsive enough that this arrangement would bother me, and I would turn Modify Leading off. That would result in a half-full (or half-empty) column.

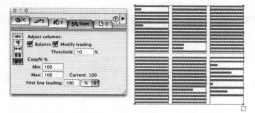

Figure 9-5: The Adjust Columns panel balances columns within limits of the text.

Enter values in the Copyfit % Min and Max fields to further control the columns. A value smaller than 100 percent results in text and leading being reduced; values above 100 percent enlarge text and leading to make the columns fit. The implication is that you give control of the text over to the program, however. If your text is set at 10-point with 2-points of leading, setting Max at 120 percent could change the text to 12-point with nearly two and a half points of leading. (The actual fit depends on the amount of text.) Expect to have the last column a line or two shorter than the other columns. If that isn't acceptable, adjust the size or shape of the text block or edit the text itself.

To add (or reduce) space above the first line of text in the column, enter a value in the First Line Leading field. Just as in the regular leading fields, you can enter a value as a percentage, an exact amount, or as an added point value. The leading value you input applies to all the columns in the row.

Paragraph rules

You can really keep columns and rows in their place by anchoring them with paragraph rules. These lines flow between paragraphs either horizontally or vertically, and break (inset), or run the full length and width of the column depending on your settings. Figure 9-6 shows a full-width rule with inset vertical rules.

Figure 9-6: Paragraph rules at work

Using paragraph rules in your text block is slightly complicated because it involves three different panels. When you select Full Height or Inset for vertical rules, and Full Width or Inset for horizontal rules in the Columns and Rows panel, nothing happens. To fix this, go to the Stroke panel, change the None setting to any type and color of stroke you want to use. If the stroke encompasses the entire block of text, go to the Object inspector panel and deselect the Display Border option.

Note It's my personal opinion that you're best off using Basic strokes, just as a matter of readability of the text. But you can use the other types of strokes as well, with the caveat that a Brush stroke encompasses the whole text block—turning the Display Border option off has no effect.

When you turn on the Display Border option, the text and rules overlap, likely impairing legibility. To overcome this, go to the Object inspector again (while the text block is selected), and enter an amount in the Inset fields.

Tabs and Margins

You can access the Text Ruler by selecting View ➪ Text Rulers. To hide the Text Ruler, select Text Rulers in the View menu to uncheck it. The units of measurement match those currently set in the document. Just as in most word-processing programs, the default tab setting is every half-inch (or three picas). These tabs (shown in Figure 9-7) are small right-pointing triangles. The left end of the Text Ruler has a split triangle that determines first and second line indents. Five types of tabs sit on top of the ruler; from left to right they are as follows:

 ✦ Left tab

 ✦ Right tab

 ✦ Center tab

 ✦ Decimal tab

 ✦ Wrapping tab

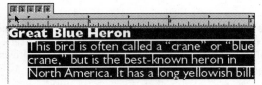

Figure 9-7: This Text Ruler shows only default tab settings. Tab icons at the top left are (from left to right) left, right, center, decimal, and wrapping tabs. Notice the left indent marker triangle has been moved to the right of the first–line indent marker triangle.

Setting tabs

Paragraphs often start with an indent. To indent a paragraph, you can enter an indent value in the Text inspector easily enough, but I like to make the indent right in the Text Ruler. It's a matter of dragging the top split triangle at the left end of the ruler to the indent location you want. The bottom split triangle indicates where the second and consecutive lines of text align. Moving this triangle moves the first line triangle as well. The rule is that the first line triangle can be moved independently, but the second line triangle maintains its relationship with the first line triangle when it's moved. To make a hanging indent, move the bottom triangle to where you want the main body of text to align, and slide the top triangle back to the left. This typesetting method doesn't require you to type a tab — or spaces — at the beginning of each line. The text automatically wraps to the correct indent.

If you click the Text tool on the page and try to set a tab, you'll be frustrated, because FreeHand doesn't work that way. With an auto-expanding text block, you can set a tab only within the width of the text you input. Create a fixed-width text block, however, and you can set the tabs and indents before typing any text.

To place a tab, click and drag a tab icon from the Text Ruler, and release the mouse when the cursor is in the clear space immediately above the ruler, or on the ruler itself. If you move the mouse above or below the ruler, the tab doesn't take. As soon as you release the mouse, tabbed text aligns with the tab. All preset tabs to the left of the tab you set disappear. A super feature of FreeHand is that a vertical guideline appears as you're dragging the tab. This guide extends the full height of the document window, making it easy to align the tab with anything above or below the text on the page. (If it annoys you, you can turn it off in Preferences ➪ Text.)

Bullets

If a shortcoming exists in FreeHand typography, it's that you can't automatically set a block of bulleted text. Fortunately, the manual process isn't that complicated. Use standard key combinations (see Bite the Bullet sidebar) to create the bullet, or choose one from a font such as Zapf Dingbats. You can also copy any graphic element and paste it in the line of text as an inline graphic. After placing the bullet, press the Tab key and begin entering the indented text. Select all the text in the block and adjust the tab setting in T Ruler. If you miss a line of text in your selection, the tab changes don't go into effect.

Typophilosophy

You are always better off if you can draw your text block to the exact size, set all the tabs precisely, and never use words of more that three characters so you won't be faced with hyphenation problems or bad line breaks. Unfortunately, that's frequently impossible. In my work, I set the text and press the Tab key where it's applicable. After I type all the text, I select the entire block of copy and arrange the tabs. This method negates a lot of adjustment as I'm typing the text. If my tabs are preset, I'm inclined to clean up the text as I'm typing so it looks nice. That's not time efficient.

Bite the Bullet

In Windows, use the CHARMAP program (click the START button, then select Programs ➪ Accessories ➪ CHARMAP). Then choose your font. You can either copy the character you select from the character map and paste it into the text at the cursor position, or use the Alt key and the numeric keyboard, and type in a bullet character (usually 0149).

Wrapping tabs

Wrapping is impossible to do in InDesign, PageMaker, QuarkXPress, or Illustrator. And, wrapping tabs from Excel or Word don't wrap when the text is imported into another program. Let's unwrap the secrets of working with wrapping tabs.

The same block of text has been used for all three parts of Figure 9-8. The top example shows the text as I typed it. Notice that after the word "Column," there is a large gap. That's due to the tab that's been inserted, and the text automatically moved to the next default tab setting. When I finished typing the word "it," I hit another tab, and that location happened to fall very close to the end of "it," so there isn't much room between words.

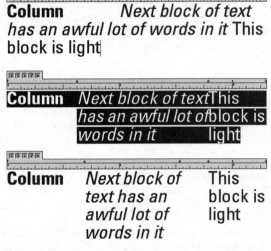

Figure 9-8: Wrapping tabs are a major strong point of FreeHand's typographic tools.

In the middle example, all the text has been highlighted and wrapping tabs have been dragged to two places on the Text Ruler. These tabs defined the width of the middle column. Unfortunately, as you can see in the middle of Figure 9-9, it impacts the third column pretty tightly. To create a space between the columns, a third wrapping tab has been dragged onto the ruler, as shown in the bottom example. I placed the insertion point just in front of the word "This" and pressed the Tab key to insert a second tab within the text. Then I arranged the tabs to suit the layout.

Note

The only drawback to the wrapping tab scheme is that all the columns that contain wrapping text are left-justified. You can't center the text or align it right-justified. I think that's a small price to pay for the convenience of a great text tool.

A FreeHand Table Project

Here's a little project so you can get your feet wet in the typing pool.

1. Open a new FreeHand document, and choose File ➪ Import, and navigate to the CD-ROM to find the file named BirdTable.rtf in the Chapter 9 folder. The font is Times, and if you are greeted with a message stating that you don't have the correct font, dismiss it by clicking the OK button. The file will be placed with a generic font. The file should look similar to the top of Figure 9-10.

2. Click anywhere in the body of the text with the Text tool, and choose Select All Control+A (Command+A).

3. Drag a wrapping tab, two left tabs, and another wrapping tab to the approximate locations shown in the bottom half of Figure 9-9.

4. Change the font in the Text inspector or at Text ➪ Font. I used Verdana. Triple-click the cursor on the top line of the table and change the font to a bold face.

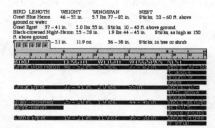

Figure 9-9: Raw tablature text and its initial alignment

5. At this point, the table works inasmuch as everything lines up, but requires more work to improve its aesthetics. Start by centering the word "BIRD" above the first column. Place the text cursor in front of the word and press the Tab key. Then drag a center tab out onto the Text Ruler so the word is centered above the column. Be aware that because the insertion point is in the top line of text, that line is being adjusted, but other lines in the table are ignored. Change all the tabs in the header row of text to center tabs and adjust them to center the header text above each column. Save the document as **BirdTable.FH10**.

To make the table more reader friendly, separate the birds with paragraph rules:

1. Select the entire block of text with the Text tool, open the Text inspector, and click the Paragraph button.

2. In the Space After Paragraph field (as seen in Figure 9-10), enter **0p6** to place six points of leading between paragraphs.

3. Select Centered from the Rules menu.

4. Depending on what you've been doing in FreeHand, several factors may have changed that will affect what you see onscreen, so we'll assume the worst case and set things back to basics. Click outside the text block to deselect it, and use the Pointer tool to select it again (as an object this time), then go to the Object inspector and select the Display Border option. This should put a stroke around the entire table, and horizontal lines between paragraphs. If you don't see them, go to the Stroke panel, select Basic, and give the stroke a color of black. A border around a table is sometimes called for — if that is the case for your tastes, you're done. If you'd rather have the table open on the sides, return to the Object inspector and deselect the Display Border option.

5. To dress the table up a bit, I decided to make a dark header bar and reverse the text. Use the Rectangle tool to draw a rectangle the same width as the table, and tall enough to make the header row of text comfortable. When it comes to a sense of design and personal taste, comfort will mean more or less space between text characters and graphic elements such as borders and boxes.

6. This rectangle will be on top of the text, so send it to the back (Modify ➪ Arrange ➪ Send To Back). Then choose the Text tool, triple-click the header row of text, and change its color to white.

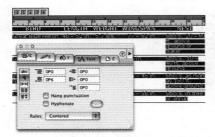

Figure 9-10: Adding space and paragraph rules to the table

7. Vertical bars would make the table easier on the eyes, so select the Line tool and draw a vertical line from the top of the header bar to the bottom paragraph rule between the first two columns. Clone (Edit ➪ Clone) the line and move it between the next two columns, and so on until all the columns are delineated, so to speak.

8. Use the Pointer tool to drag a selection box around the top points of the vertical lines. Then double-click the Knife tool icon to open the Knife dialog box. Choose Straight, and be sure that Close Cut Paths is deselected. Hold down the Shift key and drag the Knife tool across the bottom of the black rectangle.

9. Switch back to the Pointer tool and click outside the table somewhere to deselect all the lines. Drag a selection box over the top points of the lines again, and change the stroke color to white. Last, drag a selection box around the entire table and group it so you can move it around without moving tiny pieces. The final result should look similar to Figure 9-11.

BIRD	LENGTH	WEIGHT	WINGSPAN	NEST
Great Blue Heron	46 – 52 in.	5.7 lbs.	77 – 82 in.	Sticks, 20–60 ft. above ground or water
Great Egret	37 – 41 in.	2.0 lbs.	55 in.	Sticks, 10–40 ft. above ground
Black-crowned Night-Heron	25 – 28 in.	1.9 lbs.	44 – 45 in.	Sticks, as high as 150 ft. above ground
Cattle Egret	19 – 21 in.	11.9 oz.	36 – 38 in.	Sticks, in tree or shrub

Figure 9-11: A FreeHand table

If you look closely at the Text Ruler on top of the table in Figure 9-10, you'll notice that it is significantly darker than the Text Ruler in previous figures. That is because we have selected text with different tab settings. Only tabs from the top row of text appear in the Text Ruler.

Paragraph rule caveats

With paragraph rules, as with Shadow, Underline, or Outline in the text effects panel, you cannot convert the text to paths and employ your hard work. The rules (and text effects) just go away. You can draw lines on top of the paragraph rules if you really need to get rid of the font issue.

Text on a Path Project

Let's do a little experimentation with text for a logo design. This is for Habitat Alert, an organization dedicated to providing a protective environment for several types of flora and fauna, including four species of birds. One of the more prominent birds is the Great Blue Heron. A silhouette of the bird should appear somehow in the logo, perhaps incorporated into a water theme. (Keep in mind that I'm only trying to show you how easy it is to put text on a path.)

1. Start with a new FreeHand document, and name it **HeronLogo.FH10**. Import the Great Blue Heron.fh10 file from the Chapter 9 folder on the book's accompanying CD. I gave the silhouette a gradient blend of light and dark blue-grays.

2. Select the Text tool and type **HABITAT ALERT** somewhere on the page — its exact location is not important.

3. Select the text and choose a heavy, bold font. I used 24-point Gill Sans Extra Bold so I could gain some width in the typeface as well as weight. I also expanded the text's width to 200 percent in the Text inspector.

4. Double-click the Spiral tool and change the settings to match Figure 9-12.

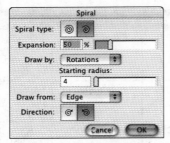

Figure 9-12: Spiral tool dialog box settings

5. Using the Spiral tool, drag a spiral approximately an inch and a half in diameter, similar to the right side of Figure 9-14. Even though the spiral's path seems to be drawn from the outside in, it actually begins at the center. You don't want the text to come from the center in this instance, so go to Xtras ➪ Cleanup ➪ Reverse Direction. With the spiral still selected, press and hold Shift while you select the line of text, and go to Text ➪ Attach To Path. If luck is with you, the text will begin on the bottom or middle left and wrap around to fit tightly inside itself, as shown on the right side of Figure 9-13. Click Save.

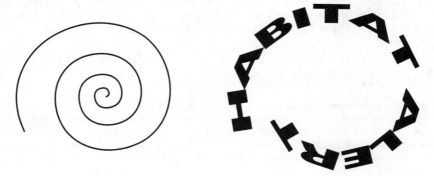

Figure 9-13: A spiral path on the left, with text attached to the path on the right

6. How about making the text look like a ripple in the water? To do that, you must flatten the ellipse/spiral the text is in. Using the 3D Rotation tool at this point is hopeless, however. It doesn't work with live text. So, select the text on a path, and choose Text ➪ Convert To Paths. Then select the 3D Rotation tool from the Xtras toolbar. Click the mouse in the center of the spiral and drag upward, holding down the Shift key to maintain a vertical constraint on the distortion.

7. To beef up the illusion more, you can add a gradient fill to the text. If you go to the Fills panel and select a gradient fill, each of the letters in the text has its own individual gradient. In this case, select Modify ➪ Join to create a compound path from the text. The gradient affects the text as a single unit. Make the gradient dark in the front (bottom), and lighter in the rear (top).

8. All that's left to do is to place the Great Blue in the center of his rippled logotype, and you're finished. Save the document. The finished logo should look similar to that shown in Figure 9-14.

Figure 9-14: A Habitat Alert logo concept using text on a path

Basic Text Styles

You can use the Font Style menu to make your font bold or italic, but depending on the font, you may not get the results you were expecting when it comes time to print the job. If it looks right on the monitor and your end use is the Web, you don't have a problem. But printing to PostScript devices can bring up a few surprises. For that reason, select a bold, italic, or bold italic style of the font you want from the Fonts menu. That way, the computer has exactly the information it needs to print the job successfully.

You also have various effects in the Text inspector at your disposal. For most purposes, I recommend that you stay away from these effects. If for any reason you must convert the text to paths, those attributes will be lost. At that point, you must attempt to come up with a way to modify the text to reflect the effect you had applied. Re-creating some effects is frustrating; others are impossible. You're much better off working with text and vectors than using the canned effects.

Inline effect project

A common text effect is inline. You can have FreeHand do the inline effect by going to Text ➪ Effect and choosing Inline from the drop-down menu. A dialog box opens, allowing you to enter the number of lines you want, the width and color of the stroke, and the width and color of the background. If you convert the text to paths, you lose those extra lines and have the basic text back. Instead, it's easy enough to make your own inline text that is just as adjustable, but permanent. As with many tasks in FreeHand, there are multiple ways to accomplish the job, and each option has its own benefits.

Note

If it's a single word or phrase that I "know" won't be changing, I usually convert the proofed text to paths right away. This serves the purpose of not having any restrictions due to font or text-based software issues, and because I'll be working with multiple graphics stacked on top of each other, the chances of introducing an extra space or something into live text is removed. If I have a hunch that the text will be changing in the future, I clone the live text and place it somewhere safe on the Pasteboard, off the page itself. In other situations, I place the live text on a separate layer and hide that layer in case of future edits.

1. Open a new FreeHand document and save it as **TextEffects.FH10**.

2. Select the Text tool, click the page, and type **"INLINE"** in a heavy bold font. Change the size to 120-points, and go to Text ⇨ Convert To Paths. This command removes any connection with fonts and text, and turns the letterforms into a group of pure vector graphics. Figure 9-15 shows the four easy steps required to make inline text — or inline anything, for that matter.

3. Convert the text to paths.

4. Give the resulting group a 6-point black stroke, and clone the group.

5. Give the new group a 4-point white stroke, and clone it.

6. Remove the stroke from the clone. Group all three graphics and you're done.

Figure 9-15: Four steps to inline text effects

Keep in mind that a path has no width dimension until it is stroked. Half of the stroke goes on one side, and half of the stroke goes on the other side of the path. In this example, you created a 1-point black outline and a 1-point white inline around the original object. You can change the width of the strokes and make them any color. To apply gradient fills, remember to create a compound path (Modify ⇨ Join) to have the gradient affect the group as a whole instead of its various parts.

Shadow effect project

To create drop shadows in Fireworks, Illustrator, or Photoshop, you can run a filter or two and the job is done. However, that's a bitmap project, and we're in a vector world. You can choose Shadow in the Text ⇨ Effect menu, but you run into a disappearance problem if you convert the text to paths.

FreeHand's Shadow text effect is simply an offset gray clone. Smudge makes clones of an object and offsets them to make you think you're seeing a true shadow effect. But if you look closely, you'll see the stair-stepped edges of the clones. That may be okay for some applications, but I prefer something closer to what I can get out of Fireworks, or the other programs. I make gradients.

Assuming you've already done the inline effect in the previous paragraphs, use that same text and apply a shadow to it. If you prefer, you can start from scratch by typing a word in a bold font and converting it to paths (and skipping the next couple steps of hiding elements):

1. Ungroup the nest of graphics you made for the inset project.

2. Select the top element and hide it (View ➪ Hide Selection).

3. Select the next level and hide it, too.

4. Select the fat bottom layer, clone it, and send the clone to the back.

5. Press the Tab key to deselect everything, and then select that fat level and hide it. You now have a fat clone in front of you. Give it an even fatter 8-point stroke.

6. Double-click the Trace tool to open its dialog box.

7. Set the color mode to 2, Grays, RGB, High Resolution, and Trace Layers: All.

8. Select Outer Edge for the Path Conversion, and move all three sliders in the bottom half of the window to the far right. Click OK.

9. Drag a selection box around the fat clone. This outlines the outline, so you have a contiguous shape instead of multiple shapes in a group.

10. In the Fills inspector, choose Gradient for the fill type, and click the Contour Gradient button (far right).

11. Drag a white swatch to the left box in the gradient color well, and create a 60 or 70 percent gray to place in the right box.

12. Move the slider back and forth until you reach a gradient effect that you like.

13. Choose View ➪ Show All to bring back all the text. It should look similar to Figure 9-16.

Figure 9-16: A soft shadow made with the Trace tool and a contour gradient

Inline graphics

Occasionally, you need to place a logo or other type of graphic within a line of text. Putting tabs or spaces in the text and pasting a graphic in the blank spot are obvious workarounds, but FreeHand provides a much easier method. In Figure 9-17, a silhouette of a bird has been placed in the middle of a block of text. If you want to work this out, follow these steps:

1. Open the file `Herons.FH10` from the Chapter 9 folder on the book's accompanying CD, and make a new page.

2. Import the `Night-Heron.rtf` file from the same folder and place it on the new page.

3. Style the text with fonts and size of your choice.

4. While holding the Shift key down to constrain the bird's proportions, drag the Night-Heron silhouette from page one onto page two, and scale it to the size you want it to be to fit within the text line.

5. Cut or copy the graphic to the Clipboard.

6. With the Text tool, place an insertion point where you want the graphic to appear, and paste the graphic.

The graphic aligns with the baseline of the line of text it is pasted in. If it's a tall graphic, such as this bird, you must adjust the leading. In this example, the baseline has also been shifted down for the inline graphic. All you need do is select the graphic with the Text tool, and adjust the baseline shift in the Text inspector. Any adjustments you make to the block of text affect the inline graphic, so you may need to replace it if you change the font size or other shape attributes such as font width. A change in the font itself doesn't affect the graphic, and its location remains fixed within the text.

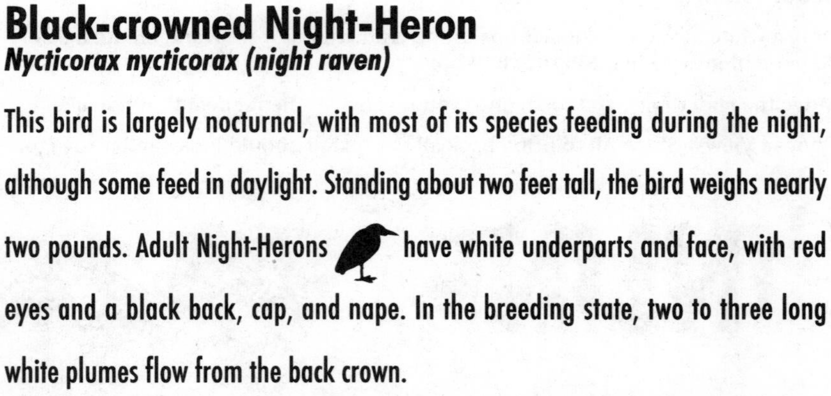

Black-crowned Night-Heron
Nycticorax nycticorax (night raven)

This bird is largely nocturnal, with most of its species feeding during the night,

although some feed in daylight. Standing about two feet tall, the bird weighs nearly

two pounds. Adult Night-Herons have white underparts and face, with red

eyes and a black back, cap, and nape. In the breeding state, two to three long

white plumes flow from the back crown.

Figure 9-17: An inline graphic places logos and artwork inside a line of text.

Placing graphics inside text

Text doesn't have to be centered, or have exact margins. Feel free to think outside the (text) box. Placing text inside graphic shapes to force a little life into your artwork is easy. However, getting the text to "work" inside the graphic requires a bit more planning:

1. Open the file Herons.FH10 from the Chapter 9 folder on the book's accompanying CD, and make a new page.

2. Import the `CattleEgret.rtf` file from the same folder and place it on the new page.

3. Style the text with the font and size of your choice.

4. Drag the Cattle Egret silhouette from page one onto page two.

5. To flow text inside this closed graphic shape, use the Pointer tool to select the text block and the graphic. Go to Text ➪ Flow Inside Path. You can align text just as you would a regular text block—justified, flush left or right, or centered.

Figure 9-18 shows an example of text inside a graphic. The text on the right has been converted to paths. Notice that the toned background has disappeared. If you want the background, just clone one and place it behind the converted text.

Figure 9-18: Text flowing inside a path can be effective in a layout.

Adding Pages

To add a page, open the Document inspector, and click the triangle in the upper-right corner of the panel. This will open the Document Options pop-up menu. Choose Add Pages from the menu. The page will be added to the document, but your view of the current page will not change. However, if you look at the page number indicator at the bottom left of the application window, you'll notice that it says you're on Page 2. You're not. To get to Page 2, you must click somewhere in Page 1, then change the page number at the bottom of the window. Conversely, you can scroll to the right until Page 2 appears. Yet another method is to click on the Page 2 icon in the Document inspector thumbnail window.

Text runarounds

Text running around a graphic can add some flavor to your artwork. The rules are simple: The graphic must not be a group or blend, and the graphic must be above (in front of) the text block. The example shown in Figure 9-19 is easy to accomplish, by following these steps:

1. Open Herons.FH10 from the Chapter 9 folder on the book's accompanying CD, and make a new page.

2. Import the CattleEgret.rtf file from the same folder, and place it on the new page.

3. Style the text with the font and size of your choice.

4. While holding the Shift key down to constrain proportions, drag the Cattle Egret silhouette from page one onto page two, and scale it to fit and ungroup it.

5. Choose Modify ⇨ Arrange ⇨ Bring To Front, and Shift-click the text block. Go to Text ⇨ Run Around Selection. A dialog box enables you to choose whether you want the text to run over or around the graphic.

6. Input a distance you want the text to be offset from the graphic in the four fields. If you choose not to put in a number, the text abuts the graphic.

7. Click OK, and the text reflows around the graphic.

8. Use keyboard arrows or the mouse to move the graphic around so text flows the way you want.

Depending on word lengths and other factors, the effect will work or not. You can resize the graphic, or change the shape of the text block, and the runaround continues to work. Move the text to the front, however, and it runs over the graphic.

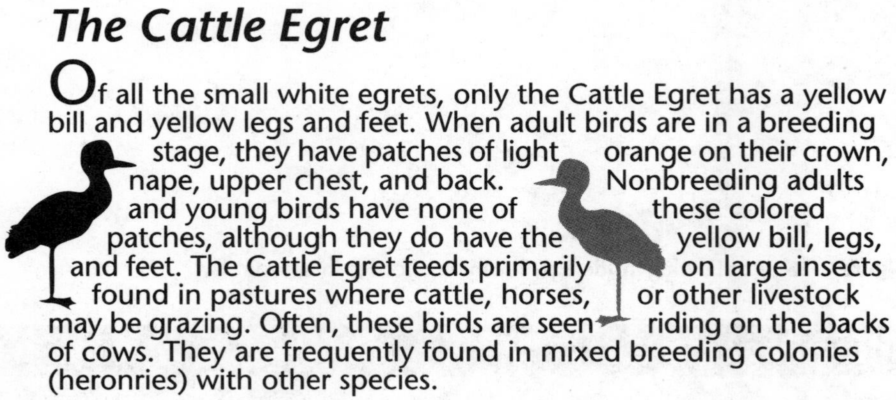

The Cattle Egret

Of all the small white egrets, only the Cattle Egret has a yellow bill and yellow legs and feet. When adult birds are in a breeding stage, they have patches of light orange on their crown, nape, upper chest, and back. Nonbreeding adults and young birds have none of these colored patches, although they do have the yellow bill, legs, and feet. The Cattle Egret feeds primarily on large insects found in pastures where cattle, horses, or other livestock may be grazing. Often, these birds are seen riding on the backs of cows. They are frequently found in mixed breeding colonies (heronries) with other species.

Figure 9-19: Text runarounds in action

The text does not run around a group. If the shape is simple to begin with, just ungroup it. When you come across a situation where an ungrouped mass could possibly cause mass confusion, draw a simple shape that's roughly the same as your grouped object. Give it a stroke and fill of None. I generally group that object with the object that I want the text to run around just to get the placement within the text fixed, and then I ungroup them. It's then a matter of selecting the new object and the text and applying the runaround.

The beauty of Paste Inside

For the last projects in this chapter, you place an image inside a block of text, and use a block of text as a lens fill. This graphic effect doesn't work too well unless you have heavy blocks of text — the heavier the better.

First put an image inside a letterform. Usually this would be a headline, but in this case, use the Habitat Alert logo: Due to font issues, the text has been set for you, then converted to paths (Text>Convert To Paths), and then each word was turned into a compound path (Modify>Join).

1. Start by opening the TextInGraphic.FH10 file found in the Chapter 9 folder on the book's accompanying CD. When it opens, you'll see the final result of the project, and the elements you need to do it yourself. You build the logo itself in a project in Chapter 11.

2. Select the black version of "HABITAT" and notice in the Object inspector that this is a composite path.

3. Import TobyhannaFerns.tif from this chapter's folder on the CD. Place it so that it covers the text, and cut it to the Clipboard (Command/Ctl+X).

4. Select the text, and go to Edit ➪ Paste Inside. (If you want to experiment a bit, hold down Opt/Alt and click in one of the letters. This clicks "through" the compound path and to the object that is pasted inside. Now you can use the mouse or keyboard arrows to move the image around inside the text.)

5. You have "greenery" for the top word; how about "water" for the bottom? Import PoconoRipples.tif from this chapter's folder. Repeat the preceding steps with the word "ALERT" and you're done. Group the letterforms to make alignment easier in the future. It should look similar to the image shown in Figure 9-20.

Figure 9-20: An image inside a text block

Let's try another technique. In this project, you use text as a lens fill to modify a graphic. The graphic can be a photographic bitmap or a piece of vector art; the technique doesn't know the difference.

1. Move to page two of TextInGraphic.FH10 to see the finished image used for Figure 9-21. Below that is a block of text that I've converted to paths and made into a compound path. If you want to try this with another typeface, you can import any of the text files found in this chapter's folder on the CD. Import one of the images from the CD, or just clone the image at the top of the FreeHand page. Place it behind the text block, and adjust (scale) the text or the image to fit comfortably. To be more precise with this technique, you should be working with live text until everything fits, and then convert the text to paths (or a copy of the text to be safe).

2. This time, you don't want a compound path, because they don't work with lens fills. So select the text group, go to the Fills inspector, and select Lens from the menu. At this point, I encourage you to experiment with the various types of lens fills and what they do to the underlying image. Some images work best with a Lighten, others with a Darken, or Transparency. In Figure 9-21, I placed a clone of the text above a Darken lens fill, and moved up and to the left a few points to make the lens fill appear as a shadow. In the top third of the text, there is no lens fill; in the middle white text is shadowed with the lens fill; and at the bottom there's only the lens fill. Exploration and experimentation are key when you're working with this type of graphic effect.

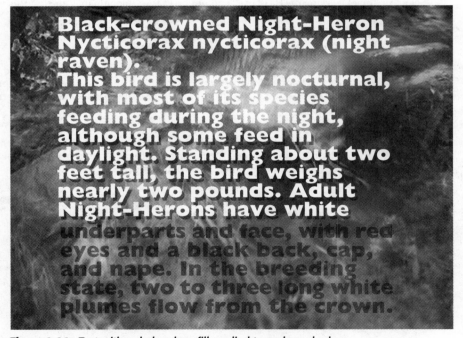

Figure 9-21: Text with a darken lens fill applied to make a shadow

Summary

Typography is very controllable and fun to work with in FreeHand and, in my opinion, is one of the program's most powerful elements. The chapter began by explaining how to get text into a layout, and basic word-processing tasks. It then explained text blocks and how you can link them and how easy it is to make multicolumn layouts. Tabs and tables were discussed, and you built a table with wrapping tabs. Separate projects taught you about basic text styles and techniques for inline text and shadows. Finally, you learned how to place graphics in the copy itself as an inline graphic, and how to use text to fill graphic shapes, how to put images into text, and how to use text as a lens fill.

Project Summary

There were several items produced in this chapter which could be used in the Habitat Alert site such as the bird table, the logo with text in it, and the text on a path logo as well as the text in the graphic. But none of these specific examples were used in the site.

✦   ✦   ✦

FreeHand and Web Graphics

FreeHand can get you well on your way to designing for the World Wide Web even if you have little knowledge of HTML programming. The program makes it easy for you to design the basic graphic look and function of a site in such a way that there's little left to do but apply finishing touches in Dreamweaver MX. Naturally, when you get the pages into Dreamweaver, you'll find lots of things to do, but you already completed the heavy lifting in FreeHand.

Turning a FreeHand Page into an HTML Page

Macromedia wants you to be able to develop Web pages in FreeHand so bad that they even have a default Web page in the Document inspector drop-down menu. This page is set to 550-pixels wide by 400-pixels tall. A page that size is fine, but if you have another size in mind, feel free to adjust it. For instance, you may be designing a banner ad or just the navigation system for a site.

To make your design time and ultimate production as worry free as possible, you should start by making a master page (or a custom template) that contains all the graphics, colors, fonts, and styles that will be common throughout your site. Continuing with your goal of workflow efficiency, you should also think about using FreeHand to generate a comprehensive layout for the site. You've probably made a sketch of how the site will flow, and therefore you know approximately how many pages will be involved. Start your document with at least that many pages. Then transfer your sketchy ideas onto the pages.

Tip

With the Page tool, it's easy to lay the pages out on the Pasteboard in a logical order, similar to a flow chart. By doing this, you can track your ideas better and decide what kind of navigational aids or graphics will make the site more user-friendly. To move the pages around the Pasteboard, click the Zoom tool and zoom to a viewing range that enables you to see all or most of your pages. Then turn on the Snap To Grid feature in the Edit menu. Select the Page tool, and arrange the pages to suit the flow of the site. It's a good idea to move your first page up to the upper-left corner of the Pasteboard so you don't run out of room later.

In the following pages, you see how easy it is to publish to the Web through FreeHand.

Export as HTML

The basic premise to HTML conversion is simple: Make a page, choose File ➪ Publish As HTML, select some parameters, and view your page in a browser. But, some additional work will result in a more polished Web page. This chapter uses files found in the Chapter 10 folder on the CD that came with this book. To begin, open the FreeHand HTML Output folder and take a look at a completed Web page layout, which was constructed completely within FreeHand 10. Inside that, you'll find three Web-page-prep00x.html pages. Double-click the 001 file's icon to open Netscape Navigator; drag it over an Internet Explorer icon to open it in that browser.

This site is just an example of different ways to make buttons or links work. Later in this section, you can make changes to the pages and publish your own HTML page. For the moment, experiment with the three word links on the right side of the page. Text was input in FreeHand and then converted to paths. Each word was then given a link as described in the instructions below. This makes for a quick-and-easy way to maintain a particular font and size, but a user must touch the graphics with the cursor to activate the links. White space (or whatever the background color is) doesn't count; you must put the cursor directly over the graphic, and I think that approach is too tough on the viewer.

Click the Act button to go to page 2. Not much changes other than color, and the appearance of the links. If you have the Lithos Bold font installed on your computer, you can view the text as it was designed. If not, you view whatever your browser sees fit. The underscore indicates a hyperlink, and the cursor changes immediately when you pass it over the text.

Clicking the Support link takes you to page 3, where I converted the text to paths, but to make the button easier to hit I placed a filled rectangle behind the text. Then I grouped the text and rectangle and applied a link. With this combination of objects, the link is easy to hit, and I maintain the integrity of my font. It's important to note that if you stroke an object, give it a fill of None, and then apply a link to that object, the cursor is active only over the stroke itself. For that reason, I delete any stroke (to avoid my own confusion) and fill the shape with the background color.

Navigation panel

Unless you have a single-page Web site, you need links or buttons on your Web pages. Those links are easy to apply through the Navigation panel (Windows ➪ Panels ➪ Navigation) as shown in Figure 10-1. This panel is described fully in Chapter 4, but you actually use the panel in this chapter. Select any object on your page and open the Navigation panel, which provides a Name field for naming the object. By naming a linked object, you can search and select that object in the Find Graphics dialog box. The Search feature is case-sensitive, so keep your naming conventions consistent.

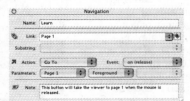

Figure 10-1: The Navigation panel links objects on your page to the entire Web.

Beneath the Name field is the Link field, where you can make a link to another page in the FreeHand site, or type a URL address to take the viewer anywhere. If you are entering your first link, the drop-down menu is empty, but each link you add is automatically added to the menu. This feature can save you a lot of typing and head-scratching when you are creating several pages that need common links. To the right of the text field is a binocular icon. Choose a link from the drop-down menu, and click the binoculars to perform a search of the entire document for items with that link. All will be selected; you can use this feature to assure yourself that each page has the correct number of links, or to make a global change to the links themselves.

Open the Web page `prep.FH10` file, and save it to your hard drive. Give it a new name. For this project, you add a fourth page and make some changes. Go to page 3, and choose Duplicate from the Document inspector pop-up menu. The FreeHand page indicator at the bottom-left corner of the application window tells you that you're on page 4, but you're really on page 3. Click the cursor anywhere on the page. (The page indicator changes to reflect your actual page view.) Then move to page 4.

This page is identical in every way to page 3, but you want to know that you've actually moved to another page in your project, so follow these steps to change the color of the major elements:

1. Click Control+A (Command+A) or choose Edit ➪ Select ➪ All; then shift+click the text block to deselect it.

2. Build a reddish color in the Color Mixer panel (see Chapter 5 for help if you need it), and add that color to the Swatches panel by dragging a swatch of it into the Swatches panel body.

3. Select Edit ➪ Find And Replace ➪ Graphics, and click the Replace tab. Then, select Fills And Strokes, and check Include Tints.

4. Choose Color from the drop-down menu, and select Black from the available colors.

5. Select the red color you just made from the Change In menu.

6. Click Apply.

All of your graphics are now red. To be able to navigate to this new page, though, you must put links on the other pages. Surprisingly, that doesn't take much time, but the following steps allow you to experiment along the way:

1. Zoom to view all four pages. Select the bottom piece of the circle graphic on page 1, and give it a fill — any color will do.

2. Select the same graphic on page 2, and give it a different colored fill, but delete the stroke.

3. Now select the bottom circle graphic on all four pages and choose Window ➪ Panels ➪ Navigation.

4. Type **Page 4 button** in the Name field, and choose page 4 from the drop-down menu in the Link field. This links all four graphics to page 4 of this site.

5. Click the cursor on an element on page 4, and choose View ➪ Fit To Page. Double-click the cursor in the text block that begins "Page 3," and when the cursor changes to the text tool, change the number 3 to **4**.

6. Select the rest of the text in that text block and type the words, **Back to the beginning on a substring**. Note that this replaces selected text in the document.

7. Select Back to the beginning, and open the Navigation panel if it's not still open. Choose Page 1 from the Link menu. Notice that the selected text is now entered in the Substring field. Set the Action to Go To, the Event to On (Release), and Parameters to Page 1 (it happens to be there by default). Leave Foreground selected.

Now you're ready to make the HTML page. This part can seem intimidating if you've never had anything to do with Web-page construction before, but only because the terminology is a little strange. If you are in this category, you can have the Wizard (Windows) or Assistant (Mac) help you through the process painlessly. The following steps do that first; then they go through it manually:

1. Choose File ⇨ Publish As HTML. The HTML Output dialog box opens as shown in Figure 10-2. The first time you open this window, you'll only have the Default choice for an HTML setting. If you save your setups, you can name them and choose for later projects.

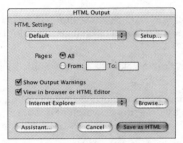

Figure 10-2: The HTML Output dialog box has basic settings for your Web page.

2. Select Pages: All; check Show Output Warnings, and check View in browser or HTML editor. Select your preferred browser from the drop-down menu, or click the Browse button to find the browser you want.

3. Click the Wizard or Assistant button (depending on the computer's operating system). The first window is an introduction to the process. After reading it, move to the next page.

4. Page 2 lets you decide whether to set up your page using layers or tables. Layers are not supported on 3.0 version browsers, and that may prevent some viewers from seeing your site as you designed it. Tables work on all browsers, but they don't support overlapping objects, and slicing may occur. Call me a rebel, but since the 4.0 browsers are now one or two generations old, I don't worry about people with 3.0 browsers. The choice is yours, though. For the purposes of this exercise, choose Layers, and move to the next page.

5. This page dictates how your vector art will be converted when the HTML page is generated. You have a choice of SWF, GIF, JPEG, or PNG. I encourage you to experiment with these settings. I found that in this particular project, PNG worked best. SWF actually lost button functionality, and GIF and JPEG both lost entire chunks of the graphics. Choose PNG, and continue to the next page.

6. You only have bitmaps for the credit cards, but you must choose a method for reproducing them. The choices are the same as with vector art, but in this instance, use JPEG. Click the arrow for the next page.

7. Page 5 tells you where FreeHand wants to place the HTML files. Because you'll probably make changes and adjustments in your pages, it's a good idea to place the folder where it can easily access it. I use the desktop. FreeHand creates a folder called FreeHand HTML Output and places all the necessary files inside. Do not rename any of these files. Move to the next page.

8. This page enables you to save your settings with a name that you can access from the menu on the first page of the HTML Output window. Name this setting **MX Bible PNG** and click the Next arrow.

9. Page 7 is a wrap-up page explaining what you've done so far and what you can still do. Read it and click the Finish button. Hold tight until we're through with the manual HTML Output setup.

   If you've made Web pages before, you can make your decisions on file types and so on without using the Wizard or Assistant. Instead, click the Setup button to open the HTML Setup dialog box as shown in Figure 10-3.

Figure 10-3: Use the HTML Setup window to choose page attributes manually.

10. There is a Setting Plus and Minus button at the top of the window. For first-time visitors, the menu reads Default, and the buttons are basically dead. Click the Minus button to delete a setting, and Plus to add a setting that you make in this window. For now, ignore the buttons.

11. Immediately beneath the buttons is the Document Root field, which was filled out by the program. Make a mental (or written) note of the folder's location, or select the Browse button to put the folder where you want it.

12. In the Layout menu, choose whether to use layers or tables to make your page.

13. In the Encoding menu, you can choose a language for the HTML encoding. For North American and British English, choose Western (Latin1). There are 17 other language choices.

14. Under Export Defaults, select the file type you want for vector art and bitmap images from their respective menus.

15. Click Apply.

16. If you want to save the settings, click the Plus button to open a dialog box in which you name the settings. Give them names, and click OK.

17. Click OK to close the HTML Setup dialog box and return to the HTML Output dialog box. Click the Save as HTML button.

18. Now Freehand creates a new untitled document and selects objects on the pages without any intervention from you. Finally everything spins to a stop, and you can continue with your work.

19. Navigate to the folder that you set up in the HTML Wizard or Assistant, or Setup page.

Now you're ready to test your new site. By default, FreeHand is set to open your browser as soon as the conversion is complete. If you've turned this option off, then open the FreeHand HTML Output folder and look inside. You'll find another folder named Images, and four pages named with a sequential number. To view the pages, double-click the –001 page and drag its icon over your browser's icon, or click File ➪ Open File to open the page in your browser. It should look and react the same as the sample file on the CD, with the exception of the changes you made and the additional page. Experiment with the different types of buttons you created to go to page 4. Note how the cursor works on page 3, where the button is actually the stroke. Test the subscript link you built on page 4. If things have gone awry, double-check your HTML output settings in the FreeHand document and export the pages again.

If you took my advice and checked the Show Output Warnings option in the HTML Output dialog box, a dialog box appears after the HTML output process is complete. This window notes every possible thing that can go wrong in your site. Most times the notes concern version 3 browser problems. You should attend to any of the errors it lists to make an error-free site. You can correct most errors more easily in Dreamweaver than in FreeHand.

You cannot change the names of any of the files inside the FreeHand HTML Output folder and expect the site to function. It won't. It's cast in stone. Code has been written that includes filenames. To make a change in a filename, you also have to go into each page and adjust link names. It's really not worth the trouble.

This short project gave you a chance to see how parts of the Navigation panel and HTML Output windows work. More importantly, you learned that you can make a quick, rough page to test basic ideas and the flow of your site before launching full-bore into Dreamweaver.

Graphic Considerations

You've read it all before, but here are the basics. Different file types are available for different end uses of the file. When it comes to working on the Web, there are four basic file types that work efficiently in one instance or another:

GIF, JPEG, PNG, and SWF. Each has a specific use, sort of like a doctor specializing in feet, lungs, or eyes.

GIF (pronounced "Jiff" or "Giff," Graphic Interchange Format) is good for large blocks of solid color. These blocks shouldn't have gradients or soft variations in color or tone. If they do, banding occurs, due to the number of colors involved in the eight-bit color file. Think of a block of red next to a block of yellow. If you create a 25-step gradient between them, you will get various shades of orange in a smooth, blended gradient. But if you only have two steps the jump between red and yellow is pretty severe, with only two shades of orange. This creates steps between the colors called banding. You can decide to have a few colors or as many as 256 colors depending on the type of artwork or project you're working on.

JPEG or JPG (pronounced "Jay Peg," Joint Photographic Experts Group) is best suited for continuous tone images. This file compression type is faithful to smooth gradients, but it leaves unsightly artifacts or blotches in large blocks of solid color — especially noticeable in reds. This type of compression results from a user-defined degradation of the image. It is the most efficient method of compression for continuous tone images, but it does so at the expense of a lot of data that is discarded.

PNG (pronounced "Ping," Portable Network Graphics) is the cream of the bitmap crop, giving up to 32-bit images and alpha channel support for transparency. But it's not supported on all browsers. Microsoft Internet Explorer 5.0 supports PNG, as does Netscape Navigator 6.0, but it has a small audience right now.

SWF (pronounced "Swiff," ShockWave Flash,) is a format for saving vector art especially for placement in Flash pages. Exporting a FreeHand file in SWF format maintains the sharpness and smoothness of vector art at any size, allowing the artwork to be magnified or reduced without image degradation — and it happens on the fly. Animations are an excellent use of SWF file export. Because you're working with vector files in the first place, SWF compression is extremely efficient, and files are quite small.

Integrating FreeHand Files with Dreamweaver MX

Problems or errors in the HTML output can be handled more efficiently in Dreamweaver, because Dreamweaver is a Web page development program; whereas FreeHand is an illustration program.

In the HTML Output window, you have the option of choosing Dreamweaver MX as the browser or HTML editor to view the final output. I suggest this option. After all, you have arguably the strongest Web page development program right there on your machine — why not use it? Dreamweaver offers everything you could want to fine-tune your pages. I suggest that you do another Publish to HTML using Dreamweaver MX as the editor. First, export the pages using tables for positioning; then publish the site again using layers. After each export, examine the site in Dreamweaver. You'll notice some features that are good, and others that are bad. For instance, using tables chops the page into four or five chunks, and all the button/link work is useless. However, layers bring everything to the page as advertised. If you export and open the pages only in a browser, you'd only see that things didn't work — not why.

Macromedia originally called FreeHand a "Web development tool." As such, FreeHand should be used as a design platform and test bed for HTML output in general — unless you're doing an extremely simple page layout.

Integrating FreeHand Files with Fireworks MX

What FreeHand lacks in the graphic bells and whistles you see on the Web today, Fireworks makes up in a big way. FreeHand doesn't have much in the way of textures and other soft-edge features that make a Web page look alive. That's the job of Fireworks, and it's quite adept at it. Each of the programs in the Studio MX is suited to a particular job and works hand-in-glove with the other four programs.

Any graphics that you develop in FreeHand can be dragged and dropped, copied and pasted, exported and imported, or even opened directly in Fireworks, because FreeHand vector drawing tools are more powerful and numerous than those in Fireworks. If you want to have airbrushed strokes, soft drop shadows, and colorful textures, you can't get them from FreeHand, but you can do the heavy lifting there, and apply the fun stuff in Fireworks. The application of various stroke styles can be seen in Figure 10-4, and the result of a path with those stroke attributes is shown in Figure 10-5. FreeHand has a larger vector-based drawing toolset that is specifically designed for illustration. I think of it as using the right tool for the job. When my illustration or layout is complete, I move it into Fireworks to make my textured panels, 3-D buttons, and rollovers with ease.

Figure 10-4: The Stroke Styles dialog box provides many variations of line treatments.

Figure 10-5: The bird has been turned into a fuzzy chick with a Hatched stroke style.

Fireworks can import native FreeHand files, EPS (Encapsulated PostScript), JPEG, TIFF, GIF, PNG, and BMP file types, but vector art should be copied/pasted from FreeHand for the best results. If your FreeHand file contains 0.5-point (hairline) strokes, they are imported into Fireworks as a 1-point line. Although this may seem like a bug, the thinnest line a monitor can reproduce is 1-pixel, or 1-point. Anything smaller either appears at 1-point, or disappears completely. Another caveat with the direct import of FreeHand files is that strokes automatically take on a round cap. The only way to maintain sharp corners on strokes is to export the files as GIF, JPEG, PNG, EPS, or BMP. Those formats provide sharp corners, but you lose the live vector editing capability available in a FreeHand copy/paste, drag and drop, or file import.

Because Fireworks is a Web-based program, it projects color in RGB. Therefore any graphics you make in FreeHand in CMYK or grayscale are converted to RGB. Oddly enough, if you choose black from the CMYK library for an object, and drop it into Flash, it retains a black appearance — 0r, 0g, 0b. However in Fireworks, that same operation results in a 90 percent gray made up of 24r, 21g, 18b.

You can take a multipage document in FreeHand and import it in Fireworks as layers or as single pages. The layers you set up in FreeHand can be imported as one flattened layer if you prefer. Conversely, you can convert the layers into separate frames to make an animation. Finally, you can maintain the layer stacking order as Fireworks layers.

Other options for importing FreeHand files are the inclusion of invisible layers (layers you've turned off), and importing the background layer with the page. If you don't choose either of these options (the default), invisible and background layers are ignored in the Fireworks import.

Another option is Render As Images. This has the benefit (or hazard) of turning everything into a single bitmap. All groups, blends, or tiled fills are reduced to a bitmap object. There's a text input field where you can enter the number of objects that must be in a group, blend, or tiled fill before Fireworks rasterizes the file. If the vector you are importing has the specified number of objects or steps it will be rasterized as a bitmap image instead of as a vector. If you don't want this to happen, remove the number from the field.

Simple button shapes are a snap in Fireworks. If you want something more complicated, it may be advantageous to set up the basics in FreeHand first; then add the bevels, highlights, shadows, and so on in Fireworks.

Another time-saver is the creation of a symbol in FreeHand that you can export into Fireworks, where you can modify it — as a symbol. All instances reflect your modifications.

Integrating FreeHand Files with Flash MX

Flash MX

The same reasons to prepare your artwork in FreeHand before using it in Fireworks apply to the graphics you need in Flash. An added bonus is the ability to create preliminary animations in FreeHand and test the ideas before fully developing them in Flash. The FreeHand layout consists of the storyboard for a Flash movie, which you can export as scenes or Keyframes in Flash. That simple feature can save you hours. The same document can be printed as a brochure or series of fliers, which can cut your production time drastically.

Another reason to use FreeHand to develop a Flash movie is your ability to maintain transparent lens fills when the file is imported to Flash. The fills become alpha color transparencies in Flash.

Symbols are becoming more powerful in the Macromedia arsenal of programs. FreeHand's symbols can be imported into Flash, providing extended editing in your movies. If you used symbols in one program, you won't lose any time working with them in the other program. The procedure couldn't be much easier. When you import or copy a FreeHand document, all the symbols from the FreeHand library are imported or pasted at the same time, and placed in the Flash document's library. The bonus is that multiple use of the same element (symbol) doesn't add any overhead to the Flash file.

FreeHand's text-handling capabilities will certainly come into play when you're designing your site. You can make styles for various text blocks in the layout and quickly change fonts, colors, and sizes to embellish ideas and concepts. The graphic search and replace can also help you make rapid modifications to your site's storyboard. When you're done, you can test the storyboard as a Flash movie with links you applied through the Navigation panel. You can print individual pages of the storyboard at high resolution to show the client, and you can e-mail the file as a Flash file for approvals or conceptual discussions. After the site is approved, it doesn't take that much more work to prepare the storyboards for printing as a multipage brochure, folder, or set of individual sell-sheets. Conversely, a group of similarly designed fliers or sell-sheets created in FreeHand can be used as the basis for storyboards.

There are a few issues to keep in mind when you're importing FreeHand graphics. In Flash, objects that overlap on the same layer react similarly to the Punch Xtra in FreeHand. The topmost object punches its shape out of anything under it. If you don't want that to happen to your images, follow this procedure:

   1. In FreeHand, place overlapping objects on separate layers.

   2. In Flash, choose File ➪ Import, and choose the FreeHand document you want.

3. The FreeHand Import dialog box opens (as shown in Figure 10-6); choose how to import (map) pages: as scenes or Keyframes; choose Layers in the Layers Mapping section.

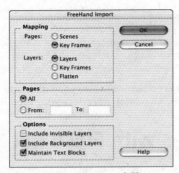

Figure 10-6: FreeHand files are imported with the help from the FreeHand Import dialog box.

4. Select the Invisible and Background layer options, and decide whether to maintain text blocks.

5. Click OK.

The drawing goes into Flash on separate layers, and overlapping objects overlap instead of punching each other out.

Blends in FreeHand can be converted to layers for animation, and based on that function, an imported blend from FreeHand converts the various steps in the blend to separate paths in Flash. If you're using a blend as a means of changing colors — not as an animation process — the addition of these paths increases the Flash file size. Keep that in mind as you're making the art in FreeHand, and try to keep the number of blends to a minimum.

Instead of blends, you may be able to use gradient fills. Here, Flash reduces the number of colors in your gradient fill to a maximum of eight. A gradient that size will be a simple color gradient fill in Flash. But, add more colors to the gradient, and Flash breaks the fill into clipping paths that look like a seamless gradient. In fact, if you choose Modify ➪ Break Apart, the gradient separates into distinct rectangles that contain a blend from one color to another. These clipping paths increase file size, and therefore file loading times, so try to keep your gradients under eight colors.

If you worked with FreeHand before, you probably encountered a box with an "X" in it when you expected to see an EPS file — the EPS preview is missing. The same holds true with Flash. If you're going to import a file that contains an EPS file, follow these steps:

1. In FreeHand, export the file in Illustrator 7 format.

2. In Flash, choose File ➪ Import, and navigate to the file you just made.

3. The Illustrator Import dialog box opens, as shown in Figure 10-7. Choose how you want the layers converted, and whether you want invisible layers.

Figure 10-7: The Illustrator Import window encountered when importing EPS files

4. Click OK.

If you have a file that has been exported from FreeHand as Macintosh EPS, MS-DOS EPS, Photoshop EPS, or Generic EPS, the file will not import. You must re-export it in an Illustrator format. Because of this, when importing pages into Flash, you may encounter an imported page on which nothing seems to happen, or find that you are missing pieces of the page. More than likely, FreeHand will have warned you, but you ignored the warning. Go back to the original document and export it again as an Illustrator (.ai) file and all will be well.

Summary

In this chapter, you learned how to make a series of pages in FreeHand as a storyboard for a Web site. You used the Navigation panel to apply links to text and graphic elements that allow the viewer to move from one page to another. Then FreeHand published the file as HTML that you could view on your browser or open in Dreamweaver for further work. FreeHand files work freely with Fireworks and Flash, and you explored how to export files to those programs. In a project, you added a page to an existing layout and made links on other pages to be able to access the new page. Then you tested your HTML handiwork in your browser.

✦   ✦   ✦

Basic FreeHand Animation

In this chapter, you learn how to make a simple animation you can embellish in Flash or use as is on your Dreamweaver Web site. First, you work with envelopes to get a taste of some fun things you can do in FreeHand. Then you move on to a more traditional approach to animation.

All About Envelopes

An envelope is a path placed around an object or group of objects. Envelopes are not magic, but you can do things with an envelope that are impossible without a lot of work any other way. A basic envelope would be a rectangular shape, but FreeHand supplies 21 shapes from hearts to diamonds and tombstone shapes. The basic rectangle looks like you drew a rectangle around your objects and added a point to the center of each side of the rectangle. But that's where the similarity ends. As you move the envelope's points, or modify the point control handles, the entire contents of the envelope distort as though made from a sheet of flexible rubber.

Envelope toolbar

The Envelope toolbar is shown in Figure 11-1. Open the Envelope toolbar by choosing Window ➪ Toolbars ➪ Envelope. If you click the icon on the left, the envelope that's listed in the menu is applied to the object you selected in the document. The drop-down menu contains the 21 presets, and any other envelopes you add. The icon with the plus sign is the Add Preset button. After you manipulate an envelope, you can click this button to name and add that envelope as a preset that you can choose during another work session. The grayed-out icon with the minus sign is the Delete Preset button. Select an envelope preset from the menu, click this button, and that preset is history. Next is the Copy As Path button which copies an envelope as a simple path. The icon with the clipboard is called the Paste As Envelope button. You use it to paste a previously copied path as an envelope around a selected object. It works like this: Draw a closed shape, and copy the path to the Clipboard. Then select an object or group of objects, and click the Paste As Envelope button. The shape you drew becomes an envelope surrounding the objects you selected.

The next two buttons are the Release and Remove envelope buttons, respectively. Clicking the Release button deletes the envelope but leaves the distortion it provided. The Remove button deletes the envelope and returns the object to its original shape. If the envelope is a preset, it remains in the menu. The last button on the right is the Envelope Map button. Clicking that button applies a grid to the envelope so you can see the distortion that is taking place.

Figure 11-1: The Envelope toolbar can float free or be attached to the Main toolbar.

Use an envelope for a logo treatment

In this short project, you use an envelope to create text with a watery wave effect. Start by opening LogoEnvelope.fh10 in the chapter11_exercise folder on the CD-ROM that comes with this book. Save the document to your hard drive. At the top of the page, you'll find the finished logo. "Alert" is supposed to look like a shadow of "Habitat." The shadow falls on water that happens to be the habitat for the herons this organization is attempting to protect. Beneath the finished logo is the starting point — the text. I converted everything to paths and applied some extreme kerning. You make some changes to the word, "Alert."

1. First, you must make "Alert" as wide as "Habitat," and give it the appearance of perspective. You could use the Perspective grid for this, but in this particular case, I thought the grid would be too extreme, so I chose the 3-D Rotation Xtra. Begin by selecting the "Alert" group and moving it so that the top corner of the "A" is under the "H" in "Habitat."

2. If rulers are not visible, go to View ➪ Page Rulers ➪ Show, and drag a vertical ruler out to the right edge of the "T" in "HABITAT." Place a horizontal guideline at the bottom of the word, "ALERT."

3. Select the "ALERT" group, and drag the bottom-right selection handle all the way to the right guideline. If you have Snap To Guides selected (View menu), the cursor will more or less "slide" along the guideline and maintain the baseline of the text object. Do not deselect the group.

4. Double-click the 3-D Rotation button on the Xtra toolbar (Window ➪ Toolbars ➪ Xtra Tools), and adjust the dialog box to match Figure 11-2.

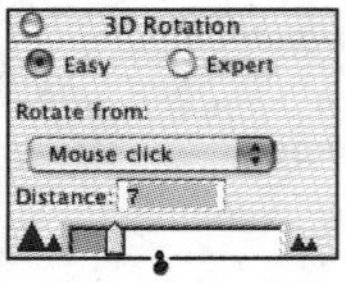

Figure 11-2: The 3-D Rotation dialog box

5. Hold down the Shift key and click (and hold) the cursor approximately at the top-left corner of the "E" in "ALERT." Drag the mouse up and watch the distortion. Stop when you think it's correct. Feel free to be creative and make the distortion as extreme as you wish. Don't worry if the word gets too thin from top to bottom, or wide from left to right. You adjust that next. Select the Pointer tool and save your document.

Now you use an envelope to make waves. You can view the completed logo animation by double-clicking `HabitatWave.swf` in the Chapter 11 images folder on the CD-ROM. Bring the Envelope toolbar into the document (if it's not there already) by going to Window ⇨ Toolbars ⇨ Envelope.

1. Start by selecting the "ALERT" group if it's been deselected.

2. Choose Rectangle from the Envelope drop-down menu, and click the Create button to the left of the menu. This applies a simple rectangular outline with eight control points. For one reason or another, each of the control points has its control handles extended. All of the points in corners are corner points; curve points occupy the middle locations.

3. Just to see what's going to happen, select the top-middle point, and drag one of the control handles up or down. Pretty dramatic, huh? Choose Undo to revert to the original envelope.

4. You want to have several waves in this design, but you can't make all those waves with a single point. So, choose Xtras ⇨ Distort ⇨ Add Points. The Xtra places a point midway between any two existing points. Choose Xtras ⇨ Repeat Add Points two more times to make a total of 15 points across the bottom and top (there are an equal number of points on each side).

5. Beginning with the second point on the horizontal path, drag and select the top and bottom points. Then skip to the fourth set of points and shift+drag and select that set. Continue with every other set of points on the envelope. You end up with eight points on the top and bottom selected.

6. Press the down arrow key twice. Assuming you haven't changed the preferences for this key, you move the points down a distance of two points.

7. Hold down the Shift key and click all the selected points on the top path to deselect them.

8. Press the down arrow key two more times. The result should look similar to Figure 11-3.

Figure 11-3: The finished distortion by use of the Envelope feature in FreeHand

9. If you want to see how the envelope is doing its job, click the Map button. You should have a view similar to that in Figure 11-4.

10. Click the Add Preset button and name this envelope **Wave 1**. Save your document.

Figure 11-4: The Map view of an envelope

Animating the logo

This could be the end of the project if you're only working for print. But why not spice it up a bit for the Web? Let's use what you've got already and make an animation:

1. Open a new document and drag and drop the "HABITAT ALERT" words onto the new document. (Don't bring the finished artwork from the top of the page.) Close the original document and save the new document.

2. Clone the distortion you just completed, and move the clone above or below the original enough to give you some room to work. Hold down the Shift key to constrain your movements vertically.

3. Use the Shift key to select all the points you previously selected and moved (every other point on the horizontal path sections).

4. Press the up arrow key four times.

5. Deselect all the points on the top row, and press the up arrow key four more times.

6. Click the Add Preset button and name this envelope **Wave 2**. Save your document.

7. Click Modify ➪ With the cloned wavy text still selected, release the Envelope by clicking the Release button in the Envelope toolbar. (Don't click the Remove button. It restores the text to its original format.) Then click Modify ➪ Join.

8. Click the original wavy text, and join it as well–remember to release the envelope here, too. (Do not join the two sets of wavy text together!)

9. Select an appropriate color for water; choose a light blue-green, for instance, and apply it to one wavy word.

10. Darken the color and apply it to the second wavy word.

11. Align the two words so the top-left corner of the initial "A" is in the same location for both words.

12. Clone the top word, and send it to the back.

13. Drag a selection box around all three words, and choose Modify ➪ Combine ➪ Blend.

14. Change the number of steps in the blend to 10 in the Object Inspector.

15. Select Xtras ➪ Animate ➪ Release To Layers. In the dialog box, select Sequence and leave the other options unchecked. Click OK.

16. Change the color of the word "HABITAT" to a dark sky blue.

17. Move the word "HABITAT" to its correct location directly above the wavy words, and place it on the Background layer. This action allows "HABITAT" to appear on all frames of the animation.

18. Turn off the Guide, and Foreground layers. The only visible layers should be the Background layer and layers containing the words "New Layer."

19. Now, go to Control ➪ Test Movie.

20. To save the file as a movie, it must be exported. Go to File ➪Export, and choose Macromedia Flash SWF.

ToolTips — What's This Thing Do, Anyway?

Some of the FreeHand icons do not readily tell you what function they perform. To help you out, ToolTips occur if you hover the cursor over the icon for a second or two — be patient, FreeHand 10 is a tad slow in showing the ToolTips. The timelag of their appearance is long enough that having them on doesn't bother most people, and they do come in very handy when you're looking for a tool that you don't usually use. Although ToolTips are on by default, you can turn them off if you want by going to FreeHand's Preferences, and opening the Panels tab. Then just deselect Show ToolTips.

In this project, three versions of the wavy word were used so that the movie will loop. If you have only up and down states, so to speak, the animation goes up, stops suddenly, and starts at the bottom again, only to repeat itself in a herky-jerky motion. In some instances, that could be exactly what you want to do. In this example, however, I wanted a smooth — fluid, if you will — motion without beginning or end.

The number of layers must be maintained between all the animated elements. If you make your initial animation with 25 steps, and then draw something else that FreeHand blends into 18 steps, you'll have 7 steps in which the second element doesn't appear on the stage at all. Keep in mind that the number of blend steps you apply in the Object Inspector must be added to the initial objects that make up the blend.

You can make this animation much more colorful if you want to give the words a gradient fill. Just remember to give all the words the same number of colors in the fill. The colors can be as different as black and white, but they must number the same. Also, blended objects must either have a stroke or not. You cannot blend a stroked object with a non-stroked object; nor can you blend a group. You can't blend two sets of objects at the same time. If you select the multiple "for" words, and the multiple "Habitat" words and attempted to blend them, you'd get a warning dialog box stating that the elements are dissimilar. Take your time, plan ahead, and you'll save time in the long run.

On the CD-ROM

A copy of the logo and animation is in the chapter11_exercise folder. The filenames are `LogoEnvelope.fh10` and `habitatwave.swf`.

Sealing the envelope discussion

During the project, you saved two envelopes. Those can be chosen at any time to be applied to any graphic you choose. You can click the Copy As Path button to copy the envelope to the Clipboard. When you paste it, you have a normal path to work with. You could use it to outline the enveloped graphic, or as a basis for a blended fill or contour gradient fill. Many uses will occur to you as you work with envelopes. Lastly, you can delete them by clicking the Remove Preset button if you know you won't need the envelope in the future.

Basic Animation

The previous animation project got its muscle from a distortion envelope, blends, and the Animate Xtra. In this animation, you rely on drawn objects instead of envelopes. Obviously, this takes a bit more time and drawing skill. This animation will be basic, in and of itself, but will take on life when you add to it in Flash.

This project (shown in Figure 11-5) is found in the chapter11_exercise folder on the CD-ROM that came with this book. Open `Flying Heron Animation.fh10` file to begin, and save it to your hard drive. The jumble of gray shapes is actually three separate birds. As in the previous animation, you want it to loop seamlessly, so the first and last states are identical, and the middle state has moved. The birds are broken down into three parts each: front wing, body, and back wing. Both wings are made in a sandwich style, with the high wing making the front and back, and the lowered state of the wing in the middle. The body could have stayed in a static location, but a bird's body rises just a bit as the wing flaps down. Besides that, it looks neater. To preview the finished movie, double-click `HighHeron.swf` on the CD-ROM.

Figure 11-5: The great blue heron in flight

You may want to work on several layers as you're building an animation of this sort, because of the multiple elements you have to deal with. But it's very important that you have all the final elements (the blends) on a single layer when you use the Animate Xtra. If you don't, the animation will not work properly. This document has all nine elements on the same layer:

1. Begin by selecting the two top wings and hiding them (View ➪ Hide Selection). You might think that something went wrong, because the wings appear to be there still, but you're looking at the end state of the animation. Select them and hide them as well.

2. Select the bottom two wings and hide them. There are only two to hide.

3. Drag a selection around the body of the bird. Look in the Object Inspector. It should say that you have three objects selected.

4. Choose Modify ➪ Combine ➪ Blend. In the Object Inspector, change the number of steps in the blend to 12. Save.

5. Select View ➪ Show All; then select the body blend and hide it.

6. Select and hide the two top front wings and the bottom front wing. You should have the far wings left on the screen. The Keyline view (choose it from the pop-up menu at the bottom of the application window) may be helpful here so you can differentiate various objects.

7. Drag a selection box around the wings on the left, and blend them as you did previously. Change the blend steps to 12. Save.

8. Select View ➪ Show All again, and this time hide the body and the blended wing.

9. Repeat the blend and blend steps operation on the right wings.

10. Select View ➪ Show All. You should have a gray mass with many holes and slices in it. Don't fret. Save the document.

11. Now for the fun part. Drag a selection box around all three blended groups, and choose Xtras ➪ Animate ➪ Release To Layers.

12. In the dialog box, select Sequence, and leave the options unselected.

13. Nothing much changes on the screen. You can tell that the blends have been disassembled into many objects (as seen in Figure 11-6), and the Layers panel has several new layers. Choose Control ➪ Test Movie.

14. Choose File ➪ Export, and select Macromedia Flash SWF for the file format. Name the file **HighHeron**. (FreeHand appends the .swf suffix to the filename). You use this file later in the Flash section.

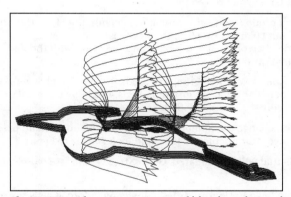

Figure 11-6: Three separate sets of blends make up the animation.

When you watch the animation, you'll see that the wings aren't perfect. To create a more precise animation, you can make intermediate steps in the animation instead of views at the extremes of movement. You'll make that decision based on accuracy versus time, money, drawing ability, and how important the image is to the overall effect of the site.

Waving Reeds project

This project won't take you much time at all, because most of it has been completed for you already in the file named Reeds.fh10 in the chapter11_exercise folder on the CD-ROM that comes with this book. Open that file and save it to your hard drive. The point of this animation is to give the appearance of a lot of action, when in fact not much is really happening. If you want to view the completed animation, double-click Reeds.swf file on the CD-ROM.

If you want something to remain on the stage throughout the animation, you must place it on the Background layer. The Background layer in this document contains four bird silhouettes, a lot of reeds, and some text. Four other groups of reeds have been placed on the Waving Grass layer, and three of them have been set up for you.

I dragged a selection box over the bottom edge of small areas of grass in the original logo concept. I cut the selection and pasted it into the document, where I converted it into a compound path (Modify ⇨ Join). Because I wanted a looping animation, I made a clone from the compound path, and modified it for the midpoint of the animation. In this case, I skewed it left or right—a little or a lot for a random look—and shortened it to make the reeds appear as if they are bending in the breeze. That takes care of the first three groups of reeds. You can do the next one now:

1. Select the group of reeds on the far right, and assure yourself that it is a compound path by looking in the Object inspector. Clone the reeds.

2. Choose the Skew tool and place the cursor at the bottom of the lowest reed. Hold down the Shift key to constrain the skewing, and move the cursor the way you want the wind to blow.

3. It will look as if the reeds have stretched instead of bent. Press the Command/Control key to switch to the Pointer tool temporarily, and grasp a top corner of the grouped reeds. Drag that corner down until the reeds look about the same length they would be if they'd been bent as far as you skewed them.

4. Select the original reed group again, and clone it. By default, the clone rises to the top of the stacking order, but I like to bring it to the front just in case (Modify ⇨ Arrange ⇨ Bring To Front). You need an original in the back and the front, with the distortion in the middle of the animation sandwich.

5. Drag a selection box around the three groups of reeds that you've been working with. If you accidentally selected an adjacent group of reeds, hold down the Shift key and deselect it. Choose Modify ⇨ Combine ⇨ Blend.

6. In the Object inspector, change the number of steps in the blend to 6 and press the Return or Enter key. Save your document. It should look similar to Figure 11-7.

7. Select all sets of reeds that will be animated. Go to Xtras ⇨ Animate ⇨ Release To Layers.

8. When the Xtra is through, go to Control ⇨ Test Movie. As before, if a section of your animation moves and snaps back into a starting position, the stacking order of the graphic elements that make up that section are out of order. Stop the animation, by closing the window, choose Edit ⇨ Undo, and make the necessary changes.

9. To prepare this animation for the Web, go to File ⇨ Export, and choose Macromedia Flash SWF as the file format. FreeHand appends .swf to the file's name. The file can be placed in an HTML page, or imported into Flash for further animating.

Figure 11-7: Four groups of reeds prepared to animate

Use of Symbols and the Library

If you plan on doing animation that involves talking heads, walking and running characters, and moving scenery, you would be wise to develop those objects in FreeHand and make them symbols. When a FreeHand animation is imported into Flash, all the symbols that are related to the project ride along and can be found in the Library. As you probably know, this can save you valuable disk space and loading time, and improve the overall performance of the movie.

FreeHand symbols work seamlessly in Flash. Once there, you can turn them into anything that Flash can use. You can make symbols into buttons, movie clips, and graphics. See the Flash section of this book for more information.

The scope of this book does not allow a discussion of traditional animation techniques. Constructing the drawing for animated characters and props is a project meant for FreeHand, and the storyboard and general conceptual work can be done there to speed up your workflow.

Summary

This chapter consists of mostly animation projects. First you learned how to work with FreeHand's Envelope feature and the 3-D Rotation Xtra to make a distortion. The resulting distortions ended up in a logo that appears to be floating on water. Then you taught a bird how to fly with a slightly different kind of animation that can easily be turned into a movie clip in Flash for some really neat effects. And last, you made the wind blow through a bog of reeds. Not bad for a drawing program!

Project Summary

Let's take a look at what you've done in this chapter that will be used in the Habitat Alert Web site. Some of the images need additional work in another section; some are ready to use in another application.

Files Prepared for Habitat Alert Web Site

Images	What Was Done	Where to Now?
HabitatWave.swf	You made a simple animation that makes the reflection of the logo look wavy.	This file will be used in a Flash animation for an e-ecard.
Reeds.fh10	Using various distortions, you made a few bundles of reeds appear to be an entire field of waving reeds.	This file will be used in a Flash animation for an e-ecard.
Flying heron animation.fh10	You made a simple animation involving three objects–a body, and two wings–that make the bird appear to be flying.	This file will be used in a Flash animation for an e-ecard.

✦   ✦   ✦

Optional Movie Techniques

◆ ◆ ◆ ◆

In This Chapter

Learning different types
of FreeHand movies

Using page and layer
animations in FreeHand

◆ ◆ ◆ ◆

Whereas Chapter 11 used FreeHand's envelopes and layer-based animations, this chapter explains page-based animations and works more with the Navigation panel to enrich the user's experience. It includes two projects that you can work through to understand the concepts better. The completed projects are on the CD that accompanies this book. The first section deals with simple rollover actions to move the viewer through the movie. The second section has a continual animation running in the background, and utilizes mouse clicks to spark the action. This movie is created in two different ways to show the differences between animation setups. The last section delves into the changes that FreeHand has brought to the drawing board.

Types of FreeHand Movies

After spending considerable time and effort on your concept, you can make your FreeHand movie in several different ways. After you decide on a method, it's a matter of producing the artwork and making a selection in the Movie Settings dialog box. The differences are defined by the way you want to create frames. You have three choices, Page, Layer, or Page and Layer.

The chief lesson in this chapter, however, is that controls you apply through the Movie Settings panel remain in effect until you change them, either during a session, or between separate movies. If you have completed a movie using Layers animation in the Movie Settings panel, and you export a movie that was built a week ago using Page and Layers animation — *without changing the settings* — the movie will not work. You must always open the Movie Settings panel, make the animation choice for the particular movie, and *then* test or export the movie. I've made a habit of labeling my Pasteboard area with the type of animation.

Page animation

By definition, making a movie with pages requires the action to move from page to page instead of relying on layers. To make the action work, you can set the frame rate slow enough to time the viewer through the movie, or you can supply interactive buttons to push the viewer along. You can apply Flash actions to elements on pages that alter the course of the movie, or you can simply have the movie run from page one to the end. When the work is complete in FreeHand, you can save the document as an SWF file, which you can place on a Web site, or a CD. Alternatively you can send it as an e-mail attachment that can be viewed with Flash Player. The FreeHand document can be imported into Flash. Each page becomes a scene or a frame, depending on how you set the attributes in the Movie Settings dialog box. With that in mind, this form of document preparation can be utilized to set up the skeletal structure of a Flash movie. When you export the final movie in SWF format, you will have a separate file (consecutively numbered) for each page in the movie. It's extremely important not to rename any of the pages, or Flash Player will not be able to find the correct links.

Layer animation

Layer animation is artwork placed on successive layers of a FreeHand document. When you export this document as a SWF file, each page becomes a scene, and each layer becomes a single frame. Just as in a page animation, you can apply Flash actions to various elements that cause the movie to stop, play, print, go to full-screen animation, load or unload a movie, start a movie, or go to a specific page and layer. When this type of movie is exported as an SWF file, you'll get a separate file for each page in the movie. Don't rename any of these pages either.

Page and layer animation

Page and Layer animation is versatile, as it uses both pages and layers to provide a rich bag of tricks to use on the viewer. Each page is a scene, and layers are individual frames. With this method, you can have multiple animations playing on different pages, or have static pages sprinkled with an animation here and there. You have the added benefit of using Flash actions on the frames or pages that enable you to let the viewer change the course of the movie. The one problem you'll have with Page and Layer animation is that Start, Stop, and Drag don't work quite the way you'd imagine; the entire page moves, instead of a single object or group. This type of movie produces a single document when it's exported as an SWF file.

Flash action concepts

There are seven useful Flash actions that you can use in a FreeHand movie. You apply these actions from the Navigation panel, in the Action drop-down menu. Select an object or group of objects in the FreeHand document, and choose the desired action from the menu. Some of the actions, such as Go To, Print, Load/Unload Movie, and Tell Target, have additional parameters that you must satisfy in the Navigation panel. These parameters appear when applicable; they include page and layer information, events, and other actions such as Play, Stop, Go To, and Print. If you're a Flash user, most of the Flash actions will be familiar. If you're new to Flash, an explanation is in order:

   ✦ **Go To** — This action takes the viewer to a particular page and layer (frame or scene) in your movie.

   ✦ **Play and Stop** — The names are pretty self-explanatory, but these commands make a movie start or stop when a particular event occurs. This event could be a mouse event, or when the movie reaches a particular frame in the movie (frame event).

   ✦ **Print** — To print frames from a movie, this ActionScript must be used to specify which pages can be printed. There's an additional section in the Movie Setup dialog box that enables you to set the quality of print output.

✦ **Full Screen** — It's polite to let the viewer see your movie at the size you make it, but if you want to take over the entire monitor you can use this to put the movie into full-screen mode. No menu bars or controls are visible; the viewer must press the Escape key to stop the animation and return the use of the monitor to normal.

✦ **Start/Stop Drag** — Using this ActionScript lets the viewer drag (or stop dragging) a specific movie clip around the movie's window.

✦ **Load/Unload Movie** — If you have a document that contains two or more pages, you can load additional movies into RAM while the current movie is playing. This can prevent unwanted delays while the movie is spooling up. Unload Movie dumps the movie from the computer's RAM.

✦ **Tell Target** — If you load another movie or movie clip while your current movie is playing, Tell Target controls them (in FreeHand 10 only). FreeHand allows only one level of loaded movies, so you can only load one movie at a time.

Now that you've got a basic understanding, you can get down to specifics.

The Page Animation Project

The concept of this animation is simple and silly. You can see the completed movie on the CD-ROM that comes with this book. The movie is called `BirdFacts101.swf` and is located in the chapter12_exercise folder along with the original FreeHand artwork. Double-click the file's icon to start Flash Player and run the movie. There are five labeled eggs at the bottom of the screen. When the cursor is over four of the eggs (a mouse-over event), the Go To Flash action moves the movie to a particular page. The last egg requires the viewer to click the mouse (an On Press event) that takes the movie to a page that has a frame event that causes six layers to play in succession. A rectangle lies directly beneath the eggs, and when the cursor is over the rectangle, the movie returns to Page 1 of the movie.

It sounds complicated, but if everything is correct, the movie works. One little mistake, and nothing happens. Working with actions follows high-school physics laws: For every action, there is an equal but opposite reaction. With a FreeHand movie, you have to apply an action to get something to happen, and apply another action to get it to stop or change. Working out the original concept is probably the toughest part. For that, I usually make a simplistic movie design, based on my pencil-and-paper sketches of the concept. Geometric shapes serve as graphics, and not a single word is typed onto the pages. I make the buttons, layers, pages, and actions work in this dummy document. When it functions the way I want it to, I use it as the blueprint for the final work. This approach cuts the work to a minimum, and I get the skeleton built before worrying about putting flesh on it.

Creating the artwork

To make the project go quickly, the artwork has been converted to symbols and is on the CD-ROM that comes with this book:

1. Open the CD and copy the BirdFacts101 Symbols file found in the chapter12_exercise folder. Paste this document into your FreeHand English/Symbols folder. To make things easy, all text in the document has been converted to paths. This solves the problem of missing fonts, but it also negates some of the choices in the Movie Settings panel.

2. Open FreeHand and start a new document.

3. In the Document inspector, change the page size to Web size (550-pixels wide by 400-pixels high).

Obtaining symbols

You learned how to create symbols in Chapter 8. For this exercise, you'll use some symbols that have been created for you. Just as in a working environment, symbols can be exchanged between artists on different computers and operating systems.

1. Open the Library (Windows ➪ Library).

2. Select Import from the Options menu on the Library panel.

3. The window should open to the English folder. Open the Symbols folder, and double-click BirdFacts101 Symbols.

4. A new window opens, showing a dozen or so symbols. Select the top-left symbol. Hold down the Shift key and click the last symbol in the window to select all the symbols. If you only want to import two or three noncontiguous symbols, use the Control (Command) key. Click the Import button.

Provided your computer doesn't crash, the library fills with this movie's symbols. The Library should look like Figure 12-1.

Figure 12-1: The Bird Facts 101 Library contains all the elements for the movie.

Layering the art

Remember that symbols are more or less "dumb" when you place them in a document. Any actions you applied to them will not work, and of course, you can't modify them other than normal transformations — no color or attribute changes. To make a symbol functional, it must be removed from its instance. At that point, actions work, but the artwork has been grouped, so you can work with it as it is, or ungroup it. Because you removed the instance, any changes you make to the symbol itself don't affect the art you just placed and released.

Now you can begin to put the page together.

1. Start by dragging an instance of Background graphic onto the document. Adjust it to fit the page.

2. Open the Layers panel, and click the Background layer to move this graphic to the background so it will be viewable in all frames.

3. Go to Modify ⇨ Symbol ⇨ Release Instance, to return the symbol to simple artwork.

4. Drag Harry Heron onto the document, and place him as shown in Figure 12-2. Since you previously selected the Background layer, the symbol will automatically go to that layer.

Figure 12-2: The basic layout for the Bird Facts 101 movie

5. Drag the Page 1 text symbol onto the page and locate it as in Figure 12-2.

6. Drag instances of Great Blue Egg, Great Egret Egg, Black-Crowned Egg, Cattle Egret Egg, and Goose Egg into position on the page. Save the document.

7. The eggs have actions already applied to them, but in their symbol form the actions are inactive. To assure yourself of this fact, select any of the eggs and open the Navigation panel; all the attributes will be blank. Select all eggs and go to Modify ⇨ Symbol ⇨ Remove Instance.

8. Ungroup the eggs that are selected.

The mechanics of Flash actions require an event to take the viewer back to a given page. In this case, you want the viewer to return to Page 1 whenever the cursor is not on an egg. Here, we have an action that has been applied to both background objects that cause the movie to stay on Page 1 when the cursor is over either of them.

If you select any egg and look at the Navigation panel, you'll see that each egg has a link to a page, and an action to cause the move to the page. Figure 12-3 shows a typical navigation setup for the eggs with a minor exception: Because there are no other pages, the Parameters field is blank in your document. When you add additional pages in the next steps, the Parameters field fills in automatically. An argument could be made that the viewer should click the egg to start the event, but I liked the idea of a mouse-over for the first four eggs, then a mouse click to drive the goose animation.

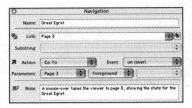

Figure 12-3: The button attached to this Navigation panel moves the viewer to Page 3.

At this point, the page should look very similar to Figure 12-2, but you still need five more pages to fill out the movie. You can Opt/Alt-drag with the Page tool to create duplicate pages, or you can use the Duplicate command in the Document inspector panel. Use whichever method you prefer to create a *single* duplicate page:

1. Go to Page 2, and drag the Great Blue INFO symbol onto the page. Place it on the Foreground layer.

2. Make four duplicate copies of Page 2.

3. Go to Page 3, drag the Great Egret INFO onto the page, and align it with the Great Blue INFO box. To help with the alignment, lock the Great Blue box, Shift + select the Great Egret box, and use the Align panel to center it vertically and horizontally. Click outside the page, select the Great Egret INFO box, and choose View ➪ Hide Selection. Then select the Great Blue INFO, unlock it, and delete it.

4. Save, and move to Page 4. Drag the Black-Crowned INFO symbol onto the page and align it as you did Page 3.

5. Repeat the process for Page 5. Go to Page 6 and delete the Great Blue INFO instance. Save.

It's time to work out some of the details of your movie. Choose a random page and check the eggs in the Navigation panel to make sure they're linked correctly. With a single egg selected, click the binocular icon to the right of the Link field. This action selects all objects on the page that are linked to that particular page, so you should see six objects selected in the Object inspector. The parameters should be complete for each link: The Links field has the page you want to jump to; the Action should be Go To; the Event should be On (Over); Parameters should be to the same page as Link, and Foreground should be in the middle field.

Now test the movie before things get more complicated. Use the Control Menu (FreeHand 10) or open the Controller panel (FreeHand 10 and MX) and select Movie Settings. Set them as shown in Figure 12-4. Note that there are no fonts in this particular movie. However, if there were, you could utilize the Maintain Blocks feature to allow the text to be edited in Flash. If you don't need to do any future editing, choose Convert to Paths to eliminate font issues. Then select Test Movie. FreeHand collects all the information, and after a few seconds, the movie starts. It should remain static until you run the cursor over one of the eggs. As soon as the cursor is over an egg, the movie should move to the appropriate page and stop until you move the cursor over the background area again, returning the movie to Page 1. When you've had just about enough excitement, close the Flash Player window to return to your FreeHand document. Correct anything that may have been wrong. You can check things out in the original FreeHand document that is on the CD-ROM that comes with this book.

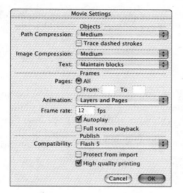

Figure 12-4: The Movie Settings panel for this movie

Final animation

You might have noticed that clicking the Goose egg leads you to a blank page. All the elements you need are in the Library. If you want to have a simple static page, you can place the Swoosh Marks and Legs Only symbols on the page with the YeeHaaHooooo text graphic. If you want to make a slightly more complicated animation, make copies of the legs and apply them to successive layers. The YeeHaaHooooo text was broken down into several smaller chunks for the movie on the CD-ROM, and placed on the same layers as the legs.

Making links

At times, you want to let your viewer print scenes from your movie. You can continue on with the movie you've built, or jump right into the FreeHand artwork (BirdFacts101.fh10) on the CD-ROM.

To add printability, you make a few modifications. First, we'll require that the viewer click the Background to return to Page 1, by changing the action in the Navigation panel from on (over) to on (press). That's not asking too much, and it solves a major problem: how to get from an egg to another object without going back to Page 1.

Getting past Page 1 is the easy part. But, how do you select a page to print? There are two easy methods for selecting a page to print, depending on how you want the movie to play. To simplify your decision-making process, think about where the user has her/his cursor on the page. To make the discussion simple, let's work on Page 2 only:

1. One method is to clone the egg and place the word "PRINT" inside it.

2. Then, with the egg selected, go to the Navigation panel and choose Print from the Action menu.

3. For the Event, choose On Press.Select Page 2 from the Parameters menu, and All in the middle. All prints the background and all visible layers. If you want to only print a particular layer, you could select it here.

The second method might not be as economical, but could enhance the users' experience by making them move to the silhouette of the bird. To accomplish this, select the bird and set the Navigation panel as in the previous method.

Testing the movie

Test the movie as before, with the Test Movie command. When you get to the Goose egg, you should see an animation (if you made one), and clicking an egg or bird prints that page. Clicking the background takes you to Page 1.

Moving outside the movie

Now that you're an accomplished movie producer, how do you get out of the movie business and into the real world? Simple. More actions. This time, go to Page 6 — the Goose page. Select the Goose egg and open the Navigation panel. Type a Web address in the Links field (remember the http:// part of the address). When the linked Goose egg is clicked, the computer starts your browser, and you go to the Web page in the link. You can go to other movies or HTML pages if you place them within the same folder as the current movie.

Exporting the movie

When you're sure that everything is working, go to the File menu and choose Export. Then select Macromedia Flash SWF as the file type and click the Export button. FreeHand creates a Flash Player file that you can place in an HTML page (Dreamweaver), or use as a stand-alone movie.

The Layer Animation Project

The idea behind this movie is to have several animations going at once, and use actions and slight of (Free)hand to make a simple game-type movie (shown in Figure 12-5). The concept is that herons and egrets have interesting eating habits and don't necessarily like broccoli. Clicking various menu items causes the heron to eat what has been clicked.

Figure 12-5: The Hungry Heron Diner movie

Instead of having you go through the building process, the document (HeronDiner.fh10) and the completed movie (HeronDiner.swf) are on the CD-ROM that comes with this book. You can find them in the chapter12_exercise/HeronDiner folder. Double-click the .swf file to see the final results before tearing into the movie's construction. Depending on your experience, you may figure out how it was done before reading about it.

Deconstructing the Diner movies

Drag `HeronDinerLayers.fh10` to your desktop from the CD. Double-click its icon to open the file in FreeHand 10. To view the movie, double-click the `HeronDinerLayers.fh10 1.swf` file in that same folder. This movie contains five pages and consists of 20 layers. Here's how it was constructed.

✦ **Reed background**—I made the area by drawing a few reed shapes consisting of a light and dark ribbon, similar to a blade of tall grass. I used the FreeHand tool to keep an organic look to the shapes. Each shape was copied, and pasted into the Graphic Hose panel (left side of Figure 12-6). When the entire set of five reeds was completed, I set the options on the right side of Figure 12-6, and randomly sewed the reeds across the background. At times, a reed is planted in an unlikely place, and has to be moved manually (which isn't too difficult). The sign is a simple rectangle with an edge added to it. The sign's legs are rectangles with other rectangles pasted inside for shadow effects.

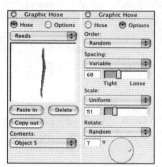

Figure 12-6: Reeds were pasted into the Graphic Hose (left) and applied with the settings on the right.

Note

If you are a true FreeHand masochist like me, you may want to build the movie yourself. If so, there is a file named `HeronDiner Symbols` on the CD. Place that in your FreeHand ⇨ English ⇨ Symbols folder on your hard drive. Start a new document, give it a size of Web, and use the symbols to build the page.

As the reeds were spread with the Graphic Hose, parts of them ended up outside of the page margins. When I was through placing the reeds, I ran a selection box across the top of the page while holding down the Alt (Option) key. Then I selected the Knife tool and in its dialog box (double-click the Knife tool icon in the Toolbox), I selected Straight, Close Cut Paths, and Tight Fit. It's a simple matter to run the Knife tool across the top edge of the page to cut off the top edge of the ragged reeds. Then hold down the Alt (Option) key again and drag a selection box just *outside* the top of the page to select the cut-off pieces. Press Delete twice to clear all the remnants. I created the right and left sides of the page in the same manner and used the same technique to clean up the ground areas on either side of the page.

✦ **The Happy Heron sign**—I made the sign from simple rectangles. The posts have shadows pasted inside them, but aside from that, it's a no-brainer. The words (Fish, Snake, Frog, Broccoli) have been converted to paths, and will be the navigation links.

The major text block is inside a rectangle with radiused corners. I gave it a Lens Fill of Lighten with a value of 66%. You can change that value according to taste and individual situations. I cloned the rectangle, and cut it with the knife in two places. The top half has a half-point stroke; the bottom has a two-point stroke. I placed text on top of the lens-filled rectangle and converted to paths to eliminate font problems. During construction, I kept "live" the text on the Pasteboard in case editing was necessary.

✦ **The snake** — I created animations one at a time on Page 6 (which was deleted when the movie work was complete). I made the frog and snake as a three-object, eight-step blend, and the fish is a 17-step blend attached to a path. The snake starts curved one way, goes straight in the middle of the animation, and curves the opposite way on the other side (by mirroring the artwork). Both the frog and snake have eight steps in their blends. (FreeHand automatically gave them 25 steps, but that would have been too much time for the movement.) To change the number of steps in the blend, go to the Object inspector. I drew a v-shaped wake with the Pencil tool (so it would remain more or less organic) for the snake as it enters on the right. In the middle position, I distorted it a tad, and distorted it again on the left side. I blended the three-object wake separately from the snake, but gave eight steps.

✦ **The frog** — The frog starts out sitting down, extends his arms and legs (legs and legs?) at the top, and sits again (a clone) at the end. All the parts of the frog (eyes, body, belly, legs, and arms) are joined to make the blend.

✦ **The fish** — I did the fish differently. First I drew it; then I applied a 17-step blend. I drew and distorted an ellipse so it looks as though the fish is traveling up and out, down deep, and across to jump again. I attached the animation to the path (Modify ⇨ Combine ⇨ Attach Blend to Path).

✦ **Ripples** — To be consistent and make everything simple, I created ripples around the signposts and the heron's legs as three objects. Each object has a different shape and color. I created only one signpost ripple, and reflected it for the other side. All have an eight-step blend to fit with the rest of the movie.

✦ **Splash!** — I drew the splash at the point where the fish leaves the water and hits it again. I selected the fish nearest the point of entry (into the air or water), noting the layer, and placed the appropriate splash art on that layer. The exit splash is made from a reflected clone of the entry splash and placed on the same layer as the fish leaving the water.

✦ **Fish underwater** — I selected all the fish under the water and gave them a tint of the above-water fish color so they would have the appearance of being under the water.

Animating everything at once

It really doesn't take all that long to make all the animations. FreeHand actually does most of the work. You can do all the animations at one time. Select all the blends, place them on the Foreground layer, and choose Xtras ⇨ Animate ⇨ Release to Layers. If you miss a blend, you will notice that when you test the movie you'll have a single frame with the blend sitting on it. It flashes by without any animation. Stop the test, and release the blend to layers. Each time you run this Xtra, be sure to select the Use Existing Layers option. Keep the Layers panel open at all times, and make sure that you don't end up with more than 17 layers (with this particular movie, your mileage may vary). If you accidentally have a blend on a different layer — for example Layer 4 — and you release to layers, the animation for that blend starts at a higher level, and additional layers are added, creating a mess. If you see numbers higher than you expect, choose Undo, and move your blend to the correct layer. Then run the Animation Xtra again. If you don't, the movie will be discombobulated when it runs, because new layers will have been added out of order.

Then test the movie. You should see ripples, a swimming fish and snake, and a hopping frog. Success! Now the real work starts. First, you explore a five-page movie that uses Page and Layers animation. Then the same movie is explained as a nine-page layers animation (that has a few added features).

The process

The point of this movie is to tell the heron what to eat. When you select an item from the menu, the heron darts his neck out and eats the selection. To save time for the demonstration, a splash image fills the screen for a single frame that implies something has happened. When the splash leaves the screen, the selection (fish, snake, or frog) has disappeared from the animation. The other two meals continue with what they were doing. The punch line for this movie appears when the user clicks Broccoli. That action takes the user to another page, where a simple five-layer animation shows the heron indicating that it doesn't like broccoli. At the end of the animation, a frame event returns the movie to Page 1. Because every page of this movie becomes a separate scene, static elements are placed on the Background (or any other layers below the Separator bar in the Layers panel).

✦ **Page 1** — The three animations (fish and its splash, snake and its wake, and frog) occupy a 17-layer animation stack. If you turn the visibility of the Background layer off, you can see all the animated objects. The movie is set up to play automatically. All the menu item buttons are linked to their separate pages, similar to the page for the Fish link shown in Figure 12-7.

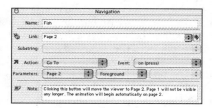

Figure 12-7: The Navigation panel settings for the Fish link

✦ **Page 2** — Page 2 is a clone of Page 1, only the objects concerned with the fish animation have been removed. Animations run from lowest layer to highest layer, with the splash graphic on the lowest layer to create the surprise element in the animation. Because you're already on the Fish page, you could change the Fish button's navigation link to make a pop-up, such as a burp, or take the viewer back to Page 1. In this movie, the buttons kept their links throughout the movie.

✦ **Pages 3 and 4** — One page removes the snake animation, the other deletes the frog animation. Both pages are cloned from Page 1.

✦ **Page 5** — Again, Page 5 is a clone of Page 1, but this time minus the heron graphic. I drew a single graphic of the bird with his mouth open, cloned it to different sizes, and placed it on layers. I used the first six layers. The last three are feathers moving a little each frame. Because you can't place a sound in a FreeHand movie, I placed the word graphic on the last few frames. I cloned the top word and placed it on the top layer (Layer 17). Then I gave it a Go To Page 1 Frame event to begin the movie over again.

If you tear the FreeHand file apart, you'll notice some red squares on the left side of the heron. I wanted them to be obvious for the project, because they're important to the functioning of the movie. One object has a Play Action Frame event for the page it occupies; the second object uses a Go To Frame event to take the movie to the bottom of the layer stack for the current page and keep the animation running on this page until another event occurs. In a real-world movie of this type, the red squares would become any one of the objects in the animation.

Layers animation comparison

In an animation such as this, you can also use masks that appear on pages to cover up an on-going animation (make the selected meal disappear). This isn't as easy or quick as the previous version, but you have more options. This version of the same movie uses the same Page 1 as the previous example, and the same basic animation for the last page, but that's where the similarities end.

✦ **Page 1** — This page is identical to Page 1 in the previous example. It is a bit more valuable in the scheme of things, however, because it contains all the visible animation for all scenes (excepting the last scene). There's a difference in the menu board, though. A new object has been added to the bottom, named Formal Attire Required. The links from the menu items are different as well. Instead of a Go To, these objects use Load Movie to move to the corresponding page.

✦ **Page 2** — Page 2 contains only a splash. Actually, there are two splashes: one on the bottom layer that is set in the Navigation panel to play on a Frame event. That action moves the movie to the next layer, which contains an identical splash. This splash has a Load Movie on Frame action that starts the movie that's playing on Page 3. So, this page is on-screen for two frames, and the second frame takes us to Page 3.

✦ **Page 3** — Page 3 has no background elements, unlike the previous version of the movie. In fact, it contains only the area in which the fish swims. An outline was drawn surrounding the fish area on Page 1. I cloned the water and beach areas and cut and pasted inside the outline. I drew a registration rectangle, cut from the page and pasted onto Page 3, in one of the corners of Page 1. Using the rectangle (with snap to guides on) I aligned the mask on the page and then discarded the rectangle. I placed the mask on the bottom layer, and then cloned it. I applied the clone to the next-higher layer and repeated the process until each layer included a mask. Had this been in a simple area without multiple graphic elements, or if I had been working with simple geometric shapes, I could have made a blend and used the Animate Xtra (Release To Layers) to distribute the mask to all the layers.

✦ **Pages 4 and 6** — These pages are identical to Page 2. They consist of the two splashes; one plays, the other uses Load Movie to move to the next page.

✦ **Pages 5 and 7** — The same concepts used on Page 3 were used here. Instead of making an outline mask, a different method could be quicker. Use the frog as an example. Select all the frog elements on Page 1. Use the Union Xtra to create one complex shape. Then use the Inset Path Xtra with a minus value to widen the shape by a few pixels to allow a little slop in the mask. Then, as before, select any elements that fall under the mask, cut them, and paste them inside the mask.

✦ **Page 8** — For the last page in this animation, the same frames were used from the other version of the movie. The problem was that the feeding heron remained on the background while the animated heron popped out of the corner. It just didn't work. So I made a mask using the technique described in the previous paragraph. I cloned it and placed it on all the layers in the Page 8 animation. The top layer has an Action of Stop, with an Event of Frame action, and the word graphic has an On (Press) event and an Unload Movie Action, which stops (dumps) the current movie, and allows the movie that's playing in the background to continue.

✦ **The Formal Attire Button; Page 9** — For a Start/Stop Drag action, I decided that the viewer could put a napkin around the heron's neck. Not very imaginative, but not too much work either. The words on Page 1 have a Load Movie On (Press) event to Page 9. I drew the napkin and placed it on Page 9 so it would show up in a clear space on the menu board. The napkin has a Start/Stop Drag action with an On (Release) event. FreeHand uses the opposite command to stop a Drag action. If you choose Press, releasing the mouse stops the dragging. At times you just can't get rid of whatever you're dragging. Try double-clicking.

Testing and exporting the movie

I have to reiterate the importance of checking the Movie Settings panel before assuming that everything is the way it's supposed to be. Use the Setup button as you Export the SWF file. If you are working with multiple movies, you will definitely run into problems. The settings stay with your FreeHand application, *not* the document. This is the first thing to look at when someone tells you that your movie doesn't work on his or her machine.

Oddball Movie Tricks

You've seen several ways to make FreeHand movies, but there are other little tricks that you can use to add some quick and cheap effects to your presentation. Remember, you can always export the FreeHand file (as an Illustrator file) and import it into Flash where you can add sound and ActionScripts.

Here's an easy way to make an animation, and an easy way to get in a lot of trouble, all at once. FreeHand's text blocks and animation work together very well. If you set a line of text, and use Release To Layers, the letters that make up the text you typed appear on the screen as though you were typing them. Type **Animation is cool!** in a 72-point font. With the text block selected, choose Xtras ⇨ Animation ⇨ Release To Layers. Choose the Build option. Now test the movie. The letters appear on the screen one at a time, disappear, and start over. Frames in the Movie Settings must be set to Layers or Layers and Pages.

That was pretty neat, but now choose the Spiral tool and draw a spiral that's about four or five inches wide. While it's still selected, choose Xtras ⇨ Distort ⇨ Add Points. Drag a selection box around the entire spiral in order to select all the points in the path. Select Modify ⇨ Split; then cut the spiral to the Clipboard. Draw a text block (larger than the spiral). Paste the spiral into the text block. Keep the text block selected, apply it to the top layer (click the Foreground layer in the Layers panel) of your previous "Animation is cool!" animation, and use Release To Layers. Keep the option set to Build, and deselect Use Existing Layers. Test the movie. The words appear as before, but as the exclamation point is placed, the spiral begins to appear on the page. This trick comes to you thanks to Ian Kelleigh (www.FreeHandSource.com).

Now you think you have it made — between FreeHand and Flash there's not much you can't do. But wait; there's more. Type **Whee** with a couple dozen e's after it. Draw a path like a roller coaster course. Attach the text to the path. Release to layers and test the movie. You can almost hear the kids screaming.

Draw a simple graphic, such as a rectangle and two circles that could be construed as a roller coaster car, and copy it to the Clipboard. Create a text block, and paste the little car in the text block as an inline graphic. Paste several more — as many as you like. Draw another roller coaster path, and attach the text to the path (Text ⇨ Attach To Path), and release to layers, with the option set to Sequence. Test the movie. Now the little car travels along the path you've drawn. The only thing holding you back is the opportunity to put this to work.

Summary

This chapter has shown you several ways to make simple or complex movies in FreeHand. You can use these techniques to test an idea that can be used in its own right, to gain client approval, or show other team members how your idea will work. Or, the movie can be exported as a SWF file as the final project. Naturally, it can be imported into Flash and embellished there. Finally, you learned a few tricks with text blocks and animations.

Project Summary

Let's take a look at what you've done in this chapter that will be used in the Habitat Alert Web site. Some of the images need additional work in another section; others are ready to use in another application.

Files Prepared for Habitat Alert Web Site

Images	What Was Done	Where to Now?
birdFacts101.fh10 (and .swf)	Mouse-over events to make an informational site	You add ActionScript to this file in Chapter 29 when you add some sound. It will also interact with a database using ColdFusion in Chapter 54.
HeronDiner.fh10	Deconstructed to show how a Layer and Page animation was built	
HeronfreestyleMovie.swf	Using techniques taught in this chapter for layer animation this flying heron was made.	You convert this animation of a flying heron into a movie clip and add it to the e-card in flash and add ActionScript and ColdFusion functionality.

✦   ✦   ✦

Printing FreeHand Documents

I s FreeHand a drawing program, a page layout program, or a Web-development program? The argument will probably be going on for years to come. All people who work with FreeHand on a daily basis will have their own point of view, and they'll all be correct to one degree or another. FreeHand can hold its own against other drawing programs when it comes to page layout features. In fact, it can hold its own against some page layout programs. In this chapter you'll learn about the ins and outs of printing or outputting FreeHand documents.

The Basics of Printing

Arguments aside, FreeHand can print with the best of them. Whether your job is destined for a slick full-color brochure, a black and white newspaper ad, or a T-shirt, FreeHand makes it easy for you to get the optimal output you need for the printer to do the job as you have designed it. There are considerations that must be resolved before getting the job underway, though. First in my mind is usually whether the job will be printed in black and white, full-color (CMYK), or spot color.

Black-and-white

Black-and-white print jobs are assumed to be the simplest and cheapest way to go. But that's not necessarily true. After all, look at your local newspaper — there's nothing simple or uncomplicated about all that black ink, especially when it comes to the reproduction of photographs. A black-and-white job is considered cheap because it uses only one ink color. But the preparation of a single-color job can be just as time-consuming and expensive for the graphic designer. It can also be as effective or even more effective than a full-color job.

Halftones

To reproduce photographs, the images must be converted to a halftone. Originally, halftones were created by placing a screen between a negative and the projected image. Where lines in the screen covered up the negative, no image was allowed to form on the negative. When light passed through the screen, an image was created on the film in a pattern of dots. When printed on white paper, a pattern of large dots creates the illusion of darkness, smaller dots, or white space on the paper build the lighter areas of the image. Today, it's all done electronically, but the end results are the same. A halftone example is shown in Figure 13-1.

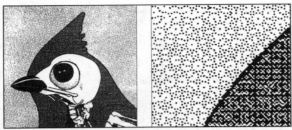

Figure 13-1: A color halftone (in black and white), and an enlargement showing the rosette pattern

The substrate is the material on which your document will be ultimately printed. A t-shirt is one kind of substrate, glass is another, and there are thousands of types and colors of paper. Different substrates require different screen resolutions. A high-gloss paper stock used for a brochure or coffee table book lets the ink dots sit on the top of the paper and dry, creating a sharp image. The absorbent nature of newsprint demands that the ink is sucked into the paper itself, causing what printers call dot-gain. It doesn't take too much imagination to see that the same halftone will print differently on different papers. If you created the halftone for a fairly smooth text stock, and then put newsprint and glossy, coated stock in the press, you'd get different results. The glossy paper would provide a light halftone because the ink isn't applied heavily enough to fill in all the white space around the ink dots. The newsprint copy would be dark and muddy because too much ink was applied and spread into white areas as the ink was absorbed into the paper.

To minimize the problems with dot-gain, paper absorption, and so on, there is a general rule about screen ruling (lines per inch, or lpi). Most newspapers are happy with 65 to 85 lpi. Medium-quality offset printers can hold dots up to 150 lpi. High-end printing presses can go up to 200 lpi and more. To get optimal results, it's best to have a conversation about the images you will be reproducing, the paper stock, and the capabilities of the press and pressman with your printer before you create halftones.

CMYK

Full-color images are produced (printed) by using shades of cyan, magenta, yellow, and black inks. The shades are created from a series of halftone dots; one halftone has been made for each of the four colors. Each halftone screen is rotated so the dots don't line up on each other. In fact, they usually make a pattern called a rosette. By mixing tints of the four colors, it is possible to build a large spectrum of color. That spectrum, or gamut, is not as large as the gamut your monitor produces, and not nearly as large as the human eye can perceive. But, it's the backbone of the printing industry right now. Several colors cannot be printed using the CMYK process. Refer to a swatch book such as the PANTONE Solid To Process book that compares inks "right out of the can" to their CMYK counterpart.

Hexachrome printing

For more adventurous people with deeper pockets, you can also reproduce your artwork with Hexachrome output. As the name implies, the process uses six colors to create a richly colored, lush image. Printing Hexachrome projects is certainly a situation that requires detailed conversations with your printer. It's beyond the scope of this book, but basically, the process uses CMYK colors, plus special orange and green inks to gain a larger, more vibrant color gamut. The colors are displayed in RGB (using your monitor's profile) and require RGB TIFFs to separate into CMYKOG. On the other hand, if you have a CMYK TIFF, it will separate as CMYK and ignore the orange and green plates. Unless Print Spot Colors as Process is selected in the Separations panel of the Print Setup dialog box, spot colors will be separated as usual (explained in the next section). If Print Spot Colors as Process is selected, the spot colors will reproduce as CMYK.

Spot colors

For all those colors that can't be printed with CMYK, ink manufacturers such as Pantone, Focoltone, Munsell, and Toyo have produced thousands of ink colors. These colors are referred to as spot colors. They are the rich blues, reds, and grays that you just can't get from CMYK. They're also fluorescent, metallic, and pastel. A black and white job can just as well be a blue and white job. After all, the service bureau or printer is going to output a single sheet of film for your spot color. Even if you had intended to print the job in a dark blue ink, you can change your mind and use a rich burgundy color instead. Of course, the printer will have a few choice words for you if he's already ordered a special ink for you. Since spot color inks are "right out of the can," they must be ordered for specific jobs. The presses must be cleaned of any ink used previously, and the spot color placed in the press and adjusted. This is extremely labor-intensive, and therefore the cost of a spot color job is usually higher than a black and white job, even though only one ink is being run. I remember a printer that had "free color specials" every day of the week. Monday it was red, Tuesday it was brown, Wednesday was blue, and so on. The customer could get the job printed in one of these colors at the same price as using black ink because the press was going to print nothing but that color all day.

Output Devices and Sources

FreeHand can output to many types of devices. The basics include desktop ink-jet and laser printers, high-end ink-jet and laser printers, and Raster Imaging Process-equipped (RIP) film and paper processors. An RIP is used to interpret the data from the computer file, and convert it into data that the printing device can utilize to get an image on a substrate. It stands to reason that you get better quality the higher up the print chain you go. Desktop printers are great for proofing jobs and making comprehensive layouts for client approval, but unless the final output will be nailed to a telephone pole or tacked to a corkboard at the supermarket, the image quality is less than optimal. Higher-end printers (ink-jet and laser) produce images that are absolutely stunning, but are used mostly for display purposes. Most of the work from FreeHand goes through a RIP at a service bureau or printing plant.

PostScript output

To properly output your FreeHand document, you should have a PostScript-enabled device. Inexpensive ink-jet printers do a super job when printing photos, but will give you jagged edges on your text and vector line work. PostScript printers are several hundred dollars more expensive than a device without PostScript. Look at it as the cost of doing business. You will need such a printer to proof separations.

PostScript is a page-description language developed and owned by Adobe. The PostScript-enabled printer receives your file after conversion by the printer driver. The driver converts your document into PostScript, and transfers that data to the printer, which generates a series of dots on the printer's imaging surface. Those dots are ultimately used to put the image on the substrate.

PostScript is device-independent, and resolution-independent, meaning that a PostScript file prints the same information from one printer to the other. Naturally, settings on individual printers will vary the output, but images from properly calibrated equipment should be virtually identical. The resolution of PostScript imagesetters reaches up to 5,000 dpi, creating extremely sharp images on substrates.

New printing processes are attempting to get rid of the old film negative method of producing printing plates for the presses. Although not widespread, these new devices are being used today. They apply the image directly on the plate, bypassing film completely. The old days of waiting for negatives to be stripped for a job are over.

PDF output

PDF stands for Portable Document Format, another process invented by those creative folks at Adobe. The most prominent PDF program is Adobe Acrobat. This format is extremely versatile, and can make a page that is viewable on the Web. You can then import it into page layout programs, and print it. In order to view a PDF file, you can download the free Acrobat Reader software (www.adobe.com/products/acrobat), but to gain the full power of PDF, you'll need the entire product.

Sadly, FreeHand doesn't make the best PDFs. There are problems with fonts and images that arise often enough that serious PDF producers don't use the File ➪ Export ➪ PDF route for PDF distribution. You should export a few PDF files so you can see if there are problems, or if the conversion works to your expectations. If you do find problems, print the file to disk as a PostScript file, then Adobe Acrobat Distiller is used to create the actual PDF. To print a file to disk, choose File ➪ Print, then in the Print dialog box, choose Output Options from the drop-down menu, then select Save As File (placement of the Save As File option varies between platforms and operating systems, but it's not difficult to find). Save it as a PostScript file, which will receive a .ps extension.

Living in the boonies as I do, I maintain a long-distance relationship with all my customers. When I need approval on a concept or a job, I make a PDF of the job at a coarse (72 dpi) resolution and e-mail it to the client. Some of my clients have not decided on a particular printer for the job at the time I finish my work, so I make a hi-res (300 dpi) PDF of the job to send along with the FreeHand files. Most printers are getting used to — and even asking for — PDF files for outputting. If you're not sure how the job is going to be printed, PDF is a safe way to go. A lot of the printers that end up with my work are still using FreeHand 7, other out-of-date software, or don't have FreeHand at all. In those situations, the PDF files work well.

Composites or separations

When you want to see what the job will look like when it's printed, choose Composite as the Output option. This option prints all of the visible layers and objects in your document. If you check the Include Invisible Layers option on the Imaging tab of the Print dialog box, you get a print of every layer in the document, whether you've turned off its visibility in the Layers panel or placed it beneath the separator bar in the Layers panel. You should always send a composite print along with the job as it heads to the service bureau or printer; they deserve to know what the heck it is you want them to do. It also helps them interpret how the job will look as they output the file.

Separations are the negatives (or positives, depending on the printing process) of each of the ink colors in your document. A black and white or single-color spot color job produces a single "sep" or image. A CMYK job gets you four sheets of images, and a CMYK plus two spot colors provides six images. Each image will have halftones (if required) and all the tones and shades of that ink in the document. To reiterate, you need a PostScript-enabled printer if you want to do professional or commercial graphics work. When you print separations, it's customary to print them as positive images, even though the final output device will probably be producing a negative. The positive image makes it easier for you to see what you've got going in the document. Use the seps to see if you have the correct combination of colors to make that orangey-gray color in the logo, or to see if the headline got knocked out of the photo as you planned.

Separations should have "printer marks" on them whenever possible. These marks include crop marks, registration marks, color bars, and the filename and date. Printer marks are found in the Imaging tab, under the Labels & Marks heading.

Trapping

If you think about the mechanics of a multiple-color print job, it's miraculous that the process works at all. A piece of paper goes in one end, and gets dragged through several rollers and has ink applied to it at various locations during its run through the press. Finally, it pops out the back end, looking pretty. The registration of the sheet to the press, the plates to the press, and everything else in these, sometimes huge, machines is of utmost importance. And, no matter how tightly the press is set up, shift happens, and misregistration occurs. When it does, the image can be just plain ugly, or it may show slight areas of white around colors that should overlap.

To negate as much of this misregistration as possible, you trap overlapping objects. The art of trapping can be as simple as asking the service bureau to do it for you, or as complicated as you want to make it yourself. Service bureaus have software that analyzes the document to find out where trapping is necessary. Then the software makes the correct adjustments required by a specific printer or press. Then when alignment goes off a little bit, no one notices. To do the trapping yourself requires a bit more work, but it puts control of the situation entirely in your hands.

Choke versus spread

Trapping is referred to as either choking or spreading. What you want to do is have the lighter of the two colors infringe into the darker color's territory. Why? Because the lighter color won't change the shape of the trapped area in the same way a dark color will. The concept of a choke is that a light color surrounds a darker area. The lighter color is made to infringe onto the darker color — choking the trapped area. A spread is the exact opposite: a light color surrounded by a dark color. In this instance, the color "spreads" into the darker area. We define the area of choke or spread relative to the printing process. If the job is to be screen printed, the types of inks, the varied substrate, and the printing process itself requires a larger trap area. Conversely, a brochure being printed on a high-quality printing press needs less trap, due to the refinement of the printing press. Any misregistration will be of a very minute amount, so you can get by with a smaller trapping value.

This encroachment of light into dark is done several ways. If the inks are extremely opaque, as they are in some screen-printing applications, the area of the choke or spread can be solid ink. Premium offset printing jobs use screen tints of the lighter color instead of a solid area of ink. This serves two purposes: First, a screen tint of the ink is less likely to draw attention to the overlapping that is going to occur; second, and not as obvious, is that a solid layer of ink over another solid area of ink tends to produce a shinier area than normal. In a trapping situation, the result is a thin outline around the trapped area, and that's not a pretty thing to behold.

For a manual choke, select the darker area and give it a Basic stroke twice the width of the trap you wish to apply. Give the stroke the same color as the lighter color — or a tint of that color. Open the Stroke inspector and select Overprint. Then open the Fill inspector and deselect Overprint. This has the effect of making the light colored *stroke* print on top of the darker color instead of knocking it out as FreeHand is set by default to do. The fill area will knock out of the light color as it should. The difference between a choke and a spread is shown in Figure 13-2.

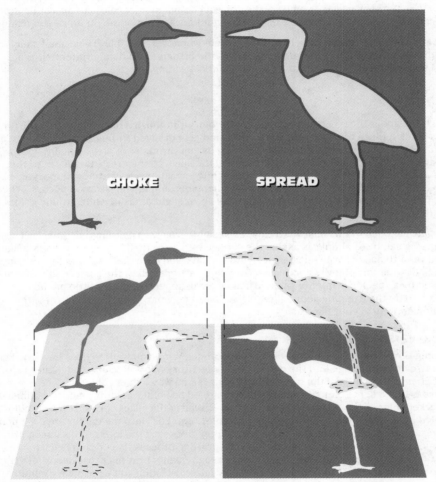

Figure 13-2: A choke on the left, a spread on the right

A spread is basically the same. Choose the light-colored object, and give it a stroke twice the width of the trap. Use the light fill color as the color for the stroke. In the Stroke inspector, choose Overprint; in the Fills inspector, deselect Overprint.

Trapping size for offset printing is screen-ruling dependent. At 65 lpi, use a 0.55 to 2.20-point rule; 133 lpi needs only 0.27 to 1.06-points, and 200 lpi requires a minimal 0.18 to 0.72-point rules for a good trap. Screen printing can be as much as a pica for large Pasteboard sign jobs, or as fine as those used for 65 lpi offset printing.

FreeHand gives you suggestions for proper trapping through the use of the Trap Xtra, or you can be very specific and do it manually where you think it's necessary.

Overprinting and knockouts

You cannot "see" overprinting on the screen in FreeHand; however, you can choose Display Overprinting Objects in the FreeHand Preference ⇨ Redraw panel. Areas that will overprint will be filled with tiny "o" shapes. It looks pretty bizarre onscreen, but lets you know that something out of the ordinary is going on. The little "o" shapes will not print, however. The difference between overprinting and knockouts is shown in Figure 13-3.

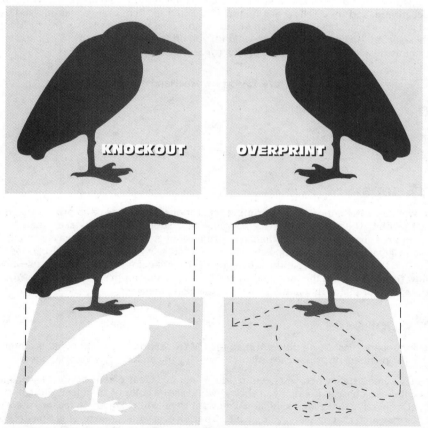

Figure 13-3: The upper object will knockout of the bottom object on the left, and overprint the object on the right.

A *knockout* is an area in a block of color that will not print. Reversed type, for instance, is knocked out of the background color, and the paper color shows through. By default, overlapping areas in FreeHand are knocked out of each other, with the highest object in the stacking order claiming dominance. Anything beneath it is knocked out. If this didn't happen, you would have many colors of ink building on top of each other, and printing would be ugly. A knock out in FreeHand is considered "hairline" registration. That is, there's less than a hairline (0.25-point) width between objects. For all intents and purposes, the objects should match completely on all sides.

Just for the record, black text is always set to overprint. And that's probably a good — no, a great — idea. You wouldn't want the printer to have to try to register body copy in reversed text areas, because if you set a headline over a bright red background, by default, the text will be typed in black, but you want to have yellow text instead. So you drag a swatch of yellow onto the fills color well, and the text turns to yellow. Beautiful, *but*, if you have turned off the Display Overprinting Objects option in the FreeHand Preferences panel, you won't know that the yellow text has not been knocked out of the red background. The job prints with a solid red background, and solid yellow text on top of it. You'll see light orange text on a red background, and you probably won't win an award for this one. With the Display Overprinting Objects selected, the little "o" shapes would tip you off (as shown in Figure 13-4), and you could simply deselect Overprint from the Fill (or Stroke) inspectors.

Figure 13-4: How FreeHand displays overprinting

CMYK seps

I can't overstress the importance of printing separations on your desktop printer before committing the job to the printer or service bureau. You'll catch so many mistakes, that the extra time it requires gives you another chance to produce an error-free job. I always send a complete set of separations and a composite with the file, so everyone along the line can see what's going on, and what I expect from the job. If you have a full-color job that doesn't use any cyan or yellow (or any other of the four colors) ink, FreeHand will not print a blank page. You only get prints of color plates that actually have an image on them.

Spot color seps

Spot color separations are no different than the CMYK versions. The end result is a film negative (or positive, or press-ready plate) to which you can have any color applied.

There may come a time when you need to print white ink. Clear plastic bottles, bags, and other containers come to mind. If you choose white as the color of an object, though, you won't get a negative that reflects the area you want to be white. For some reason, there's no white color swatch that actually prints white. To trick everyone, choose a light pastel color from the Swatches panel, and rename the color White, or Prints White. It will look a odd on the monitor, but when it's output, the printer will have a negative to use to make the plate that uses white ink right out of the can. If the white area bleeds, I generally go one step further and type "PRINTS WHITE" on an edge of the white area. I convert the text to paths, and use the Union Xtra to make it part of the image. It's my insurance policy that the printer isn't going to print baby blue or fluorescent red in that space.

Printing in FreeHand 10

Print dialog boxes vary depending on the operating system. This section of the book was done on a Mac operating with OS X 10.2, so what you see on your monitor may be arranged differently, but the controls are basically the same from platform to platform, OS to Os.

The Print dialog box

When your type has been set, your drawing drawn, and your traps choked or spread, it's time to print. Go to File ➪ Print, and you'll be faced with the powerful Print dialog box as shown in Figure 13-5. It provides the following options:

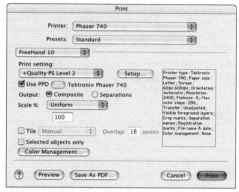

Figure 13-5: The FreeHand Print dialog box

✦ **Print setting** — You have a choice of Normal, Draft, Hyphen, and Quality PS Level 2. These settings provide preset conditions for printing. Most of the setting differences are located on the Imaging tab. Select a document to print, and in the Print dialog box, click the Imaging tab. Then change the Print setting at the top of the window. Notice the variations that are created by switching from one to another. Draft produces the lowest-quality output, and Quality PS Level 2 provides the highest-quality output. Even after you make a selection, you can change any of the attributes.

✦ **Use PPD** — The PPD is the PostScript Printer Description file that provides intimate information about your printer to the computer. This file tells your machine what kind of resolution, page sizes, line screen rulings, and screen angles the printer uses when outputting a file. Checking this option opens a navigation box for you to find the PPD for the printer you want to use. The name of the printer will then be displayed in the space after the Use PPD buttons. You can change the PPD in the Settings dialog box.

✦ **Output** — This section gives you two choices: Composite or Separations. Take your pick. Override this setting in the Setup dialog box if you decide to use a different printer.

✦ **Scale %** — You have three choices of the size you want your image printed. Uniform prints the document at whatever size you type in the field. The aspect ratio of the page is maintained. Variable enables you to stretch or squeeze one dimension or the other. Type the scale percentage of the width and height in the appropriate fields. This distorts the image. The last choice is Fit On Page. If you choose this option, FreeHand automatically scales the document proportionally so that it fits comfortably on the page size you have selected. This is suitable for documents that are larger than the paper you can print. Crop marks and other printer marks are included in the reduced print if you elect to have them print at all.

✦ **Tile** — If you are printing a document that is larger than your printer can accommodate on a single sheet of paper, you can choose to tile the document. You have additional choices of Automatic or Manual tile. If you choose Automatic tiling, FreeHand decides the best way to cut up the document and then prints as many pages as necessary to complete the image. Each edge of the page has small registration marks to which you can trim to ensure perfect registration. It becomes a matter of taping and/or gluing the pieces together at that point. If you tile a document, you can tell FreeHand how much of an overlap you would like to have on the pages.

Manual tiling is just a bit different. For this option, you move the Zero Point to where you want the bottom-left corner of the printed sheet to be. You must manually move the Zero Point for the next print, and so on. This can be useful if you want to print a particular area of a large page, although the Print Area tool does the same job from the desktop, and it isn't confined to a particular page size or shape.

✦ **Selected objects only** — You may have multiple objects on a page, but be interested in printing only one or a group of them. Just select them, and check this box. Only the selected objects will print. You can still tile, change the scale, or make any other adjustments to the printed sheet.

✦ **Color Management** — The fine art or black science of color management is a toughie. It's beyond the scope of this book. My recommendation is that unless you have your scanner, monitor, and printer all correctly color managed, that you leave this selection set to None. You will have fewer surprises when printing if you do. (Conversely, if you are serious about your work, take the time to create profiles for all your devices, and use color management to your benefit.) In this dialog box, you have the options of choosing Adjust Display Colors, where you adjust your monitor by calibrating it with the Display Color Setup, shown in Figure 13-6; Color Tables, Kodak Digital Science, or Apple ColorSync (on a Macintosh only).

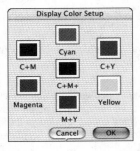

Figure 13-6: The Display Color Setup window

The Setup window

The Setup window offers more choices and decisions for you. You see a thumbnail preview of the printed page, among other things. You arrange many printing attributes in this dialog box. To begin with, you can change the print setting and PPD at this point (and change it again back in the Print dialog box if you're really unsure of yourself or change your mind). You can choose UserPrep files — files that are workaround files that stretch the limits of some high-end PostScript devices. There are several UserPrep files included with FreeHand that provide PostScript code to print tiled, pattern, or gradient fills. These files are not effective on most desktop or PCL printers.

At the bottom of the preview, you can change the page currently showing as a thumbnail. You can also change the view to your choice of Preview, X-Box, or Keyline. The right side of the Setup window is divided among several attributes under three tabs.

The Separations tab

The title of this tab tells you that this is the logical place to start if you're printing separations, but there's more information available. First, you can change from Separations to Composite (and change back again in the Print dialog box). The following options are available:

✦ **Print Spot Colors As Process** — This option turns all your PMS or other ink colors into CMYK for printing with standard inks. With this setting, you can produce your project with "live" spot colors in the document, and change them to output in CMYK configuration for printing. Keep in mind that spot colors will not be converted to the exact color when printed as process colors. This button provides the same function as changing your spot colors to CMYK in the Swatches panel, only in this location it's not permanent — colors will stay as spot in the document.

✦ **Ink Window** — This next space fills up with all the colors that are going to print in your document. If you have spot colors, they show up here. When you click the Print Spot Colors As Process button you only see Cyan, Magenta, Yellow, and Black. Click it again and all the spot colors appear in the list again.

There are letters and words at the top of this window. The P stands for print. If there is a check mark in this column, that ink color will print. If you don't want to print a particular color, uncheck it. The O stands for Overprint; use this with care. It causes the selected ink color to overprint every other color. Nothing knocks out of it. You're better off choosing Overprint in the Fill/Stroke panels for individual objects. Angle refers to the screen angle of half-toned fills. FreeHand has default settings (standard in the printing community) that you shouldn't monkey with unless your printer gives you specific instructions. But you can specify the screen angle of a spot color to fit with CMYK angles, or for specific applications such as screen printing. The Separations heading lists the ink name, which will be printed on the output if you choose to have printer marks on the document (found in the Imaging tab).

✦ **Halftone screen** — Depending on the PPD you've chosen, you will have the option of setting the halftone screen luring and resolution in this field.

✦ **Transfer function** — This option tells the printer how to have the PPD interpret and print grayscale images. Unadjusted makes no change in the gray levels. Normalize is for PPDs that have a Normalize function and causes a smooth transition from white (0% black) to solid (100%) black. Posterize trims the grays to four levels and is used mainly on black and white printers.

✦ **Spread size** — Here you set the distance your fills and strokes will spread to compensate for misregistration. You can choose from the available selections, or type in a suitable number.

The Imaging tab

This tab (Figure 13-7) provides even more options, but you have set most of them when you chose your print setting. They're all modifiable, however:

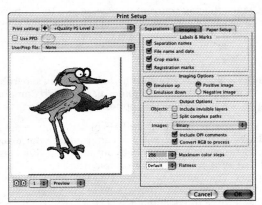

Figure 13-7: The Imaging tab of the Setup section of the Print dialog box

✦ **Labels & Marks** — Labels and marks are necessary for the printer to print the job reliably. Check these boxes to include separation names, filename and date, crop marks, and registration marks. If you leave this information off of your separations, the printer will not be able to create any kind of alignment.

✦ **Imaging Options** — Depending on the printing process, you may want to have film or paper negatives or positives produced. The printer may want the output right reading or wrong reading. Select these options here and include emulsion up or down, and positive or negative image. Standard offset printing practices require right-reading-emulsion-down film (RRED) so that would be Emulsion Down and a Negative Image. But if you are printing paper separations to accompany a composite print with the job, a Positive Image would be in order. Ask your printer what he wants.

✦ **Output Options**

• **Objects** — Often you want invisible layers to print. Here's where you put the check mark to do just that. Invisible layers include layers you've turned off in the Layers panel and anything below the separator bar in the Layers panel. If your document is complicated, choose Split Complex Paths. This option cuts paths into smaller sections that the printer can deal with more easily, and lessens the chances of a PostScript error.

• **Images** — This options tells the computer how to send bitmap data to the printer (or include it in an export file). None uses Open Pre-Press Interface (OPI) comments to relink to a higher-resolution image. ASCII creates a data file from the image file as ASCII characters. This makes large and slow-printing files, but is cross-platform. Binary (Cross Platform) encodes the images in binary form readable by Windows or Macintosh computers. Binary (Macintosh) files are also encoded as binary, but it creates a small Mac file that causes PostScript errors on Windows machines.

Check the Include OPI Comments box to include Open Pre-Press Interface comments an application uses to relink to higher-resolution images at the time of final output.

The Convert RGB to Process option prints RGB colors as RGB if you deselect it. Leaving it selected converts RGB colors to CMYK. If you print separations, RGB image colors are converted to CMYK or CMYKOG.

✦ You have the option of setting the maximum color steps in a graduated or radial fill. The choices are Default (the PPDs), 126, or 256. You can enter your own number here if you prefer.

✦ Flatness determines the number of straight segments used to define a curved path. Default is what the PPD wants to use; 3 and 10 are the preset choices. You can type any number, but small numbers provide more points along the path and can cause the printer to choke. Anything over 10 will probably give you a visible distortion as the curve becomes a series of straight lines. If you choose to set the flatness for specific objects in the Object inspector, those settings override anything you do in this panel.

The Paper Setup tab

The third tab in the Setup triptych shows you the paper size and its orientation. It's usually filled out by the time you get here, but you can make changes for the following options:

✦ **Paper size** — Depending on the PPD you've chosen, you'll have a choice of paper sizes. You can choose Custom to input the sheet size yourself. If you want to rotate the sheet by 90 degrees, put a check in the Transverse box.

✦ **Orientation** — FreeHand chooses the orientation of the sheet based on the document size and shape, and the paper that you selected in the Paper Size menu. If you're printing tiles, or using Fit To Page, you can change the orientation by making the selection here.

Printing Project

If you want to put all your eggs in one basket, it's easy enough to do in FreeHand. That's what we'll do with this project. The Habitat Alert letterhead, envelope, postcard, and business card will all be in one document. Obviously, you could (and maybe should) have each of these pieces in separate documents, but that would be like working in Illustrator. Begin by going to the chapter13_exercise folder on the CD-ROM that came with this book. Drag the Chapter 13 Symbols document into the `FreeHand\English\Symbols` folder on your hard drive. The symbols enable you to build these individual projects in short order. Start FreeHand, and open a new document. Name it Habitat Collaterals. If you're feeling particularly lazy, there are color versions of the various symbols in the library. Use them instead of going through the coloring process, or if you need the experience, just follow the instructions.

Letterhead

The default page size in FreeHand is a letter-sized page, so start with the letterhead. Open the Library (Windows ⇨ Library), and choose Import from the pop-up menu at the top-right of the Library panel. When the navigation window opens, choose the Chapter 13 Symbols document you copied earlier. When that window opens, select all the symbols and click the Import button. The Library should be filled with symbols. Save the document.

1. Select View ➪ Page Rulers ➪ Show.

2. Set the units of measure to inches at the bottom of the FreeHand window; then drag a horizontal guideline to the 10.75-inch mark (just a quarter inch beneath the top edge of the page.

3. Place another horizontal guideline .75 inches from the bottom.

4. Then drag the Habitat Alert Logo symbol onto the page, aligning the top of it to the guideline.

5. Open the Align panel (Windows ➪ Panels ➪ Align) and set the horizontal menu to No Change, and the vertical menu to Align Center. Put a check in the Align To Page box, and click Apply (Align).

6. Click the Text tool on the page and type, **108 Las Palmas, Oxnard, California 93035 205-884-7335** in a sans-serif font such as Arial. Press Alt+0149 (Option+8) to insert a bullet. To ensure that the text will be on one line, use an auto-expanding text block (explained in Chapter 9), and click the Center align icon in the Text inspector. Repeat Step 5 to center the text block on the page.

7. Triple-click the text to select it all, and change the font size to 9. Open the Text inspector and click the double-arrow button. In the field near the "A" with the arrows beneath it, type **200** to stretch out the text. (FYI, you didn't have to have the text selected with the Text tool for this — selecting the text block with the Pointer tool would apply the same changes.)

8. The address line looks a little wimpy, so beef it up by going to Text ➪ Convert Case ➪ Upper.

9. The letterhead lacks color, so modify it. Start by removing the symbol instance (Modify ➪ Symbol ➪ Release Instance). Then ungroup it twice.

10. Open the Swatches panel, and choose PANTONE Uncoated Pastels from the Options pop-up menu at the top-right of the panel.

11. Choose PANTONE 9441; then hold down the Shift key and select 9503. Close the window.

12. Give "ALERT" and "For" a fill of PANTONE 9441. Choose PANTONE 9503 as the fill for "HABITAT" and the address line. Group HABITAT ALERT.

13. Select the Zoom tool and draw a selection box around the logo and address. Go to View ➪ Custom ➪ New. Name the new view Letterhead. The top of the letterhead should look similar to Figure 13-8.

Figure 13-8: The two-color letterhead design

Envelope

You can't have a letterhead without an envelope, so add a new page (Document inspector ➪ Options ➪ Add Pages). In the Add Pages window, enter B for the number of new pages, and follow these steps:

1. Click the current page; then click the next page triangle at the bottom left of the document window (or choose Page 2 from the pop-up triangle).

2. In the Document inspector, click the landscape button, and change the page size from Letter to Custom, and enter 9.5 inches wide by 4.125 inches tall (standard #10 envelope size). Press Enter (Return).

3. Choose View ⇨ Fit To Page, or click the Fit To Page button if you installed it in the main menu.

4. Drag a horizontal guideline to a quarter inch below the top of the envelope, and a vertical guideline a quarter inch from the left side. Place a second vertical guideline at the 3-inch mark, and another horizontal guideline a quarter inch above the bottom.

5. Clone the logo from the letterhead, and drag it onto the envelope page. Place it in the top-left intersection of the guidelines.

6. Hold down the Shift key and use the Pointer tool to select the bottom-right corner point of the logo. Drag up and to the left until the logo meets the 3-inch guideline. Save the document.

7. Drag an instance of Great Blue Heron from the Library onto the page, and place it in the bottom left intersection of the guidelines.

8. Release the instance of the bird, and ungroup it twice. Then apply a gradient fill using the two pastel colors in the Swatches panel.

9. Hold down the Spacebar+Command/Control keys to access the Zoom tool, and drag around the logo and heron silhouette on the envelope.

10. Create a new view, named **Envelope**.

11. Go to the View menu at the bottom-left corner of the document. Hold down the triangle and choose Letterhead from the menu.

12. Select the text and copy it.

13. Choose Envelope from the View menu, and paste the text at the feet of the bird.

14. Change the text paragraph alignment to flush left, and place a carriage return after the street name. Abbreviate "California" to "**CA**" and delete the bullet and phone number. Save. The artwork should look similar to Figure 13-9.

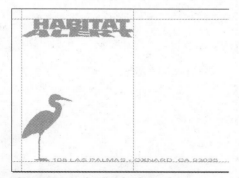

Figure 13-9: The finished envelope

Business card

If the company requires only a single business card, it's a simple procedure to create a single business card-sized page. However, the usual routine is to have multiple business cards for a company. You don't want to spend a lot of time and energy creating a unique card for each person in the company, so it's a good time to let FreeHand go to work for you. For this project, you make a business card layout that prints 10 cards on a letter-sized page.

There are more than a couple ways to accomplish the multiple-card layout. You could make each card. You can arrange the key, non-changing elements, and do a step-and-repeat method to fill the page. You could make a single card and turn it into a symbol that could be placed into a quick grid. You could make one business card and use a lens fill to make the multiple layout. And, you could set up a master page from the last couple choices that could be used for each new group of names.

In this instance, it makes the most sense to make a single card and use a Lens fill to create the layout. Then you can make the layout into a master page:

1. Go to Page 3 of the document. In the Document inspector, change the dimensions to 2 inches wide by 3.5 inches tall. Check that the page orientation is portrait.

2. Use the View menu or the button in the main menu to choose Fit To Page. Open the Library if it's closed.

3. Create a new view of the page, and call it **Card**.

4. Drag guidelines to 3/16-inches from all four sides.

5. Using the method you prefer — drag a symbol, or copy or clone elements from the other pages — place and scale the various elements on the page as shown in Figure 13-10.

Figure 13-10: The finished business card layout

6. Change the expanded width of the address text to 155% in the Text inspector. Then adjust the leading for the address to solid, or 8-point. Put three points of leading (11-point) between the address and phone number.

7. When working with these text blocks, drag the text block from one guideline to the other to maintain accurate center-alignment of the text.

8. Clone the address text and move it beneath the bird. Triple-click the text to select it all, and type in a name. Then give the person a title and reduce the title text to 7 point. Change the name to bold, and adjust the leading to solid, or 8 point. Save.

9. Select the Rectangle tool and draw a rectangle over the card you built. Make the rectangle the exact size of the card — from border to border.

10. Drag a selection box around the entire card layout, and drag the selection onto the Library, creating a symbol. If you want to name the symbol, double-click its icon in the Library and type the new name.

Now you have a single card and a symbol of the card. Let's get to the business of multiple imaging. Start by moving to Page 4 of your document:

1. Change the page orientation to landscape (in the Document inspector) and choose the Fit To Page view.

2. Drag vertical guidelines in to one-half inch from left and right sides of the page, and a horizontal guideline at the 4.25-inch mark.

3. Drag an instance of the business card symbol onto the page, nestle it at the intersection of the left and horizontal guidelines.

4. Clone the card, hold down the Shift key, and drag the cloned card beneath the top card. If you have Snap to Guides selected, the card locks into place when it hits the guidelines.

5. Select both cards and open the Transform panel. Type **2** inches in the X field, and **zero** in the Y field. Type **4** in the Copies field, and click Apply. This puts eight more business cards in perfect registration onto your page, as shown in Figure 13-11.

Figure 13-11: Set up 10 business cards in minutes!

6. Save. Then select all the cards on the page and remove their instance. Ungroup twice. Save again.

7. Now it's a matter of changing the names and titles on the cards. You can drag guidelines down to mark the top of the name text block, and other guidelines to separate the cards, but it's really not necessary.

Brochure

This brochure will be used as a direct mail piece and also placed in brochure racks for tourists to pick up. The standard for this type of piece is a letter-sized piece, letter-folded in thirds. Usually, these brochures are vertical in nature, and we'll stick to that.

1. Begin by turning the next page to a landscape orientation. Note that I didn't give you a page number. FreeHand is a little squirrely about its numbering techniques. Pages don't always fall in numerical order, so you have to pay attention to what you're doing. That's one of the reasons for the custom views — page numbers aren't necessary.

2. Place guidelines a quarter inch inside each edge.

3. Here's a tricky way to get column marks in a hurry. Select the Text tool and drag a text block the width of the guidelines. The height doesn't matter.

4. Go to the Text inspector and click the next-to-the-bottom column icon.

5. In the Number of Columns field, type **3**. This field is not labeled, but it's the top left field.

6. The next field on the right indicates the space between columns. Type **0.5** inches. When you press the Return or Enter key, you'll have three equal columns on the page without ever looking at the rulers or picking up a calculator.

7. Drag vertical guidelines out to each of the column markers. The page should look similar to Figure 13-12. Now delete the text block. Save.

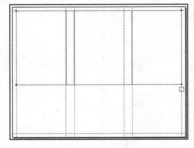

Figure 13-12: A quick and painless three-column layout

8. The edges of the brochure will bleed; the brochure is printed on paper larger than the finished size. Ink is printed outside the brochure's borders. When the printed job is dry, the printer trims the paper to the final size, letting the printed surface go right to the edge of the brochure. It costs more, but the effect is worth the extra money in most cases. So, in the Document inspector, enter **1p0** in the Bleed field to give a bleed margin of a pica.

9. Select the Page tool. Click the brochure page, hold down Shift+Alt (Shift+Opt), and drag a copy of the page to the right. When it's clear of the original page, let go of the mouse. Save.

Now you have the skeletal beginnings of a brochure. The Library contains most of the elements you need to flesh it out. By having these elements in the Library, you are able to build other documents — flyers, notices, and Web pages — without recreating all the details or making them from scratch.

Element placement

Rather than put you through a tedious explanation about how to paste the various elements into the layout, you can use Figures 13-13 and 13-14 for the placement. The body text is called `MumboJumbo.rtf`. The three photos are in a folder named `BrochurePix`, and that's all in the Chapter 13 folder on the CD-ROM that comes with this book. The finished set of pages for letterhead, envelope, business cards, and brochure is on the file named Chap13project.fh10, on the CD. If you open this file a Locate File dialog box opens. Navigate to the `BrochurePix` folder and select the image name in the title bar of the dialog box. Repeat for each image.

Printing the documents

Each of the jobs you've done in this project has different printing requirements. This type of project isn't something that you just click the Print button and head for the water cooler. Size and orientation of the different pages is the main concern. The letterhead, envelope, and business card jobs are spot color; whereas the brochure is CMYK. A commercial printer experienced with FreeHand can work from this multipage file. If your printer isn't familiar with FreeHand, you might be better off providing separate files for each job.

FreeHand does some strange page-numbering things on the Pasteboard, so before printing to your laser printer or ink-jet, select an object on the page you want to print, and take note of the page you're on in the bottom-left corner of the application window. Then choose that page in the Print dialog box. Except for approvals or proofing purposes, there's no need to print the single business card. You can use the Page tool to drag that document below the rest of the pages to take it out of the numbering loop (at least put it at the end of the page list).

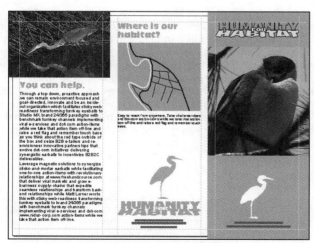

Figure 13-13: The brochure's inside panels

Figure 13-14: The outside of the brochure

The letterhead, envelope, and mass business card must have their orientation checked before printing to prevent wasting a lot of paper and time. If you are going to print Avery preperforated business card stock, its orientation is portrait, not landscape as you made the layout. You can either change the orientation of the actual layout to a vertical page, or you can be careful to make the change in the Print dialog box.

The brochure uses the same colors as the letterhead, but in the brochure, those colors were converted to CMYK. If the company has deep pockets, or logo colors are critical, you could use spot colors with the CMYK; it's not uncommon.

Print Area

The Print Area feature is new in FreeHand 10 and provides one more tool to aid you in printing specific parts of a document. You can install its button in the main menu where it is easy to click, or choose it from the File menu. Either way, the cursor turns into a crosshair that you drag across the document to select what you wish to print. If you've used the Page tool to abut pages, the Print Area tool will select objects on adjacent pages and print them. You can also type notes near pages or between them on the Pasteboard. Anything within the Print Area selection will print. It's perfect to show thumbnails of a multipage job. Arrange the pages with the Page tool, and drag a Print Area selection box. Then print with Fit On Page enabled. All umpteen pages, complete with notes or labels you've placed on the Pasteboard, print on the same sheet of paper.

Preparation for Output

Whether you will be taking the job to a printer in a strip mall, large commercial printer, or magazine, those companies have certain requirements. The most common comment you'll find with smaller companies is that they don't have a current version (FreeHand 10 or FreeHand MX), or have the program at all. They'll ask you to put it in some other format. Macromedia has bent over backwards to accommodate nearly everyone in this respect.

What the service bureau needs

I've worked with large service bureaus who want the job as a PostScript file, and others that want the native FreeHand file. I've also had many ask me for Illustrator files and even JPEGs. When they ask for a JPEG for a print job, I usually hang up the phone, but for most other needs, I ask them what version of what program they'd like to have. All you have to do is go to File ⇨ Export, and choose from the long list of file formats there. Most are self-explanatory, but a few can use some clarification.

If you're providing a PostScript file, the onus is on you to have everything just right. When this file is output, no one does anything to it but make sure it comes out the other end of the machine. If you've chosen spot colors but really wanted CMYK, you're out of luck, and you'll pay for it. This is one instance where proofing the job on your desktop printer is absolutely necessary. The PostScript file contains all the fonts in the job.

When you choose File ⇨ Export, the default is to export the file as a Macromedia Flash SWF file. The default save location is in the FreeHand 10 folder. Be sure to check which type of file you're creating, and where it's going — each time.

Some of my clients don't know where the job will be printed at the time I'm through with the artwork. To cover all the bases, I put the original FreeHand 10 file along with exports of the same job in FreeHand 8, Adobe Illustrator 8, and a PDF. I have even throw in a Quark EPS just to be sure. When I do all of these, I convert all the text to paths before making any of the exports (except for the older FreeHand file). Then I make all the exports, and choose Undo to put my live text back into the FreeHand 10 document.

Exporting to Adobe Illustrator

The largest problem with exporting to Illustrator is that type goes haywire. I've exported files to Illustrator that had entire blocks of text disappear, letter or word spacing is off, or Illustrator just works with type differently, but line breaks are all different, and text blocks shrink or grow. To solve this, it's best to convert all the text to paths. That fixes the text problem, but if a typo is discovered, the printer or service bureau will have a chore to repair it. Some of us can steal a letter here and there to clean up some spelling, but if you don't have anything to steal, you'll have to try to replicate the font. Best advice: read your text backwards. Misspelled words jump out at you when you aren't reading the words in context. Then read it again in a few minutes for content. Run FreeHand's spell checker, and have someone else proofread the text as well. At the least, you will have discovered 99 percent of the text errors before converting to paths.

Multiple-page documents are converted into consecutively named single-page documents for Illustrator. You'll have to name them something intelligent, such as "Flyer Front," and "Flyer Back" to know which page will be worked on.

Since the printer/service bureau is asking for an Illustrator file, assume that they'll be able to clean up any other minor things that happen in the export process.

Exporting to PDF

FreeHand has a PDF export, but many people have problems with the resulting files. Missing clipping paths from Photoshop TIFFs and font issues are some of the problems. Common advice is to create a PostScript file (choose the Output Options tab in the Print dialog box, check the Save As File box; then choose PostScript as the format) and then use Adobe Acrobat Distiller to create the actual PDF file. That requires an additional program, but it's bulletproof. Whichever method you choose, it's safest if you convert the text to paths.

EPS exports

There are several flavors of EPS you can use to export a document from FreeHand. When you want bulletproof, the Quark EPS method seems to get the best results if you're handing the file off to someone else. If you are running a Mac, and the file must go to a Windows environment, use the MS-DOS EPS format, or the other machine will not show the document. The most common comment about EPS files is that when the file is placed, only a box with an "X" in it appears on the page. It prints fine, but there is no preview, therefore nothing to see on the screen. The two EPS types just mentioned solve the problem, although on a Mac, the MS-DOS EPS has a very ugly black and white preview. You're better off using the Macintosh EPS format. If you have any fonts in the EPS file, do yourself and everyone else a huge favor and convert them to paths. Otherwise, you must send the necessary fonts along with the EPS, and it's just too easy to forget or lose them.

Collect for output

Unlike with Adobe Illustrator, when you want to gather fonts and graphics together to bundle for the printer, FreeHand offers a one-click solution. Well, almost one-click. Choose File ➪ Collect For Output, and you'll be prompted to Save; then a dialog box appears enabling you to choose the information to be saved in a document information page. A dialog box opens where you can name the document information file, and lets you choose where to save the information. It's best to create a new folder. When you click Save, the program pulls all the fonts and graphics used in the document, makes a copy of the live file, and places all that data in the location you set. All that's left for you to do is to put the data on a suitable media. One wacky note, though. If you have a space character in front of the name of your hard drive, Collect For Output doesn't work. Don't ask why; change the name of your hard drive.

Summary

This chapter helped you learn the ins and outs of printing from FreeHand. Terms such as knockout, spread, and choke were discussed, and overprinting was explained. You found out that bleeding costs you money, but it is not necessarily painful. In the projects, you learned how to make a multipage document that contains a letterhead, envelope, business card, and brochure. These documents utilize symbols to streamline the layout process. Then you learned what the service bureau or printer needs to finish the job for you, and you learned a little about various export options.

Project Summary

Files Prepared for the Habitat Alert Web Site		
Files	*What Was Done*	*Where to Now?*
Chap13project.fh10	A two-color letterhead design where you added and formatted text	The Printer
	An envelope with the logo and address added.	
	A Business Card which was then made into a symbol and used for a multiple card layout	
	A three column brochure	

Introducing
FreeHand MX

This chapter is being written to the third beta build of FreeHand MX. Therefore, there are many things that remain to be discovered: Some will be pleasant surprises, others may be glitches. But from what Macromedia has done so far, it looks like it will be a solid release. That said, there are many more things to say about this latest version — in all, Macromedia's marketing department targeted nearly 50 new features or improvements. If you have the program already, then jump in! If you are just thinking about the upgrade, this chapter should have you reaching for your credit card or checkbook.

FreeHand MX in Broad Strokes

The first thing you'll notice when you initially start FreeHand MX is the location of panels — what used to be known as palettes — along the right side of the screen. On a Windows machine, they snap in and out of your workspace as you need them. Individual panels can be removed and floated on the desktop and nested with other panels, regardless of platform. Then you're likely to notice that the Toolbox has been modified. Tools of a feather are nested together, and you have to hold the cursor down on one tool to open the group of tools that are available. Most of the Xtras have been grouped into the Toolbox as well. You'll also see a few new tools: Output Area, Extrude, Action, and Connector, to name a few. Beyond the abilities you're given with these new tools, the main thrust of the upgrade is the way you can have multiple strokes, fills, and effects on a single object. Draw an object once, and add squiggly lines, drop shadows, Gaussian blurs, and glows. Then do it again. Each attribute is added to an Object "tree" that you can edit by moving branches up and down the tree, or removing them altogether.

Gradient fills get a big boost, too. Any gradient fill can have one of three new modifiers applied to it that reflect, duplicate, or fit the object precisely. The gradient is editable directly within the document with a set of control handles that is new in FreeHand MX. Rounded corners on rectangles are definitely easier with the tricks the Subselect tool can do with a rectangle, and ellipses can have precise sections of their arcs removed. Polygons are editable beyond belief now. You can make changes in stars or straight-sided polygons live, on the object, or through modifications in the Object panel.

You can import a SWF file and make it part of your FreeHand page and then export the page with the SWF embedded in it. During all that, you can click a button to open Flash, where you can modify the SWF file. It's automatically updated in the FreeHand document.

There are too many new elements to mention so briefly. The following pages provide greater detail about everything that is available at the time of writing.

Features You May Not Notice

There are some new features in FreeHand MX that won't be apparent because they're either working in the background or they're part of the new MX way of working. If you have experience with FreeHand, you may think some tools are missing, but they've just been moved to a new location.

Image alpha channel support

If you're a Photoshop user, you know that an alpha channel is a black and white layer that allows the display of transparent areas, opaque areas, and the shape of an object. Previous versions of FreeHand did not work well with bitmaps containing alpha channels. That's now a thing of the past. You can import documents with alpha channels, and you can also export your own alpha channels. This isn't an answer to all your problems with alpha channels, but it's a good start. If you import a bitmap from Fireworks or Photoshop that has an alpha channel, everything will look and function as you would expect when you have the Display Alpha Channel option turned *off* in the Object panel. Turn that option on, however, and white areas in your alpha channel act as masks, and those portions of the image appear as "normal." It's as though you used the Punch Xtra on the image. Black areas in the alpha channel let the pixels become missing in action and transparent. Keep in mind these are the black and white areas of the alpha channel, not the image itself. You can apply live effects, such as shadows, beveling, and so on, to the image whether Display Alpha Channel is on or off. FreeHand is a vector-based drawing program, so you shouldn't be surprised that you cannot edit the alpha channel on an imported bitmap.

Now for the good part: You can make a mask in FreeHand and place it on the Background layer (or any other nonprinting layer beneath the separator bar). Export the file as a TIFF, PSD, PNG, or GIF, and the mask becomes an alpha channel when opened in Fireworks or Photoshop. Keep your head about you, though, if you're creating masks in multiple programs. In Fireworks, white areas of the mask become transparent areas in the image, but in FreeHand (and Photoshop) black areas are transparent. You can create gradient fills or grayscale blends to make the mask. Use it to set a line of text that you want to have set in the background color of your Web page when you haven't decided what color that will be yet, or will change it occasionally. Make the mask and leave the area transparent so the background color shows through.

PDF export updates

FreeHand's PDF export produces Adobe Acrobat formatted files that support CMYK, RGB, grayscale, and monochrome bitmaps. Some things haven't changed. For example, you can't export custom or PostScript fills or strokes, arrowheads, or textured fills. Text effects (underscore, inline, shadows, and so on) and overprinting are ignored. Any EPS images are ignored unless they have a TIFF preview. In that case, the TIFF preview is exported instead of the EPS. Alpha channel transparency is lost. FreeHand can also open PDF files, but be prepared to do a little work. Text blocks may be separated into individual blocks; reconnect them using common text tools and techniques. Sometimes the page show up as a single object with graphics pasted inside. Choose Edit ➪ Cut Contents to edit everything normally.

Save Location Default enhancement

FreeHand 10 saddled users with a default location for new files when they were saved. Now, FreeHand MX uses the application folder as the default location for a brand new document. If you navigate to another folder and save the file, successive saves or save as commands will place the file into the new folder–not the application folder. On the Mac, FreeHand is now in complete sync with the General Controls Panel settings.

Output Area

Previous versions of FreeHand had a Print Area tool. This feature has been upgraded and is now called the Output Area tool, and it is part of the Tools panel. Selecting the tool changes the cursor by adding a dashed-line rectangle to the Pointer tool. Drag a selection on the document to print only that area. The area is defined by a red dashed outline with solid red handles on the sides and corners of the rectangle. The selection can go across several pages, or include only a tiny section of a single page. Move the cursor over one of the bounding edges to turn the cursor into a grabber hand. Then you can move the Output Area anywhere in the document. Resize the rectangle by selecting and dragging any of the corner points. The Output Area rectangle will remain in view until you deselect it by clicking the Output Area tool on the desktop. The rectangle itself does not print.

If you drag a selection through a text block and across a graphic, it prints as though the area were cut out with a pair of scissors. Anything on the pasteboard is printed, so between pages you can place notes, alternate graphics, or comments about the page or layout. You must select Print Output Area in the FreeHand MX Print dialog box (Figure 14-1). There you have the further option to show page borders that may be in the selection area. These options are not available unless you've created a selection with the Output Area tool.

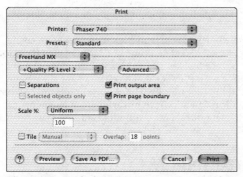

Figure 14-1: The Output Area options in the Print dialog box

Output Area also works when you are exporting certain types of files. Those file types include all the flavors of EPS, plus SWF, PDF, and PSD. Even if you have made a selection, the entire document will be exported in other file formats.

Printing news

You can see the changes FreeHand has made in the Print dialog box for Macintosh OS X in Figure 14-1. It is assumed that you will be printing a composite image, but if you need separations, all you need to do is click the Separations button. The Advanced button replaces the Setup button used in previous versions of FreeHand, and contains the same information (see Chapter 13 for that discussion).

New Page button

It's a really small thing, but the addition of the New Page button in the bottom-left corner of the application window is welcome. A single click adds a new page to the document. The button lies between the pop-up Page selector and the View Mode menu; its icon is a dog-eared document with a plus sign. When you click it, a new page the same size and orientation of the page you're currently working on is created. If you want a button to duplicate a page, you can install one in your Main menu or Tools panel through Windows ➪ Toolbars ➪ Custom ➪ Pages. That button has been there for a while, but is generally overlooked.

Swap object for symbol

If you've ever made a symbol in FreeHand that you would like to use to replace objects that are already in place in your document, this little addition will be good news for you. Select an object or instance in the document (or a group of them), and then choose a symbol in the Library. Click the Swap Symbol button at the bottom of the Library, or choose Swap from the Library's pop-up Options menu, and all the elements become instances of the chosen symbol. The swapped symbol assumes the size and aspect ratio of the object or instance that was selected. For instance, if you had a symbol that was a perfect circle, and you swapped it in place of a capital letter "I" the circle would become a tall ellipse. There's no way to maintain the aspect ratio. Along the same line of reasoning, if you modified an object with the 3D Rotation tool — for example, turned a rectangle into a trapezoid — and then swapped that object for a circular symbol, the symbol fits itself to the bounding box of the object. In this case, not a trapezoid, but the rectangle that the trapezoid occupies.

Pantone libraries updates

PANTONE colors can be confusing if you are sharing FreeHand files with someone using an older version of FreeHand. You may specify a PANTONE color in CMYK values that doesn't match what your colleague has, and the program has set the values in both cases. You might blame Macromedia, but the responsibility lies with PANTONE. Over the years they have constantly striven to keep up with computer and ink technology. Thankfully, FreeHand MX has the latest and greatest range of PANTONE colors: 14 separate libraries from Hexachrome to metallics, pastels, and solid to ProSim EURO. Of course, Macromedia retained libraries from Munsell, TOYO, and the DIC Color Guide.

Mac-specific features in FreeHand MX

FreeHand 10 was the first drawing application to be completely OS X-ready. Unfortunately, as hard as both Apple and Macromedia worked, neither were really ready for prime time. However, Macintosh OS X 10.2 and FreeHand MX have had a year to work out many bugs. For one thing, FreeHand adopted the Carbon Event Manager, which increases the overall efficiency of the operating system. In the Classic Event Manager, applications are forced to poll the operating system for events. If there weren't any events available at the time for the application, the polling process was wasted CPU time. With the Carbon Event Manager, the application goes to sleep until an event is ready for it. The application uses only as much time as necessary, and the responsiveness of the operating system increases.

FreeHand is placed inside an Application Bundle, which gives FreeHand access to the localization and internationalization tools that OS X makes possible. However, the application seems less complex to the user. Under previous versions of the OS, it was really easy for a user to drag the FreeHand application away from vital resources (such as shared libraries and support files). Now you'll have a tougher time finding a way to separate the application from support files because they're hidden inside the package.

There were a few fixes in the printing department as well; all of these items have been fixed in FreeHand MX. When running FreeHand 10 on OS X, FreeHand cannot tell the difference between a PostScript printer and a non-PostScript printer when the printer is chosen in the Print dialog box. The Print Preview had a marquee that was low and to the left, giving an erroneous preview. Clipping paths with curves had unnecessary flatness when printed to a non-PostScript printer. Finally, if you accessed the Print Setup dialog box several times, a bug in OS X caused a crash. Fixes and the new look make FreeHand printing more streamlined and easier for newer users to comprehend.

Central European and Simplified Chinese font support

FreeHand 10 had a bug in Windows 2000 and higher that disallowed Baltic, Central European, Cyrillic, Greek, and Turkish font sets. This bug has been eliminated so the fonts are available now. Additionally, FreeHand supports Simplified Chinese.

Open documents

For power users who want to test the bursting strength of their computers, FreeHand MX lets you open more than a dozen documents at one time.

Resizable file dialogs

On both Windows and Macintosh machines you can resize the Open, Save As, Import, Export, Export Again, and Send (Windows only) dialog boxes. It's nice to be able to read entire filenames at times, or make the box smaller to see something of a reference on the desktop. All you have to do is grab the gripper corners in the right bottom of the dialog boxes. The Save As box on the Mac must be expanded to reveal the gripper corner.

Spell Checker change

You probably won't perceive a difference, but FreeHand has changed to the WinterTree Dictionaries for the spell-checking feature. This provides consistency across the entire Studio MX product line.

Toolbox reorganization

Macromedia spent quite a bit of time assessing the Toolbox, and which tools should be more accessible than others. You may have to look a little farther for some tools if you're a FreeHand veteran. Novice or veteran, the reorganization makes sense, and after a session or two you won't have trouble finding things. Some tool groups have changed from FreeHand 10, and others remain the same. Any tool icons that have a small downward-pointing triangle in the bottom right have other tools nested. Just hold down the mouse, and the other tools pop up. Select these tools by dragging the mouse over the needed tool and letting go of the mouse. If you use a digital tablet, you slightly drag the mouse on a tool icon to open the other tools in the set. This can take a bit of getting used to, as it's easy to slide the pen tip over a tool that activates the pop-up menu. When that happens, you must choose a tool before the menu will go away.

The Pen tool is nested with the Bezigon tool. The Line tool is nested with the Arc and Spiral tool. The Pencil tool nests with the Variable Stroke Pen tool and the Calligraphic Pen tool, and the Rectangle and Polygon tools are nested together. The Scale tool is grouped with other transformational tools: the Rotate, Skew, and Reflect tools. The Freeform tool is connected to the Roughen and Bend tools. The 3D Rotation, Fisheye Lens, and Perspective tools are nested; the new Extrude tool is hooked up with the Smudge and Shadow tool; and the new Blend tool is grouped with the Chart tool, Mirror tool, and Graphic Hose tool.

In addition, any of the tools that have an inverted "L" shape in the top-right corner of their icon have a dialog box connected with them that is activated by double-clicking the tool icon.

JPEG thumbnail preview

Windows users and artists operating Macs on OS X have the option of choosing JPEG or BMP as a file format for Export thumbnail previews. These previews are shown in the Open menus; the size of the preview can be adjusted by the user. If you choose to have JPEG thumbnails, you can further adjust the quality of the image in the top of the Preferences ➪ Export window as shown in Figure 14-2.

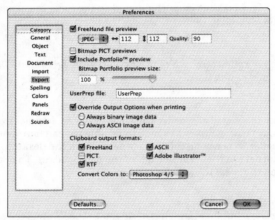

Figure 14-2: The Mac version of the Export Preferences thumbnail preview controls

Drawing Changes in FreeHand MXThere are whole new ways of looking at the way you draw in FreeHand MX. Smart Cursors have raised their IQ, and you don't need the Shift key to constrain a path or regular object any more. Vector and bitmap effects are very useful for the personalization of your drawing style, or just to add a little pizzazz to your work. The new Object panel and new effects do have a learning curve, but it's short, and once you get the hang of it, you'll really enjoy the way the program flows.

Pointer activity

A small circle appears near the pointer when it is within selection distance of a path. When a mouse-click will select a point on a path, a black square appears near the pointer cursor. The range that determines when the cursor will occur is called the Pick Distance, and can be changed in the Preferences dialog box. Distances from 1- to 5-pixels are usually sufficient, but you're best off with a setting of 3 pixels for Pick Distance and Snap To Distance.

Auto Constrain

You don't have to hold down the Shift key to constrain ellipses to circles, rectangles to squares, and straight lines to 45-degree increments any longer. With the new Auto Constrain feature, all you have to do is drag the cursor close to a 45-degree angle, and simple geometric shapes become circles or squares. As you near a 45-degree angle, the cursor is accompanied by a large, blue dot, and you have a perfect circle or square at that time. The line tool snaps to 45-degree increments, and the dot occurs at the end of the path.

If you change the constrain angle (Constrain has moved to File ⇨ Document Settings ⇨ Constrain), the dot still occurs when the cursor reaches 45-degrees from its starting point, but the object is auto-constrained to the angle you set. Holding down the Shift key provides circles and squares on the constrained angle. You must hold down the Shift key to constrain the Line tool to a custom angle.

Anti-alias view

For quite a while Macromedia has heard people ask for an anti-alias view for vector objects. Finally, it has been implemented in FreeHand MX. The old Flash Anti-alias view had a few problems in the integrity of the paths it showed. Flash Anti-alias is no longer in the program. The Anti-alias option can be turned on or off (Enable Anti-alias) in the Redraw section of the Preferences dialog box on Windows or Mac OS X machines. However, it is not available for OS 9 Macs.

Vector Live Effects

One of the new classes of effects in FreeHand MX is called Vector Live Effects. Any object or live text can be given these effects, including Bend, Duet, Expand Path, Ragged, Sketch, and Transform. You'll be using these when you want a freer look to your work. For a great place to start experimenting, import the Vector Effects from the Styles panel. All these effects are contained within the new Properties ⇨ Object panel and can be combined for even more creative appearances. I encourage you to tear the default effects apart so you can see how they work and why. Here's what the individual effects do:

✦ **Bend** — On a geometric shape or free-form object, each point in the object gains control handles creating an inner curve between points, with an equally severe outer arc, as you can see in Figure 14-3. This object started out as a circle, then the Bend was applied, and the object ungrouped. The top point of the circle was raised, and a control handle was extended to the right.

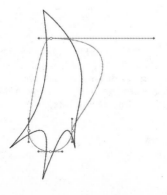

Figure 14-3: Notice where the Bend's points are in relation to the final line. The line with the live points on it will not print.

In Figure 14-4, you see a circle, a square, and the word "FreeHand." The Bend effect has a negative value on the circle, square, and text on the top line. The circle, square, and middle text (in the right half of the figure) all have a positive bend. The bottom text has a positive bend, but the X-distance has been shifted to the right. The values used here are pretty extreme at 50 or –50. You can get some good-looking effects with other values. Notice how the fills go to the original graphic's edges, not the vector effect's edge.

Figure 14-4: The Bend effect is great for creating an exciting starburst, comet trail, or bug splat.

✦ **Duet**—Essentially, this is the Mirror tool used as an effect. Figure 14-5 shows a leaf shape (selected) with the Duet effect applied with the settings in the Object panel. It's important to note that the Copies field has an input of 5. You might think, then, that there should be six leaf shapes in the figure, but FreeHand makes the first copy directly beneath the original path, leaving the original path available for other transformations and effects. Change the X and Y values to precisely locate the copies.

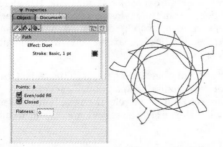

Figure 14-5: The Duet effect multiplies your artwork.

✦ **Expand Path**—This effect is similar to the way the Expand Path Xtra works, except it's in the Object panel and therefore can enjoy other effects added to it. Figure 14-6 shows the circle and square with a Direction of Both, the Width is 8-points, and the square is filled with a light gray tone. Note that the fill goes to the original shape, not either of the paths. The text is set to Outside Only, with a width of 2 points.

Figure 14-6: The Expand Path effect

✦ **Ragged** — To get this effect in FreeHand 10 or earlier, you added points, and used the Roughen Xtra. Now it's easier to apply from the Object panel instead of navigating menus or searching for Xtra buttons, and you have the advantage of making multiples for a really rough look. In Figure 14-7 all elements but the top text have a Size of 10 and a Frequency of 10. The top circle has been given a Rough edge, and 1 copy. The top square has a Smooth edge, but 3 copies. Moving to the lower circle, you see a Smooth Uniform edge, and a fill. The bottom square is Rough, with 3 copies, and is also filled.

Figure 14-7: The Ragged effect

The text at the top is Rough with a Size of 4, a Frequency of 15, and 1 copy. The middle text is Smooth, and the bottom text is Smooth Uniform. Regular Uniform creates almost star-like shapes.

✦ **Sketch** — This effect is one of the more versatile, in my opinion. I tend to be pretty tight in my illustration, and this will certainly loosen up my style. The circle in Figure 14-8 has an Amount of 10, with just 1 copy, and has been made Open. The same values were applied to the square, but it was filled. Notice how the odd-even fill takes over, and how random the square's sketchiness is. Text was given an Amount of 7, and set to Closed. Values above 7 (on this bit of text) made the type unreadable, but this would suffice for a grunge look.

Figure 14-8: Loosen up your artwork with the Sketch effect.

✦ **Transform** — Choosing this effect brings the Transform panel into the Object panel. You can rotate, skew, scale, move, and mirror your selection here. The results are the same as if you had created the transformation with the Xtra, only they're tied to all the other effects within the panel. See Figure 14-9 for an example of how the Transform effect can be used. This simple illustration involves scale, skew, move, rotate, and multiple copies.

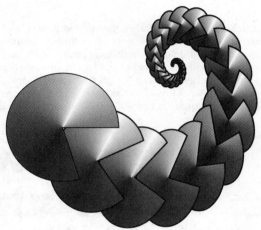

Figure 14-9: You can get carried away with the Transform effect.

Raster effects

You can apply multiple effects to an object with vector or raster effects. You can only apply an effect to multiple selected objects if they have the same type of stroke and fill. The objects can have any type of fill (or they all have no fill) as long as they all have a fill. The fill can be basic or a gradient. All the objects must have the same type of stroke (or no stroke), but it can be of any weight or color. To get around these limitations, you can select several objects and group them. Then you can apply effects, but if you ungroup the group, all the effects are lost and must be re-created from scratch.

When you click the Effects button in the Object panel, you'll see that the Effects menu is divided into a top and bottom half. Vector effects own the top half (explained above). Raster effects dominate the bottom. Here, you can add effects that were available only through Photoshop or Fireworks (or Illustrator) before. These effects include drop shadows, inner and outer glows, blurring, sharpening, bevels, and embossing. The names of these effects have no relationship to the vector effects of the same names. These effects must be rasterized on export and print. Unlike vector art, rasterized artwork is resolution dependent, and you have to determine the output resolution of the document. You handle this through the entries you make in File ➪ Document Settings ➪ Raster Effects Settings. There, you select a resolution of 72-, 144-, or 300-dpi, and have the option to choose Optimal CMYK Rendering. In order to work more freely without the wait for screen redraws, you can set the resolution at 72-dpi while you're working, and change it to 300-dpi if you are going to print the document. The screen image is pretty coarse at 72-dpi, but with a Gaussian blur on a large object, the redraw time can be reduced significantly. Because FreeHand users are not used to this type of effect capability, it may take some getting used to.

✦ **Bevel and Emboss** — You have a choice of inner and outer bevels and embossing and the style of edge: smooth, flat, rippled, and so on. Examples are shown in Figure 14-10.

Figure 14-10: Examples of the types of bevels and embossing you can apply

✦ **Blur** — If you feel the need to blur a vector object or a bitmap, you can use a simple blur or a Gaussian blur just as you would in Fireworks or Photoshop. This image "editing" can be done on a TIFF or EPS that you created with the Convert To Image command, as well as imported on graphics. Figure 14-11 shows standard and Gaussian blurs.

Figure 14-11: Make people think they need glasses with blur effects.

✦ **Shadows and Glows** — Where would we be without drop shadows these days? Now you can apply them plus inner and outer glows and shadows. You can even choose a color for the shadow, which makes it easier to create seamless effects on top of bitmaps or other colored objects. See Figure 14-12 for shadow examples.

Figure 14-12: Live shadow and glow effects

✦ **Transparency** — This feature is similar to the Transparent Fill feature, but now you can create gradient masks, and feathering. See some of these effects in Figure 14-13.

Figure 14-13: Transparency effects including a gradient mask on the text

New tools and tool changes

The action of the Pen tool has changed significantly, including a path preview. A digital tablet will allow you to have pressure-sensitive drawing again (it was inoperable in FreeHand 10 on a Mac). Brush attributes have been enhanced, and there's a new Eraser tool that's pretty neat. The new Blend tool supplies greater control over blends between objects, and rounded corners have never been easier to make. There's a new Cone gradient fill for some really neat effects, and a whole new way of working with polygons. The list goes on and on. Let's start with the drawing tools.

Pen tool changes

The Pen tool still has "Smart Cursors," but they've been simplified substantially from FreeHand 10. The first feature you'll want to check out is the Pen Preview. Double-click the Pen tool icon in the Toolbar to find this option. When it's selected, a blue path follows the cursor from the last point placed, in a rubber band fashion, showing you how the path will look if you click the mouse to add a point. If you're experienced with Bézier curves, this may annoy you. Turn it off. However, if you like a preview of coming events, leave it on.

When you have the Pen tool selected and there is not a path with a point selected, the Smart Cursor shows an "X," indicating that you will be starting a new path when you place the next point. After the first point, the cursor is the normal pen point until you move the cursor over an existing path. At that time, the cursor gains a small open circle. If you have View ➪ Snap To Objects on, the cursor creates a large circle on the path itself, indicating that you will be placing the point exactly on the path. Moving the Pen cursor over an existing point places a black square near the cursor regardless of whether the path is selected or the Pen is drawing a path.

If you have Snap To Objects or Snap To Point on, the cursor changes from an "X" icon to a buttonhole icon until the cursor is out of the snap-to range. At that point, the buttonhole disappears and you won't see it again. The buttonhole indicates that the path will close with the next mouse click. With either of the two snap-to options turned on, the buttonhole cannot show up again because the hierarchy of the Smart Cursors puts the buttonhole cursor beneath Snap To Point or Object cursors. So, if you want to know — visually — that you're about to close a path, you must have both snap-to options off.

The modifier keys have changed as well. To add a point to a path, you must hold down the Alt (Option) key, which adds a plus sign to the cursor. If you want to remove a point, pressing the same key creates a minus sign beside the cursor, and a click deletes the point, leaving the rest of the path as it is. If you select a path and click the Pen tool on the path without the Alt (Option) key, you start a new path. If you want to add or adjust Bézier curve handles, hold down the Alt (Option) and Control (Command) keys at the same time, and drag from the point or adjust the handle.

Calligraphic stroke

Although this sounds as if it belongs in the Toolbox, it doesn't. Instead, it can be a part of any stroke you draw with any tool. You can think of it as a variation on the brush, but it does much more. This new addition is located in the Object ➪ Stroke menu. Click the stroke branch of the tree, and choose Calligraphic from the stroke type menu. The Stroke panel looks like Figure 14-14.

Figure 14-14: The Calligraphic Stroke offers many options with just the default selection.

With the default stroke, you have the world's best digital "Speedball" D-style pen point, but the fun doesn't stop there. By changing numbers in the vertical and horizontal scale fields, you can change the width and height of the stroke's shape. Rotate the thumbwheel to change the angle of the stroke. Figure 14-15 shows the same drawing with variations in scaling and angle of the default stroke.

Figure 14-15: Variations are quick and painless with the Calligraphic Stroke.

To see some of the fun stuff, create a simple (single) shape and copy it to the Clipboard. Open the Calligraphic dialog box and click the Paste button. The graphic you just drew is now the stroke you will draw with. You can apply the stroke to anything you draw, even as the outline to text that you converted to paths. Figure 14-16 shows examples of what you can do with calligraphic text outlines. The top example is the text in Century Schoolbook Bold Italics. The second version has the default Calligraphic Stroke applied with a value of 5 for both width and height, and an angle of 135 degrees, giving the text a "Speedball," hand-lettered appearance. The third example shows an angle of 0-degrees, and 100 for width and height. The stroke has gray color, and the fill was applied (black) and moved above the stroke in the Object panel. This version appears as if you had applied the Expand Stroke Xtra to the text. The bottom text has the same setup as the one above it, only the angle was changed to 135 degrees, and both values are set to 100.

Handlettered

Handlettered

Handlettered

Handlettered

Figure 14-16: Simple examples of the Calligraphic Stroke on text

One value of using this method on an object or text is that you can get a fluid, almost organic look to the stroke without duplicating the path itself. Another reason to use the Calligraphic Stroke is to get the artwork away from a "computer generated" look. The option of pasting your own shapes into the stroke panel makes it even more personal and something you can work into your drawing style.

Brush enhancements

Admittedly, FreeHand 10's brushes had problems in the corners. The code that made the brushwork caused the brush to overlap itself in tight corners, which brought the odd-even-fill into play, causing unsightly corners. FreeHand MX has fixed the corners to a large degree. Figure 14-17 shows a shape with tight corners, and you can see how well the brush (the brushes shape is shown in the center) conforms to the outer path.

Figure 14-17: Brushes hug the corners tighter in FreeHand MX.

Eraser tool

What if you had a tool that would cut through a vector object and instead of slicing the paths, actually removes a swath of the object? Now you have this in the Eraser tool. It has a user-defined width, and when you pass it over a selected vector object, it cuts the path in two places, and heals the cuts, retaining the fill and stroke attributes. Figure 14-18 shows three ways the Eraser tool can be used with a Wacom graphic tablet. The pressure-sensitive settings are shown above the three different ways the tool works. Starting outside the object and cutting into the object makes a simple closed path. By holding down the Alt (Option) key, you can constrain the tool to a straight path. In the middle example, the pen started with greater pressure than when it ended, causing the wedge-shaped cut resulting in two separate objects. The right example used pressure sensitivity to cut a hole inside the object. When you release the mouse, the object becomes a compound path. If you choose Modify ⇨ Split, you would have three separate shapes in this example.

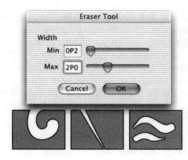

Figure 14-18: The Eraser tool is versatile. From left to right, it created a single closed path, a pair of closed paths, and a composite path.

The Eraser tool can be used in its most simple application to cut an object into two pieces with a straight constant-width path. You can also use it to make a jigsaw puzzle with pieces that can be removed. It works only on vector paths (open or closed), however, so if you want to apply some special effects on text, you have to convert it to paths first.

Blend tool

Blending has changed in FreeHand MX. The Modify ⇨ Blend command still works as it did previously. But, with the addition of the Blend tool, you may not use the menu command much anymore. Select the Blend tool and click an object. Then click a second object. They automatically blend together (with a default of 25-steps). Click another object and the blend continues between the last two objects. The objects can have any kind of fill, stroke, or effect (both vector and raster) and the blend works. Although, place a drop shadow on one object, and have no effect on another object, and use the Blend tool to create a blend. The entire blended group has the drop shadow, excepting the object that had no effect in the first place. As with a "normal" blend, to dismantle the blend, you must ungroup it. That leaves you with the original two objects, and a single group with the blended steps. If you want to make changes in the objects, delete the middle group, make the modifications, and run the blend again.

But wait, there's even more! If you use the Modify ⇨ Blend command, the object on the bottom of the stacking order always remains at the bottom of the blend. With the Blend tool, the object you select first goes to the bottom of the blend, regardless of its stacking order in the document. As shown in Figure 14-19, the objects that are being blended have a special set of point indicators, including one that indicates a key point that is connecting to a corresponding key point in the other object. When the blend has been done, you can Alt (Option) select an end object, and move the key point to another point on the object. This simple addition to the process solves many problems with blends twisting and turning the wrong way.

Figure 14-19: Key points appear and can be moved when objects are selected with the Blend tool.

Extrude tool

You can extrude any FreeHand shape, including live text in FreeHand MX. After the extrusion is complete, double-click in the center of the object to bring up an encompassing circle. The circle has a small triangle shape that indicates the zero point. When you first click and drag outside the circle, the object rotates around the axis pointing to the vanishing point. Click inside the circle and drag to cause the object to tumble. At that point, the vanishing point still applies, but you control movements in a hit-and-miss way. However, as you can see in Figure 14-20, there are text input fields for the vanishing point, the three axes' rotation coordinates, object placement, and length of the extrusion. The three buttons show various attributes for object (this panel), lighting, and bevel/twist.

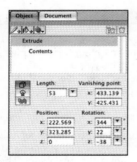

Figure 14-20: The Extrude panel determines many factors of the extrusion.

If you have multiple objects that you've extruded and would like them to have the same vanishing point, select all the extruded objects and choose Modify ⇨ Extrude ⇨ Share Vanishing Points. A new vanishing point will appear under the cursor when you click it on the page. All the objects will point to the new common vanishing point. Lighting on an extrusion is limited, but adequate, with two sets of nine light sources each. You get to choose all you want, as long as you want only two lights, but you can vary the intensity of each light. Figure 14-21 shows a few objects with fairly simple extrusions, including live, editable text and a hole through an object. Effects, such as glows and shadows, are based on the entire outline of the object and its extrusion, so realistic drop shadows may have to be constructed as a separate object beneath the extrusion.

All objects must be filled before making the extrusion, or you end up with a wireframe rendering. At the time of this writing, you cannot change the color of an object after it has been extruded. Choose a fill color before using the Extrude function, or the object will only consist of any stroke you have applied. If the object has a fill and a stroke, only the face of the original object will have a stroke, the extrusion will just have a shaded fill. Bitmaps can't be extruded. Instead, take the bitmap and the extrusion into Fireworks and distort the bitmap to fit the face of the extrusion. Then bring the distortion back into FreeHand and place it on the extrusion.

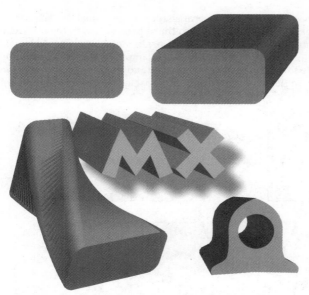

Figure 14-21: Examples of extruded objects and live text

Simple Object manipulations

Although we could have discussed this topic in the Panels section, it has more to do with drawing than with organization. Use the Rectangle tool to draw a rectangle. Choose the Subselect tool (white pointer) and select the rectangle. A diamond-shaped point appears at the corners of the rectangle. Click and drag those points to make instant, symmetrical rounded corners. That would have been enough for me, but Macromedia took it a couple steps further in the Object panel. Choose the Rectangle item in the Object panel, and notice the corner options you have to choose from (Figure 14-22). Keep Uniform selected (default) and any changes you make in the panel are applied to each corner. Deselect it to make individual corner changes. The eight fields indicate the radius of the corners. Padlock icons allow or prevent changes to corner adjustments. The nicest touch is the group of icons in the center that enable you to make "innie" corners instead of radiused corners.

Figure 14-22: The Rectangle information panel allows individual corner development.

As shown in Figure 14-23, a rectangle can take several shapes. The original rectangle is shown in the top left. Rounded corners have been added with the Subselect tool in the top-right example. In the bottom left, Uniform was selected and an inside radius was created by clicking one of the corner buttons in the Rectangle panel. The last example on the bottom right has had various adjustments made through the Rectangle panel, and the rounded corners were modified by entering numbers in the panel and using the Subselect tool to move the corner points.

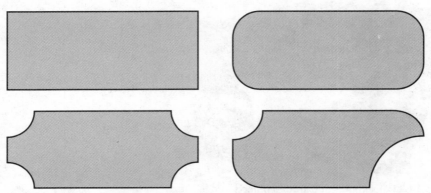

Figure 14-23: Rounded corners are really a snap in FreeHand MX.

The Rectangle isn't the only simple object that you can manipulate. How about ellipses? If you draw an ellipse in FreeHand MX and then choose the Subselect tool, a diamond and square handle show up on top of each other at the top of the ellipse. Click the mouse on them and drag left or right to take a wedge out of the ellipse, but leave a containing shape. It's as if someone stole a piece of pie. If you want, you can deselect the Closed option and just remove an arc from the ellipse. But what good is all of this going to be to you? Well, beyond making pie charts, Pac Man characters, or fortune cookies, you can use other information available in the document window. Figure 14-24 shows an ellipse and the Object panel fields. All the good names for things were taken, so the two points on the ellipse that you are able to move are called the dot and the diamond, after their shapes. In line with the standard Cartesian alignment, zero is the center point on the right side of the circle. The dot is vertical (by default); therefore in the Arc text field, the number is 90 degrees. The diamond is also vertical by default, but here it has been rotated midway to the zero point by entering 45 in the diamond Arc field. Under the Dimensions heading, "x" and "y" indicate the coordinates of the bottom-left corner of the ellipse's bounding box; "w" and "h" are the dimensions of the ellipse in the current document units of measure. If you are a technical illustrator, it won't take you long to work out the details of using this panel to the utmost.

Figure 14-24: Elliptical modifications are easy to handle through the Object panel.

Polygonal controls

Okay, your appetite for simple object manipulation has been whetted, here's the main course. Click and hold the Rectangle icon in the Toolbar and select the Polygon tool when it appears in the pop-up menu. If you double-click this icon, you get the standard Polygon dialog box where you can change the number of sides/points and shape of the polygon. But you don't have to use this dialog box if you don't want to. Instead, draw a polygon on the page and change the number of points to 10 in the Object panel. The Object panel displays a new set of parameters that you've never seen before. In fact, these parameters are so new that they don't even have names–it's like the "artist formerly known as Prince." As a substitute for names, the outer point of a polygon receives a diamond icon, and the mid-point between outer points has a dot icon. What the heck, I think it's pretty safe to say that most artists are visually oriented, and we don't need names for things anyway. Choose the Subselect tool and click the polygon to make the diamond and dot icons appear on the polygon itself. When a single diamond or dot is clicked and dragged with the mouse, the entire array of diamonds or dots move as a unit. You can extend them, bring them toward the center, or rotate them at will. As you do so, changes are updated in the Object panel, and if you know exactly what you want to do, you can input numbers in the diamond and dot text fields to create change in the polygon.

But wait, there's more! Just because a polygon's point starts life on the outside of the shape doesn't mean it has to stay there. The dot points can be dragged outside the diamond points to extend the size of the polygon in one simple click and drag. Obviously, the diamond points can be dragged inside the dot points as well. When you rotate the points so they overlap each other, a complex shape is created, and you can invoke or deselect Odd And Even Fill to create even more complex designs (see Figure 14-25). The diamond and dot control is effective even after skewing, scaling, or rotating the polygon.

You've seen that you can add points and shift them around. What else is new? How about radiused corners—or fillets? Notice the corner icons at the bottom of the diamond and dot columns in the Object panel. By placing numbers in these fields, you can turn outside corners into blunt ends, and sharp inside corners into smooth, transitional paths.

Figure 14-25: Twelve-point polygons with different settings in the Object panel

Connector lines

If you are the organized type, or you need to show the relationship between elements, the Connector tool will be the highlight of FreeHand MX. It's simple to operate. Select the Connector tool, click an object, and click another object. A connector line joins the two objects with a straight-lined path to which you may apply arrowheads to either end, as with any other path. The tool has its limitations. All lines are right-angled between objects, there are no "angled" lines available, whether you utilize the Constrain feature or not. The connecting line will be "dog-legged" unless both objects are centered on each other (see Figure 14-26). Working with regular shapes, such as rectangles and circles, provides the best results, because the connecting lines start and end at the center of the bounding box of each object. Therefore, if you have an irregular-shaped object, the connecting line may not contact the edge of the object itself. You use this tool to draw map callouts, labels, and organization charts, but because the connector lines pass between pages, you can also use it to show the progression through a FreeHand HTML site setup.

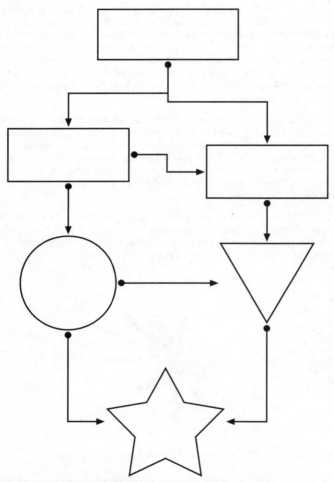

Figure 14-26: Connector lines make organization a snap, but precise alignment is necessary.

Gradient fill handles

Say good bye to the old thumbwheel for gradient fills, and say hello to the new Show Fill Handles option on the Pointer and Subselect tools. Double-click either of those tools to set the option for both tools. Then when you add a gradient fill to an object—and have Fill: Gradient (Linear, Radial, and so on) selected in the Object panel — a new fill handle shows up over the filled object.

A dashed line connects the two handles. One handle has a small black diamond. Click and drag this handle to move the entire range of the gradient around the object. The second handle is a black square, slightly larger than the diamond handle. This handle can be moved around the object, but it maintains the diamond handle as its center point. The square handle can be moved away from the diamond to stretch the amount of gradient, or moved toward the diamond to shorten the width of the gradient. But best of all, you can move the square handle *around* the diamond handle to change the direction of the gradient. This means you can see the path of the gradient and make visual decisions instead of the old hit-and-miss adjustments of the thumbwheel.

Gradient fill enhancements

If you like to use gradient fills, FreeHand MX has some additional toys to play with, called Behaviors. These attributes control the way the gradient fills an object, and they come in four flavors: Normal, Repeat, Reflect, and Auto size. It helps if you turn on the Show Fill Handles option for the Pointer and Subselect tools so you can see what's going on with the various behaviors.

If you choose Normal (the default), the gradient is business as usual. You can move the Gradient Fill handles around to change the way the gradient looks. Auto Size brings the control handles to a zero setting where the gradient is aligned to the page horizontally and vertically. There are no fill handles to work with, only the center point, but you can it move it within or outside the object. The Repeat behavior causes the gradient to begin and end at the terminus of the gradient fill handles. The handles can be rotated and moved around the document in a normal manner. Finally, the Reflect behavior (shown on the sphere in Figure 14-27) adds a reflection to the darker end of the gradient. Add a drop shadow and you've almost got 3-D.

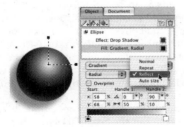

Figure 14-27: The Gradient Fill Behaviors enhance gradients with a mouse-click.

Multiple attributes

For the life of FreeHand, a path is drawn, then stroked and filled. If you wanted to do something else with the path you had to clone or copy and paste the path before you could make modifications. Things have changed in FreeHand MX. Now when you draw a path, it's only the beginning. You can apply multiple strokes, fills, and raster and vector effects all from the same path, through the controls in the Object panel. Unless it changes from the beta state of the program, gradients rotate with an object when transformed — that is, if you've decided to use the gradient indicative of a light source, the light source rotates as you rotate the object, so you have to adjust the gradient handles.

It's a matter of selecting the path in the Object panel and choosing various attributes. Then you can add a path or add a fill to the original path and place different attributes on it. Do it again and again until you have it right. When you're done, it's just a single object with all the effects you've applied to it. Figure 14-28 shows a path with several attributes. Alongside the path is the Object panel showing how the Object tree looks. Notice that the glows and shadows are fully transparent and react naturally to the Cone gradient beneath the sphere. The really nice thing about the multiple attribute arrangement is that you move only one object. There's no grouping, joining, or anything else. If you see an attribute you don't like, select it in the Object tree and click the Trash icon. None of the other attributes will change.

Figure 14-28: You can add multiple attributes to fills and strokes in the Object panel.

Reposition while drawing

Adobe Photoshop has let you reposition a selection before committing it to the Pasteboard for a couple years now. It's really easy to get used to. Just drag your selection with any of the selection tools and while the mouse is down, press the Spacebar. Any further movements of the mouse drag the selection; they don't change the shape of the selection until you release the Spacebar.

Snap To Objects

Before, you could only snap a point to another point, using Snap To Point. Now you'll be able to align objects and points perfectly to each other, anywhere along a path. Hover the Pen, Bezigon, or Line tool over a path, and the cursor gains a small circle, and a large dot appears on an object. This dot indicates that the next point will be placed directly on the path of the object beneath the cursor. The snap distance is 8 pixels by default. To change it choose Preferences ➪ General — you're best off with a setting of 3. The feature gets even better when you select an object somewhere on its path and move the object over another path or object (see Figure 14-29). The same circle and dot appear, showing you exactly where the objects will intersect. You can turn Snap To Point on or off in the View menu. The range that determines when an object snaps to a guide or an object is set under the Snap To Distance field in the Preferences ➪ General dialog box. The default is 8 pixels.

Figure 14-29: Align objects and points anywhere on a path with Snap To Objects.

Using panels

Of all the improvements to FreeHand, changes to the panels are the most evident and possibly the most useful — especially if you work on a small screen. All the panels are contained (at least when you first open the program) in a single panel that runs the full height of the right side of the monitor. It looks similar to the rest of the Studio MX setup. But, there's one great advantage if you're on a Windows machine, in that there's a tiny box and triangle in the separator bar that contains the panels. Click that triangle, and all the panels fly off the monitor completely, leaving only the 6-pixel-wide separator bar running down the right edge of the screen. Click the triangle again, and the whole shebang flies out. There are five panels, including Properties, Assets, Layers, Mixer and Tints, and Answers. You can move them up and down the stacking order by grabbing the gripper buttons on the left side and dropping the panel where you want it. A white triangle hides or shows the contents of the panel when clicked.

To remove a panel from the main group, grab the gripper buttons and drag the panel onto the desktop. If you want a tabbed panel out on its own, or included within another panel grouping, choose Group (name of tab) With from the panel Options menu and choose the new location. If you attempt to move a tab, you'll see a window with specific instructions on how to move the tabbed panel. You will quickly tire of this message; there's a box to check to halt its appearance.

Properties panel

This panel separates FreeHand MX from any previous version. Within it, you'll find the Object and Document panels. Document is no different than in previous FreeHand versions. But the Object panel gives you a whole new way to work. At the top of the panel you'll see the Add Stroke, Add Fill, and Add Effect buttons.

If nothing is selected in the document, Default Drawing Style will be the top entry in the Object panel. Directly beneath that is the stroke or fill that you've made part of your default setup. Whatever you draw next reflects these attributes. If you want to change the stroke attributes, click the Stroke entry in the attribute tree. That brings up everything to do with strokes: type, color, width, cap, and so on. Anything you select here shows up in the attribute tree. If your object lacks a fill, click the Add Fill button, and the Stroke attributes go away to make room for the Fills attributes. Again, your selections appear in the tree, including a color swatch. Double-clicking the swatch alternately opens the Mixer panel or the Swatches panel so you can change colors quickly.

On the right end of the panel are two trashcan icons. To utilize them, you must select an attribute in the attribute tree. Clicking the Remove Branch button deletes everything on the selected branch. This could be fill color, Gaussian blur, and a drop shadow, leaving a sketched, six-point Rhodamine Red stroke (if that's how you had it set up). If you wanted to remove only the drop shadow, you would select that item in the tree and click the Remove Item button. Everything else would remain.

Answers panel

All the Studio MX applications now have an Answers panel as standard equipment. They snap, dock, and zip with each other, and are linked to Macromedia's Web site for the latest information on the program. Basically, there's nothing on your machine — it's all on the Web, so an Internet connection is a necessity.

Styles panel

If you're a power-user and utilize styles, you're going to fall in love with the way you create styles in FreeHand MX. It's sort of a mix between the way it used to be done and symbol making. Graphic styles can include any and all of the following: Stroke, Fill, Object Halftone, and Effect. To begin with, the Styles panel is located within the Assets panel by default. You can move it out of the panel. The panel can be viewed in three different modes: Compact List View, Large List View, and Previews Only. Compact List View is basically the old Styles view — a small icon and the name of the style. It's great if you work with many styles. The Large List View has icons about four times larger than the Compact view, and also has the style name. Previews Only is a grid of large icons without names. The icons show stroke and fill for graphic objects. The larger two modes show "Aa" in the font you've chosen for the style.

Starting with text styles, all you have to do to make a style is select a text block that contains the text attributes you desire, and drag it onto an empty spot on the Styles panel. If you want a name for the style, you must be in the Compact List or Large List view; double-click the generic Style-1 text and type in your own style name. Text styles contain everything you can apply to text in the Text panel. A Text style ignores vector or bitmap effects that you applied in the Objects panel. You'll have to do a three-stage operation for those effects: set the text and make a Text style; then convert the text to paths; then apply the vector or bitmap effects and create a style from that.

Graphic styles are different. Because everything you do to an object is shown in the Objects panel, you can create a style from there easily. Either select an object on the page and set attributes in the Objects panel, or set the attributes with nothing selected. Then drag the Preview swatch at the top of the Objects panel onto the Styles panel. The Preview swatch shows a compilation of all the attributes you want for a given object. You can also select New from the Style panel's Option menu to add the style. If you created an object that you want to use as a style, you can select the object and drag it onto an open area in the Styles panel. The object won't go anywhere, but its attributes become a style.

Applying the style is a no-brainer. Select an object and click the style in the Styles panel. And, if you have a style or group of styles you want to be able to access in other documents or share with other artists, you can export them through the Styles Options menu. Think about using styles in your designing stage, by making various attributes into styles and using them throughout your production. Then if you need to make global changes, it can be done very quickly by changing the style.

The easiest way to redefine a style is to drag the new style object onto an existing style in the Styles panel. Additionally, you can drag the Preview swatch onto an existing style, or select the top-level entry in the Objects panel and choose Redefine from the Styles panel Options menu. This opens a dialog box enabling you to choose a style to redefine. You could get confused if you have nothing selected in the document, and you click on a style. Its attributes appear in the Objects panel where you can modify them. This *does not* change anything in the style. When you're through with the modifications, redefine a style or make a new style.

FreeHand MX Movie Considerations

Yes, you can make movies in FreeHand. No, they probably won't be as slick as anything you can do in Flash. But, FreeHand allows you to tie down the basics of a movie that you can take into Flash and polish into the award-winning masterpiece you want to make. The new Action tool helps you define links in your movie or Web page, and you can import Flash movies to become part of FreeHand movies.

Action tool

Creating navigation actions can't get much easier than this. Choose a view that shows all the pages involved in your movie, and select the Action tool. Click an object that will be the "trigger," and then click the object page. Making a link in this manner creates a "Go To" or "Print" action between the trigger object and the page. An arrow/box icon and wavy line between the items show the origin object and page, as shown in Figure 14-30.

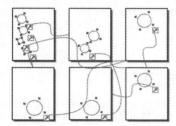

Figure 14-30: This simplified example of the Action tool shows page relationships.

Improved SWF performance

There is a behind-the-scenes improvement when you export a file in SWF format. FreeHand MX takes less time to do the SWF export than FreeHand 10. It will not affect anything you do or see onscreen, or the outcome of the movie.

SWF import/re-export

You can have a SWF movie clip as part of a FreeHand MX page. Furthermore, you can export the document as a SWF file, and the imported SWF will be a part of the file you export. You might well ask, "Why?" but if you need client approval on movies, backgrounds and so on, this is an elegant solution. Say you have a Web site under development that includes a small movie, such as a banner ad, and you want the client to see the movie on various colored backgrounds. In this instance, you would place the imported SWF on a master page and create several child pages with different background colors or various scenes. All you would need to do is create a simple object such as a button shape, and use the Action tool to link the button to another page. Your client can make a sound decision based on your presentation.

Another example would be a static background element and the SWF file at different sizes or locations on the page. Going beyond these examples, you may need to make a slide presentation and want to print several frames (slides) to make a brochure or handout. Then again, maybe you want a frame of a movie to print for packaging or an instruction booklet. By selecting the frame(s) you have in mind from the field at the bottom of the Object panel, you can easily print them individually instead of running the movie in Flash and stopping it for screenshots. Then, you may want to select a particular frame of the movie as a still shot for a Web page. Select the frame in the Object panel, and export it as a JPEG. Selecting a frame in the Object panel displays that frame in the document.

The preview frame for the movie is user-chosen, and can be printed, or exported in a rasterized version or as vectors. As explained in the following section, you can edit the SWF in Flash with the Flash jump button (Launch/Edit Flash MX). The movie is automatically regenerated and updated in FreeHand.

Simplified movie settings dialog

Movie Settings has moved from the Control menu in FreeHand 10 to the Windows ⇨ Movie menu in FreeHand MX. Instead of an entire menu to itself, the movie settings are handled in a pop-up menu. The Toolbars menu contains the Controller, which you can float on the document, or nest in with other panels. Its functions have not changed.

The Movie Settings dialog box changed significantly. Export Options now provides a choice between Single or Multiple pages, and Animated or Flattened layers. Icons beneath the Layers and Pages title show the effects of your choices. A new Movie Property has been added: Size To Match Contents, and Optimization terminology has been simplified. The basic functions are the same, but it's easier for novices to get a handle on the process.

Interaction Between MX Programs

Macromedia comes close to having the look and feel of one large program with the Studio MX. If you're comfortable in one MX program, you won't feel lost in another because the user interface is so similar. Naturally, each program has its own purpose, and the tools and menus are different. But, the common user interface is easy to get around in.

Fireworks MX

Fireworks PNG Importer

FreeHand and Flash have played well together for their last couple versions, but now Fireworks can play too. A bitmap that's been imported to FreeHand can be edited quickly by clicking the new Fireworks jump button at the bottom of the Object panel. When you save a Fireworks PNG document, and import it into FreeHand, you can edit it with all the vector tools that FreeHand offers and modify the effects that Fireworks has applied. Unfortunately, any texture effects you applied from Fireworks styles are lost in the translation. You have a basic fill instead. When you're finished in FreeHand and take the document into Fireworks again, you could be in for another unwelcome surprise if you want to put that style back to work. Applying a style to an object that has a (FreeHand) glow effect causes the new (Fireworks) style to go to the outer dimensions of the glow.

Flash MX

Launch/edit Flash

If you have used original Flash file to create an SWF file that you've imported into FreeHand, a quick edit mode is available. Click the imported SWF file in the FreeHand document; then go to the Object panel. At the bottom of the panel you'll see the new Flash jump button. Click this button and Flash opens. You will be prompted to search for the original FLA file. After the document opens in Flash, the top of the window says Edit From FreeHand. Do any editing necessary, and click the Done button. You'll return to FreeHand with the newly edited movie in place, even if you rename the movie in Flash.

There are important considerations when working with Flash and FreeHand. It all has to do with the development and introduction of multiple products from a single manufacturer. First there was FreeHand 10, which allowed SWF export to Flash 5. Then Flash became Flash MX, which could understand FreeHand 10 files, but had no clue what a FreeHand MX file would look or act like. Finally, we have FreeHand MX, which would like to play nice with Flash MX, but can't because Flash doesn't understand FreeHand MX. What all this amounts to is that if you want to use a FreeHand file in Flash MX, you have to export it as a FreeHand 10 file. Then everyone gets along. At the time of writing FreeHand MX is still in its beta stage, but there is a Flash updater that is planned to ship with FreeHand MX that will allow Flash to read FreeHand MX data.

Summary

In many respects, this chapter is the toughest because it covers all the new components of FreeHand MX. But you learned all about the new, all-important Object panel and how you can apply multiple effects to objects and that the effects are *both* vector and bitmap. You learned that the Pen tool has changed, and the Blend function has been modified. The Extrude tool was explained, and so were the workings of the Polygon tool and the way the Subselect tool interacts with simple shapes to create rounded or indented corners. You found out that you can import an SWF file, modify it in Flash, and re-export it as part of a new SWF file. Most of all you learned that once you start working in FreeHand MX, you won't want to go to any other drawing program.

✦　　✦　　✦

Mastering the Power of Macromedia Fireworks MX

Getting Around
in Fireworks

Fireworks is an integral part of the Macromedia Studio MX Web-development workflow. In Fireworks, you can design spectacular text effects as editable vectors, or you can utilize its powerful bitmap functions. This new version has added powerful bitmap tools, like dodge, burn, smudge, sharpen, and blur. Design your text right on the screen, complete with kerning, leading, paragraph leads, and more. If you've used Fireworks before, you'll really appreciate the improvements to the pop-up menu editor. You'll love it even if you've never used it! For a full list of new features, check out Chapter 2.

It's now much easier to move between vector and bitmap modes. Just select a vector or bitmap tool — Fireworks is smart enough to know what mode you need to be in and makes the switch automatically.

Working with bitmaps and vectors together is a huge advantage in Fireworks. You can have vector shapes filled with bitmap images, or you can place vectors over a bitmap and integrate them. The possibilities are endless.

In Macromedia Studio MX, Fireworks helps you design, optimize, slice, and export all the images you need for any project — all while playing very nicely with its companions programs, FreeHand 10 (MX), Dreamweaver MX, Flash MX, and ColdFusion MX.

Introducing the Fireworks Workspace

When you install Macromedia Studio MX and open Fireworks MX for the first time, you are presented with a Welcome Screen, as seen in Figure 15-1. You can click the various links to learn more about graphic design, what's new, or the Web Design button (which takes you through a tutorial). The Macintosh user's workspace is a bit different. On the Macintosh platform, panel groups float.

Cross-Reference Installation instructions are in Chapter 1.

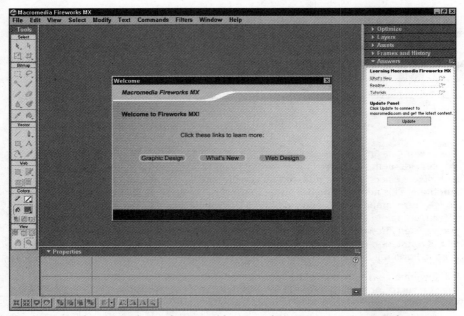

Figure 15-1: The Fireworks workspace with a new document open in a Windows PC environment

Working with the Document Window

When you open a new file (File⇨New), you are opening a document window. Inside the document window is the canvas. The canvas is the area in which you work.

To open a new document:

1. Click File⇨New

2. In the New Document dialog box, type in the desired height and width of your canvas.

3. The default resolution is 72 dots per inch (dpi), which is appropriate for using on the Web. You can adjust this number if you need to if you are designing for something other than the Web.

4. Choose whether you want a white canvas, a transparent one (depicted by a grid of gray and white squares) or choose a custom color.

5. Click OK when you've filled out all the options.

To modify the canvas after the document window is open:

1. Click Modify⇨Canvas and choose one of the available options.

   • Image Size adjusts the selected image.

   • Canvas size adjusts the canvas size without changing the size of any of the document's elements.

- Canvas color allows you to change the canvas color, from white to transparent to a custom value.

- Trim Canvas is used like a crop, to remove extra space around the content of the document.

- Fit Canvas adjusts the canvas to fit around all content in the document window, including images that overlap or which are outside the canvas area. The canvas expands or contracts to fit the content.

- Rotate 180%.

- Rotate 90% CW (clockwise).

- Rotate 90% CCW (counterclockwise).

To open and arrange multiple document windows, follow these steps:

1. Open the documents you want to work with.

2. Click Window⇨Cascade. This option makes it easy to select each image.

3. Click Window⇨Tile Horizontally if you prefer a horizontal positioning.

4. Click Window⇨Tile Vertical to line the documents up vertically.

To open a copy of an opened document window, follow these steps:

1. Select the document you want another duplicate window opened for.

2. Use the keyboard shortcut Control+Alt+N (Command+Option+N). A new document opens at the same magnification as the first one. You can zoom in and do detail work and view the results in the overall image in the original document.

3. Close the second document. You'll notice that you aren't asked whether you want to save changes.

4. Click the Preview tab to see how your document will look in a browser. You can also click on 2-Up or 4-Up to compare optimization settings.

Cross-Reference You will learn more about comparing optimization settings in Chapter 23.

Working with the Panel Layout

The use of docked panel groups is new to Fireworks MX. The docked panels are locked into the interface for Windows users and free floating on a Mac. There are also some new terms to learn, some missing panels to discover, and some new panels to explore. The most notable addition in MX is the Property inspector. Many functions that were previously accessed only by panels are now accessed from the Property inspector.

Those familiar with earlier versions of Fireworks will notice that the Stroke, Fill, Effect, Object, Tool Options, and Color Table panels are gone. The Property inspector replaces the functions of these panels. Two new panels, Answers and Align, have been added, bringing welcome features!

Figure 15-2 shows the areas common to many panels. Clicking the little white arrow (expander arrow) opens the panel.

Figure 15-2 The Layers panel, marked to show the new names and features of all the panels in Fireworks

Customizing the panel layout

You may dock, undock, close, or rearrange panels within a group anyway you want. To move a specific panel into a different panel group, follow these steps:

1. Click the Options menu of the panel you want to move.

2. Click Group (panel's name) with, and select the panel group you want to move it to.

To make a new panel group, follow these steps:

1. Click the Options menu of the panel you want to make a new group for.

2. Hover your mouse over Group (panel's name) with and click on New Panel Group.

The New Panel Group option effectively undocks a specified panel. You may reposition or close it as desired.

To rename a panel group, follow these steps:

1. Click the Options menu of the panel you want to rename.

2. Click Rename Panel Group and enter a name.

To dock a panel, follow these steps:

1. Select the desired panel from the Windows menu. The new panel opens below all current panels.

2. Click and drag the Gripper (little dots on top-left side) and drag the panel into position.

3. Release the mouse when the solid blue line indicates the location where you want the panel to be docked. In Figure 15-3, the bottom solid line marks where the panel was. The top solid line (blue) shows where it will be docked when you release the mouse.

4. To close a panel group, click its Options menu and select close Panel Group. The panel group will remain closed unless you open it again using the Window menu. If you want it docked, you have to dock it again.

If you want to rearrange the order of panels within a group, simply regroup it with the same group using the same method used to move a panel to a new group. This action has the effect of placing that panel last in the group. With a little forethought, it is easy to arrange your panels in your preferred order.

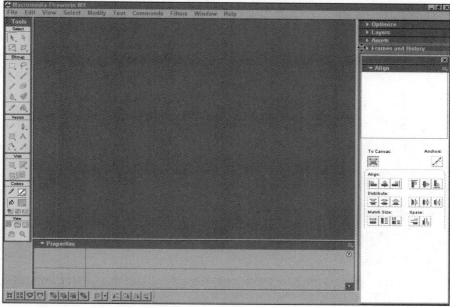

Figure 15-3: The solid line indicates where the panel will be docked.

Features common to most panels

This is a list to show you some of the features that you'll find in the various panels (Figure 15-4). You'll work with specific panels throughout the Fireworks section as you learn how to use the wide array of tools.

✦ You'll find an options pop-up menu for each panel, which you access by clicking the little icon in the top-right corner of the panel. This menu contains additional options relative to that panel.

✦ Slider controls are present in many panels. When a number is required for a percentage or size, you can click the down arrow and then click and drag the slider to select the number. You can also type in the amount. If you choose to type in a number, you need to press Enter/Return to accept the setting.

✦ A Color box is present whenever a color option is available. When you see a color box (square with a color in it) and you want to change a color, simply click the color box and choose a color from the swatches panel with the Eyedropper tool. Alternatively you can use the Eyedropper to select a color from anywhere in the workspace. If you know the hexadecimal number you want to use, you can type it into the Color panel that opens when you click the color box. If you type in the number, you need to press the Enter/Return key. You may also access the system picker by clicking the color wheel or choose to remove all color by clicking the square with the red slash mark.

Figure 15-4: Typical panel features

Examining the Menu Bar

The Menu bar is located below the Title bar (top of the application). The Menu bar contains 10 different categories. Much has changed in the menus since previous versions of Fireworks. For example, the new Edit menu replaces the Insert menu of earlier Fireworks versions. A new Select menu has been added to contain the many bitmap selection options. The Xtras menu has been renamed to Filters.

File menu

The File menu contains options to open, close, save, import, and export files. The most notable change in the File menu is the Reconstitute Table feature. You may now open an HTML document and "rebuild" the images and HTML code in a Fireworks document — even when you don't have the original PNG file.

Edit menu

The Edit menu contains many new features, from options to cut, copy, or paste, to cropping and replacing. Other options, to build or add buttons and other graphics, are hidden as sub-menus beneath the Insert and Libraries options.

View menu

The most notable change in the View menu is the amount of additional magnification options. There are many more preset zoom options available.

Tip

You can always return to 100 percent by double-clicking the Zoom tool in the Tools panel.

This menu also has the options to view the rulers, guides, and grids. If you want to use guides you must have the rulers visible. Once the rulers are visible you click and drag in the ruler and pull down (for horizontal) or drag from the side ruler for vertical guides. Once you have guide visible you can double-click on it to open a dialog box where you can set a specific coordinate.

Select menu

The Select menu is new to Fireworks MX. Some of the options were formerly in the Edit menu and most were formerly in the Modify menu in previous versions of Fireworks. Notice that you can now modify your bitmap selections from the Select menu as well as save one selection per document.

Note

If you are a Photoshop user, you understand that a selection can be saved. In Fireworks the selection does not get saved to a separate channel or location that you can see — Unlike Photoshop, where you may save many selections that generate separate, modifiable channels, Fireworks can only save one selection, which is not readily accessible, except through the Restore Selection option.

Modify menu

The Modify menu contains a lot of options to modify your canvas and objects, including alignment and transformation functions. There are several changes to the Modify menu. All options pertaining to the canvas are now grouped under the Canvas menu item.

Pop-up menus are now available in the Modify menu (formerly in the Insert menu). Merge Down is new to Fireworks MX and causes the selected objects to be flattened into the bitmap object that is below the lowest selected object. The Flatten Selection option does the same thing that Convert to Bitmap did in Fireworks 4. The animation options are also accessed through this menu. You'll be using the options in this menu frequently throughout the Fireworks portion of this book.

Text menu

The Text menu contains options for working with text — from setting character formatting to attaching text to paths to converting to outlines. Although Fireworks MX text is typed onscreen and edited with the Property inspector, you can still access the Text Editor from the Text menu. Alternatively, you can access the Text Editor right-clicking (Control+click) any text in your document to access a contextual menu.

New Feature

In Fireworks MX, text is now typed directly into your document.

Commands menu

The Commands menu contains the following powerful options for managing and using Fireworks:

Flash MX

✦ The Manage Saved Commands option lets you organize commands you made in the History panel.

✦ The Manage Extensions option lets you work with extensions. Fireworks MX includes extensions, which you can download and install. You can also use Flash to design Fireworks panels and functions. The Align panel was made using Flash.

✦ The Arrowhead command is in the Creative category; you'll find an Arrowhead command to add a variety of arrow shapes to one or both ends of a path. Also included is the new Fade command. It's masking in one step. Or you can automatically add a variety of picture frames using the Add Picture Frame command.

✦ The Dashed Line command, also in the Creative category, enables you to add a dashed line instantly. This dashed line even wraps nicely along squared edges.

✦ The inset gray line below this line is a list of the commands you made yourself or saved from someone else.

✦ The Data-Driven Graphics Wizard works together with XML to add additional functionality for calling images.

✦ The Document options enable you to distribute all the objects in a document to separate layers. This and the Reverse Frames option both come in handy when designing animations. You can also hide or lock layers.

✦ The Panel Layout Sets are commonly used arrangements of windows and panels based on monitor resolutions. You can also customize and save your own layouts if desired. Panel Layouts are powered by JavaScript.

✦ The Reset Warnings dialog box resets all the "Don't Show Again" warning dialog boxes so that they appear when needed. This is useful when you turn off warnings and decide you want them back.

✦ Resize Selected Objects does just that. It opens a very easy-to-use interface that enables you to resize objects visually. If you press Shift and select multiple objects, they will all be resized.

✦ The Web option enables you to create a shared palette, which makes a custom color palette from a folder of images. You can set the maximum number of colors you want. This is a fast way to develop a custom palette of indexed colors. You can also choose to select or set blank alt tags.

Filters menu

The Filters menu was formerly named Xtras. The top portion of the menu contains various filters that you can apply to an image. Most of these filters (and more) can also be found in the Effects menu. You can apply filters and effects to vectors and bitmaps, but when a filter is applied to a vector object via the Filters menu, it converts the vector to a bitmap. Once saved, filters are not editable. The same adjustments applied through the Effects menu is a "Live Effect" and is always editable, even after saving, closing, and reopening the document.

Cross-Reference   You use Live Effects in Chapter 16.

Fireworks MX ships with Eye Candy LE and Alien Skin Splat LE. These two plug-ins don't expire and contain a sampling of the filters that ship with the full versions. The rest of your third-party demos appear at the bottom of the list. You may add to the list by importing filters and effects via Preferences.

Window menu

The Window menu gives you access to all the panels in Fireworks. Some of the most frequently used panels are already docked in the panel group area of your workspace. For instance, the Styles, URL, and Library panels are all in the Assets panel group set. You can customize your panel groups to fit your work style.

Using Fireworks Toolbars

Fireworks has two toolbars: the Main toolbar (which isn't open by default) and the Modify toolbar, which is open by default just below the Property inspector. The toolbars provide instant access to numerous functions.

The Main toolbar

The Main toolbar displays the most commonly accessed menu functions. To open the Main toolbar choose Window➪Toolbars➪Main. When the toolbar opens, it docks below the Main toolbar for easy access. Figure 15-5 shows the Main toolbar and its icons.

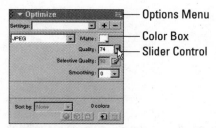

Figure 15-5: The Main toolbar open and docked below the Menu bar

The Modify toolbar

The Modify toolbar, shown in Figure 15-6, gives you a quick way to group, arrange, align, and rotate objects. This toolbar is open by default and is located just below the Property inspector.

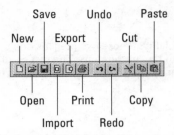

Figure 15-6: The Modify toolbar

Tools panel

All Fireworks drawing and editing tools can be accessed from the Tools panel. Figure 15-7 shows the many tools available.

New Feature The Bitmap and Vector tools are grouped together; this is new to Fireworks MX. There is also a section for the tools that can be used with bitmaps and vectors.

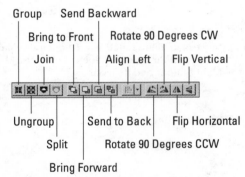

Figure 15-7: The Tools panel

New Feature You can now access fill and stroke option menus by clicking the color boxes in the Tools panel. These options can also be accessed in the Property inspector. The way you access these properties depends on the object you selected.

The Property Inspector

The Property inspector in Fireworks is very much like the one in Dreamweaver. (See Figure 15-8.) The Property inspector is below the document window. You can click the expander arrow to open and close it. The Property inspector is context-sensitive, meaning that its contents change based on which object you select in the Document window. Select any tool and look in the Property inspector. Click another tool and notice the change.

New Feature The Property inspector is a new addition to Fireworks MX. It replaces the Effects, Objects, Tool Options, Stroke, Fill, and the Color Table panels.

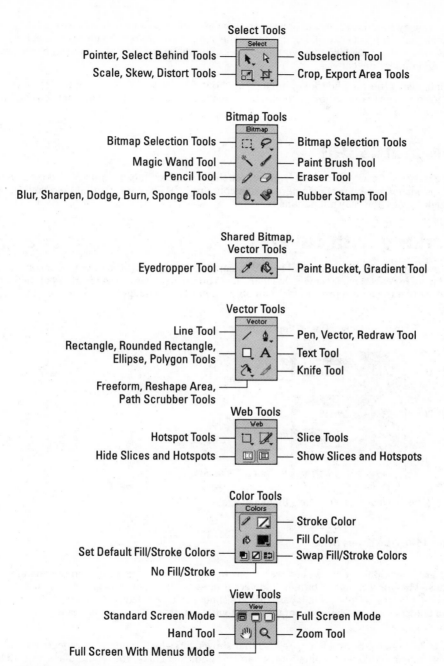

Select Tools

Pointer, Select Behind Tools ——— Subselection Tool
Scale, Skew, Distort Tools ——— Crop, Export Area Tools

Bitmap Tools

Bitmap Selection Tools ——— Bitmap Selection Tools
Magic Wand Tool ——— Paint Brush Tool
Pencil Tool ——— Eraser Tool
Blur, Sharpen, Dodge, Burn, Sponge Tools ——— Rubber Stamp Tool

Shared Bitmap, Vector Tools

Eyedropper Tool ——— Paint Bucket, Gradient Tool

Vector Tools

Line Tool ——— Pen, Vector, Redraw Tool
Rectangle, Rounded Rectangle, Ellipse, Polygon Tools ——— Text Tool
——— Knife Tool
Freeform, Reshape Area, Path Scrubber Tools

Web Tools

Hotspot Tools ——— Slice Tools
Hide Slices and Hotspots ——— Show Slices and Hotspots

Color Tools

——— Stroke Color
——— Fill Color
Set Default Fill/Stroke Colors ——— Swap Fill/Stroke Colors
No Fill/Stroke

View Tools

Standard Screen Mode ——— Full Screen Mode
Hand Tool ——— Zoom Tool
Full Screen With Menus Mode

Figure 15-8: The Property inspector

The Property inspector lets you change settings by adding a value in text boxes (such as the size of a font) or by using a slider. If you use the slider, you can see the changes onscreen right away. If you type in values, you must press Enter (Return for a Mac) to accept the settings and update the canvas.

You'll be using the specific tool options throughout the Fireworks section of this book. You will discover the many options and functions available via the Property inspector as you use the various tools.

The Status Bar

At the bottom of every document, you will see the Status bar. Information about the document size and magnification is shown here. It also contains VCR-like controls that help you navigate through frames and play animations.

Working with Layers

A layer is a powerful organizational tool. You can arrange objects (bitmap or vector) on separate layers for easier management. In Figure 15-9 you can see many of the features of the Layers panel. Notice the icon representations of objects, paths, and images.

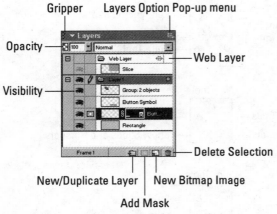

Figure 15-9: The Layers panel

Most graphic applications use layers, but Fireworks works with them in a unique manner. Because Fireworks contains bitmap and vector objects, each object is given its own list layer. Object list layers are placed in layers that are similar to Layer Sets in Photoshop. It's easy to move objects from one layer to another and to add, name, and arrange as many layers as desired.

Notice the Frame 1 button in Figure 15-9 that shows you which frame your objects are on. If you are making rollovers, animations, or storing additional files, you would place objects in different frames. It's a great way to keep track of what is on which frame.

The Frames panel and the use of frames are discussed in Chapter 22.

The Web layer

The Web layer is a special layer in Fireworks and remains at the top of the layers list. You cannot delete, move, or rename it, and there's only one. It has a very unique function — this layer stores *only* information about slices and hotspots.

Slices and hotspots are Web objects. The primary function of a slice is to name, optimize, and define separate graphics from an entire document. A slice may also contain references to a JavaScripted behavior.

Fireworks, by default, names slices using a seemingly cryptic naming scheme. You can customize the automatic naming by editing the HTML Settings (File⇨HTML Settings). Better yet, give your slices specific names. You can double-click the slice for any slice or hotspot right in the Web layer and name it there or select it and use the Property inspector. The name will be used on export. Keep in mind that Web files can't contain spaces or special characters in their names. Fireworks supplies the file extension based on your optimization choices.

In Chapter 23 you see how to hide specific slices and why it's a great time-saver to do so.

Adding layers

A new layer is an empty layer with no content. Layers are added above the layer that is currently selected. There are several ways to add new layers, choose one of the following methods:

✦ Click the New/Duplicate Layer icon; it is a yellow folder located at the bottom of the Layers panel.

✦ Click Insert ⇨ Layer.

✦ Click the Layers Options menu and choose New Layer.

Duplicate layers

A duplicate layer contains the same content as the selected layer you duplicated. To duplicate a layer, select a layer, click the Layers Options menu, and select Duplicate layer. When the Duplicate Layer dialog box opens choose where you'd like the layer to be inserted. (See Figure 15-10.) You can also change the number of duplicate layers you want to add.

Figure 15-10: The Duplicate Layer dialog box

Delete a layer

You can delete a layer by using one of these methods:

✦ Select the layer you want to delete and press the Delete key on the keyboard.

✦ Click and drag the layer on top of the trashcan icon.

✦ Select the layer (to select multiple layers or objects press Shift and click) and click the trashcan icon.

Opacity settings in layers

In Figure 15-8, near the top-left corner is an icon with gray and white checks and the number 100 grayed out. This is the opacity setting. You can adjust the opacity for each individual layer and for each individual object on a layer. To change the opacity, select the layer (or object), and type in the opacity number you want or use the slider to adjust the opacity amount.

 New Feature The Opacity can also be set in the Property inspector.

Showing/hiding layers

To show or hide whole layers (or objects) click the eye icon of any layer or object. If the eye is on, the layer or object is visible in your document. If you click it again it toggles off the visibility.

Lock layers

To lock a layer, click the box to the left of the layer's name. The picture of a lock icon indicates the layer is locked. After a layer is locked, you can't alter anything in that layer. You can't even select it. To lock or unlock all the layers, open the Layers Option menu and choose the appropriate action.

Name a layer

To name a layer or an object, double-click the layer or object name and rename it in the dialog box that opens. If you use the Layers Options menu to add a new layer, a dialog box opens where you name the layer at the time of insertion.

Single layer editing

Single layer editing enables you to work on only one layer without affecting other layers. To use Single Layer Editing mode, open the Layers Options menu, and select Single Layer Editing. After that action, you can select or edit objects on only the current layer.

Share a selected layer

When you develop an animation you will frequently want some of the same images in every frame. The Share a Selected Layer option can be a real time-saver. If you have repeating elements on a layer that you want on all layers, all you have to do is to select the layer, open the Layers Options menu, and choose Share this Layer.

Setting Preferences

Fireworks offers many preferences you can set and/or change in. Figure 15-11 shows the Preferences dialog box. Open the Preference dialog box by clicking Edit ➪ Preferences. Table 15-1 lists the different preference categories and options. From opening documents to adding effects and filters, it pays to set up your preferences!

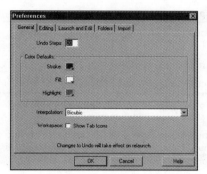

Figure 15-11: The Preferences dialog box

Table 15-1: Preferences

Category	Preference Options
General	Undo Steps (Enter the number of undos you want)
	Color Defaults (Fill, Stroke, Highlight color options)
	Interpolation (The scaling of pixels method)
	Workspace - Show Tab Icons (Turned off by default, when checked icons will be displayed on the panel tabs.)
Editing	Precise Cursors (Check if you want Precise Cursors.)
	Delete Objects When Cropping (If selected, cropped objects get deleted.)
	Turn Off Hide Edges (When unchecked the marquee is not visible.)
	Display Striped border (Check this if you want the visual clue of a border for a bitmap image.)
	Show Pen Preview (Shows a preview of the next path segment.)
	Show Solid Points (When checked, the point of a selected object is hollow and an unselected objects points are solid.)
	Pointer Tool Options
	Pick Distance (How close the pointer is to an object to select it)
	Snap Distance (Determines how close an object needs to be in order to snap to a grid)

Continued

Table 15-1: *(continued)*

Category	Preference Options
Launch and Edit	When Editing from External Application (When external Macromedia applications can't locate the source PNG file it will use the preferences you set here to determine how to handle locating the PNG file.)
	When Optimizing from External Application
Folder	Photoshop Plug-ins (Browser to locate the folder you keep your Photoshop compatible plug-ins in)
	Textures (Choose a folder with texture images.)
	Patterns (Choose a folder with pattern images.)
Import	Photoshop File Conversion (Choose whether to convert layers as objects or new frames and whether you want to share layers between frames.)
	You have the option of maintaining text appearance which changes the text to a bitmap (uneditable) image. Or you can choose to keep the text editable. It looses any effects applied that are not compatible with Fireworks.
	You can choose to flatten all the layers and import as a single object bitmap image.

Keyboard Shortcuts

Five sets of keyboard shortcuts are available. The Macromedia Standard is on by default. You can customize Fireworks with your own shortcuts. A custom shortcut is added to (or changed in) one of the existing sets. When defining new shortcuts you can't use any modifier keys, such as Control, Shift, Alt, Command, or Option.

Follow these steps to customize your keyboard shortcuts:

1. Choose the set of shortcuts you want to customize.

2. Click the Duplicate Set icon and name your new set.

3. Name the new set.

4. Select an item to change. Type in a new key combination in the Press Key field. For PC users, the key combination must contain the Control key; for Macintosh users, it must contain the Command key. Many combinations are taken but you can override an existing shortcut.

5. Click Change.

Note   If you enter a keyboard shortcut that is already in use, a warning box lets you know.

Customizing your keyboard shortcuts to accommodate the way you work can be a fantastic timesaver.

Summary

In this chapter you explored the Fireworks workspace. You learned how to use the new panel groups as well as the new Property inspector. We also discussed how to make your own custom keyboard shortcuts so you can make Fireworks work the way you want it to.

✦　　✦　　✦

Applying Color

Fireworks MX is built specifically to output images to view on a monitor screen. Since Fireworks is a Web graphics program, you will not find print-related topics (color separation, halftone, and so on) because they aren't used on the Web. For print applications, use FreeHand 10 from the Macromedia Studio MX package.

But with Web graphics, there are still variables involved that affect the way your images are viewed by others. The viewer's monitor, video card, and settings determine how many colors can be viewed. In the not very distant past, the average monitor displayed 256, or *indexed* color. Statistics now show that most monitors can view thousands, if not millions, of colors.

Windows and Macintosh have different Gamma settings, used to adjust white point settings and to keep midtones from appearing too dark. The Windows system uses a white point setting of 2.2, which is also standard for television. Macintosh systems default to a setting of 1.8. Images appear lighter on Mac systems and darker and more saturated on PCs.

Tip Choose View ➪ Macintosh Gamma or View ➪ Windows Gamma to see how your images will appear on a computer with the other operating system.

Operating systems and browsers can also affect the quality of your images.

Tip AOL browsers are notorious for recompressing your images. I checked the AOL Web site and as of July 21, 2002, they have a statement that says they are caching system send images through a compression manager. AOL users can disable this caching compression but it's on by default. What this means is that AOL recompresses your carefully compressed images. Often times this results in very bad-looking images.

Choosing Color in Fireworks MX

To choose a color, click a color box in the Property inspector or Tools panel. There are many color boxes in Fireworks. A color box is available for any feature that has a color choice (such as canvas color) and for characteristics such as fills and strokes. A color pop-up window opens (Figure 16-1). Move the cursor to a color and click. The color window uses a preset swatch group called Color Cubes by default. You may change, add, and delete colors from the color window.

Tip   PC users can sample a color anywhere in the Fireworks environment by simply passing the Eyedropper cursor over a color and clicking. PC users can however sample a color from anywhere including the desktop by clicking and dragging the cursor and releasing the mouse to sample a color. Mac users can sample a color anywhere including the Windows desktop by simply passing the eyedropper cursor over the desired color and clicking.

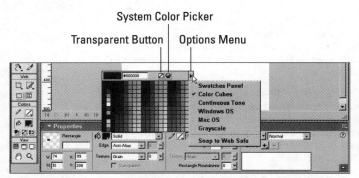

Figure 16-1: Clicking a color box opens a color pop-up window. There are additional options available in the Options menu.

To use custom colors, click the System Color Picker icon (see Figure 16-1). The Color dialog box in Figure 16-2 opens. You may enter RGB (red, green, blue) or HSL (Hue, Saturation, Lightness) values, add a color to the palette, or select a color from the color field. Notice that if you click a color, the sliding bar shows variations of the color you selected. This is a great way to choose a lighter or darker version of a color.

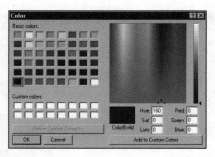

Figure 16-2: The Color dialog box that opens when you click the System Color Picker icon

Note   System Pickers vary for the Macintosh platform but the methods are similar.

Click the Color palette's Options menu to access the following options:

✦ **Swatches panel** — The panel you have set up or customized in the Swatches panel (Window ➪ Swatches).

✦ **Color Cube** — The default swatches, which are Web-safe.

✦ **Continuous Tone** — The color swatches are arranged by tone.

✦ **Windows OS** — The color swatches for the Windows OS.

✦ **Mac OS** — The color swatches for the Mac OS.

✦ **Grayscale** — The 256 Grayscale swatches.

✦ **Snap to Web safe** — If this option is selected, any color you sample is snapped to the nearest Web-safe color.

Caution

If you use the Eyedropper to sample a color from an object but you notice the color shifts, and you want to use the actual non-Web-safe color, be sure that Snap to Web safe is unchecked.

Cross-Reference

Chapter 23 shows how to optimize image colors precisely and export the color palette as a custom swatch set.

Customizing the Swatches panel

The color cube display you see in the color pop-up window is the default found in the Swatches panel (Window ➪ Swatches). It uses 216 Web-safe colors defined in Hexadecimal notation. You can add to the Swatches panel by mixing your own custom colors in the Color Mixer (Window ➪ Color Mixer) or by using the Eyedropper tool to sample a color.

Loading saved color palettes

If you have a custom color palette you would like to add, be sure it is a GIF file or an ACT file. ACO files can be loaded as well (refer to the following Tip). To load a saved palette, follow these steps:

1. In the Swatches panel, open the Swatches Options menu, and choose Add Swatches.

2. Select the appropriate file (a saved ACT or GIF file), and click OK.

Adding swatches extends the existing palette. If you want to use only a saved palette, you need to choose Replace Swatches; when you choose Add Swatches, the swatches are added to the bottom of the current panel.

Tip

You can force Fireworks to use Photoshop ACO files, too. Use the Swatches panel options to choose, Add, or Replace Swatches. In the dialog box, locate the folder where you know a Photoshop ACO file resides. In the File box, type "***.aco**" and press Enter or Return. You should see your ACO files. Choose the file you want, and click Open. Be aware that the palette may not be organized and displayed the same as it is in Photoshop.

Understanding Web Color

It's important to understand that monitors represent color as RGB — Red, Green, and Blue. The hexadecimal system is the standard way to specify RGB color for use in HTML documents. Hexadecimal values use base-16 mathematics, not the standard base-10 counting system. The 16 values used are 0, 1, 2, 3, 4, 5, 6, 7, 8, 9, A, B, C, D, E, F. A color is defined using three sets of two-digit numbers. You won't have to know how to convert RGB into hexadecimal unless you want to; however, you should understand the difference in the numbers when you see them. You'll begin to see how the hexadecimal coding system works as you learn more about using Web-safe colors.

Export the current export palette

Fireworks MX makes it easy to save a palette of the colors in the file you have open, which is a valuable tool when multiple designers are working on the same site design. By using a custom palette of colors, everyone involved can use the approved colors.

To export a palette, follow these steps:

1. Open any file.

2. Be sure the Export File Format is set to GIF in the Optimize panel. If you don't see the colors, click the Rebuild button.

   The Optimize panel is covered in Chapter 23.

3. Open the Swatches panel if it isn't already; open the Swatches Options menu, and select Current Export Palette. You'll see the current colors in the Swatches panel.

4. Click the Swatches Options menu, and select Save Swatches. Save anywhere you'd like. Fireworks saves in the ACT (Active Color Table) format.

Cross-Reference

Note If the option Current Export Palette is grayed out and you have an Export File format of GIF or Animated GIF, WBMP, PNG 8, TIFF8, BMP8, click the Rebuild button to show the colors in your image. The Current Export Palette option becomes available.

Web-Safe Colors

When the majority of monitors could display only 256 colors, a Web-safe color palette was generally used when adding color to flat color images, such as backgrounds, text, logos, and vectors you drew as well as buttons. The Web-safe palette of 216 colors displays in the major browsers without dithering and displays the way you designed it. *Dithering* means combining colors to produce alternative colors (not to be confused with the Web dithering option in Fireworks MX, which dithers Web-safe colors). You can recognize Web-safe colors by their hexadecimal numbers, which contain three sets of 00, 33, 66, 99, FF, or CC. To make it easy to use Web-safe colors, Firework's default color picker in every color box uses the Web-safe palette.

When designing a Web site for the masses, you want it to look its best for the widest audience possible. This is where the 216 Web-safe color palette comes into play. These 216 colors don't degrade on a monitor that can display only 256 colors. Many designers today are not as concerned about this problem as they were a few years ago, because more and more people are upgrading to better system monitors with better video cards, supporting millions of colors. However, good monitors are less expensive and more available in the United States than in many other countries that are online, so this reasoning does not necessarily apply to the global audience on the Web. The choice to use Web-safe colors or not is up to you, but keep in mind that a lot of new "consumers" are buying computers mainly to get online. Many of these new users can barely use their mouse, much less check and change their monitor settings.

 Tip

If you want to sample a color and automatically convert it into a Web-safe color, simply hold the Shift key as you sample.

Also, if you click in a color box and decide you don't want to change a color, you can press the Esc key on your keyboard to close the color palette.

Finding non-Web216 colors

You can easily check an entire document or project log (see Chapter 21 for how to use the Project log) for Web-safe colors within Fireworks by using the Find and Replace feature. To begin the search, follow these steps:

1. Open the Find and Replace panel, shown in Figure 16-3, by choosing Edit ➪ Find and Replace (Control+F (Command+F)).

Figure 16-3: The Find and Replace panel

2. Choose Search Files and locate a file you want to check for Web-safe colors.

3. In the Find area, choose Non-Web216.

4. More options appear. In the Apply area, you have the choice of applying the color change to only the Fill, Strokes, or Effects, to all the Fills and Strokes, or to All Properties.

5. Click All Properties.

6. Click the Find button. The document you chose opens and the first area with a non-Web-safe color is highlighted. Click Replace. If you want to, automatically accept all the changes instead of accepting one at a time.

7. Click Replace All.

This tool is quite a time-saver if you have a Web site you are upgrading for someone, or one that you want to convert to Web-safe colors.

Using the Color Mixer

Fireworks offers several color models from which you can choose. The default color model is the Web-safe one: Hexadecimal RGB (Red, Green, Blue) values based on a range of values from 00 to FF. You can change color models by accessing the Color Mixer (Window ➪ Color Mixer), opening the Color Mixer Options menu, and choosing another color model. Table 16-1 shows the available color models.

Table 16-1: Color Models

Color Model	Description
RGB	Includes up to 16.7 million 24-bit colors. Each RGB component has a value from 0 to 255 where 255-255-255 is white.
Hexadecimal	RGB Hexadecimal values, uses a hexadecimal value from 00 to FF, where 00-00-00 is black and FF-FF-FF is white.
CMY	Print designers may be more comfortable using a CMY (Cyan, Magenta, Yellow) model. It's not the same as CMYK but similar, it doesn't have the additional black component.
HSB	Hue, saturation, and brightness. Hue has a range of degrees of 0-360. Saturation uses a percentage of 0-100 percent where 100 percent is pure white. Brightness has a range of 0-100 with 0 being black.
Grayscale	256 tones from absolute white to absolute black.

Working with Strokes

Strokes are easy to add to vector objects. If you used a previous version of Fireworks, you would have accessed the various stroke options in the Stroke panel. That panel has been removed. You can now access the functions by using the Property inspector or the Tools panel. Figure 16-4 shows the Stroke area in the Property inspector.

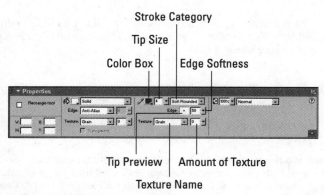

Figure 16-4: The Stroke panel

You can add a stroke to any vector object you've drawn or to any path. You can see the change right in your document. The stroke setting that is current in the Property inspector is used on the object or path you have selected or are drawing. If you change the properties, you can see the change on the screen. In Fireworks, if you type in a property, you need to press the Enter/Return key or click in a blank area to activate the change. But if you use a slider control to change a property, the change is automatic.

Take a look at the various stroke categories. Go to the Property inspector and click the down arrow for the Stroke Category to access the various stroke categories (Figure 16-5). As you pass your cursor over each stroke name, additional options for each stroke type are displayed.

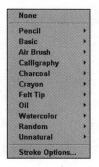

Figure 16-5: The Stroke categories

You add strokes from the Property inspector. The various options are visible only when you select an object (not a bitmap image), or when you select one of the Vector tools. To add a stroke, follow these steps:

1. Open a new document (File ➪ New).

2. Select the Rectangle tool and draw a rectangle on your canvas, any size and any color.

3. Select a stroke from the Stroke Category, or select None if you want no stroke at all. Choose Basic, Hard Line.

If you want to remove a stroke, click the color box next to the pencil icon and click the white square with the diagonal red line. Alternatively, you can choose no stroke from the Tools panel. Just below the Fill icon you will see the middle icon is the white square with red diagonal line.

Each stroke in the Stroke category has variations available in the Stroke name area.

4. To adjust the Edge Softness, use the slider control. 0 is a hard edge and 100 is a soft edge

5. Click the color box to select the color you want to use.

6. Adjust the Tip size using the slider or type in a number. Remember, if you type in a number, you must press the Enter/Return key to accept the change.

There are many other properties you can alter for a stroke. Accessing all the properties for strokes is an exercise in drilling down through all the various menus.

Stroke options

You can access the stroke options using one of these methods:

✦ Click the Stroke Options category in the Stroke Category pop-up window.

✦ Click the Stroke Options button, which is visible when you click the stroke color box in the Tools panel.

Figure 16-6 shows the pop-up window for the stroke options. You can change the category here, as well as the tip size. You can also add texture. The Centered on Path (default) option offers the additional choice of having the stroke on the inside or the outside of a path. The last option is the Fill over stroke, which draws the fill over the stroke. If your object has an opaque fill, the part of the stroke that is inside the path is blocked. If the object has a fill with any transparency the stroke may blend with the fill edges inside the path.

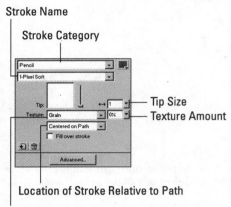

Figure 16-6: The Stroke Options pop-up window

There is also a button labeled Advanced Options. Figure 16-8 shows the Edit Stroke dialog box. Clicking Stroke Options and then on the Advanced button opens the Advanced pop-up menu, which gives you access to three tabs: Options, Shape, and Sensitivity. The best way to discover the power of the advanced settings is to experiment.

Options category

Figure 16-7 shows the Edit Stroke Options dialog box, where you set the ink amount, the spacing, the flow rate, and the texture options. If you change the number of tips you want to paint with to more than one, the variations and spacing options become available. The preview of the changes you've made appear at the bottom of the dialog box.

Shape category

Figure 16-8 shows the contents of the Shape tab. You have a lot of control here by altering the Size, Edge, Aspect, and Angle. When you get the shape just right, click Apply to your current stroke, and then click OK.

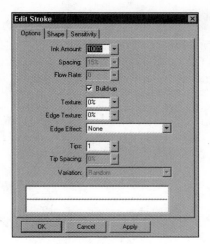

Figure 16-7: The Edit Stroke Options category

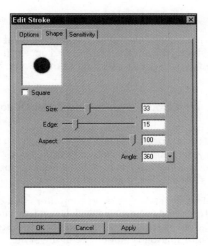

Figure 16-8: The Shape category options

Sensitivity category

Figure 16-9 shows the Sensitivity category, where you can choose a stroke property such as Size, Ink Amount, or Saturation from the drop-down menu of properties to be affected. In the Affected By options, choose the degree to which sensitivity data affects your current stroke. Preview in the panel window; click Apply, and then click OK when you are satisfied.

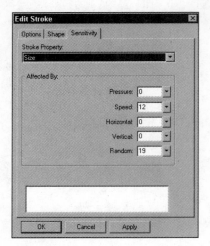

Figure 16-9: The Sensitivity category options

Saving strokes as styles

After you start experimenting with strokes, you'll probably come up with some you want to save and reuse. You can save a stroke as a style, which you can then add to and access from the Styles panel. You learn how to add to and change the Styles panel later in this chapter.

To save a stroke as a style, follow these steps:

1. Open the Styles panel (docked in the Asset panel group), and from the Styles Options menu, choose New Style.

2. Check the features you want to save for the style. For instance, when working with text you may not want to save the font style, so you would uncheck that option. If you check font, when you apply the style, it uses the font information. If the Font option is not checked, only the stroke, fill, and effects are applied to any text or object.

When you choose to save the font information, the style works on computers that don't have the font installed. This applies for textures and patterns as well. If you use a custom texture or pattern in a style and you want to share your style, you don't have to send a separate texture or pattern file. The information is embedded in the style.

3. Enter a name and click OK.

That's all there is to it. The new style is added to the bottom of your Styles panel for use on any object.

Adding Fills

The Fill area in the Property inspector (or Tools panel) works very much like the Stroke area. You select the type of fill you want, the color, the type of edge, and a texture if you want one. Figure 16-10 shows the Fill area of the Property inspector.

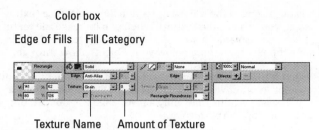

Figure 16-10: The fill area of the Property inspector

You can add fills in a several ways. You can choose to use any of these methods or a combination of methods:

✦ Fills are added automatically to a closed path.

✦ You can add fills via the Fill box in the Tools panel.

✦ You can add fills via the Fill box in the Property inspector.

✦ You can add a fill by using the Paint Bucket tool.

✦ You can add a gradient fill by using the Gradient tool (in the Paint Bucket tool fly-out).

Note

Everything in the Property inspector is context sensitive. You need to have a vector object or a vector tool selected in order for the fill options to be visible. For a bitmap image, the Paint Bucket tool or a bitmap selection needs to be made to see the fill options.

To fill an object, text, or path, follow these simple steps:

1. Open a new document (File ➪ New) that is 800 × 500 with a white canvas.

2. Select the Rectangle tool and draw a rectangle that is 100 pixels high and 800 pixels wide.

   Tip

   You can draw a rectangle any size, enter the desired height and width into the Property inspector, and press the Enter/Return key to activate the change.

3. Access the Fill Category Options menu (in the Property inspector or Tools panel) and select Solid.

4. Click the color box to change the color. The example uses #999933 from the custom swatches.

5. In the Edge area, click the drop-down arrow and make a selection. Anti-Alias, which helps smooth the edges, is the default. A Hard edge gives a sharp edge, but will be jagged on any curves; the Feather option can soften the edges a great deal depending on the amount of feather you use. When the Feather option is selected the Amount of Feather option becomes available.

6. If you want a texture, click the arrow to access the Textures pop-up menu, and choose a texture from the list. For this example, click Line-Horiz 4 and move the Amount of Texture slider to 25%.

7. Save your file. I saved a copy for you as well. To find all the Habitat Alert source files navigate to the habitat_alert_start folder on the CD-ROM.

Notice the *Other* option, which is discussed in the following section. If you select a texture, you have to increase the opacity so you can see the texture. When you increase the texture amount, a Transparent option becomes available. If you click Transparent to select it, the objects or image below (assuming there is something below your object) show through.

Note

A word on transparency: This is not a true transparency; it will appear transparent only over the object you are using in Fireworks. In other words, you can't export the object alone and expect it to be transparent in the browser. At this time, only a PNG32 file will do this, but unfortunately all the browsers do not support this format.

None

Using no fill at all is an option. There are two different ways to use no fill. The Tools panel contains a white square with a red slash mark. The ToolTip calls it *No Stroke or Fill*. Click it to remove the fill from a selected object. You can also click the fill color box in the Tools panel or Property inspector and click the white box with a red slash, which appears near the top-right of the Color pop-up window. The ToolTip for this one calls it *Transparent Button*.

Solid

The fill category of Solid fills your object with a solid color. The default is a 100% fill, but you can alter the percentage in the Property inspector by changing the Opacity (to the left of the Blend Mode).

Web dithering

Web dithering expands your Web-safe color palette greatly. Dithering was originally used when only the GIF format was available, and photographs with millions of colors were being used for the Web and being viewed with monitors using 256 colors. The process of dithering involves taking two or more pixels of different colors and positioning them to produce a pattern. This pattern tricks the eye into seeing a different color. This technique works well with GIFs, but with photographs you lose a lot of detail when many colors blend. The best path to take is to use the JPEG format for photographs and the GIF format for vectors and images containing few colors.

This technique of combining two colors or more into a new one is called dithering, producing a hybrid-safe color. In Fireworks it is called Web Dither. Web Dither contains two Web-safe colors in an alternating 2 pixel × 2 pixel pattern producing a third color. With this technique, you have 46,656 Web-safe "designer" colors. Don't worry. Fireworks provides you with a simple-to-use interface. To use the Web Dithering feature follow these steps:

1. In the Property inspector, open the Fill Category menu and choose Web Dither. Click the color box to see the Web Dither menu shown in Figure 16-11.

Figure 16-11: The Web Dither pop-up menu

2. For more options, click the color box from the Fill area in the Tools panel, and then click the Fill Options button. Figure 16-12 shows the Fill Options window. Notice that edge options are now available. These are already available in the Property inspector, so an extra click isn't needed to access the edge options.

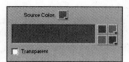

Figure 16-12: The Fill options pop-up that opens when the Fill Options button is clicked

3. The first color well on the top is the current fill color. Click the color well to choose a non-Web-safe color or type a Hexadecimal number, or select a color with the Eyedropper.

The color you see in the large color area is the color that will be applied to your object. Fireworks automatically selects the best Web-safe colors to mix to obtain the closest color to the one you choose. You can, however, click in either color box on the right and choose a different color.

You can see the two different colors side by side that Fireworks has chosen to pattern (the first two colors below the original color well), and then the reverse of these colors just below it. To see the Hexadecimal numbers, simply move your mouse over the color and the number will appear. Sometimes it's fickle, so simply move your mouse over again until you see the number. This is the pattern being used to produce the best match possible, which can be seen in the large color area. If the area you want to fill is selected, it automatically fills with the new color.

You don't have to use the color that Fireworks has chosen to blend with; you can choose your own colors to mix if you are feeling adventurous. Fireworks does a great job of automatically finding the best possible match to the color you want to be Web safe. If you move your mouse over the fill color from the Info palette, you see two different RGB settings — one for each Web-safe color used to achieve a new Web-safe color.

Using patterns and textures as a fill

You can use patterns and/or textures to fill with. Most images can be used as a pattern or a texture. As long as an image is a 32-bit image in a BMP, PNG, GIF, JPEG, TIFF, or PICT (for the Macintosh) file format, you can have an instant pattern. You are limited only to what you can hold on your hard drive or on CD-ROMs. You see later in this section how to utilize this almost limitless resource.

Filling with patterns

The use of a pattern in a path object increases the range of options you have as a designer, making flat, uninteresting objects come alive. Although many preset Patterns are available in Fireworks, the Other option in the Fill Options menu opens the door to limitless patterns. To use a pattern follow these steps:

1. Select the object you want to fill.

2. In the Property inspector, from the Fill Category, choose Pattern.

3. Click in the Fill color box, and access the Pattern Name list.

4. Choose any pattern you want. If you want to use a pattern from an image on your hard drive or CD-ROM, scroll to the bottom of the list and select, Other.

5. If you choose Other, browse to an image file, select it, and click Open.

Note

If you want a pattern to be permanently added to the Pattern Name drop-down list, simply place the image file in the Fireworks MX\Configurations\Patterns folder. The path name may vary depending on the OS you are using, so look around for the Patterns folder.

Editing patterns

After you apply a pattern (or gradient), you can move, rotate, skew, and change the width of a pattern. When an object that has a pattern (or gradient) fill is selected you see handles. As you pass your cursor over a handle, you see the rotation icon (Figure 16-13). You can click and drag to rotate. Or you can click the circle in the center and drag to a new location. By clicking and dragging on the solid point, you can adjust the handles.

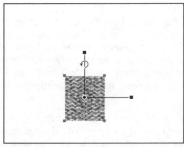

Figure 16-13: A pattern-filled object, which is selected revealing the adjustment bars

Adding textures

Textures can be added to any fill, modifying the brightness of the fill but not the hue. You can use any PNG, GIF, JPEG, BMP, TIF, or PICT file as a texture. When an image is used as a texture fill, its grayscale value is used. To add texture, follow these steps:

1. Select any object containing any fill, gradient, or pattern.

2. In the Property inspector, click the down arrow for the Texture Name to access the Texture Name list. Choose one of the included texture files or click Other to select a file of your own. The texture shows in the Texture list only for this document, it's not a permanent addition.

Note

If you want a texture to be permanently added to the Texture Name list, simply place the image file in the Fireworks MX\Settings\Textures folder.

3. Adjust the percentage of opacity, which determines the amount of the texture that is applied.

Cross-Reference

In Chapter 15 refer to Edit Preferences — save an additional texture file, and tell Fireworks where to find it.

Using gradient fills

A gradient is a blend of two or more colors. Gradients are often used to produce lighting effects, to give the illusion of depth, and to provide an interesting blend of colors. They are also used as terrific backgrounds and as a fill for transparency masks when working with bitmaps (see Chapter 19). In this section, you learn how to use gradient fills and how to edit them to suit your needs.

Tip

Gradients are best used in images that you plan to export as JPEG files. Many colors are needed to make a nice smooth transition of colors. Gradients often appear banded (noticeable lines) in a GIF image.

Fireworks MX ships with 11 types of gradients and 13 preset gradient color patterns. But, the number of alterations and variations is almost endless. The best way to describe the 11 types of gradients is to show you a small sample of each. Figure 16-14 shows a representation of each. From left to right, they are Linear, Radial, Ellipse, Rectangle, Cone, Starburst, Bars, Ripples, Waves, Satin, and Folds.

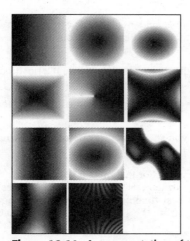

Figure 16-14: A representation of the gradient options

After you choose the type of gradient you want, you can change the preset colors, add additional colors, and even add transparency. Click in the Fill color box to access the Edit Gradient dialog box (Figure 16-15).

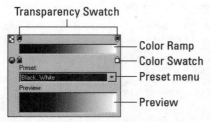

Figure 16-15: Edit Gradient window

To fill using a preset gradient follow these steps:

1. Select an object you want to apply a gradient to.

2. From the Fill category in the Property inspector, choose one of the gradient options.

3. Choose the color combination you like from the Preset gradient color sets, or use the gradient that is the default.

Note

The default gradient fill color is a combination of the current color of your stroke and the color of the Fill tool.

If your object is selected, it is automatically filled with the gradient. Test each of the presets and all the different gradient types to get an idea of how each one looks and performs.

Tip

If you are using a gradient fill in a GIF image, you may see banding. To help minimize this effect, add a small blur to the fill.

Altering gradients

This is where the real power of the Gradient tool becomes evident. Adjusting the pattern's center, width, and skew can customize gradients. To alter a gradient's position, follow these steps:

1. Follow the preceding steps for filling with a gradient. To alter the gradient's position, click the object to make it active; the gradient handles appear.

2. To change the position of the gradient, drag the circular handle to adjust the gradient's starting point.

3. Move the cursor over the control handles until you see the rotate cursor. You can now drag the handles to a new location

Tip

It is sometimes difficult to adjust a gradient, which is small. For instance, if you want a vertical gradient, the gradient handles need to be perfectly straight. Holding the Shift key doesn't help. What does do the trick is to adjust the handles larger than needed, then shorten them. Another way to fill vertically is to use the Gradient tool from the Tools panel, and click and drag while pressing the Shift key, to apply the fill.

Editing gradient colors

Existing colors in a gradient preset can be changed, deleted, moved around, or new colors can be added with ease by following these steps:

1. Draw a rectangle and fill it with a gradient style you prefer.

2. Click the Fill color box to access the Gradient Edit window.

Note

If you access the gradient fill by clicking the Fill color box in the Tools panel, you need to click the Edit button to access the Gradient Edit window.

3. To change any of the colors, click the color swatch and choose another color.

4. To add another color, place your cursor anywhere below the color ramp where you want another color added. A plus (+) sign appears next to your cursor; click and choose a new color.

5. To move the position of any of the colors, click and drag the color swatch to the new location.

6. To delete a color, click and drag the swatch toward the bottom of the panel.

You have plenty of control when it comes to gradient colors. You can sample colors from other images with the Eyedropper tool — just as you can when selecting solid fills — to produce some interesting color combinations. You make a custom gradient using the colors you find in an image.

Adding Transparency

New Feature

The ability to add transparency to your gradients is new to Fireworks MX.

To add transparency to a gradient, follow these steps:

1. Fill an object with a gradient of any color and style.

2. Click the Fill color box in the Property inspector.

3. Click one of the transparency swatches (Figure 16-15) and move the slider to the opacity you want. You can adjust both the swatches as well as add additional ones in the same way you added color swatches.

Saving gradient colors

After you have meticulously produced a new gradient, you may want to use it again later. Unfortunately, your custom gradient is good for only your current document.

You can save the gradient type and colors as a style. Any repositioning you may have done won't be saved. To save as a style, follow these steps:

1. Open the Styles panel (Assets Panel group or Windows ➪ Styles).

2. From the Styles option menu, choose New Style. The New Style dialog box opens; name the gradient, choose which properties to save as a style, and click OK. Your new gradient style is added to the bottom of your Styles panel.

Note

If you save properties such as text, anytime this style is applied it changes the font, font size, or text style depending on which options you choose. If you want only the effects to be applied to any other object or text, leave the text options unchecked.

Using the Styles Panel

Macromedia Fireworks ships with a number of styles. Styles are presets that you can apply to an object with the click of a button. You can edit preset styles, or you can make your own styles. The Style Panel is shown in Figure 16-16.

To apply a style to an object, follow these steps:

1. Select the object to receive the style.

2. Open the Styles panel (Window ➪ Styles).

3. Scroll the list of styles and click one.

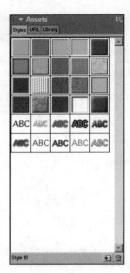

Figure 16-16: The Styles panel

Modifying styles

After you apply a style you, might want to change it. If you open a previously saved object with a style applied, you can change it. To modify or edit a style, follow these steps:

1. Select the object with a style applied.

In the Property inspector you can see whether the object has any effects. (Many styles contain effects.) Any Live Effects applied show up in the Effects list. If so, click the Edit and Arrange Effects icon, and alter the settings to your liking. If you want to see what the object would look like without a particular effect, you can turn off the view by clicking the eye icon next to the effect. Only the view is turned off, the effect is still there. To turn it back on, just click the eye area again. If you want to delete an effect, click it and then click on the minus sign.

2. Any fills applied are shown in the Property inspector. Click in the Fill color box to edit the fill.

3. Any strokes settings are also shown in the Property inspector. Edit them just as you would edit any other stroke.

Saving styles

If you have an object to which you have applied a custom fill and special effects that you want to keep and reuse again on another object, you can save it as a style. You can use styles you save as well as those in the Style panel for the pop-up menus that Fireworks can make. See Chapter 20 for more on making instant pop-up menus. To save a style, follow these steps:

1. Select the object you want to save the effects as a style for.

2. Open the Styles Options menu and choose New Style. Name your style.

3. Select the options you want to save as a style. Remember if the style is attached to a font; you don't have to choose Font. If you do choose Font, the same font is applied when you apply the style. If you don't choose Font, the style effects are added to whatever text to which you are adding the style.

The nice part about making a style out of text and saving the font is that the font is embedded and can be used on any machine.

4. Click OK.

Importing and exporting styles

When you make new styles, you can export only one or make several and export them as a set. To import or export styles, follow these steps:

1. Open the Styles panel (Window ➪ Styles).

2. Open the Styles Options menu, and choose either Import Styles or Export Styles.

3. A window opens where you can locate and choose the file to import or choose where to save the export.

There are quite a few additional styles in the Fireworks folder of the Macromedia Studio MX installation disc.

4. Click Open or Save.

Effects versus Filters

If you compare the Filters menu to the Effects panel menus, you will notice that mostoptions are available in both menus. The main difference is that, after you use the filters menu to apply a filter, it is permanent. If you use the Effects menu, it remains editable. Basically, the Filters menu is for bitmap images (pixel-based images) and the Effects menu is for vectors (mathematically rendered) images. But the Effects menu is really much more. Effects are actually Live Effects, which means that you can edit or remove the effect. You can even use most of the Live Effects on a bitmap image. But if you try to use the Filter menu on a vector object, it converts the vector to a bitmap and then applies the filter. Whenever possible, use the Effects menu, which gives you the choice of editing.

You work with the Filters menu in Chapters 19 and 21.

Change an image's color using live effects

Using Effects to change colors sounds unusual, but it's quite powerful and offers a lot of flexibility. The logo for this sample is from www.graphic-design.com. If you have a logo like this on a Web site and decide to change the color of the ampersand or the text itself, it could be a huge pain to redo, especially if the logo were more ornate than this one. Another roadblock could be that you are doing a redesign, and you don't have access to the original file, and a custom font was used. With the following techniques, it doesn't matter. You'll be able to change the colors, quickly and easily:

1. Open design.jpg from the chapter16_exercise folder on the CD-ROM.

2. Using the Pointer tool, select the bitmap, and click the plus sign in the Property inspector to open the Effects list.

3. Click Adjust Color ➪ Color Fill.

4. Click the Color box and choose a bright blue. In the same window, choose a Blending Mode of Hue. Notice how only the ampersand changes.

5. Click the Edit and Arrange Effect icon (little I with blue circle) to access the Color Fill options, and change the Blending mode to Screen to colorize with variations of the blue you choose.

 Note   All these colorizing samples can be seen in the Color section.

Many circumstances require that you use a grayscale image. You might be given a grayscale image, or you might need to convert a color image into grayscale.

Convert a color image to grayscale

It's pretty easy to convert a color image into grayscale; you just need to know were to find the function. To convert a color image into a grayscale one, follow these steps:

1. Open coloredflowers.jpg from the chapter16_exercise folder (or any image you'd like).

2. Choose Commands ➪ Creative ➪ Convert to Grayscale.

 Note   Notice there is also a command to convert to a Sepia Tone image.

3. You can now export this image as a JPEG image. This image is ready to colorize in the following section.

 Cross-Reference   You learn all about exporting in Chapter 23.

Colorize a grayscale image using Live Effects

You now see how easy it is to obtain the extremely popular effect of one-color images. They are one color with many tones. To colorize an image in this fashion, follow these steps:

1. If you closed the grayscale flowers image, that's okay. You can open the flowers.jpg image from the chapter16_exercise folder.

Tip   When you applied the greyscale (or sepia) effect, Fireworks generated a Hue/Saturation Live Effect. If the file hasn't been closed, you can click on the Edit and Arrange Effects icon (the little I) and make changes also. Or add a second Hue/Saturation effect.

2. Select the image.

3. Click the plus sign in the Effects area of the Property inspector.

4. Click Adjust Color ➪ Hue and Saturation.

5. Move the sliders to get the color you want

6. Experiment with lowering the opacity.

7. Change the Blend Modes and see the interesting effects you can achieve.

Tip

You can also use the Adjust Color ➪ Color Fill to select a specific color and then adjust the opacity to suit.

Scanning into Fireworks

You can use the scanner to scan images and send them to Fireworks. It just needs to be TWAIN-compliant for Windows users or support Photoshop Acquire plug-ins for the Macintosh. This applies to digital camera image transfers as well.

To access a scanned image or digital photos from a camera, you use the Import function of Fireworks. This function opens the image as a new document. If you are on a Macintosh, you need to be sure that the Acquire plug-ins are in the Fireworks folder or change your preferences (Edit ➪ Preferences) to point to the location of the plug-in. To import an image, follow these steps:

1. Follow the scanner manufacturer's instructions, connect it to your computer, and be sure it's plugged in.

2. If you haven't installed the drivers for your scanner, do so now.

3. Click File ➪ Scan ➪ Twain Select, if this is the first time you are using the scanner; otherwise select Twain Acquire. If this is your first time, select your scanner from the list and click OK.

4. Click File ➪ Scan ➪ Twain Accquire. Your scanner software opens. You can now apply your settings and scan.

5. The imported image opens as a new Macromedia Fireworks document.

Removing artifacts from a black-and-white scan

A common thing people run into when they scan a line drawing is a lot of gray noise or trash in their image. It's really simple to correct in Fireworks. I have a scan of a drawing that Ron Rockwell sent me (author of the book *FreeHand 10 f/x & Design* [Paraglyph, 2002] as well as the FreeHand section of this book) that you can use for practice.

1. Open tonyline.tif from the chapter16_exercise folder.

2. Zoom in to the right side of the steak, or anywhere you see a lot of gray particles.

3. Select the image, choose Filters ➪ Adjust Color ➪ Levels.

4. In the Levels dialog box, click the Select Highlight Color Eyedropper tool (on the right).

5. In the document, click a gray spot.

6. Click OK to close the Levels dialog box. Notice the spots disappear!

Tip

You can darken some of the black lines using the Levels dialog box as well. Zoom into the curve of the apron below the elbow that is holding the steak. Notice the lighter spots of color, which are caused by the fact that the drawing was made with a felt pen. Select one of the lighter squares using the Select Shadow Color Eyedropper tool and click OK.

7. Export the image when you are satisfied.

Summary

In this chapter, you learned a lot about using the color functions in Fireworks. You learned not only how to use fills and strokes but how to make customized strokes and effects and save them as styles. You learned how you can use custom swatches, which really become important in a shared work environment. You also learned how to import scanned images into Fireworks and how to remove flecks from a scan. You saw first-hand how powerful Live Effects could be in colorizing an image.

Project Summary

This section takes a look at what you've done in this chapter that you will use in the Habitat Alert Web site. Some of the images might need additional work in another section or they might be ready to use in another application.

Files Prepared for the Habitat Alert Web Site

Images	Where to Now?
ha1.png	This is the beginning of the layout for our Habitat Alert site. You use it again as you add shapes and more images prior to exporting.

✦   ✦   ✦

Drawing Like a Pro

In this chapter you master the vector tools to draw complex and simple shapes, add borders, make rounded corners and triangles. You learn how to edit and customize your shapes.

A great deal of Fireworks power lies in its ability to produce a wide range of vector objects. Or rather, the ability you have using the vector tools to produce practically anything you'd like. The following section gives you more insight into the benefits of using vector objects versus bitmap images.

Using Vector tools can be quite intimidating to many people. This is especially true for the Pen tool and manipulating handles, which alter the shape of an object. If you find yourself getting frustrated while learning the tools, take it in small chunks. To help you master the vector tools, I've included several movie tutorials for you on the CD-ROM so that you can see how to use them in addition to reading about them. You'll get plenty of practice along the way. You will be making quite a few different shapes in this chapter and learning how to edit what you've drawn.

Understanding Paths

Every path has at least two points to yield a line segment. A path can be open (a line) or closed (lines connecting). In Fireworks, an object is also a *path*, a "vector" path. Whereas bitmap images use *pixels*, a series of little squares with color to depict the image, much like a mosaic. Vectors use mathematical calculations. A path starts at X, Y and ends at A, B. Because of the mathematical nature of vectors, they are very flexible. A vector object can be stretched to a larger height and width and still maintain its image integrity. As the object increases or decreases in size, Fireworks recalculates the math necessary to render a great-looking image. It's this quality that makes vector objects so popular for use in animations and Web page graphics. The ability to scale a vector drawing is also beneficial if you design a logo that you want to print. The logo can be scaled down for Web use and scaled up for print.

FreeHand MX

The logo you've made for the Habitat Alert site will be printed from FreeHand where the printing capabilities exceed those of Fireworks. It's one of the benefits of owning Macromedia Studio MX; you utilize the strengths of each application.

In This Chapter

Using vector tools and the Pen tool

Understanding Bezier curves

Editing paths

Vector Tools

To use the vector tools in Fireworks, you simply need to select one. In previous versions of Fireworks, you had to switch between vector and bitmap mode. It's all seamless now. As soon as you choose a vector tool, you are automatically in Vector mode. Figure 17-1 shows the area of the Tools panel that contains the vector tools. Refer to Figure 17-1 for a detailed listing of each of these tools.

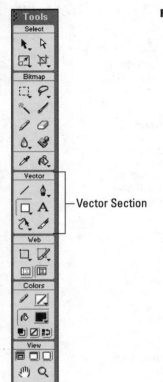

Figure 17-1: The Tools panel showing the Vector tools area

—Vector Section

Note

The Eyedropper tool and the Fill tool can be used in both Bitmap and Vector drawings so they are placed in the Tools panel between the bitmap and vector areas.

The vector tools include Line Tool, Vector drawing tools (Pen, Vector Path, Redraw Path), the shape tools Rectangle tool, Ellipse tool, Rounded Rectangle tool, and Polygon tool. They also include the Text tool, Freeform, Reshape Area, Path Scrubber tools, and the Knife tool.

When a vector object is selected you can add various properties to it including strokes, fills, or effects from the Effects menu.

Using the vector shape tools

The vector shape tools are easy to use. For example, you'll use the Rectangle and other simple shape tools on a regular basis for making buttons.

Every object you draw with a vector shape tool contains a starting point and an ending point to plot the path of a line. With the vector shape tools, those points are automatically placed. You can edit the points for vector shapes at any time, although you may be prompted to ungroup a shape first. Holding down the Shift key while adding the shape constrains it to a perfect square or circle; while holding down Shift, press the Alt (Option) key to start the shape from the center point out.

Rectangle tool

The Rectangle tool is often used to build buttons and shapes. When you select the Rectangle tool, you have many options available in the Property inspector, as shown in Figure 17-2.

Figure 17-2: The options available in the Properties inspector when the Rectangle tool is selected

> **Note**
>
> Select any of the tools in the Tools panel and check the Property inspector for its properties. Many tools need you to set their properties prior to using the tool.

After you draw a rectangle, you have more options available in the Property inspector to alter the width and height, the X, Y coordinates, and the ability to add effects. You may also add fills and strokes.

> **Note**
>
> In Fireworks, rectangles are grouped objects. This becomes important to know when you want to use certain tools that require an ungrouped path.

No stroke is the default if you are starting with a new document, as shown in Figure 17-2. The red line through the circle next to the pencil icon indicates no stroke. But if you've used any tool with a stroke in the same document, the default stroke is the last one you used, except with the Pencil tool.

Drawing a triangle

Like most things in Fireworks, there are many ways to accomplish the same task. One method of drawing a triangle is with the Rectangle tool.

1. Select the Rectangle tool and draw a rectangle in your document. If you want to constrain to a perfect square then press the Shift key as you draw.

2. With the Subselection tool (white arrow), select the rectangle. The warning in Figure 17-3 opens. Click OK. A rectangle has to be ungrouped prior to editing.

3. Click one of the of the lower corner points to select it; then press the Delete key. Figure 17-4 shows the resulting triangle.

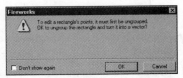

Figure 17-3: The warning that opens when you use the Subselection tool to select the rectangle

Figure 17-4: A point deleted resulting in a triangle

4. You can reposition it by using any of the Transform functions that give you the Rotate option as shown in Figure 17-5. (I selected the Scale icon from the Tools panel.)

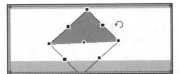

Figure 17-5: The triangle being rotated

Rounded Rectangle tool

The only difference between the Rectangle tool and Rounded Rectangle is the default of the roundness. The default rectangle roundness for the Rectangle tool is 90 degrees, and the Rounded Rectangle always remembers the last roundness setting used.

Ellipse tool

The Ellipse tool has the same options available as the Rectangle tool except for Rectangle Roundness. If you want a perfect circle, press the Shift key as you draw your ellipse.

Polygon tool

In Fireworks, you can draw equilateral polygons ranging from a triangle with three sides to a polygon with 360 sides. The Polygon tool always draws from the center out. If you want to constrain the shape to a 45-degree angle, hold down the Shift key and drag the shape.

The Polygon tool does have a few options that the other shape tools don't have. When you select the Polygon tool the Properties inspector (Figure 17-6) includes Polygon or Star shape options. You can choose the number sides, and the Angle you want, or leave Automatic checked. But, if you draw the polygon first, these options are not available. You must choose the shape, sides, and angle prior to drawing the shape.

Figure 17-6: The options of the Polygon tool prior to drawing the shape

Line tool

The Line tool only draws a straight line with two points. If you want to constrain the line in 45-degree angle increments, hold down the Shift key and drag the shape. You can choose the stroke type, size, color, and texture prior to drawing. All the options in the Property inspector become available after you draw a line or lines. Practice using the Line tool by drawing a zigzag line:

1. Select the Line tool and be sure you have color for the stroke different than the canvas color.

2. Press the Shift key to constrain to 45-degree increments to a line as shown in Figure 17-7.

Figure 17-7: The first line drawn

3. Press the Shift key and draw another line as shown in Figure 17-8. Pull out a guideline to help position and size your lines (View ➪ Rulers). Then drag a guide from the ruler.

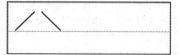

Figure 17-8: The second line drawn

4. Place the lines together to form an upside-down *v*. With the Pointer tool, draw a selection around the two top points (or choose Select ➪ Select All) and choose Modify ➪ Combine Paths ➪ Join (Figure 17-9).

5. To continue with the zigzag line, choose Edit ➪ Clone (or Alt [Option] and drag a copy) and use the arrow keys to move into position. Repeat until the line is the size you want.

6. When your line is as long as you'd like, choose Select ➪ Select All; then choose Modify ➪ Combine Paths ➪ Join to make it one object as shown in Figure 17-10.

Figure 17-9: The lines joined together

Figure 17-10: The completed zigzag line

Tip

Another easy way to make a zigzag line is to use the Text tool. Choose an M in a font with pointed peaks, such as Lithograph. Adjust the Kerning and you'll have a line. Since it's the Text tool, you can also attach this to a path and use it as a border.

Vector path drawing tools

The drawing tools enable you to draw any shape you want. If you have a digital drawing tablet, now would be the time to use it. It's much easier to draw freeform lines with a drawing pen than it is with a mouse.

Pen tool

With the Pen tool, you don't actually draw a line; you plot the points, as you would when drawing a dot-to-dot picture. Each click places a new point and between each point, a line segment is added.

The Pen tool has two kinds of points: a Corner point, which has at least one straight segment, and a Curve point, which has at least one curved segment. To see first-hand the difference between these two types of points, follow these steps:

1. Open a new document (File ➪ New) and use a size of 300 pixels by 300 pixels. Check to be sure the line has a color assigned to it. In the toolbar near the bottom in the Color section, click the color well next to the pencil icon and choose a color.

2. Select the Pen tool and click the canvas; go straight across the page a few inches and click again. A line connects the two points you added. Continue clicking anywhere on the canvas. No matter where you click, the lines keep connecting the dots.

3. Close your first practice document and open a new one (File ➪ New); any size is fine, but 200 pixels by 200 pixels gives you a little room in which to practice. Select the Pen tool and click the canvas; click again a few inches away, and then go down the page a bit and click and drag. See what happens as you drag? The line is curved, as shown in Figure 17-11. It takes practice to get used to working with a curved line.

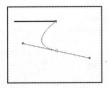

Figure 17-11: A curved line using the Pen tool

Cross-Reference See Part II of this book on FreeHand for even more Pen tool practice. There are also some movies and tutorials on the CD-ROM for more practice.

When you draw with the Pen tool and drag to form curved points, Bezier control handles are added to the path. Control handles control the shape of the object.

Shapes form closed paths; a line that does not make an enclosure is considered an open path. To end an open path, double-click the last point or choose Edit ⇨ Deselect. To form a closed path, click the starting point. As you move your cursor to the starting point, look for a small circle to appear beside the arrow. The circle indicates that clicking will complete a closed path. Most tasks with the Pen tool have these small indicators to let you know how clicking will affect a point.

Vector Path tool

The Vector Path tool is similar to the Brush tool; it draws like a paintbrush. But the result is still a path containing points. A path with a stroke applied can be edited like any other path.

Bezier Curves

A Bezier curve (pronounced bezz-ey-aye) is based on mathematical calculations. The name comes from Pierre Bezier, who in the 1970s formulated the principles on which most vector objects are now based. The theory is that all shapes are composed of segments and points. A segment can be straight, curved, or a combination of both straight and curved. A combination of two or more points joined by a line or a curve is referred to as a *path*.

A straight line is a line that joins two points using the shortest possible distance. A curved line is controlled by the position of the points and the control handles, which manipulate them. Figure 17-12 shows two paths with the same position of points; notice how different the same path can be made by manipulating the control handles.

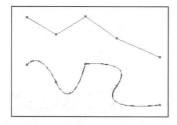

Figure 17-12: A path with straight segments and one with Bezier curves added

No limit exists to what you can do to a Bezier curve by adding, deleting, moving, and manipulating the points of a path.

Drawing a Bezier curve

To draw a Bezier curve, follow these steps:

1. Open a new document (File ⇨ New). Select the Pen tool and click anywhere on your canvas to set the beginning point of the path.

2. Move your cursor and click somewhere else on the canvas to set the second point of the path. Notice how a straight line automatically connects the points.

3. Move the cursor again and click to set another point, only this time hold the mouse button down and drag a bit in any direction. As you drag, a curve will form. You can click anywhere to place another point.

4. Double-click to end the path. Notice that a control handle is attached to the curve you formed, as shown in Figure 17-13.

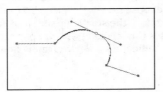

Figure 17-13: A curve with the control handles visible

Using the control handles of a Bezier curve

After you've drawn a Bezier curve a smooth curve is formed. Manipulating either control handle affects the line segment. Pulling on a handle increases the tension for that line segment. To make adjustments with the control handles, use the Subselection tool and click a point on the path. When the cursor is near a point, it changes to a white arrowhead, which indicates the point can be selected. When you click a point, the solid square turns into a hollow square. Bezier handles are usually visible when you select a point that is a Bezier curve. To practice manipulating Bezier curves using Bezier control handles, follow these steps:

1. Select the Pen tool, click to place three points in a row, and then double-click the ending point of the path (Figure 17-14).

Figure 17-14: A straight line with three points drawn

2. Select the Subselection tool. Click the middle point; it will turn into a hollow square. If no handles appear (and they won't on this straight line), press the Alt (Option) key and drag the middle point down. When you release the mouse button, a control handle is visible. Figure 17-15 shows what your curve should look like as a result of holding down the Alt (Option) key and pulling down on the middle point.

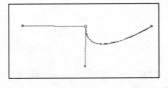

Figure 17-15: A curve added to the straight line

3. Press the Alt (Option) key on the same point and drag straight up. Figure 17-16 shows the results.

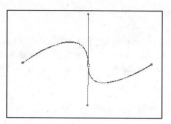

Figure 17-16: Another curve added by dragging the other control handle

When working with Bezier curves, it takes practice to get a feel for what direction to pull and turn to get the desired shape. Practice by clicking and dragging the top control handle to the right and down. You can move it up, down, and all around.

Be sure to watch the movie tutorial in the Movies folder on the CD-ROM called `bezier.mov`.

Editing with the Pen Tool

So far in this chapter, you have learned how to draw paths and how to connect the beginning and ending points. Sometimes, you will need to join multiple paths that you have drawn, or you may want to break apart a path. The Pen tool is used to join multiple paths, close a path, and continue a path you have drawn.

Closing a path

If you try to fill a path object and nothing happens, or the fill doesn't go just inside the path, producing very strange results, your path is probably not closed. If this happens, you need to join the path, or join multiple paths to close the path. To close a path, follow these steps:

1. With the Pointer tool, select the path you want to close.

2. Select the Pen tool, move your cursor over one of the end points of the path (when you are near the end point, a little *x* will appear in the lower-right corner of the cursor), and click the end point once. A little arrow appears in the corner of the cursor, indicating you can now select a closing point.

3. Move your cursor to the closing point and click it once. The path is closed. You don't have to use only one point to close a path. If the ending point is not near, you may want to place points along the way and then select the closing point.

Continuing a path

Adding to a previous path is similar to closing a path, except you don't have to close a path to add on to it. If you want to add on to a previous path, follow these steps:

1. With the Pointer tool, select the path you want to add on to.

2. Select the Pen tool, move your cursor over one of the end points of the path, and click the end point once. If you want the next line segment to be curved, click and drag.

3. Move your cursor to the next location in which you want to add a point and then click once; continue clicking to add points until you have the path you want.

Joining paths

After you draw multiple paths, you can join them together using the Pen tool. This may sound like the same thing as closing paths, and it is almost the same procedure; the difference is that you don't have to close the joined paths. To join paths together, follow these steps:

1. With the Pointer tool, select the path you want to join.

2. Select the Pen tool, move your cursor over one of the end points of the path, and click the end point once.

3. Move your cursor to the end point of the other path you are connecting to and click once. You can combine as many paths as you like in this way.

Adding and deleting points

If you want a path to change direction, you may need to add at least one point. Use the Pen tool to add points to an existing path:

1. Select the path using the Pointer tool.

2. Click once on the line segment using the Pen tool to add a corner point. To add a smooth curve point, click and drag to pull out the curve control handles.

Using the Vector Path tool often adds more points than are necessary for the shape desired. Extra points can make a shape or path look choppy or not as smooth as you might want. To remove points, follow these steps:

1. Select the path you want to edit with the Pointer tool.

2. Select the Pen tool. Move to the point that you want to delete. When the minus sign appears beside the cursor, click once on the point.

3. Another way to remove unwanted points is to choose Modify ⇨ Alter Path ⇨ Simplify and then type the number of points you want removed and click OK. Although this option doesn't give you precise control, it is a fast way to make simple changes.

Using the Pen tool to edit a shape

The shapes used in the Habitat Alert site are complex and use Pen tool techniques and the Path Combine features shown in the following section.

Adding guides

Before altering the shape we need to set up some guides to use. To set the guides, follow these steps:

1. Navigate to the `habitat_alert_final\designfiles\Fireworks` folder and open the `ha1.png` file. Or open the `myha1.png` file from the `habitat_alert_start\designfiles\Fireworks` folder if you saved it there in Chapter 16.

2. You'll be using guides for this exercise. Enable rulers by choosing View ⇨ Rulers. To place a guide, click in the horizontal ruler area and drag into the document to place a guide, which is green by default.

3. To position the guide precisely, double-click the guide to open the Move Guide dialog box. Type in **24** for the Position and click OK. Set the following guides:

- Horizontal: One at 74 and one at 100
- Vertical: One at 231 and one at 160

Editing a shape

We are going to add a curve to the left side of the blue rectangle for the Habitat Alert site. To alter the shape of the rectangle, follow these steps:

1. Select the blue rectangle and ungroup it (Modify ➪ Ungroup or Control (Command)+ Shift+G).

2. Select the rectangle with the Subselection tool.

3. Click the Pen tool to select it. Place your cursor over the guide at 160 and the bottom horizontal guide at 100 and click to place another point (Figure 17-17). Add one at the 231 intersection as well.

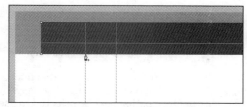

Figure 17-17: A point being added to the intersection of the guide at 160 and 100

4. Using the Subselection tool, Shift+select the bottom-left point and the one directly to the right of it (at the 160 guide). Using the keyboard up arrow, press Shift and press up arrow two times. Release the Shift key and press up arrow five more times. You moved only two points up to the guide at the position of 74 as shown in Figure 17-18.

Pressing the Shift key as you press the arrow keys moves in increments of 10 pixels.

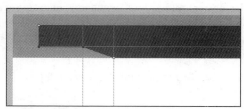

Figure 17-18: The two bottom left points moved up 25 pixels

5. You want to add a bit of a curve to the straight diagonal line. Using the Subselection tool, press the Alt (Option) key and click toward the 231 guide. Press Alt (Option) and click the lower point and drag toward the 160 guide a tiny bit. Refer to Figure 17-19 to see where the handles are dragged out to for the proper shape.

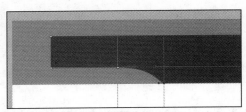

Figure 17-19: The curve added by using the Alt (Option) key and dragging the handles to form the curve shape

Tip

It can be difficult to pull the correct handle, especially when using the Atl+drag (Option+drag) method to pull a handle from an existing corner point. Use the Pen tool instead. As you move the Pen tool over the point, you see a minus sign. Click and drag a short distance to pull out control handles, following the exact direction of the line. Then press the Alt (Option) key while editing a handle with the Subselection tool to form the desired curved line segment.

6. Save this in the `habitat_alert_start\designfile\Fireworks` folder as `myha2.png`.

Reshaping Paths Using Path Operations

Join, Split, Union, Intersect, Punch, and Crop are all Boolean operations that may be used to create quite interesting and complex paths — both closed and open. Choose Modify ➪ Combine Paths to access these options. One or more paths must be selected to use the Combine Paths operations.

Union

The Union option is used when you want to merge two or more paths. This operation combines selected paths into a single path, removing overlapping points. To use the Union operation, follow these steps:

1. Shift+select one or more objects with the Pointer tool.

2. Choose Modify ➪ Combine Paths ➪ Union.

The Union operation helps you work smarter, not harder — when it would require a complex Pen tool to build the desired graphic, use simple shapes with the Union operation instead. For example, to build a shape shown in Figure 17-20, use a rectangle and circle, combining their paths together with Union.

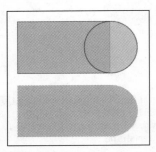

Figure 17-20: Two shapes joined by using the Union command

To make a shape with both rounded and square corners (or ends) such as you see in
Figures 17-20 and 17-21, follow these steps:

1. On a new canvas draw a rounded rectangle with a roundness of 50 with no stroke and
   any color fill. The size of this sample is 180×60.

2. Draw a rectangle that is 180×20.

3. Position the rectangle over the rounded rectangle. Choose Select ⇨ Select all; then
   choose Modify ⇨ Combine Paths ⇨ Union. The shape is shown in Figure 17-21.

Figure 17-21: A shape with rounded and squared corners

Join

The Join operation isn't the same as connecting paths together into one continuous path
using the join techniques with the Pen tool. When you use Join, overlapping areas are joined
into one path.

Intersect

The Intersect operation works the opposite of the way Union works. Whereas Union throws
away the overlapping area, Intersect keeps it and throws away the rest.

Crop

The results of using the Crop operation look the same as the results of using the Intersect
operation. Use Crop to delete portions of a selection of objects outside of a specific region.
For example, Figure 17-22 shows three circles that overlap. Using Crop, you would use the top
circle as the cropping area (region) and keep only those parts of the lower two circles that
fall within the region. The crop object disappears.

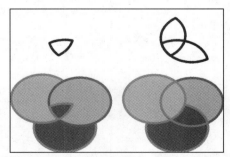

Figure 17-22: Intersect (the image on the
left) keeps only the area common to the
intersection. Crop (the image on the right)
uses the top circle as the cropping region
and only keeps the parts of the lower two
circles that are within the region.

Punch

Use Punch to build complex, compound shapes. Punch uses the top object to remove a portion of the bottom object. In the Punch process, the top object disappears.

To use the Punch operation, follow these steps:

1. Select both objects with the Pointer tool. The punching object must be above the object to be punched.

2. Choose Modify ➪ Combine Paths ➪ Punch.

Build the layout interface

The interface used in the project layout uses Combine Paths operations to form complex shapes. When the shapes are completed, effects are added to create depth and visual interest. To build the interface, follow these steps:

1. Open the ha3.png file from the habitat_alert_final\designfiles\Fireworks folder (or open your copy of myha3.png if you saved one).

   This file includes shapes you can use in the Combine Paths operations. The large, green, rounded rectangle was made using Union to form a single shape.

2. In the Layers panel, click the green rounded rectangle and copy it (Ctrl [Command]+C). Click the eye icon to turn off its visibility.

3. Click the blue shape and paste (Ctrl [Command] +V). This should place the copy above the blue shape as well as the document. If it doesn't, drag the green shape above the blue shape in the Layers panel.

4. Shift+select both objects and choose Modify ➪ Combine Paths ➪ Intersect. The results are shown in Figure 17-23. This operation added a curve to the top of the blue rectangle.

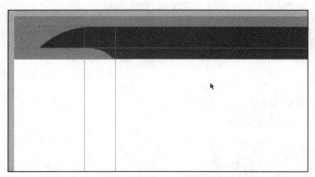

Figure 17-23: A curve added to a rectangle by using the Intersect command

5. Make a copy of the blue shape (the Intersect command changed the name to Path) and paste it. Double-click the bottom one and rename it **blueshadow**. Rename the top path to **blueshape**.

6. Select the blueshadow and remove the texture by moving the slider to 0% in the Property inspector.

7. Click the Effects menu and choose Shadow and Glow ➪ Drop Shadow using these values:

   - Distance: **5**
   - Opacity: **85%**
   - Softness: **6**
   - Angle: **323**

8. Draw another rectangle and use these values:

   - Height: **45**
   - Width: **800**
   - x: **-35**
   - y: **74**
   - Fill: **White**
   - Stroke: **None**

9. Copy and paste the blueshape. In the Layers panel, move the white rectangle below the top blueshape. Shift+select the top blueshape and the white rectangle and choose Modify ➪ Combine Paths ➪ Punch.

   Keep in mind that the punch object disappears in the operation. If you need to keep the shape you plan to use as a punch, make a copy.

   Figure 17-24 shows the result of the punch. The shape is named white shape to identify it. Notice that it sits below the original blue shape.

10. Select the Line tool and use a color of #003366. Press the Shift key and drag a line across the entire document. Use the Property inspector to set its Y coordinate to **120**.

11. Select the white shape object and apply the effect Shadow and Glow ➪ Drop Shadow using these values:

    - Distance: **3**
    - Opacity: **65%**
    - Softness: **2**
    - Angle: **315**

12. Copy the original circle in the Layers panel.

13. Click the top path object and paste. You can turn off the visibility of the original circle. You need to cut off the top and right sides of the circle for the design.

14. Draw a rectangle to cover the top of the circle down to the dark blue line you drew earlier (Figure 17-25). In the Property inspector enter these values and press Enter/Return:

    - Width: **414**
    - Height: **126**
    - x: **-13**
    - y: **-5**

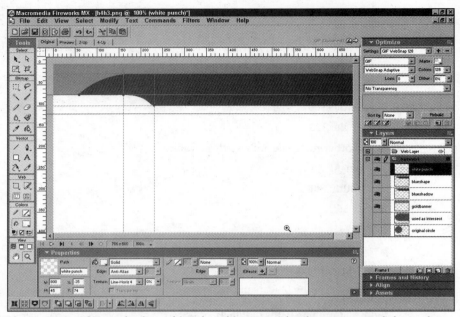

Figure 17-24: The result of punching the white rectangle. The Layers panel shows the shapes and layers you should have at this point.

Tip

Change the fill color of the rectangle to make it easier to see what it covers.

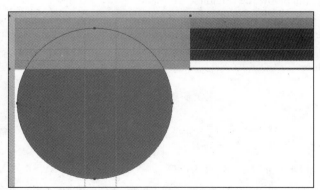

Figure 17-25: A rectangle drawn over the top portion of the circle

15. Shift+select the rectangle and the circle and choose Modify ⇨ Combine Paths ⇨ Punch.

16. Draw another rectangle over the right side of the circle, up to the guide at 231. Be sure it is large enough to cover all the circle to the right of the guide. Shift+select the rectangle and circle, and choose Modify ⇨ Combine Paths ⇨ Punch.

To finish the interface:

17. Select the blue shape and copy. Select the circle shape and choose Edit ⇨ Paste Attributes to apply the textured fill to the circle shape.

18. Add a new layer. Name it **circlepics**. Move the circle shape to the new layer.

19. Copy and paste the circle shape. Select the bottom copy and from the Effects menu add a Shadow and Glow ⇨ Inner Shadow effect using these values:

    - Distance: **1**

    - Opacity: **100%**

    - Softness: **4**

    - Angle: **315**

    - Check Knockout

20. Copy and paste the object to make the effect darker. Shift+select both inner shadow objects and group (Ctrl [Command] +G). Name the newly grouped object inner shadow.

21. Save your file as `myha4.png` into the `habitat_alert_start\designfiles\Fireworks` folder you saved on your hard drive.

Summary

In this chapter you learned how to use vector drawing tools and designed unique shapes using Combine Paths operations. Using these new skills, you completed the interface for the Habitat Alert page layout.

Project Summary

You built the base interface for the Habitat Alert site.

Files Prepared for Habitat Alert Web Site

Images	What Was Done	Where to Now?
Ha4.png	You made the shapes for the sites layout design.	The layout is now ready for the rest of the site images to be added to it.

✦   ✦   ✦

Designing Spectacular Text Effects

Macromedia Fireworks MX makes it possible to design spectacular text graphics. You can control the fill and stroke of the path, apply live effects, and even make the text follow a specified path. You'll even see how to use your text object as a mask to build text from bitmap images!

In this chapter, you explore the text tools and use the Property inspector to control the appearance of the text. Experienced Fireworks users should read this chapter carefully — the tools and methods used to add text have changed since earlier versions of Macromedia Fireworks.

Working with the Text Tools

Macromedia Fireworks MX enables you to work with text in new ways. In earlier versions of the application, The Text Editor was used to manipulate text, choosing font settings and adjusting alignment, kerning and other options. In Fireworks MX, text is handled on-canvas and the text properties, which include many new options, are applied via the Property inspector.

Use the Property inspector to set the font, size, color, leading (space between lines), kerning (space between letters), and alignment of your text. You may also choose text orientation and paragraph options, such as paragraph spacing and indentation (see Figure 18-1).

The Text menu contains many of the options available from the Property inspector. It also provides access to the Text Editor, if you prefer to use it. You must first create a text box to access the Text Editor as you'll see shortly.

The Text menu also contains a few special text-handling techniques, including tools to attach and control text along a path. Fireworks also offers a Spell Checker in the Text menu.

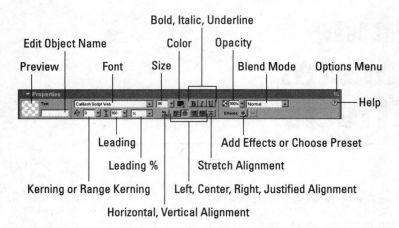

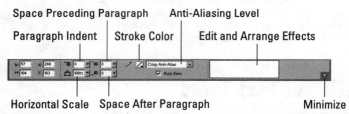

Figure 18-1: The Property inspector contains tools for controlling text and paragraph properties.

Adding text to a document

To add text to your document, select the Text tool and click the canvas. Click and drag if you want to build a text box that constrains the width of the text block. Type to add the desired text. You may select your font and size and other values prior to typing or wait until after you add the text. To set text properties after you've added text, select the text using the Pointer tool and adjust the settings in the Property inspector. Use the Pointer tool to move and position your text. To edit an existing text block, double-click with the Pointer tool. The Pointer tool changes to the Text tool, inserted into the text block at the point you clicked.

Controlling text spacing

After you select the Text tool or some text, you'll see the various options available. Some are common options, such as alignment and paragraph indents that you've probably used before, but there are also several options (presented in the following sections) that you may not be familiar with.

Kerning

Kerning determines how close letters are to each other. Kerning enables you to add more or less space between characters. Place your cursor between the characters you want to adjust and move the slider to set your spacing. You can go from 1–100 or -1–100.

Range Kerning

To use Range Kerning, select the letters or text that you want to change. Entering a new value affects all the text selected.

Leading

Leading is used when you have multiple lines of text and want to control the space between the lines. The percentage of leading you choose is based on a percentage of the text size. If you choose 100%, you get a single-spaced line. Choosing 200% creates a double-spaced line.

Baseline Shift

Bottoms of most text are normally aligned. But what happens when you want to add a trademark symbol, subscript, superscript, or a footnote? You can place letters above or below the default baseline. A negative value places the word or letter below and a positive value places it above.

Horizontal Scale

Horizontal Scale stretches or shrinks the selected text. Move the slider up or down to adjust the scale. The default is 100%.

Enhancing text

Text in Fireworks is flexible. By default text contains a solid fill and no stroke. But you can add a stroke just like you can any other vector object. Select it and choose the stroke size, type, color, and texture. Strokes are outlines and textures are added to fills. You can also alter the stroke orientation. To select the stroke's color, you click the stroke color box. In this dialog box at the bottom a drop-down menu gives you the choice of putting the stroke outside the path, inside the path, or centered on the path. There is also a Fill Over Stroke option that draws the fill over the stroke.

You can select text and the select one of the Transform tools to scale, skew, and distort. Even after transforming it, it will still be editable. You can highlight one letter and make it larger or change its color, baseline, or stroke. This can produce some interesting text. Figure 18-2 shows text using the techniques discussed in this section.

Using text as a placeholder

Many times a designer will design a layout in Fireworks to present as a mockup to the client. To simulate how the text will look in the Web site, you can use a text block for the mockup. It's a good idea to use the font that you'll use in Dreamweaver, such as Verdana or Helvetica. Set the edge of the text to Alias because that's the way HTML text is formatted. You'll want to simulate the real look as much as possible. If you use anti-alias text, stylized and so on, the clients will be disappointed when they see the HTML text because it won't look like the mockup.

Figure 18-2: Text (from top to bottom) with a stroke, kerning, scaled, rotated, distorted, and using a baseline shift

Converting text to a path

Text in Fireworks is editable at all times, whether it is grouped, transformed, or has applied effects. Editable text is powerful, but there will be times that require converting editable vector text objects to vector paths. You want to convert text to a path to two common reasons:

✦ You are giving a file to someone and they may not have the fonts used in the file.

✦ You want to edit the appearance of the text in a way that requires manipulation of one or more letterforms.

Text may be scaled, skewed, distorted, or rotated using the Transform tools, but you cannot make any changes to the individual letters themselves. To modify a letter in the font, you must first convert the text to paths using Text ⇨ Convert to Paths. Words converted to paths are grouped to make it easier to keep the letters together. To access individual letterforms, select the text and choose Modify ⇨ Ungroup (Figure 18-3). To edit a letterform, select a letter with the Subselection tool.

Figure 18-3: Converting normal text to paths enables you to modify the text outlines. Here, the letter X is selected with the Subselection tool to reveal its points and line segments.

Using text as a punch

Use Modify ⇨ Combine Paths ⇨ Union to convert several text letterforms to a single path. This saves time and effort when you want to cut text from another image or object.

When the text paths are converted to a single path, it may be used like a cookie-cutter. To use text as a cookie-cutter, follow these steps:

1. Open a new document 500 × 300 with a white background.

2. Draw a rectangle to fill the canvas. Add a fill using a color different than the canvas.

3. Type some text to use as a cookie-cutter. A thick font, like Arial black, works best.

4. Select the text and choose Text ➪ Convert to Paths. Each letter now is a path. Select the grouped letters with the Pointer tool and choose Modify ➪ Ungroup.

5. Shift+select each letter with the Subselection tool and choose Modify ➪ Ungroup. To form a single path from all the letters, choose Modify ➪ Combine Paths ➪ Join.

6. Shift+select the text and the rectangle with the Pointer tool and choose Modify ➪ Combine Paths ➪ Punch.

7. The punched object is a compound path. You may add effects or manipulate the points of the object, if desired.

Setting Type on a Path

Fireworks contains options to place text on an open or closed path. To place text on any path, select the text and the path. Choose Text ➪ Attach to Path. The alignment properties of the text will affect where the text attaches to the path, relative to the path's points.

✦ When the text is left-aligned, attaching to a closed path places the text to the right of the left-most point. Attaching to an open path places the text after the first point.

✦ When the text is right-aligned, attaching to a closed path places the text to the right of the left-most point. Attaching to an open path places the text before the last point.

✦ When the text is center-aligned, attaching to a closed path distributes the text over the right-most point. Attaching to an open path distributes the text over the center-most point.

✦ When text is stretched or justified, the left-most point is the starting point.

In this exercise you place text along the top and bottom of a circle in two independent operations. To do this, the circular path must be cut in half to form two arcs and the direction of the bottom type will be reversed:

1. Open the shelllogo.png from the chapter18_exercise folder on the CD-ROM.

2. Select the Ellipse tool and draw an ellipse around the image. Use a fill of None and a 1-pixel black stroke. Position the ellipse around the image.

3. Create a text object with the word **Shell**. This exercise uses the following settings; you may use any font you prefer:

   • Font: Tarzan

   • Point Size: 62

   • Color: Black

   • Edge: Smooth Anti-Alias

4. Add another text object with the word **Seekers** and move the text to the bottom of the circle. The position really doesn't matter yet (see Figure 18-4).

Figure 18-4: An ellipse around the image and the text in place for the logo

5. Select the ellipse and use the Knife tool to cut a straight line, holding the Shift key as you slice horizontally. In Figure 18-5 the arc is moved down a bit so you could see the cut, but it will be moved back into position.

To move one of the paths, Shift+click (with the Pointer tool) on the path that will remain in place to deselect it, leaving only one path selected. Use the arrow key to nudge the path or move it using the Pointer tool.

Figure 18-5: Paths prepared for the text

6. Shift+select the top text and ellipse and choose Text ➪ Attach to Path.

7. You may edit text that is attached to a path, just as you can edit any text object. Select the text and change its leading to 20% (Figure 18-6).

8. Repeat Step 7 for the bottom text (see Figure 18-7).

9. The bottom object's text is upside down. Choose Text ➪ Reverse Direction (Figure 18-8). Now the text runs above the path of the arc, creating a crowded look.

Figure 18-6: The top text attached to a path

Figure 18-7: The text is upside down on the bottom half.

Figure 18-8: The text is too high up on the arc.

Note

Knowing that the text is going to be placed upside down, you could select the bottom path and flip it to reverse the direction of the path before attaching the text. To flip, first select the path; then choose Modify ➪ Transform ➪ Flip Vertical.

10. Use Baseline to adjust the text on the path. In order to get access to the Baseline option, the text must be selected first. Set Baseline to -30 and modify the Leading to 20% in the Property inspector (Figure 18-9).

Figure 18-9: The bottom text is altered and in position.

Filling Text with an Image

Although this effect isn't difficult, it is one that is useful. The text itself won't remain editable but any of the effects applied to it will be. To fill text with an image, follow these steps:

1. Open an image file. Use `flower.tif` from the chapter18_exercise folder if you don't have an existing image file.

2. Type a word using all caps. Use a solid or thick font.

3. Move the text over the part of the image you want to show inside the text.

4. Select the image and cut (Control [Command]+X).

5. Select the text object and choose Edit ➪ Paste Inside or use the shortcut Control+Shift+V (Command+Shift+V).

   Pasting an image inside text is the same as using an image as a mask. A mask is one or more objects that are grouped in a special way.

Cross-Reference This technique works for any vector object, not just text. See Chapter 19 for more information about masking.

All masked images display a "cloverleaf" set of four dots in the center of their group. Grab the cloverleaf to position the image within the text.

Adding Special Symbols

To add special symbols to your text, such as a copyright, trademark, or an em dash, you must use key combinations for the computer platform you are using. On a PC you type the keycode into the keypad of your keyboard.

Table 18-1 shows the key combinations for commonly used characters.

Table 18-1: Character Key Combinations

Character	Windows	Macintosh
Copyright	Alt+0169	Option+G
Em-Dash	Alt+0151	Shift+Option+Dash
Trademark	Alt+0153	Option+2
Degrees	Alt+0176	Option+0
Cent	Alt+0162	Option+4
Pound (currency)	Alt+0163	Option+3
Euro	Alt+0128	Shift+Option+2
Registered Mark	Alt+0174	Option+R
Greater than		Option+. (Period)
Less than		Option+, (Comma)
Divided by		Option+/

Altering Paths

Here are two techniques you can use to achieve effects that you can only achieve with bitmap objects in other image editing programs.

This exercise shows you how to use the Alter Paths functions:

1. Open a new document that is 450px wide by 150px tall. Set the canvas color to blue.

2. Add some large-sized text and style it. This example uses size 88pt Futura Book, filled and with a linear Spectrum gradient.

3. Make a copy of the text object. Use the Layers panel eye icon to hide one of the text objects. Figure 18-10 shows the text and the Layers panel with the two objects.

4. Select the text and choose Text ➪ Convert to Paths.

5. Choose Modify ➪ Ungroup; then choose Modify ➪ Combine Paths ➪ Join. Now choose Modify ➪ Alter Paths ➪ Expand Stroke. Enter 3 for the Width and click OK.

6. Add a drop shadow using the default settings. Figure 18-11 shows the result.

7. Click the eye icon in the Layers panel to hide this text and click to turn on the copied version.

8. Select the text, make a copy, and paste. Select the bottom text and change the fill to black.

9. Now with the black text selected, choose Text ➪ Convert to Paths; then choose Modify ➪ Ungroup, and choose Modify ➪ Combine Paths ➪ Join.

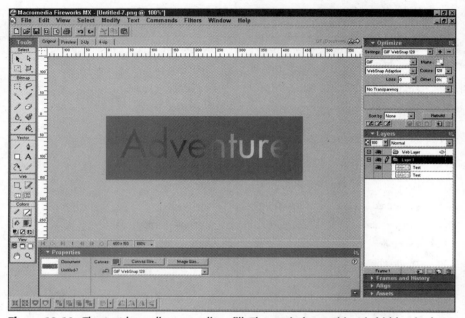

Figure 18-10: The text has a linear gradient fill. The copied text object is hidden in the Layers panel.

Figure 18-11: The Expand operation applied to the text

Cross-Reference

See Chapter 17 for a better understanding of Combine operations, if needed.

10. Choose Modify ➪ Alter Paths ➪ Inset Path. The Inset Path dialog box opens. Click Outside for the direction and enter **3** for the width. Click OK.

11. Be sure the black text is below the other text object. Add a drop shadow to the black text object (Figure 18-12).

Figure 18-12: The text size increased using the Inset Path command

You expanded the size of the text by a pixel amount, without increasing the spaces around the letterforms. Scaling or adjusting the text size also increases the amount of space between the letterforms. This technique is a great way to add custom bevels and effects to your text or objects. A copy of this exercise is in your Chapter 18 images folder. Try turning off the visibility of the Inset Path text and turn on the Expand Path text to see yet another effect.

Power Text Mask, *by Japi Honoo*

I have spent a lot of time developing a process of making a futuristic skin to apply to a shape. It's done totally as a vector and remains editable. You'll be able to change the object's properties such as color, texture, and effects.

There is a bit of masking being done in this tutorial. If you need to know more about masking refer to Chapter 19.

To learn how to do some amazing things in Fireworks, follow these steps:

1. Open a new document (File ⇨ New) and use a width of 560 and a height of 200 with a white canvas color.

2. Select the Text tool and use an appropriate font and size. I used the following values:

   Font: Garamond Bold

   Size: 230

   Color: #36524F

   The text size slider only goes to 99 but you can type in a number and press the Enter/Return key.

3. Type the word **bible** in lowercase letters.

4. With the text selected, choose Text ⇨ Convert to Paths.

5. In the Property inspector access the Effects menu and choose Bevel and Emboss ⇨ Inner Bevel and use these values:

   Bevel Edge Shape: Smooth

   Width: 35

   Opacity: 100%

   Softness: 10

   Angle: 135

   Button Preset: Raised

6. From the Effects menu (Property inspector) choose Adjust Color ⇨ Curves and enter 43 for input and 25 for the output. Notice the point added to the curve.

   It's important to use the Effects menu and not the Filters menu. Curves used from the Filter menu convert your vector object into a bitmap.

7. Access the Effects menu and choose Adjust Color ⇨ Brightness and Contrast. Type in 9 for Brightness and 29 for Contrast.

8. Add the Brightness and Contrast effect one more time using the same values.

9. Access the Layer Options menu and click Duplicate Layer. Enter 2 for the Number and click the After Current Layer option to select it. Click OK to close the dialog box.

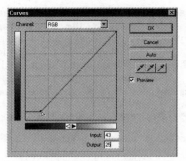

The Curve dialog box with the input
and output settings adjusted

The text converted to paths, an inner bevel effect,
and the brightness and contrast effect added twice

10. Rename the layers, name the top layer Text1, the next Text2, and the bottom one Text3.

11. Select the Text3 layer and ungroup the object (Ctrl [Command]+Shift+G). Notice how the effects are removed after you ungroup the object.

12. Chose Modify ➪ Alter Path ➪ Inset Path. In the Inset Path dialog box, enter these values:

    Direction: Inside

    Width: 2

    Corners: the icon on the right

    Miter Limit: 10

    Click OK

13. While the object is still selected, group it (Ctrl [Command]+G).

14. Repeat Steps 5–8 to add the bevel, curve, and brightness effects back to this copy of the text.

Adding the gold skin

To add gold skin to the text, follow these steps:

1. Click the eye icon in the Layers panel next to the Text3 and the Text1 layers to hide them.

2. Click the Text2 layer to select the object.

3. Click a fill color box and change the color to #9F8146.

4. To add guides to the document, be sure your rulers are visible; then drag out four horizontal guides. Double-click each guide and set these locations:

35.

98.

134.

161.

5. Draw two rectangles between the top two guides and the bottom two guides as shown here. Fill both rectangles with white.

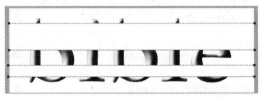

Two rectangles drawn over the text and filled with white for use as a mask

6. Shift+select the rectangles and copy (Control/Command+C) and paste into the Text1 layer.

7. Back in the Text2 layer, group the two rectangles and then shift+select the text object.

8. Choose Modify ➪ Mask ➪ Group as Mask.

The rectangles are above the text object prior to applying the mask.

9. Add a drop shadow by accessing the Effects menu and choosing Shadow and Glow ➪ Drop Shadow using these values:

Distance: 2

Opacity: 80%

Softness: 3

Angle: 300

10. Turn the visibility back on for the Text1 and Text3 shapes.

The text object with the gold skin applied using a mask

Apply the gray skin

To add the gray skin over the text, follow these steps:

1. Hide the visibility of Text2 and Text3 layers.

2. Select the grouped text object inthe Text1 layer and change the color fill to #000000 (black).

3. In the Property inspector, select a texture of Metal; move the percentage slide to 50%.

4. You don't need the two brightness and contrast effects for this layer. In the Effects list you can select the effect name and then click the minus sign to delete it or do it the way I like to use. Click the check mark, and an x that disables the effect appears. It's still there if you decide to use it.

The Property inspector showing the metal texture added and two effects disabled

5. Select the top rectangle; in the Property inspector make it 4 pixels shorter (about 59 pixels high). Press the down arrow key twice.

6. Select the bottom rectangle, in the Property inspector; make it 4 pixels shorter (about 23 pixels high). Press the down arrow key twice.

7. Group the two rectangles.

8. Shift+select the rectangles that are on top of the text and the text. Choose Modify ➪ Mask ➪ Paste as Mask.

9. Make all the layers visible and you have some pretty snazzy text

10. Select the Text3 layer and add a drop shadow using a color of #333333 and the default settings.

11. If you want a background, draw a rectangle over the document in Text3 layer and drag it below the text. Fill with a pattern. I used a marble image. This is the final result (see the color section). This file is saved as bible.png in the Chapter 18 images folder.

The futuristic text on a background

Summary

You learned to use the Text tool, setting text values using the Property inspector. You also learned how and why to convert text to paths. Adding to your skills with text, you experimented with text on a path and saw how to add special symbols to your Fireworks documents. You also learned how to paste an image inside paths created with text. Finally, you explored altering paths using a converted text object.

✦   ✦   ✦

Working with Bitmap Images

◆ ◆ ◆ ◆

In This Chapter

Understanding the
selection tools

Using bitmap tools

Fading an image into
the background

Cutting an image from
its background

Using a bitmap mask

◆ ◆ ◆ ◆

Photographs are comprised of pixels, the smallest component part of a bitmapped image (which is also known as a raster image in some programs). Pixels are little squares of color resembling a mosaic composition. Editing pixels involves adding, removing, or coloring individual pixels. Fireworks MX devotes a whole section of tools just for working with bitmap images.

The pixels are what distinguish a bitmapped image from a vector image, which consists of paths, a line with at least two points. Because vector objects (called *objects* in Fireworks) are made up of a series of lines they are fully scalable. Pixel images lose detail as they are scaled up because each image contains a set number of pixels. When you scale a bitmapped image up, Fireworks has to guess which pixels need to be resampled to "fake" the detail in the increased space. This stretching of pixels results in what is known as a "pixilated image." You can identify pixilated images by the obvious squares that can be seen or by the blurring of detail. The bigger the image is stretched the worse it will look.

In previous versions of Fireworks there was a bitmap mode and a vector mode that you needed to switch between. In Fireworks MX, you don't change modes; everything is automatic. The Tools panel is divided up into sections. The top portion contains the bitmap tools; if you select a bitmap tool, you are in bitmap mode. If you open a bitmap image, you are in bitmap mode. But as soon as you select a vector tool, the mode changes.

Figure 19-1 shows the new Tools panel with the pointer pointing at the Bitmap section. A thin line just below the bitmap tools divides the section with the Eyedropper and Paint Bucket/Gradient tools. You can use this section in both bitmap and vector modes.

Figure 19-1: The Tools panel showing the placement of the Bitmap tools

Opening Bitmap Images

The bitmap images you use will probably come from your scanner, digital camera, or other applications. If you already have images that you want to open, you can open them directly using the File ➪ Open command or you can import them into an open document by choosing File ➪ Import. When you import an image, you'll see an icon that looks like a corner. You can simply click your canvas to place the image or you can click and drag to conform the imported image to a specific size.

You can scan directly into Fireworks or open images from a digital camera directly in Fireworks by following these steps:

1. Connect the digital camera or scanner to your computer.

2. Install the software drivers that come with your camera and/or scanner.

The scanner and camera need to be twain compliant for Windows or support Photoshop Acquire plug-ins for Macintosh. Fireworks looks for the Photoshop Acquire plug-in in the Fireworks plug-ins folder for the Macintosh. You do not need to own Photoshop to use the Photoshop Acquire plug-in.

3. The first time you use the camera or the scanner you'll need to choose File ➪ Scan ➪ Twain Select and choose your scanner.

4. Now choose File ➪ Scan ➪ Twain Acquire to open your scanner application.

A Bit About Bitmaps

Just in case you are coming from a "vector-only" world, here is a quick course in pixel-based images. Photographs are comprised of pixels, the smallest component part of a bitmapped image, also known as a raster image or, in Fireworks, an image object. Pixels are little squares of color resembling a mosaic composition. Editing pixels involves adding, removing, or coloring individual pixels.

The pixels are what distinguish a bitmapped image from a vector image, which consists of paths, a line with at least two points. Because vector objects (called objects in Fireworks) are made up of a series of lines they are fully scalable.

Pixel images loose detail as they are scaled up because each image contains a set number of pixels. When you scale a bitmapped image up, Fireworks has to guess which pixels need to be resampled to "fake" the detail in the increased space. This stretching of pixels results in what is known as a "pixilated image." You can identify pixilated images by the obvious squares that can be seen or by the blurring of detail. The bigger the image is stretched the worse it will look. On the other hand if you have a bitmapped image larger than needed, you can scale it down, resulting in the same amount of pixels in a lesser area, producing a sharper image with more detail.

To create your own bitmap image, you can select and draw with the Brush tool or the Pencil tool in the Bitmap section of the Tools panel. You can add bitmap drawings to a vector object if you want to. The change of bitmap to vector mode is seamless, and Fireworks handles it behind the scenes so you don't have to switch modes.

Using the Selection Tools

The selection tools are the real power behind working with bitmap images. Selections enable you to edit particular areas of an image. The selections tools include the Marquee, Oval, Lasso, Polygon, and the Magic Wand tools. These tools are available only when you are editing bitmap images. Selections are made to isolate problem areas or to select a specific portion of an image. If you are editing, only what is contained inside of the selection is affected. A selection also enables you to copy or cut only what is contained in a selection. You can apply effects and filters to specific selections. By defining a selection, you protect the rest of the image from change.

Note If you've made a complex selection or any selection that you may want to use again in your image, you can save it (as you'll see later in this section). You can also make a selection in one layer and then copy and paste the selection into another layer.

Using Marquee Tools to Make Selections

The Marquee tools are used to make a specific selection in an image. Selections are useful for copying specific areas but more importantly they are useful for making alterations to an image. Making a selection constrains any changes to the selection area only. To make a selection, follow these steps:

1. Open any bitmap image (a JPG, GIF, or TIFF for instance).

2. Select the Marquee tool. (Click the little arrow to access the Oval Marquee if you want it.)

3. Choose the properties you want in the Property inspector. For practice, change the Edge to Feather and enter 10 for the Amount of feather. Leave the Style as Normal (Figure 19-2).

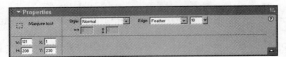

Figure 19-2: The Property inspector showing the Marquee properties

You must make set the properties prior to drawing the selection. Once it's drawn you can't change any of the properties except for Feather, which can be done using the Select ➪ Feather.

4. Click and drag to make your selection.

5. Select the Paint Bucket tool and fill the selection.

6. Press Control/Command+D to turn off the selection.

The Marquee tool properties you set remain unchanged the next time you use the tools, so be sure you change them prior to drawing your selection.

Adding to and subtracting from a selection

You can make more than one selection in your document or you can add onto the current selection. To add onto the selection put your cursor just inside the selected area and hold the Shift key and drag with one of the selection tools to enclose the new area, ending inside the current selection. To add a totally new selection in a different area, simply press the Shift key and make the selection. You can use the Marquee tools or the Lasso tools to define the area or areas you want to add to the selection.

Subtracting from a selection is just as easy as adding to a selection. The difference is you press the Alt (Option) key as your drag to define the area you want to subtract.

Moving selections

You can move a marquee by using one of these methods:

✦ Press the arrow keys of your keyboard to nudge the selection 1 pixel at a time or press the Shift key and nudge it 10 pixels at a time.

✦ With the Marquee tool selected, you can place your cursor in the selection and click and drag to a new location.

When moving a marquee selection be sure that a selection tool is selected. If you try to move a selection with the Pointer tool selected, you will move the selected portion of the image (i.e., cut). Also, make sure you click and hold as you move the selection. A simple click will deselect.

Saving and restoring selections

Some selections are complex and you may want to save them. When working with some special effects you may want to call up your selection again. To save and restore a selection follow these steps:

1. Choose Select ⇨ Save Bitmap Selection.

2. To restore the selection, choose Select ⇨ Restore Bitmap Selection.

It's easy to save and restore a selection, but there is a caveat. You can save only one selection per document. If you save a second one, it overwrites the first one.

Floating selections

So far you've seen how to make selections and move the selection itself. To build composite images many times, you need the ability to alter a part of an image and copy it, move it, and so on. If you want to move the selection and its contents follow these steps:

1. Make a selection.

2. Select the Pointer tool (or press Control [Option]) and drag to a new location. This moves the selection and its contents to a new location. It also removes the selected pixels from the original image.

3. To leave the pixels in place and move a copy only, you need to copy and paste and then use the Pointer tool (or any Marquee tool) to move the selection.

Using the Magic Wand

The Magic Wand tool works differently than all the other selection tools. The Magic Wand tool makes selections based on color. You determine the range of color in the selection by setting the tolerance. To set the tolerance of the Magic Wand tool, select the Magic Wand tool, and then in the Property inspector adjust the tolerance value. The higher the value, the more colors will be added to the selection. The Magic Wand works well for large areas of similar color.

Polygon

You use the Polygon Lasso tool by placing points around a selection area. Each time you click, the points are connected. Place points very close together in curved areas. After you define your selection area, double-click to close at the starting point.

Selection Commands

There are several options for altering the edges of your selection. From the Select menu, you can choose to feather the edges, contract, expand, smooth them, or add a border. In each case, you enter the value in pixels that you want to affect in the dialog box that opens with each selection.

An option you may use frequently is Select Inverse. For example, if you have a colorful background you want to eliminate, but the object to remain has a lot of similar colors, it may be easier to select the object (Figure 19-3) and then choose Select ⇨ Inverse. This selects the area around the original selection. You can then delete the background area or blur it out of focus (Figure 19-4).

Figure 19-3: The focal point is selected.

Figure 19-4: The selection is inversed and a Gaussian blur is added to only the background.

Blur Tool Group

In the bitmap portion of the Tools panel you'll see what looks like a water drop. This group of tools includes Blur, Sharpen, Dodge, Smudge, and Burn. These tools work well for smaller areas that need repair or a quick focused touchup.

Blur

After you select the Blur tool, you have a good bit of control in the Property inspector. You can adjust the softness of the edge, choose the size and shape (round or square), and determine the intensity or the amount of blurring that is applied. The Blur tool is great for smaller areas that you need to blend into a composite image, to help blend pattern changes, or even to blur out sensitive parts of an image.

For large areas needing to be blurred, such as a background, the Gaussian Blur filter found in the Filters or Effects menu does a more efficient job than the Blur tool does.

Sharpen

The Sharpen tool helps bring detail out in an image. It can't make a truly bad photo clear however. It can reduce blurring if you blurred a bit too much or add detail back to the edges of a blurred area. It's great for bringing focus back to things like eyes, hair, and other details of an image. Once you select the Selection tool you have the same properties available as the Blur tool. Practice with the Intensity setting to get a feel for what setting you need. You'll know you sharpened too much when you begin to see odd colors showing through.

Dodge

The Dodge tool is new to Fireworks MX. If you use the Dodge tool carefully you can gently lighten or desaturate an area. Figure 19-5 shows the properties available for the Dodge tool. Notice the Range pop-up menu. You can adjust the Shadows, Midtones, or the Highlights settings. Try each to see its effect.

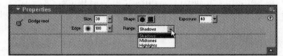

Figure 19-5: The properties available for the Dodge tool after the tool is selected

Burn

The Burn tool works the opposite of Dodge, that is, it adds darkness. The Burn tool has the same properties as the Dodge tool.

Smudge

The Smudge tool smears paint and can be useful for those coming to Fireworks from a traditional paint background. You can make your strokes more organic looking. The following list describes the properties for the Smudge tool:

✦ Size, Shape, and Edge are the same as they are for the Blur tool.

✦ The Pressure setting determines the intensity of smudging.

Using the Rubber Stamp

If you do a lot of image repair, you'll use this tool often. The Rubber Stamp tool copies one area of an image onto another area. It's frequently used to remove unwanted portions of an image (such as an old boyfriend/girlfriend) or to make repairs, perhaps scratches, blemishes, and so much more. Anywhere you need to make a touch up, the Rubber Stamp can probably do the job. It does take some practice to get the hang of it so that you don't produce noticeable patterns. You'll find that textured areas are the toughest to repair because of distinct patterns. You can remove utility wires from a photo, a car, or other undesirable elements using the Rubber Stamp. The Rubber Stamp tool is indispensable for those of you who work often with bitmap images. To get a feel for how the Rubber Stamp works, do the following:

1. Open any bitmap image.

2. Select the Rubber Stamp tool from the Tools panel.

3. When you determine the size of the stamp, keep in mind it is the sampling area as well as the area you are repairing. If the size is too large you may copy more than you want.

4. Also adjust the edge softness. The higher the setting, the softer the edge.

5. If you want to sample pixels from the composite image, in other words, objects that overlap each other and/or on different layers, select the Use Entire Document option.

6. Now that you finished the settings for the sampling area, you need to set the sampling point. To do this, press the Alt (Option) key and click in the area you want to sample.

7. Before you begin to stamp, you need to choose either Source Aligned or Fixed. Set the Opacity slider to control the amount of paint you are copying. This is especially important when you are working on textures or patterned areas. You'll get a better blend of textures if you paint in a building process.

Note

The Aligned option means that the sampling spot is aligned with the Rubber Stamp tool and will move horizontally and vertically. No matter where you move your cursor the sampling point stays in the same alignment with the cursor. If you uncheck Source Aligned, the sampling point is taken from one spot as you click. You can click anywhere and copy from the same spot. But if you drag, the sample source moves horizontally or vertically in relation to the sample point.

8. Click the area you want to cover with the sampling area. You can also click and drag but be careful of making a distinct pattern. For this reason I usually click when making repairs to a smaller problem area.

Masking Images

How to fade one image into another is one of the most asked questions in the Macromedia Fireworks forum, and it's one of the easiest things to do. If you make collages, montages, image compositions, you'll use the masking features of Fireworks frequently. A mask *masks off* portions of an image, thereby determining which areas are opaque and which areas are transparent. Masks are used to blend one image into another or to isolate an area to be removed from an image.

Note

Bitmap masks in Fireworks are similar to layer masks in Photoshop. And Photoshop layer clipping paths are similar to Fireworks vector masks.

In Fireworks, a mask object is what you use to apply transparency. The mask object resides above the image to be masked; a mask isn't applied directly to the image. A mask object contains a fill, which affects the pixels of the image or object that is being masked. The fill color or texture determines how much of an image shows through the mask. In the areas of a mask that are white, the underlying area is totally visible. In solid black areas, the image is totally invisible. The varying degrees of gray determine the amount of transparency.

Note

If you have used previous versions of Fireworks, the white and black are reversed from what they used to be. In Fireworks 4, white is invisible and black is visible. Although if you open a Fireworks 4 file with a mask in it, Fireworks MX will normally make the change without your intervention.

Fading an image into a background

To fade an image into a background texture, follow these steps:

1. Open a new canvas that is 800 × 400.

2. Draw a rectangle to cover the canvas and fill with #BACBF9. Add a texture of Line-Horiz3 at 30%.

3. Navigate to the chapter19_exercise folder and Import (File ➪ Import) the `Black_Caped_Poster_Boy1.jpg` image.

4. Place the cursor in the top-left corner and drag to fill the rectangle by about two-thirds its size

5. To blend the image into the background, draw a rectangle to cover only the image.

6. Choose a Fill Category of Linear (in the Property inspector). Move the Texture slider to 0.

7. Click the Fill color box for the gradient options. From the Preset list choose White, Black.

8. In the Layers panel press Shift while you select the rectangle and the image.

9. Choose Modify ➪ Mask ➪ Group as Mask. Notice how the white areas of the rectangle are opaque and the black area is transparent. This image is a bit too transparent, so you'll want to edit it.

10. In the Layers panel click the little pen icon of the mask to make the gradient handles visible (or use the Pointer tool to select).

11. Drag the circle handle to the right and drag the square handle near the edge of the picture (Figure 19-6). If you drag the square handle out too far it shows the edge of the image. You can close the document or save it.

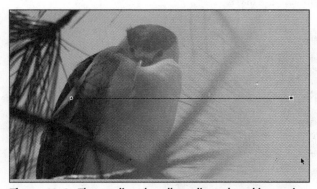

Figure 19-6: The gradient handles adjusted, making a nice fade into the background texture

 Note   You can use any kind of gradient you'd want for this type of mask. You can rotate the gradient as well. You can even use another image as the mask object. This technique is flexible and has a lot of possibilities.

Super fast mask shortcut

Now that you know the basics of applying your own mask, I'll show you a shortcut. Fireworks MX contains a command called Fade Image that offers a variety of instant masks. To make a quick mask, follow these steps:

1. Open the `Black_Caped_Poster_Boy1.jpg` image again from the Chapter 19_exercise folder.

2. Deselect the image and in the Property inspector click the canvas color box. Sample the blue color from the image background to make the canvas blue.

3. Select the image.

4. Choose Commands ➪ Creative ➪ Fade Image. Figure 19-7 shows the dialog box that opens. Notice the different fade options available.

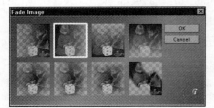

Figure 19-7: The various fade options available in the Fade Image dialog box

5. To compare this to the technique you used previously, choose the second one from the left in the top row. This option fades to the right.

6. Now you can adjust the gradient handles to get the fade you want. Figure 19-8 shows that you achieved the same effect as doing it yourself by drawing and filling the rectangle and applying the mask.

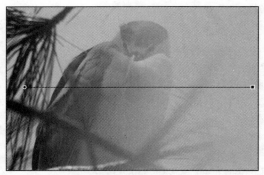

Figure 19-8: The left-to-right fade image option from the Fade Image command applied to the image

Cutting an image out of a background (vector mask)

Another common use of a mask is to cut an image out of its background. Fireworks provides two ways to do this, a bitmap mask or a vector mask. Using a vector mask offers the most flexibility. Because the mask is a vector object, it has points, which you can manipulate into a perfect fit. Plus, if you make a mistake, you don't look at all of your selection like you would with a Selection tool. Follow these steps to make a vector mask to cut an image from its background:

1. Open the `Black_Caped_Poster_Boy1.jpg` image again from the Chapter19_exercise folder.

2. Select the Pen tool and set the fill to None for now. To see your path, set the stroke to 1-pixel soft and a color of red.

3. With the Pen tool, click around the bird and cut through the chest above the branch (Figure 19-9). Click and drag to form the curves and adjust the bezier handles as needed.

Figure 19-9: The bird image with a path around the area to remain

See Chapter 17 for more details on using the Pen tool and bezier curves.

4. Change the stroke to None and the fill to white. Set the fill edge to Feather and a value of 3 pixels.

5. Press Shift while you select the vector path and the image.

6. Choose Modify ➪ Mask ➪ Group As Mask (Figure 19-10).

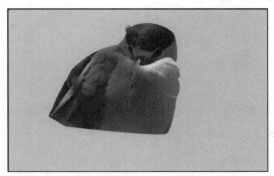

Figure 19-10: The vector mask applied to the bird with the background removed

7. You can still edit this mask to make adjustments. In my sample the bottom line is rough and uneven. To edit the mask, click the little pen icon in the mask in the Layers panel. You'll notice yellow points.

8. Select the Subselection tool and you can move the points to where you want.

9. Save now if you'd like to keep this image, otherwise leave it open for the next exercise.

Using Paste Inside (vector mask)

You can also use any vector shape and paste an image into it. Because this is the technique we used for the Habitat Alert site you'll learn how to do it here. You can practice using the site files. The bird you've been practicing on is the bird for the homepage. But this time you'll access the image from the root folder.

Note If you haven't copied the habitat_alert_start folder onto your hard drive, do that now.

To get the bird image into the circle shape of our homepage, follow these steps:

1. You'll need to open the ha4.png file. If you have done the previous chapter and have it saved in the habitat_alert_start folder on your hard drive then you're ready. Otherwise you can get a copy from the habitat_alert_final\designfiles\Fireworks folder.

2. Open the Layers panel. In the circlepics layer, select the circle and copy and paste it two times. This produces three copies of the circle object.

3. Pull a horizontal guide (choose View ➪ Rulers if you don't have them on), double-click on the guide, and set it to 289.

4. Draw a rectangle to cover the top of the circle shape to the bottom guide, and cover the entire circle horizontally (Figure 19-11). You will be removing the top portion for this copy of the circle

Note To make drawing to a guide easier be sure the Snap to Guides option is on. (File ➪ Snap to Guides).

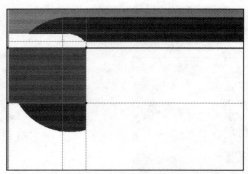

Figure 19-11: A rectangle drawn to cover the top of the circle

5. Shift+select the rectangle and the top shape in the Layers panel.

6. Choose Modify ➪ Combine Paths ➪ Intersect. If you turn off the view of all the objects in the circlepics layer except the top image you just intersected, you will see you have only the top part of the shape. This is the shape that the bird image is going to go into.

7. Choose File ➪ Import and navigate to the habitat_alert_start\designfiles\Fireworks folder and open the same image you've been practicing on, the Black_Caped_Poster_Boy1.jpg.

8. Place your cursor in the top-left corner of the circle shape and drag past the shape by about 50 percent (Figure 19-12) and click.

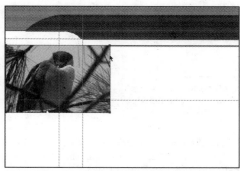

Figure 19-12: The image imported and placed above the circle shape

9. Select the Scale tool and drag the bottom-right corner up to fit to the guide placed at the bottom of the shape (Figure 19-13).

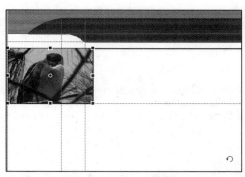

Figure 19-13: The image scaled to fit horizontally

10. Select the image and cut it (Control [Command] +X).

11. Select the adjusted shape (layer name of Path) and choose Edit ➪ Paste Inside.

12. Draw a rectangle over the bottom portion of the other copy of the circle shape as shown in Figure 19-14.

13. Shift+select the rectangle and the circle shape and choose Modify ➪ Combine Paths ➪ Intersect.

14. Double-click the new shape in the Layers panel, and name it **circle bottom**.

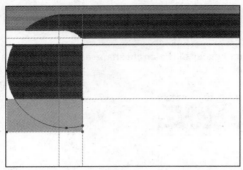

Figure 19-14: The rectangle drawn over the bottom of the circle shape to use as an intersect command

15. Drag the inner shadow to the top of the stack of objects; then drag the circle bottom below it. Finally drag the masked image and below that drag the shape containing the background. The Layers panel should look like Figure 19-15.

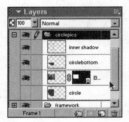

Figure 19-15: The stacking order in the Layers panel

16. Select the masked image and from the Effects menu choose Adjust Color ➪ Auto Levels. A copy of this file up to this point is saved in the habitat_alert_final\designfiles\Fireworks folder as ha5.png. You can save your copy as myha5.png into the `habitat_alert_start/designfiles/Fireworks` folder.

Using a Bitmap Mask

Users of other image-editing software may have a tendency to use bitmap masking first because that is how other applications handle masks. Because you do use bitmap masking at times, this section demonstrates its use, but vector masks are much more flexible after you learn to use the Pen tool. Whereas bitmap masks throw away or delete pixels forever, a vector mask masks only the pixels, and you can regain them at any time. However, bitmap masks can offer a fast solution in some cases and be the only solution if you can't handle bezier curves to make precise selections.

For a quick vignette (an image with a feathered edge), follow these steps:

1. Open `Black_Caped_Poster_Boy1.jpg` image again from the Chapter19_exercise folder.

2. Select the Oval Marquee tool, and in the Property inspector, set the Edge to Feather and a value of 40 pixels.

3. Draw an ellipse around the bird.

4. To remove the background, choose Select ➪ Inverse.

5. Press the Delete key and choose Modify ➪ Canvas ➪ Canvas Color, and make the canvas white. Figure 19-16 shows the result.

Figure 19-16: A vignette made from the bird image

Note You can achieve this same effect by using the vector Oval tool (for a vector mask) with the edge set to Feather and 40 pixels. Drag around the bird, fill with white, and Shift+select the oval and the bird, and group them as a mask.

Painting a mask

The more useful purpose of a bitmap mask is the ability to paint the mask on, which comes in handy for the Pen tool challenged users. To paint the mask, follow these steps:

1. Open the bird again. You can choose File ➪ Open Recent (or File ➪ Revert if your document is still open) and choose the image from there.

2. Select the bitmap image and in the Layers panel, click the Add Mask icon on the bottom of the panel to the right of the New/Duplicate Layer icon.

3. Zoom in close to the head area of the bird.

4. Select the bitmap Brush tool. Set the stroke to black. Set the size to 1000, Air Brush, and an Edge of 0.

5. Use the large brush to erase the background area, staying away from the edges, as shown in Figure 19-17.

6. Set the brush size to 10 and an edge of 50. Paint in as close as you can to the head without erasing detail.

7. Set the brush to size 5 and lower to paint in the fine detail (Figure 19-18). To paint fine detail, a digital tablet would be easier than a mouse. I find it easier to use a Pen tool if no tablet is available.

8. Leave this image open for the next exercise.

Figure 19-17: The background removed with a large brush

Figure 19-18: The fine detail is painted in with a white canvas added.

Saving a mask

If this were a precise or custom mask that you spent a lot of time making, you might want to save the mask for use in other images. The method presented here removes your mask, so if it's an image you want to keep, be sure you save it prior to doing this exercise. Follow these steps to save this mask:

1. Using the bird image you masked the background out of, click the mask icon in the Layers panel (black and white) and drag it below the image (or another layer). As you drag, you see a slight flicker at the edge of the layer, release then. Figure 19-19 shows the mask removed from the bird and now as a separate object.

2. To save just the mask, delete the image object. Now only the mask is left. Save this with a different filename. Figure 19-20 shows what just the mask looks like.

Figure 19-19: The mask separated from the image as a separate object in the Layers panel

Figure 19-20: The mask ready to be saved for later use

Note You can import Photoshop images with masks, and they are fully usable and editable in Fireworks.

Working with the Filters Menu

The options in the Filters menu are applied to bitmap images. If you try to use an effect from the Filters menu on a vector object, the vector is converted to a bitmap object prior to using the filter. The difference between using the Filters menu and the Effects menu is that the Effects menu uses *Live Effects*, which remain editable where the Filters menu converts everything to a bitmap and is not editable. For instance, for the Habitat Alert site we added a drop shadow to the banner rectangle using the Effects menu. This is a *Live Effect*, which can be edited. Most of the Live Effects can be applied to a bitmap and still remain editable. But as soon as you use the Filters menu there is no editability other than undo. You'll use *Live Effects* in the Expert Tutorial in this chapter.

Using the Blur filters

The Blur and More Blur tools are good for cleaning up an image. It'll erase small dust and scratches, and then you can sharpen the image again. With the Gaussian Blur, re-sharpening doesn't work very well. But the Blur and More Blur filters give you no control at all over the amount of blurring. You get what they are preset to and that's it. I find the Gaussian Blur filter to be the most useful Blur filter for larger areas or more intense blurring. You can set how much blur to add. If you use the slider to adjust the amount, you see the effect in your document. If you type in an amount, you'll have to accept the changes, press enter, or click on the slider to preview it.

Note Motion blur is also useful. It is a plug-in that comes with Eye Candy 4000LE.

Using the Sharpen filters

Similar to the Blur filters, the Sharpen and the Sharpen More filters are automatic adjustments with no choices available; even the Sharpen tool in the Tools panel gives you intensity options and more. What the sharpening filters do, especially the Unsharp Mask filter, is increase the sharpness of an image by working with contrast. The contrast is emphasized in an image based on the selections you make in the Unsharp Mask dialog box. The following options are available:

✦ **Sharpen Amount** specifies the intensity, determining the effect neighboring pixels have on one another. The Sharpen Amount is affected by the Radius and Threshold amount as well, so you may have to adjust those settings. The best settings for the Sharpen Amount are between 50% and 100%.

✦ **Pixel Radius** is similar to a feather and determines how many pixels are evaluated. The larger the number you select the more pronounced the contrast. The Pixel Radius settings range should be .5% to 1.5% of the dpi of the image.

✦ **Threshold** determines which pixels are affected. Which pixels are affected is based on the number of levels of difference in the surrounding pixels. If the number of levels is greater than the threshold, sharpening is applied based on the settings for Radius and the Sharpen Amount. The higher the Threshold number, the fewer pixels affected.

Adjusting color

This section looks briefly at each option for adjusting color, and gives instructions for some of the easier options. You use these various tools from the Filters menu or the Effects menu throughout the Fireworks section. You work with bitmaps in this section, but you can use these following functions from the Filters menu (bitmap only) or from the Effects menu (bitmap and vector).

Auto Levels

Levels adjust the tonal range of an image. If detail isn't visible, levels can often bring it out. Auto Levels is like most automatic tools, you have no control.

Brightness and Contrast

The Brightness and Contrast option is a quick way to adjust an image's appearance. After you choose Brightness and Contrast, the Brightness and Contrast dialog box opens. If you move the sliders to the left or right, you can view the changes in real-time on the canvas. When you get it the way you want, click OK.

Curves

Curves adjust tonal values like levels do, but in a different visual way. You can select a specific channel and adjust the Input and Output values just like you can in Levels. Some people prefer one method over the other. Levels show you a histogram; whereas curves show you the curve.

Hue and Saturation

Hue and Saturation is a great way to change the color of an image. Let's say you have a button you really like and would like to use it, but it's red and you need teal. All you need to do is select the object, choose Filters ➪ Adjust Color ➪ Hue and Saturation. As you move the sliders, the color changes. You can add contrast, lightness, or color. If you click the Colorize option, you can change an RGB image to a two-tone image or add color to a grayscale image. Be sure to check the Preview option so you can see the effect on the canvas as you move the sliders. When you get the color you want click OK.

Invert

The Invert filter changes each color in an object or image to its inverse on the color wheel. For example, applying Invert to a red image changes the color to light blue. To use the Invert filter, select an object, choose Filters ➪ Adjust Color ➪ Invert.

Levels

Levels are used to make tonal corrections in images. The Auto Levels option isn't a bad one to try until you learn how use the shadow points and histogram of levels.

Plug-ins

Plug-ins are third-party filters that you can use to achieve all kinds of great effects. In Chapter 21, you'll get a chance to use the ones that ship with Fireworks MX and take a look at some of my favorites.

You'll find demos of Alien Skin plug-ins on the CD.

Expert Image Composition, *by Japi Honoo*

In this tutorial you learn to combine various unrelated images to form a composition. You see how to combine bitmap and vector images in the same composition. You use a variety of techniques, such as Blend Modes, Curves, drawing tools, multiple effects, and more. When you are finished you will have a stunning work of art. This project teaches the following skills:

✦ Preparing the main image subject

✦ Adding a second image

✦ Adding a vector drawing

✦ Adding texture

✦ Adding text on a path

When designing Web pages, writing articles, or simply trying to convey a concept, you will probably turn to imaging to fully communicate your topic. The theme of the artwork in this exercise is "New Economy Assault." It fuses an image representing an assault with an image of a motherboard. In keeping with this theme, you add a vector drawing of blood, which you blend into the composition. You also add special text effects and blending modes to really change the look of the composition.

The end results of the project in this tutorial are twofold. First, it helps you learn how to take bitmap images and blend them together to present a theme. And second, it helps you learn to apply various, multiple, Live Effects. The following image shows how your image will look when you are finished.

Preparing the main image subject

Many Web sites use imaging to evoke emotions. When I found this image taken by Olaf Starorypinski (www.orsphoto.com), I was inspired to make this composition. In this exercise I show you how easy this composition was to create, but don't forget to use your imagination!

1. Open jon.png from the chapter19_exercise folder. You can use any image you like, just find one that inspires you, the size and subject is not important but the feelings it invokes are. This image sample is black and white, but if you have a colored image, convert it by choosing Command⇨Creative⇨Convert to Grayscale.

2. In the Layers panel, double-click Background and rename it **Photo**. Double-click the bitmap and name it **Jon**.

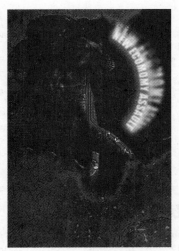

The completed project sample

Brightness and contrast added
to the image

3. The first thing you will do to the image is to add brightness. I show you two different methods and you can choose the one you prefer. Or you can try both and see the final results and then decide.

Although this is a bitmap image, you can still use the Effects list instead of the Filters menu. By using the Effects list, you can use multiple effects and turn off one or more to try different options. After you decide what you like best, you can delete the one you don't like or leave it turned off.

Click the plus sign in the Property inspector to access the Effects list, choose Adjust Color ⇨ Brightness/Contrast. Use these settings:

    ✦ Brightness: 20

    ✦ Contrast: 33

This adds stronger light to the body, particularly in the center, as shown in the following image.

4. In the Property inspector, uncheck Brightness/Contrast.

5. Click the plus sign in the Property inspector to access the Effects list. Choose Adjust Color ⇨ Curves. The following figures shows the shape of the curve and the results of adjusting the curve for the image. Apply the following settings:

    ✦ Input: 92

    ✦ Output: 168

    ✦ The lightening effect is less subtle: use the curves and leave more detail

6. In the Property inspector, uncheck Curves, and click to check Brightness/Contrast. Try this option first and toggle back and forth as you progress. You can leave both effects for now.

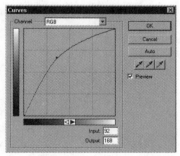

The shape of the adjusted curve

The results of adjusting the curve
for the image

Adding the second image

The second image you add is a photo of a motherboard; the color isn't important. This image was chosen for its line detail. When you are looking for images to use in a composite, look for ones that add interest, detail, and texture to your final piece. Things like the color aren't important because it is so easy to alter them.

1. In the Layers panel, click the yellow folder to add a new layer. Double-click it and name it **Motherboard**. Lock the Photo layer (click to the right of the eye icon).

2. Choose File ➪ Import and navigate to the chapter19_exerciseimages folder. Select motherboard. jpg and open it. Click the top-left corner of the canvas to place the image.

3. In the Layers panel, change the Blend Mode to Multiply and lower the Opacity to 78%.

 The Layers panel showing the Opacity and Blend Mode settings

The image with the Blend Mode changed to Multiply and Opacity lowered a bit

4. To brighten the motherboard, access the Effects list in the Property inspector and choose Adjust Color ➪ Brightness/Contrast, and use these settings:

   ✦ Brightness: –35

   ✦ Contrast: 45

5. To make the motherboard black and white, access the Effects list in the Property inspector and choose, Adjust Color ⇨ Hue/Saturation with these values:

   ✦ Hue: 0

   ✦ Saturation: –100

6. Next you need to define the lines of the motherboard more to make it more closely resemble a drawing. To do this you need to alter the curve. From the Effects list, choose Adjust Color ⇨ Curves.

You need to add two additional points to this curve. (It currently has a beginning and end in the corners.) Click two times on the line; the location doesn't matter. Leave the bottom-left point alone; then click the second point on the line and add the Input and Output values in the following list. Repeat for the third and fourth points.

   ✦ Second Point (from bottom left) — Input: 81; Output: 250

   ✦ Third Point — Input: 118; Output: 78

   ✦ Fourth Point (top right) — Input: 211; Output: 246

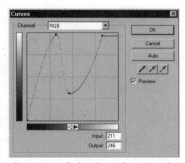

The Curve dialog box showing the new
curve with three points

The image with the contrast/brightness
and the adjusted curves

7. Lock the Motherboard layer and turn the visibility off for both Photo layer and the Motherboard layer.

Add a Vector Drawing

Since the theme of this composition is "New Economy Assault," I thought adding bit of blood would be appropriate for this design. Don't get squeamish now — it's only vectors.

1. In the Layers panel, add a new layer and name it **Blood**.

2. If you are pretty good with the Pen tool, make a shape like you here.

   If you need some assistance in making the drawing, you can use a tracing image. Choose File ➪ Import and select `tracing.jpg` from the chapter19_exercise folder. Lock this image.

The shape of the blood spots

3. Lower the opacity of the shape and with the Pen tool (be sure to have a stroke), begin to click around the shape. Click and drag for the curve areas. Deselect after the first shape, and then draw the second shape.

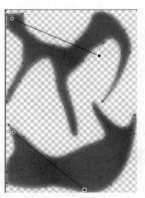

The shapes traced

4. Unlock the blood image tracing image and delete it. Your two paths should be in the Blood layer.

5. Select one of the paths. In the Property inspector, in the Stroke Category, select Pencil, 1 Pixel soft. Click in the Color well and in the Swatches box type **Hex #FF6600**. (Or you can select it. It's a shade of orange.)

6. From the Fill Category pop-up menu, select Satin. Click the color well to access the Gradient Edit window. Click the first color chip, type the Hex number **#E52700**, and press Enter/Return. Click the color chip on the right and type **#FF6500** and press Enter/Return.

7. From the Effects list, select Blur ➪ Gaussian Blur, enter a value of **4.1**, and click OK.

8. To apply the same settings to the second shape, I'll give you a shortcut. Select the object that is colored, choose Edit ➪ Copy (Control [Command] +C). Select the second shape and choose Edit ➪ Paste Attributes.

9. To get a look at what you now have, turn the visibility back on the Photo and Motherboard layers. Select the Blood layer and change the Blend Mode to Color.

The blood shape with the Blend Mode of Color applied

10. Lock the Blood layer. If you want to check your progress so far, you can compare your file to the Layers panel shown here.

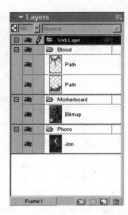

The Layers panel up through Step 10

Add Texture to the composition

Texture images always add depth and character to a composition.

1. Add a new layer and name it **Texture**. Turn the visibility off of the other layers.

2. Choose File➪Import and navigate to the chapter19_exercise folder, select texture.jpg file, and open it. Click the top-left corner of the canvas to place the image.

3. To make the texture black and white, access the Effects list in the Property inspector, and select Adjust Color ➪ Hue/Saturation. Use the following settings:

   ✦ Check Colorize

   ✦ Hue: 0

   ✦ Saturation: 0

4. To define the edges a bit more, access the Effects list again. Choose Adjust Color ➪ Brightness/Contrast and enter these values:

   ✦ Brightness: –75

   ✦ Contrast: 55

A dramatic reduction in brightness

5. In the Layers panel, lower the opacity of the Texture layer to 80%, and change the Blend Mode to Lighten. Turn the visibility back on for all layers.

Adding the title

You now add a title, which is curved to the right side of the composition.

1. Add a new layer and name it **Text**.

2. Select the Ellipse tool and draw an oval. In the Property inspector change the Width to 177 and the Height to 200. The color isn't important.

3. Select the Text tool. In the Property inspector, apply the following settings:

  ✦ Font: Impact (Arial will do as well)

  ✦ Size: 20 and Bold

  ✦ Color: white

  ✦ Kerning: 5%

  ✦ Center Alignment

  ✦ Type the words **New Economy Assault**

The composition with all the image layers complete

The text so far

4. Access the Effect list, choose Blur ➪ Gaussian Blur, and enter a value of **1**. Click OK.

5. Go to the Effect list again and choose Shadow and Glow ➪ Glow. Enter the following settings:

   ✦ Color: white

   ✦ Width: 4

   ✦ Opacity: 53%

   ✦ Softness: 9

   ✦ Offset: 0

6. Select the text and shift+select the oval. Choose Text ➪ Attach to Path. (I choose to curve the text to emulate a shield.)

The text attached to the path

7. With the text selected, choose Edit ➪ Clone and use the right arrow key on the keyboard to move the duplicate text as shown in the following figure.

8. Choose Text ➪ Convert to Paths (Control/Command+Shift+P).

The cloned text moved

9. Choose Modify ➪ Transform ➪ Distort so it looks like the following image. Double-click to accept the transformation.

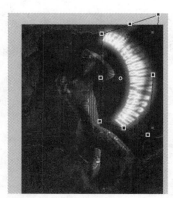

The text distorted

10. From the Effects list, choose Blur ➪ Gaussian Blur, enter a value of **2.8**, and click OK. Then choose from the Effects list, Sharpen ➪ Unsharp Mask and use these settings:

✦ Sharpen Amount: 58

✦ Pixel Radius: 4.1

✦ Threshold: 0

11. Change the Layer blend Mode to Luminosity.

Well, that's all there is to this image. Now you can see how versatile the Live Effects are and the great effects you can get using the different blend modes and masking effects.

Summary

In this chapter, you learned how to make selections and use the various bitmap editing and painting tools. You also learned how to mask an image. Although the most powerful and flexible masking is done using vector masks it was a bitmap image you masked. You also saw that bitmap masking may come in handy now and then. You also learned how to make a composite image.

Project Summary

Let's take a look at the skills you performed in this chapter that you will also use in the Habitat Alert Web site.

Files Prepared for Habitat Alert Web Site

Images	What Was Done	Where to Now?
ha4.png	You edited the circle shape and added the bird image using masking techniques and Combine Paths commands.	
ha5.png	This is the saved copy of the page that you edited in this chapter.	It is now ready for the buttons to be added and then the design can be sliced. The logo has also been inserted into this document. The logo was made in FreeHand and enhanced in Fireworks.

✦   ✦   ✦

Designing Navigational Elements

This chapter provides descriptions of several of the Web-page navigation solutions that Macromedia Fireworks MX offers: the extremely popular pop-up menus (which are easier to use than ever), navigation bars, and disjoint rollovers.

Understanding Navigation Solutions

Enabling users to navigate your Web site easily is of utmost importance when designing a site. Users get frustrated when they arrive at a page and can't figure out how to get to where they want to go. Fireworks MX offers many navigational solutions — you simply choose the best method for your Web site.

Simple rollovers — buttons with up and over states (described in more detail later) — are the most widely used type of JavaScript buttons on the Internet. Fireworks gives you several methods to create rollovers, using frames or symbols.

A *disjoint rollover*, sometimes called a *remote rollover* or a *multiple-event rollover*, is much like a simple rollover but is designed to trigger an image swap in a location other than the button itself. Each button can change this area to provide additional information to the user.

A *navigation bar* is a cohesive group of buttons with three or more "states" that are tracked. The tracked states of the buttons help the users understand where they are in the site. Navigation bars are especially useful in frames-based sites, where a single navigation page can be used in one frame to change the content in another frame.

A more sophisticated navigation system uses *pop-up menus*. Pop-Up menus, which are all the rage these days, can be made quite easily with the Fireworks MX Pop-Up Menu Wizard. However, pop-up menus involve a few technical considerations. The pop-up menu tutorial in this chapter digs into the issues and offers solutions.

Using Buttons

The following are the four different states of a button:

✦ **Up** — The default appearance of the button as first seen by the user.

✦ **Over** — The way the button looks when the user passes the mouse pointer over it. The Over state alerts users that this button is "hot," meaning that it leads to another page when clicked.

✦ **Down** — The appearance of the button after it has been clicked, which often appears as if the button has been pressed down. In Macromedia Fireworks, you can set the Down state to be active on the page the user is clicking to and designate the button as the current page (it's the default setting).

✦ **Over While Down** — The appearance of the Down state button when the mouse pointer moves over it.

The quick-and-easy way to add multiple states to a button is to use the Button Editor (which is described in the next section). The Button Editor is designed to help you make up to four different states of the same button in one location. Using it is the easiest, fastest, and most efficient way to make multiple-state buttons.

Most Web navigation buttons use JavaScript to power their interactivity. Using the Button Editor, you can build these buttons without knowledge of JavaScript. Fireworks MX generates the necessary JavaScript code for you automatically. You can choose to produce from two to four states for a button, and easily change the appearance of each state. Any button produced with the Button Editor is automatically a Symbol. When you want more than one of a button, simply drag another Instance onto the canvas from the Library.

Another important feature of the Button Editor is that when you alter the text on the Up state button, the text is automatically updated for the other states as well, eliminating the need to change the text on all four buttons.

Using the Button Editor

When you make a button using the Button Editor, the behaviors for the different states of the buttons are automatically added according to the choices you make. The JavaScript for the buttons is exported with the button.

The following are the steps involved in creating and modifying a button with the Button Editor:

1. Open the `btn_quiz.png` file.

2. Double-click the instance (a copy of a symbol) of the button. An instance is indicated by the arrow in the lower-left corner. The Button Editor opens. Figure 20-1 shows your button in the Button Editor.

   The Button Editor has several different tabs. When you click one, Fireworks gives you a description of what the corresponding state does. The Up state tab should be the active one, if it isn't, click it to open it.

   New Feature

   If you've already used Fireworks, you will notice an extra button: Import a Button. Click it. Figure 20-2 shows the Import Symbols: Buttons dialog box. These are the buttons found in the button library, which ships with Macromedia Fireworks MX. These symbols can also be accessed by choosing Edit ➪ Libraries ➪ Buttons. It is possible to add buttons you design into the Button Library later in this chapter.

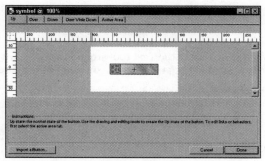

Figure 20-1: The instance of the button symbol opened for editing in the Button Editor

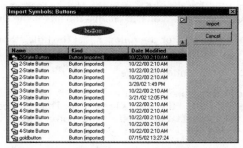

Figure 20-2: The Import Symbols dialog box for buttons

3. To center your button, select the button. Open the Align panel if it isn't already (Window ➪ Align). Click the To Canvas button. (It's orange when selected.) In the Align area click the Align horizontal center and Align vertical center icons.

Notice the button is centered under the cross (+) symbol. Buttons have registration points, which are the center of the button for alignment purposes. The cross serves as the button registration point, the point where each state of the button will be aligned.

Note When you are in the Button Editor, open the Frames panel (Frames and History panel group) and notice that four frames are present, one for each available state of your button. Now look in the Layers panel. Notice that a slice has been added to the Web layer. All this happened automatically.

To add text in the Up state:

1. Select the Text tool and type the text you want on the button. Remember that the text is fully editable and can easily be changed later.

2. Type **Home**. Use any font and size that looks good on your button. We used Lithos Regular and a size of 14 for this example.

New Feature In previous versions of Fireworks, adding text at this point would mean a new symbol would be generated every time you altered the text. Not so anymore. Enter text for one of your buttons. Add effects and color change as you desire for every state of the button.

3. Click and drag to visually align your text.

You can use the Center Text function, but be aware that the text is centered only in its text box not to the object. To center the text you can use the Pointer tool to place it visually, or you can draw a text box using the Text tool around the clear area; then type the text. Using this method, when you click the Center icon, the text is centered.

Follow these steps to alter the Over state:

1. Click the Over tab.

2. Click the Copy Up Graphic button to put a copy of the Up state in the Over state's editing box.

For any of the button states, you can import a button, draw a unique button, or drag a button from another document, instead of using the Copy Graphic Up/Over/Down button. Be sure to keep the images the same size and center for a smooth rollover.

3. Select the button and ungroup it (either use the icon in the Modify toolbar or press Shift+Control+G (Shift+Command+G)). Now you can change the fill for the Over state.

4. For this button you won't change the text for the rollover, just the little star in the square. Click the star and change the Stroke to a color of #CC0000. Regroup the button.

5. Leave the Include Nav Bar Down State option checked.

A common rollover effect is to add a stroke, glow, or a Live Effect. Be sure the button, or text if you have any, is selected so that the effects are added. The great part is that when you change the text on the symbol later, the effects are automatically applied to the new text!

To alter the Down state, follow these steps:

1. Click the Down tab.

2. Click the Copy Over Graphic button.

3. Make any changes to the appearance you require. For the Habitat Alert button we are making, use these values: choose a color of #B08B00 for the star; change the fill of the small rectangle to #CC0000.

If you want to see all the buttons at one time, click the Onion Skinning check box.

If you want to assign an Over While Down state to the button, which isn't as widely used as the other three states, click its tab, click the Copy Down Graphic button, and make your changes. No changes were made for the Habitat Alert button.

4. Click the Active Area button to see a slice added to your document automatically. The Active Area is set to Automatic by default and generates a slice large enough to cover all the button states. There is one slice for all four-button states; you can change the size of the slice by dragging the slice points.

In previous versions of Fireworks there was a Link Wizard in the Button Editor. It's been removed and you now can easily add links and alt text right into the Property inspector.

5. Click the Done button when you are finished with all the states of the button. An instance of the button is automatically placed in your document, indicated by the little arrow in the corner.

6. Save this file as btn_quiz.png. Since this image will be used in the Habitat Alert site it is being saved in the following folder: habitat_alert_final/designfiles/Fireworks.

To add more buttons to your document, drag them from the Library panel (in the Asset panel group) by clicking and dragging either the button symbol or the name of the symbol onto your document. Alternatively you can Alt+click and drag (Option+click and drag) a new copy of the instance. Figure 20-3 shows the symbol in the Library panel.

Figure 20-3: The button symbol added to the Library panel

You can easily preview your new button by clicking on the Preview tab in your document window, pass your mouse over the button and click on the button to see the different states. Figure 20-4 shows the preview tab selected and the rollover effect.

Figure 20-4: The rollover state of the image as seen in Preview

Flash MX

This button's PNG file can be imported into Flash where the text can be changed. It will maintain it's texture and the rollover effects in Flash.

Using symbols, instances, and libraries

Symbols are automatically generated when you use the Button Editor. A button symbol encapsulates up to four different button states and moves as a unit. You can convert any object into a symbol. If you have a custom button designed, you can make it into a symbol, to use over and over, as you'll see later in this chapter. There are three types of symbols in Fireworks.

✦ Graphic symbols — Basically any object you'd like to use multiple times.

✦ Button symbols — Graphics intended for use as a button with two or more states. Button symbols are generated in the Button editor, which also automatically applies a slice.

✦ Animation symbols — Contain all the frames and timing of an animation. A completed animation including links is contained in the symbol.

Symbols are editable. When you make a symbol it is stored in the Library panel (in the Assets panel group) and an instance is placed on the canvas. An instance is a copy of a symbol.

Button Facts

Buttons have some common characteristics and abilities. This is a handy list of button features.

✦ You can make a graphic or text object into a button.

✦ You can convert a graphic or a text object into a button.

✦ You can import buttons from the Button library or from others.

✦ You can make one button symbol and drag instances of that symbol from the Library.

✦ To edit a symbol you simply double-click an instance on the canvas or the Library to open the Button Editor. You can also change its properties in the Property inspector.

✦ You can edit the Text on a Button without affecting other instances of the same symbol. This also does not break the link to the original symbol. Symbol color, effects, and so on can all be edited and filter down through all instances.

✦ You can edit the URL and target without affecting other instances of the symbol.

Once you have a library of symbols, you can drag additional instances of them from the Library panel (Window ➪ Library) onto your canvas. The "child" Instance maintains a link to the "parent" Symbol. An instance is marked with a dotted box and corner arrow.

In most cases, double-clicking an instance opens the appropriate editor and changes are made globally to all instances. However, there are some techniques you can apply to an individual instance that do not affect the symbol. You may use the transform tools or alter the opacity on individual instances. You may also add effects on an instance-to-instance basis.

There are two types of libraries. The default library is generated when you first convert an object into a symbol, and it includes the symbols. The library is saved with the document. When you re-open the document, the library is available for that document only. You may easily export a set of symbols from the library for use in other documents, or even save them into the libraries that are accessible in any document in Fireworks.

The following are the steps involved in exporting symbols from the library:

1. Open the Library panel.

2. Click the down arrow to access the Library Options menu. Choose Export Symbols.

3. Select the symbols you want to export. If you want them all, choose Select All. If you want several in a row, Shift+click. For non-contiguous selections, press Control+Click (Option+Click) on the desired symbols. When you are done, click the Export button.

4. Name your library and choose where to save it, then click Save.

Tip

For libraries you think you may use often, save them or move them to the Fireworks Library folder, which is in Macromedia\Fireworks MX\Configurations\Libraries (for Windows 2000, your location may vary). By placing your file here, it can be accessed by choosing Edit ➪ Libraries submenu. Any new libraries you export into the libraries folder will be available the next time you start Fireworks.

To import a library:

1. Open the Library panel.

2. Access the Library Options menu and choose Import Symbols.

3. Locate the saved library and choose Open.

4. The Import Symbols dialog box opens with the list of symbols in the library. Choose one or more and click the Import button.

Making a button symbol

It's easy to make a button directly in the Button Editor or convert an existing button into a button symbol and edit it in the Button Editor. As stated earlier, a button symbol encapsulates up to four different button states and moves as a unit. Instead of spending lots of time reproducing similar buttons, you simply have to place a symbol onto your canvas and edit the text and link.

I find it easier to design my button first. So in this exercise you will convert a button graphic into a button symbol.

The starting and finished buttons (quiz.png, btn_quiz.png) are in the chapter20_exercise folder on the CD-ROM.

1. Navigate to the CD ROM chapter20_exercise folder and open the quiz.png file.

2. To convert this graphic into a symbol:

   a. Choose Select ⇨ Select All.

      If you don't select all the objects, only the part that is selected will be converted to a symbol.

   b. Click on Modify ⇨ Symbol ⇨ Convert to Symbol.

   c. In the Symbol Properties dialog, select Button as the Type, and click OK.

      As soon as your button is converted to a symbol, it is placed in the Library (Assets panel group).

3. You can save this file now as btn_quiz.png. Save it in the habitat_alert_start\designfiles\Fireworks folder if you copied it to your hard drive. Otherwise a copy is in the habitat_alert_final folder.

Editing button symbols

Editing the buttons you have made is quite simple. There are multiple parts of a button, which can be edited as follows.

To edit the text:

1. Select the text you want to edit.

2. In the Property inspector you can change the Text, add a Link, and enter Alt text.

   This works only if the button symbol has text on it.

To change the button characteristic:

1. Double-click to open the Button Editor.

2. Click the tab for the state or states you'd like to alter and make your changes.

3. Close the Button Editor when you are done.

Note
When you edit an original symbol, if it's been used in other documents, you can update all instances simultaneously by choosing Update from the Library pop-up menu (F11). If you try to edit an imported symbol, a warning will open telling you that an edit will break the link to the original symbol.

When you edit an instance of a button, it breaks the link with the original object, allowing you to make changes in the new document without affecting any documents containing the original symbol. To update an imported button, open the Library pop-up menu in the Library panel and choose Update.

In Fireworks MX, you can now also edit the active area, which is really the slice directly in the document. Be sure the Show Slices and Hotspots view is turned on. You can drag the red lines to the size you need.

You could still edit the Active Area via the Symbol editor but it's so much easier to do it in the document itself. This technique however will change the slice size of all instances in the document.

Tip
To change the slice of individual instances you'll need to make a copy of the symbol. In the Library panel click on the Library Options pop-up menu and click on Duplicate. You can now change the slice or any other part of the new symbol. It's no longer attached to the original however.

Adding a button to the button library

As promised, you will now learn how to add your own special buttons to the button library that ships with Fireworks MX. You can even make your own custom named libraries if you'd like.

1. Open btn_quiz.png from the chapter20_exercise folder on the CD-ROM, or use your own button.

2. You need to open the file that contains the library of button symbols that is included in Fireworks. The location of the file will depend on your operating system. Locate your Macromedia Fireworks MX program files and locate the Libraries folder (it's FireworksMX ⇨ Configurations ⇨ Libraries on Windows 2000).

   a. In this folder you'll find Buttons.png. Select it and Open.

   b. A dialog may open asking you to Change Fonts or Maintain Appearance. Click on Maintain Appearance.

   Notice in the Layers panel how each button in the library is its own object but all the buttons are in one document (Figure 20-5). Don't be intimidated by all the slices you see. You can click on the Hide Hotspots and Slices icon in the Tools panel if you'd like.

3. Select your button in the Library panel and drag an instance of the button and drop it onto the open Button Library.

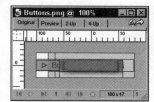 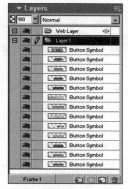

Figure 20-5: The buttons library as seen in your document and in the Layers panel

4. Center the button by using the Align panel.

   In the Library panel you'll see your button added (Figure 20-6).

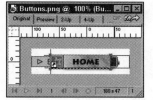

Figure 20-6: The new button added to the buttons library

5. To give the button a descriptive name, double-click the button name in the Library panel (mine said symbol) and change it. I named mine goldbutton.

6. Save the file.

Creating Interactive Images

There are a variety of behaviors you can add to an image to make it interactive. Rollovers are one of the most popular behaviors. JavaScript rollovers all work the same way: when a cursor passes over one graphic, a trigger is activated. A number of behaviors or actions can be assigned to this trigger, such as replacing the current image with another or displaying a graphic or text in another location of the Web page. The trigger is always a hotspot or a slice. Then there are other behaviors, such as disjoint rollovers, pop-up menu, bar and navigation bar behaviors, which all perform different functions.

Making a rollover image

A simple rollover is one image that is replaced (or swapped) with another image on demand. It's quite easy to build a rollover in Fireworks using the Behaviors panel. A simple rollover has an image in Frame 1, which is swapped for an image in Frame 2. In Fireworks, the button states are always on specific frames: the Up, Over, Down, and Over-Down states are Frames one through four, respectively. This section covers adding simple rollover and other behaviors using the Behavior panel instead of the Button editor. I prefer using the Button Editor for button rollovers but there are some people who prefer to use the following method.

Designing the Up and Over states of a button

This tutorial shows how to make one of the buttons for the Habitat Alert Web site. You'll build both the Up and the Over state of the button. The remaining buttons are made using the same method but altering the button size where needed.

1. Open the ha4.png file from the chapter20_exercise folder on the CD-ROM.

2. Using the Text tool, type the word **LEARN** (refer to Figure 20-7 for placement). Use a font that will fit the area. Here I used:

   • Font: Lithos Regular (an Adobe font)

   • Size: 12

   • Color: #666600

   • Range Kerning: 7

   • Anti-aliasing Level: Smooth Anti-Alias

Figure 20-7: The first button text added to the site interface

The remaining text links and positioning can be seen in Figure 20-8.

Figure 20-8: The rest of the main navigation text added to the layout

3. Open the Frames panel and click to Frame 2. This is where you will make the Over state of the text navigation.

   The rectangles around two of the links are already in place in this file to show you the effect you are going for. You'll see how to remove the bottom of each rectangle in a little bit. Each link was done the same way, then the cut rectangles edge was butted up against each other.

4. Draw a rectangle anywhere below the navigation and set its size to 60 × 20.

5. Set the fill to none and use a Basic, 1-pixel Hard stroke using #003366 for the color.

6. We only want a three-sided rectangle without a bottom for the rollover, to cut the bottom off the rectangle:

   a. With the rectangle selected, use the Knife tool to drag horizontally across the bottom of the rectangle. You want to cut off approximately 3 pixels (Figure 20-9).

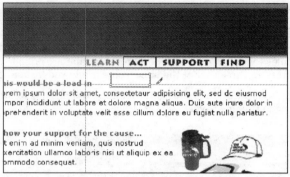

Figure 20-9: The Knife tool after it sliced the bottom of the rectangle

   b. Click on the canvas to deselect.

   c. Use the Pointer tool and select the bottom portion you sliced and delete it.

Note

   The sliced portion won't be a separate object until you deselect then reselect. Alternatively you can use the Pointer tool and Shift+click on the portion you want to keep (this deselects it) then press the delete key to remove the unwanted portion.

   d. Use the Subselection tool and Shift+click both of the bottom points of the sides and use the up or down arrow key until the height is 17.

   7. Click on Frame 1.

Adding the Swap Image behavior

You need to have a slice or a hotspot in order to attach a behavior; we'll be using slices for this exercise.

   1. In the Frames panel, click on Frame 2.

   2. Select the three-sided rectangle around the LEARN button next and click on Edit ➪ Insert ➪ Slice.

   3. Add a slice to each text link as seen in Figure 20-10.

Figure 20-10: Slices added to each text link

4. It's a good idea to give your slices unique names. To name the slice:

   a. Select the slice over the LEARN button.

   b. Type **btn_learn** in the Slice area of the Property inspector (see Figure 20-11). When naming files for export there are certain things that are not allowed such as special characters and spaces. But the underscore is allowed instead of the space.

Dreamweaver MX

If you name all the buttons with btn in the front then they will be easy to locate in a list of images as you'll see in Dreamweaver.

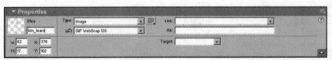

Figure 20-11: The LEARN slice is selected and given a unique name in the Property inspector.

Note

If you don't assign your own names for slices Macromedia Fireworks will do it but its naming system is a bit cryptic. You can set up your own naming system if you'd like in the HTML Setup, Document Specific dialog box (File ➪ HTML Setup).

5. Open the Behaviors panel (Window ➪ Behaviors) and click the plus (+) sign.

6. Click on Simple Rollover.

7. In the Behaviors panel you'll notice the onMouseOver Event is added. Double-click on it. A dialog box opens as seen in Figure 20-12 explaining that the Over state uses whatever you have in Frame 2.

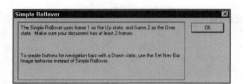

Figure 20-12: The Simple Rollover dialog box

8. Click on Preview in the document window and pass your mouse over the link to test it.

Cross-Reference

You will optimize this image and add a few more slices for a special menu that will be made in Dreamweaver in Chapter 23. You will also learn a couple of different ways to export the text navigation and the benefits of each method.

Making a disjoint rollover image

A disjoint or remote rollover allows you to trigger image replacement in one or more locations — the swapped image need not be the same as the triggering image. With a disjoint rollover, a user moves the mouse pointer over a graphic (usually a button) and may trigger a rollover in the graphic but also in a different, remote location. A group of buttons can trigger different images in the remote location. This is useful because a single area may display lots of different information depending upon which button is active. Disjoint rollovers are typically onMouseOver events. To produce the disjoint rollover, follow these steps:

1. Open the `disjointstarter.png` file from the chapter20_exercise folder on this book's CD-ROM (Figure 20-13).

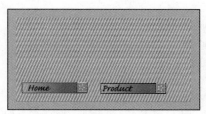

Figure 20-13: The images used in this exercise

2. Select the slice object that will trigger the remote image swap. In this exercise you will use a blue button labeled Products. This is the same version as the gold button you made earlier in the chapter, except that the fill is transparent. Notice that you can see the texture of the page behind the button. The gradient fill was added using 50% transparency for the right and left markers in the gradient edit pop-up.

Cross-Reference

See Chapter 16 to learn more about using gradient transparency.

3. This button is a symbol. Symbols automatically apply button behavior and include a slice. If you are using a static button or have built your button using the document frames, add a slice now. To add a slice, select the button's graphics (be sure to get all of them), choose Edit ➪ Insert ➪ Slice.

As the user passes the cursor over the Products button, two things will happen: the button graphics will change and an image will appear above the button.

4. To set up this behavior:

   a. Open the Frames panel, in the History and Frames panel group.

   b. Click the Frames panel options to access the menu and select Duplicate Frame. Add one frame after the current frame.

5. With Frame 2 selected go to the Layers panel and click the eye icon on for Layer 2 bitmap image. By keeping the image hidden in Frame 1 it is only visible in Frame 2. Figure 20-14 show the image added to the second frame.

Cross-Reference

Exporting the image as a GIF is discussed in Chapter 10.

Figure 20-14: An image added to the second frame for the swap image behavior

6. Select the slice tool and draw a slice to cover the area. You can see in Figure 20-15 that the slice is larger than needed.

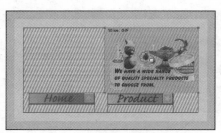

Figure 20-15: A slice added to cover the new content for Frame 2

If you have several different buttons that use the same swap area, you only need a single slice. Be sure to make the slice large enough to encompass the largest image for the area.

If you click Frame 1, you will see the empty frame; if you click Frame 2, you will see the image added.

7. Adding the behavior to make it work is easy—you will use a drag and drop method:

   a. With slices visible, click on Frame 1. Slices may be toggled on and off from the Toolbar or in the Web Layer.

   b. Select the Products button. You should see a little circle in the center and a pointing hand, which turns to a fist when you click and hold.

   c. Click, hold and drag with the fist, moving to the slice area above the remote graphics. A line is added showing the link (Figure 20-16).

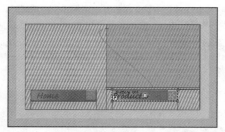

Figure 20-16: The drag and drop method being used to add the Swap Image behavior

   d. A Swap Image dialog box opens, which should default to Frame 2. To select a different image, click the More Options button, select a different image file, then click OK.

   It's possible to use an external file as well. For example, if you have graphics that have been previously exported, you may select them by browsing to their location. This is a method often used when the remote area includes animation.

e. The `Restore Image onMouseOut` option is checked by default. It's used to undo the swap when the mouse cursor moves away. If it isn't checked, check it.

f. To see that the behavior has been added, open the Behaviors panel (Window ⇨ Behaviors). Figure 20-17 shows the Swap Image behavior added.

8. To view your new disjoint rollover, click the Preview tab to enter the preview workspace. Move your mouse pointer over the button graphic. You can toggle the slices to hide them to get a better view of the graphics.

Figure 20-17: The Swap Image behavior added

Multiple Buttons using the same remote area

This is a variation of the disjoint rollover you just did. The sample design is using three separate button images. You could just as easily use buttons with rollover effects if you'd like. Below the buttons is one large slice for the remote or disjoint rollover. I've provided a starter file for you.

1. Open the `disjoint_multiple.png` file from the chapter20_exercise folder on the CD-ROM. Notice the buttons have slices already and the large empty slice below the buttons.

2. Open the Frames panel Options menu and click on Duplicate Frames. Type in or scroll to three frames after the current one.

3. Select Frame 2 and type in some text below the Home button as seen in Figure 20-18.

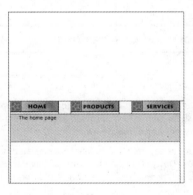

Figure 20-18: Text added below the Home button in Frame 2. This text will only be visible when the mouse cursor rolls over the Home button.

4. Repeat Step 3 for the remaining two buttons.

5. To add the behavior:

   a. Click the first button slice to select it. Use the drag and drop icon and drag it to the remote slice and release the mouse button.

   b. When the dialog box opens, choose Frame 2 if it isn't selected already.

   c. Repeat for the second button only use Frame 3 (Figure 20-19).

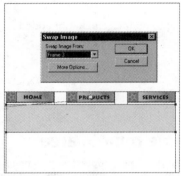

Figure 20-19: Frame 3 being used for the second buttons rollover

   d. Repeat for the third button but use Frame 4.

6. Click the Preview tab and mouse over the links.

Table 20-1 shows a list of behaviors and what they do. The behaviors all are applied in a similar manner as the rollovers.

Fireworks behaviors are compatible with Dreamweaver.

Dreamweaver MX

Table 20-1: Behaviors and Descriptions

Behavior	Description
Simple Rollover	Swaps an Image on Frame 2 with an image on Frame 2.
Swap Image Restore	This restores a swap image on another frame back to its default appearance in the relevant frame (usually Frame 1). You can change the event that triggers the behavior by specifying a mouse event.
Set Nav Bar Image	The Set Nav Bar behavior has several other behaviors associated with it. You can choose to use Nav Bar Down, Nav Bar Over, and/or Nav Bar Restore. You can choose to add these behaviors individually or add all at once using the Set Nav Bar Image behavior.
Set Pop-Up Menu	This behavior will present you dialog boxes that allow you to automatically build a pop-up menu. You attach the behavior to a slice or hotspot.
Set Text of Status Bar	This behavior is used to add text to the status bar of a browser window.

Making an Image Map

An image map is often used when it is inconvenient or difficult to slice up a graphic into individual elements. By default, only one link may be placed on an image. With an image map, you can designate several clickable "hotspots" or areas in a single image, allowing more than one link to be added to the image. You can even add behaviors to the hotspots. Hotspots are defined with drawing tools that build rectangles, ellipses, or polygon coordinates. An Image map is easily made in Macromedia Fireworks and can be copied or exported for use in HTML pages.

A common use for an image map is a navigational line across a page. Figure 20-20 shows the bar we will add hotspots to. A hotspot is the area that is "hot" when a cursor goes over it. A hotspot is an area that is clickable.

Use the following steps to create an image map in Macromedia Fireworks MX:

1. Open `imagemap.png` file from the chapter20_exercise folder (Figure 20-20).

Figure 20-20: A navigational line that will have hotspots added to it

2. Select the Rectangle Hotspot tool. If you click and hold on the corner of the tool icon you'll see that there is a Circle and a Polygon shape available as well.

When you make a Polygon shape, the shape area is the "hotspot," although it will still be sliced as a rectangle.

3. Draw a rectangle over the Home word as seen in Figure 20-21. It will have a blue overlay when the hotspot is drawn.

Figure 20-21: A hotspot is added to the word Home

4. In the Properties inspector add the link name and the Alt tag as seen in Figure 20-22.

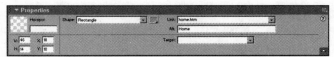

Figure 20-22: The Property inspector showing the Link and the Alt tag added

Foolproof Pop-up Menus, *by Kim Cavanaugh*

First introduced in version 4 of Fireworks, the pop-up menu feature has been one of the most popular, and troubling, new additions to Fireworks. While pop-up menus have been greatly improved in Fireworks MX, they can still present quite a challenge. Much like making a soufflé, it's easy enough to mix the ingredients together. However, once things get popped into the oven, or in this case, into your Web site, things can go wrong in a hurry if you don't have good understanding of the rules for the implementation of pop-up menus.

Before beginning to use pop-up menus then, take a look at the components that comprise them. You'll have much more success if you have a good understanding of the separate components that need to work together to make these dynamic objects function correctly.

The first component of the menu system is the graphical object where all the JavaScript behaviors are attached. Designed in Fireworks, the images are the easiest part of the recipe to put together. Simply decide on the appearance that you want and design away. Once you're ready to put the menu into the page Fireworks will use an HTML table to hold all the pieces of the image together and provide the code to attach the triggers to each image.

The second part of the pop-up menu is contained in the <head> of each document that uses the menu. This JavaScript can be quite large, and will often add 25 to 30K of file weight to your page. The JavaScript in the head controls the function of the pop-up menus and accounts for browser issues so that the menus will function in as many browsers as possible.

The third part of the menus is a small bit of script that resides in the <body> of the document and is responsible for calling, or causing an external script to function.

Finally, Fireworks will generate an external script that loads the layers themselves into the page and controls their appearance. This file, named "mm_menu.js" is the key to the appearance of your menus.

When all four of these objects are working in concert pop-up menus function exactly as expected. Most problems with the menus result from a failure to keep these objects working in the proper relationship or when changes are made with one part of the system without taking into account the effect the change has on the other components. In this tutorial you'll have the opportunity to see one method for ensuring that your menus function correctly every time and how you can plan ahead so the inevitable changes you'll need to make later on don't cause the entire menu system to fall flat.

In this tutorial you'll be designing a menu system for a fictional chamber of commerce for the equally fictional town of Poinciana Key, Florida. As with any navigation system you'll want to consider the structure of your Web site before you begin building the pages and how the different sections of the site will be linked together. When using pop-up menus in particular it's important to keep the relationship of your files and folders in mind as you build the objects. While you can use relative links to the pages in your site as will be done here, absolute links often work much better if you want to create multiple subfolders and employ templates to control the appearance of the individual pages.

With all of that in mind, let's get started.

1. In the chapter20_exercise folder on the CD-ROM, locate the file called menu_sample.png. This simple sample file has been designed to take a little of the work out of the setup of the menus and contains five buttons with slices applied to them.

    The process of building the menu objects themselves is really quite easy. Fireworks MX provides a dialog box with four tabs that allow you to set the content, appearance, advanced properties, and location of the menus:

2. To begin building your menus select the slice over the Lodging button on the far left of the canvas and then click the Behavior handle (little circle) that appears in the center of the slice. From the available options that appear select Add Pop-up Menu.

3. Once you've made this selection the Pop-up Menu Editor will launch. The Editor has four tabs at the top to allow you to set the properties of the menu objects. By default the first tab that will be active is the Content tab. This is where the text that will appear in the menu is set along with the link to the page that will open when the menu object is selected.

4. For this tutorial set the text area and links as listed below. You can also refer to the illustration below to see how they have been applied.

Abel's Motor Lodge	abels.htm
Baker's Family Motel	bakers.htm
The Green Turtle Inn	green_turtle.htm

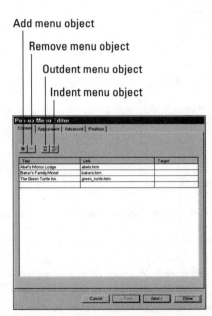

Add menu object

Remove menu object

Outdent menu object

Indent menu object

The Pop-up Menu Editor when it first opens.

5. At the bottom of the Editor locate the Next button and click it to move to the next tab, where you'll set the appearance of the menus.

Examine the contents of the Appearance tab to orient yourself to the features found. As you see there are a number of ways to set the appearance of your menu objects. The first choice to make is whether to use HTML elements in the menus or to use images. Generally speaking, since HTML will produce slightly faster page load times that type of menu is preferred. Remember that the JavaScript alone will require at least 25K of file weight and in order to get your pages to load as quickly as possible you'll want to be conservative with your menus wherever possible. However, feel free to experiment with the various settings that can be changed to affect the way your menus appear. As you make each change note that Fireworks provides a preview of how the menu will appear when the menu first appears (Up state) and how it will appear when the mouse passes over it (Over state). For the illustrations that you'll see as this tutorial progresses the menu styles have been set to HTML.

Set text appearance

Set menu type

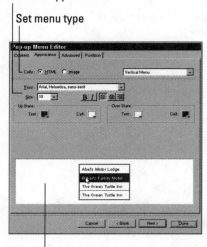

Menu Preview

The Appearance tab where you set the
font attributes, type of menu, and cell colors.

Tip

The styles that are used in the image option for the menus are the same ones that appear in the Assets panel. A great way to customize the appearance of your menus is to create and save a custom style. Once the style is saved it will become available as an option in the Pop-up Menu Editor.

6. Once you've set the appearance of your menus click the Next button again to move to the Advanced tab. You can leave these settings at their defaults for now or experiment with the ways they affect your menus.

Notice the features such as the ability to modify the amount of time that the menu appears (Menu Delay), the amount of space that surrounds your text in an HTML cell (Cell Padding), and options for setting the borders and shadows for HTML elements of a menu. Note that there are fewer options available if you choose the image setting for your menus.

Caution

Setting the Menu Delay at settings smaller than 500 will often cause menus to fail in some older versions of the Netscape browser.

7. The final tab controls the location of your menus and gives you the option to fine-tune where they will appear in relation to the slice they are attached to. For this exercise click the second button from the left so the menu will appear directly below the button and aligned to the right. Note that Fireworks MX also allows you to provide precise pixel-level control of the menus by specifying exact X and Y coordinates as well.

8. With all of your settings complete, click the Done button, save your file. Time to see how this first object appears in a live browser.

9. Select File⇨Preview in Browser (or press F12) for a preview of the navigation bar with its first menu attached.

10. If you find that you're not happy with the look of your menu simply select the slice again and choose Edit Pop-up Menu from the menu that appears when the behavior target is clicked.

Tip

Getting the menu looking the way you want with the first set of menus will save you a great deal of time later on. Since Fireworks will remember all the settings you apply as you move on to the next slice, setting your menu appearance now will let you zip through the rest of the tutorial.

Adding a menu to the additional buttons

With the first menu set, it's time to move on to the additional slices and apply the menus. Since Fireworks will remember the appearance and advanced settings you've applied, you need only enter the text, links, and set the menu's position for the remaining items.

1. Follow the guide below for setting the text and links for the additional buttons in your menu:

Restaurants

The Greenhouse	greenhouse.htm
Marker 98	marker98.htm
Angelo's Ristorante	angelos.htm

Boating

Glass Bottom Tours	glbottom.htm
Sunset Sailing	sunset.htm
Mullins' Boat Rentals	mullins.htm

Fishing

Back Country Charters	backcountry.htm
Deep Sea Adventures	deepsea.htm
Lazy Day Sportfishing	lazyday.htm

Diving

Diver Down Dive Shop	diverdown.htm
Lady Luck Dive Boat	ladyluck.htm
Coral Seas Diving	coralseas.htm

Tip

Remember to save as you work and to preview your menus often in a browser.

Now that the appearance of all the menus and the content that is to appear in each is set, it's time to move on to the actual export of the menu, and it's time to move on to the site and prepare it for their use.

To prepare for this tutorial you'll need to create a new folder on your computer as the root folder for the Web site, along with one subfolder to place the images in.

2. Choose a location on your computer's hard drive or on the desktop and create a new folder called pksite for our fictional town of Poinciana Key. Open that folder and create a subfolder called menu_images.

3. Before exporting the file one additional change needs to be made for this file. Return to Fireworks and select File ➪ HTML Setup.

4. In the dialog box that appears check the box labeled "Include HTML Comments" on the General tab. You'll see in a few minutes why this is helpful for implementing your menus.

5. With the groundwork out of the way it's now time to export the menu into the Web site. Choose File ➪ Export to open the Export dialog box.

The Export dialog box

6. Change the name of the file to **pkmenu** in the File Name field and navigate to the folder you created in the previous step. Be sure that you check the option to put the images in a subfolder and select the folder called "menu_images" as the location for all of the images.

Note

While this simple menu will not create a great number of images, it's best to always use the images subfolder option when creating pop-up menus.

7. Match your settings to those in the illustration and click the Save button to export all of your files.

8. At this point you can save your file and exit Fireworks as you move on to Dreamweaver to complete the project.

Adding the menu in Dreamweaver

1. In Dreamweaver choose Site➪New Site and define your site for this exercise.

Cross-Reference

If you are unfamiliar at this time with defining a site refer to Chapter 32 in the Dreamweaver section.

2. Set the name of the site as Poinciana Key and navigate to the pksite folder you created previously and set it as the root folder.

3. Once Dreamweaver completes the survey of your site's files, open the Site panel and review the files that were created when your menus were exported.

Your site files should match those you see in the Site panel illustration. Note that in addition to the HTML file that was created and the image files, the all-important file called "mm_menu.js" has also been placed into the root folder.

Site panel showing the files within the defined site of Poinciana Key

Of course this site has no real Web pages in it as of yet, so your first job is to create new files that match the filenames that were set in Fireworks.

4. Start by setting a home page for this site by right-clicking the root folder at the top of the site structure and choosing New File from the context menu. Name this file index.htm.

Once your home page is established, refer back to the filenames that you assigned in Fireworks and create a new file for each page, keeping all of the files in the root folder.

This tutorial uses a flat site structure where all of the pages are contained in the root folder. While you can use a more traditional site structure where individual pages are contained in subfolders of the site, the only practical way to link to your files in that situation is to use absolute URLs.

The four components of the pop-up menu

You'll recall from the introduction to this tutorial that there are four components that must be taken into account when using the pop-up menu feature:

✦ JavaScript in the head of the document

✦ Graphical images

✦ The call to load the JavaScript

✦ The external file called mm_menu.js that controls the appearance of the menus

The next steps you'll take will use each of these components to ensure that your navigation system works every time and is easy to upgrade and change as the needs of your site grow.

1. Double-click the file called pkmenu.htm in the Site panel.

This will open the HTML file that was created when you exported the menu file from Fireworks. All of the components you'll need for your menus are in this file.

The graphical objects are contained in a table that Fireworks created and can be converted to a Library item for re-use. While this Library item won't contain any JavaScript, it's useful to convert it so that any changes that only affect the appearance of your menus can be easily updated.

2. Click the edge of the table so the re-size handles appear and the table is listed in the Property inspector as a Fireworks Table.

3. Once the table containing the buttons is selected, select Modify ➪ Library ➪ Add Object to Library.

4. Name the new Library item "menu bar." Leave this file open as you move to the next step. The next object to create is a template file where you'll complete your final assembly of the menu and define the structure of your pages.

5. Choose File ➪ New and in the New File dialog box choose Template as the category and set the file to be an HTML Template.

6. Click the Create button to generate your template.

7. Choose File➪Save to save the template and name it PK Main. You can ignore the warning about the lack of editable regions.

Since you'll want to see things actually happening, set up the template file with some simple tables to insert the content for the site as well as the menus.

8. Insert a single table with 2 rows and 1 column at the top of the template page, followed by a second table with 1 column and 1 row below it.

9. Select the second table and right-click the table and choose Templates ➪ New Editable region. Name this editable region "Content".

In the example you see in the template illustration shows that an image placeholder has also been added at the top of the template for a banner.

Banner (468 x 60)

Content

The template file showing the area that the pop-up menu will be added to

10. Save the template file when you are done. The menu will be added in the area below the banner.

11. To put the graphical objects into the template, all you need to do at this point is drag the Menu Bar library item from the Library into the cell below the banner placeholder.

12. Set the alignment of the cell to Center by selecting that option in the Horizontal alignment field of the Property Inspector. That's one object down and three more to go.

13. Return to the pkmenu.htm file and switch to Code View or Split Code view and locate this bit of script that is located in the body of the document:

```
<script language="JavaScript1.2">mmLoadMenus();</script>
```

14. Copy the script and return to the template and switch to Code view. Paste the script in the first open line after the opening body tag. When you are finished the section of your page where the body tag begins should look like this:

```
<body>
<script language="JavaScript1.2">mmLoadMenus();</script>
<table width="95%" border="0">
```

It is important to place this script directly after the opening body tag to ensure the menus function correctly in Macintosh browsers.

15. Back to the pkmenu.htm file for one more copy and paste routine. This time the script you need is in the head of the document. If you chose the option to use HTML comments previously you'll find the script easily enough. The key here is to capture all of the script beginning with this section:

```
<script language="JavaScript">
<!--
function mmLoadMenus() {
     if (window.mm_menu_0726104544_0) return;
```

and concluding with this section:

```
     //-->
</script>
<script language="JavaScript1.2" src="mm_menu.js"></script>
```

16. Copy the entire section and return to the template file.

Do not copy the comment when completing this action. It is there only as a marker to let you know where to begin copying. In fact, attempting to copy and paste the comment will cause the operation to fail.

17. As you'd expect the goal is to paste the JavaScript into the head of the template file. Locate the closing head tag, move one line above it, and paste the script into place. That's three objects, and now for the final component.

In order to test your template, or to allow any menus in subfolders of your site to function correctly, you must place a copy of the mm_menu.js file into the folder where the pages are located.

18. In the Site panel, right-click the mm_menu.js file and select Copy from the context menu. Right-click the Templates folder and choose Paste.

19. Save your template and preview in a browser. With all of the steps completed your template will preview and you'll be ready to apply it to the pages in your site.

20. You can finish up by opening the pages in your site and choosing Modify ⇨ Template ⇨ Apply Template to Page. As the template is applied to each page you'll be able to preview in a browser and see that the menus are functioning correctly. Finally! Mission accomplished!

While the method demonstrated here may seem incredibly laborious, it is one that is proven to work every time and to be easy to update as the needs of your site change. By following this method you'll also avoid some problem areas that are known to crop up from time to time when using pop-up menus.

In order to apply changes, you would essentially repeat the process. Note that it is not recommended that the file be edited from Dreamweaver. In brief, the correct method for making changes is as follows:

1. Open the source Fireworks PNG file and modify as necessary.

2. Re-export the file to the same folder in your site and overwrite all files.

3. Delete the existing Library item, taking careful note of the item's name.

4. Open the Fireworks HTML file and select the table containing the graphical objects.

5. Convert the table to a Library item, using the same name as you had previously assigned. Update the library items in the site.

6. Open the template file and delete the script in the head of the document.

7. Copy and paste the script from the Fireworks HTML file into the template.

8. Replace all instances of the mm_menu.js file that you've copied into your site structure.

9. Update all files created from the menu.

Thus, Fireworks pop-up menus are create by an incredibly sophisticated bit of technology that is deceptively easy to use. While building the menus is easy enough, there are so many quirks and strange turns that can happen along the way to implementing them that it is best to take a methodical approach to their use. In this tutorial you have seen one method for ensuring that your menus will function correctly and that the inevitable changes you'll need to make as your site's needs change will be easy to implement.

Summary

In this chapter you learned how to utilize the power of symbols, instances, and libraries, including how to add your buttons to a library and even make your own custom libraries. Then you discovered the great tool, the Button Editor, which automatically, adds frames, a slice, and code to your buttons. On top of all this you saw how to make several different types of navigational elements by using Macromedia Fireworks behaviors. In brief, we've covered the following:

✦ Symbols, instances, and libraries

✦ Using the Button Editor

✦ Making custom libraries

✦ Making a simple rollover and disjoint rollover

✦ Making a navigation bar

Project Summary

The following tables outline what you've done in this chapter that will be used in the Habitat Alert Web site. Some of the images will need further work in another section or will be ready to use in another application.

Files Prepared for Habitat Alert Web Site

Images	What Was Done	Where to Now?
quiz_btn	You learned how to make the different states of a button using the Button Editor.	This button is ready to use in Dreamweaver or Flash. It's going to be imported into Flash for use in a quiz interface.
btn_learn	You added this text image including an Over state.	This will be optimized and exported in Chapter 23. They will be inserted in Dreamweaver a couple of different ways.

✦   ✦   ✦

Automating Your Workflow

Designers spend many hours developing the graphics and layout of a Web site. Whether you are building the entire site in Fireworks as a mockup or just the graphics you'll love the automation feature available to you. There comes a time when Web sites must be updated, whether it's a color change, text change, or links have changed. You'll find that what could be a very time-consuming task can be done easily in Fireworks primarily because of the editability features of Fireworks. You'll find several ways in which to make repetitious jobs easier and quicker by using a batch process or making commands out of frequently used steps. You can also speed up tedious jobs, such as changing text, colors, or links, by using the Find and Replace feature.

Using Find and Replace

The Find and Replace feature in Fireworks can save you from a lot repetitious tasks when you need to make changes to an image, document, or even a file. To access the Find and Replace panel, choose Edit ⇨ Find and Replace (Figure 21-1).

In the first field you choose what to search. You have the following options:

+ Search Document
+ Search Selection
+ Search Frame
+ Search Project Log
+ Search Files

The second field drop-down menu contains the options for the type of searches you can make. Each option lists additional choices to narrow down the specific search. The options are as follows:

+ Find Text
+ Find Font
+ Find Color
+ Find URL
+ Find Non-Web216

Figure 21-1: The Find and Replace panel

Using the Project Log Panel

The Project Log panel is in the same panel group as Find and Replace panel. After you perform a Find and Replace, the action is recorded in the Project log. It shows the filename, the frame, or layer with the date and time of the modification. You can double-click the filename in the Project Log to check the file.

Some of the other functions of the Project Log include:

✦ Export Again, which repeats the last export overwriting the previous one

✦ Add files to Log, which you use to navigate to and select the files you want to add

✦ Clear Selection, which removes the selected listings in the log

✦ Clear All, which removes all entries

The files in the Project Log can be used in a batch process. To print a copy of the log, open the `Project_Log.htm` file located in the First Run folder of the Fireworks MX application folder. Choose File ➪ Print from the browser window.

Fireworks Commands

Commands are recordings of what you do in your canvas. These actions or steps are recorded in the History panel, which is in the Assets panel group. To make your own commands, follow these steps:

1. Perform the steps involved in a task that you think you might want to repeat again in another document or to another object.

2. Open the History panel.

3. Select the last step in the History list. (This step contains all the previous ones.)

4. Click the down arrow to access the History options pop-up menu, choose Save as Command, and name your new command.

Note

Sometimes the last step in the History doesn't work as a command. If you save as a command and it doesn't work, try again by Shift+selecting all the steps and saving again. Be sure to test your command.

That is all there is to making a simple command in Fireworks. The History panel shows the steps or actions you've taken; if anything is below the line in the History panel it probably will not record properly. You may need to repeat some steps or perform an action in a different way to be able to record it and save it as a command. Commands can include other commands. For instance, you can run a command, perform a few more actions, and save all the steps, including running the command, as a new command.

Creating a Command to Add a Border to Bitmapped Images

In this section, you make a command that adds a 2-pixel border around bitmap images. These images are full documents and have to have extra canvas to accommodate a border. To make this command, follow these steps:

1. Open `flowers1.tiff` from the chapter21_exercise folder.

2. In the Property inspector, from the Effects menu choose Shadow and Glow ⇨ Glow.

3. Use these settings:

   - Width: 2
   - Color: Black
   - Opacity: 100%
   - Softness: 0
   - Offset: 0

4. Choose Modify ⇨ Canvas ⇨ Fit Canvas, which expands the canvas by two extra pixels all the way around.

5. Open the History panel in the Frames and History panel group (Figure 21-2).

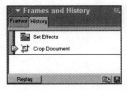

Figure 21-2: The actions performed on this document. The Fit Canvas command is actually a crop action.

6. In the History panel, Shift+select both actions.

7. From the History Options pop-up menu, choose Save Command.

8. Name the command **2pxborder** and click OK. The command is instantly available in the Commands menu. You use this command in a batch process later in this chapter.

9. Close the image without saving it.

Extending Fireworks

You can also make commands by writing your own JavaScript. The major functions in Fireworks are JavaScript-based; therefore they can be changed according to the way you work if you can write JavaScript code. This topic is beyond the scope of this book, but you can find out more about writing your own JavaScript commands at the Macromedia Web site (www.macromedia.com/support/fireworks/extensibility.html).

Support for extending Fireworks has been sparse up until now. Fireworks MX enables developers to use an SWF interface for Fireworks extensibility. You'll see several of the new commands made with this method in the Commands folder. The Arrowheads, Image Fader, and Nav Bar Builder are just a few. Also the Align panel is made this way. If you are interested in writing extensions for Fireworks, go to www.macromedia.com/support/fireworks/extensibility.html.

Using a Batch Process

A lot of tasks required to develop a Web site are repetitive and tedious. You can automate some of those tasks using a batch process. You can use a batch process for setting optimization settings, for sizing or resizing images, and even for running commands in conjunction with other batch functions.

To run a batch process, follow these steps:

1. Select File ➪ Batch Process. You do not need to have a document open to use batch process.

2. The Batch dialog box opens. Navigate to the batch folder inside the Chapter 21 folder. You won't see any files listed because they aren't PNGs.

3. In the Files of Type field, choose All Files. The list of files appears.

4. Figure 21-3 shows the Batch Process dialog box with All Files selected. You can select an image and click Add. You want all the images, so click Add All. Notice the filenames are all in the blank white area under the file types. You can also choose to add files from a project log or ones that are open as well.

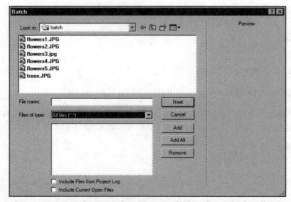

Figure 21-3: The Batch process dialog box with All Files showing

5. Click the Next button. Figure 21-4 shows the Batch options available.

Figure 21-4: The Batch options that are available

6. Select Export and click the Add button. The Export settings field becomes available. Choose JPEG smaller file. If you wanted to customize the settings, click the Edit button.

7. You aren't going to scale, but click the drop-down menu and check the options. You can scale to a specific size, area, or percentage.

8. To run the 2px border command in the batch process, click the plus sign next to commands and select 2pxborder. (It's available only if you made it in the exercise earlier in this chapter.)

9. Click the Add button.

10. After you finish setting the batch options, click Next.

11. This dialog box lets you pick how and where to save the processed files. The options are as follows:

    • Save in the same location as the originals. (If you do, a new folder is generated.)

    • Choose Custom location, which you can then browse to select.

    • Backups, if selected, give you the options of overwriting existing or making incremental backups.

    • Save Script enables you to save the batch configuration you just set up.

12. If you copied the files from the CD to your hard drive, you can choose same location; otherwise browse to a new folder. When your selections are made, click Batch. You'll see a progress window. When it's complete, click OK.

13. Open the flower1.jpg from the location in which you saved it to check out the changes. It is now a JPEG image with a black border.

Creating Commands in Fireworks, by Stephen Grosvenor

With the release of Fireworks MX and with the plethora of new features within Flash MX, extensibility is about to become a hot topic within the Fireworks community.

Because of the ability to write commands in Fireworks, users of all skill levels can share time-saving scripts, interesting effects, and tricks with the rest of the community . This tutorial will show you how to get your ideas in motion, how to plan the process flow of your command, how to design, and how to create Fireworks MX commands.

What's the main work involved in designing interface, layouts, Web sites, or just interesting designs? Repetition, pure and simple repetition of mundane or step-orientated tasks. These tasks suppress creative flow and take a lot of the time away from the design process. Many tasks in Fireworks MX consist of three or more steps. These tasks can be easily converted to commands that help relieve the monotony of those procedures, and free up more of your time for creative design. Fireworks MX, with the help of Macromedia Flash MX, makes this possible.

This tutorial guides you through the basic process of creating a user-based command. The command created here is an SWF file, exported from Macromedia Flash MX. The steps to design a command — create the script, design the interface in Macromedia Flash MX, test for bugs, install in Fireworks MX — may involve some investment of time, but the long-term rewards will make the effort worthwhile.

Understanding Fireworks MX commands

A command in Fireworks MX is essentially a script. A script tells Fireworks MX to carry out a particular action or series of actions. Flash-based Fireworks MX commands are essentially these scripts wrapped in a Flash file for ease of use or when user input is required.

Nearly every action you take in Fireworks MX — from moving an object on the canvas to creating button symbols — is powered by Fireworks MX scripting. You have access to this script and it can be manipulated in Macromedia Flash MX to design forms for receiving user input and creating instructions for Fireworks MX to carry out. While creating the architecture and designing the commands, you are simply harnessing the scripting capabilities of Fireworks MX and the scripts that it produces as you work.

The ability to create these kinds of commands comes under the general heading of extensibility. More background information about extensibility in Fireworks MX can be found in Extending Fireworks MX, available in PDF format from Macromedia (www.macromedia.com/support/fireworks/extensibility.html). This documentation can help you understand the scripting concept and the Fireworks MX Application Program Interface (API) routines, as well as guide you in the development of more complex commands.

Creating the command: Back to basics

Now you can turn to the basic steps involved in the command-creation process. Like most process-based activities, creating a Fireworks MX SWF file command requires careful planning and investigation prior to starting to draft the command, interface, and code requirements.

Define the purpose of the command

All user-input commands start with a goal and then go through an initial planning stage. This is actually the most important part of the process, and after you finish with that, you're practically finished.

One of the most important parts of creating a user-input command for Fireworks MX is to distill in your mind the purpose of the command. Most of the goals for commands I create are usually spawned from a direct requirement to carry out a task, which would fall into the following categories:

✦ The process takes a long time to complete manually.

✦ The process consists of many tedious steps.

More often than not, you can consolidate several laborious steps into one simple command; if those steps are actions you perform on a daily basis, you end up saving a considerable amount of time.

In this tutorial, the command's goal is to take a single object on the canvas, and duplicate it many times in a random fashion within your active canvas. This command would be useful if you needed to bring an unordered and random factor into your design. Having to place copies 20 or 30 times manually into the canvas by copying, pasting and creating a random placement of your objects would take a long time. Therefore this command fits into the "tedious" category: It carries out a mundane task quickly and effectively enabling you to get on with other parts of the design

The following figure shows a glimpse of the command and what you end up with after you have created it.

The interface of the command that you will create with this tutorial

Note

For a sneak preview, locate the `randomizer.mxp` file in the `chapter21_exercise` folder on the CD-ROM. Double-click the file to launch the Extension Manager and follow the instructions for Fireworks MX installation. To test it, open a document in Fireworks, place and select an object on the canvas, and choose Commands ➪ Randomizer. Click the button with a check mark. You see the object that you selected on the canvas duplicated many times within the canvas. Reapplying the command a subsequent time on the same object yields differing results, as the command is set to use random values.

Process flow for developing your first command

After you know specifically what you want your command to accomplish, you create a "process-flow" or requirements list. You'll want to identify the goal, the interface components within the command (such as menus, buttons, sliders, dials, text areas and so forth), and the scripts that the command needs to communicate with Fireworks MX. Because a picture is worth a thousand words, the following figure shows a process diagram for the implementation of this command:

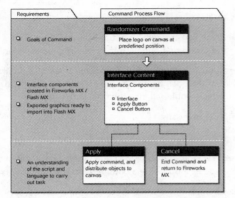

Process Flow for creating the Randomizer command

The following table shows the steps involved for a command and then the implementation.

Steps for command	Implementation for this command
Set goal	Place a selected object onto the canvas multiple times in random positions
	Determine user interface components needed (some may be created in Flash MX, others in Fireworks MX and imported into Flash MX)
	General background
Apply button	
Cancel button	
Identify script and language needed to carry out task in Fireworks MX	Apply command to execute code and duplicate selected object multiple times within the active document
Cancel to end command and return to Fireworks MX	

Following the review of the process flow for your command, you may need to reconsider certain aspects of the command, such as the interface, number of controls required, code requirements, or other facets required for a successful and usable command.

Important points for Fireworks MX command creation

Never underestimate the power of the interface and how it can affect the users experience when using your command. The larger the group of people you intend to distribute the command to, the greater the degree of usability testing required, and more thought required in the planning phases of the command's life cycle. On the other hand, if you are distributing to a small team of internal graphic designers, and the command doesn't go outside of the company, less stringent usability testing is required.

The following simple rules will help you when creating commands for distribution to groups of users:

✦ **Keep it simple** — Don't confuse users with a barrage of hidden or cryptic menus. Present them with the options they will need to execute the command. successfully.

✦ **Keep it clean** — Don't over clutter the interface with several complicated menus. This will confuse users. If you have suboptions that can be used for your command, place them in an options-type menu that can be accessed when and if the optional items are needed. A clean interface invites the users' curiosity and they'll be more likely to explore its possibilities and have a better user experience.

✦ **Keep it focused** — Make the command easy to use, as well as useful.

Prior to embarking on getting your hands dirty with the code, and testing functionality within Fireworks MX, you should create a composition of how the interface will look. Include all the options that you need displayed and available to the user. If you place too many options on the screen, and it looks too busy, attempt to tuck these options away in quick and easily accessible option menus.

The Fireworks MX History panel

While you are actively carrying out functions in Fireworks MX, Fireworks MX is tracking your actions and recording them in the History panel.

These actions that are recorded in the History panel are scripts or series of nested scripts telling Fireworks MX what it is supposed to be doing. You can use these recorded actions as the building blocks for creating your commands.

Effective use of the History panel

If you're wondering where you will get ideas for your command's scripts, the History panel is a best place to start.

Whilst you are carrying out actions within Fireworks MX, try to watch the History Panel. We will be using the History Panel within this tutorial to review scripts involved in placing objects into the canvas and moving them around.

Follow these steps to access the scripts within the History panel for the actions you are about to carry out:

1. Create a new document.

2. Create a vector object (either rectangle or circle) within your active canvas. Move the object to another point on the canvas.

   Examining the History panel, you can see that the History panel has two entries: the Rectangle tool and Move entry will form the building blocks for the command you create (see the following figure).

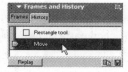
Examining the History panel for building blocks for your command

   Even though you have just created a vector object on the canvas, you are not interested in this entry within the History panel, because the command you will create is involved in moving objects around the canvas in a random fashion.

3. Select the Move entry on the History panel. Then click the Options pop-up menu at the top of the panel. In the pop-up menu, select Copy Steps (see the following figure).

Copying steps from the History panel

4. Now you can paste the Fireworks scripts and API calls into a text editor. After pasting the step into NotePad (Windows) or BBEdit (Macintosh), you see the nude script that is used to interface with Fireworks MX.

5. Save this file and name it **randomizer_basic.txt.**

Tip

Keep an eye on the History panel for potential useful commands. Copy the steps and keep the text files in a library or series of libraries. You'll always be able to see the complete steps traced out in Fireworks MX.

Getting down and dirty with the exported scripts

Examining the script yields important information about its function, and how it can be modified to create a useful command within Flash MX.

For example, the following script is moving your selection by specific x and y coordinates across the canvas. If you were to just use this script on an object on your canvas, it would move it to X:32 and y:1. You obviously don't want to do this, because you want to introduce a random factor into the equation.

```
fw.getDocumentDOM().moveSelectionBy({x:32, y:1}, false, false);
```

Also, you need to be able to copy the selection, paste it, and apply random movement to it. With this in mind, you need to return to Fireworks MX, and the vector object you just created and moved on the canvas in previous steps. then you need another snippet of script:

1. Select the vector object previously created within the active document

2. Press Control+X (Option+X) to cut the object from the canvas. Press Control+V (Option+V) to paste it back to the canvas.

3. Within the History panel, select the cut and paste steps, and repeat Steps 3 and 4 from the previous exercise (see the following figure).

4. Save the file as **randomizer_additional.txt.**

Copying additional copy and paste steps from the history panel

This may seem like a pointless exercise, but what it is actually doing is cutting and pasting the object and propagating the History panel with the necessary scripts to aid in your command-creation process.

Armed with this script analysis, you can move on to the next stage in the design of your SWF command: Macromedia Flash MX. There you create the interface and assign the scripts.

What you now have are the building blocks to your command: the scripts exported from the Fireworks MX History panel. You need to create a functional script that will run from within a Flash MX command.

Chapter 24 begins the Flash portion of this book. If you are unfamiliar with using Flash you may want to get comfortable with it before continuing the next portion of this tutorial.

Stitching the command together in Flash MX

You assembled the necessary scripts from Fireworks MX and created a process flow for the command. Now you need to create the Flash MX command using your building blocks.

Create the interface within Flash MX

To start, launch Macromedia Flash MX. Then open the `Randomizer_Start.fla` file (located in the FLA folder in the downloadable tutorial files).

The premade items in this tutorial file act as the basics for creating the command. Of course, when you create your own custom commands, you will have your own images, buttons, and resources already created for the command.

Setting the scene in Flash MX

Within the file you just opened, you will see a blank canvas with only the non-interactive elements of the command (the logo). You need to build the interface, adding design and functional elements. after the user interaction elements are added, you can assign the scripts to those elements (see the following figure).

The empty interface of randomizer_start.fla within Flash MX

Setting up the Apply button

At this point in the creation process, the only things that you need to add to the interface are the Apply and Cancel buttons. To further enhance the command, you could add sliders, dials, and other interface components:

1. In the main Timeline, select the Elements layer.

2. The Apply and Cancel buttons are within the Library, choose Window ➪ Library to open the Library panel.

3. Double-click the Buttons folder in the Library to open it. Drag the button named Apply onto the Stage, and place to your liking (see the following figure).

Adding the Apply button from the Library panel in Flash MX to the active Stage

4. Click the Apply button to select it.

5. In the Instance Name text box on the Property inspector, name the instance of the button **apply**.

To preserve the original tutorial file, rename this FLA file as **your working copy** and save your file to another folder.

6. Press F9 to open the Actions panel.

7. As you are using a button you need to add triggers to capture the execution of the command. The event handler in this instance is the release of the mouse button. On the Actions panel, click the View options button, and select Expert Mode. Add the following code in the Actions panel:

```
on (release) {

}
```

This code forms the basis for the button trigger, and your specific code goes in between the two curly brackets to create the behaviour for the command (see the following figure). You carry out the same function later in the tutorial for the Cancel button.

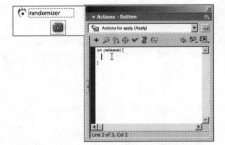

Adding the ActionScript to the Apply button

Adding Fireworks MX functionality to the button

To add functionality to the button, you need to add Fireworks MX API routines into the ActionScript, including all necessary parameters. As an example of this, the Fireworks MX API call is the following:

```
moveSelectionBy({x:100, y:100}, false, false);
```

This script tells Fireworks to move the currently selected item by 100 pixels along the x axis and 100 pixels along the y axis. You can replace these numbers with parameters to suit your needs. To produce a truly random effect, these need to be replaced by random values. What you are now going to do is to add certain API calls to your Flash MX movie.

To make this a dynamic effect, you need to be able to apply the effect across the whole of the canvas, whatever the width and height of the canvas. To do this, you need to retrieve the width and height of the current document. In the Actions panel, you can add a Fireworks MX API call to retrieve that information. This particular API call cannot be retrieved via the History panel, but is available from the Extending Fireworks MX documentation available from the Macromedia Web site. The first line of the following code is a JavaScript-compliant comment that contains information about what the line(s) of code below it are created to do. Always try to comment your code, so you can quickly understand what its doing when you may come back to it.

```
// Get the width and height of the current document
    docWidth = MMExecute("fw.getDocumentDOM().width;");
    docHeight = MMExecute("fw.getDocumentDOM().height;");
```

The second and third lines are Fireworks MX API calls, which are nested within a container which is then passed to Fireworks MX for execution.

You could translate this code to read like this:

```
MMExecute("...Fireworks MX API routine and parameters...");
```

The nested API call is as follows:

```
fw.getDocumentDOM().height;
```

This retrieves the height (in this example) of the current document, whereas the previous line retrieves the width of the document. Both are assigned to variables within the *Apply* button for later use.

You now need to create a number of iterations of the selected object on the canvas that you want to apply the effect. The following code snippet sits below the code you just entered within the Actions panel.

```
//The two Parameters below are used to create an array of objects
    //X Iterations
    xNumber = num=Math.ceil(Math.random()*15);
    //Y Iterations
    yNumber = num=Math.ceil(Math.random()*15);
```

This produces a random number (rounded up) between 1 and 15 for both variables xNumber and yNumber, so it will produce a random number of duplicates across and down within the active canvas. Using the hard-coded value of 15 here produces between 2 and 225 random objects on the canvas later in the tutorial. The number here does not have to be 15, it is used to illustrate the command within Fireworks MX. The following figure shows the code in the Actions panel.

Note

You have hard coded the values here to produce a random number of objects. You could also have user input controls, such as text boxes, dials, or sliders, to control these values.

Adding the ActionScript to the Apply button to get the document height and width, and to assign random values to variables

So far you have retrieved the active document's width and height, assigned these to variables, and assigned two random numbers between 1 and 15 for the number of times the command is to be repeated.

You now need to begin the process of duplicating the selected object on the canvas and moving to a new position. This can be simplified in the following steps.

1. Cut selected object from canvas.

2. Start a loop based on number of Y iterations and create random values for X and Y placement of objects based on document width and height.

3. Start a loop based on number of X Iterations. Create random values for X and Y placement of objects based on document width and height.

4. Paste your selection.

5. Move your selection to random position.

6. Close the X loop.

7. Close the Y loop.

8. Write an End command and return focus to Fireworks MX.

9. With the Apply button still selected, paste the following line of code that you exported earlier from the History panel below your last line of code within the on (release) event trigger to cut the selected object from the canvas, noting how you encapsulate it within the container MMExecute(""); to pass the information to the Fireworks API.

```
//Cut the selected object
    MMExecute("fw.getDocumentDOM().clipCut();");
```

Next you need to create a nested loop that takes the variables assigned earlier and creates between 1 and 15 objects on the x axis and between 1 and 15 objects on the y axis.

First create the y loop. With the Apply button selected, and beneath the last line of code added in Step 4 within the Actions panel, add the following code:

```
for (y=0; y<yNumber; y++) {

}
```

This code tells what is encapsulated between the curly brackets { } to be executed while y is less than yNumber (the random number you created earlier). Every time you step through the loop, the variable y is incremented by 1 by the command y++.

Now add the following code into the mix, to create the x loop within the existing y loop (see the following figure):

```
for (x=0; x<xNumber; x++) {

}
```

You should end up with the following nested loop:

```
for (y=0; y<yNumber; y++) {
    for (x=0; x<xNumber; x++) {

    }
}
```

Adding the ActionScript to the Apply button to create
a nested loop based on random variables

The reason for creating a nested loop, is that the number of x and y iterations of duplication will usually be and both loops will need to be able to carry out the actions and FW API calls contained within.

Now that the basics of the loop are constructed, you need to create variables to hold the position of the object and deine where to place it on the canvas. To do this, you will assign a random value based on the document width and height to work out the relative x and y positions for the object. The setting of these random values needs to be recreated every time the loop is parsed so that they are unique values.

Within the first curly bracket of the y loop, add the following code:

```
//Create random placement within Y loop for X and Y co-ordinates to
place objects
    xPlacement = num=Math.ceil(Math.random()*docWidth);
    yPlacement = num=Math.ceil(Math.random()*docHeight);
```

This code creates a value from 1 to your maximum document height or width for x and y values. Later you use these new variables (xPlacement, yPlacement) to randomly move your object on the canvas.

Repeat adding this code within the opening curly bracket of the x loop, renaming the comment accordingly to reflect which loop it is for (see the following figure).

```
▼ Actions - Button
  Actions for apply (Apply)
  + ⋄ ⊕ ⊕ ∨ ≡ ⊕                                                    ⋄ 82. ⊡.
  12    //Start Looping
  13    for (y=0; y<yNumber; y++) {
  14        //Create random placement within Y loop for X and Y co-ordinates to place objects
  15        xPlacement = num=Math.ceil(Math.random()*docWidth);
  16        yPlacement = num=Math.ceil(Math.random()*docHeight);
  17        for (x=0; x<xNumber; x++) {
  18            //Create random placement within X loop for X and Y co-ordinates to place objects
  19            xPlacement = num=Math.ceil(Math.random()*docWidth);
  20            yPlacement = num=Math.ceil(Math.random()*docHeight);        I
  Line 20 of 28, Col 47
```

Adding the ActionScript to the Apply button to dynamically assign random
values to the variables xPlacement and yPlacement

Add the following line to the Actions panel just below the code you added earlier for the x loop.
This code pastes your object to the active canvas:

```
MMExecute("fw.getDocumentDOM().clipPaste('ask user', 'vector');");
```

Now that you have pasted the object to the canvas, you need to move it based on the random x and
y parameters you create within the x and y loops. Add the following code below the line you added
above.

```
MMExecute("fw.getDocumentDOM().moveSelectionBy({x:"+(xPlacement)+",
y:"+(yPlacement)+"}, false, false);");
```

This is essentially the script that you exported from the History panel earlier, but with the random
values from the x and y loops.

Your command is nearly complete. All that remains for the Apply button is to insert the close the
command, as follows:

```
// End command and release system resources
FWEndCommand(true, "");
```

This line of code occurs at the end of the code stream and returns the user to the active document
after executing the command. The following figure shows the final ActionScript for the Randomizer
command.

Note

There is an alternative option for this code, which is changing the `true` value to `false`. This option
means that the user stays within the command. The double quotes that you see at the end can contain a string of text, or a variable and are useful for feeding alerts to the user.

Creating the Cancel button

Finally you add the Cancel button. After establishing the event handler, you need to add only a single line of code. This API call carries out the task of exiting the command and returning focus to the
main Fireworks MX environment.:

1. Select the elements layer.

2. Open the Buttons folder in the Library and drag an instance of the Cancel button onto the
   Stage. Give this Cancel button an instance name of **cancel** in the Instance Name text box on
   the Property inspector.

3. Select the Cancel button on the Stage. Press F9 to open the Actions panel. Switch to Expert mode.

4. Add the on (release) code as you did in step 7 of the Apply button section.

Final ActionScript for the Randomizer command within the Actions panel of Flash MX

5. Add the following code to the Actions panel:

```
// End command and release system resources
FWEndCommand(true, "");
```

Now that you have isolated the requirements for the command, isolated code from the History Panel, and created a hybrid ActionScript / Fireworks MX API code routine within Flash MX, its time to test your command.

Adding error checking

Not every command you create will need error checking within it. However for this particular command, you need to check that two conditions exist for the interface to appear. These are as follows:

✦ There is an open document within Fireworks MX.

✦ There is an active selection within that document.

With the first frame of the movie selected, press F9 to open the Actions panel and switch to Expert mode. Add the following code:

```
//Error Checking Functions
//Steven Grosvenor (c) 2002 www.phireworx.com
//Check for Active Document
function documentchecker() {
    anyDoc = MMExecute("fw.documents.length;");
    if (anyDoc == 0) {
        FWEndCommand(false, "Sorry, you need an open document to
run this command");
    }
}
//Check for Active Selection
```

```
function selectionchecker() {
    previewinfo = MMExecute("fw.documents.length;");
    if (anydoc>0) {
        var previewnumber = MMExecute("fw.selection.length");
        if (previewnumber == 0) {
            FWEndCommand(false, "Sorry, you must have an active
selection to run this command");
        }
    }
}
documentchecker();
selectionchecker();
```

These two functions (documentchecker and selectionchecker) check for an active document and an active selection within that document and are called when the command is selected from the Commands menu within Fireworks MX. These two functions use the following built-in Fireworks API routines:

```
fw.documents.length;
fw.selection.length
```

The results of these API routines are fed back into the function to create conditional checks for the correct conditions to carry on and present the interface to the user. If the conditions are not met, the user is presented with an alert created by the the FWEndCommand within Fireworks MX. The alert informs users that they need an active document or an active selection. The following figure shows the final Error Checking added to the command.

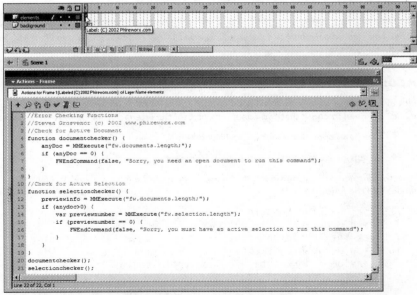

Final Error Checking added to the command for completion of user experience

Exporting your command and testing in Fireworks MX

After creating the code for the command, it's time to test your creation by exporting the command as an SWF file directly to Fireworks MX's command folder:

1. In Macromedia Flash MX, save your working copy FLA file. Then choose File ➪ Export Movie.

2. In the Export Movie dialog box, navigate to and select the Configuration ➪ Commands folder in the Fireworks MX application folder.

3. Name the file **Randomizer.swf**. Click Save.

4. In the Export Flash Player dialog box, use the default settings, making sure to select Flash 6 for the version (see the following figure).

Exporting your Flash MX command into the Fireworks MX command folder

5. Click OK. The SWF file is now located in within the Fireworks MX application.

Testing your command

You are now ready to take you newly created Randomizer command for a test run within Fireworks MX.

1. Launch Fireworks MX. Create a new 400 × 400 pixel document (with default settings).

2. Create a new vector object on the canvas, and with the object selected choose Commands ➪ Randomizer. The Randomizer interface should now appear.

3. Click the Apply button. Your selected object is duplicated and thrown around the canvas in a truly random manner (see the following figure).

If you appear to be having problems, or your command isn't working, check your code and the settings for the text input boxes against the code and settings in the `Randomizer_final.fla` file (located in the source file's FLA folder).

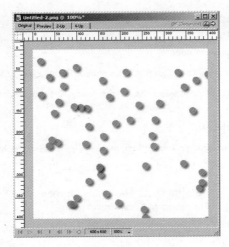

The Randomizer command in action within Fireworks MX

Resources

You should become familiar with the Extending Fireworks MX documentation before creating commands for public distribution. A good solid understanding of JavaScript and Flash MX ActionScript will stand you in good stead for creating appealing and useful commands.

For help with packaging a command as an MXP file for the Macromedia Extension Manager, see, "Creating and Submitting New Extension" (in the Extension Manager's Help menu) and the "Macromedia Extension File Format" document (PDF).

Enhancements to this command

Using the following ideas, the History panel, and a little perseverance, you can create exciting and useful commands within Fireworks MX:

✦ Input for x and y iterations (text input, dials, sliders, and so on)

✦ Random scaling

✦ Random rotation

Summary

In this chapter you learned several different techniques to automate your workload in Fireworks. You learned how to use the Find and Replace panel for things such as text, fonts, and colors. You also saw how easy it is to make a command by making one yourself. The command you created was then used as part of a batch process that automated a couple of tasks into a process that you applied to an entire folder of images with the click of a button. The tutorial introduced you to making extensions for Fireworks.

✦   ✦   ✦

Designing
Animations

Animations are often used to communicate an idea; unfortunately they are sometimes used for no practical purpose and end up only annoying users. The challenge you face producing animations is to get the illusion of motion in as few frames as possible to keep the file size to a minimum. If an animation takes too long to download it can take away from its intended purpose.

You probably remember using a flipbook as a child, a book containing many images, which appeared to move as you flipped the pages with your thumb. That's the basic foundation of GIF animations, many images shown in sequence to give the illusion of motion—minus the thumb.

The decision to use a GIF animation or another technology, such as Flash, is a decision you have to make. Some of the determining factors will be your audience and the intended purpose of the animation, along with your budget and the frequency in which you produce animations. One of the major benefits of using Fireworks to produce GIF animations is the cost factor—no additional purchase is required for specialized software. If you produce only a limited number of animations or only short or small ones, Fireworks MX is more than suitable for the job. Another benefit to using GIF animations is the fact that no additional plug-in is required to view the animations, and the learning curve for creating them is extremely short. Incorporating a GIF animation into an HTML Web page doesn't require any special coding. You insert them just as you would any other image. Some of the drawbacks include a limited color palette of 256 colors, making GIF animations unsuitable for gradients, 3-D, or photographic animations, larger file size, and no streaming capabilities. Because all the frames of the animation need to be downloaded in the browser before it plays properly, the first time it runs, it may look jerky.

Working with Symbols and Instances

Understanding symbols and instances in Fireworks is the foundation of producing animations. Symbols represent an object, a group, or a text block. A symbol may contain many objects, layers, and frames. A symbol can be a graphic, an animation, or a button; each of these symbols is discussed in this section. When you convert an object into a symbol, you access the original symbol from the Library panel. Symbols are extremely useful when you want to reuse the same elements. In

Fireworks symbols are necessary, not optional, for producing GIF animations. Symbols are similar to what other programs call "sprites." They animate independently and can be used multiple times throughout an animation.

Instances are copies of a symbol. After an object is converted into a symbol, the object in the document is replaced with an instance. The original symbol is stored in the library and accessible through the Library panel (Assets panel group). Wherever a symbol is used in the document it is a copy or an instance of the original symbol. If you edit the original symbol, every instance is automatically changed to the edited version, streamlining your workflow.

Types of symbols

There are three kinds of symbols:

✦ **Graphic** — This option is used for objects that appear multiple times in your animation.

✦ **Animation** — An animation symbol can play an animation independent of another animation.

✦ **Button** — Button symbols contain different states such as Up, Over, Down, and Over While Down.

Creating a new symbol

To make a new symbol, follow these steps:

1. Choose Edit ➪ Insert ➪ New Symbol (Control+F8/Command+F8).

2. The Symbol Properties dialog box (Figure 22-1) opens. Type a name for your symbol, choose the type you want, and click OK.

Figure 22-1: The Symbol Properties dialog box

3. The Symbol Editor window opens. This is where you can draw (import or drag in) either a vector object or a bitmap object. Draw a rectangle of any color for use in the following exercises. Close the Symbol Editor when you are done.

You now have an instance of the rectangle on your document, which is indicated by the little arrow in the bottom-left corner. The actual symbol now resides in the library of this file.

Convert an existing object to a symbol

To convert an existing object to an animated symbol, follow these steps:

1. Select an object.

2. Choose Modify ➪ Symbol ➪ Convert to Symbol, or press the keyboard shortcut, F8.

3. The Symbol Properties dialog box opens. Name your symbol, choose the type, and click OK.

Add animation selections

Now that you have a symbol, you are ready to animate it. To do this, choose Modify ➪ Animation ➪ Animation Settings to open the Animate dialog box as shown in Figure 22-2.

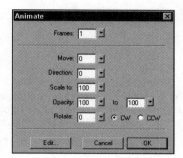

Figure 22-2: The Animate dialog box

The following options are available:

✦ **Frames** — Type in the number of frames you'd like in the animation. The slider only goes to 250 but you can type in any number you want; the default frame amount is 5.

✦ **Move** — Move determines the amount of movement in pixels that each object will move. The value range is from 0 to 250 pixels; the default is 72.

✦ **Direction** — The amount in degrees that the object will move. The value range is 0 to 360 degrees.

✦ **Scaling** — The percent change from the beginning to the end of the animation. The default is 100 percent scaling, which keeps the animation at its original size up to 250 percent of the original size.

✦ **Opacity** — The percentage of the opacity from the beginning of the animation to the ending opacity of the animation. Use this to do the fade in and out effects.

✦ **Rotation** — The amount in degrees that the symbol rotates from the beginning to the end. The values range from 0 to 360 degrees; 0 is the default. You also have the option of having the animation rotate CW, clockwise or CCW, counter-clockwise.

Click OK and accept the default settings. Notice the motion path — the blue line with green, blue, and red dot — added to your animation. You see how to adjust that later in this chapter.

Editing symbol properties

After you add the animation properties, you have access to them in the Property inspector. You can also access the Animate dialog box by choosing Modify ➪ Animation ➪ Settings. If you want to edit the appearance of the symbol, double-click it and open the Symbol editor.

Editing symbol motion paths

An animated symbol when selected shows a bounding box and a motion path, which is attached to it. This path indicates the direction in which the symbol will move. The green dot indicates the starting point, and the red dot indicates the ending point. The blue dots in between represent the frames within the path. You can change the Move and Direction values by dragging the handles in the bounding box in your document. You can move the green handle to change the beginning point and the red one to change the ending point. To constrain the movement to 45-degree increments, hold down the Shift key as you drag. See Figure 22-3 to view a symbol with a motion path.

Figure 22-3: A motion path of a symbol

 Tip   You can preview an animation in the Fireworks workspace without having to open a browser. There are VCR-like controls on the bottom of the document window. Click the white right-pointing arrow to play. To preview an animation in preview mode, click the Preview tab in the document window, and then click the Play button.

Working with Frames

The Frames panel is where most of the action is when producing animations. What is on each frame determines how the animation plays. By default, the Frames panel is docked with the History panel in the docked area. The Frames panel is the "control center" for your animation production. From the Frames panel you can add, delete, move, duplicate, use Onion Skinning, and set the looping options. Figure 22-4 shows the Frames panel.

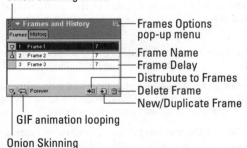

Figure 22-4: The Frames panel with labeled icons

Adding and deleting frames

To add frames, you can add one at time or enter a specified number of frames. If you have too many frames or if you decide you don't like or need a particular frame, you can delete one.

To add one frame, click the New/Duplicate Frame icon. To add multiple layers, access the Frames Options pop-up menu (Figure 22-4) and choose Add Frames.

When deleting a frame you delete all its content, with the exception of a frame that has been distributed to Frames. The deleted frame containing a shared frame doesn't affect other frames that are using the shared frame. To delete a frame or frames, select it by clicking the frame or shift+clicking multiple frames and using any of the following options.

✦ After the selection is made, click the trashcan icon to delete.

✦ Click and drag the frame/frames on top of the trashcan icon.

✦ Choose Delete Frame from the Frame Options pop-up menu by clicking the down-pointing arrow in the Frames panel.

Moving and duplicating frames

Moving frames works the same way as moving layers; you click and drag the frame to the desired position. If you double-click the frame name, you can rename it. In Fireworks MX, you can give your frames unique names. Moving the frames does not change the names or the numbers assigned.

Duplicating frames is a good way to save time by altering only the elements changing in each frame. To duplicate a frame, select the frame you want from the Frames Options pop-up menu; then choose Duplicate Frame. Figure 22-5 shows the positioning options. Choose where you want to place the duplicate frame.

You can actually duplicate multiple frames by Shift+selecting then using the Duplicate Frame option from the Frames Options pop-up menu. This saves a lot of time when you want to reverse your animation. The only thing is, the last frame isn't duplicated, but duplicating that one extra frame when you've got a lot of frames is still a timesaver.

Figure 22-5: The Duplicate Frame dialog box

Reversing the order of duplicated frames

If you have an animation that for instance moves to the right and you want it to slide back to the left you can reverse the order of frames. Make duplicate frames of the range of frames you want to reverse then choose Commands ➪ Document ➪ Reverse Frame Range. A dialog box opens asking for the first frame you want to reverse. Enter the number and click OK. Another window opens, and you enter the last frame you want to reverse and click OK.

Sharing layers across frames

The ability to share layers across frames is an important one. When you have a repeating element, such as a background image, it is very inefficient and time consuming to have to insert it into every frame. Sharing layers across frames automatically places the contents of the selected layer onto every frame present and to all frames added. There is one caveat though; it is an all or nothing proposition.

Note If you have an animation where at some point you don't want the layer shared, you'll need to draw a rectangle over the shared part to cover it and then add your new content.

To share a layer across all frames, follow these steps:

1. In the Layers panel, select the layer you want to share.

2. Access the Frames Options pop-up menu and select Share This Layer.

3. Repeat for any other layer you want to share.

Tip You can also double-click on the layer name and check the "Share Across Frames" option.

Distributing to frames

You can distribute multiple objects on one layer to individual frames. A good use of this command is to animate text. You can break your text apart then place each letter in a separate frame to animate. Shift+select all objects in the Frames Options pop-up menu and choose Distribute to Frames. Each object is placed on a separate frame.

Onion Skinning

The Onion Skinning option comes in handy when you need to place an object in one frame in alignment with an object on another frame, or if you need to add to or subtract from an object appearing on another frame. Using Onion Skinning is like placing tracing paper over the individual frames: you can see through to the other frames. One advantage of using the Onion Skinning feature is that you can select the faded objects on frames other than the selected one and edit them. To use Onion Skinning follow these steps:

1. Set up a quick file to use just to experiment with onion skinning.

   Draw a shape in your document.

   In the Frames Options pop-up menu, select "Add Frames" and type in 2 and select "At the End".

   Select Frame 2 and add another shape.

   Select Frame 3 and add another shape.

   Select Frame 1 again.

2. Click the Onion Skinning icon, Figure 22-6 shows the Onion Skinning options.

Figure 22-6: The Onion Skinning options

3. Choose Before and After. In Figure 22-7 you see an icon that resembles an elongated hourglass, indicating which frames are using Onion Skinning. If the No Onion Skinning option was selected this icon is collapsed and looks closed on the selected frame. To try it, click the Onion Skinning icon and choose No Onion Skinning.

Figure 22-7: The elongated hourglass shows which frames are affected by onion skinning.

4. If you tried the No Onion Skinning option, go back and change it to the Before and After option again. In the Frames panel click the gray square to the left of Frame 3. Notice how the icon expands to include this frame as well. If you click the Onion Skinning icon, the option automatically changes to Custom.

5. Click any of the objects. You can edit any of the frames, not just the object in the active frame. The frames made visible because of Onion Skinning are faded.

Looping

Looping sets the amount of times your animation will repeat. You can have it play over and over again indefinitely, choose a specific number of times to loop, or not to loop at all. No looping simply means the animation plays one time and stops. To set the looping options, click the GIF animation looping icon (Figure 22-4) next to the Onion Skinning icon, and select No Looping, a number, or Forever. No Looping is the default.

Note

When you preview an animation in the browser, the looping you set doesn't take effect until you export the animation.

Frame delay

The frame delay determines how long each frame is visible before the next frame appears. The delay settings are specified in hundredths of a second. A setting of 10 means 10 one-hundredths of a second. A setting of 100 means a one-second delay before the next frame appears. To set the delay settings, double-click the last column in the Frames panel where you see a number. Enter the delay time you want and click outside of the dialog box to close it. You can also Shift+select multiple frames and from the Options pop-up menu choose Properties to change the Delay time. Be sure to check the Include When Exporting option to have the delay change take effect.

Tip

To avoid jittery animations, try setting the first frame a bit longer than normal, which allows extra time for the rest of the animation to load. The biggest drawback to this trick is that when the animation loops there is a longer delay than normal each time. This isn't a problem in some animations.

Tweening

At first glance, tweening looks the same as the motion paths you saw in the Symbols section at the beginning of this chapter. Tweening is a traditional term indicating a starting point and an ending point that you produce; the computer generates the steps in be*tween*. (Hence the term *tweening*.)

Tweening in Fireworks is performed on two or more instances of the same symbol. The same symbol is a key factor, but you can trick it, as you discover in the second exercise.

Note   The types of tweening available in Fireworks are position, opacity, scale, rotation, and effects. You cannot do shape tweening, which is a gradual changing of one shape into another, where your starting point is one graphic and the ending point another. You can achieve a type of shape tween by using the Transform option and altering a shape by choosing Modify ⇨ Transform ⇨ Skew.

Applying a multiply tween

In this exercise, you do a fade effect by applying a tween with opacity, position, and scale by following these steps:

1. Open a new document (File ⇨ New). A size of 300 pixels by 300 pixels will work.

2. Select any one of the drawing tools and draw an object: a circle, star, or something similar.

3. With the object selected, choose Edit ⇨ Insert ⇨ Convert to Symbol (F8) and choose Graphic symbol. The symbol is added to the library and an instance is in your document, which is indicated by the little arrow in the corner.

4. For the second symbol, you can press Alt (Option) key. Click and drag a copy to the desired location to produce a duplicate instance and the ending point of the tween.

5. Select only the ending point instance of the symbol, choose Modify ⇨ Transform ⇨ Scale, and drag one of the corners to increase the size.

6. To change the opacity, select the starting instance, and in the Layers panel move the opacity slider to 0. This makes the beginning instance invisible and gradually increases to 100 percent at the ending instance.

7. Shift+select the beginning and ending symbol instances, choose Modify ⇨ Symbol ⇨ Tween Instances, and check Distribute to Frames. In Figure 22-8, you see the Tween Instances dialog box showing the default frames of 10. You can change this. Be sure to check the Distribute to Frames option, which places each in-between instance on its own frame. If you neglect to check this option, all the in-between instances will be in the same frame.

Figure 22-8: The Tween Instances dialog box

Note   This exact same effect can be achieved using only one symbol by converting an object to a symbol (F8) and choosing Animation. In the Animate dialog box, set the Opacity to 0-100, alter the scale, and set the direction. You can adjust the direction by adjusting the motion path if you need visual help in setting the direction.

Using Numeric Transform

Transforming the size of an object can produce interesting effects. You can use the Numeric Transform option to change the size of an object frame by frame or to distort the shape. All you have to do to access the Numeric Transform dialog box is select the object you want to transform and choose Modify ⇨ Transform ⇨ Numeric Transform and enter in the parameters you want.

Tween Live Effects

Tweening Live Effects is a method that cannot be produced using the Animated Symbol dialog box. This exercise demonstrates the technique of tweening Live Effects. To tween Live Effects, follow these steps:

1. Open a new document (File⇨New). A size of 300 pixels by 300 pixels will work.

2. Select any one of the drawing tools and draw an object, a circle, star, or something similar.

3. Convert to a symbol (F8) and drag out another instance of the symbol.

4. Here is where things start to change. Select the beginning instance and click the + sign in the Property inspector to access the Effects menu. Choose Adjust Color ⇨ Color Fill. Select a color you like but be sure it is different from the ending symbol.

   Note

   You may be wondering at this point how this can be done, that is, creating tween symbols that are different. You may recall that tweening can only be performed on two instances of the "same" symbol. If you were to try and tween these two instances right now it would not work. To make the two instances the same, the same effect has to be applied to both or all symbols that will be tweened.

5. Select the ending instance from the Effects menu. Choose Adjust Color ⇨ Color Fill. This is where you fool the symbol into thinking it is the same. The same effect is added; move the opacity slider to 0 and no "visible" effect is applied.

6. Shift+select the beginning and ending symbol instances, and choose Modify ⇨ Symbol ⇨ Tween Instances. Accept the default frames, check the Distribute to Frames option, and click OK. Play your animation to see the gradual color change.

Note

You can use more than two instances of a symbol when tweening. If you place instances in other locations, the tween follows a path according to the stacking order. The closest to the canvas is the beginning point of the tween. Just remember that when you tween Live Effects, you must apply the effects whether they are invisible or not to every instance. You can make transformations such as width, height, skew, opacity, and blending modes separately to individual instances.

Importing and Exporting Animated GIF Images

Getting the image ready to export is pretty easy. The main thing you'll want to concentrate on is optimizing the images so you get the smallest file size possible. Chapter 23 discusses the many optimization options. And importing an animated GIF image is the same as importing any other image.

Importing

You can import GIF animations from other programs or users into Fireworks, where they can be edited or deconstructed for learning purposes. If you import an existing GIF animation into a current document, it looses its Frame Delay settlings, and it becomes a symbol of the current document. If you want to retain the delay settings of the original GIF animation, open it instead of importing it.

To import a GIF animation follow these steps:

1. Choose File ➪ Import.

2. Locate the file and click Open. You can navigate to the chapter22_exercise folder and import the `chesire.gif` if you'd like.

3. The cursor turns into a corner shape. Click in the document to place it. Any additional necessary frames needed are added.

Exporting

To export your animation with motion, you need to be sure that you have set it as an Animation GIF. Open the Optimize panel and choose Animated GIF. The Optimize panel is also the place to reduce your colors as much as possible to reduce the file size. Chapter 23 discusses how to optimize in more detail. To export as a GIF Animation follow these steps:

1. Choose Animated GIF in the Optimize panel.

2. Choose File ➪ Export.

3. In the Export dialog box, name the animation, choose where you want to export, and click Save.

Your animation can be used in Flash and further edited there. To export as a Flash SWF file, follow these steps:

1. Choose File ➪ Export.

2. Choose where you want to save the file.

3. Type in the name of your animation.

4. Click the down arrow under Save as type, and select Macromedia Flash SWF.

5. Click the Options button, choose the options you want, and click OK.

6. Click Save.

Animating Images for the Web, by David C. Nicholls

We're all familiar with the myriad of animated GIF banners that populate many Web sites. Most of them look the same because it's difficult to think up a novel animated GIF. Designers simply blink text on and off or move image objects about, often because they're working to a limited file size for the average animated page banner specification. But it's not necessary to follow the usual routine. In fact, it's a good idea not to do so, because most Web site visitors ignore the usual animated banners in the same way they ignore many TV commercials. Thinking up a way to attract the viewer's attention is important but not easy.

By completing this tutorial, you learn skills associated with the following tasks:

   * Creating a series of layers with graduated fades

   * Distributing these layers to frames and building the animation

   * Optimizing and saving the animated GIF

I'll also show you how to do these same things in earlier versions of Fireworks, which lack the transparent gradient fill capability.

Some designers resort to Flash to produce complex moving images. However, not all visitors have Flash players installed in their browser, and it's hard to resist the temptation to create really intricate animations, resulting in large files and slow downloads. This section demonstrates that you can create an interesting animation by using the simple animated GIF, which works in all browsers and doesn't have too large a file size.

In this tutorial, I show you how to draw a cat and give you plenty of practice with the Pen tool and manipulating curves. You also learn how to use masks and utilize the new gradient transparency to enhance your animation. You then add the frames and settings to make the cat fade in and out and still maintain a reasonable file size for a fast-loading animation.

Designing the animation

The designing of the animation usually consumes more time than the actual animating does. Thought and preparation are required to produce a good quality and effective animation.

The concept

This is the hard part — thinking up an animation that's interesting and at the same time avoiding a large file size. The trick is to think outside the nine dots. In this example, I have no particular client in mind, just the intent to do something different. I've chosen the Cheshire Cat which appears (and disappears) in the story Alice in Wonderland by Lewis Carroll.

A bit of background. In her adventures in Wonderland, Alice meets a host of strange characters. One of these is a talking cat — the Cheshire Cat. As it talks to Alice, it disconcertingly starts to disappear, leaving only its grin. You're going to animate this disappearing act.

Preparing the vector drawing for animation

We have supplied you with a vector copy of a cat but you'll first need to convert it to a bitmap. This may seem odd, but there's a reason. One of the possible animation options is to have the cat disappear to a background pattern. For this, the components of the cat need to be filled with a solid color, so that it initially covers the background pattern. However, as some of the cat body parts aren't completely closed vector shapes, the fill process doesn't fill the whole animal, and bits of background show through. It would be possible to join all the vector shapes into a single closed vector object and fill the result. But this would involve more fiddling than just turning the cat back into a bitmap requires.

1. Open the `vector_cat.png` image (chapter22_exercise folder).

2. In the Optimize panel, change the export file format, to TIFF24.

3. Choose Modify ➪ Canvas ➪ Canvas Color, and make the canvas white if it isn't already.

4. Choose Export, name your file, and save it. A copy is in the Chapter 22 image folder named `cat.tif`. You have not made changes to the original vector file since you saved it with a new name.

5. Now open your saved image (or use `cat.tif`). Then open the saved vector file again (`vector_cat.png`) if you've closed it.

6. In the `vector_cat.png` file, select the grin group, and convert it to a bitmap by choosing Modify ➪ Flatten Selection.

7. Copy the flattened selection and paste the grin over the cat bitmap (the `cat.tif` you opened). Position the copied grin over the bitmapped one.

8. The cat has two grins now, because you need one to remain as the rest of the cat fades away. For the moment, hide the second grin. (Click the appropriate eye icon in the Layers panel.)

9. Select the Magic Wand tool, and in the Property inspector, apply the following settings:

   · Tolerance: 32

   · Edge: Anti-alias

10. In the Layers panel, select the bitmap layer. Using the Magic Wand tool, select the area outside the cat's body.

11. Delete the selection using the Delete key, and change the Canvas color (Modify ➪ Canvas ➪ Canvas Color) to transparent. Now you have a solid cat on a transparent background.

12. To set the cat on a textured background, deselect the current selection (Ctrl/Command+D), use the (vector) Rectangle tool, and draw a rectangle that covers the entire canvas.

13. In the Property inspector, set these values:

   · Stroke: None

   · Fill: Solid, mid-gray (#666666)

   · Texture: Hatch 5 and the percentage to 40%.

14. In the Layers panel, drag the new filled vector rectangle below the cat image. The cat should now appear against a patterned background, as in the following image.

You can use any other sort of background — for example a bitmap image — but this texture is a simple way to demonstrate a cat fading to a background. This choice of background pattern also turned out, by trial and error, to be quite efficient when converted to a GIF.

Bitmap cat with background

Fading the cat

You want to make the cat slowly fade, starting at its hind end, with the fade gradually covering the whole animal, moving toward the head, and finally leaving only the grin.

There are three main ways to do this. One, which works in both Fireworks 4 and Fireworks MX, is to use a Mask group. The second, which works in MX only, is to overlay the cat with a white-to-white radial transparent gradient. You can apply the latter to an outline of the cat and overlay only the cat, or to a rectangle covering the whole canvas.

The third way, and by far the most interesting is possible only in Fireworks MX. First you select parts of a bitmap according to transparency information in a gradient fill vector object. Put another way, you create a vector object, fill it with a suitable gradient with variable transparency, and use that transparency information to selectively etch away a specific bitmap (the cat) while leaving everything else (the background) unchanged. Using this method, you can make the fading bitmap images very quickly and easily and is the method this tutorial explores in detail.

Because the third method actually uses the same techniques as the first two, I'll show you those options as well and then build upon each one. This way, you learn to do all three at once.

Fireworks MX with instructions for Fireworks 4, Mask Group Method

Fireworks enables you to create a vector object with a black-to-white gradient fill (linear, radial, ellipse, and so on) and apply it as a mask to the image you want to fade. A simple approach is to draw a rectangular vector object that covers the entire window, set the fill to radial, the colors of the gradient to black and white. Then you select the rectangle and the cat beneath it and apply as mask (Modify ⇨ Mask ⇨ Group as Mask). The cat pixels remain where the mask gradient was white and fades completely where the mask was black. You have to adjust only the location of the black and white parts of the mask rectangle to suit the intended fade. (In Fireworks 4, black areas are visible and white are transparent. It's the opposite in Fireworks MX.) You start with a background, but you won't be using it in the end.

1. Open the TIFF image of the cat with a background (bitmap_cat.tif).

2. Using the Rectangle (vector) tool, draw a rectangle that exactly covers the cat image frame. If the fill was already set to solid, the cat disappears beneath a rectangle, which appears in the color you set the fill to (most likely white, but it will be whatever you left it at last).

3. Next you set the Fill to Radial, and edit the fill (click the Fill color box) so that the right end of the fill spectrum is black and the other is white. You want the rectangle to be white in the center and black at the edges. (Note: The reverse is true for Fireworks 4). Accept the settings shown in the following image.

Setting the gradient colors

4. Select with the Pointer tool. The fill handles appear on the black bullseye. Drag the circular handle about half-way up toward the top-left corner, and the square handle down to the bottom-right corner as seen here.

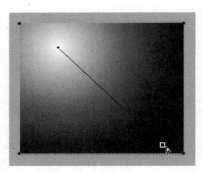

The gradient mask with the circular handle moved

5. Now for the masking. In the Layers panel, select both the rectangle object and the cat (shift+click in the Layers panel). Group them as a mask by choosing Modify ⇨ Mask ⇨ Group as Mask.

   Part of the cat reappears where the white parts of the rectangle were. But it's not centered where you want it.

6. Using the Pointer tool, in the Layers panel, select the vector mask with a pen icon on the right in the grouped objects. A yellow line appears around it when selected. When you do this, the fill handles reappear over the cat.

7. Drag the circular handle over the cat's grin and the square handle in from the bottom-right corner. As you move the square handle, you see the effect of the mask change. Play with the location of the square handle to make different parts of the cat fade out. You'll immediately see how you can create a gradual fade by progressively moving the square handle from the bottom-right corner in an anticlockwise spiral inwards toward the cat's grin.

That's all that is necessary to build the various animation frames using the Group as Mask process. Next you look briefly at the transparent gradient overlay process.

Transparent gradient overlay method

The previous method of masking works, but if you have Fireworks MX the method demonstrated in this section utilizes gradient transparency. It is the method you would use if you were using a background image.

1. Instead of creating a black-to-white radial gradient, fill in the rectangle as you did previously, and then set both color chips in the Gradient pop-up menu to white.

2. Click the opacity chip on the left and set the opacity to 0% (transparent), leaving the opacity on the right end at its default 100%. This action fills the vector rectangle with a radial white fill with varying transparency. Sitting over the top of the cat bitmap, it partly fades it to white. The only problem is, it also hides part of the background pattern as you see here.

Transparent gradient overlay

If you were building an animation of a cat fading to a plain white background, the background being partially faded wouldn't be a worry, and the technique would be fully effective. Which leads you to the third way to fade the bitmap: You use the transparency information in the white rectangle as a means of etching away the bitmap.

Etch-away-the-bitmap method

Now you use the transparency information to selectively etch away a specific bitmap (the cat) while leaving everything else (the background) unchanged. This is actually very easy to do.

1. In the Layers panel, select the cat bitmap.

2. Press and hold the Control (Command) key. Click the white rectangle in the Layers panel (on the actual thumbnail). As you do this, a small rectangular cursor appears. This action selects part of the bitmap, which shows as a selection border on the bitmap image. In fact, the pixels are not all selected equally, but according to how transparent the same location is in the white rectangle as seen here.

Selection marquee

3. Hide the white rectangle layer (eye icon in the Layers panel). Repeat Step 2 and Press the Delete key; then press Ctrl (Command) +D to deselect. As if by magic, the bitmap fades into the background exactly as you need as seen here.

The cat faded to background

The location and extent of the fade effect in the bitmap is controlled by the transparency gradient in the white rectangle. This is an effective way to fade images, and you should work through it carefully to master it.

Creating the animation

So let's get down to the task of creating the animation. The first thing you need to do is to work out the number of frames you want. Some animations use a lot of common content between frames, which means a small file size for a given number of frames. Animations where most of the details change from one frame to the next will have a large file size for the same number of frames. This animation is a fade, so it's an intermediate case.

The compromise that's necessary is to strike a balance between a smooth fade and a small file size. You can experiment with this, but set the first target at 12 frames and see how large the animation is.

You also start with a white background to minimize detail in the GIF and, thus, file size. (The textured background adds significantly to file size, even though it looks good.)

1. You start with the bitmap cat PNG file, which should have the following layers, from the top: the second grin (hidden, but now make it visible again); the white rectangle with the transparent gradient fill; the bitmap cat image; and the background texture rectangle (hidden, and keep it hidden). The Layers panel should appear as shown in the following image.

The Layers panel

   2. Turn off the visibility of the background pattern rectangle, and make sure the Canvas color is set
   to white (Modify ➪ Canvas ➪ Canvas Color).

The process from here on in is purely mechanical — to create a series of bitmap cat images that fade
progressively in toward the cat's nose. The first frame is the model for the subsequent frames. Here's
the sequence:

   1. Select and duplicate the cat bitmap image (Control (Command) +Shift+D or Edit ➪ Duplicate).
   Hide the duplicate image in the Layers panel: This is your reference cat image, which you use as
   the source for all the fading frames.

   2. Enlarge the window to about twice its default size; select the white rectangle, and using the
   Pointer tool, drag the square fill handle down and to the right, off the canvas, for a distance of
   about twice the length of the cat.

   3. Select the visible cat bitmap image. Hold down the Ctrl (Command) key (see image) and click
   the white rectangle thumbnail in the Layers panel, as before.

The bitmap cat selected

   4. Press the Delete key and deselect the image. Rename the modified bitmap frame 2, and temporarily hide it.

   5. Repeat the process, duplicating the original bitmap again. Select the white rectangle and drag in
   the square fill handle inwards toward the cat's nose, and a little upwards. Then repeat the "etching" process, naming the modified bitmap frame 3, and so on.

   You might have noticed that this process uses only one layer (the white rectangle) to create all
   the frames and that you adjust it step by step as you go. You use copies of the original cat bitmap
   as source material for the frame.

   Keep this process going until you have moved the white rectangle fill handle through a succession
   of shorter lengths, in a slow counterclockwise arc, fading each successive duplicate of the original
   cat bitmap, until the fill handle is close to the cat's eyes. Adjust the change in the fill handle
   length and position so that you finish up with 10 progressively faded bitmaps.

   6. When you have frames 2 through 11 done, save a safe copy of the file; then delete the white
   rectangle, which has served it purpose. (Select it and press the Delete key.)

   The original, unfaded bitmap, the 10 progressively faded bitmaps, named frames 2 through 11,
   and the grin, are the raw material of the animation. One is the basis of each frame. Every frame
   also needs a copy of the spare grin, because you don't want that to fade with the rest of the cat.
   The final frame will be the grin by itself.

What you must do next is distribute the bitmaps to different frames. Fireworks animates an image by swapping from one frame to the next in a specified time. You can view the different frames using the Frames panel. Initially, there is only 1 frame, the one you have been working in, and you need 12 for the complete animation. These are created automatically when the layers are distributed to frames.

1. You start with the Layers panel open, showing the grin at the top layer, followed by layers named *frame 10, frame 9*, and so on, with the original unfaded bitmap cat on the bottom layer. These should all be visible (the eye icon showing). If not, make them so. If the background texture rectangle is present as the bottom layer, hide it. Next, select all the layers (except the background rectangle) by clicking on each in sequence while holding down the Shift key.

2. The next step is to distribute these 12 layers each to a separate frame. Open the Frames panel, and, with the 12 objects still selected, click the Distribute to Frames button (arrow and film-strip icon, lower right). Each layer has been moved to its own frame.

3. In the Frames panel, select Frame 12. The grin layer is the only image visible in the frame. Click the grin image to select it. Then, in the Frames panel, click the panel Options pop-up menu (top right), and select Copy to Frames. In the pop-up box that opens, accept the default to copy to all frames. This action sends a copy of the grin to every other frame.

4. The main part of the animation is done. Under the main image window, you will see the animation controls. Click the forward arrow and watch the animation preview. The frame duration defaults to 7/100 second, but it performs better if you set the delays on the first and last frames longer. In the Frames panel, select Frame 1, double-click the 7 in the second column, and set it to 50. Set the delay for Frame 12 to 100 in the same manner. Now preview the animation again. This gives quite a nice animated vanishing cat. If you had created more frames — to make the fade more gradual — the effect would be smoother, but at the cost of a larger file size. Which brings us to exporting.

Exporting the animation

You now export the animation.

1. First you must decide whether the animation is going to cycle through once, more than once, or indefinitely. For trial purposes, it is probably best to select Forever. To change this, in the Frames panel, click the loop icon at the bottom left of the panel. This opens a pop-up menu to set the animation repetition.

2. With this chosen, you export the animation as an animated GIF. In the Optimize panel, select Animated GIF in the Export File Format drop-down list. Use the following settings:

   · Web Snap Adaptive

   · No dither

   · No Loss

   · No Transparency

   · 128 colors

3. Export the file as normal (File ➪ Export) and save with an appropriate name. The resulting file size is about 55K for Web Snap Adaptive and 128 colors, and 27K if you want to export as Web216.

4. These are both too large for practical use as a Web animation, but there is a way to reduce the file size. You have a very large cat! The image you've been working on is around 300 × 250 pixels, which is much larger than needed on a Web page. If you reduce the size to 150 × 125 pixels (Modify ➪ Canvas ➪ Image Size), the file sizes reduce to 10K for the two options. This is much more acceptable.

5. As a final step, it's worthwhile to preview the animation in a browser to see exactly what it looks like and to check the timing and looping. Choose File ➪ Preview in Browser and select the browser you prefer.

And there you have it — a vanishing Cheshire Cat. There's only one more problem. Where do you use a vanishing Cheshire Cat, except on an Alice in Wonderland Web site?

Note for the Alice in Wonderland purists: The Cheshire Cat that Alice meets actually disappears completely after a while. If you want to follow the cat's behavior to the letter, add a final completely blank animation frame after the grin-only frame.

Modification

If you want to use the background texture, select Frame 1 in the Frames panel, make it visible, and select the Background Texture Rectangle. Then in the Frames panel, using the Panel Options button, copy to frames as before. This copies the background rectangle to each frame, but as it is copied to the top layer in each frame, it is necessary to select each frame in turn in the Frames panel, and in the Layers panel, to drag the background rectangle layer to the bottom.

If you were to export now, the file size would be about 68K. If you change the Optimization parameters to Web 216, with a dither of 100%, the file would be around 61K. If you reduce the cat, as in Step 4 in the previous section, the file will be about 22k.

There is another animation Expert tutorial — "Animated Banner," by Japi Honoo — in the Bonus Tutorial folder on the CD-ROM. In that tutorial you create a banner for the Habitat Alert Web site.

Summary

In this chapter you learned how to use the animation tools in Fireworks. You explored the Frames panel and made symbols, used instances, and accessed the Libraries panel. You also learned how to edit the animation, add tweening effects, and use Live Effects.

✦   ✦   ✦

Slicing and Optimizing

This chapter explores how to slice (divide) your designs and apply optimization settings. Slicing an image or document is one of the most important things you will do in Fireworks. The decisions about whether to slice your document, where to slice your document, and how to slice your document all contribute to how, and sometimes whether, users view your Web pages. Slicing when needed allows for better and specialized optimization to decrease file size. Using slicing techniques, which ultimately reduce the file size, is vital to the final display of your project if you have an image that fits the profile of images needing slicing.

After your slices are defined, you learn how to optimize them. Optimization, or getting your image to the smallest possible size while retaining an acceptable quality, is one of the most important factors in determining how fast your Web page loads. Not only can you export with GIF and JPEG images in the same document, but you can actually apply different settings to specific areas of a JPEG image.

After the images are sliced and optimized, you will discover the many methods and options available in Fireworks for exporting your images or entire Web pages.

Working in the Web Layer

The Web layer is the special layer that contains all the hotspot coordinates and slices that you've made in your document. Everything on this layer is shared across all layers, meaning that if a slice or hotspot encloses elements that are actually on different layers, the slice or hotspot is active on each layer. The slice or hotspot activates the behavior you have assigned to it. You can't delete the Web layer and you can't add another one.

To Slice or Not to Slice?

Before beginning to slice your images, you need to understand why it needs to be sliced, or whether it needs to be sliced at all. Many people mistakenly believe that slicing increases loading speeds. This usually isn't so; in most cases, the page actually takes longer to load because there are more hits to the server since every slice is being requested from the server. Slicing does make the page "*appear*" to load faster, because the user can see parts of the image before the whole thing loads.

Many reasons exist to slice an image:

✦ If an image is over 20K, it needs to be sliced to form the perception that it's loading faster.

✦ If you need to export some slices as JPEGs and some as GIFs, or GIF animations within the same image, slicing is the best way to go; that way some of the slices can be a different format to suit your needs.

✦ If you want to attach behaviors, such as rollovers, to an area, it has to be a slice or hotspot object.

✦ Slices help the loading of your Web pages when you have a logo or other repeating elements in the Web site if you place the same slice on every page using the repeating element.

When you have a logo or element that is repeated often within your site, be sure that the element or slice is linked to the same image file. That way, after the server retrieves it one time, it is in the browser's cache. If you use the same image and put it in different folders, the server has to fetch it each time.

Another wonderful advantage of slices is that if you need to update one section or slice, you don't have to redo the whole image. For instance, suppose you have a complicated sliced image that you have optimized, sliced, exported, and incorporated into every page on a large site. You then discover that one of the major slices contains a misspelled word. You can simply fix a copy of the one sliced image, optimize it, export it, and upload it to replace the image with the error.

Slicing Tools

The slicing tools are the Rectangle and Polygon tools. The Rectangle Slice tool works the same way as the other Rectangle tools in Fireworks; click and drag over the area you want to define. The Polygon Slice tool also works the same way as the other Polygon tools in Fireworks; click a starting point and click to add points to define a shape.

You can define a polygonal shape with the Polygon Slice tool, but the polygonal shape cannot be exported as a polygon shape. All slices are rectangular, without exception. Fireworks automatically adds as many rectangles as necessary to maintain your defined polygon shape. These rectangles fit together with the polygon shape enclosed.

Using the guides

Before you actually begin to slice an image, you need to set up a few aids for yourself. Using guides is an efficient way of defining your slices. Before placing your guides, you need to know how you plan to use the images in your layout. For the Habitat Alert site I know I want the logo as a separate image, the buttons will be exported as a whole, the bird area as an image, the entire circle area as an image, the home button as an image, and the top-left corner of the curve as an image. The area behind the logo will be used as a tiling background.

Guides not only provide a visual aid, but also aid your selection if you have the Snap To Guides option checked, allowing selections within a set amount of pixels (determined by you) to snap to the guide automatically.

Note

In the Dreamweaver section you will define a site and add folders for the sites structure. On the CD is a site folder you can use for the exercises in this chapter. Save the habitat_alert site to your hard drive, then continue. We've had to set up these different folders since this book is not necessarily read in a linear fashion.

To set up guides, follow these steps:

1. Open `ha6.png` file from the `habitat_alert\designfiles\Fireworks` folder. To enable the guides, the rulers have to be visible. From the menu bar, choose View ➪ Rulers.

2. Choose View ➪ Guides ➪ Snap To Guides.

Note

You can set your own preferences regarding how the Snap To Guides function responds. Choose Edit Í Preferences and click the Editing tab. In the Snap Distance dialog box, enter the number of pixels from the guide your object needs to be before it snaps to the guide. To change the color of the guideline, choose View ➪ Guides ➪ Edit Guides, and change the color.

3. To place guides, click in the vertical ruler area and drag a guide into your document. The guide will not be visible until you begin to pull it onto your document, at which point you will see a green line, which is the default color. In this document you will also see red lines but disregard them for now. They are slicing guides generated because of the button slices made using the Button Editor.

Note

If you pull a guide onto your canvas and you don't see it, it is probably because you pulled off the canvas. Be sure that you drag into the canvas area, not above or below it.

4. To set precise positioning of the horizontal guide, double-click it and type **74**. Repeat for a second guide except change its position to **117**. This places the guide at the top of the dark line and shadow of the header area.

5. Pull a vertical from the left side ruler. Double-click and set its position to **230**. Repeat except position the second vertical guide at **498**. Figure 23-1 shows the guides in place. They've been bolded for illustrative purposes to distinguish them from the red slice guides.

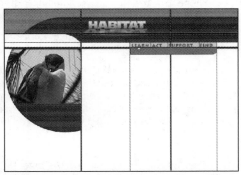

Figure 23-1: Four guides placed to aid in slicing the document

6. Save. A copy is saved in the chapter23_exercise folder and is named `ha_guides.png`.

Defining the slices

Slices are needed to export specific images or parts of images in a document. A slice (or hotspot) is also needed when you want to add a behavior. One of the biggest advantages of defining a slice is that you can individually optimize each slice. This means that you can have JPEG and GIF images in the same document. You can also use different compression settings for each image if desired.

To begin slicing the Habit Alert layout, follow these steps:

1. To begin slicing, select the Rectangle Slice tool (to the right of the Hotspot tool) from the Tools panel.

2. Place your cursor in the top-left corner and drag a rectangle to the first horizontal and first vertical guide.

   A green overlay appears when a slice is drawn. You can toggle this view on and off by using the icons in the toolbar located at the bottom section, labeled, View.

3. In the Property inspector in the Slice field, replace the name that is automatically placed and use **banner_left**. The size should be 230 × 74.

   Fireworks automatically names a slice according to the row and column that it's in. You can change the naming convention by choosing File ➪ HTML Setup, the Document Specific tag. Or you can give your slice unique names via the Property inspector.

4. Draw another slice below the one you just made. This one is 230 × 45. Name the slice **location**.

5. Draw a slice to cover the entire bird area to the bottom of the blue circle. The size is 230 × 265. Name the slice **circle_btm**. Do you notice that all the slices on the left have been 230 pixels wide? This is because they will all be placed in a column in Dreamweaver that is 230 pixels wide.

6. For the logo slice, draw from the top of the blue area to the second vertical guide but go below the horizontal guide to get the entire logo and blue area. The size should be 267 × 78 and the name should be **logo**.

7. Draw a new slice over the bird (which is also over the circle_btm slice) starting at the guide set at a position of 117. The size should be 230 × 170. Name it **circlepic0**.

8. Select the image just below the buttons and choose Insert ➪ Slice. Repeat for the image below it.

Every time you define a slice, Fireworks automatically places red lines where additional slices could be to slice the whole page. As you make additional slices the red lines change. You could stop slicing after a few slices and allow Fireworks to use its own guides (the red lines) to slice the rest of the image. In the Exporting section you see an option called Include Areas Without Slices, which slices your document according to the areas defined within the red lines.

Background image slice

Now you need to make a slice for the tiling background image behind the logo. I usually draw it a bit wide and adjust the width in the Property inspector. Follow these steps to make the slice for the background.

1. Draw a thin slice from the top of the banner to a bit below the dark line under the buttons.

2. In the Property inspector set the size to 10×27.

3. Name this slice **banner_bg**. Figure 23-2 shows all the slices you made.

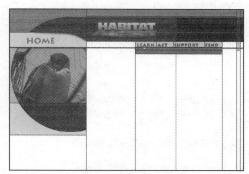

Figure 23-2: The Habitat Alert document with the slices visible

Exporting various images using one slice

The top slice under the buttons is the top of a menu that will be made in Dreamweaver. Each button has the white arrow below it. These images will be placed in a separate frame to be exported as separate images in the exporting section.

1. Select the sm_top_learn image (the one with the white arrow) and note its x and y coordinates.

2. Open the Frames panel and select Frame 2.

3. Choose File ➪ Import and navigate to the habitat_alert\designfiles\Fireworks folder. Select the sm_top_act file and click Open.

4. To position the image exactly, enter the coordinates in the Property inspector (x: 377, y: 119).

5. From the Frames Option pop-up menu, select Add Frames. Enter **2** and use the After Current Frame option. Click OK.

6. Repeat Steps 3 and 4 for Frames 3 and 4, inserting the sm_top_support image in **Frame 3** and the sm_top_find image in Frame 4.

7. Save your file. A copy of this file is saved as ha_sliced in the chapter23_exercise folder.

Adding URLs and Alt tags to sliced images

Many designers believe that every image with a link should contain an Alt tag. You should include alternate text on logo images with or without a link, so that while the image is loading, the users can see what is coming, or if they have images turned off, they can read a description of what is there. The text you put in the alternate text area is what the user sees before the image loads or when the mouse is placed over the image. This text might expedite browsing, because the users might find a link they want via the Alt tag and click it before the page is finished loading.

Note   Alternate text also makes your site more user-friendly for those using text readers. Some search engines also place importance on the content of the Alt tag.

To add alternative text or URLs to your images, follow these steps:

1. Open the ha_sliced document from the chapter23_exercise folder. Select the slice named logo.

2. In the Property inspector you will see the Link and Alt fields. Type **www.habitat_alert.org** for the link and **Take me Home** for the Alt (Figure 23-3).

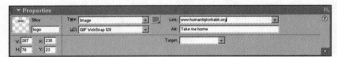

Figure 23-3: The link and alt information added in the Property inspector for the location slice

Note   You can add alternate text in the Alternate Image Description box (File⇨HTML Settings, Document Specific tab). This alternate text applies to the entire image, not just a slice. Use this option when there are no slices. To add alternate text to slices, or hotspots, enter it in the Property Inspector for the individual slices.

3. You use targets if you are developing a framed site. You can choose from the following targets choices:

   - **_blank**—Loads the linked document in a new, unnamed browser window.

   - **_parent**—Loads the lined document in the parent frameset or window of the frame that contains the link. If the frame containing the link is not nested, the linked document loads into the full browser window.

   - **_self**—Loads the linked document in the same frame or window as the link. This target is implied, so you usually don't need to specify it.

   - **_top**—Loads the linked document in the full browser window, thereby removing all frames.

4. None of the other slices need a link because the buttons will be linked in Dreamweaver. Save your file if you like. A copy is in the chapter23_exercise folder named ha_sliced_done.png.

HTML text slices

When you have an image selected, a Type field Type in the Property inspector offers two choices: Image and HTML. The purpose of HTML slices (formerly called Text slices) is to have a slice area in which you can enter HTML text. You can type HTML text from within Fireworks or in your HTML editor. To define an HTML slice, follow these steps:

1. Select the slice you want to reserve for text.

2. In the Property inspector, choose HTML from the Type pop-up menu. If you want to add HTML text from within Fireworks, click the Edit button and the Edit HTML Slice dialog box will opens so you can type the text to enter.

You can also add the text in an HTML editor. That's all there is to it, the slice color turns a darker green and a label of HTML slice replaces the Slice label.

Note

Text boxes have no borders, cell padding, or cell spacing, which places your text against the edge of the area. If there is a bordering image or background, it will be unsightly. To solve this spacing problem, insert blank text images before and after the text box, or insert slices before and after the text box. The extra text boxes or slices can then be filled with the background color or background image in Dreamweaver or the editor of your choice.

Optimizing Images

The technology for high-speed Internet connections is improving every day, but the majority of Internet users still use modem connections. Users in most U.S. urban areas enjoy all kinds of options for high-speed connections, but most rural areas don't yet have that option, nor do a lot of other countries. When you get used to using high-speed connections, it can be really easy to forget that you are privileged and that many users don't have such access. Maybe sometime in the near future file size won't be a concern, but for now it is. You should keep in mind that the larger the file or combination of files on a Web page the longer it takes to load. The connection speeds determine how long each file takes to load.

Optimization, or getting your image to the smallest possible size while retaining an acceptable quality, is one of the most important factors in determining how quickly your Web page loads. Not only can you export with GIF and JPEG images in the same document, you can also apply different settings to specific areas of a JPEG image.

Note

The file types currently available for the Web include the PNG format, but all browsers do not yet support this format, so you may want to hold on using that one just yet.

Previewing Images

Previewing an image's optimization settings is vital, and Fireworks makes it easy. You can view one setting or up to four different optimization settings, including different file formats. You can see the changes each setting will make on the file size and the appearance of the image.

The Preview tab

The preview displays your image as it will look in a browser. The Preview tab in your document window shows only the current view (a selected slice or the entire document if there isn't a selection) with the current optimization settings applied.

The 2-Up and 4-Up tabs

The 2-Up and the 4-Up tabs are used for viewing the effects of the optimization you are applying to an image or slice. The 2-Up tab shows you the original image and another one alongside it with optimization settings you have selected. This is a good way to determine how far you can go in optimizing and still have an image that looks acceptable.

Which view you see in your preview depends on whether or not a slice is selected. A selected slice shows in preview as it will display in a browser; the other areas will be dimmed. If no slice is selected, there will be no dimmed areas.

The 4-Up tab offers the most flexibility. You can view the original image and three other settings as well. To change the optimization, select the pane you want to change. In the Optimize panel change the setting; do this for each of the three views. You can mix the file formats as well so you can compare JPEG and GIF settings. You will be able to see the results in each view panel. If you look at the bottom of each view, you can see the file type, quality (or dither and colors for GIF), file size, and approximate time required to load the image in a browser (see Figure 23-4). Since this is a photo it is best optimized as a JPEG. Take note that the GIF file is considerably larger.

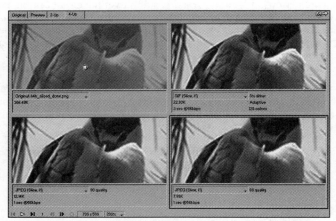

Figure 23-4: The 4-Up view showing a GIF and two different JPEG optimization settings

The Export Preview dialog box

In Figure 23-5 you can see the Export Preview dialog box (File ➪ Export Preview). The settings available are the same as those in the Optimize panel and include a few from the Optimize Options pop-up menu.

Figure 23-5: The Export Preview dialog box

You'll notice that there are a few other options, such as the File tab, which enables you to scale your image, and the Animation tab, which enables you to make a few changes to the timing and looping of an animation. Optimize to Size (Figure 23-6) has an arrow pointing to the **Optimize to Size** icon and the **Optimize to Size** dialog box open. You can type in a maximum file size you want your image to be and it will be optimized accordingly.

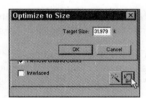

Figure 23-6: The Optimize to Size dialog box open

Optimizing GIF Images

Quite a few different settings are available in optimizing a GIF image. You can select which indexed palette and the number of colors you want to use, and more. Figure 23-7 shows the Optimize panel with a file format of GIF selected. The bottom row of icons are used to change or lock specific color swatches you choose to alter.

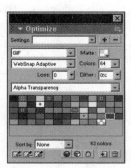

Figure 23-7: The Optimize panel with a file format of GIF

The indexed palette

GIF images are limited to 256 colors; the indexed palette you choose determines which of the 256 colors are included. You can lock a specific color before you reduce colors if you want to ensure that it doesn't get removed.

The Indexed Palette drop-down menu contains nine preset indexed palettes plus a Custom option. Each palette makes a different palette of colors available. You can customize each palette and save it with a unique name. The following list shows a few of the most used palettes:

✦ WebSnap Adaptive palette is the default palette for indexed color in Fireworks. Any color that is not Web safe is automatically evaluated and snapped to the closed Web-safe color, plus or minus seven values. It doesn't guarantee that all the colors will be Web safe but it's close.

If using only Web-safe colors is important to you, you can use the Find and Replace feature to locate any color that is not Web safe and change it.

✦ Adaptive palette finds a maximum of 256 colors. It's not a preset color set, but the best 256 colors for your image. This technique may contain a mixture of Web-safe and non–Web-safe colors.

✦ Web 216 converts all colors in the image to the nearest Web-safe color.

The Matte option

The Matte option is available for all the file formats. On the right side of the Optimize panel you see the label of Matte. Notice the color box; gray and white checks indicate that it is set to transparent. The Matte option enables you to export your image slice as though it has a background color — without changing the canvas background color. This option is particularly important when you want to use the exported image in an environment different than the one it was designed in or when you are planning to use the image on a variety of different-colored backgrounds.

There is no transparency in a JPEG image so there will always be a background color. Click in the Matte color box and use the Eyedropper tool to select a color. You can select a color from the image itself. For GIF images with transparent backgrounds you'll want to use a Matte color that closely matches the background on which the image will appear. Images that have an anti-alias edge (most do) will blend in with the background color. I'm sure you've seen "halos" or color around images. This is caused by an image exported from one colored background and placed on top of another. If you always keep your source PNG file, fixing this problem is a matter of resetting the matte color and exporting a new image.

Reducing colors

You can reduce the size of your image file by reducing the amount of colors used. Choose a number from the Maximum Number of Colors pop-up menu. You can also reduce colors from the Color Table. If you choose a color amount from the Maximum Number of Colors pop-up menu and the number is less than the number actually present in your image, Fireworks deletes colors based on the least-used colors in the image.

The color table area of the Optimize panel displays the color swatches of the colors in your image. If you don't see the swatches or if you make a change to the optimizations settings, click the Rebuild button in the lower-right corner. An updated table of colors is displayed. The Rebuild button is visible only if the colors in the color table don't reflect the most current settings you've chosen.

Using the color table gives you greater control over which colors get eliminated. You can lock specific colors so they don't change; you can have colors automatically shifted to Web-safe colors, or change the color. To make alterations to the colors, click a color to select or Shift+click to select multiple colors and then change the color, delete, snap to Web-safe, or lock. Figure 23-8 shows the labeled icons that enable you to make these changes as well as the swatch feedback showing the status of each color.

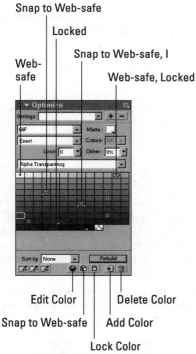

Figure 23-8: The color swatches showing the various feedback icons

Setting transparency

Transparency is available for GIF and PNG files. The choices for transparency are Index Transparency and Alpha Transparency. The difference is often confusing. To see the difference first hand, follow these steps:

1. Open a new document that's 300 × 300 with a white background.

2. Select the Rectangle drawing tool and draw a square filled with black.

3. Draw another square in the center of the white one and fill it with white.

4. From the Optimize panel, be sure Matte is set to None, and choose Index Transparency.

5. Click the Preview tab so you can see the results (Figure 23-9). The Index Transparency setting removes the background color. But this option removes not only the background but also any other areas that contain this color. Notice that the white box in the center is also gone.

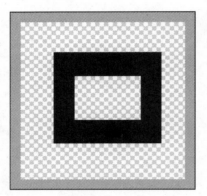

Figure 23-9: The white background and white center are both removed using index transparency.

Only one color can be used for the matte or background color automatically. You can however add or subtract additional colors to the index or alpha transparency by using the various eyedroppers in the lower-left corner of the Optimize panel. Click the appropriate eyedropper; then click the color. You'll need to reselect the eyedropper each time you want to add or remove a color to the transparency.

6. Because the removal of color from other areas isn't usually acceptable, another option exists: Alpha Transparency, which removes only the background colors, as shown in Figure 23-10.

When choosing Alpha Transparency, the view may not always show properly. Try clicking No Transparency first and then reselecting Alpha Transparency.

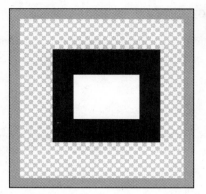

Figure 23-10: When you want to remove the background color only and not the same color from the image, use Alpha Transparency option.

Dithering

Dithering gives the illusion of new colors by varying the pattern of dots of color. The downside is that it increases the number of color changes in a horizontal row, which also increases the file size. You apply any percentage of dither you feel is needed to help a GIF image look better. If you have an image that is best suited as a JPEG but you need transparency; dithering may help make the image look better. It can also help in an image with a gradient fill for which you need transparency. Dithering can also be used when you reduce the color palette below what is actually in the image. By adding dithering, you can smooth out the colors. To determine the best options, use the preview mode and experiment with the settings. Try adding more colors and no dither or less colors and more dither and compare image quality versus file size.

Loss

Loss is the amount of compression used. GIF images normally have no loss of image detail because they use loss-less compression. But you do have the option of using compression even in a GIF image; it produces some distortions in your image however. The higher the loss setting, the higher the distortion.

Interlacing

Interlacing is an option for GIF files you are exporting for use on the Web. You can access this option only in the Export Preview (File ➪ Export Preview) or from the Optimize Options pop-up menu in the Optimize panel. When a file is interlaced it appears "blockie" or blurry, until it loads, enabling the user to see a blurred copy while the image is loading. The alternative is to not use the interlacing object, in which case, the user sees nothing until the entire image loads. The drawback to using interlacing is that the image needs to load fully before it becomes clear.

Optimize the Habitat Alert logo and other GIF slices with the following steps.

1. Open the ha_sliced_done.png file from the chapter23_exercise folder and select the logo slice.

2. Select the 2-Up tab.

3. In the Optimize panel, choose GIF file format.

4. Choose Alpha Transparency.

5. Select the Add Color to Transparency eyedropper and click in the background area of the logo slice. Because the striped background will be a background image, you don't need the stripes and blue area in this image. Every little bit helps when reducing image file size.

6. A stripe will still be present after adding the first color to the transparency. Using the Add Color to Transparency eyedropper again, click the remaining stripe color to remove it.

7. Change the Matte color to #003366. The logo will look like Figure 23-11.

Figure 23-11: The Habit Alert logo seen in preview mode after the optimization settings are made

8. Shift+select all the slices except the bird image and the buttons; then click the Preview tab.

9. In the Optimize panel set the following settings:

   • File Format: GIF

   • Indexed Palette: Web Snap Adaptive

   • Colors: 64

   • Matte: None

   • Transparency: No Transparency.

10. Shift+select each button and use these settings:

- File Format: GIF
- Indexed Palette: Web Snap Adaptive
- Colors: 16
- Matte: None
- Transparency: Index Transparency

11. Shift+select the two slices below the buttons using these settings:

- File Format: GIF
- Indexed Palette: Web Snap Adaptive
- Colors: 4
- Matte: None
- Transparency: No Transparency

12. Save as **ha_gif.png.**

Optimizing JPEG Images

There aren't many choices to make when optimizing JPEG images but there is still a lot of flexibility. Selective JPEG compression is a special feature available only for JPEG images. It's used to set higher optimization to selected areas of an image. Following is a brief explanation of each option for JPEG images. Figure 23-12 shows the Optimize panel for JPEG images.

Figure 23-12: The Optimize panel with a File Format of JPEG chosen

Don't JPEG a JPEG image; it looses information each time and gets considerably worse after the second time. JPEG is good for 24-bit color depth, no less.

Quality

The quality setting determines how much compression is applied to the image. Be sure you check in the Preview mode. It's a good idea to zoom in a bit to see the artifact effect on your image. Go as low as you can and still have an acceptable-looking image.

Smoothing

When you lower the quality setting you may see visible artifacts depending on how low you went. The Smooth option adds a bit of blur to blend the image. You loose some image sharpness but it may be a compromise you are willing to make when a small file size is a must. The Smooth setting ranges from 0 to 8 with 8 being a higher degree of blur. You can then apply an Unsharp filter if you'd like, using either Effects menu or the Filters menu.

Sharpen JPEG edges

The JPEG compression works best on photographs, gradients, and drop shadows. But you may have incorporated areas of text or perhaps used some smoothing. To bring back the edge detail, open the Optimize Options pop-up menu and select Sharpen JPEG Edges. This, however, adds to the file size.

Progressive JPEG

The Progressive option is similar to GIF interlacing. The image appears "blockie" and gradually clears. The drawback is that it is not supported by older browsers (before Netscape 2 and IE 3) and shows a broken image.

Selective JPEG compression

You can optimize the background of a JPEG image at a lower-quality setting to emphasize the foreground image. Or you can use a lower setting for most of a document and select the areas that appear a bit block-like and blurry, which occurs when a JPEG image has been compressed too much and optimized at a different setting. To use selective JPEG compression, follow these steps:

1. Open `selectivejpeg.png` from the chapter23_exercise folder. This image doesn't need to be sliced but it could use some Selective JPEG compression.

2. Click on the 2-Up preview tab and choose JPEG from the Export File Format pop-up menu. Zoom in to see the effects of the JPEG artifacts better.

3. Click the bitmap image to make it active. If you are in the habit of locking background layers be sure that you remember to unlock it. Click the Preview tab in the Document window so you can see the results of lowering the JPEG compression.

4. In the Optimize panel, lower the Quality setting all the way to 40. I know the text and shadow look horrible (Figure 23-13); you fix that in a moment, but the gradient still looks good.

5. Click the Lasso tool (or you can use the Marquee tool) and draw around the area you want to compress at a higher quality setting. To use the Lasso tool, you have to return to the Original tab so you'll have to remember where you want to outline. If there is more than one area, press Shift and make your next selection.

If you have more than one area to use selective compression on, they must all be selected now or you will have to start over and make your selections again, including all the areas that need the Selective JPEG compression applied. These selections are going to become a JPG mask, and there can be only one per document.

Figure 23-13: The image with the JPEG quality lowered to 40

6. Select Modify ⇨ Selective JPEG ⇨ Save Selection As JPEG Mask. As a default, the mask will be a pink color.

7. You can set the Selective settings from the menu bar by choosing one of these methods:

   • Modify ⇨ Selective JPEG ⇨ Settings

   • Click the pencil icon in the Optimize panel to the right of the Selective Quality field.

8. Check Enable Selective Quality and enter a quality value in the Selective Quality field. You can change the overlay color. Since there is text, I checked the Preserve Text Quality option (Figure 23-14).

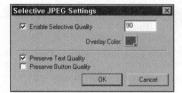

Figure 23-14: The Selective JPEG Settings dialog box

9. A Quality of 90 looks about perfect (Figure 23-15). You could compromise and go to 80 or 85. You can't really see the JPEG artifacts when it is zoomed out. Only you can determine whether the trade off of quality and file size is worth it.

Figure 23-15: The image with the quality setting of 90% and zoomed in to 200%

Note The figures you see here are zoomed in at 200%; even using a quality of 80, it looks good at 100%.

10. To edit the JPEG mask, you can delete and start over by choosing Modify ⇨ Selective JPEG ⇨ Remove JPEG Mask, or if you want to add to or subtract from the current mask, go to Modify ⇨ Selective JPEG ⇨ Restore JPEG Mask As Selection. With the selection active, you can use the Shift key and draw another area or add on. If you want to delete a portion, hold down the Alt (Option) key and draw around the area to remove.

11. Save the mask by choosing Modify ⇨ Selective JPEG ⇨ Save Selection As JPEG Mask.

Much of the optimization process is trial and error; choose your settings, preview, and repeat until you get an acceptable image.

Understanding Exporting

Before you begin exporting, it's important to have your site structure set up. Setting up your folders locally in the same way that they will be uploaded saves you many headaches. If you are using Dreamweaver and save your site files in one folder and then move the file to another folder, all the links to your images are broken, so it's better to save in the same folder that the file will ultimately be in.

When you choose to export images as well as the HTML of a Fireworks document, the images and the HTML file (containing a table that places all the image slices back together) are generated.

If you export from Fireworks and expect to insert the Fireworks code into a Dreamweaver document, the HTML file and the images must be saved in the same folder as the file into which you will insert the Fireworks code. Otherwise all your image links will be broken. For example, a simple site structure might be a site folder called Bookstore with a subfolder of images and another subfolder called assets. If your site's HTML/HTM files are kept in the Bookstore folder, you would want to export your Fireworks document containing the HTML document into the Bookstore folder and designate that the images be exported to the images folder.

Export Wizard

The Export Wizard is especially helpful to new users who are not familiar with optimizing images. The Wizard can help you decide which format to use and help you decide on the settings to use. To use the Export Wizard, follow these steps:

1. Open an image to export and choose File ⇨ Export Wizard. Figure 23-16 shows the opening dialog box for the Export Wizard. If you had a file size limit you could select the Target Export file size option and enter a number.

2. Select the Select an Export Format option and click Continue. The next dialog box asks how to handle frames if there are any. The choices are as follows:

   - Animated GIF
   - Javascript Rollover
   - Single Image File

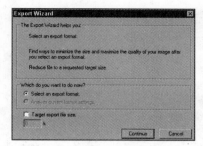

Figure 23-16: The Export Wizard opening dialog box

3. Choose the appropriate option if you have any frames; then click Continue. The next dialog box asks what the destination of your image will be. The options are as follows:

   - The Web
   - An image editing application
   - A desktop publishing application
   - Dreamweaver

4. Select The Web and click Continue.

5. The Analysis Report dialog box opens with recommendations for your selected image. If there is more than one option, such as JPEG and GIF, click Exit.

6. The Export Preview window opens showing you both GIF and JPEG. The first image shown is the smallest. You can decide which one looks best. You can change the optimization settings in this dialog box. You can also click the File tab and alter the scale size or the crop size if a crop selection is made. The Animation tab enables you to alter some of the animation settings.

7. When your image is ready to export click the Export button.

Continue with the export. The next section, "General exporting options," details how to complete the export.

General exporting options

The Export dialog box is present each time you export an image no matter which exporting method you choose. This section looks at the various options for exporting (Figure 23-17).

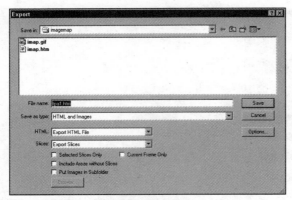

Figure 23-17: The Export dialog box

To export, follow these steps:

1. Select an image and use one of these methods to open the Export dialog box:

   - Choose File ➪ Export.

   - Click the Quick Export icon (the round Fireworks icon with an arrow in the top right of the document window) and choose the appropriate application to which to export.

   - Choose File ➪ Export Preview; optimize and click the Export button.

   - Right (Control)+click an image and choose Export Selected Slice.

   - Use the Export Wizard and click the Export button from the Export Preview dialog box.

2. Navigate to the folder you want to export to. If you are developing a site it's a good idea to export into the root folder of the Web site.

3. Name your file.

4. Select the type of file from the selections in the drop-down menu. The options are as follows:

   - **HTML and Images** — This option exports the image, JavaScript, and the code necessary to place everything into a table.

   - **Images only** — This option exports only an image or selected images with no HTML or JavaScript code.

   - **Dreamweaver Library (.lbi)** — A Library folder is necessary to export into. The HTML and images will be exported as a Dreamweaver library item.

   - **CSS Layers (.htm)** — This option exports images, layers, and frames as CSS layers that can then be used in Dreamweaver.

   - **Director (.htm)** — Export buttons and rollovers as Director cast members.

   - **Layers to Files** — Exports each layer as a separate file.

- **Frames to Files** — Exports each frame as a separate file.

- **Lotus Domino Designer** — Exports rollovers and buttons as image wells.

- **Macromedia Flash SWF** — Export animations or maintain vectors by choosing this option.

- **Illustrator 7** — Exports as a vector image but may loose effects applied depending on the application in which it is opened.

- **Photoshop PSD** — A native Photoshop format. You can choose to maintain editability or appearance.

5. If the HTML field is active, choose to export the HTML file or to copy it to the Clipboard.

6. The bottom portion of the dialog box has several important options spelled out here:

   - **Selected Slices Only** — When selected, only the slices you have selected will be exported.

   - **Include Areas without Slices** — When selected the areas of the image that are not specifically defined by a slice are also exported. They are sliced according the automatic slicing guides (red lines).

   - **Current Frame Only** — If selected, an image with multiple frames exports only the current frame. If unselected, all frames are exported and the filename ends with f2, f3, and so on.

   - **Put Images in Subfolder** — If selected, the Browse button is active so you can browse to a subfolder or make one to store the images in.

   - Option button opens the HTML setup dialog box, which is detailed in the next section.

7. Click Save when you are finished.

HTML setup

You can access the HTML Setup dialog box by choosing File ➪ HTML Setup or by clicking the Options button in the Export dialog box.

The General tab

The Export panel includes an Options button with more options. Click it to open the HTML Setup dialog box. The General tab is where you choose the application you will be using the code in, the extension of your choice, whether to add comments, and whether you want everything in lowercase.

The Table tab

The Table tab (see Figure 23-18) has some important options. The Space with options includes 1-Pixel Transparent Spacer, which is probably the most often used option because it generates a transparent image as a space holder. When you export, you will notice one file called `spacer.gif` when you look in the folder to which you exported. This is a 1-pixel by 1-pixel transparent file that is used as a spacer to keep a table's structural integrity. This spacer is known by several names and is frequently called a shim or a transparency.gif.

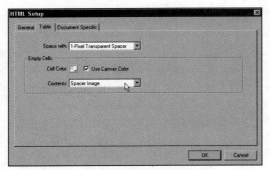

Figure 23-18: Table options tab

You can also choose to export using a nested table, which places one table into another table. This sort of table layout does not require spacers. Or, you can choose to export only a table with no spacers at all. It will probably be fine in Internet Explorer, but Netscape Navigator often does not hold the table's integrity if empty cells exist. To help prevent the presence of an empty cell, you could also choose Non-breaking Space instead of Spacer Image for the Contents option.

In Netscape if a nonbreaking space is used instead of a transparent image, the table doesn't show any background image or colors.

If your table has an image in every cell, Single Table–No Spacers works just fine.

Document Specific tab

This tab enables you to set the naming conventions to use for automatically naming exported images. This is also where you make the selection necessary if you are exporting a nav bar with multiple pages.

Exporting HTML and images

Use the HTML and Images option when you want to export an entire document as a Web page or when you want to export an image that has a behavior attached. To export an image as a generic HTML and Images file follow these steps:

1. Open the `ha_sliced_done.png` image from the chapter23_exercise folder. This is a sliced and optimized file. This isn't the way you are going to export for the Habitat Alert site but you can practice on it.

2. Choose File ➪ Export. In the Save in box, choose a place on your hard drive to save this exercise.

3. In the Save as Type field, choose HTML and Images.

4. In the HTML field choose Export HTML file.

5. In the Slices field choose Export slices.

6. Check Include Areas without Slices.

7. Check Put Images in Subfolder. Don't browse for a folder, a new folder named images will be automatically added.

8. Click on Save.

Exporting images only

You can export one slice or you can Shift+select multiple slices to export by following these steps:

1. Select a slice or slices.

2. Choose File ⇨ Export.

3. Navigate to the location to which you want to export.

4. Name your file.

5. In the Save as Type box choose Images Only.

6. In the Slices box, choose Slices Only; uncheck the Include Areas without slices option.

7. Click Save.

Exporting the Habitat Alert layout

Most of the slices in our Habitat Alert layout are exported using slices only. You also export the navigation later in the chapter using another method.

Note In the Dreamweaver section you will define a site and add folders for the site's structure. On the CD is a site folder you can use for this exercise.

To export the slices, follow these steps:

1. Open the `site_layout.png` file from the `habitat_alert\designfiles\Fireworks` folder. You are using the site file found in the root site so that when you edit in Dreamweaver, it knows where to locate the source file.

2. Right-click on the bird image only. (Be sure the slice name is circle0 and not circle_btm.) Choose Export Selected Slice.

3. The Export dialog box opens. Export into the habitat_alert folder you saved to your hard drive. The path is `habitat_alert\html\sharedimages\circlebirds`.

4. This option automatically has the Selected Slices only option checked.

5. The Frames option is active because there are other bird images being stored on other frames. They will be getting a random script applied to them in Dreamweaver. Uncheck the Current Frame only option because you want to export all the images.

6. Click Save.

Note Open the circlebirds folder and notice the naming of each image. The images in the frames each have a frame number after them. You may want to change the names. We changed ours to circlepic1, and so on.

7. Repeat for the Location slice (Home) and save in the `habitat_alert\ htmlsharedimages\locations` folder.

8. Repeat for the main navigation buttons and the gold boxes below then. When selecting small slices, zoom in so you can select them. Export to the `sharedimages\mainnavs` folder. Again you may want to rename the images in the frames. The images in the frames will be used in Dreamweaver as rollovers.

Because you exported including all the frames, a few blank images will be generated where the frame is empty. Just delete these.

9. Zoom in and select the banner_bg slice. It's the long thin one on the top right. This is your background slice. Repeat Steps 2–6, except check the Current Frame only option.

10. Select the circle0 slice and cut it (Control [Command] + X). Then export the slice under it named circle_btm into the backgrounds folder. Paste the circle0 back into the document.

When a slice overlaps another, you need to move it to export the entire slice below it. Turning off the top slice in the Web layer doesn't do the trick. By cutting and pasting the top slice, you ensure that it's replaced in the same location.

11. Shift+select the logo and the banner_left slice and export to the `sharedimages` folder.

Exporting with the Export Area tool

The Export Area tool is located on the pop-up menu of the Crop tool. This tool is similar to the Crop tool in the way it defines an area but it doesn't affect the original image. To export using the Export Area tool, follow these steps:

1. Open the `site_layout.png` file from the `habitat_alert\designfiles\Fireworks` folder you saved to your hard drive.

2. Select the Export Area tool and drag around the main navigation buttons only. Use the handles to adjust the size. Don't get the gold slices below or the line with shadow.

3. Double-click when the area is defined.

4. Choose File ➪ Export.

5. Navigate to the `navbuttons` folder in your root folder and open it.

6. Name the file **navigation_buttons_fw.png**.

7. In the Save as Type box, choose HTML and Images. In the HTML box, choose Export HTML file.

You can use any export option you'd like, depending on the type of image you are exporting. Since you have JavaScript attached you are using the HTML and Images.

8. If you want the images put in a separate folder, check that option and click the Save button.

Exporting as a Library Item

If you want to use your image as a Library Item in Dreamweaver follow these steps:

1. Select a slice or area. (See Export area.)

2. Choose File ➪ Export.

3. In the Save as Type box, choose Dreamweaver Library. A message opens telling you to have a Library folder in the root. Click OK.

4. In the new window that opens, if you don't have a Library folder, click the Create New Folder icon (the solid yellow folder) and name it **library**. Click Open. Otherwise navigate to your Library folder.

5. In the Slices field, choose Export Slices and check the Put Images in Subfolder box.

6. Export into the Library folder.

Exporting to Macromedia Flash SWF

Flash MX

It seems like only yesterday that GIF animation was the option of choice for animations, but Flash has quickly become the favorite choice for full-featured animation. Based on a recent survey, which revealed that 96.4 percent of all Web users already have the Flash player, many more Web sites are featuring Flash animations instead of GIF. One of SWF or Flash animation's greatest appeal is the small file sizes.

You can export Fireworks images as Flash SWF files, or you can use a native Fireworks PNG file and import it into Flash. For instance, if you apply a gradient transparency in Fireworks you have to export the transparent object over the area you want to appear transparent. But the same image imported into Flash has true transparency and can be placed on top of any object.

To export as Flash SWF, follow these steps:

1. Open the document you want to export and make the appropriate selections.

2. Choose File ➪ Export.

3. In the Save as Type box, select Macromedia Flash SWF.

4. Click the Options button to set your export options. Figure 23-19 shows the Macromedia Flash SWF Export Options dialog box.

Figure 23-19: The Macromedia Flash SWF Export Options dialog box

5. The following object and text options are available; select the ones you want:

- **Objects: Maintain Paths** converts paths into editable Flash paths.
- **Objects: Maintain Appearance** converts paths into bitmapped images.
- **Text: Maintain Editabiltiy** converts Fireworks text into text that is editable in Flash.
- **Text: Convert to Path** converts the text into a bitmap.

6. If you are exporting a JPGE image, select the quality setting you want.

7. Select All Frames or only the frames you want to export.

8. The last option is to set the Frame Rate per second.

9. When you are done with your selections, choose OK and the choose **Save** in the **Export** dialog box.

SWF exports from Fireworks can be used as they are for Web viewing or inserted into Dreamweaver or another layout editor without even using Flash. But the real purpose of the ability to export as a Macromedia Flash SWF file is to reuse the artwork you made in Fireworks in Flash.

Vector content remains vector in Flash if you choose the Maintain Paths and Maintain Editability options. But many actions you can take in Fireworks are lost when exported for use in Flash. Some of the things that are not compatible with Flash include Live Effects, Opacity (objects with opacity become symbols with an alpha channel), and blending modes. Masks, slice objects, image maps, and behaviors, such as rollovers, are lost as well. Other features lost are things such as feathering, layers, and some text formatting. Anti-aliasing isn't maintained on export. But this isn't a problem because Flash automatically applies it to documents itself. If you keep in mind that the main reason to use a SWF export from Fireworks is to reuse the art then you will do fine.

Exporting to PSD

PSD is the native file format of Adobe Photoshop. If you want to open your Fireworks PNG files in Photoshop, or share your files with someone who will use Photoshop, you can export a Fireworks file as a PSD file. When you export as a PSD, you have the option of exporting with better editability over appearance or better appearance over editability. But keep in mind that Fireworks paths are always converted to bitmap images. To export for Photoshop, follow these steps:

1. Select an image to export and choose File ➪ Export.

2. From the Save as Type box, select Photoshop PSD.

3. In the Settings area you have four options:

- **Maintain Editability over Appearance** will place each object on a separate layer and the effects will remain editable. It will convert text into editable text. Effects that don't have an equivalent in Photoshop will be discarded.
- **Maintain Fireworks Appearance** converts objects into layers and renders the effects and text into images.

- **Smaller Photoshop File** flattens all the objects and layers into one layer, producing a smaller file size.

- **Custom** enables you to select separate setting options for objects, effects, and text.

4. When you are done making your selections, click Save.

Exporting as vectors

You can use Fireworks vectors as paths in FreeHand, Illustrator, or Flash. You maintain only the path, a solid fill, and stroke. Any effects will be lost. To export a vector shape for FreeHand, Illustrator, or Flash, follow these steps:

1. Select an image and choose File ➪ Export.

2. In the Save As Type box, choose Illustrator 7.

3. Click the Options button. Figure 23-20 shows the Illustrator Export Options dialog box.

Figure 23-20: The Illustrator Export Options dialog box

4. If you want to keep the elements on individual layers, select Export Current Frame Only. If you want each frame on a separate layer, select Convert Frames to Layers.

5. To make the export completely for FreeHand, choose FreeHand Compatible.

6. Click OK.

7. Click Save to complete the export.

Exporting to CSS layers

You can export Fireworks object and images, layers, and/or frames as CSS layers. By using CSS layers in Dreamweaver you can overlap and stack layers on top of one another, make them visible or invisible, or even move them, which you can't do with normal Fireworks HTML output. To export to CSS layers, follow these steps:

1. Select the object or images you want to export and choose File ➪ Export.

2. In the Save As Type box, choose CSS Layers.

3. In the Source area, choose from the Fireworks options: Fireworks Slices, Fireworks Layers, or Fireworks Frames.

4. The Trim Images box, which trims any excess canvas around objects you are exporting, is checked by default.

5. If you want the exported images in a subfolder, check the Put Images in Subfolder option.

6. Click Save to export.

Export layers or frames as separate files

You can export all the layers or all the frames of a Fireworks document as separate files. To export layers or frames as separate images, follow these steps:

1. Open the image you want to export and choose File ➪ Export.

2. From the Save as Type box, choose Layers to Files or the Frames to Files.

3. Leave the Trim Images option checked if you want to automatically trim the images to fit the objects on each layer (or frame).

4. Click Save.

Summary

In this chapter, you learned how to slice an image or document. You also discovered how to optimize your images. You learned which images are better suited to GIF and which ones are best suited to JPEG. After your images were sliced and optimized you moved on the many options available for exporting the images. You discovered how to export for compatibility in a variety of other formats, such as Flash SWF and Dreamweaver Library items.

Project Summary

The following tables outline what you've done in this chapter that will be used in the Habitat Alert Web site. Some of the images need further work in another section; others are ready to use in another application.

Files Prepared for Habitat Alert Web Site		
Images	*What Was Done*	*Where to Now?*
site_layout.png	This is the source file used to export the images needed in the site. It has the guides in place and the images sliced and optimized.	These images will all be placed into the layout in Dreamweaver.

Additional Site Assets from Techniques in This Chapter

Additional Images	Techniques Used	Where to Now?
adtab.gif and ad.gif	These images are used for a small banner ad in the site. It was sliced and optimized as a GIF.	Banner will be added in Dreamweaver.
storethings.gif cards.gif printme.gif	These images are used on the home page of the site, a link for the store, credit card image, and a print image. The slices for these images use the Insert ➪ Slice method.	These will be added with the final site design in Dreamweaver.
location_learn location_act location_support location_find	Using the same technique as the section titled, "Preparing for various images to be exported using the same slice," images for the location slice were added to the Frames panel. During export, the Current Frame only option was toggled off.	Inserted into a Dreamweaver template.

✦   ✦   ✦

Unleashing the Power of Macromedia Flash MX

Navigating through Flash MX

The Flash MX workspace is similar to Fireworks MX and
Dreamweaver MX. So if you are new to Flash MX but familiar with
one of the other applications, you will get acclimated quickly. The
work area in Flash is called the Stage whereas in the other applications its called the Document Window. Even if you are new to using
the Macromedia Studio MX applications, the new interface is intuitive
and easy to use. You'll be zipping around the panels and tools in no
time at all. In this chapter, you explore the main interface features
and where to find the tools you'll need. The Flash MX interface has
changed dramatically since version 5. The panel system is streamlined and a Property inspector has been added, which gives you
access to what used to be nine different panels, in one location. As
you select a tool, the Property inspector changes to reflect the properties of the selected tool.

Using the Flash MX Interface

When you first open Flash you'll notice the panel groups. In Windows
they are docked to the right of the interface. On a Mac they float as a
group on the right. Windows users can undock the panels if they like.
Both platforms enable you to rearrange the grouping of panels and
determine which panels are open in the interface by opening the various panel Options pop-up menus and choosing where to move them
or to close them. To undock a panel or panel group, drag it by its
gripper and rearrange. Drag back to the panel area until you see a
highlighted line and release the mouse button to dock a panel. Panels
are also accessible by using keyboard shortcuts. After you arrange
the panels the way you want them, you can save the configuration
by choosing Window ⇨ Save Panel Layout. Figure 24-1 shows the
Flash MX interface.

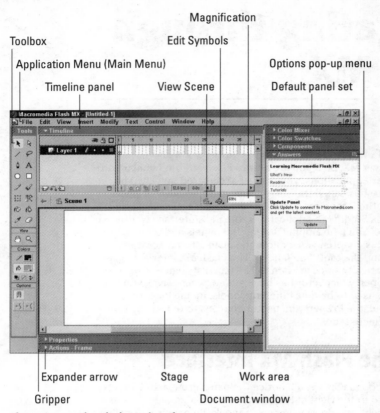

Figure 24-1: The Flash MX interface

 Note   Windows has two toolbars available that the Mac doesn't: the Main toolbar, which contains icons for commonly used toolbox items and panel options, and the status bar, which provides a description of the selected tool. These are off by default because many of the items are redundant. But the tool descriptions and icons may be helpful to new users.

The Property Inspector

The Property inspector is new to Flash MX and is similar in function to the one found in Dreamweaver. As you select a tool or object on the Stage (the large white area that you work in), the Property inspector changes to reflect that item's properties. You can leave it docked at the bottom (or floating in Mac) or close it and access it as needed by choosing Window ➪ Properties. Although it's used so frequently you'll probably want to click the Expander arrow to close it when it's not in use.

The Property inspector replaces nine panels: Stroke, Fill, Character, Paragraph, Text Options, Instance, Effect, Frame, and Sound. That's a lot of panels you no longer have to shuffle. Figure 24-2 shows the Property inspector with the Pen tool selected.

Figure 24-2: The Property inspector when the Pen tool is selected

Tip

The expander opens and closes a panel, but you can actually click anywhere on the gray bar to open and close a panel.

The Toolbox

The Toolbox is organized into four main sections. At the top are 16 Flash tools, the second category is the View tools, the third is the Color area, and the fourth is the Options area, which displays tool-specific modifiers. Figure 24-3 shows the Toolbox.

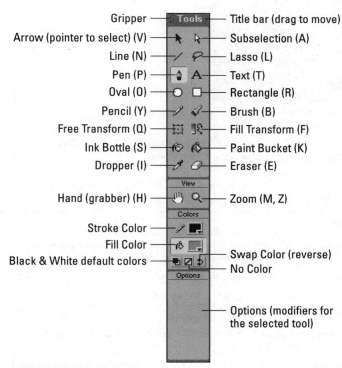

Figure 24-3: The Toolbox

Tip

When using the tools in the Toolbox always check the Options area (bottom of the Toolbox) and the Property inspector for modifiers. You'll find that at times there are different options in each area depending on the tool selected.

The Document Window

A new document opens automatically when you launch Flash MX. You can open additional documents by choosing File ➪ New or File ➪ New From Template — a new feature to Flash MX. Figure 23-4 shows that there are seven categories of templates and each one contains Category Items. These are great starter templates for a variety of projects.

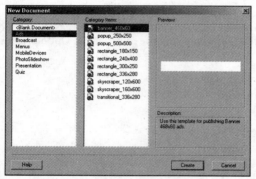

Figure 24-4: The template documents that ship with Flash MX

The View menu contains options that control various functions within the Document window. Table 24-1 shows a listing of the options and their functions.

Table 24-1: The View Menu Options

Option	Description
Goto	There is a submenu of scenes in the current movie. You can also access this menu from the Edit Scene icon in the Document window.
Zoom In	Increases the scale of the Stage by 50 percent.
Zoom Out	Decreases the scale of the Stage by 50 percent.
Magnification	Various view size options.
Outlines	All shapes are shown as outlines only. This option does not affect how your movie exports, only how you view it.
Fast	Anti-aliasing and dithering are turned off to speed up the display. This option does not affect how your movie exports, only how you view it.

Option	Description
Antialias	The edges of shapes and lines are dithered to make them look smoother. This option does not affect how your movie exports, only how you view it.
Antialias Text	Smoothes the edges of text. You can use only one Anti-alias option, either for text or for shapes. This option does not affect how your movie exports, only how you view it.
Timeline	Shows or hides the timeline even when it's docked.
Work Area	The gray area around the Stage can be used when this option is turned on.
Rulers	Toggles the ruler's visibility on and off. If you are going to use guides, rulers have to be turned on.
Grid	You can choose to show the grid (which doesn't export), or to snap to grid, or edit grid from this menu. When you choose the Snap to Grid option, items snap to it even if it's invisible.
Guides	Rulers need to be turned on for guides. Drag a horizontal or vertical guide from the rulers. Submenu options are Show Guides, Lock Guides, Snap To Guides, and Edit Guides.
Snap to Pixel	This option aligns items to the x and y coordinates to be in whole-pixel increments. A 1-pixel grid appears when the Stage is magnified to 400 percent or higher.
Snap to Objects	When you move an item from its origin point, it snaps into alignment with items already on the Stage.
Show Shape Hints	Shape Hints are used when tweening shapes.
Hide Edges	Hide Edges hides the selection pattern without affecting the selection.
Hide Panels	Hides or unhides all visible panels. You can also use F4 or the Tab key.

Change Document Properties

To change the properties of your Flash document choose Modify ➪ Document. The Document Properties dialog box opens, as shown in Figure 24-5. You can alter the size by typing specific dimensions or by clicking the Print or Contents buttons to match the size of either. You also change the background color, frame rate, and ruler units from this dialog box. Many of these properties can also be changed right in the Property inspector.

Figure 24-5: The Document Properties dialog box

Active Window Focus

Focus is the part of the application that is active. In Flash MX it is possible to have more than one window/panel active. To make a specific panel or window active click it. Then when you return to the Stage to edit an item, you need to click it to return the focus to it.

Keyboard Shortcuts

Flash MX ships with keyboard shortcuts that were designed for it. But you can also choose to use a set of shortcuts for applications, such as Fireworks, Photoshop, and others. Or you make your own custom set. To customize your own shortcuts, follow these steps:

1. Choose Edit ➪ Keyboard Shortcuts.

2. You can use the current set or choose one from the Current Set drop-down menu.

3. Click the Duplicate set icon (first one to the right of the Current Set field), enter a new name, and click OK. By making a duplicate you prevent overwriting the original shortcut file.

4. Choose one of the categories listed in the Command area. Click the plus sign (+) to expand the category to its associated commands. Choose the command you want to add or change.

5. In the Shortcuts area click the minus sign to remove (it will be grayed out unless there is a command already associated with it) or click the plus sign to add a new shortcut.

6. When adding a new shortcut or changing a current one, the Press Key field is active. Enter the key combination you want to use for the shortcut by pressing the keys on your keyboard. Press the Control (Command) key and a letter or number. If it's already used or if you press an invalid selection, you see a warning message.

7. Click the Change button, and then click OK.

Understanding Layer/Folder Basics

You'll work with layers when you learn about the Timeline in Chapter 27. In this section, you won't be exploring the entire Timeline you need to understand the basic concept of layers for most everything you do in Flash. Layers help you separate and organize pieces of your content and actions. The way you use layers will depend on your own workflow and work habits. It's a good idea to separate different parts of your movies onto separate layers; otherwise you'll be amazed at how quickly you can loose things. This section shows you how to name layers and gives you some organizing tips.

Figure 24-6 shows the various options for layers and folders in the Timeline.

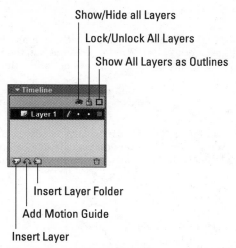

Show/Hide all Layers

Lock/Unlock All Layers

Show All Layers as Outlines

Insert Layer Folder

Add Motion Guide

Insert Layer

Figure 24-6: Layer and folder options and functions

Adding layers and/or layer folders

There are several ways to add a new layer in Flash. You can choose one of the following:

✦ Insert ➪ New Layer or Insert ➪ Layer Folder from the main menu.

✦ On the bottom-left corner of the Timeline, click the icon with the plus (+) on top of the document for a new layer or the icon with the plus (+) on top of the folder for a new layer folder.

✦ Right-click (Control-click) the layer name and choose Insert Layer or Insert Folder from the context menu.

All new layers/folders are added to the top of the selected layer/folder.

Deleting layers or layer folders

To delete layers (or folders), select the layer or layer folder you want to delete and click the Delete Layer (Layer Folder) icon, which is the Trashcan, or Right-click (Control+click) and select Delete Layer or Delete Folder from the context menu.

Moving layers/folders

To rearrange a layer or folder, click and drag it to the new location. Objects on the top layer hide objects on the layer below it. Not all objects are obscured; only those directly below what's on the layer above it. This doesn't affect the way your movie plays. The timeline and frames you use control what appears in your movie and when it appears.

Visibility

You can turn off the visibility of each individual layer by clicking the dot in the column below the eye icon. If you want to hide or show all the layers, click the eye icon. A red X in the layer indicates the layer's visibility is turned off. The visibility of the layers does not affect the way the movie plays.

Locking layers/folders

You can lock a layer, layers, or folders to prevent editing. This is particularly handy when you are tracing items. You can lock the layer you want to trace so you don't accidentally alter it. To lock all layers, click the lock icon. To lock individual layers, click the dot in the column below the lock icon.

Naming layers/folders

It's a good idea to get in the habit of naming layers and folders. To name a layer or folder, double-click the layer or folder name and type the new name.

Selecting layers/folders

Layers and folders are selected in several different ways. You can select a layer by clicking the layer name. If you select a frame, the layer it is on is automatically selected. If you select an action, the layer it is on is selected. Also, if you select an object on the stage, the layer it is on is automatically selected.

Organizing with Layers and Layer Folders

If you are an experienced Flash user, you probably already organize your layers. It's a good idea to get in the habit of placing certain kinds of content and actions on separate layers. The following sections explain some of the most commonly used Flash layer names and functions. You'll develop your own naming system, which best suits the way you work.

Content layers and layer folders

Content layers are layers or layers in folders that hold your art and things such as buttons, text, or sound. As you work through this Flash section, you'll see that the authors put almost everything on its own separate layer. For example, a background image is on one layer, buttons on another, actions on another, and so on.

Actions

Actions are bits of *ActionScript* code similar to JavaScript that add functionality to your movies. You'll discover that actions are the power behind Flash, they allow you to communicate to different parts of your movies. If you keep all of your actions on a layer named actions, you'll be able to locate them easily.

Guide layer

If you right-click (Control+click) the layer name, you see the Guide option. This is a layer where you can keep any guide you want to use. For example, you can set up guidelines for your movie and store them on this layer. You can also use shapes, such as a rectangle, that you want to arrange other objects around or maybe a bitmap image of a mockup to use as a guide. Content you put on the guide layer does not export with the movie.

Motion guide

In Chapter 27, you learn how to make motion tweens using a motion guide. In short, when you select a tween object and right-click (Control+click) and choose Motion Guide, the object is added above the layer the tween is on. When it's added, it is added as a Guide layer. The name will be Guide plus the name of the layer for which it's a guide. An arch icon appears before the guide name indicating that it's a motion guide. You draw the path you want the motion to follow in the Guide layer. This layer doesn't export with your movie.

Importing Files into Flash

Flash is compatible with many of the popular image file formats. Table 24-2 shows some of the files you can easily import. Chapter 25 discusses how to directly import assets into your movies Library.

Table 24-2: Image Formats for Flash Import

File Type	Extension	Description
Adobe Illustrator	.ai, .eps	These files import as vector graphics unless they contain bitmap images.
Bitmap images	.bmp, .jpg, .gif, .pct, .pict, .tiff	These are flattened images without layer or transparency information.
PNG	.png	This format supports alpha channels. Png files imported from Fireworks into Flash maintains layers, vectors, and transparency.
PSD	.psd	These are Photoshop native files. Effects that are not compatible will not import properly, but you can choose to maintain layers and editability.
QuickTime Movie	.mov	This is a video format by Apple computers.
FreeHand	.fh7, .fh8, .fh9, .fh10, .fh11	This is a vector-based format that maintains editability and many effects in Flash.
Toon Boom Studio	.tbp	These vector files preserve layers, scenes, sound, and more. There is a trial version on the CD-ROM.

Summary

In this chapter, you learned how to navigate through the Flash environment and how to find the various tools and panels. You learned how you can customize your own keyboard short-cuts. You also learned layer basics and saw a general list of file formats that you can import into Flash MX.

✦   ✦   ✦

Designing Visual Content

The visual content is the most important part of your Flash movie; it conveys your thoughts, concepts, ideas, and company image. ActionScripting can add the magic. The drawing tools in Flash MX are robust, and you'll be looking at some of them in this chapter. Some of the tools are so similar to FreeHand or Fireworks tools that this chapter doesn't repeat information but it does include cross-references so you know where to look for details that have already been covered in the book. You'll be looking at a new tool called the Free Transform tool and the Envelop modifier, which warps and distorts shape as well as using text. You can create three types of text boxes in Flash and you'll look at each one of them. As you'll see in this chapter, there are a lot of ways to work with, manipulate, and arrange objects with Flash.

The Drawing Tools

The drawing tools are located in the top portion of the Toolbox. Most shapes you draw will probably have a fill and a stroke. In Flash once you draw a shape that has a stroke, you can then select the fill and the stroke separately.

Fill and stroke basics

You start by drawing geometric shapes using the Rectangle or Oval tools (the instructions work for either Oval or Rectangle tools).

1. Select the Rectangle tool from the Toolbox or press R. Notice the Property inspector shown in Figure 25-1.

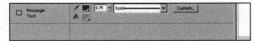

Figure 25-1: The Property inspector showing the properties for the Rectangle tool

2. In the Property inspector click the Stroke color box to select a color for the stroke. Select a number (pixels) for the stroke width. If you want a custom stroke, such as a dotted line, click the Custom button. You'll notice a lot of different options for the stroke's appearance.

3. Click the Fill color box to change the color of the fill. You can also choose one of the preset gradients at the bottom of the Swatch panel that opens. Later in this chapter you learn about using gradients and bitmap fills.

4. To edit a shape, select the Arrow tool, and click the rectangle's center. A dotted pattern indicates that the fill is selected. You can now change the fill or even delete it.

5. With the Arrow tool, click the edge of the rectangle and notice that a portion of the stroke is selected. On a rectangle there are four strokes not one. If you want to change them all, you need to Shift+select all four.

6. If you want to select the entire object, including fill and strokes, double-click the object. You can group the object to edit or move it as one item by choosing Modify ➪ Group, or Control (Command) +G.

Note   You can also change fills and enter an RGB number in the Color Mixer (Window ➪ Color Mixer). This panel is one of the ones that opens by default when you first install Flash.

FreeHand

FreeHand MX   In FreeHand and in Fireworks, when you place one object on top of the other, each object remains separate. One covers or obscures the other but both objects exist in their entirety. In Flash, if you place an object without a stroke on top of another object of the same color, they become one object when you deselect. If the objects are two different colors, the one you place on top cuts out the portion of the object below it, acting like a cookie cutter.

Rounded rectangles

Rounded rectangles are great for buttons and other interface objects and they are easy to make. But you need to set the options prior to drawing the shape. Select the Rectangle tool and in the Options area of the Toolbox; you see the Round Rectangle Radius option. When you click it a dialog box opens where you type the amount of the radius. Selecting 100 makes a pill shape, and selecting 30 makes a slightly curved corner.

Using the Pencil tool

The Pencil tool works much like a traditional pencil, a freeform line. But with the Pencil tool using a few tricks can make your drawing smoother or sharper. Select the Pencil tool and notice the Options area of the Toolbox. You can choose one of three options (Straighten, Smooth, Ink) prior to drawing. Or you can select the line and then apply one of the options, which are:

✦ **Straighten** straightens all the curves in a line.

✦ **Smooth** smoothes out angles, but you have no control over how much smoothing occurs. Practice with each setting to see how they respond.

✦ **Ink** leaves the line just as you drew it.

You can also select a line and change the stroke properties in the Property inspector.

Using the Brush tool

The Brush tool is similar to the Pencil tool in that it's freeform. The line you draw with the Brush tool is a stroke and as a stroke you can apply the different stroke attributes, such as dotted lines and so on, from the Property inspector.

Prior to using the Brush tool to affect an object already drawn, you had to select the object first. When you select the Brush tool in the Options area, you see the top icon for Paint Modes, which leads to the following options:

✦ **Paint Normal** — No selection is required and you use the Brush tool like a paint brush.

✦ **Paint Fill** — The stroke is applied to all areas of the selected fill.

✦ **Paint Behind** — The stroke is drawn behind the selected object.

✦ **Paint Selection** — Applies the stroke to only the selected fill area.

✦ **Paint Inside** — Doesn't paint over an existing object's border but remain inside the fill area.

The differences can be seen in Figure 25-2.

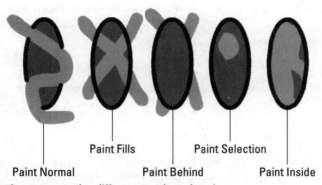

Figure 25-2: The different Brush tool options

The next icon in the Options area of the Toolbox is the Brush size; the last one is Brush Shape. You can also adjust the size by entering a pixel amount into the Property inspector.

Using the Pen tool

The Pen tool is what I'd consider the main drawing tool in Flash. It gives you the greatest control and flexibility. The Pen tool in Flash works like the one in FreeHand and in Fireworks. You place points, and they are connected by line segments. These line segments can then be altered or curved by adding and manipulating Bezier or tangent handles. For detailed instructions on using the Pen tool refer to Chapters 6 and 17.

In the Movie folder on the CD is a tutorial called Bezier curves, which shows you how to use the Pen tool and manipulate the curves. It's made using the Fireworks Pen tool, but it works the same way in Flash.

Using the Ink Bottle tool

The Ink Bottle tool affects only a stroke's color, width, and style. To use the Ink Bottle tool, follow these steps:

1. Draw a stroke.

2. Be sure nothing is selected on the Stage; then select the Ink Bottle tool from the Toolbox.

3. In the Property inspector, click the stroke color box and choose a new color. Change the stroke height and/or style.

4. Click over any stroke.

Using the Paint Bucket tool to fill an object

You saw a little bit about editing fills in the "Fill and stroke basics" section earlier in this chapter. In this section, you learn how to use and edit gradient and bit fills. To use the Paint Bucket tool, follow these steps:

1. Draw a rectangle. It fills with the currently selected color. It will have a stroke only if you currently have a stroke selected.

2. To change the fill, deselect the rectangle by clicking anywhere on the blank part of the Stage.

3. Select the Paint Brush tool from the Toolbox.

4. Click the area to fill.

Tip   You can also change the fill and stroke of a solid fill (not gradient or bitmap) in the Property inspector after you select the object.

Using gradient fills

A gradient fill changes from one color to another gradually. You can have two or more colors and you can adjust the position of the colors. Gradients are mixed in the Color Mixer panel (Window ⇨ Color Mixer). To use a gradient fill, follow these steps:

1. Click the expander arrow to open the Color Mixer (Window ⇨ Color Mixer).

2. Select an object to which to add the gradient fill.

3. In the Color Mixer, open the Fill Style drop-down menu, and choose Linear or Radial. Figure 25-3 shows the Color Mixer with Linear selected. Notice the color ramp that appears with two color markers. The one on the left is white and the one on the right is black by default.

Figure 25-3: The Color Mixer with Linear fill style being selected

4. The default gradient of white to black is added. You can easily change the color by clicking either of the color markers. When you select one, the Color Proxy icon below the color box is activated. You click the color box to choose a new color for the selected marker.

Tip   If you don't want to make a new gradient but use one in the Swatches panel, instead of using the Color Mixer you can choose any preset gradient or one you've saved from the Fill color box on the Toolbox.

5. To add another color, place your cursor below the ramp and you'll see a plus (+) sign near your cursor. Click to add another marker. Choose your color and add as many markers as you want. Move the markers around by dragging them.

Tip   If you choose the gradient fill prior to drawing your shape, it will be filled automatically with the gradient you selected.

6. To save a custom gradient to the Swatches panel, click the Color Mixer Options pop-up menu and choose Add Swatch. Now you can choose this gradient directly from any color fill box when the Swatches panel opens.

7. A feature unique to Flash is the ability to lock the gradient fill. This means you can have multiple objects filled with a continuous gradient. To fill continuous objects with a gradient, follow these steps:

   a. Choose a gradient or make your own.

   b. Select the Paint Bucket tool.

   c. In the Toolbox, click the Lock Fill icon in the Options area of the Toolbox.

   d. Fill one object, then the next. Notice how the gradient continues into the second object (Figure 25-4).

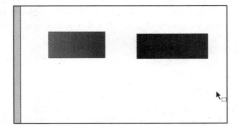

Figure 25-4: The gradient is filled in the left rectangle and continues into the right rectangle.

Fireworks MX

Fireworks has an additional ramp in the Gradient editor for transparency. In Fireworks you see the transparency only if the object is exported over the object it sits above. But you can import the Fireworks PNG into Flash and the transparency is true. In other words, you can move the object with Fireworks transparency settings around your stage and see through to underlying objects.

Filling with bitmap

In the Fill Style drop-down menu of the Color Mixer along with the Linear and Radial options for the Gradient there is a Bitmap option. This option enables you to fill with an image. To fill with an image, follow these steps:

1. Select an object.

2. Choose Bitmap from the Fill Style drop-down menu in the Color Mixer.

3. Navigate to the location of the image you want saved. Select it and open it. This image is added to your Library and shows up in the Color Mixers Bitmap Fill window. You can select any image from this window to use as a fill. To get additional images into your Library use the File ⇨ Import to Library method of adding images to use as fills.

Fireworks MX

It's a good idea to optimize your images in Fireworks prior to using them in Flash. Flash applies optimization but Fireworks is more robust and offers you much more control.

4. With a bitmap selected from the Bitmap Fill window you can use the Paint Bucket tool to fill.

5. To edit the fill's appearance you can use the Fill Transform tool, which you learn about in the next section of this chapter.

Cross-Reference

For more information about using Web-safe colors and a more detailed description of using the Swatches panel, refer to Chapter 16.

Using the Fill Transform tool

The Fill Transform tool is new to Flash MX. In previous versions it was a Paint Brush tool option; now it's a tool on its own. The Fill Transform tool is used to adjust the position and size of gradients and bitmap fills. To use the Fill Transform tool, follow these steps:

1. Select the Fill Transform tool.

2. Click an object with a gradient or bitmap fill. After you click the object, you see a bounding box. Figure 25-5 shows a bitmap, linear, and radial fill with the various Fill Transform handles. As you pass your cursor over each square around the box cursor tips indicate the function. You can perform any of the following functions:

   • Rotate the fill

   • Adjust the fill's width

   • Adjust the fill's height

   • Skewing the image

   • Scale proportionately

- Enlarge or make smaller a linear gradient by dragging the square handle in the center

- Change a radial gradient's position by dragging the first circular handle just below the square one

Fill Transform for a linear fill

Fill transform for a radial fill

Fill Transform for a bitmap fill

Figure 25-5: Different Fill transform options

Using the Eraser tool

Using the Eraser tool is easy enough; you select the tool and drag it over the areas you want to erase. Several options control how the eraser performs. When you select the Eraser tool from the Toolbox, these additional options are available in the Options portion of the Toolbox:

✦ The Eraser Mode drop-down menu includes

- **Erase Normal** — Erases any fill or style
- **Erase Fills** — Erases only fills
- **Erase Lines** — Erases only strokes and lines
- **Erase Inside** — Erases within a shape
- **Erase Selected Fills** — Erases only fills that are selected first

✦ Faucet deletes any fill and/or stroke selected.

✦ Eraser Shapes offers shapes and sizes from which to choose.

Utilizing the Text Tool

In Flash, you can use Type 1 PostScript fonts, TrueType fonts, and bitmap fonts (Mac only). You'll find that for PCs the TrueType fonts are most reliable and that the PostScript fonts can be problematic for both the Windows and Mac platforms. Be sure to test all fonts on your machine and also from a server, preferably on a computer that may not have the same fonts installed to test in real-world situations. If the user doesn't have the font and you haven't taken that into consideration, your design could fall apart. Later in this chapter, you learn how to ensure that everyone sees your movie exactly the way you want it to look.

To use the Text tool, follow these steps:

1. Select the Text tool.

2. Start typing on the Stage. Notice the text box that the text is in. There are three types of text boxes available:

   - **Extending** — The default. This box extends as you type.

   - **Fixed** — A fixed text box does not extend horizontally. To make a fixed text box, use the Text tool and click and drag until the outline shows the size you want. Text in a fixed text box automatically wraps vertically.

Tip

You can also adjust the width by pixels in the Property inspector after you've made the fixed text box. Select it and change the Width property.

   - **Input** — This text box is used for user input or for dynamically generated text from a database. To add an input text box, you change any text box's property in the Property inspector as shown in Figure 25-6.

Figure 25-6: A selected text box being changed to an input text box

Note

An input text box is used for the Flash interface for the Habit Alert site, and a dynamic text box is used on each e-card to accept the user input for the cards.

Setting text properties using the Property inspector

The text properties are similar to the rest of the Studio MX applications but there are some exceptions. You take a look at each of the Property inspectors for static text, dynamic text, and input text. Figure 25-7 shows the Property inspector when you use the default of Static text.

Figure 25-7: The Property inspector for static text

Some of the fields include

   ✦ Character Spacing, which is also known as kerning. This option enables you to add or delete space between characters.

   ✦ Character Position is also known as Baseline shift. This option determines where the bottom of the text sits.

   ✦ Change Direction of Text changes the text's orientation horizontally and vertically.

   ✦ Rotate text.

✦ URL field.

✦ Selectable button is used when you want the user to be able to select, copy, and paste your text.

✦ Use Device Fonts allows Flash to use an appropriate font from the user's system.

✦ Format button, when clicked, presents a dialog box where you can enter line spacing and margin information.

Dynamic text properties

Figure 25-8 shows the Property inspector when Dynamic Text is selected. The first thing to notice is that there is an Instance Name field. You name the instance in the Property inspector. By naming it, you can reference it when you begin to add ActionScript.

Figure 25-8: The Property inspector as it appears when Dynamic Text is selected

The other changes to the Property inspector include

✦ **Line Type** — You can choose whether you want single, multiple lines, or multiple lines without a wrap. The definitions for these options are

  • Single line — One line of text without any wrapping.

  • Multiline — Multiple lines of text that wrap.

  • Multiline no Wrap — Multiple lines that don't wrap unless the Enter/Return key is pressed.

✦ **Variable** — An additional field to enter a unique name so you can code the dynamic text to go to the right text box.

✦ **Render Text as HTML button** — You can retain certain HTML tags, such as bold, italic, underline, font, color, paragraph, and font size.

✦ **Show Border Around Text** — This adds a border around the text box.

Note

When you choose to show a border you'll see it in Flash, but if you choose not to you'll see a dotted border around the text box in Flash, but it doesn't export with your movie.

✦ **Character button** — This is used to enter information about font embedding.

Caution

The more characters you embed, the larger the file size will be.

Inputting text properties

The Input Text properties are similar to the dynamic text properties. The difference is that input text goes from the user's browser into a database and dynamic text goes from the database on a server to the user's browser. There are two additional options in the Property inspector (Figure 25-9) when you choose Input Text:

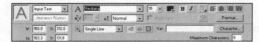

Figure 25-9: The Property inspector when Input Text is selected

✦ **Password** — In the Line Type drop-down menu there is an additional option of Password. This option displays the onscreen text as asterisks for security. You need to add the ActionScript to pass the information, however. This option only affects the onscreen view of the entered text.

✦ **Maximum Character field** — In this field, you can limit the number of characters users can enter into the input text box.

Breaking text apart

Breaking text apart into individual letters can be useful. By breaking them apart, you can edit the individual letters, but more importantly, you can animate the letters.

Caution

After text is broken apart it is no longer editable as text, and the file size is larger.

To break text apart, follow these steps:

1. Select a block of text.

2. Choose Modify ➪ Break Apart. Each letter can be manipulated separately.

3. If you want to alter the individual letters, select one and choose Modify ➪ Break Apart again.

4. Select the Subselection tool, and select the letter you broke apart again. You'll see each point of the letter, which you can alter.

Using the Align Panel

The Align panel is shown in Figure 25-10. From this panel you align objects to each other and the stage. To access the Align panel, choose Window ➪ Align (Control(Command)+K). The panel contains the following sections:

✦ **Align** — On the left you have the horizontal alignment with the options of Align Left Edge, Align Horizontal Center, and Align Right Edge. The button on the right shows the vertical options: Top Edge, Align Vertical Center, and Align Bottom Edge.

✦ **Distribute** — The left set of options are Distribute Top Edge, Distribute Vertical Center, and Distribute Bottom Edge. The set on the right side includes Distribute Left Edge, Distribute Horizontal Center, and Distribute Right Edge.

✦ **Match Size** — The options are Match Width, Match Height, Match Width, and Height.

✦ **Space** — The options are Space Evenly Vertically, and Space Evenly Horizontally.

✦ **To Stage** — The option is Align/Distribute to Stage.

Figure 25-10: The Align panel

Using an Object's Envelope

Envelopes are new to Flash MX and are used to warp ungrouped objects. They don't work on grouped objects, symbols, gradient, text, or bitmaps. But if you Shift+select multiple objects, envelopes work. To use an object's envelope, follow these steps:

1. Select an object/s (don't group them).

   To use an envelope for text refer to the "Break Apart Text" section to make the text into a shape first. Then Shift+select each letter before Step 2.

2. Choose Modify ➪ Transform ➪ Envelope.

3. You'll see two kinds of handles, square and circular (Figure 25-11). You can manipulate the points using the square handles. The circular handles are tangent handles (Bezier).

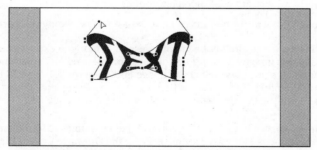

Figure 25-11: The envelope with the handles manipulated

4. If you decide to remove the envelope effect, select it and choose Modify ➪ Transform ➪ Remove.

Editing Bitmap Images

In Flash you can draw only vector images but you can work with bitmaps by importing them from other applications. For a discussion of bitmap and vector images refer to Chapters 6 and 19. You can optimize in Flash, but you have many more optimizing features in Fireworks. It's a good idea to optimize prior to importing into Flash.

To import bitmap images, choose File ➪ Import to place the image on Stage and in the Library. Or choose, File ➪ Import to Library to place it in your movies library.

To edit an imported bitmap, choose one of these options:

✦ Right-Click (Control+click) it and choose Edit with Fireworks.

✦ In the Library panel right-click (Control+click) the name, and you also have an option named Edit with... where you can navigate to a different editing application.

✦ Click the Edit button in the Property inspector.

Converting a Bitmap into a Vector

If you want to convert a bitmap image in Flash to a vector, you can do this by tracing it with the Trace Bitmap command. You can get some pretty good traces. However, the better the trace the larger the file. But it's a great way to produce a quick vector image from a bitmap.

To trace a bitmap, select it and choose Modify ➪ Trace Bitmap. The Trace Bitmap dialog box opens and displays the following options:

✦ **Color Threshold** is the number of colors that will be used. Flash averages the colors to limit the number. The lower the number the more colors used and the larger the file size.

✦ **Minimum Area** — This value is the radius that Color Threshold uses to describe adjacent pixels. The smaller the number, the more detail.

✦ **Curve Fit** — Determines how smooth the curves are. If the bitmap has smooth curves, select Very Smooth; if there are a lot of angles choose Very Tight.

✦ **Corner Threshold** — Similar to the Curves Fit except it refers to only the corners.

Caution
When you import a JPEG file it has already been compressed. When you export your Flash movie, Flash compresses this image again. JPEGS that are compressed multiple times frequently result in artifacts. To avoid this, select the image and open the Library (F11). From the Library Options pop-up menu choose Properties. The Bitmap Properties dialog box opens; choose Lossless from the Compression drop-down menu, and click OK.

Traces often have far more curves than you need for an acceptable image. To reduce the number of curves in the trace, choose Modify ➪ Optimize. From the Optimize Curves dialog box, choose the amount of Smoothing you'd like and click OK. A window opens telling you how many curves you started with, how many you have now, and the percentage of reduction.

Summary

In this chapter, you learned what the Flash tools do and how some of the Flash drawing features differ from FreeHand and Fireworks drawing tools. Various types of fills and strokes and editing methods were discussed. You saw how to work with bitmaps in Flash and how to convert one into a vector image.

✦   ✦   ✦

Symbols and Libraries

Symbols are the main reason that file sizes in Flash can be kept to a minimum. Symbols are usable elements that are stored in the Library with other assets, such as sound and video. When a symbol is produced it is automatically added to the Movies library. You can drag an instance (a copy) of the symbol into your movie as many times as you'd like. Libraries can be shared between movies and even be made available to all movies.

Understanding the Library

The Library contains all the symbols for your movie. When you make a Movie Clip, button symbol, or graphic symbol, they all are automatically added to the Library. You can also import bitmaps, sound, and video files. Every Flash movie has its own library, but you can drag a symbol or other asset from open Flash movie into another. To open the Library, press F11. Figure 26-1 shows the Library with various assets. Notice the different icons that represent the type of asset in the Library. The icon appears first, then the name of the item, then the type. You can change a name by opening the Library Options pop-up menu and selecting Rename.

Importing into a library

You can import any graphic, image, sound, or video file into your current movie's library by choosing File ⇨ Import to Library. The asset is added to the Library. You can then add it to your movie as many times as you want. You can also access items, such as sound, from the Library without placing them on the Timeline by using ActionScript.

Cross-Reference You learn how to access sound from the Library using ActionScript without placing it in the Timeline in Chapter 29.

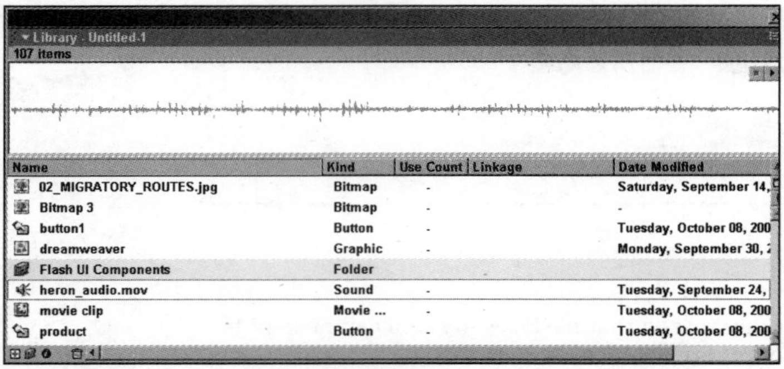

Figure 26-1: A library showing various icons, names, and types

Using libraries

Your symbols or other assets are automatically added to the movie's Library when you produce them or when you drag one from another library. To add sound, bitmaps, vectors, or QuickTime to the Library, you import them into your movie.

To use a symbol or other asset from the Library, you simply drag an instance (a copy) of the symbol or asset to the stage.

Sharing libraries between movies

If you have more than one movie open, you can drag assets from one to another. But if you don't have other files open and don't need them open, you can still borrow the assets of another movie by opening its library. Choose File ⇨ Open as Library, navigate to the file that has the library you want, select it, and click Open. Only the Library opens, not the whole file. This is similar to the way common libraries work except it's more a use-as-you-need method rather than having the library permanently available.

Common libraries

There is another type of library, a common library. If you choose Window ⇨ Common Libraries there are three options. These are libraries that are common and available to all movies. If you have a library in a movie that you want to make into a common library, save your Flash file with a descriptive name and place into the Libraries folder of the Flash program on your hard drive. You can delete this file anytime you decide you don't want it any longer. As soon as you drop the file into the Libraries folder it is available in Flash. You don't have to close and reopen the program.

Using Symbols

There are three types of symbols: Movie Clips, buttons, and graphics. When you make a symbol, it is automatically stored in the movie's Library. To insert the object into the movie, you drag instances of it onto the Stage from the Library. When an instance of a symbol is placed on the Stage, there is little to no increase in the file size.

You can alter these instances to appear differently when in fact they are still an instance only of the original symbol. The movie has to call the symbol only once; then Flash stores information about any size, color, or transparency changes you've made.

Symbols also save you a great deal of time if you have to edit them. When you edit the original symbol, all instances are changed automatically. You'll love this if you've ever had to change an element in a large Web site without symbols.

After you start making symbols, you should develop your own (or a company) naming convention. The symbols must be named so you can reference them when adding ActionScript. Because symbols are stored in the Library, it's vital that you understand how to use the Library.

You can convert an existing object on the Stage into a symbol by choosing Insert ➪ Convert to Symbol. When the Convert to Symbol dialog box opens (Figure 26-2) name your symbol and select the type you want.

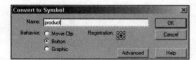

Figure 26-2: The Convert to Symbol dialog box

If you want to add a new symbol, choose Insert ➪ New Symbol, and the same dialog box opens. Name it, choose the type, and click OK. The symbol is now in the movies Library. You can drag the symbol onto the Stage.

Movie Clip symbols

Each Movie Clip symbol has its own timeline and layers. Movie Clip movies can be used in a single frame on the main Timeline. One of the best advantages of Movie Clips is that they play independently of the main Timeline. Because you can add actions to Movie Clips, there are infinite possibilities. You can generate dynamic animation, such as an object that moves during playback when the user presses keys on the keyboard.

Movie Clip is one of Flash's predefined objects. Movie clips can be instances, but they can also be objects. As an object they have characteristics you can access and control. Some of the properties you have control over govern appearance, for example transparency, visible or color, size, and position.

To convert an object into a Movie Clip, choose Insert ➪ Convert to Symbol, name it, and select the Movie Clip option. To convert a movie on your Stage into a Movie Clip, follow these steps:

1. Select any frame (of the movie you want to make into a Movie Clip) that doesn't contain a Keyframe and choose Edit ➪ Copy Frames (Control+Alt+C[Command+Option+C]). Alternatively you can right-click (Control+click) and select Copy Frames.

2. Choose Insert ➪ New Symbol (Control+F9[Command+F9]) to convert the movie into a symbol. The Symbol Properties dialog box opens.

3. In the Symbol Properties dialog box, choose Movie Clip.

4. After Step 3 the Stage is empty, because you are in Symbol Editing mode. In the top-left corner, you see Scene 1, but the name of your movie is in white, indicating you are in the Symbol Editing mode. The Stage and Timeline you see are both for the current symbol. Select the first frame of the Timeline and choose Edit ➪ Paste Frames (Control+Alt+V[Command+Options+V]).

5. Double-click the layer 1 name and give it an appropriate name.

The Movie Clip is now in the Library ready to be inserted in the main Timeline of a movie.

Empty Movie Clips

You can use an empty Movie Clip when you don't want graphics. Empty Movie Clips can still have actions attached to them. They are similar to invisible buttons (later in this chapter). Empty Movie Clips can have instance names so you can control them with ActionScript. To make an empty Movie Clip, follow these steps:

1. Choose Insert ➪ New Symbol.

2. Give the symbol a name.

3. Choose the Movie Clip behavior and click OK.

4. Return to the main scene.

5. Drag an instance of the Movie Clip from the Library to the Stage. A white dot on the Stage represents the empty Movie Clip.

Button symbols

Button symbols are popular and useful for navigation buttons. You can add sound, animation, and actions to button symbols. To make a button symbol, follow these steps:

1. With a new Flash movie open, choose Insert ➪ New Symbol. In the Symbol Properties dialog box, choose the Button behavior, and click OK.

2. You are now in Button Edit mode. Take a moment to look at the Timeline (Figure 26-3). Notice the Up, Over, Down, and Hit tabs. Up is the default. Draw a button, drag on a button graphic, or import one.

Figure 26-3: The Button Symbol editor

3. Select the frame under the Over tab, and choose Insert ➪ Keyframe (F6). Change the button's appearance for the Over state.

4. Repeat Step 3 for the Down state.

5. Select the frame under the Hit state, and choose Insert ➪ Keyframe (F6). The user can't see what you draw here. Draw a rectangle large enough to cover the button, otherwise

only the text will be the "hit" area. The hit area is the area in which the action assigned will be triggered when the mouse passes over it. In this case, it's a rollover.

6. Notice your button is a symbol in the Library. If you didn't name your button in the Symbol Properties dialog box, you can do it now by double-clicking the symbol name and giving it a suitable name. Click Scene 1 to return to the main movie. To use your button, drag an instance from the Library to the Stage.

You can test your button by choosing Control ➪ Enable Simple Buttons.

Invisible button symbols

Invisible buttons are not a separate or different kind of symbol. Because they are used so frequently as "hit" areas they need to be mentioned. An invisible button is a hotspot to which you can assign actions. You put them over other objects. Because they are a transparent blue color, you can position them easily.

In the Bonus Tutorial folder on the CD-ROM a tutorial folder named "FLA_369" uses invisible buttons to rotate a product 360 degrees.

To make an invisible button, follow these steps:

1. With a new movie open (or your current movie) choose Insert ➪ New Symbol. In the Symbol Properties dialog box, choose Button behavior and click OK.

2. Select the frame below the Hit tab and choose Insert ➪ Keyframe (F6).

3. Draw the shape of your invisible button. The color of the fill makes no difference and a stroke or no stroke makes no difference. It is added to the Library.

4. Click Scene 1 to return to your main movie. You can drag the invisible button from the Library onto the Stage.

5. Click on the Control menu and check to see that the Enable Simple Buttons option is unchecked.

6. The invisible symbol is invisible in the Library so drag the name onto the Stage. But once on the Stage it isn't invisible to you, so you can easily position it.

Graphic symbols

Graphic symbols have the least capabilities in Flash. They are great for repeating static elements or for simple animations. You cannot add actions or attach sound to a graphic symbol. To make a graphic symbol, follow these steps:

1. With a movie open, choose Insert ➪ New Symbol. In the Symbol Properties dialog box, choose the Graphic Behavior and click OK.

2. You are now in Symbol Editing mode. You can draw, drag, or import the content for the symbol. It will be added to the Library.

3. To return to the main Timeline, click Scene 1. Drag an instance of the graphic symbol onto the Stage wherever you want it, and as many times as you want to.

Editing symbols

To edit a symbol do one of the following:

✦ Double-click the symbol instance on the Stage.

✦ Double-click the symbol icon to the left of the symbols name in the Library.

✦ Click the arrow for the Edit Symbols icon on the stage and symbol bar, and select the symbol you want to edit from the list.

Above the Stage is the scene and symbol bar. Notice after you double-click a symbol or choose it from the Symbol list that you'll see the symbol name on the bar as shown in Figure 26-4.

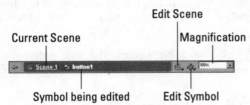

Figure 26-4: The bar above the stage showing the scene and/or symbols in the edit mode

Summary

In this chapter you learned how to make and add symbols to your movies and into the movie's Library. You also learned how to use a library from another movie and how to import additional assets into your current Library.

✦   ✦   ✦

Animating a Movie

Animation is the appearance of movement. It's the effect of movement or changes made over time that makes your images appear to move. Using Flash for animation is much like making traditional animations where each movement or change is drawn. But Flash offers even the traditional animator some fantastic timesavers such as being able to "tween" images. By drawing only the starting and ending image you can have Flash produce all the "in between" images for you.

Beginners and experienced animators alike are using Flash every day to produce some visually stunning animations. In this chapter, you learn the basics of how to add movement to your images.

Working with the Timeline

The Timeline controls all the timing, which determines how long your movie plays, when it plays, what plays, and basically everything involved in producing your Flash movie. What the viewer sees from the time the movie starts to when it stops is determined by where you place the content on the Timeline.

The Timeline sits on top of the stage area of your movie. Figure 27-1 shows the Timeline, which sits on the top of the stage by default.

You can reposition the Timeline by clicking and dragging the gripper. It comes in handy to be able to move the Timeline when you have two monitors; then you can move the Timeline off the stage altogether onto a separate monitor. It's a great way to view all the layers at the same time.

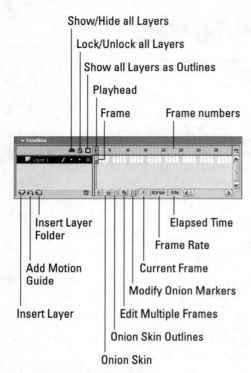

Figure 27-1: The Timeline

Frames and Keyframes

To make an animation, you use the Timeline to control the timing of your images. When a series of images varies slightly from page to page, these images will to move as you flip the pages. Images are placed in frames, and each time a major change occurs in the animation, an image is placed in a keyframe, as you'll see in some of this chapter's exercises.

When you begin to build an animation the first frame is automatically an empty keyframe. This is designated by the hollow circle you see in Frame 1 (Figure 27-1). After you place content into this empty keyframe, it becomes a keyframe and is indicated by a solid black circle. The remaining frames are all placeholders containing the same content as the keyframe until you add another keyframe. Whenever you want to make a major change in position, shape, or color, you need a keyframe. Think of keyframes as "I need another sheet of paper" to draw the next position.

For a simple demonstration of keyframes and frames, follow these steps:

1. Select Frame 1 in the Timeline.

2. Draw anything on the stage. Move the red playhead and notice that whatever you have on the stage is in all the frames.

3. Click in Frame 10.

4. Choose Insert ➪ Blank Keyframe (F7).

You could also choose Insert ➪ Keyframe (F6). Which action you need to perform depends on what you are going to do. If you are adding to or moving the current keyframe's content and want its content to remain, choose Keyframe. But if you want to remove the content of the current frame totally, choose Blank Keyframe.

5. Draw a new shape. Now as you move the playhead you see your first shape in Frames 1-9 and the new shape in Frame 10 (Figure 27-2).

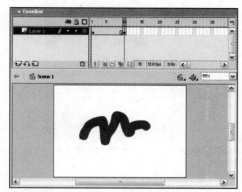

Figure 27-2: New content added to the stage in Frame 10

Of course this isn't an animation yet but it's vital to understand the difference between frames and keyframes.

Frame-by-Frame Animation

Frame-by-frame animation is the traditional way of making animations such as cartoons. Every frame has a slightly different image on it to produce the appearance of movement. This is a long and tedious process but at times the only way to achieve the desired results. For a frame-by-frame animation, every frame is a keyframe and the image changes slightly in each frame. To get a better feel for a frame-by-frame animation, follow these steps:

1. Open a new document.

2. Choose File ➪ Import and from the Chapter 27 folder select HighHeron.swf. Click the stage to place it. This is an animation that was created in FreeHand.

3. Click Frame 1 and notice the content (Figure 27-3). Move the playhead to Frame 2, Frame 3, and so on. The position of the bird and wings changes in every frame, thus the need for a keyframe. You'll also notice that every frame has a solid black dot indicating that it is a keyframe.

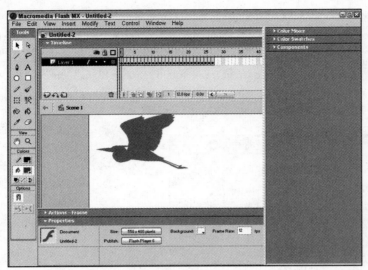

Figure 27-3: A frame-by-frame animation showing the Timeline with keyframes for each movement change

Frame-by-frame animations produce larger file sizes because each frame contains different content. In the following sections, you learn about tweening. Tweening reduces the file size because it uses symbols that are altered to achieve movement. Because of the use of symbols there are fewer actual objects for the browser to download. It's this reusable content that makes Flash so powerful.

Onion skinning

The onion skin feature is a great way to see the "pages" of your animation. It's used to assist you in placement of objects in your keyframes. You can see a faint image or just the outline of the other frames.

To turn the onion skin option on, click the icon at the bottom of the Timeline. In Figure 27-4 you can see the onion skin option is turned on, but for this bird it would be difficult to use it for placement. If you use the Outline option, click the Onion Skin Outlines icon as seen in Figure 27-5. The position of the bird is much easier to see in this case. If you want to see the frames after the selected keyframe, click and drag the little hollow circle near the selected frame.

Frames per second

The frames-per-second setting determines how many frames play in a second's time. If you make it too low, the animation is choppy when it plays. If you make it too fast, it may begin to drop frames on slower machines, producing a choppy movie. For the Web, it's a good idea not to go over 15 FPS. The default in Flash is 12 FPS, which is compatible with older computers with low processing speeds.

Figure 27-4: Frame 10 is selected and the onion skin option is turned on.

Figure 27-5: Frame 10 is selected and the onion skin Outline option is turned on.

If you want to slow down an animation you would add more frames. To speed it up, use fewer frames. You can change the FPS settings using one of these options:

✦ In the Timeline, double-click the FPS box to open the Document Properties dialog box. Change the FPS setting and click OK.

✦ Choose Modify ➪ Document to open the Document Properties dialog box. Change the FPS setting and click OK.

✦ Press Control/Command+J to open the Document Properties dialog box. Change the FPS setting and click OK.

Adding frames

If you need to add more frames, choose one of the following methods:

✦ Insert your cursor where you want to add a frame and choose Insert ➪ Frames.

✦ Insert your cursor where you want to add a frame, right (Control)+click, and choose Insert Frames.

✦ Insert your cursor where you want to add a frame, and press F5.

✦ To add multiple frames shift+select and press F5 (or one of the other methods for inserting frames).

Deleting frames

If you want to speed up a portion of your animation or delete unnecessary frames for optimization purposes, choose one of the following methods:

✦ Select a frame or shift+select multiple frames, and choose Insert ➪ Remove Frames.

✦ Select a frame or shift+select multiple frames, right/Control+click, and choose Remove Frames.

✦ Select a frame or shift+select multiple frames, and press Shift+F5.

Reversing frames

Reversing frames comes in handy if you want to change the direction of an animation. To accomplish this, follow these steps:

1. Select the frames (Shift+select) you want to reverse.

2. Choose Edit ➪ Copy Frames.

3. Select the frame you want to put the reverse animation into and choose Edit ➪ Paste Frames.

4. To reverse the order, shift+select the pasted frames and choose Modify ➪ Frames ➪ Reverse.

Labeling a keyframe

When you want to add ActionScript you'll need to reference your keyframe. You could just use the frame number but it's much more difficult to remember. You can name only keyframes not frames. To label a keyframe, follow these steps:

1. Select the keyframe you want to label.

2. In the Property Inspector, enter the name in the Frame field on the left.

3. Look in the Timeline and notice a little red flag over the keyframe you added a label to.

Note

Flash enables you to label a frame in the Property inspector, but it's deceiving. If you do this and check the Timeline, the label is applied to the previous keyframe, not the selected frame.

Table 27-1 shows some frame and keyframe shortcuts.

Table 27-1: Frame and Keyframe Shortcuts

Command	Shortcut
F5	Add static frames
F6	Add a keyframe
Shift+F5	Delete frames
Shift_F6	Delete keyframes
F7	Add a blank keyframe

Changing the pivot point

If you want to give your animation an anchor point other than the center, you need to change the pivot point. To do this, follow these steps:

1. Open the head.fla from the Chapter 27 folder. This object has already been converted into a symbol.

2. Select Frame 2 and add a keyframe (F6).

3. Select the symbol on the stage (head object); then select the Free Transform tool. Notice the hollow circle in the center. This is the pivot point. To see how the object would rotate as it is now, place your cursor outside the object until you see the curved line with two arrows and then drag to rotate. Notice in Figure 27-6 that the object rotates from the center point.

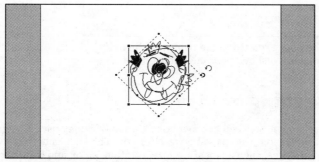

Figure 27-6: The pivot point in the center and rotated to the right

4. Choose Edit ➪ Undo.

5. To move anchor or pivot point, simply drag the hollow circle to a new location. For this exercise, drag it to the bottom center. Now rotate toward the left and notice the difference (Figure 27-7).

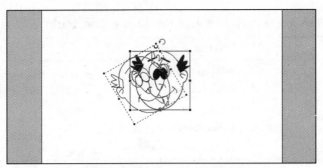

Figure 27-7: The pivot point moved to the bottom center and rotated to the left

6. Select Frame 3 and add a keyframe. Select the Free Transform tool and rotate to the right. Press Enter/Return to play the simple animation. Figure 27-8 shows the animation with onion skin option turned on.

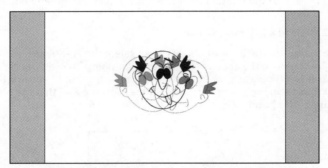

Figure 27-8: The object rotated to the right with the onion skin option turned on to show the rotated movement

Motion Tweening

Motion tweening is movement between two symbols. Motion tweening uses a beginning and an ending symbol. Flash fills in the steps in-between for you. The shapes between the two symbols are based on changes, such as location, size, rotation, color, and transparency, you make to the symbols. The two symbols have to be the same, but you can change characteristics. Because there are only two keyframes and two symbols involved, you save on file size.

The basic steps to make a motion tween are simple:

1. Open the head.fla file from the chapter27_exercises folder. It's a symbol that is in Frame 1.

2. Select Frame 20, add a Keyframe (F6), and move the symbol to a different location.

3. Select Frame 1 and in the Property inspector choose Motion from the Tween drop-down menu (Insert ➭ Create Motion Tween). Notice the line with an arrow in the Timeline from Frame 1 to Frame 20. This indicates the motion has been added. A dotted line indicates an improperly working tween.

Move the playhead over the frames and notice all the intermediate shapes Flash added. It's really that easy to add motion to two symbols. After you select a tween type, the Property inspector changes and offers several more options, as shown in Figure 27-9.

Figure 27-9: The properties available for a motion tween

Notice that you can set rotate and ease options, which determine the acceleration and deceleration of the tween. The ease setting determines whether the object moves slower or faster. A setting of 0 is a constant rate of movement; a negative value eases into the animation slowly at the beginning and faster at the end. Just how slow or fast depends on the amount you enter. A positive value is just the opposite; the animation begins fast and slows down at the end.

Making an e-card using motion tweening

We used motion tweening extensively for one of the e-cards for the Habitat Alert site so you can learn how to use motion tweening by making a simple e-card. This is based on a small, animated banner that Japi Honoo made (Bonus Tutorial on the CD).

Because the banner made in Fireworks used vector graphics (made in FreeHand), they were easily resized for use in Flash.

1. Choose Modify ➭ Document, change the Width to 600 × 400, and click OK. You can also do this in the Property inspector. If you can't see the document properties, click on the stage.

2. Choose File ➭ Import and navigate to the chapter27_exercise folder and select ecard1_bk.gif and open it.

3. Double-click the layer name and name it **background** (Figure 27-10).

4. Add a new layer and name it **goldleft**. You are going to add some gold herons that move from the left of the stage and stop when they are on top of the blue herons. Then repeat for the right side.

5. Choose File ➭ Import to Library and navigate to the chapter27_exercise folder and select goldheron.png. The Fireworks PNG Import Settings dialog box opens. Choose to import to a new layer and to keep paths and text editable, and click OK (Figure 27-11).

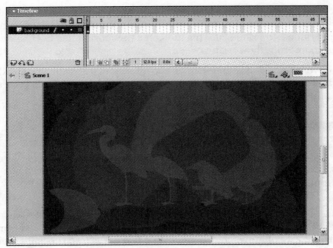

Figure 27-10: The background image in place and the layer renamed

Figure 27-11: The Fireworks PNG Import Settings dialog box with the settings used

6. When you import the Fireworks file as a Library item, it is automatically made into a symbol. Choose Windows ➪ Library to open the Library panel.

7. Drag a copy of the goldheron symbol onto the stage. Notice that the keyframe on this layer has a solid black dot because you added content.

8. Position the gold heron directly on top of the blue herons and note the *y* coordinate of 143.3 in the Property inspector. Use your left arrow key to move the birds to the left of the stage and off of it as shown in Figure 27-12.

9. Select Frame 25 and insert a keyframe (F6). You no longer see the background. You need to extend the Timeline for your background image. In the background layer right-click the first frame and choose Insert frame (or press F5). Now drag the little hollow white rectangle to Frame 25. The gray line extends to Frame 25.

10. Back in the goldheron layer with Frame 25 selected, drag the goldheron symbol from the left of the stage, and position it exactly on top of the blue herons (x: 98.5, y: 143.3). You now have one symbol in Frame 1 and one in Frame 25. Now all you need to do is add the tween.

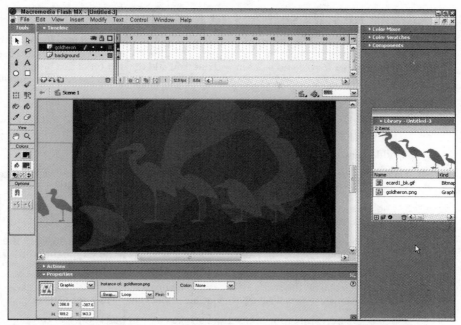

Figure 27-12: The gold herons added to the second layer and moved off the stage

11. Select the first keyframe and choose Insert ➪ Motion Tween. Press Enter/Return to see your animation. Lock the heronleft layer.

12. Add a new layer and name it **goldright**.

13. You want this animation to play at the same time as the left heron layer, so select Frame 1 and place a goldheron symbol from the Library off to the right of the stage with a y coordinate of 143.3.

14. Select Frame 25 and press F5 to insert a keyframe. Place the symbol on the right on top of the blue herons. Select Frame 1 and add the motion tween (Insert ➪ Create Motion Tween). Press Enter/Return to play the animation. Figure 27-13 shows the Timeline so far.

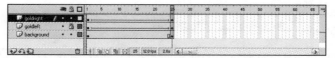

Figure 27-13: The Timeline showing both motion tweens added

Only one motion tween can be on a layer.

15. Save the animation. A copy is saved for you in the chapter27_exercise folder named `ecard1_gold.fla`.

Adding opacity settings to a motion tween

Motion tweens are good for more than simple motion. You can also change the symbol's properties, such as color and opacity, as well as transformations. The Habitat Alert e-card uses a simple text animation that moves and fades in and out. You add the first bit of text here; then you can inspect the finished file to see how the same techniques were used to finish the animation.

1. Open `ecard1_gold.fla` if you closed it.

2. Click in the background layer and insert (F5) 14 frames to extend the background to Frame 40.

3. Add a new layer and name it **saveit**. Lock the goldright layer.

4. On the saveit layer, select Frame 26, and add a keyframe (F6). You want the text animation to begin playing after the gold herons have moved into position.

5. Choose Insert ➪ New Symbol. Name it **saveit**, choose Graphic, and click OK. The Symbol Editor opens.

6. Select the Text tool. Change the font to Arial Black with a size of 96. Click the color box and type a hex number of **7A9ABA**. Using lowercase letters, type the words **save it into the Symbol editor**.

7. I want a stroke on the text so it'll have to be broken apart. With the text selected, choose Modify ➪ Break Apart. Repeat one more time, you'll see little dots in the text.

8. Select the Ink Bottle tool, and set the stroke color to black. Click at the edge of each letter to give it a black stroke (Figure 27-14). Click inside the "a" and the "e" to stroke the centers.

Figure 27-14: The stroke being added to the text

9. Return to Scene 1 and drag a copy of the symbol onto the stage (x: 126, y: 240).

10. Select Frame 40 and insert a keyframe (F6), which has a copy of the text in it. Since you want to fade the text to almost invisible, select the text. In the Property inspector in the Color drop-down list, choose Alpha and change the opacity to 20%.

11. Select Frame 26 and choose Insert⇨Create Motion Tween. Move the playhead and notice how the text fades.

12. The next word starts from a fade on the same frame as the words "save it" and goes to full opacity. Add three more frames to the background layer. In the saveit layer, select Frame 41 and insert a new keyframe.

13. Choose Insert ⇨ New Symbol and use the same font type, except change the color to **999933**. Break it apart and give it a black stroke. Return to the stage and drag a copy to the center of the "save it" text.

14. Select **or** and change the color to Alpha and 20%. Select **or** and choose Edit ⇨ Copy.

15. Add a new layer and name it **or**. Select Frame 41 and add a keyframe. Choose Edit ⇨ Paste in Place. This pastes "or" in the same position as the previous layer. The text is now ready for you to add another symbol to it and apply a motion tween. You can find the finished file, named `ecard1.fla`, in the chapter27_exercise folder.

Tween Along a Path

Flash has a special layer called Motion Guide. This layer is used as a guide path for your animation to follow and is not exported with your animation. You can make the path using any of the drawing tools, or you can import an EPS or AI file format to use. If you choose to import a file, you'll need to ungroup the object first.

To add a Motion Guide layer that contains a path for your symbol to move along, follow these steps:

1. Make a simple motion tweened animation. In Frame 1, draw a circle and choose Insert ⇨ Convert to symbol. Add a keyframe to Frame 10. Select Frame 1 and choose Insert ⇨ Motion tween.

2. Click the Add Motion Guide icon in the Layers area. This action places a guide layer above the animation layer. The name is Guide Layer (plus the layer named it is above).

3. Select Frame 1 of the Motion-Guide layer, and use any drawing tool to draw a path. Figure 27-15 shows the animation so far.

4. To attach the animation to the path, select Frame 1 of the animation. Look in the Property inspector and be sure the Snap option is checked.

5. Select your object and drag, placing the registration point (circle) at the beginning of your path, as shown in Figure 27-16.

6. Select the last keyframe. Click and drag to place the registration on the end of the path.

   If the registration point doesn't appear, click the circle with cross hairs and click and hold for a second or two, then drag it to position.

7. Press Enter/Return to play the animation.

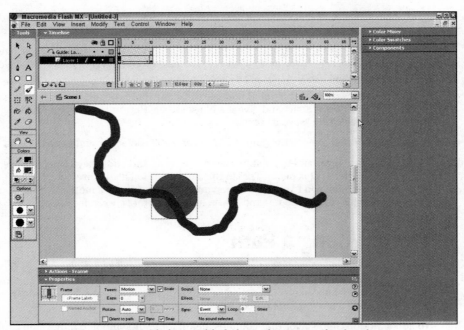

Figure 27-15: A Motion-Guide layer added above the tweened animation and a guide drawn

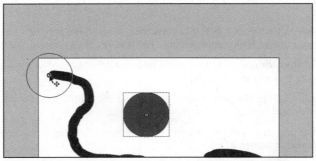

Figure 27-16: The object placed with its registration point at the beginning of the Motion Guide

Shape Tweening

Shape tweening follows the same steps as motion tweening with a few exceptions. You can't shape tween a bitmap, a grouped object, movie clips, or text blocks unless you break them apart first. If you are going to tween more than two objects, they all have to be on the same layer. If the shapes are complex, you can control the resulting tween by using shape hints.

1. Open shape.fla. Select Frame 20 and add a keyframe (F6).

2. Add a new layer.

3. Select the Pen tool and in the Property inspector change the fill color to black and the size to 4.

4. Click the head image, where the center of a smile would be, and draw a short line. If you press Shift while you click the second point, you get a straight line, as shown in Figure 27-17.

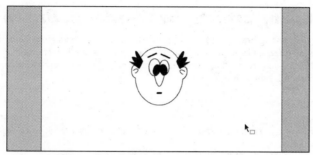

Figure 27-17: A dot added to Frame 1 for the beginning of a shape tween

5. Select Frame 20 and add a keyframe. Select View ➪ Rulers and pull a guide down on top of the line you drew for the mouth. You can use this to position the full smile. Delete the short line.

6. Draw a full smile. The easiest way to draw a smile is to click the first point for the top of the left side of the smile, click the top-right side, and drag to form the mouth curve as shown in Figure 27-18. Be sure the smile is on top of the guide.

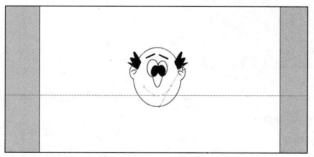

Figure 27-18: The mouth drawn using the Pen tool

7. To add the shape tween, select Frame 1 and go to the Property inspector and choose Shape from the Tween drop-down menu. For this exercise, you don't need any other options, but take note of the following options available for a shape tween:

   • **Easing** — Positive values of 1 to 100 ease out the tween. Changes occur quickly at the beginning and ease out toward the end. To ease in, you choose a negative value.

- **Distributive mode** — This is an option in Blend drop-down menu. Use this option when you don't want to preserve any of the straight lines or curves.

- **Angular** — This is an option in Blend drop-down menu. Angular mode preserves the corners and straight lines in the in-between shapes.

8. Press Enter/Return to play the animation.

Flash MX Masking Effects, *by Charles E. Brown*

This section presents an interesting project employing techniques I use to introduce a Flash site. You use some text and masking effects. I have purposely set this up using only basic techniques. There are, of course, more sophisticated ways to do some of what you do here. You learn some fundamental principles using the techniques I show in this exercise.

Setup

We are going to start by laying out some ground work for our small project. I think you will find these steps useful for other projects.

1. Create a new movie and use the Property inspector, or choose Modify ⇨ Document (see the following figure). For this example, I use the following settings:

   · Canvas Size: 600 pixels wide and 400 pixels

   · Background Color: #0000FF

2. Select the Text tool and use the Property inspector to set the text characteristics. As an example:

   · Font: Arial Black Font

   · Size: 40 points

   · Color: Black

3. Type the text, **Macromedia Studio MX** (or any text you choose).

   Press esc.

4. Using the Align panel, center the text on the stage.

Flash animations can become pretty complex. You should properly label all layers and objects.

5. Double-click the Layer 1 label at the beginning of the timeline. Name it **Introduction Text**.

6. Using the Align panel, center the text object on the canvas.

Creating the mask

Creating a mask is like taking a piece of cardboard, cutting a hole in it, and putting it in front of your text. The hole can be any shape and size. Flash gives you the ability to move the cutout. The example used here to illustrate this principle is simple. Use a circle:

1. Create a new layer above the text and call it **Mask** (see figure).

2. Draw a white circle, with no stroke, and make it 60 pixels high and 60 pixels wide. Make sure it is off the left side of the stage and that its center point is approximately centered with the text.

3. Create a keyframe for both layers at Frame 40 (see figure).

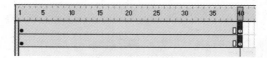

4. Make sure you are in Frame 40. Shift + click to keep the movement straight, while you drag the circle to stage right (see figure).

5. Create a Motion Tween in the Mask layer. When you test it, it will look like a white circle going across the text.

6. Right-click the Mask layer and select Mask. Several things should happen: the text and circle looks like it has disappeared, and the Text layer indents under the Mask layer. The indented layer is the Masked layer. In addition, the layers are locked. Locking the layer is essential for the mask to work properly.

7. Try running the animation. You should see the text appear in the circle cutout as it moves across the Stage.

Edit the mask

Now that we have the basics set up, let's do a little editing to make more happen.

1. To edit your mask, unlock the layers.

2. Place a keyframe in Frame 60 for both layers (see the following figure).

3. Create a second motion tween (discussed earlier in this chapter), if necessary, and back track the circle mask to have it stop halfway over the text (see figure).

4. Lock your layers, and test the animation again.

5. If all is working well, unlock the layers again.

6. Place keyframes in Frame 80.

7. Select the circle graphic and the Right click to select the Free Transform tool.

8. Using the graphic handles, enlarge the circle so that the dimensions are approximately 600 pixels wide by about 400 pixels high. This size fills most of the Stage, leaving rounded corners (see figure).

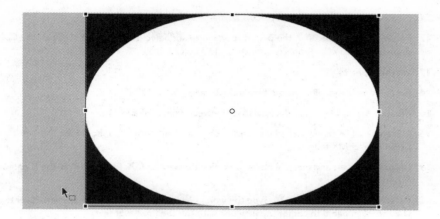

9. If necessary, create a motion tween between Frames 60 and 80.

10. Lock your layers and test your movie again. You should see the mask move from left to right, back to the center, and then enlarge to reveal the entire text.

More text animations

Now that the text is introduced, you are going to create some additional text animations. First, move the existing text up:

1. Unlock the layers and hide the Mask layer (click the eye icon column to hide the layers visibility) so you can get to the text easily.

2. On the introductory text's layer, create a keyframe at Frame 90. I am not going to extend the Mask layer any longer because you will not be using it again. If, later on, you want to use the mask again, you need to expand that also.

3. Select the text box, and press the Shift and the up-arrow key to move your text up 10 pixels.

4. Create a motion tween.

5. Before you test your movie, make sure you relock your layers and unhide the mask. Bring additional text into play.

6. Create a new layer called **Dreamweaver MX** and place it below the introductory text layer by dragging it down. Notice that it is indented below the masked layer. This will not hurt anything, but if you want to create a normal indentation, choose Modify ➪ Layer. Select Normal. Notice that you can change several Layer properties using this dialog box. Click OK.

7. Make sure the new Dreamweaver MX layer is selected. Press F6 to make Frame 90 a keyframe.

8. Select the Text tool,.type **Dreamweaver MX** below the Macromedia studio MX text and center it. Make the text size 20 points. You can use the Align panel to center the new text against the original text.

9. To create a fade in effect, convert your new text into a graphic symbol. Call your new symbol **Dreamweaver**.

10. Making sure the Dreamweaver symbol is selected, open the Color drop-down list in the Property inspector, and select Alpha.

11. Select the two text layers, and place a keyframe at Frame 110.

12. Return to the Frame 90 in the Dreamweaver layer and select the text symbol. Open the Color drop-down list in the Property inspector, and select Alpha.

13. Set the Alpha to 0%.

14. Go to Frame 110, select the symbol, and set the Alpha to 100%.

15. Create a Motion Tween in the new Layer between frames 90 and 110.

16. Make sure all layers are locked and turned on. Play your movie. You should see the words Dreamweaver MX fade in.

17. Unlock the layers and create a new layer called **Fireworks MX**. Place it below the Dreamweaver MX layer.

18. Insert a keyframe at Frame 110. Type the words **Fireworks MX** below the Dreamweaver text. Use the Align panel to center the new text with the Dreamweaver text.

19. Extend the three text layers by putting keyframes in Frame 130.

20. Create a motion tween in the new layer.

21. In the Property inspector, select the Rotate Property. Select CW for clockwise rotation, and set the number of rotations to 3.

22. Just setting a rotation is interesting. However, it is not a very graceful way to bring in the text. Make certain you are still on the keyframe of Frame 110 of the new layer.

23. Open the Transform panel. Set the dimensions to 0.0%. If you have Constrain checked, both settings should be set to near 0; 1.0 is fine.

24. Click Frame 130. The Transform panel should show 100%. Leave it at that.

25. Test your movie again. You should see the last text rotate in.

26. Create a new layer at the bottom and call it **Flash MX.**

27. Insert a keyframe at Frame 130.

28. Select the Fireworks MX text box, and click Copy.

29. Select the new keyFrame at Frame 130.

30. Select Edit ⇨ Paste in Place. Theoretically, you have the same text on two locations in the exact spot.

31. Extend each of the 4 text layers by extending the timeline to 150. Add a keyframe at 150.

32. Select Frame 150 on the new Flash layer and press the Shift and press the down-arrow key 3 times to move the text down 30 pixels.

33. Create a motion tween on the new layer. You should now have Fireworks MX in two places (see figure).

34. Create keyframes for the text layers at Frame 170.

35. Select Frame 150 in the Flash layer. To create some text effects, you sometimes need to break the text to its root level.

36. Place another keyframe at Frame 151 to distinguish animations.

37. Go to Frame 170 in the Flash layer. Double-click the text and change it to **Flash MX**.

38. Choose Modify ➪ Break Apart twice.

39. Return to frame 151 andChoose Modify ➪ Break Apart twice to break this text apart also.

40. Using the Property inspector, create a shape tween between Frames 151 and 170. Shape tweens should be used when changing a shape, color, or shape while moving. Shape tweens do require a bit more computing power and should be used sparingly.

41. You may want to move the text slightly to the right while morphing the shape.

42. Test your new movie now.

Finishing touches

We now need to add one finishing touch to our movie. You have one problem yet. Your movie will just continue moving. Here is a quick technique for stopping the movie. Here is a quick ActionScript to stop the movie.

1. Create a new layer and call it **ActionScript**.

2. Select Frame 170 and place a keyframe there.

3. Choose Window ➪ Actions, or Press F9.

4. Your panel should say Actions for Frame 170 of Layer Name ActionScript.

5. Click the plus sign in the Actions panel; then click Actions ➪ Movie Control ➪ Stop. Close the Actions panel. Notice that a lowercase "a" appears in the keyframe.

6. Now export the movie using File ➪ Export Movie. Choose a name and a location and click Save. You can now play your movie using the Flash Player.

You just learned some simple techniques for creating stunning effects. And you barely used any programming whatsoever. Try experimenting with some variations of these techniques.

A copy of the finished file is in the `chapter27_exercise` folder and is named `mask.fla`.

Summary

In this chapter, you learned the differences between frames and keyframes as well as how to use and edit them. You then discovered how easy it is to make a motion tween and saw some of the variations you could make, such as following a path or tweening opacity. Making shape tweens was just as easy and powerful.

Project Summary

Let's take a look at what you've done in this chapter that will be used in the Habitat Alert Web site. Some of the images need additional work in another section; others are ready to use in another application.

Files Prepared for Habitat Alert Web Site

Images	What Was Done	Where to Now?
ecard1.fla	You made the beginnings of a simple e-card using motion tweens.	You add ActionScript to this file in Chapter 29 when you add some sound. It will also interact with a database using ColdFusion in Chapter 54.
ecard2.fla	Using the same techniques taught for motion tweening the grass of the second e-card was animated.	You convert an animation made in FreeHand of a flying heron into a movie clip and add it to the e-card. You also add ActionScript and ColdFusion functionality.

Using Flash ActionScript

Flash MX uses ActionScript (a scripting language) to add interactivity to your movies. ActionScript is used for things such as navigation, arcade type games, puzzles, sound, banners, and communicating with a server for things like chat or e-commerce activities, such as login and registration. ActionScript is a powerful yet relatively easy scripting language to learn.

ActionScript is based on JavaScript, which is an object-oriented language, so if you know JavaScript you will learn ActionScript quickly. JavaScript controls objects in the browser; ActionScript controls the objects in a Flash movie. An object only knows about itself and only does things that relate to itself. Because each object is separate it is reusable and it can be used as often as needed.

An object allows programmers to define the data type of a data structure as well as functions that can be applied to the data structure. As a result the object includes both data and functions. Because of this, objects can inherit characteristics from other objects. Object-oriented programming is easier to modify because you can create modules that don't need to be changed every time a new type of object is added because the new object can inherit from existing objects.

Flash MX uses a syntax called dot syntax, which is similar to the format programmers are familiar with. Not only will a programmer be more comfortable using the dot syntax, using it adds a lot more power and flexibility. The dot syntax is a scripting language that adheres closely to the same specifications that are based on JavaScript. It's an object-oriented programming language with code that looks like this:

```
object.property=value;
or
object.methods();
```

In this statement four things need defining: the object, properties, values, and methods. For example, a Movie Clip object has properties (characteristics) that can be changed. The data that goes with the properties is the value. A dot separates a clip instance from its property, its nested clip instances, and its variables.

Like any new language you are trying to learn, there is a learning curve. You have to learn a few rules of the language. You'll have to learn to speak Flash's language, which is ActionScript. If you tell Flash to "move the ball," it can't comply if it doesn't understand. You have to tell it how big the ball is, how far to move it, and where to move it to. Some information Flash needs is which direction it should it move it and how long should it keep moving. Thinking through the specifics of what you want to happen is the first step to making your Flash movie — before you write any code.

Because ActionScript is such a huge topic it's impossible in the scope of this book to even cover a minute amount of the possibilities. We will go over the basics and some of the more common actions in this chapter. There is a large project which allows you to experiment first hand with using actions.

There are two additional tutorials in the Bonus Tutorials folder. There are also links to various Flash resources on the Links page on the CD.

If you are serious about ActionScript I highly recommend you purchase *Macromedia Flash MX ActionScript Bible*.

The Actions Panel

Everything that happens in Flash is the result of an event that causes a script to execute. There are three kinds of events: keyframes, mouse, and clip. These events also correlate to the areas you can place the scripts, which are keyframes, button instances, and clip instances.

Interactivity begins with an event being performed, such as a mouse click that results in something happening, a behavior or action. You can apply many actions in Flash, but for them to execute, you must tell them how to act. This telling is done by an event handler such as on (rollover) or on (release).

The Actions panel makes adding commands easy. You select the action you want or type your own code in (in Expert mode). The Actions panel is in your interface by default when you install Macromedia Studio. Click the expander arrow to open the panel. If you close and then open the Actions panel, choose Window ➪ Actions (F9). The name on the Actions panel varies depending on which event handle is selected. For instance if you have a frame selected, the panel would be called Frame Actions. If you select the object, the panel would be called Object Actions. In this book, it is referred to as the Actions panel.

Normal mode is the default. You'll see a list of actions grouped in categories or "books" in the left pane of the Actions panel. To switch to Expert mode, click the little blue arrow on the right side, and select Expert Mode or select Normal Mode or Expert Mode from the Actions Options pop-up menu. The keyboard shortcut is Ctlr+Shift+E (Command+Shift+E). In Expert mode, you can type or copy and paste custom code into the right pane of the Actions panel. You can also combine your custom code with the pre-built actions by double-clicking the action from the left pane or dragging the action into the right pane.

The Actions panel (Figure 28-1) in Flash MX has a new look and several new features. A brief outline of the various areas and functions follows.

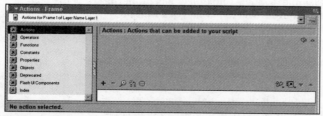

Figure 28-1: The Actions panel

✦ **ActionScript toolbox** — An entire library of actions arranged in categories. Double-click an action or drag it to the Script pane to add it.

✦ **Script pane** — The scripts you add from the ActionScript toolbox or type in Expert mode are displayed in the Script pane.

✦ **Parameters pane** — In Normal mode only, you'll see optional parameters for selected actions when they are available. The triangle in the top-right corner expands or collapses the Parameters pane.

✦ **Add/Delete an Action statement** — Select the action statement you want to work with and click the plus sign to add an action statement and the minus sign to delete an action statement.

✦ **Move Selected Action Statement** — The up and down buttons are used to change the order of statements.

✦ **Insert Target Path** — When referencing a button or Movie Clip instance, use this button to determine the relative or absolute path.

✦ **Jump menu** — Because the Actions panel is context sensitive, the jump menu changes its information based on the selected element.

✦ **View Option menu** — Toggles between Normal and Expert modes. You can also turn on line numbering from this menu.

✦ **Launch ActionScript Reference** — Provides instant access to a built-in ActionScript reference library.

✦ **Script Pin button** — You can choose to "pin" a script to the Script pane. It remains viewable at all times while you select other objects.

✦ **Normal mode** — Generally new users who don't know a lot of ActionScript use this mode. Actions are created by choosing menu selections from the ActionScript toolbox.

✦ **Expert mode** — You type your own ActionScript in Expert mode.

Tip

You can switch back and forth between Normal and Expert modes as needed. But if there are errors in your syntax (code) then it can only be edited in Expert mode.

Flash Pre-built Actions

When the Actions panel is open, you can add actions in several different ways. You can open the appropriate book, and double-click the action you want to add (it will be added to the right pane) or you can click and drag the action over to the right pane. You can click the plus sign (+) and choose from that list. After you make a selection, the code is automatically added to the right pane. You can choose Expert mode from the Options pop-up menu and type your own actions or use a combination of pre-built and hand coding.

In the Actions toolbox and in the Actions folder you'll see additional folders for Movie Control, which contains actions such as **goto, on, play, stop, stopAllSounds**. There are additional folders inside the Actions folder and at the same level as the Actions folder as well, such as Movie Clip Control, Variables, printing, and more. Dividing the actions into specific folders makes it much easier for you to locate the ones you want. In addition to the Actions folder, other categories such as Functions and Properties are available.

Note There is a new category of actions in the Actions panel called Deprecated. These are actions that are being phased out.

The best way to see what the actions do is to select an action, and in Normal mode a description will show in the Parameters pane. In Expert mode hold your cursor over the action and a description will appear.

Another way to learn about the various actions is to use the built-in Reference panel. To use it, select an action and then click on the Little book with a question mark on it icon. It's located on the right side of the Actions panel next to the Debug and the View options icons.

Color coding

A new and helpful feature for people trying to learn how to code ActionScript is color coding. The colors can assist you in learning code. Keywords and identifiers are dark blue; comments (which are ignored by Flash) are gray, and anything between quote marks are blue. If you forget to close the quotes, what you typed remains gray until you close it. At times, code hints appear to help you write your syntax. Code coloring is a preference, so if you want to use it choose Edit ➪ Preferences ➪ ActionScript Editor tab (Figure 28-2). It's on by default. You can uncheck the option or change the default colors.

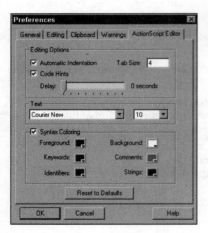

Figure 28-2: The ActionScript Editor tab of the Preferences dialog box, where you can change the color-coding colors or toggle it on or off

Tip Keywords are case-sensitive. For instance if you type **goToAndPlay**, the code would not turn blue because it's not accurate. You have to type **gotoAndPlay**.

Adding an action to a frame

Let's take a look at the **goto** action in the Movie Control folder of the Actions category. This action is basic and easy to use and understand.

ActionScript is written into the Flash Action window in the Actions panel either by using menus (on the left) or by choosing Expert mode (Options pop-up menu) and typing your own syntax. ActionScript is added to frames, buttons, or objects.

To add ActionScript to a frame, follow these steps:

1. With a new movie open, draw a simple rectangle on the stage and select the frame to receive the ActionScript.

2. Open the Actions panel.

3. In Normal mode, click the Actions book to open it; then click the Movie Control to open it. Double-click **goto**. Double-clicking adds the syntax to the right pane. You can also drag the action into the right pane (white area). An alternative way of selecting the action is to click the plus (+) sign and choose from the menu there; the syntax is automatically added to the right pane. Figure 28-3 is how it looks in Normal mode.

You add code below any existing code in Normal mode by clicking the existing statement to highlight it then double-clicking an action from the actions list to add the code. You can drag code to rearrange or even copy and paste it.

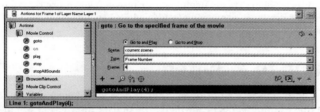

Figure 28-3: The Actions panel in Normal mode showing the goto action added

4. Switch to Expert mode. Figure 28-4 shows what the same code looks like in Expert mode.

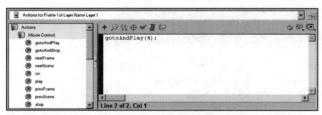

Figure 28-4: The Actions panel in Expert mode showing the goto action added

This statement says to go to and play a specified frame, which is indicated by a number in the parenthesis. The other variation of the **goto** action is **gotoAndStop**, which goes to a specified frame and stops. These actions are frequently used with buttons.

Actions that contain parameters that you need to specify have the parameter choices in the parameters area above the script window. For instance, the **goto** action has parameters but the **play** action doesn't.

The parameters for **goto** are

✦ **Scene** — You can choose various scenes.

✦ **Type** — You choose the frame number, frame label, expression, next frame, or previous frame to be the target of the action. The choices are self-explanatory except for Expression. Expressions are used to assign targets of **goto** actions dynamically.

✦ **Frame** — This area varies depending on which Type you select. If you choose Frame, you enter the frame number here. If you choose Frame Label, you enter the label name.

✦ **Go to And Play** or **Go to And Stop**.

Note   You can edit code in Expert mode by selecting any portion of a statement and edit it. But be sure to check your syntax for accuracy.

A practical use for the **goto** action is a simple preloader. A preloader indicates that a movie is loading and how much time is left. This is useful if your movie takes more than a few seconds to open. Often a preloader contains something (audio, video) to entertain the user while he or she waits for the movie to load.

Add an Action to a Button

If you attach the same **goto** action to a button symbol, the code will vary slightly. The event (which is `release` in this example) specifies which type of user interaction will make the action occur. You can change the event by selecting the `on (release)` line of code and choosing a different event from the Event list as shown in Figure 28-5.

Figure 28-5: The on (release) line of code selected and the Parameter area open showing the list of events

Usually with a button you want the click to take the user somewhere, such as to another page. There are two different options: you can go to another frame within the same movie or to a different HTML page outside of the Flash movie. You can access another frame of the movie by using the **goto** action. To use a hyperlink instead, you would use the **getURL** action, by following these steps:

1. Select a button symbol.

2. Open the Actions panel, open the Actions book, open the Browser/Network folder, and then double-click **getURL**.

3. You see the following code:

```
on (release) {
    getURL ("");
}
```

4. In the Parameters area, type the URL in the URL field. You see the address added to the syntax between the quotation marks as you type. If you want to use an expression to produce a value for the URL, click the box next to the URL file and enter your information.

5. In the Window field, select the target for the URL to open into from the following choices:

   - **_self** — Targets the window and frame where the movie is currently playing

   - **_blank** — Targets a new browser window

   - **_parent** — Targets the current window, but replaces only the frameset where the movies is playing

   - **_top** — Targets the current window and replaces all framesets with the new URL

6. In the Variables field, choose from the following:

   - **Don't send** — This is the default and best used when there is no transfer of data.

   - **Send Using GET** — Use when transferring a small amount of data such as a small form.

   - **Send Using Post** — Use when transferring larger amounts of data.

Add an Action to a Movie Clip

Adding an action to a Movie Clip is similar to adding to a frame or a button. In this exercise, you add the ActionScript to one of the e-cards being made for the Habitat Alert Web site. You can get the starter file (ecard2_start.fla) from the `chapter28_exercise` folder on the CD-ROM. Take a moment to look at each frame. You'll notice that Frame 1 contains a cartoon heron and some eggs. If you open the Library (F11), you'll see that each egg is a Movie Clip symbol. Click Frame 2, and you'll see a text area with information about the Great Blue Heron. Continue to check the other frames. Each one has text added for the various eggs. What you will be doing is adding ActionScript with the corresponding text to each egg. The text will appear when the user clicks the egg. The last frame for the goose egg is a joke, as in being goosed. (In Chapter 29, you learn how to add a squawk sound to the goose link.) To add the ActionScript to the e-card, follow these steps:

1. Open the `ecard2_start.fla` file from the `chapter 28_exercise` folder.

2. Select the first large egg marked Great Blue Heron.

3. Open the Actions panel (F9) and use Normal mode.

4. In the Actions toolbox, open the Actions category and the Movie Control category. Double-click the **on** action.

5. Notice the Script pane and that `on (release)` has been added. You want the frame to change on rollover. In the Parameters pane the only parameters available are events. Select Roll Over and deselect Release.

6. The ActionScript in the Script pane has changed to

```
on (rollover) {
}
```

7. Now you need to tell the ActionScript what you want to happen on rollover. In this case, you want it to go to Frame 2 and stop so you can read it. To do this, double-click the **goto** action in the Movie Control category of the ActionScript toolbox.

8. In the Parameters pane, click the **Goto and Stop** radio button. In the Frame field enter the number **2**. The script now looks like this:

```
on (rollover) {
gotoAndStop(2);
}
```

9. The rollover works, but what happens when the user moves the cursor away from the egg? As it is now, nothing happens. You want the movie to return to Frame 1 when the cursor moves off the egg. Select the curly bracket ({) in the last line of code in the Script pane.

10. Double-click the **on** action again. In the Parameters pane, select Roll Out and deselect Release.

11. Double-click **goto**, select **Goto and Stop**, and enter **1** in the Frame field.

12. Test the movie (Control+Enter [Command+Enter]).

    The movie plays through all the frames. You have correctly entered the ActionScript for the rollover, but now you need to have the movie stop at Frame 1. Select Frame 1 and double-click the **stop** action in the Movie Control category. Now test your movie. Mouse over the first egg and then move your mouse away.

13. Repeat for the remaining eggs adding a **stop** action to each frame of the movie. For the second egg (Great Egret) you want to go to Frame 3. The goose egg goes to Frame 6. Remember that the first **goto** is going to the frame that holds the text for that particular egg.

Movie Clips

This section looks at using Movie Clips, embedding Movie Clips inside Movie Clips, and accessing or giving instructions to these various Movie Clips.

Note   When you export your Flash movie it becomes a SWF file. You can incorporate these movies into other movies you are developing in Flash. The movie can be imported and converted into a Movie Clip with its own Timeline. Or you can use ActionScript to tell Flash to load an external SWF movies into your movie at run time.

Before you look at the awesome power of using Movie Clips let's discuss loading movies into your main Flash movie. You can have multiple Flash movies, which play at the same time in your main movie. This is accomplished by using different levels for each movie. For instance, the main movie (the root) is level0 (zero), the bottom level. You would then use the **LoadMovie** action from the Actions, Browser/Network book to open another movie. The movie you wanted to open would need to be on another level such as level1, so it plays on top. If you try to open this second movie and it is on level0, it would replace the original movie. You can only have one movie per level.

The big advantage of using Movie Clips over loading movies is that a Movie Clip runs independently of the main movie. Movie Clips have their own Timelines and actions and constitute mini movies. You have a lot of control over a Movie Clip. You can change its color, position, and even make it disappear (transparency). You can also use duplicate Movie Clips and control them by assigning them different instance names.

Movie Clips are controlled by the instance name (set in the Property inspector). You add ActionScript to a Movie Clip by referencing its instance name. You can also have a Movie Clip inside of a Movie Clip. Let's look at how to communicate with your movie clips in Flash. The main Timeline is by default the root. So for instance if you wanted to add a **play** action it would look like this:

```
on (release) {
     play();
}
```

There is no need to add the word root. But we have a Movie Clip called mymovie1. If you want to assign the **play** action to mymovie1 then the code would look like this:

```
on (release) {
     mymovie1.play();
}
```

The addition of mymovie1 tells Flash that the Movie Clip is being played rather than the root. The dot is similar to the slash in a paths address.

Let's say we have another Movie Clip named mymovie2, which is inside the first Movie Clip. To access the embedded Movie Clip the code would look like this:

```
on (release) {
     mymovie1.mymovie2.play();
}
```

Your first Movie Clip, mymovie1, is the parent of mymovie2. If you want to communicate to mymovie1 from mymovie2 the code would be

```
on (release) {
_parent.play();
}
```

Now if you wanted to communicate with the main Timeline from within the Movie Clip the code would be this:

```
on (release) {
     _root.play();
}
```

Understanding Objects

Objects are a collection of *properties*; all properties have a name and a value. Objects have changeable and accessible characteristics that you set by using ActionScript. Objects in Flash have different meanings. There are graphical objects, user-defined objects, and built-in objects. Graphical objects are drawings, photos, or text. The object is not only the image but the instructions that go along with it for its properties and/or methods. For instance a box has properties of height and width.

An instance of a symbol has to be placed on the Stage to have an object action applied to it. Actions are not applied while in Symbol Editing mode. A few of the built-in objects follow.

The Array object

A list of options to choose from is frequently used as a menu and powered by JavaScript. You can do it in Flash using the Array object. The method of the Array object is **New Array** with an optional argument for array length. For example, you have a customer list with a list of names such as

```
Name ="Sally";
Name2="Gerald";
Name3="Sue";
Name4="Hank";
```

A new Array would appear as

```
customers=New Array(Sally, Gerald, Sue, Hank);
message="Thank you for your order" + [3];
```

The result of this small piece of code is

```
Thank you for your order Sue. The number 3 indicates that the third
name in the list should be used, which is Sue.
```

The Color object

The method of the Color object is **SetRGB**. This sets the color of the color object. The argument is `0XRRGGBB`. The zero x `(0x)` is an escape code for hexadecimal values and is always used prior to the hexadecimal values. You replace the `RRGGBB` with the hexadecimal values of the color you want to use. You can find the hexadecimal values in the Mixer panel.

There are two ways to manipulate the color attributes of a Movie Clip instance: the hexadecimal value and the RGB code. The RGB values are in decimals from 0 to 255 and translate to 0 to FF in hexadecimal.

Math objects

The math objects access trigonometry functions. All the math objects prepare read-only values and are written in all capital letters. The trigonometry functions of sine, cosine, and tangent, logarithmic, mathematical, and constant are beyond the scope of this book. `math.round` is just what it sounds like; it rounds to the nearest integer.

You code looks like this:

```
math.round(this.getBytesTotal()/1000)
```

This code means to round off the calculation of the objects total size property (`this` refers to the object you are editing) to the nearest byte giving the total number of kilobytes of the object. The total bytes in this case it will be the size of a movie, which is a song. At the end you add `/1000`, which tells Flash to divide by 1000, so you get the number of kilobytes instead of bytes.

The Movie Clip object

Movie Clip is one of Flash's predefined objects. Movie Clips can be instances, but they can also be objects. As objects, they have characteristics you can access and control. Some of the properties you have control over include appearance, such as transparency, visible or color, size, and position.

Using Properties

Properties are attributes of objects. Each instance of an object can have different properties. Movie Clips, frames, and symbols have properties that you can control through ActionScript. You can control changes, such as position, color, transparency, and so on.

In Flash MX, Movie Clips are no longer the only objects to which you can assign instance names. You can give instance names to buttons, text, and video. When you select the object, you type the instance name in the Property inspector.

To set a property, follow these steps:

1. Select a Movie Clip.

2. Open the Actions panel.

3. Select the Properties book and choose the property you want to control. Add it to the right pane by double-clicking your choice.

4. In the Parameters area type an expression. You can choose from the following:

   ✦ _visible — Visibility is either true or false.

   ✦ _x or _y — The x, y coordinates of the object.

   ✦ _droptarget — The target path of a dragable Movie Clip that must be dropped on a specific target.

An example of changing properties of a Movie Clip would be to move a clip by a specified number of pixels. Let's say you wanted to move the mymovie2 Movie Clip by 20 pixels. The first thing to do is locate the clip. Then you set the new value (more on setting values in the "Variables" section). The **getProperty** action does this. To move the mymovie2 Movie Clip (remember this is inside mymovie1) by 20 pixels, follow these steps:

1. Select the frame or object you are attaching the action to. In Normal mode open the Movie Clip Control book in the Actions toolbox and double-click on **getProperty**.

2. In the Parameters pane there is a drop-down list of properties to choose from; select the x.

3. Click in the Target field, then click the Insert a Target Path icon and select the Movie Clip you want to target.

4. For the value, check Expression, then type 20 into the Value field. So if you want to move mymovie2 over 20 pixels the code would be

   ```
   getProperty("mymovie2.mymovie2","_x") + 20
   ```

If you try to enter this code directly into the setProperty value box, it wouldn't work. If it's entered in the value box, Flash thinks it's a value and it isn't. Flash needs to perform a calculation to determine the value (expression), so check the Expression box by the value of the **setProperty** action. You can see how you can save a lot of time once you understand how to write ActionScript. It would be much easier to write this line of code rather than use the Normal mode.

Variables

Variables are the information containers of ActionScript. The container is the variable's name, which remains constant, but the content can change. Variables can record user input and evaluate whether a condition is true or false.

Flash remembers data and the label that identifies the data. The data and its label make up the variable. Every variable has a name, which is used to access the data it contains. To put information into the container (variable) the formula is as follows:

```
variable Name = Value
variable Name is the name of the variable and value is the data, for
example:
message="Hi";
```

Message is the variable name, the text (Hi) is the value, and the equal sign (=) is the assignment operator. It assigns the right side to the variable on the left side. In this example, the value is text. The value can also be mathematical. Your code can be attached to a frame, keyframe, button, or Movie Clip.

To set or declare a value, you can type the variable's name or use an action. The set variable action is in the Variables book. Double-click **set variable** to see a message telling you that the variable has to be named. In the value box, I typed Joyce. The syntax reads as follows:

```
MyName = "Joyce";
```

Note   Declaring or setting the variable is a good habit to get into, but if you don't, Flash does it automatically. If you come from a programming background you can name your variables with var prefix. Setting the variable yourself lets you make your own naming conventions.

Variables are stored in the target where they are declared. So if you have TitleName="Macromedia Studio MX Bible" in a Movie Clip named mymovie1 and in the Movie Clip named mymovie2, there won't be a problem.

Movie Clips can share variables by using target paths that describe where they are. If you recall in the ActionScript overview, you used mymovie1 and mymovie2 Movie Clips with mymovie2 inside of title. If you want to change the value of TitleName in the Movie Clip mymovie2 from the main Timeline (root or level0) the code would look as follows:

```
_level2.mymovie1.mymovie2.TitleName="New Value"
```

Tip   When first learning how to write your own code, you can set an option to check the syntax for you by choosing Check Syntax from the Actions panel Options pop-up menu. If an error is found, an Output dialog box opens and any errors are described. When you are first beginning to write code, you should check it often by pressing Control+Enter (Command+Return). If you are still having problems with your code, you can use the Debug option by choosing Control ➪ Debug Movie.

Data types

Data type is the kind of information that a variable element can hold. There are prime data types (string, number, and Boolean) which have a constant value. Then there are reference data types (Movie Clip and objects) which have values that can change. This list describes the different data types.

- ✦ **Strings**—A string consists of text or numbers or both enclosed in quotes (""). When using numerical calculations, the quotes are not present in the code. The quote marks indicate a string. If you were to use numbers such as "6" + "2" it would be interpreted at 62.

- ✦ **Boolean**—Variable values that are either true or false. Boolean values are used in either/or situations such as a toggle switch.

- ✦ **Number**—Number data types are any values (or expression values) that refer to numeric values in Flash. Number data does not contain quotes around it in the syntax.

- ✦ **Movie Clip**—Movie Clips are symbols, and they are the only data type that refers to a graphic element.

- ✦ **Object**—Objects have properties and each property has a name and value. The value can be any data type including the object data type.

Flash UI Components

A new panel in Flash MX is named Flash UI Components. These components are similar to what used to be called Smart Clips, but they've undergone some changes. You can edit the components and even change their appearance. They have skins that are components of the component. You can also make your own components or get more from the Flash Exchange. To use the components, drag them to the Stage. Check the Property inspector. This is where you can add your specific parameters and change the properties. To begin using components for the first time, choose Help ➪ Tutorials, and select Introduction to Components.

Making a Puzzle Using ActionScript

The puzzle you are going to make can be used in any Web site requiring a puzzle. You'll see in the project that it's easy to use the same puzzle and code and simply change the image (if it's the same size). The puzzle pieces you will be using were made in FreeHand, and the file is provided for you. The finished project is shown in Figure 28-6.

Figure 28-6: The finished puzzle project

Making the puzzle pieces

To make a puzzle out of the heron image used on the Habitat Alert's homepage, follow these steps:

1. Open a new Flash movie. Double-click Layer 1 and name it **puzzle base**.

2. Choose File ⇨ Import, navigate to the `chapter 28_exercise` folder, and select `puzzle1.jpg`. Because this folder has another puzzle with a number Flash thinks they may belong together and gives you a message asking if you want to import as a sequence. Click No. Move the image off the Stage.

3. Choose File ⇨ Import, navigate to the `chapter28_exercise` folder, and select `puzzle.FH10`. In the FreeHand Import dialog box, choose Flatten and accept the defaults.

4. Zoom out so you can see the entire puzzle. Use the Arrow tool to draw a selection around the puzzle shapes (marquee select), and group (Control+G (Command+G)).

5. Choose Edit ⇨ Select All. In the Align panel be sure the To Stage button is not selected (very important), and click the Match width and height button. Now select the To Stage button; then click the Center Horizontal and Center Vertical buttons (top row).

6. These puzzle shapes, which were made in FreeHand, are horizontal and vertical lines that are grouped. Select the outline of the puzzle and ungroup it. Figure 28-7 shows how it looks ungrouped. The blue rectangles you see each represent a group for each horizontal and vertical row.

Figure 28-7: The puzzle's horizontal and vertical lines that are still selected after the first ungroup

7. Ungroup again. The result after ungrouping will look like Figure 28-8. Notice the little dots in the lines, which show they are now ungrouped. Do not deselect yet.

   Once they are ungrouped and you deselect, the puzzle will be behind the bird image.

Tip

8. Choose Edit ⇨ Select All (Control (Command)+A).

Figure 28-8: The puzzle pieces
aligned and ungrouped

9. With everything still selected, choose Modify ➪ Break Apart. You see a shadowed, dotted overlay on the puzzle (Figure 28-9). When you deselect and select each puzzle piece
   (centers not outlines), the individual pieces should be indicated by the dots. I say
   should be because it's possible you will have pieces connected, and this can be quite
   trying. See the sidebar, "Troubleshooting the Puzzle," to see what causes pieces to be
   connected and how to fix the problem.

Figure 28-9: The dotted image after
the pieces have been broken apart

10. Save your file.

Troubleshooting the Puzzle

When you design the puzzle shapes you have to be careful that there are no openings. Each of
the horizontal and vertical lines must touch the edges. Even if they touch, you may have to adjust
them. Don't let any lines overlap the bounding shape. I had to fix the puzzle shape (the one supplied doesn't need adjusting). Test in Flash; alter them again where the shapes were connected,
then edit, and so on.

Converting to Movie Clips and naming instances

You will now change the 16 puzzle pieces into separate Movie Clip symbols.

1. Select the top-left piece, and choose Insert ⇨ Convert to Symbol (F8).

2. For the Behavior, select the Movie Clip and name it **MC1**, and click OK.

3. Repeat for each piece ending with **MC16**. Notice that you can no longer see the puzzle shapes.

4. Although you can't see the shapes, the puzzle outline is still in your movie and you need to remove it. Open the Movie Explorer (Window ⇨ Movie Explorer). Be sure the Show Graphics, Buttons, and Movie Clip button is selected (second from the left). The Movie Explorer is shown in Figure 28-10.

Figure 28-10: The Movie Explorer with the Movie Clips button being clicked

5. In the Movie Explorer, select MC1 from the puzzle base layer, and shift+select all the Movie Clips through MC16. Choose Edit ⇨ Cut (Control+X [Command+X]).

6. On the Stage marquee, select the puzzle shapes and delete them.

7. Choose Edit ⇨ Paste in Place to return your puzzles pieces. Lock the puzzle base layer by clicking the dot below the lock icon in the Timeline.

8. Select the puzzle base layer, and click the plus sign to add a new layer on top. Double-click the new layer's name and name it **pieces**.

9. Select Frame 1 of the piece's layer, and choose Edit ⇨ Paste. (The pieces are still in memory because you have recently cut them.) The pieces are now on the new layer.

10. Move the pieces off the image in the puzzle base, in other words, to the white area. Be sure none of the puzzle pieces touch the puzzle base image (Figure 28-11).

11. Now you need to set the instance names and target for the puzzle pieces. The name and target coordinates will be used when you add the ActionScript. The puzzle targets are the location of each piece in the puzzle base. Lock the pieces layer.

12. Unlock the puzzle base layer. In the Movie Explorer, select the Show Frames and Layers button at the top. In Layer one select MC1.

Figure 28-11: The pieces moved off to the side

13. In the Property inspector, type **base1** for the instance name. Repeat for the rest of the pieces, ending with **base16**. Notice in the Movie Explorer that the instance name has been added. Figure 28-12 shows the Property inspector. The instance name for the first piece is shown. The x and y coordinates for this instance name are now the target that will be used to identify where the puzzle piece belongs.

Figure 28-12: The Property inspector showing the instance name and x, y coordinates of the first puzzle piece

14. Check to be sure that the Pieces layer is locked; then in the Property inspector, choose Alpha from the Color drop-down menu, and type **40%** or select it with the slider.

Dragging the pieces

You are going to enable the user to drag the puzzle pieces in the puzzle pieces layer by using the press and release mouse events of buttons. To set up the puzzle pieces, follow these steps:

1. Unlock the pieces layer and lock the puzzle base layer.

2. Open the Actions panel (F9). Select the MC1 puzzle piece. Select Expert Mode from the Options pop-up menu, and type the following code:

```
on (press) {
this.startDrag();
}
on (release,releaseOutside) {
this.stopDrag();
}
```

This code makes the enables the user to drag a puzzle piece. Next you must determine whether the puzzle piece is in its proper place. You need to determine whether the puzzle piece is over the puzzle target. You are going to utilize one of the Movie Clip properties called _droptarget. The __droptarget command returns the name of the object on the stage that the puzzle piece you have selected is over.

3. After `this.stopDrag();` press Enter/Return and add the following code:

```
if(eval(this._droptarget)==_root.base1){
this._x=_root.base1._x;
this._y=_root.base1._y;
}
```

This piece of code checks to see whether the item you are dragging is on top of the base1 instance on the stage. If it is in the right place, it sets the x and y positions of the piece to the base instance on the stage. The piece snaps into place when it's close to the correct location. The finished code will look as follows:

```
on (press) {
this.startDrag();
}
on (release,releaseOutside) {
this.stopDrag();
if(eval(this._droptarget)==_root.base1){
this._x=_root.base1._x;
this._y=_root.base1._y;
}
}
```

Next you add a bit more code to make the puzzle piece snap back to its original location if it's in the wrong place. If you use the Movie Explorer to select each puzzle piece from the pieces layer you will be able to see the x, y coordinates in the Property inspector. This way you won't have to write them down when you edit the ActionScript for each piece. Just look at the Property inspector and type the coordinates to the code.

4. In the Actions panel while the MC1 (base1) piece is selected, highlight the last two curly brackets (}) and overwrite with the following code:

```
} else {
setProperty (this, _x, 115.3);
setProperty (this, _y, 69.0);
}
}
```

This bit of code is saying that if the puzzle piece isn't dropped here return it to these x, y coordinates. The `else` statement is checking to see whether the drop target is correct, or else (if it isn't) returns the piece to its original location. Replace the x and y coordinates in the two setProperty lines with the x and y coordinates that are shown in the Property inspector.

5. Save your file and test the movie (Control ⇨ Test Movie). You should be able to select the first puzzle piece you just added ActionScript to and place it over the correct target in the puzzle base. The puzzle piece should snap into place. If it's in the wrong location, it snaps back to its original location. If there are errors, you will be notified in a dialog box. The most likely errors to occur are typos. Check your code carefully.

6. The easiest way to add the script to the rest of the pieces is to copy this code and then select each piece and paste into the Script pane. Change the base name number and the x, y coordinates for each piece. Save the file. A copy is saved for you named `puzzle1.fla`.

7. Save and test your movie. You can change the base layer to an Alpha of 0 if you don't want it visible at all.

Multiple puzzles

You are going to make a Flash movie with two buttons so you can have multiple puzzles. The first thing you do is change the puzzle picture; then you load the puzzle of choice from the main movie.

For any image you want to swap with this puzzle (that's right, swap, no additional coding required) you need another image the same size as the original image. `puzzle2.jpg` is in the same puzzle folder with the first bird puzzle; use that one. To swap the image, follow these steps:

1. Open `puzzle1.fla` from the `chapter28_exercise` folder if you've closed it.

2. Choose Modify ➪ Document and change the background color to **#66CC99** (a light green).

3. Open the Library panel and right-click (Control+click) the first bird image and choose Properties. In the Properties dialog box, choose Import, and select `puzzle2.jpg`. Click OK. That's all there is to it, you now have a new puzzle (Figure 28-13).

Figure 28-13: The bird puzzle changed into a different puzzle

4. Save the puzzle as **puzzle2.fla** and test the movie. You can close this file.

5. Open a new Flash movie and choose File ➪ Import to Library. Select the heronbutton, drawingbutton, puzzle1_thumb, and puzzle2_thumb images from the `chapter28_exercises` folder and click Open. All four images will now be in the Library.

6. Use the Text tool and type **Click the button for the puzzle you'd like to build** and center it at the top of the Stage. I used the font of Verdana and size of 18.

7. Drag the buttons and images from the Library (F11) to the stage and arrange as shown in Figure 28-14. As you can see there is plenty of room to add more images.

8. Select the heron button and choose Insert ➪ Convert to Symbol. Select a Button behavior and name it **heronbutton**. Click OK. Repeat for the drawing button.

Figure 28-14: The interface for selecting the puzzles

9. To load the movies by selecting a button, select the heron button, open the Actions panel, and choose Expert Mode. Add this code to the heron button and then the drawing button (change the filename on each):

```
on (press) {
loadMovie ("puzzle1.swf", 0);
}
```

The puzzle loads into level 0 and overwrites the interface file. If this movie is embedded into an HTML file, you can use named anchors so that the browser's back button works. The next step shows you how to add a named anchor.

Cross-Reference Embedding Flash movies is covered in Chapter 41.

10. Select the first frame and in the Property inspector in the Frame field, type **interface**, and select the Named Anchor box.

11. Save your file as **puzzleinterface.fla**.

Load into the same window

With this example the puzzle loads into the same window as the thumbnails instead of overwriting them. You accomplish this by loading the puzzles into different levels.

1. Open puzzle`interface2.fla` from the `chapter28_exercise` folder.

2. Open `puzzle1.fla`. With both layers unlocked, choose Edit ➪ Select All, and click the Free Transform icon. Drag one of the corners in and press the Shift key to constrain. Check the Property inspector and make it about 270 × 180, anywhere close will work. This size will fit on the bottom of the interface for the puzzles.

3. Save as **sm_puzzle1**. Repeat for `puzzle2.fla` and save as **sm_puzzle2**.

On the
CD-ROM

A copy of the small puzzles are on the CD-ROM if you'd rather skip Steps 2 and 3.

4. In the main movie (puzzleinterface2.fla) select the heron button, and open the Actions panel in Expert Mode. Type the following code:

```
on (press) {
loadMovie ("sm_puzzle1.swf", 1);
}
```

This code tells Flash to open the bird puzzle file in level 1. When a movie loads into the same level, it replaces the current movie. When it loads into a different level, the main movie is still present. Select the drawing button and add this code to the Actions panel in Expert Mode:

```
on (press) {
loadMovie ("sm_puzzle2.swf", 1);
}
```

Figure 28-15 shows the buttons on the bottom of the Stage in level 0 and the heron puzzle loaded on level 1.

Figure 28-15: The buttons visible while a movie is loaded

Summary

In this chapter you learned various ActionScript terms and techniques. You became familiar with the Actions panel in Normal and Expert modes. You learned how to attach actions to various objects and performed some advanced ActionScripting in the puzzle project. You also saw how to load movies onto different levels.

Project Summary

The following table shows what you did in this chapter that will be used in the Habitat Alert Web site.

Files Prepared for the Habitat Alert Web Site

Images	What Was Done	Where to Now?
ecard2.fla	ActionScript was added to make a rollover or swap image effect when a button is clicked.	In Chapter 29 you learn how to attach sound, and this file needs sound added.
puzzle1.fla puzzle2.fla	You added ActionScript to make the pieces dragable, snap to position, and snap back if the wrong position.	This is ready to be used with the interface2.fla file.
interface2.fla	You added ActionScript to load the movie into a different level.	This is ready to be embedded into an HTML file in Dreamweaver.

Working with Sound

Adding sound to your Flash movies can certainly enhance them, but if used improperly they can irritate and even chase away visitors. When sound is used judiciously, it can convey your message in a way that is memorable. Using sound effectively also means understanding that you need to edit the sound files to make them as small as possible and still maintain the sound's integrity. Sound files can add a tremendous amount of download time to a file. Flash MX enables you to do some minor sound editing, but if you use sound frequently you'll want to get a sound editor to do the job. A few recommendations are made in the editing section of this chapter.

Sound Files

The type of sound files you can import depends on your operating system. For instance Windows supports WAV files and Macintosh supports AIFF, but Windows and Macintosh both support MP3. There are additional sound types that may be compatible with your operating system.

When working with sound there are some terms you will see frequently, and it's important to understand what they are.

✦ **Sample rate** — In a digital recording, the computer examines the sound wave and takes snapshots of its amplitude. The snapshots are called samples, and the speed at which they are taken is the sample rate. In most consumer's digital audio, the sampling rate is 44.1khz or 44,1000 samples per second. The sample rate is used to describe sound along the x-axis.

✦ **Bit depth** — Measures sound along the y-axis. Bit depth is either 8- or 16-bit for digital audio. 16-bit offers more clarity and truer sound.

✦ **Panning** — You can assign left and right channel information for stereo sound. Stereo is played through two simultaneous channels, and each channel has a unique position. Mono is a single channel and is best used for dialog or sound effects.

Importing sound files

You need to get the sound files into the Library of your movie; to do this, follow these steps:

1. Navigate to the chapter29_exercise folder and open `ecard1.fla`.

2. Choose File Import to Library.

3. Navigate to the location of your sound files. Select one or multiple files and open. To practice, navigate to the chapter29_exercise files and select `heron_audio.mov`.

4. Press F11 to open the Library panel. You can see that your sound file is now added. Leave this file open for the next exercise.

Adding sound to the Timeline

It's a good idea to add a new layer for your sound because it makes it easier to identify. Plus if you have multiple sounds in your movie, you'll need to put each one on its own layer. To add sound to the Timeline of a movie you can practice on one of the e-cards for the Habitat Alert site. To add sound to the Timeline, follow these steps:

1. Select the forever3 layer and add a new layer. Name this layer **sound**.

2. Select Frame 1 of the sound layer.

3. In the Property inspector on the far right is a Sound field. Click the drop-down menu and you will see the `heron_audio.mov` file you imported. Select it.

4. The Effects menu and Edit button in the Property inspector are activated. You won't be adding effects now but be aware that they are here and available. You'll be using the Edit button in the next section of this chapter.

5. In the Sync field, click the arrow to open the menu, and choose Event. The options are:

   • **Event** — This is the default selection and is best used with shorter sounds.

   • **Start** — This is similar to Event. The Start option starts the sound and plays it entirely. If used on a button, the sound plays only once, and only one instance of the sound can play at a time. This means that if you happen to mouse over another button while the sound is playing, another instance will not begin to play at the same time.

   • **Stop** — This stops sounds that were cued using the Event or Start options. For streaming sync, you need to determine how many frames you want to have no sound in and then remove the appropriate number of frames (Shift+F5) for the part of the animation you want silence in.

   • **Stream** — This option locks the movie's frame rate to the playback of the sound. This is not recommended for looping sound but is great for scored music, lip sync, multitract, and component audio.

6. Enter the number of times you want your sound to loop in the Property inspector.

7. Save your file. A copy of this file is saved in the habitat_alert_final_designfiles\ Flash folder as `ecard1_sound.fla` in the final site file folder. Leave this file open for the next exercise.

Editing Sound Files

In Flash you can edit where a sound begins and ends as well as adjust volume and create fade ins and outs by following these steps:

1. For practice you can use the file from the previous session or navigate to the `habitat_alert_final` folder and the `designfiles\Flash` folder and open the `ecard1_sound.fla` file.

2. Select Frame 1 of the Sounds layer to activate the appropriate properties in the Property inspector.

3. Click the Edit button. Figure 29-1 shows the Edit Envelope dialog box.

Time In   Time Out

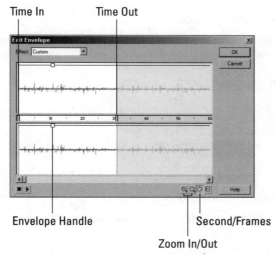

Envelope Handle   Second/Frames

Zoom In/Out

Figure 29-1: The Edit Envelope dialog box

4. Drag the Time In control for the start point and the Time Out control for the end point.

5. Use the envelop handles to adjust the volume for fade in and fade outs. You can also choose a preset from the Effects menu.

6. Choose a loop.

7. Click Play to test.

8. Click OK.

For further editing you'll need to use a sound-editing program. You can use a command called Normalize to boost the sound (use a setting between 96 and 98), which you can then adjust the volume in Flash. Prior to using a sound file you'll need to check for any dead space at the beginning and end of the file and remove it. The dead space adds a pause before the sound plays plus it adds to the weight of the file. If you want or need pauses, it's better to program them in rather than leave dead space in your file. Of course there are a lot of other reasons to edit your file. The actual editing of files is beyond the scope of this book.

A couple of sound editing programs to check out are Cool Edit 2000 (`www.syntrillium.com/cooledit/`) and Sound Forge (`www.sonicfoundry.com/`).

Adding Sound to a Button

You can enhance the effect of a button with an appropriate sound. When the user mouses over or clicks the button they will hear the sound you attached. To add a sound to a button, follow these steps:

1. Import the sound file/s into the Library (File ⇨ Import as Library).

2. Select the button symbol.

   Making button symbols is covered in Chapter 26.

3. Click the Edit button in the Library panel and notice the Timeline change. You can now see the Up, Over, Down, and Hit states of the button (Figure 29-2).

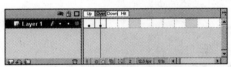

Figure 29-2: The Timeline for the button symbol

4. Add a new layer and name it **sound**.

5. Select the Overstate and add a Keyframe (F6).

6. In the Property inspector, select the name of your sound file from the Sound drop-down menu.

7. Select the type of sync you want.

8. Choose an effect if you want.

9. Return to the main scene and test the button by choosing Control ⇨ Enable Simple Buttons. Pass your mouse over the button to hear the sound.

Stopping Sounds

A sound plays until the frames run out or until the looping option you set runs out. But you can program a sound to stop at other times by following these steps:

1. Select the frame in the Sound layer where you want to stop the sound.

2. Add a Keyframe (F6).

3. Select the sound filename from the Sound field drop-down list in the Property inspector.

4. From the Sync menu click on the Stop option. Now when the new Keyframe is reached the sound will stop.

Stopping All Sounds

To stop all sounds in a button or frame, follow these steps:

1. Select the button frame or another frame with sounds.

2. Open the Actions panel (F9).

3. Click the Actions folder; then click the Movie Control category.

4. Double-click the `stopAllSounds` action to add it to the script window. Or you can use Expert mode and type **stopAllSounds()**;.

Exporting and Compressing Sound Files

If you have more than one sound file per movie, you'll want to set the compression for each individual file because you may be able to compress some more than others. Sound files can add a tremendous weight to your movie, so you need to compress and edit carefully for the best effect and impact. If the movie takes too long to load many people on modem connections simply won't wait. To set the compression settings for a sound file, follow these steps:

1. Open the Library panel (F11).

2. Select a sound file.

3. Right-click (Control+click) and select Properties. Figure 29-3 shows the Sound Properties dialog box.

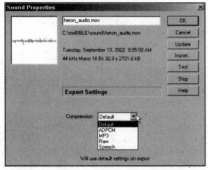

Figure 29-3: The Sound Properties dialog box

4. Click the Update button if you edited the file outside of Flash. Click the Test button to hear any changes you've made.

5. From the Compression drop-down list, choose a compression type. The options are

- **Default** — This applies the settings you have set in the Publish Settings dialog box. You can change the Publish Settings to change the default.

   Publish Settings is covered in more detail in Chapter 30.

- **ADPCM** (Adaptive Differential Pulse-code Modulation) — Normally used for short sounds.

- **MP3** — CD or near CD quality. Used for music, dialog, and long sounds. A quality setting of 20 or above gives you the option of stereo channels or mono. The quality setting of Fast is best compression, but the worst quality. Medium is better than the fast compression. Best is the least compression, but it gives you the best quality for music or sounds that are important.

- **Raw** — This option applies no compression at all.

- **Speech** — This is new in Flash MX and is meant for human speech. If you select this option but export for Flash 5, it will be converted to ADPCM.

- **QuickTime** — This option is used when you are going to export as a QuickTime movie instead of a Flash movie.

6. Click the Test button to hear the sounds.

7. Click OK when you are done.

Using Sound Objects

So far you've attached sound to the Timeline. By using Sound objects you can use ActionScript to access the sound even if it isn't in the Timeline. A Sound object is a predefined ActionScript object, which contains the information about the movies sounds and its properties. Objects have properties, which are variables that contain data. By attaching a Sound object to a sound you can pass information from it to the sound. The Sound object has methods (which can be applied to unique instances of the object), which send and retrieve information about your movie and its objects. The Sound object has methods, which set and check values, panning, play, and stop actions. Sound objects can control the following:

✦ All sounds loaded in the current movie

✦ All sounds currently available in the Flash Player

✦ Sounds in a specific Movie Clip

✦ A specific sound the object is attached to

The generic constructor for a Sound object is

```
SoundObjectName=new Sound("targetInstance");
```

In Chapter 26, you learned about Movie Clip objects and in Chapter 28 you learned about the Array, Math, and TextField objects. The Sound objects (as well as the Color and Date objects) are a bit less forgiving than the others and require formal rules. The sound object needs to be instantiated using a constructor function such as the following one:

```
newObject(); for sound it's newSound();
```

Using newSound() doesn't really do anything. You need to store the object in a variable. By using mySound=newSound() you create a new instance of the Sound object and place it into the variable mySound. mySound can be referred to by its properties or by using a method (mySound.someProperty or mySound.someMethod()). The thing to remember is that you need to instantiate an object and place it in a variable before you can do anything with it.

Attach the Sound to the Sound Object

By using ActionScript you can access the sound from the Library, but sounds in the Library won't export by default with the movie unless they have been placed onto the Stage. You can override this by setting the Linkage properties. The sound then loads with the movie. To set the Linkage and attach the sound, follow these steps:

1. Open the ecard3.fla file from the chapter29_exercise folder.

2. Import the heron_audio.mov file to the Library (in the chapter29_ exercise folder).

3. Select the sound in the Library panel.

4. Right-click (Control+click) and select Linkage.

5. In the Linkage Properties dialog box, give it a unique identifier. (We used soundID.)

6. Leave the Export for ActionScript box checked.

7. Click Ok and leave the file open.

   Now you are ready to attach the sound to a sound object. An object can only have one sound attached. Use the attachSound method to attach.

8. Select the top layer and add a new layer. Double-click to rename it and name it **sound**.

9. Select the first Keyframe of the Sound layer, and open the Actions panel (F9). In Expert mode, type the following code:

```
heron=new Sound();
heron.attachSound("soundID");
heron.start(0)
```

This creates a new instance of the sound object named heron and attaches the sound using the identifier you added in the Linkage dialog box. (We used soundID.) Then you tell the sound to start.

Summary

In this chapter, you experimented with adding sound. You saw how to get sound into your movie's library, how to add it to a Timeline, and how to add effects. You also saw that you could do minor editing of sounds within Flash itself. Sound objects were introduced, and by using ActionScript you were able to control the sound in a movie. You added the sounds to the ecards for the Habitat Alert site.

Project Summary

No Habitat Alert pages were created or modified in this chapter, but you will use many of the extensions in other chapters to create features for the site. You could also build object tools for items used repeatedly for the site.

Files Prepared for the Habitat Alert Web Site

Files	What Was Done	Where to Now?
ecard1.fla	You added a sound to the Timeline.	You will program this to use ColdFusion and access a database.
ecard2_squawk.fla	You added a squawk sound event to Frame 6.	You will program this to use ColdFusion and access a database.
ecard3.fla	You added a sound object and attached the sound.	You will program this to use ColdFusion and access a database.
Ecard4.fla	You added a Sound layer to the Timeline and used a fade out effect for the sound.	You will program this to use ColdFusion and access a database.

✦   ✦   ✦

Publishing Your Flash Movies

You are probably ready at this point to get some of your newly generated movies onto your Web server. The first thing you need to do is consider the size of your SWF movie file and its performance. In this chapter, you'll learn how to check your syntax and use the Debugger to help you locate any errors in your movie.

You learn a series of tips and tricks to optimize your images. It is beyond the scope of this book to teach you all the finer points of optimization, but the tips should help point you in the right direction so you know what areas to check. It should also show you where you need to brush up on your skills and where you need more specific information.

Optimizing Flash Movies

Carefully optimizing the individual elements in your movie and following some of the tips listed here will help you reduce the size of your SWF movie.

Bitmaps

It's a good idea to use large bitmaps as static background images only. It's not a good idea to use large bitmaps in an animation because of the large size of the files. You can, however, use small bitmaps sparingly and animate them with a motion tween.

You get better results if you edit your bitmaps in Fireworks before you place them into Flash. The difference in file size may not be much, but every little bit helps; plus you have more control and optimization options in Fireworks. For instance, with the new Selective JPEG Compression feature, you can optimize portions of an image at a higher setting and optimize less important areas at a lower setting.

Keep in mind that when you export your Flash movie, Flash compresses your image again. JPEGs that are compressed multiple times frequently result in artifacts. To avoid this, select the image from the Library list (before you make it a symbol). From the Options pop-up menu, choose Properties. The Bitmap Properties dialog box opens. Choose Lossless from the Compression drop-down menu, and click OK.

Traced bitmaps

If you trace complex images, the file sizes may be considerably larger than the original bitmap version because of the complex curves. You can simplify the curves to make it less complex. Always check the file size to determine whether you need to redraw portions of the traced bitmap or even perhaps use the bitmap itself depending on the use of the image.

Animations

When making animations, it's best to use symbols as much as possible and then use tweens on the symbols. If you animate frame-by-frame, each keyframe has to load. If you animate using a motion tween or a guided motion tween, only the symbols have to load.

Symbols

You get small file sizes if you tween symbols instead of using large groups of objects. If you ungroup your elements, there are fewer paths involved for Flash. Plus in a symbol if there are no groups, any effects you apply are applied to the symbol as a whole instead of to groups within the symbol.

Paths

When you make vector images in FreeHand or other vector programs, simplify the paths as much as possible while maintaining the integrity of the paths. Vectors you make in Flash should have the paths optimized as well (Modify ➪ Optimize).

Fonts

Fonts are embedded and the outlines are exported with your Flash movie. But Flash does not necessarily support all fonts. It's easy to do a quick test to see if the fonts you want to use are acceptable. Choose View ➪ Antialias Text. If the text appears jaggy, it isn't compatible. If the text you need isn't design critical you can use device fonts: _sans, which is similar to Arial and Helvetica, _serif, which is similar to Times Roman, and _typewriter, which is similar to Courier. These fonts are the top three in the font drop-down list of the Character panel. You reduce the file size by using device fonts, because they use the closest font match from the user's system, so there is no embedding of fonts in the movie.

Gradients

Solid fills add the smallest amount to your file size. Gradients should be used sparingly. Flash can do gradients up to eight colors; after that the additional colors are broken up into separate shapes, which adds to your file size.

Alpha versus Tint

When you add an Alpha effect to a symbol, it increases the file size. Tint adds less if it'll do the trick for you. Try to limit the number of Alpha effects you have in the same symbol.

Layers and folders

Layers and folders are a great way to keep your movies organized: images on a layer, buttons on a layer, actions, and so on. Use all the layers and folders you want or need. They do not add to the finished SWF movie file size.

Sound

You should optimize each sound separately, as discussed in Chapter 29. Edit your sound to the absolute minimum to get the best sound at the lowest file size. Remember to edit out any dead space. If you use sound frequently, you may want to invest in a good sound-editing program.

If you want streaming sound, place it in the main movie Timeline and not in a Movie Clip. The reason being, in the main Timeline, the sound begins at the appropriate frame and plays immediately. If it's in a Movie Clip, the entire file has to load before play begins.

On the Flash tab of the Publish Settings dialog box you can compress audio streams and audio events separately so you can have a higher quality for music and lower quality for sounds that go with buttons.

Debugging

The most frustrating part of making a Flash movie is when you choose Control ➪ Test Movie and it doesn't work. The most common error is incorrect spelling. When writing your ActionScript, you need to take extra care to spell things correctly each time you use them or reference an instance or a Movie Clip. It's important to check your movies frequently so you don't get to the end of a large project and discover it isn't working. It's a good practice to check and debug after each stage of your movie.

Fortunately, Flash provides some tools for tracking down additional problems. It's easy to forget to select a frame in an action's layer and attach a button action to a frame that doesn't contain a button; this, of course, will return an error when you test your movie.

Following is a short list of troubleshooting tips to be aware of as you develop and test your movies:

- ✦ Check your syntax often. In the Actions panel, use the Check Syntax button.

- ✦ Use capitalization where needed. For instance `gotoandplay` won't work because it needs to be `gotoAndPlay`. Capitalization is important.

- ✦ Include semicolons at the end of statements.

- ✦ Use curly braces to enclose the statements of handlers and loops.

- ✦ Be sure your target path is correct.

- ✦ Be sure all Movie Clips and buttons are instances and have unique instance names.

- ✦ Be sure all variables and functions have unique names.

Debugger panel

In the Debugger panel, you can monitor Movie Clip instances, variables, and properties. The Flash Debug Player is automatically installed. This player opens the Debugger. To use the Debugger press Shift+F4 or choose Window ➪ Debugger. To activate the Debugger, choose Control ➪ Debug Movie. Figure 30-1 shows that you can see the contents of the movie and that it is paused by default. Click the green Control button in the Code View menu to continue.

The top portion of the Debugger panel is the Display list with the absolute path and nesting of all the current Timelines including all Movie Clips. You can also access properties and variables from their respective tabs. The Watch tab lets you monitor specific variables on any Timeline.

Debug from a browser

You can now access the Debugger panel to debug your movie from a Web browser. If you choose Debugging Permitted in the Publish Settings Default tab options, you can access the Debugger panel from the Debug Movie environment or from a browser that has the Flash plug-in. (You need to install the Flash Debug Player plug-in or ActiveX control. You can find it in the Players folder of your Flash MX application folder.) You should also require a password so others can't access the Debugger.

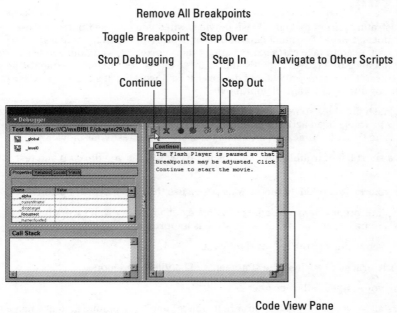

Figure 30-1: The Debugger panel

Remote Debugging

Being able to debug your movie while it's live on the server is new to Flash MX. You can debug movie variables, which communicate to and from a server to insure that the information is being exchanged properly. To use this feature, you need to enable remote debugging and then activate it from a remote location. To enable remote debugging, follow these steps:

1. In Flash, choose File ⇨ Publish Settings.

2. Click the Flash tab (Figure 30-2).

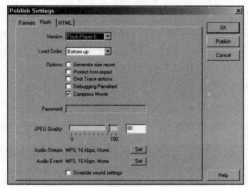

Figure 30-2: The Flash tab of the Publish Settings dialog box

3. Check the Debugging Permitted option.

4. Enter password information if you want users to have to enter a password to use this feature.

5. Click the Publish button. This produces a file with an .swd extension. This file is needed to perform remote debugging.

6. When you are done, click OK.

7. Upload the .SWD file, SWF file/s, and HTML to your server. The SWD and SWF files need to be in the same directory.

8. Before debugging, open Flash and press Shift+F4 to open the Debugger.

9. From the Debugging Options pop-up menu, select Enable Remote Debugging.

To activate remote debugging, follow these steps:

1. Use a browser or the stand-alone Flash player to open your movie from the remote location by entering its URL.

2. In the Remote Debugging dialog box, choose one of the following:

   • **Select Localhost** if the debug player and Flash MX are on the same machine.

   • **Select Other Machine** if the debug player and Flash MX are on different machines. Enter the IP address of the machine running Flash MX.

3. Click OK.

4. Enter password information if needed.

5. Click OK. The Debugger is activated.

Using Breakpoints

This useful feature is new to Flash MX; it enables you to pause a script to examine each line and its effect in your movie. Once paused, you may see additional bits of data. The line of code will be in the right side of the Debugger panel. If the line of code is in a function, you see variables, which are specific to the paused function, listed under the Local tab.

To set and/or remove breakpoints in the Debugger panel, follow these steps:

1. In the Code View box (the large area on the right showing the code), select the line of code in which you want to set or remove a breakpoint.

2. Choose one of the following options:

   • Click the Toggle Breakpoint icon above the Code View pane.

   • Right-click (Control+click) the line of code and select Set/Remove Breakpoint.

3. You can now move through each line of the movie by using the following buttons located above the Code View pane:

   • **Step Out**—When the line of code is inside a function, this command steps outside of the currently enclosed function.

   • **Step In**—This advances to the next line of code.

   • **Step Over**—This skips a line within the function.

Output Window

When you test your movie, the Output window automatically opens and lists any errors. Whenever you test your movie, even if there are no errors, a menu item is added to the menu bar as shown in Figure 30-3. Debug is added with additional menu options.

The other options in the new menu are explained as follows:

✦ **List Objects**—You can use List Objects in test movie or in Debut Movie modes to obtain a list of every element present on the stage. This can be extremely helpful in checking target names. Figure 30-4 shows an Output list.

✦ **List Variables**—Again, if you are in Test Movie or Debug movie mode, you can access a list of all variables in your movie and see their locations and values.

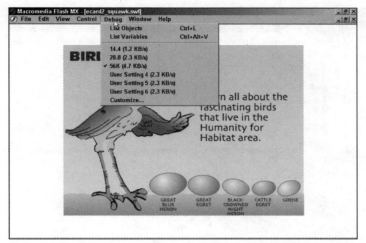

Figure 30-3: The Test Movie command with a new menu bar with Debug menu in it

Using a Trace Action

Use a `trace` action to get a report about specific parts of your movie. Your queries are answered in the Output window. You can track things such as dead handlers, Movie Clip parameters, target paths, and so on. You can add a trace action to send the value of an expression to the Output window during Test Movie or Debug Movie modes. Select an object or frame in the Timeline, and open the Actions panel. You enter the `trace` action into the Actions panel like any other action. For instance, let's say you have an instance of a circle on stage with properties of color and an X position and you want to check the properties, you would type the following into the Actions panel in Expert mode:

```
mycircle = new circle (0x660000, 40);
trace (mycircle.color); //the trace return in the Output window would
be 660000
trace (mycircle.xPosition);  //the trace return would be 40
```

If you don't get a return, you know to check for errors.

Bandwidth Profiler

With the Bandwidth Profiler, you can determine how long it will take users with modems to load your movie. In the Profiler you can simulate how long it will take a user to see your movie using different modem or cable speeds. To use the Bandwidth Profiler, follow these steps:

1. Open the `ecard2_squawk.fla` file from the `chapter30_exercise` folder.

2. Choose Control ➪ Test Movie.

3. Choose View ➪ Bandwidth Profiler (Figure 30-4).

Figure 30-4: The Bandwidth Profiler

4. From the Debug menu, choose the modem speed or custom speed you defined to simulate.

5. Go to View ➪ Show Streaming. You see a simulation of the time it will take for your movie to load.

Publish Settings

You can access Publish Settings by choosing File ➪ Publish Settings. After your settings are all done, you can click the Publish button in the HTML tab if you want your movie in an HTML page or choose File ➪ Export for an SWF movie. The following options are available:

✦ **Format tab** — The default tab that opens is Format. The Flash (.swf) and HTML (html) are checked by default. SWF is the only format that maintains full functionality of your movie and ActionScript.

✦ **GIF** — GIF is used primarily for images with a lot of flat color and when you want a transparent background. Its main limitation is the fact that it supports only 256 colors. When you check the GIF option, a GIF tab is added to the Publish Settings dialog box.

The options in this tab enable you to format your Flash movie into a static GIF image or a GIF animation, which can be used if a user doesn't have a Flash player installed.

✦ **JPEG** — JPEG is best used on images with more than 256 colors, such as photographs. Although gradients don't have that many colors, they also look better as JPEGs. Gradients in a GIF usually have banding, but as JPEGs they look great.

Full details of the JPEG options are covered in Chapter 23.

JPEG images are compressed and then decompressed when they are opened. This means that although the file size is small more memory is needed to decompress the image in the browser than for a GIF image.

When you select the JPEG option, a JPEG tab is added to the Publish Settings dialog box. From this tab you can make some adjustments to the image. For example you can change height and width, the quality, and whether you want to use the Progressive option.

Note The JPEG options in the Publish Settings area do not override the settings you chose for the individual image in the Library under Properties. These settings are for static JPEG images you may want to export to the Flash movie.

✦ **PNG** — PNG (Portable Network Graphics) was developed as an improvement over GIF and JPEG, which it is, if all the browsers actually supported its wonderful features. Its biggest advantage is that you can have transparency and lossless compression. Unfortunately these features are not fully supported yet in the major browsers. Until they are, the PNG format will not be used widely on the Internet. The PNG settings in this tab also apply to exporting a static image of your Flash movie.

✦ **Windows Projector** — Choose this option if you want to export your movie as a stand-alone projector for use in Windows.

✦ **Macintosh Projector** — Choose this option if you want to export your movie as a stand-alone projector for use on a Macintosh.

✦ **QuickTime** — Starting with QuickTime 4, there has been built-in support for Flash SWF files as well as something called a Flash track. Flash can import QuickTime movies, add Flash content and then export the whole movie as a QuickTime movie. If you want to publish your Flash movie as a QuickTime movie, check the QuickTime option in the Format tab and make the appropriate selections.

Note Real Player was supported in Flash 4 but not in Flash MX.

✦ **Flash tab** — The Flash tab offers a lot of control over your movie settings. The following list looks at each option separately.

• **Version** — Choose the version of Flash Player you want your movie to be compatible with. Be aware that new features of a version will not be compatible with older Flash Players. The new features in Flash MX will not be present in the Flash 5 Player.

• **Load Order** — If you check this option, you can determine how your frames load. Bottom up, which is the default, loads in ascending order: the lowest layer displays first, then the second, and so on. If you select Top, the frames load in a descending order.

• **Generate Size Report** — The size report can be quite useful in determining problem areas in bandwidth concerns. If you check this option, the Publish command exports a Simple Text (Mac) or TXT file (PC).

• **Omit Trace Actions** — If you used trace actions while you were developing your movie, check this option. The Flash player ignores any trace actions used in ActionScripting. The trace actions open the Flash Output window for debugging purposes.

- **Protect From Import** — If you check this option, it protects your Flash SWF file from being downloaded and imported into Flash. But Macromedia Director can import and use even protected SWF files. Some hacker utilities can get at a protected file as well. SWF files can be read in NotePad to see variables names and values. Because of this, you should never include sensitive information, such as passwords, in your source file. The bottom line is, that protecting your movies helps discourage the general audience from using your movies. Those who know how and are determined to steal your work can do so.

- **Debugging Permitted** — With this option checked, you could access the Debugger panel from the Debug Movie environment or from a browser, which has the Flash plug-in. (You'll need to install the Flash Debug Player plug-in or ActiveX control. You can find it in the Players folder of your Flash MX application folder.)

- **Compress Movie** — The move is compressed to reduce file size and download time. This new option to Flash MX works only in the Flash 6 player.

- **Password** — If you checked Allow Debugging, which can be accessed from an Internet browser, you should check this option so that the Debug Movie panel can only be accessed with a password.

- **JPEG Quality** — The slider from 0-100 determines the JPEG compression applied to bitmap images. The higher the value you choose, the less compression applied. This setting doesn't override the choices made in the Library.

- **Audio Stream** — The display you see listed is the current audio compression scheme for Audio Stream. If you click the Set button, you can alter the compression scheme. Like bitmap properties, the Audio Stream settings do not override the compression value if any compression other than the default is applied in the Sound properties dialog box in the Flash Library.

- **Audio Event** — The display listed is the current scheme for Audio Event. The Set button enables you to alter the settings. Audio Event works very much like Audio Stream.

- **Override Sound Settings** — This option enables you to override any settings you made to the Sound properties in the Flash Library.

✦ **HTML tab** — The settings in this tab control the way Flash publishes its movie to an HTML page. A lot of the options in this tab are self-explanatory if you understand how HTML works.

The first option, Template, gives you options to choose from such as Flash Only for Pocket PC or Image Map. Make a selection; then click the Info button, which gives a description of the option and a bit of instruction. It would be a good idea if you haven't done so yet, to check out the info buttons on each option to familiarize yourself with everything you can do.

Make any other size, playback, quality, or alignment changes you want and click OK when you are done.

Exporting Your File

After you have optimized your movie, debugged it, checked the download speeds in the Bandwidth Profiler, and set your Publish Settings, you are ready for the export.

After setting your Publish Settings the export is one step: File ➪ Export. This exports your movie as an SWF file. If you want your movie to automatically be an HTML page, choose File ➪ Publish. The HTML file with your Flash movie embedded is generated automatically.

If you also selected other options, such as QuickTime, on the Format tab of the Publish Settings, these formats will be generated when you choose File ➪ Export Movie or File ➪ Export Image.

Summary

In this chapter you learned how to optimize your Flash movies to reduce the file sizes as much as possible so your movies load faster in the user's browser. You explored many of the settings available and the export options you can use.

✦　　✦　　✦

Developing in Macromedia Dreamweaver MX

Understanding the Dreamweaver Environment

◆ ◆ ◆ ◆

In This Chapter

Learning Dreamweaver's bars, windows, and inspectors

Using docked and grouped panels

Customizing your workspace

◆ ◆ ◆ ◆

Dreamweaver MX is a feature-rich, professional Web design and development program. Its tightly integrated environment enables you to design, build, and manage Web sites and Internet applications with easy-to-use visual design tools and a customizable coding environment that supports current and next-generation 509 technologies for static Web sites or server-based Web applications. Dreamweaver's Features and tools are supported by panels that you can group and dock as needed. Design and Code view options enable you to work in a comfortable environment. A single-click option lets you change views at any time. Contextual menus and panel options provide convenient access to tools and may be supported with custom keyboard shortcuts. Program preferences enable you to select specific settings for your workflow, from opening new documents to previewing work in progress. Dreamweaver is also extensible, which means you can add new objects, behaviors, and commands to add new tools, features, and functions to your application.

In this chapter you'll become familiar with the Dreamweaver MX workspace, which is the basis for using all the tools available in Dreamweaver MX.

Choosing a Workspace Layout

If you are a Windows (PC) user, when you start up Dreamweaver MX for the first time, you see a dialog box for choosing a workspace from three options, as shown in Figure 31-1.

The Dreamweaver MX workspace uses a Multiple Document Interface (MDI), where you can open all documents, toolbars, and panels within a single application window. A dock of panel groups is placed along the right edge of the application window, with any opened document to the left. Menus, bars, and inspectors are distributed above and below the opened document windows. This is the recommended layout and is the one shown in the help documents.

The HomeSite or Coder-Style workspace is similar, but places the panel groups along the left edge in a layout that both HomeSite and ColdFusion users will find familiar.

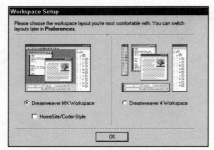

Figure 31-1: Windows users can choose from three workspace options.

The third workspace option is the Dreamweaver 4 workspace—also called "the floating panel" layout. Each document appears in its own floating window. The panels are all docked as groups along the right edge, but the docked groups and panels are not locked into an application window. You can reposition all components to float freely.

Note   The Dreamweaver 4 workspace is the only workspace available to Macintosh users.

All the workspace layouts allow for adjustments. You can place the dock on either side, and you can configure certain bars and panels to change their size and position. Windows users may opt to change the workspace via the program preferences at any time.

To change the Windows workspace, follow these steps:

1. Choose Edit ➪ Preferences or press the keyboard shortcut Control+U.

2. Select the General category, if not already in that screen.

3. Click the Change Workspace button.

4. Select the desired layout.

5. Click OK.

Bars, Windows, and Inspectors

The Dreamweaver Document window is where you design, code, and edit your Web pages. You use the bars and inspectors surrounding it to add, modify, and manipulate your pages and the elements they contain.

Dreamweaver MX menus

Standard program/application menus, as shown in Figure 31-2, provide access to Dreamweaver MX's tools, features, and functions. Each menu offers a related set of options, as discussed in the following list:

Figure 31-2: The application menus

✦ File and Edit menus give you options to create, save, preview, and edit pages and page elements.

✦ The View menu offers items that are also on the Document bar (see the following paragraphs) and can be used to view and edit rulers and grids.

✦ The Insert menu mirrors the Insert bar, with options that match the toolsets.

✦ To edit page properties or elements, including table structures, use the Modify menu.

✦ The Commands menu contains tools with special functions; you can download and install new commands, or build your own with the History panel.

✦ The Site menu contains management and publishing options.

✦ The Window menu provides access to and helps organize all the panels in Dreamweaver MX. It also lists all open documents.

✦ Finally, the Help menu offers access to resources for using Dreamweaver MX, including tutorials, help files, and support links.

Bars and inspectors in Dreamweaver MX provide access to tools, functions, and properties for developing Web pages.

The Insert bar

Located below the application menus, the Insert bar (Figure 31-3) is a panel of different toolsets, from a common set containing basic editing functions to specialized sets like frames, forms, and special characters. Click a toolset tab to bring those tools to the forefront. Each toolset contains icons, text, or icons and text, depending on your preferences' settings. By default, only icons are displayed, but if you hover over a tool, a ToolTip lists its function.

Figure 31-3: The Insert bar

The Document bar

Along the top edge of the document window, the Document bar (Figure 31-4) contains buttons for accessing and controlling views. In Dreamweaver, you can build your pages in a visual Design view, in Code view, or in a Split view environment. Each view offers its own advantages depending upon your preferred method of working. To select a view, click its button. Views also include a Live Data view, which you use when building Web applications connected to a data source. Other views include the Remote Web server, and the local view of the Web browser in Preview mode or when debugging in a browser.

Show Code View

Show Design View

Live Data View

Show Code and Design Views

Figure 31-4: The Document bar provides access to all views.

The View menu (main application menu) offers a way to hide or display elements in your pages, based on your view choice. When Design view is selected the View menu options include Table, Frame, Layer borders, and an option for displaying icons for invisible elements. Grayed out options are not available. In Code view, Word Wrap and Line Numbers are some of your choices. These choices also include code indent and syntax coloring. Split view offers Design and Code view options.

The Document window

Depending on your workspace layout and computer platform, your documents open in an application window (Windows, integrated layout) or as floating, separate windows (Windows or Macintosh, Dreamweaver 4 layout). By default, Dreamweaver opens a new, untitled document each time you start the program, but you can disable this option in your preferences. When you disable it, the program starts up with only the docked panels (Windows only, integrated layout) or Site Window (Windows or Macintosh, Dreamweaver 4 layout) showing. To disable the new, untitled document on startup, follow these steps:

1. Choose Edit ⇨ Preferences.

2. In the General category, check the Show Only Site Window on Startup box.

3. Click OK.

The Status bar

Along the bottom of the Document window, the status bar (Figure 31-5) contains the Tag selector, Window Size selector, and Download Speed indicator. Although you will barely notice the selector at first, as you build your development skills, you will come to rely on this feature's powerful functions. Web documents are based upon a Document Object Model (DOM), which is based on tags that tell the browser how to display the content in the page. The Tag selector reveals some of this model by showing you the relationship of your cursor or selection point to the `<body>` tag. Web browsers display elements between opening and closing `<body></body>` tags.

Figure 31-5: The Tag selector

You can select any tag that is part of the display by clicking it in the Tag selector. In complex table structures, this makes tag selection and editing a snap.

Tip Selecting the <body> tag selects everything on your page.

Use the Window Size selector to mimic the browser window size to ensure that your pages fit your planned target dimensions. The Download Speed indicator gives you a rough estimate of how long it will take to download the page code and graphics, based on your modem configuration and connection speed. You can modify these settings in the program Preferences menu (Edit⇨Preferences). To modify a setting quickly go to the Window Size menu (Figure 31-6) by clicking and holding over the small black arrow there.

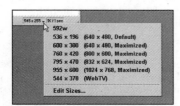

Figure 31-6: Edit window size options and download speeds

The Property inspector

To work with each HTML tag's attributes, use the Property inspector, shown in Figure 31-7. By default, the Property inspector is docked along the bottom of the Document window. The inspector is contextual, meaning that its contents change based on the currently selected tag. If you cannot find the Property inspector, you can access it via the Window menu or press Control+F3 (Command+F3).

Figure 31-7: The fields in the contextual Property inspector change with the page element selected.

The Property inspector is your primary tool for setting element attributes. Be sure to click the small white arrow at the bottom-right edge of the inspector to expand the panel fully. Depending upon the element selected, you can enter values, choose from menus populated with options, and browse or point to specific files in the Site panel (window in the floating layout). Press Tab to move among fields.

Tip When entering values for tag properties, get into the habit of pressing the Return or Enter key afterwards. This action updates the document and ensures that the value is accepted.

Using Docked and Grouped Panels

You access most of Dreamweaver MX's functionality through panels that are grouped and docked along the right or left edge of the application window. You can enable all panels from the Window menu, but many are on and visible by default. To view the panels in a group, expand the group with the expander arrow (little white triangle on the top left side). Close to minimize the group and hide the panels.

You can hide or show groups at will. To hide all groups temporarily, choose View ⇨ Hide Panels or press F4. Disable the Hide Panels option to bring the panels back.

Tip

PC users can click the button incorporated into the border between the document window and the panel groups. This "slides" the dock to the right or left (depending upon the workspace) to allow expansion of documents. To slide it back into place, click the button again. Dragging this border widens or narrows the dock's width.

Grouping the panels makes sense because there are so many of them, but don't feel locked in by the default arrangement; you can group individual panels and reposition, close, or create new groups to contain your panels. Additionally, you can float one or more panels. To regroup any panel, use its Panel Options menu located at the top, to the right of the panels title bar, as shown in Figure 31-8. Choose GroupSite With [panel name] and select one of the 12 listed panels. The repositioned panel joins the group of the selected panel.

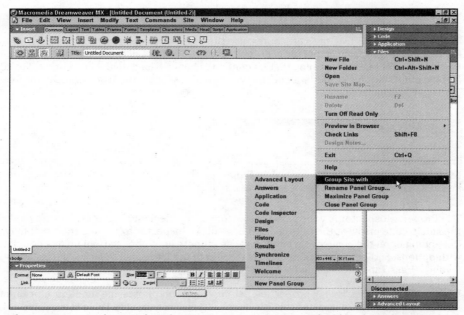

Figure 31-8: Use the Panel Options menu to regroup a panel within a group or to rename, close, or maximize the current group.

Tip

To arrange the panels within a group, select and group a panel with the same group until the panels are repositioned as needed.

To close a group of panels, use the Panel Options menu to choose Close Panel Group. To close a specific panel, you have to first create a new group with the panel using the panel options. Choose Group Site With [panel name] New Panel Group; then click Close Panel Group.

You can also use the Gripper (the textured area at the left side of each group's title bar) to pull the panel away from the dock. You see a blue highlighted area as you move the group around. To create a separate, floating panel, wait until you don't see the highlight, then release. This forms a floating panel.

Other options for modifying the default grouped panels include the following:

✦ **Renaming groups** — Using the Panel Options menu to choose Rename Panel Group.

✦ **Repositioning Groups within the Dock** — Use the Gripper to drag, move the group until the highlight appears in the desired location; then release.

✦ **Help** — Click this option to trigger the Using Dreamweaver Help files, opened to the proper directions for the panel in question.

Answers and reference panels

Depending upon the site you plan to build, you will use some panels and not others. All the panels are covered in the following chapters, but the Answers and Reference panels stand alone in function.

Answers

New to Dreamweaver MX, the Answers panel provides single-click access to tutorials, TechNotes, extensions, and more. Click the Update button to link to the Macromedia Web site and download the latest content.

Reference

The Reference panel is a great way to expand your Web development knowledge. If you want to know more about a specific tag, select it in a document, and then click the Reference button in the Document bar to open the Reference panel. The panel contains concise guides to different technologies, including Cascading Style Sheets (CSS), ColdFusion (CFML), HTML, JavaScript, Active Server Pages (ASP), Java Server Pages (JSP), Sitespring, and Accessibility. Other ways to access the Reference guide for a specific tag include choosing Help ➪ Reference or pressing Shift+F1 with a tag selected in Code view or in the Tag selector.

The Files panel

The Files panel contains two of the most important panels, Assets and Site. These panels are covered in depth in the next chapter, but it's important to note here that this group should not be closed. You'll be using both panels extensively.

Cross-Reference

The Site panel for the PC is the same as the Site window on the Macintosh. This panel is covered extensively in Chapters 32 and 45.

Modifying Preferences and Keyboard Shortcuts

You can increase your productivity in Dreamweaver MX by setting program preferences and creating keyboard shortcuts. Preferences provide a way to determine default behavior for the way Dreamweaver opens, codes, and publishes your pages.

Keyboard Shortcuts are a great way to speed up page development. The default shortcut set used is the Macromedia Standard Set but, using the Keyboard Shortcut Editor (Figure 31-9), you can choose from a HomeSite (PC) or BBEdit (Macintosh) set, a Dreamweaver 3 set, or opt to create your own custom set, starting with one of the first three as a base set. You can modify most of the menu options, including menus on the Site Panel (PC), Code Editing, Document Editing, and the Site window.

Figure 31-9: The Keyboard Shortcut Editor

To use the Keyboard Shortcut Editor, follow these steps:

1. Choose Edit ➪ Keyboard Shortcuts. (Be patient, it may take a while to load the shortcuts.)

2. When the dialog box appears, choose from an existing set.

3. Duplicate the set by clicking the first of the four buttons to the right of the Current Set menu.

Note The default sets cannot be edited, and you will be prompted to make this custom set if you try to do so without first duplicating it.

4. Name the set and click OK; then wait for the custom set to load.

5. Select the location of the menu command you want to edit by choosing it from the Commands menu.

6. Expand the appropriate menu and select an existing menu option.

7. In the Press Key field, add your new key combination.

Note For the PC, the key combination must include the Control key; for the Macintosh, it must include the Command key.

8. To accept the new combination, click the Change button.

Tip To avoid endless attempts to find a combination that hasn't been used, print out the preferred keyboard set. Click the Export Set as HTML button (the third of the four buttons) and save the page as HTML. In a browser, open and print the page to list all the existing keyboard shortcuts.

Summary

In this chapter, you learned the different ways to customize your Dreamweaver layout, from modifying panel groups to creating your own custom keyboard shortcuts. In the chapters to follow, look for cross-referenced notes to show you even more options for improving your workflow by altering the Dreamweaver workspace.

✦   ✦   ✦

Starting a Web Site with Dreamweaver

The basic approach to building a Web site is to build pages on your local computer's hard drive, then transfer a folder with all the site's content to a Web server to make it publicly available. Dreamweaver MX includes features to help you in this process, from structuring the files and folders to publishing static or dynamic Web content.

It all starts with defining a site. In this chapter, you tell Dreamweaver where you want to store your Web files and folders and learn to manage them using the Site panel.

Defining a Site

Defining a site gives Dreamweaver information about a project's root folder. A root folder is the outermost folder that contains all the elements of a Web site. There are two kinds of root folders, local and remote. The *local* root folder lives on your computer's hard drive. The *remote* root folder lives on a Web server — usually on a different computer — connected to the Internet or a local network. You may have more than one remote folder set up: one where you test and another for publishing.

There are two important steps to defining a *static* site in Dreamweaver MX. A third step is required for defining *dynamic* (data-driven) sites:

✦ Locating the local root folder that stores all the site elements

✦ Entering the Web server access information for the remote site

✦ Specifying an application server model

Additionally, you may set up different testing servers used in dynamic development prior to publishing. Next we will define the site for the Habitat Alert Web site. Then in the ColdFusion portion of this book you will set up the testing server.

Local info

Copy the habitat_alert_start folder from this book's CD-ROM to your hard drive. Be sure to unlock the files. To add local information, name your site, and show Dreamweaver where the root folder is located on your computer's hard drive.

Note
Because this book may not be used in a linear fashion you will be provided the site folder for each chapter of the Dreamweaver section where needed. You'll need to define a new site (or edit the path for the local root folder) for each chapter.

Follow these steps to define your site:

Tip
There are two modes you can use to set up your site, Advanced and Basic. Use Advanced if all you want to do is begin to build a site and worry about publishing later.

1. Choose Site ➪ New Site from the application menus. Click the Advanced tab.

2. Click the Local Info category if it isn't already selected (blue highlight). Enter **Habitat Alert** for your site's name in the Site field.

3. Click the Browse for Folder icon (Figure 32-1) beside the next field. Locate the folder where your site files are contained.

Note
If you are starting a site from scratch, create a new folder where you plan to place all your Web files, folders, and other assets.

4. Leave everything else default.

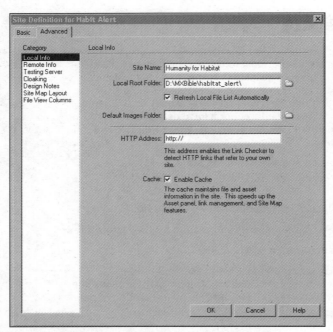

Figure 32-1: Name your site and select a root folder.

Basic Site Setup Wizard

Dreamweaver MX features a new Site Setup Wizard that you may find helpful. Basic mode asks simple questions to elicit the right information for your site:

1. Choose Site ➪ New Site from the application menu.

2. Select the Basic Tab to use the wizard.

3. Enter your site's name. This is a name you can use later to select a site from the Site panel's Site menu. Try to keep your site names short. Also, some characters are not allowed. They are /, |, \, :, ?, *, <, and >.

4. Click the Next button.

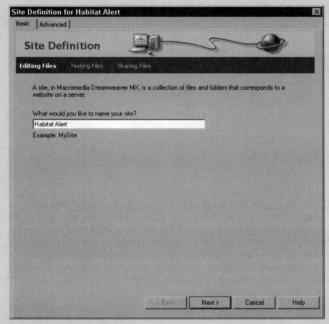

Basic Site Setup Mode

5. If building a static site, select the first option in Editing Files, Part 2. A dynamic site uses the second option. Click Next.

6. Select the first, recommended option to Edit locally, then upload to a server when ready in Editing Files, Part 3.

Continued

Continued

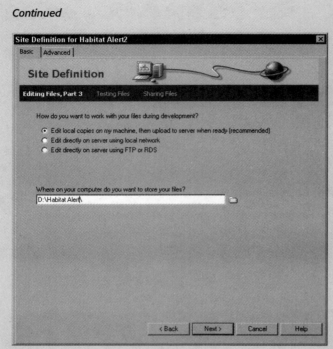

Select where you will store files locally.

7. Click the Browse for Folder icon and locate and select the local root folder of your site. Click the Next button.

8. Choose None from the menu on the Sharing Files screen. This is equivalent to Server Access in Advanced mode, Remote Info. To add remote information, you choose your method of transferring files to a remote Web server or local, networked Web server. This chapter presumes you will leave this set at None. Click Next.

9. The Summary page shows you the information you supplied. Click Done.

Remote info

Building a site presumes that somewhere, somehow, someone will see the site. There are many different ways to publish a site, from uploading to a Web server connected to the Internet to burning the site to a CD for local browsing.

Click the Remote Info category in the Site Definition dialog box. Figure 32-2 shows where remote information is added. You need not add any information about how you plan to publish your site to start building it.

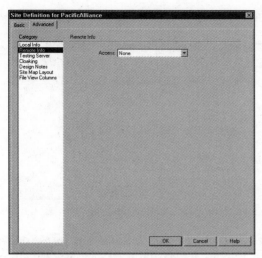

Figure 32-2: Information about the Web server is added in the Remote Info category.

More detail about the publishing portion of Site setup can be found in Chapter 45. If you are building a dynamic site, see Chapter 46 to learn how to set up your site with server applica-tion information.

Click OK to close the Site Definition window.

Working with the Site Panel

After you define your site, you use the Site panel to add files, assets, and even new folders to the root folder. Press F8 to open the Site panel in the Files dock group.

Mac users don't have a Site panel. They have a Site window.

Figure 32-3 shows both portions of the Site panel, as seen on a PC. While docked, the Site panel displays a single view controlled by the View menu.

✦ Local View displays the root folder and all its contents, all local and networked hard drives, and any mounted media, such as floppies or CD-ROMs.

✦ Remote View shows the root folder structure on the remote Web server.

✦ Testing Server shows the root folder on a separate testing server when defined.

✦ Map View displays the local root folder as a flowchart of folders and files, based on how pages are linked together.

Expand/Collapse

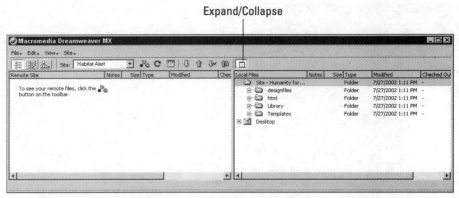

Figure 32-3: Click the Expand/Collapse icon to view local and remote together.

When expanded, the Site panel has its own menus. The icons at the left side (below the menus) are the button equivalents of the View menu when the panel is docked. The Site menu offers access to all defined sites.

Cross-Reference

The icons to the right of the Site menu deal mostly with publishing and are covered in more depth in Chapter 45.

The Site Window

Macintosh users have a Site window, which contains the same features as the Site panel. To expand or collapse the window, click the small white arrow at the bottom edge of the window.

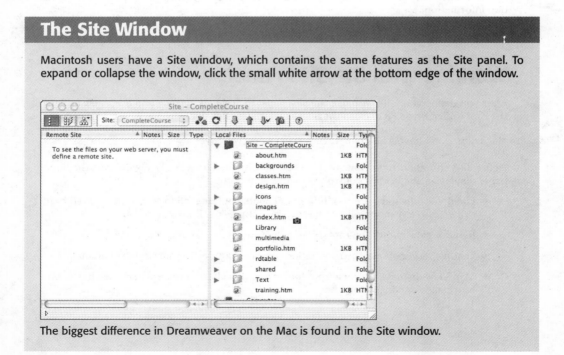

The biggest difference in Dreamweaver on the Mac is found in the Site window.

Navigating the root folder

Use the Expand/Collapse buttons (arrows for Macintosh) to open and close folders. To open a file, double-click its icon.

Fireworks MX

If the icon represents an image, double-clicking it launches Macromedia Fireworks. If double-clicking does not launch Macromedia Fireworks, use the File Types/Editors category in your Preferences to set Macromedia Fireworks MX as the primary editor for PNG, GIF, and JPG file types. You can also right-click (Control+click) a graphic's icon, choose Open With, and locate the Macromedia Fireworks MX program.

To move a file or folder, select and drag its icon. When you move files or folders with relationships to other files in the site, Dreamweaver prompts you to preserve the links and update the site.

Creating new files

There are different ways to create new files for your site such as using the File menu of the Application toolbar or the Site panels File menu. You'll be looking at each method in this section. All site files must be saved within the root folder or its subfolders.

To add a new page to a defined site using the Application toolbar File menu, follow these steps:

1. Choose File ⇨ New, this launches the Gallery (Figure 32-4) of prebuilt files of all types, a new feature in Dreamweaver MX.

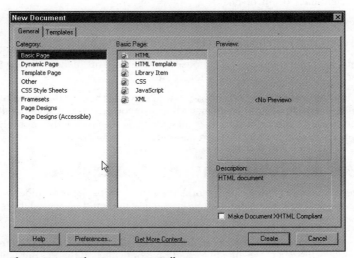

Figure 32-4: The Document Gallery

About Index

Web servers are configured to recognize certain extensions (mime types) and automatically load a file if it is named correctly. Have you ever navigated to a folder using a Web browser and seen a listing of all the files and folders in that directory? The listing is a dynamically generated page or *index* of the folder's contents. If the directory lives on a Web server, you wouldn't want the general public to see its contents. After all, designing a Web site is about controlling how users access your content. Name your page's index (or, in some cases, default) to supercede the dynamic index.

The extension used with index depends on the type of site you are building and the requirements of your Web server.

Cross-Reference

See more about the Gallery in Chapter 37.

2. Choose Basic Page; then click the Create button.

3. Save the new file as **index.htm** in the site folder you are working on.

Contextual menus

Another (easier) method of creating new files and folders in your site root bypasses the Gallery and uses a contextual menu. Dreamweaver is full of easy-to-use context menus accessed with a right-click (Control+click).

1. Right-click/Control-click the root folder of the humanityforhabitat site in the Site panel.

2. From the context menu, choose New Folder and name the folder **html**.

3. Now right-click the html folder, and choose New Folder. This places the new folder within the html folder. Name the new folder **site**.

4. To add a new file, right-click and choose New File. Name the new file **index.htm**. This method is easier than using the File menu because you create and save the file at the same time. Because it is critical to have all your site's files inside the root folder, this method prevents accidentally saving a file to the wrong location.

Adding files and folders with the File Explorer

The File Explorer (Site panel, File ➪ Open) works the same way as the root folder. Add, move, rename, delete, or open files from your computer and any mounted or shared disks or media using the File Explorer.

Tip

When you move files from shared disks or mounted CD-ROMs, you copy the selected files. Manually copying files from a CD results in locked read-only files on the PC, but when you use the File Explorer, the files are not locked!

Setting Target Browsers

In the next chapter, you build basic page layouts. To view your work in progress, you preview pages locally in a Web browser. When you planned your site, you set browser targets — now set Dreamweaver to use those target browsers to preview your pages. To add a Preview browser, follow these steps:

1. Choose File ➪ Preview in Browser ➪ Edit Browsers, or Edit ➪ Preferences; then select the Preview in Browser category. Both methods take you to the Preview category in the Preferences.

2. Add (+) a New Browser.

3. Browse to locate and select the browser that you determined the majority of your visitors will be using. PC users should find browsers in their Program files. Mac users may have them in the Applications folder.

Tip

Ideally, you will have, locally or on another machine, a copy of the target browsers running so that you can test your pages during development. The more complex and mission-critical your site, the more important it is to test early and often.

4. The Name field is auto-populated, but alter the name to reflect the version of the browser you chose.

5. Set this browser as the Primary Browser; then click OK.

6. Repeat the process to add a secondary browser.

Note

PC users can run only one version of the Internet Explorer browser but can have multiple versions of other browsers. Mac users can run multiple versions of all browsers.

To preview a Web page in your primary browser, highlight it in the Site panel (window) and press F12. Ctrl+F12 (Command+F12) previews the selected page in the secondary browser. These shortcuts are automatically set up when you define the primary and secondary browsers.

Cross-Reference

You may add as many browsers as necessary for your site. See Chapter 31 to find out how to add a shortcut.

To access other browsers without a shortcut, choose File ➪ Preview in Browser, and select the browser or use the same option in the contextual menu, which you access by right-clicking a file in the Site panel/window.

Select Internet Explorer 5+ for your primary browser. Add Netscape 4+ for a secondary browser. Add Netscape 6+ as a third browser target.

Summary

In this chapter, you learned about site planning and how to set up your site in Dreamweaver by defining a local root folder. You learned to work with the Site panel to manage files and folders. Finally, you set up Dreamweaver to preview your pages in progress using your target browsers.

Project Summary

The following table describes what you accomplished in this chapter in the creation of the Habitat Alert Web site.

Files Prepared for the Habitat Alert Web Site	
Images/Folders/Pages	*Where to Now?*
html folder	This is your domain's default folder that all files go into. You use the same file structure locally so all our links work once uploaded.
site folder	The site folder will contain the other folders of this site; it will be used throughout the Dreamweaver section.
index.htm	This is the home page and will be used to insert graphics and the home page layout into. The next step is to add a background image for the top banner area.

✦   ✦   ✦

Building a Simple Page

In the previous chapter, you learned how to create and open a new
document. Here you see how to add and format content to control
how that content appears in the page. This chapter covers the basics
of simple page layouts from page properties to HTML structural
markup. Text and images are easily added and formatted using the
Property inspector and Tag editors, which enable you to insert empty
tags or wrap selected tags around your content and control dimensions, colors, and alignment of page elements with a few clicks. You
can even edit and optimize your images in Macromedia Fireworks
directly from Macromedia Dreamweaver.

Setting Page Properties

Setting the Document Title and other page properties will control
how a user views your page in a browser. If you don't set these properties, browser and platform-specific values are used by default. Use
the Page Properties dialog box to apply the settings used by the
entire document.

To access Page Properties (Figure 33-1), choose Modify ➪ Page
Properties (Control+J (Command+J)). When you have selected values, the OK button closes the dialog. You can choose not to accept
the new values by clicking the Cancel button. Clicking the Apply button forces the page to update while the dialog box is still open. Keep
in mind that Apply presumes you accepted the values. Canceling
after applying does not revert the properties to default settings.

Tip

You can always use Edit ➪ Undo or the History panel to back step.
Dreamweaver remembers 50 history steps. You can control the number of steps Macromedia Dreamweaver remembers in the General
category in your preferences (Edit ➪ Preferences).

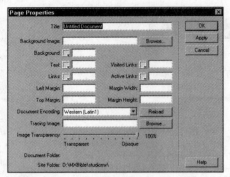

Figure 33-1: The Page Properties dialog box sets the properties of the <body> tag.

The document title

The document title appears in the title bar of the Dreamweaver Document window and most browser windows. Unlike many programs, in Dreamweaver the filename used when you save a page and the document title are not one and the same. Setting a document title is not required but is highly recommended; since most search engines on the Web catalog titles and display them in search results. Effective titling of your pages can improve a user's chance of finding your site.

Dreamweaver adds "Untitled Document" between the <title></title> tags in the head of the page when it is saved. Add a new title in the Title field of the Page Properties dialog box.

A Title field is also available in the Document bar in Design view.

Adding a background image

You can make your pages more visually interesting with the use of a background image — a special type of image that is displayed *beneath* the content of your page. Background images tile or repeat horizontally or vertically based on the dimensions of the image and the current width and height of the document window.

Fireworks MX

See Chapter 23 to learn how to make your page background image. Background images can also be used in table cells, as covered in Chapter 34.

Note

Because you may not be working through the chapters in chronological order, we will not provide instructions on adding files to the root folder you created in Chapter 32. Instead you'll need to define a new site for each site folder in the chapterXX_exercise folder.

Before doing this exercise copy the Habitat Alert folder (in the chapter33_exercise folder) onto your hard drive. Then define the folder as a new Dreamweaver site (refer to the "Defining a Site" section in Chapter 32).

Hint: If you already have another Habitat Alert site defined, then choose the Edit Site option in the Site panel of the Site Definition drop-down menu and change the path to the Local Root folder.

To add a background image to the index page of the Habitat Alert site, follow these steps:

1. Double-click the index.htm page to open it (html\site\index.htm).

2. Choose Modify ⇨ Page Properties.

3. Type **Habitat Alert** for the title.

4. Click the Browse button and navigate to site\sharedimages\backgrounds\ banner_bg_4html.gif, select it. and click OK.

5. Click in the color box for the Background and choose white.

   Background refers to the *page* background color, although a background image may supply the actual color(s) displayed.

   It is recommended that you always set a background color for your page, especially if you use a background image that is dark with light or white text. Choose a color that is close to the background images color. If your image is not found, the page color ensures that the text is still readable.

6. Leave the text and link fields blank. You will be adding this using CSS in Chapter 36.

   By default, browsers display all text in black. Links also have default color settings. If the user has not visited the link's destination, the link is displayed in a vivid blue. Visited links default to purple and when the user clicks a link, most browsers change the link color to red while the mouse is being clicked.

7. Set all the Margins to 0.

   Margins cause page elements to be offset from the edges of the browser window. To control the margin offsets of your page, add specific values to override the default browser settings. The top and left margins show Internet Explorer settings; Margin Width and Height are Netscape-specific.

8. Click the OK button to close the Page Properties dialog box.

9. Save the file.

Choosing Color in Dreamweaver MX

The Color button is used throughout Macromedia's MX programs. In Dreamweaver, click the button to access the color picker. Click any of the 216 colors in default Color Cube palette to select a color. You may also type in a specific hexadecimal value in the field next to the current color swatch. To remove a color, remove the hex value or (easier) click the Default color (no color) button. To choose colors other than those shown, click the Color Wheel button to access your system's color picker. You may also sample color from anywhere in the program.

To sample color outside of the program on the PC, first click the Color button with the pointer tool; then click again and keep the mouse pressed. Move the cursor outside of the application window and release when over the desired color. This presumes that you are not working in maximized mode. Macs may sample colors outside of the program without the extra step.

The color button opens a color palette.

The Color palette's panel options offer other color palettes and controls whether Macromedia Dreamweaver "snaps" your sampled color to the nearest Web-safe value.

Creating the mission statement page

This is a simple page that you later learn to control with JavaScript behaviors. Before doing this exercise copy the Habitat Alert folder (in the chapter33_exercise folder) onto your hard drive. Then define the folder as a new Dreamweaver site (refer to the "Defining a Site" section in Chapter 32).

Hint: If you already have another Habitat Alert site defined, then choose the Edit Site option in the Site panel of the Site Definition drop-down menu and change the path to the Local Root folder.

1. Open `mission_statement.htm` from the Find folder (`habitat_alert_start\html\site\find\mission_statement.htm`).

2. Press Control+J (/Command+J) to open Page Properties.

3. Set the properties using the values listed in Table 33-1.

4. Click OK to accept the values and close the dialog box.

5. Save the file.

Table 33-1: Habitat Alert Page Properties

Property	Value
Title	Mission Statement
Background Image	find/images/vert_stripe.gif
Color	#FFFFFF (white)
Text	#003366 (blue)
Links	#666600
Visited links	#666633
Active links	#006699
Left margin, Margin Width	100, 100
Top margin, Margin Height	0, 0

Inserting Images

Images are an important, though not required, part of your site. They set a mood and provide clarity to your content. The basic Web image file formats are GIF and JPEG, although other file formats are viewable in newer browsers. It is safest to stick with GIF and JPEG. You may add images to your page via the Insert bar's Common toolset, the Insert ⇨ Image menu option, or by using the Assets panel.

Fireworks MX

See Chapter 23 for more information about Web image file formats.

Use the Property inspector to modify an image's attributes. Add Alt Text to your images to provide additional information and to aid accessibility.

Tip

If you accidentally distort an image by clicking it or dragging one of its handles (the small black dots that display when an image is selected) don't worry. The W (Width) and H (Height) fields display the current image size. If the value bold, the image has been distorted. Click W or V once to restore the value.

The Assets panel

Images are site assets. The Assets panel provides access to all the site's images without opening folders. Since folders are a great way to organize your site, the Assets panel can save you lots of time looking for a specific image — it displays images in alphabetical order, without listing the folder structure. Dreamweaver tracks any image inserted and adds the correct path structure.

The Assets panel is located in the Files group. Click the Assets tab to activate the panel and click (if necessary) the Images icon (Figure 33-2) to view all image assets. To insert an image into your page, place your cursor where you want the image, and select the correct image from the Assets panel. Right-click (Control-click) and choose Insert or use the Insert button at the bottom of the panel.

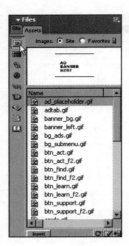

Figure 33-2: Right-click (Control-click) to insert an image.

 Double-clicking an image in the Assets panel opens Fireworks MX. This is good, if you want to edit the image; but it can be annoying if you accidentally double-click when you really wanted to insert.

Fireworks MX

Adding images to the mission statement page

Before doing this exercise copy the Habitat Alert folder (in the chapter33_exercise folder) onto your hard drive. Then define the folder as a new Dreamweaver site (refer to the "Defining a Site" section in Chapter 32).

Hint: If you already have another Habitat Alert site defined, then choose the Edit Site option in the Site panel of the Site Definition drop-down menu and change the path to the Local Root folder.

To add images to the mission statement page of the Habitat Alert defined site, follow these steps:

1. Open mission_statement.htm from the Find folder if you've closed it. Place your cursor into the page just before the text content; then open the Assets panel to Image assets.

2. Select logo_white_top.jpg, right-click (Control+click) and Insert (or click the Insert button in the Assets panel). Press your right arrow key to deselect the image and move to the right of it.

3. Locate and insert nav_map.gif.

4. Press the right arrow key to deselect the image then press the Enter/Return key two times to add two paragraph spaces.

Tip   Press Shift+Enter/Return to add a single space or line break. To view line breaks in Design view, edit the Invisible Elements category of your Preferences. Check the Line Breaks box and click OK to close the dialog box. Then, in Design view, access the Document bar's View Options ➪ Visual Aids ➪ Invisible Elements. This forces Macromedia Dreamweaver MX to use an icon to represent the line break. Don't worry that it disturbs the layout, as that is only temporary and will not occur in a browser.

5. Insert `mission_statement.gif`.

6. Save the page and preview it. Keep it open for later. Figure 33-3 shows the results so far in Internet Explorer.

Editing images with Fireworks MX

Use the integration between Macromedia Dreamweaver and Macromedia Fireworks to edit an image.

Before doing this exercise copy the Habitat Alert folder (in the chapter33_exercise folder) onto your hard drive. Then define the folder as a new Dreamweaver site (refer to the "Defining a Site" section in Chapter 32).

Hint: If you already have another Habitat Alert site defined, then choose the Edit Site option in the Site panel of the Site Definition drop-down menu and change the path to the Local Root folder.

You can easily perform simple edits to the width or height of an image with the current Web file with the following steps:

1. Open the `mission_statement.htm` if you closed it.

2. Select the `m_s.gif` image. This image is a bit large; so make it smaller.

3. Click the Edit button in the Property inspector to launch Fireworks MX, which asks whether you want to open the source image or edit the current Web file, click No.

4. In Fireworks, click Modify ⇨ Canvas ⇨ Image Size.

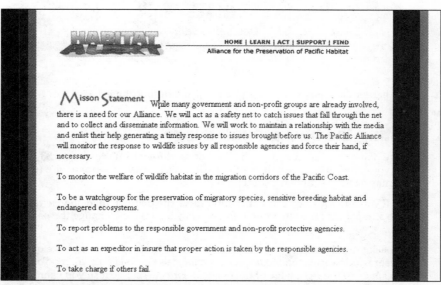

Figure 33-3: Images added to the mission statement page

5. Type **166** into the top width field. The height changes automatically because the Constrain Proportions option is checked.

6. Click OK.

7. Click Done.

8. Return to Dreamweaver and click the Reset button in the Property inspector to reset the size of the image.

9. To optimize the image — edit its palette, format, or transparency — select the image in Dreamweaver; then choose Commands ➪ Optimize Image in Fireworks. This places you in the Fireworks Export Preview window in (Figure 33-4). You can close the window without making any changes.

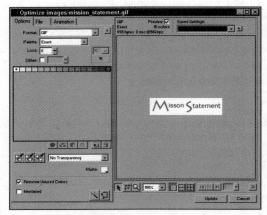

Figure 33-4: Dreamweaver to Fireworks, at your command

See Chapter 23 to learn more about editing and optimizing images.

Editing the background image

Before doing this exercise copy the Habitat Alert folder (in the chapter33_exercise folder) onto your hard drive. Then define the folder as a new Dreamweaver site (refer to the "Defining a Site" section in Chapter 32).

Hint: If you already have another Habitat Alert site defined, then choose the Edit Site option in the Site panel of the Site Definition drop-down menu and change the path to the Local Root folder.

The background image, vert_stripe.gif, repeats along the right edge of the page if the browser window is expanded because the image's width is only 700px. To avoid this, add extra space to the right edge of the image in Fireworks. Because you cannot select and edit from the Property inspector, follow these steps:

1. Choose File ➪ New and create a new Basic Page.

2. Insert vert_stripe.gif into the page.

3. Select the image and click the Edit button. Use the current file, if asked (click No).

4. In Macromedia Fireworks MX, choose Modify ⇨ Canvas ⇨ Canvas Size.

5. Click the top, left anchor button (Figure 33-5) and change the Width value to **1600**. Click OK.

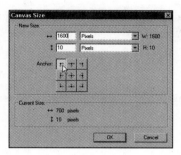

Figure 33-5: Select the top-left anchor to add additional space to the right of the canvas only.

6. Choose Modify ⇨ Canvas ⇨ Canvas Color and set the color to White. Click OK and click Done.

7. You can close the new document in Dreamweaver without saving. Dreamweaver lets you know that your page is not saved — just click OK for any warnings.

8. Save the `mission_statement.htm` page in Dreamweaver, and preview it (Figure 33-6). With the wider image, the browser window must wider than 1600px for you to see the stripe repeat.

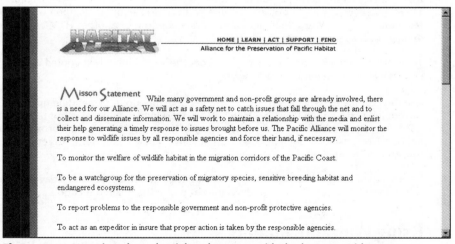

Figure 33-6: No stripe along the right edge, even with the browser wide-open

Note What you just did was a trick to change the original GIF background image in the `mission_statement.htm` page. That's why you didn't need to save the new HTML page.

Adding Text Content

Much of your site's content will likely be text. It's easy to add text to your pages by typing. Dreamweaver adds the underlying HTML code. You can format the text using the Insert bar, Text menu, Property inspector, or a Tag Editor.

Text selections

You can swipe through a word or paragraph to select text, but Dreamweaver offers the following easier options:

✦ Double-click to select a single word.

✦ Triple-click to select an entire paragraph.

✦ Double-click the first word and press Shift to limit your selection. Click the last word of the desired selection.

✦ To select a single line of text, move your cursor to the left edge of the text block. When the cursor changes from the I-beam text cursor to a white arrow, click. Shift+click another line to select it and all lines between the first and last line.

Copy and paste functions

If you have existing content, you may want to copy and paste it into your Dreamweaver page. There are several ways to do this: the one you should use depends upon where your copied text comes from — Word documents, a browser window, or another HTML or text document opened with Dreamweaver.

Fireworks MX

To use text from a Fireworks file, copy it from the Text Editor. Text copied directly on the screen will not paste into Dreamweaver.

Use the Edit menu to access basic Copy and Paste functions. Depending upon the source of the copied text and the view in which you are working, you may also opt to use the Copy HTML and Paste HTML functions. For example, if you copy text from a browser window or another Dreamweaver document, in Design view choose Paste HTML to remove any formatting applied to the text.

Tip Here's a quick way to move text from one opened Macromedia Dreamweaver document to the other: Make your selection; then drag and drop into the desired location on the target page.

Using Word documents

If your content exists as Word documents, use Dreamweaver's Import Word and Clean Up Word HTML functions to speed up page development. To use Word content, save the Word page as an HTML page into your site, or choose File ➪ Import ➪ Word HTML. When importing, Dreamweaver automatically uses Clean Up Word HTML to let you modify and remove Word's proprietary markup, reducing the amount of code in the page. When opening a Word document, you access Clean Up Word HTML from the Commands menu.

Using Block Formatting

The most basic HTML tags control the layout of text (and images) in the page. Macromedia Dreamweaver offers different options for adding markup to format your content into blocks. The Text menu, Property inspector, Insert bar/Text toolset, and Quick Tag Editor give you options to apply formatting, such as paragraphs, headings, lists, and more.

The Quick Tag Editor

To access the Quick Tag Editor, press Ctrl+T (Command+T) until Wrap Tag <> is displayed (Figure 33-7). To create a paragraph, type **p** between the brackets; then press Enter.

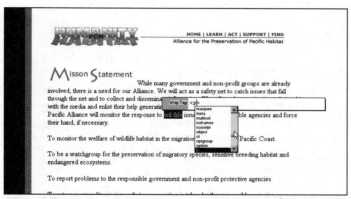

Figure 33-7: Wrap Tags around a selection with the Quick Tag Editor

The Quick Tag Editor can edit, wrap, or insert HTML. To cycle through these options, press Control+T (Command+T) until the desired function appears. If you are not sure which tag you want to add with the Quick Tag Editor, wait briefly, and a list of HTML tags is displayed. Choose a tag and press Enter. More Tag Hints may be displayed to add attributes to the selected tag. Press Enter again to close the editor.

Tip

To prevent images from separating when the browser window is sized smaller, use the Quick Tag Editor to wrap <nobr></nobr> around the line of images.

Formatting the mission statement page

Before doing this exercise copy the Habitat Alert folder (in the chapter33_exercise folder) onto your hard drive. Then define the folder as a new Dreamweaver site (refer to the "Defining a Site" section in Chapter 32).

Hint: If you already have another Habitat Alert site defined, then choose the Edit Site option in the Site panel of the Site Definition drop-down menu and change the path to the Local Root folder.

This exercise gives you a chance to use many of Dreamweaver's basic tools:

1. Skip over the first block of text.

2. The next six text blocks should form a bulleted list. Select all six paragraphs and click the Unordered List button on the Property inspector (Figure 33-8). You could also activate the Text toolset in the Insert bar to choose ul.

3. Place your cursor into the line with Government Agencies and format as Heading 4 with the Format menu (click arrow to see options).

4. Select the next six blocks and format them as a Unordered list (bullets).

5. Format "Non-Profits" as Heading 4.

6. Select the next 13 items and format them as a bulleted list.

7. Save the page, preview it, and keep open for additional exercises.

Horizontal rules

Add a horizontal line between page elements to separate them visually. Follow these steps to insert a horizontal rule into the mission statement page:

1. Place your cursor at the end of the first paragraph, and choose Insert ➪ Horizontal Rule.

2. The Property inspector offers control over width, thickness, shading, and alignment, but you can access other attributes through the Tag Editor.

3. In the Property inspector set the Width to 400px, the Height to 1, and uncheck the Shading box; then save and preview (Figure 33-9) the page.

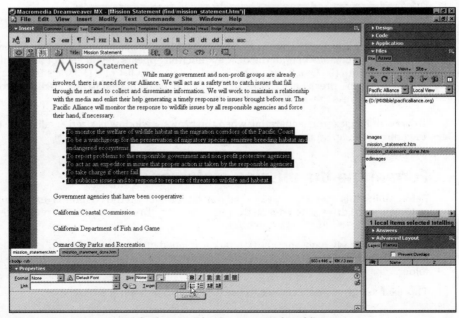

Figure 33-8: Six paragraphs formatted using an unordered list

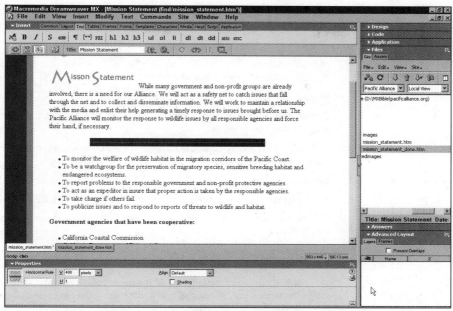

Figure 33-9: Formatted paragraph and lists, separated by a horizontal rule

Block alignment

By default the text in all paragraphs, lists, and other block elements aligns horizontally to the left, as do images. You can alter that value by placing your cursor into a block and using the Alignment buttons on the Property inspector, or by choosing Text ⇨ Align. The options are Left, Center, and Right.

Tip

To align all the text in the entire page of paragraphs and other block elements, choose the `<body>` tag; then click the desired alignment icon.

Floating images in a text block

To wrap the text in a paragraph around an image inside the same block follow these steps:

1. In the `mission_statement.htm` file, select the Mission Statement image.

2. Click the arrow for the Align menu and click Right. Table 33-2 shows the results of each align option.

The Align menu floats the selected image, adjusting the remaining content to the selected image, and places an `align="value"` inside the `<img>` tag.

Table 33-2: Float Image Options

Menu Option	Result
Default (Baseline)	Aligns the bottom of the image to the baseline of the current line of text or the bottom of any other image in the block.
Baseline	See previous entry.
Top	The top of the image is aligned with the top of the tallest *object* in the current line, whether text or image.
Middle	The middle of the image is aligned with the current line and any other text is pushed below the image.
Bottom	Same as Baseline.
Text Top	The top of the image is aligned with the tallest character in the current line.
Absolute Middle	The middle of the image is aligned with the middle of the text or object in the current line.
Absolute Bottom	The bottom of the image is aligned with the descenders that fall below the current line.
Left	The image is aligned to the left edge of the current block and aligned to the top of the current line. All remaining text flows along the right side of the image and wraps below the image.
Right	The same as Left, except the image floats to the right edge of the block and content flows along the left side of the image.

Cross-Reference See Chapter 34 to understand how to create more complex image and text layouts. Using the Align menu to float an image may not offer a solution for the layout you desire.

Character Formatting

This section covers basic character formatting through the use of Font tags. Font tags are deprecated in the W3C[1] HTML 4.0 specification in favor of using Cascading Style Sheets (CSS) and should be used only when you are targeting extremely old browsers (prior to version 4). The tools used to apply font formatting Macromedia Dreamweaver MX are found on the Property inspector or in the Text menu. If you must use font formatting across many pages, make the work easier by using the HTML Styles panel in the Design group.

---

[1] The World Wide Web Consortium (W3C) develops interoperable technologies (specifications, guidelines, software, and tools) to lead the Web to its full potential. W3C is a forum for information, commerce, communication, and collective understanding. See www.w3c.org.

Font face

By default, browsers render text in the Times New Roman or Times typeface. You can specify your own font. However, the user viewing the page must actually have the font you specified installed on their machine for this to work. For that reason, it is best to specify a list of fonts, selecting system fonts if possible. Dreamweaver's font lists use system fonts and provide several categories of serif, sans-serif, and monospaced faces. To choose a font family, follow these steps:

1. Select a block element, such as a paragraph or other tag using the Tag selector. You can also make a text selection.

2. Set font face, using the "A" menu in the Property inspector, or choose Text ➪ Font ➪ , and select from the fonts shown.

Font size

The HTML specification offers limited font-sizing options. You can choose an absolute size using a value between 1 and 7. Or, set a relative size, which places a plus (+) or minus (-) sign before the same 1-7 size options. A relative size looks to the size of the current block element and adds or subtracts a size (or two) to come up with a new value *relative* to the current default font size selected by the viewer.

Here's the tricky part:. Sizes 1-7 are equal to XXS–XXL. There is no size 0 or size 8; so, if you set a paragraph to use Size 4 text, then make a selection within that paragraph and size it to +6, it will not equal size 10. To make things worse, browsers set their own point sizes for each of the sizes; therefore, text in one browser may appear larger than in another.

Using basefont

Most, but not all, modern browsers recognize the `<basefont>` tag. Use Insert ➪ Tag to insert `<basefont>` with the Tag Chooser. Place the `<basefont>` tag just after the `<body>` tag.

Cross-Reference
Text inside tables may not render using the basefont settings. You might need to apply font tags to the content in each table cell. See Chapter 34 for more details.

PC versus Mac Font Sizing

By default, browsers render text using their defaults, which vary from browser to browser, causing great consternation for designers who want to control the layout of their pages. The browser also uses point-based values, editable by the end-users in their browser's preferences, to display text. For example, Netscape 4*x* browsers on the Macintosh platform default to 12-point text for most elements. Internet Explorer browsers on the PC use 16-point text for the same default size.

To make things worse, point sizes are rendered at different resolutions on Macintosh and PC. Macs use 72dpi (dots per inch); whereas PCs use 96dpi. Roughly, this means that 12-point text on a PC shows up at about 75 percent of that size on a Mac. It's easy to see how frustrating HTML character formatting can be.

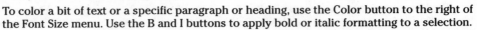

Font color and style

To color a bit of text or a specific paragraph or heading, use the Color button to the right of the Font Size menu. Use the B and I buttons to apply bold or italic formatting to a selection.

To add color to some of the text in the mission_statement.htm page, follow these steps:

1. Select the `<body>` tag with the tag selector and use the Property inspector to apply the Verdana category at Size -1.

2. Select the first `<h4>` heading and set its size to default by choosing None from the Size menu. Set its color to #999933.

3. Repeat step 2 for the second heading.

4. Save and preview the page.

Using HTML Styles

Use the HTML Styles panel (Figure 33-10) to set up macros for commonly used paragraph, lists, and other block formatting. To create an HTML style, select an element that contains block and/or font format options; then click the (+) button at the bottom of the panel, or choose New from the panel's Options menu.

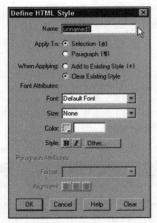

Figure 33-10: The HTML Styles panel

Dreamweaver auto-enters any existing values into the appropriate panel fields. You can add or modify any value. Give the new style a name and click OK to accept the settings and create the style. This results in a new item in the panel.

To apply an HTML style, select an element and click the panel item.

Caution

Modifying an existing style does not update elements that use that style. To update elements that use the style, reapply it.

Summary

In this chapter, you learned the basic tools in Dreamweaver for adding text and images to your pages. You learned how to use the Insert bar and menu, Property inspector, and Tag Editors to apply block formatting, including line breaks, paragraphs, headings, and lists. You learned how to align your content and to float an image in a text block. Finally, you learned the limitations in HTML character formatting while using Macromedia Dreamweaver to apply font face, size, color, and style options to your text.

Project Summary

Let's look at what you did that will be used in the Habitat Alert Web site.

Files Prepared for the Habitat Alert Web Site		
Files	*What Was Done*	*Where to Now?*
Mission_statement.htm	You inserted images, add bulleted lists and a horizontal line.	This page will later be used as a pop-up window.

✦   ✦   ✦

Using Tables for Complex Layouts

◆ ◆ ◆ ◆

In This Chapter

Understanding the basics of tables

Integrating Fireworks HTML in Dreamweaver

Building a Modular Layout

Using great table tricks

◆ ◆ ◆ ◆

Simple block formatting is often not enough to display your content properly. HTML tables offer a greater degree of control for placement of text and images through the use of rows and columns in fixed and relative widths. They are especially important when it comes to displaying dynamic data in Web applications.

Web pages have grown increasingly complex and the HTML table has become the tool of choice for the Web designer/developer. Although originally intended only for the display of raw data, tables offer other options, but such table tricks come with more than a few caveats — not all browsers render tables as suggested by the World Wide Web Consortium's (W3C) HTML 4.0 specifications.

In this chapter, you see how to work with Dreamweaver MX table tools and learn solutions to the most common browser issues to build complex, but consistently rendered, pages. You also see how to modify the table(s) structures used in Fireworks HTML exports.

Understanding Table Basics

A table is a grid that uses rows and columns to form cells — the intersection of a row and column. The table expands to hold content, and certain rules guide that expansion. You can set a fixed, specific width in pixels, or use a relative, percentage-based width that expands or collapses with the width of the HTML document in the browser window.

A typical table uses the `<table><tr>` and `<td>` tags, sometimes incorporating the `<th>` to indicate a table heading cell. Each tag has its own properties, controlled in Dreamweaver MX through the contextual Property inspector. Browsers, notably Netscape 4*x*, have specific requirements for rendering a table, and the property values you supply to the browser may or may not display consistently between different versions and on different platforms. Learning to build cross-platform, cross-browser tables is the key to developing complex page layouts.

Table Types

There are four table types, defined by the way that each behaves when viewed in a browser.

✦ **Fixed-width tables** control the width of text content, to provide multicolumn text, or to force images together. A fixed-width table uses a pixel-based width. Text content within the cells of this table type wraps to maintain the table's width. However, if you place "hard" content with a total width wider than that set to the containing table, the cells and table expand to accommodate it. A fixed-width table forces a horizontal scrollbar to appear along the bottom edge of the browser window when that window is smaller than the width of the table. This scrollbar enables the user to see all the table content by scrolling. And, if the total height of the content expands the table vertically, a vertical scrollbar appears.

✦ **Relative/percentage-width tables** display content that adjusts to the width of the browser window. Use a relative table to display content that adjusts to the width of the browser window. A table with a percentage value for its width is said to be *relative* because its size adjusts according to the *document's size* within the browser's window. When the browser window is expanded, the table expands and vice versa. A relative table doesn't force a horizontal scrollbar *unless* the percentage value is set to greater than 100%. An exception to this rule occurs when the total width of the table's hard content, such as images, media, or other tables, is greater than the width of the browser window.

✦ **Fit to data tables** do not use a table width. Use this table to have the table collapse around the content, whatever its size. Different browsers render this table type in different ways. Be sure to test your page in your target browser(s) to see whether this table behaves as expected. Fit to data is most often used for dynamic content or when using the Insert Tabular Data tool in Macromedia Dreamweaver.

✦ **Hybrid tables** are percentage-based tables with at least one fixed-width column. This table is also knows as an AutoStretch, stretchy, or fluid table because the table and one or more of its columns stretch to fit the browser window while the remaining column(s) remain set to a specific width. This table type has the advantage of relative sizing with the control of fixed-width columns, but beware: its development and consistent rendering can be tricky.

 See the sidebar "Building the Hybrid Table in Standard Mode" to learn how to build the hybrid table used in the Habitat Alert's homepage.

✦ **Nested tables,** while not specifically a table type, enable you to place tables inside the cell of another table to form a *nested* table. Avoid excessive nesting of tables, as they slow down the rendering of your page in browsers. An occasional nested table is fine, but using multiple tables for modular page construction or through the use of Cascading Style Sheets (CSS) often works better.

Inserting a Table

You can insert a table into your page using one of these methods:

✦ Click the Insert Table tool from the Insert bar's Common or Tables toolsets.

✦ Choose Insert ➪ Table.

✦ Press Control+Alt+T/Command+Option+T.

This opens the Insert Table dialog box (Figure 34-1) where you can choose the number of rows and columns and set the table's width, border, and other properties.

Figure 34-1: The Insert Table dialog box

You can work with your table in Design or Code views. Most of the tools used for tables are the same in both views. Figure 34-2 shows the views for a simple inserted table. The nsbp; seen in the code (Figure 34-3) represents a non-breaking space. Macromedia Dreamweaver places these in each cell of the inserted table to prevent the cells from collapsing. Many browsers require some sort of content in a cell to display certain cell properties.

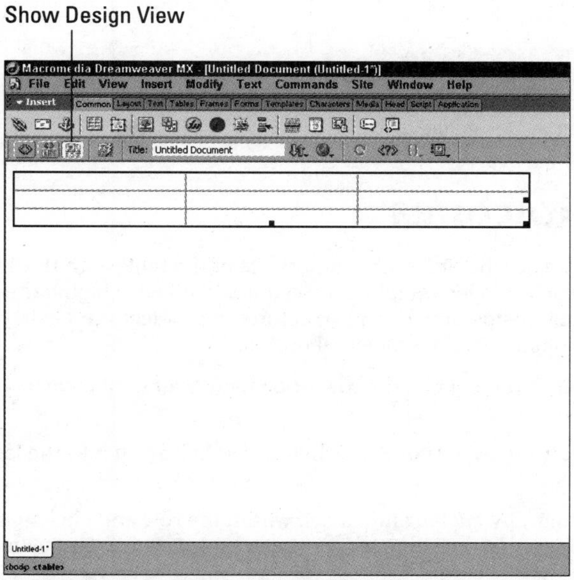

Show Design View

Figure 34-2: What you see in Design view is powered by the HTML in Code view.

Tip

It's a good idea to view the table code often if you are not familiar with HTML code, as this will increase your coding skills greatly.

Show Code View

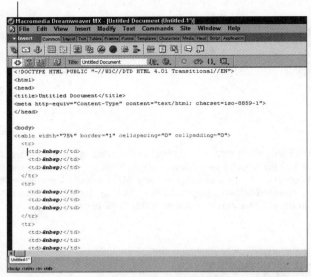

Figure 34-3: In Code view, the non-breaking spaces in each cell in the code hold the cells open in Design view.

Selecting Table Structures

To work with tables, you need to select the different components of the table with the Tag selector and edit the tag's properties. A selected table, row, column, or cell is highlighted. To select the table, first click anywhere inside of the table structure; then select the `<table>` tag (Figure 34-4). To select a row or column, you have several options:

✦ Move your cursor to the left or top edge of the row or column, wait until an arrow cursor appears, and click.

✦ Shift+click into the first cell (of a row or column); then shift+click again into the last cell (of the row or column).

✦ Select a row (but not a column) by clicking into a cell within the row and clicking the `<tr>` tag displayed in the Tag selector. There is no column table tag to select using this method.

Moving around in tables is easy. Use the Tab key to move from left to right, top to bottom, and to jump from cell to cell and row to row. Press Shift+Tab to move in the opposite direction. Pressing the arrow keys also moves you through the cells, but content within cells may make it necessary to use a key more than once to get to the desired location.

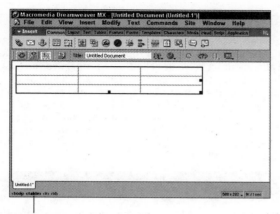

Table tag

Figure 34-4: Selecting the <table> tag selects the entire table. The selection is indicated by the thick black border.

Modifying a Table Structure

You can modify the number of rows and columns or adjust the width, height, border, and other properties for a table in the Property inspector or, in some cases, the Modify ⇨ Table menu options.

Select the <table> tag; then enter new values in the Rows and Columns fields to add or remove rows and columns. You can also modify the table tag and properties by hand in Code view or by using the Tag editor. Add new rows or columns by clicking Modify ⇨ Table ⇨ Insert Rows, or in the Columns dialog box. To remove a row or column, select it; then press Delete (Backspace), or use the Modify ⇨ Table ⇨ Delete options.

Setting table width and height

To control the width of a table from the Property inspector, select the table tag, enter a value into the Width field (W), and choose the table type from the drop-down menu. Table heights are seldom used because actual content in the table's cells determines the total height of the overall table.

Caution

Although Dreamweaver contains a feature to drag the borders of a table for sizing the table, rows, or columns, I don't recommend using it. This feature does a lot more than is obvious while you are using it, such as setting values in unexpected places that will later interfere with your layout.

Modifying rows and columns

Because each part of the table controls specific properties, you must select the proper tag to access the properties of the tag using the inspector. Use the Property inspector to set widths, heights, and horizontal and vertical alignment for rows or cells. Some properties, such as horizontal or vertical alignments, are shared by the row and cell tag (Figures 34-5 and 34-6). When the values are the same, you should set the values using the `<tr>` row rather than the `<td>` cell. This writes the values to the row so you don't have to write them in each cell, reducing excessive coding to create a smaller download. That being said, you can set a row's properties and then override them in a single cell by setting different properties to that tag. Simply select the specific cell by clicking into it; then set new properties.

When to Use a Table Structure

In some cases, you'll use a table to display data, either in static form or dynamically from a data source. But the majority of your tables will be used as solutions for placement of content. For example, you cannot place two small images directly to the side of a larger image without using a table.

Tables make tricky layout possible.

Of course, it is possible (even easy) to overuse tables and to build overly complex table structures. Your goal should be to build the simplest table structures possible. The following good rules to follow are covered in-depth later in this chapter:

✦ Avoid *nesting* too many tables — placing a table inside of another table and so on.

✦ Build modular tables to avoid overly complex row and column spanning.

✦ Don't attempt to build one big table that holds everything.

✦ If you can position elements without a table, you can put the same elements in a single table cell.

✦ Do the math; be sure that column widths add up to match the table's width.

✦ Provide every column's width; this is the secret to getting Netscape 4x browsers to behave!

Finally, keep in mind that *you* are the logic behind the tools, whether working in Dreamweaver or any other Studio MX program.

Fixed-width tables use pixels values for column widths. By default, the value you add in the Cell Width field is in pixels and it is not necessary to specify it. Percentage-based tables generally use percentage values for column widths. To set a cell's width to a percentage value, type the percentage sign after the value without adding any space between the number and sign.

Figure 34-5: A cell selected makes the cell properties available in the Property inspector (notice the table icon in the left corner showing the approximate location of the selected cell).

Figure 34-6: A selected row showing the properties available in the Property inspector

Working with Fireworks HTML

With few exceptions, pages exported from Fireworks MX use table structures for layout. User-defined slices build complex rows and columns that are exported as one big table by default. To keep the complex structure from falling apart, an extra row is added along the top of the layout, and *spacer* GIFs — formed from a 1 × 1 transparent pixel image — are stretched to the column's required width.

Fireworks MX

See Chapter 23 for options and more information about how Fireworks MX exports HTML.

Because Fireworks cannot export all types of tables, it's likely you will want to modify the table structure and add HTML text content, links, and other elements inside of Dreamweaver. You can open and modify Macromedia Fireworks MX pages in Macromedia Dreamweaver MX. The simpler your layout in the Fireworks page, the easier this is to do in Dreamweaver. When your design's slices are too complex, it is often easier to rebuild the page layout in Macromedia Dreamweaver rather than try to modify it.

No graphic application's HTML features match those found in Dreamweaver. For professional, fine-tuned, and modular pages, it is *always* better to build the HTML in Dreamweaver rather than rely on Fireworks to export the entire page. Later in this chapter, you see how to rebuild a page layout and bring in carefully planned exported HTML from Macromedia Fireworks MX.

Opening a Fireworks page

To use Fireworks pages in Dreamweaver, export the page and images (from Fireworks) into a folder, and in Macromedia Dreamweaver define a new site using that folder as the site root. You can, of course, export the page into an existing Dreamweaver site. Figure 34-7 shows the Habitat Alert page as exported from Macromedia Fireworks and viewed in Macromedia Dreamweaver.

Figure 34-7: Basic page and complicated table structure exported from Fireworks MX

Modifying a Fireworks table

The table structure of the page illustrated in Figure 34-7 is actually far more complicated than the final page structure used for the Habitat Alert site, because Macromedia Fireworks creates a separate cell for each slice. Since cells form the grid of rows and columns, and Macromedia Fireworks (by default) uses one table to contain everything, the table is very complex and contains 11 rows and 11 columns, as marked by the dotted lines in Figure 34-7. The code is long and complex, with many *spans*. A span is formed by merging cells and should be avoided unless absolutely necessary. Unfortunately, Macromedia Fireworks tables make excessive use of spans, as shown in Listing 34-1.

Listing 34-1: **Code for the Fireworks HTML file**

```
<html>
<head>
<title>pacificalliance.gif</title>
<meta http-equiv="Content-Type" content="text/html;">
<!-- Fireworks MX Dreamweaver MX target.  Created Sat Jul 27 09:03:54 GMT-0700
2002-->
</head>
<body bgcolor="#ffffff">
<table bgcolor="#ffffff" border="0" cellpadding="0" cellspacing="0" width="680">
<!-- fwtable fwsrc="typical_export.png" fwbase="pacificalliance.gif"
fwstyle="Dreamweaver" fwdocid = "742308039" fwnested="0" -->
  <tr>
   <td><img src="images/spacer.gif" width="231" height="1" border="0"
alt=""></td>
```

```
    <td><img src="images/spacer.gif" width="19" height="1" border="0"
alt=""></td>
    <td><img src="images/spacer.gif" width="112" height="1" border="0"
alt=""></td>
    <td><img src="images/spacer.gif" width="15" height="1" border="0"
alt=""></td>
    <td><img src="images/spacer.gif" width="62" height="1" border="0"
alt=""></td>
    <td><img src="images/spacer.gif" width="51" height="1" border="0"
alt=""></td>
    <td><img src="images/spacer.gif" width="43" height="1" border="0"
alt=""></td>
    <td><img src="images/spacer.gif" width="51" height="1" border="0"
alt=""></td>
    <td><img src="images/spacer.gif" width="53" height="1" border="0"
alt=""></td>
    <td><img src="images/spacer.gif" width="43" height="1" border="0"
alt=""></td>
    <td><img src="images/spacer.gif" width="1" height="1" border="0" alt=""></td>
  </tr>
  <tr>
    <td><img name="banner_left" src="images/banner_left.gif" width="231"
height="74" border="0" alt=""></td>
    <td rowspan="2" colspan="9"><img name="logo" src="images/logo.jpg"
width="449" height="102" border="0" alt=""></td>
    <td><img src="images/spacer.gif" width="1" height="74" border="0"
alt=""></td>
  </tr>
  <tr>
    <td rowspan="2"><img name="location_" src="images/location_.gif" width="231"
height="45" border="0" alt=""></td>
    <td><img src="images/spacer.gif" width="1" height="28" border="0"
alt=""></td>
  </tr>
  <tr>
    <td rowspan="2" colspan="3"><img name="btn_left" src="images/btn_left.gif"
width="146" height="21" border="0" alt=""></td>
    <td rowspan="2"><img name="btn_learn" src="images/btn_learn.gif" width="62"
height="21" border="0" alt=""></td>
    <td rowspan="2"><img name="btn_act" src="images/btn_act.gif" width="51"
height="21" border="0" alt=""></td>
    <td rowspan="2" colspan="2"><img name="btn_support"
src="images/btn_support.gif" width="94" height="21" border="0" alt=""></td>
    <td rowspan="2"><img name="btn_find" src="images/btn_find.gif" width="53"
height="21" border="0" alt=""></td>
    <td rowspan="2"><img name="btn_right" src="images/btn_right.gif" width="43"
height="21" border="0" alt=""></td>
    <td><img src="images/spacer.gif" width="1" height="17" border="0" alt=""></td>
  </tr>
  <tr>
    <td rowspan="3"><img name="circlepic0" src="images/circlepic0.jpg"
width="231" height="171" border="0" alt=""></td>
```

Continued

Listing 34-1 *(continued)*

```
  <td><img src="images/spacer.gif" width="1" height="4" border="0" alt=""></td>
 </tr>
 <tr>
  <td colspan="9" bgcolor="#ffffff"><img src="images/spacer.gif" width="449"
height="91" border="0" alt=""></td>
  <td><img src="images/spacer.gif" width="1" height="91" border="0"
alt=""></td>
 </tr>
 <tr>
  <td rowspan="2" colspan="6" bgcolor="#ffffff"><img src="images/spacer.gif"
width="302" height="118" border="0" alt=""></td>
  <td rowspan="4" colspan="3"><img name="shop_items"
src="images/shop_items.jpg" width="147" height="170" border="0" alt=""></td>
  <td><img src="images/spacer.gif" width="1" height="76" border="0"
alt=""></td>
 </tr>
 <tr>
  <td rowspan="3"><img name="circle_btm" src="images/circle_btm.gif"
width="231" height="94" border="0" alt=""></td>
  <td><img src="images/spacer.gif" width="1" height="42" border="0"
alt=""></td>
 </tr>
 <tr>
  <td rowspan="2" bgcolor="#ffffff"><img src="images/spacer.gif" width="19"
height="52" border="0" alt=""></td>
  <td><img name="creditcards" src="images/creditcards.jpg" width="112"
height="19" border="0" alt=""></td>
  <td rowspan="2" colspan="4" bgcolor="#ffffff"><img src="images/spacer.gif"
width="171" height="52" border="0" alt=""></td>
  <td><img src="images/spacer.gif" width="1" height="19" border="0"
alt=""></td>
 </tr>
 <tr>
  <td bgcolor="#ffffff"><img src="images/spacer.gif" width="112" height="33"
border="0" alt=""></td>
  <td><img src="images/spacer.gif" width="1" height="33" border="0"
alt=""></td>
 </tr>
 <tr>
  <td valign="top" bgcolor="#ffffff"><p></p></td>
  <td colspan="9" valign="top" bgcolor="#ffffff"><p></p></td>
  <td><img src="images/spacer.gif" width="1" height="116" border="0"
alt=""></td>
 </tr>
</table>
</body>
</html>
```

When you place content into the table cells, to add text, you must first remove the spacers in the cells. Select and delete them; then add your text by typing or copying content and pasting it into the cell. Figure 34-8 shows how the overly complicated table structure might react to additional content.

It is possible to edit the table structure to simplify its layout prior to adding text and other content to prevent problems like the one in Figure 34-8. The idea is to simplify the content area, as seen in Figure 34-9, by *merging* rows and columns.

Images are first deleted; then a logical selection of cells are selected and merged to form a single, main content cell. Choose Modify ⇨ Table ⇨ Merge Cells or use the Property inspector's Merge Cells icon, shown in Figure 34-10.

Content is replaced inside the newly merged cells, as shown in Figure 34-9.

Controlling the alignment of content within table cells is a key factor to having your design lay out properly. Click a cell (or row) and use the Property inspector to vertically align the images and text (content) within a cell (or row). The default horizontal alignment for table cell content is Left. The default vertical alignment is Middle. When two cells sit in the same row, uneven amounts of content can cause the other cell's content to realign. Setting the vertical alignment of the cell or row to Top in the Vert menu forces each cell's content to start at the top of the cell.

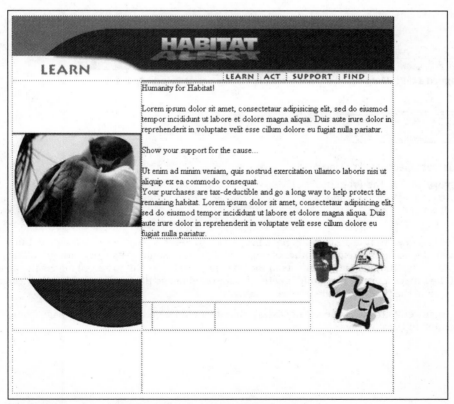

Figure 34-8: The table falls apart when HTML text is added.

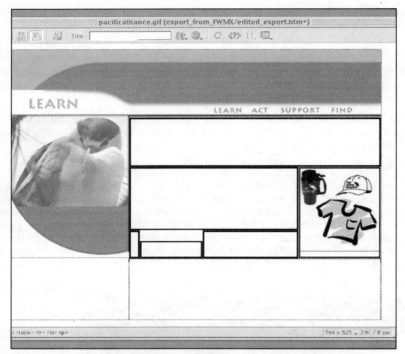

Figure 34-9: Merging all of these cells forms an easier-to-edit space.

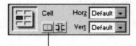

Merges selected cells using spans

Figure 34-10: The Property inspector's Merge Cell and Split Cell icons

You still need to title and modify page properties to get this page close to finished, but it is at least able to accept text and other HTML content within some of its cells without falling apart. Adjusting the margin offsets in the page properties (set all to zeros) places the design in the top-left corner. You could create a background image tile to place behind the design to continue the blue and gold stripes to the right.

So many edits to this page are necessary that it would be better to build the page from scratch in Dreamweaver MX.

Building a Modular Layout

Using multiple tables to lay out your content is superior to using a single, complex table structure. The table code is less complex, and it is easier to modify your page regions without disturbing every section of the page. Plus the page will begin to load faster. When you have one large table nothing will display until the browser has read the last table tag. So by using smaller tables they will load one at a time and appear to load faster.

Figure 34-11 shows a more desirable table layout for the Habitat Alert site. Because the site specifications call for a "stretchy" or fluid behavior to fit more target monitor widths, hybrid table structures are stacked to create a modular design.

Building a hybrid table

There's nothing hard about building a fluid table that renders consistently in all browsers, when you know the secrets. In the Habitat Alert layout, you build three tables.

 Save the Habitat Alert34 folder from the chapter34_exercise folder to your hard drive. Define a new site. Hint: If you already have another Habitat Alert site defined, then choose the Edit Site option in the Site panel of the Site Definition drop-down menu and change the path to the Local Root folder.

1. Open the Site panel (F8 makes the Site panel active) and open the html folder, and the site folder. Then double-click the `index.htm` file to open it.

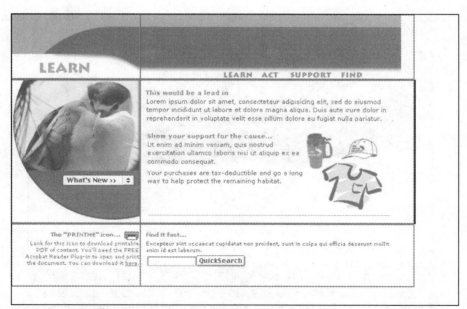

Figure 34-11: Modular tables make this page layout easier to build and modify. The table border is for demonstration purposes only.

Cross-Reference   All the margins have been set in Page Properties to zero, and the background image was added in Chapter 33.

2. Insert your cursor into the page and add a table with the Insert Table tool. Set the table to use 1 row, 3 columns, and a width of 100%. Set Border, Cell Padding, and Cell Spacing to zero (Figure 34-12). Click OK.

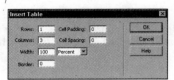

Figure 34-12: The Table dialog box with the settings for the first table in the index page of the Habitat Alert site

3. Place your cursor into the first cell and use the Property inspector to set its width to 230. This is a pixel value by default.

4. Select the `<tr>` from the Tag selector, and set the vertical alignment for the row, to Top using the Vert menu options (Property inspector). Click in the first cell.

5. Use the Assets panel to insert `banner_left.gif`.

6. Press right arrow to move to the right of the image's tag then insert `location_home.gif`. Total the height of both images. You'll see that together they are 119px. (Don't worry if the table cells jump around and change sizes. You fix that shortly.) Press Tab to move into the next cell.

7. Insert `logo.gif` and note its dimensions (208 × 47). Figure 34-13 shows the table and images so far.

8. Press Tab to move to the next cell.

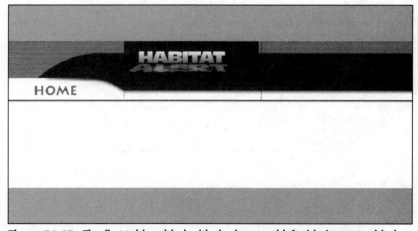

Figure 34-13: The first table added with the logo and left side images added

Note

If you are using Windows 2000 or XP, you may have to reselect the image to place the keyboard's focus back in the document.

9. Insert `spacer.gif`, go to the Property inspector, and set the spacer's width to 300px and its height to 102px.

10. Move to the right of the image by pressing right arrow, and add a line break.

11. Add `spacer.gif` and set its dimensions to 20×17. The spacer will keep the buttons off the right edge of the browser window when you align the cell's content to the right.

12. With your cursor still in the last cell, go to the Property inspector and change the Horz setting to Right. Do not use the paragraph alignment buttons to set alignment!

13. Set the last cell's width to 400px.

So far you have set the width of two columns using fixed pixel values, but earlier you learned that percentage-based tables generally use percentage values. When pixel values are used for column widths in a relative table, that makes it a hybrid table; therefore, at least one column must use a percentage value to allow for stretch in the table. Because you cannot know what the fixed width would need to be in the user's browser window, it makes sense to use a value that will take up all of the remaining space available. That value is 100%.

14. Set the middle column's width to 100%, manually adding the percentage sign. To select the middle cell, select the logo graphic; then click `<td>` in the Tag selector (Figure 34-14).

15. Save and preview your page.

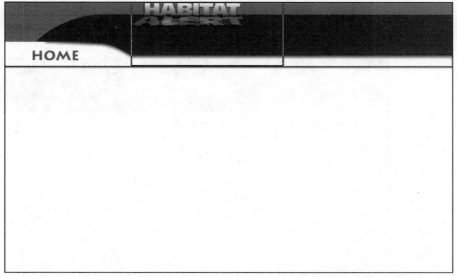

Figure 34-14: The first table with the cells set, spacers added, and the logo inserted

The logo isn't positioned properly. To force the logo to align properly, follow these steps:

1. Select the logo and press left arrow to move in front of the image.

2. Add a line break; then press up arrow to move to the new line that is now above the logo.

3. Add another spacer image, setting its dimensions to 190 × 34.

4. Select the logo image and add 10px to its Hspace value. It looks much better now, as shown in Figure 34-15.

5. Save and preview in both target browsers.

 Note   Hspace (horizontal space) places white space before and after an image. Vspace (vertical space) does the same, only it places the space above and below.

Stacking tables

By default, tables will stack. You do not have to place line breaks or paragraph returns between tables to place one table below another. In fact, adding a line break may actually cause unwanted space between your table structures.

 You'll now add the table that holds the bird image and the main content in the Habitat Alert layout.

1. To build the next table, click the page below the existing table, and click the Insert Table icon to add another table.

2. Give the table 1 row, 2 columns, and set its width to 100%. Set border, padding, and spacing to zero.

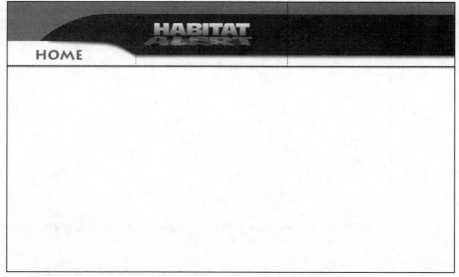

Figure 34-15: The logo in a better position

Now you can see the advantage to using modular, stacked tables. If you had to build a single table to hold three columns for the top portion and two columns for the remaining structure, you would be forced to span columns by merging two columns into one. Although this would work, it offers less flexibility in the long run because it is unnecessarily complex. Two tables are simpler, and they load faster. Keep it simple with stacked, modular tables.

Using a table cell background image

Almost all major browsers recognize the use of background images in table cells. The Habitat Alert layout uses a graphic in the background to form the bottom of the circle below the heron image. The heron image is inserted into the cell and sits at the top of the cell, over the background image. This forms a more flexible layout that you can use in other pages, replacing the heron image with a form or other HTML content.

Although it's possible to apply a background image to the table, Netscape 4x browsers will not render it. In fact, Netscape 4x browsers have several documented problems with background images, covered more in-depth in Chapter 36.

To set the background for the second table's first cell in the Habitat Alert homepage, follow these steps:

1. Place your cursor into the first cell, and click the Browse for folder icon next to the Bg field in the Property inspector.

2. Locate `circle_btm_plus.gif` in the sharedimages\backgrounds folder of your site. Don't worry about what you see onscreen; you're not finished!

3. The image appears to tile horizontally because you haven't yet set a width for the table cell. Set the cell's width to 230px.

4. Use the Asset panel to insert `circlepic0.jpg`.

5. Tab to move to the next cell. Set this cell's width to 100% to create the stretchy cell for this hybrid table. This prevents the horizontal tiling of the background image in the first cell.

Without the heron image, the fixed width cell would collapse because the 100% width set to the second cell is *very* powerful. When working with hybrid tables where you do not have a foreground image to force the fixed cell to remain open, use a spacer GIF, setting the width to the desired column size.

Using a minimum cell height

You can't set the maximum height of a table. The same is true of table cells and rows. You can, however, set the minimum height, and a spacer is not necessary to hold it open.

Although you fixed the tiling problem, the background image's bottom portion is not visible because the cell isn't tall enough to display it. Follow these steps to correct the problem:

1. Select the heron image; then use the Tag selector to select the cell (`<td>`).

2. Set the height of the cell to 300px.

3. Select the `<tr>` row and set the vertical alignment to Top, using the Vert menu options. Save and preview.

Tip   Before you apply a background image to a table cell, be sure you set up the image to behave properly. Remember, background images tile, repeating horizontally and vertically. The circle graphic used here has lots of white space added to the bottom — roughly 2,800px to prevent vertical tiling — much like the edit made to the Mission Statement's page background image in the previous chapter.

Coloring a table cell

This trick can be used horizontally or vertically but the example shown from the Habitat Alert layout uses a cell in a table row to form a colored line that stretches as the document widens in the browser window. Not all browsers support coloring horizontal rules, and it would be nearly impossible to get the rule to align properly.

In this set of steps, you use a background color in a table cell to create a 1-pixel line that stretches with the right column of the page.

1. To place some quick content into the right column of the second table, open the content.htm file and copy it all. Then close the document and paste into the index.htm file.

2. Insert your cursor below the second table in the Habitat Alert homepage. If you cannot easily place your cursor below the page content, click into the last cell, and select the `<table>` tag, using the Tag selector. Press right arrow to move outside of the table.

3. Insert a new table. Give this table two rows and two columns, and set the width to 98%. Set the border, padding, and spacing to zero.

4. Click the second cell of the top row; then scroll to see the top of the page. Use the Bg color picker to sample the darker gold color (#999933) from the banner area (or the bird's belly). Be sure to use the Bg color picker found below the Bg field. If you hover over the color picker, a ToolTip should say Background Color.

5. Click the first cell of the top row. Set this cell's width to 230px and add a spacer Gif, setting its width also to 230px. Leave the spacer's height set to 1px.

6. Click the second cell again and set its width to 100%. Although this table's width is 98%, you still use a 100% value for the stretchy column. Remember, relative values are relative to their container. The 98% value set for the table takes up 98% of the *document*. The 100% value in the stretchy column takes up 100% of the remaining width in the *table*.

7. Add a spacer Gif to the gold cell. Click the `<table>` tag in the Tag selector to force the page to update; then save and preview the page. Figure 34-16 shows the nice, single-pixel line that sits along the bottom of the main content area and stretches to the right when the browser window is expanded.

8. Place your cursor in the second cell of the second row and set the Horz setting to Center.

9. In the same cell, type `home | learn | act | support | find`.

10. Save and preview your page.

Tip   Create the vertical divider between the words using the pipe character. To add one of these cross-platform characters, type a backslash while pressing Shift.

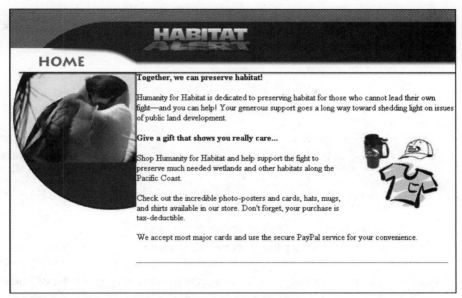

Figure 34-16: A line added to the bottom of the content area

Inserting Fireworks HTML

To finish the Habitat Alert homepage layout, you make use of another integration feature between Dreamweaver and Fireworks. The Insert Fireworks HTML option enables you to take an exported Fireworks page and insert its table structure into an existing page. To use this feature wisely, crop Fireworks files down to a specific structure, save the file as a component of the design, and export the page and images as you would any other file, saving them into the defined Dreamweaver site.

Fireworks MX

The steps described previously were covered in Chapter 23, where you exported the rollover navigation buttons for the Habitat Alert layout.

You can even edit the Fireworks HTML page in Macromedia Dreamweaver prior to using the Insert Fireworks HTML button!

Tip

Because Macromedia Fireworks creates a separate cell for each image, the button table for the Habitat Alert layout is overly complex—separate table cells are not needed to have buttons sit side by side. In fact, no table is needed at all. In this example, inserting the Macromedia Fireworks HTML creates a nested table, not necessary and again, overly complex. Remember, your goal should be to build the simplest structures possible for your layout.

1. Open the page `navigation_buttons_fw.htm` from the site folder. This is the page exported from the cropped button file in Chapter 23. Code in the head of the page tells Dreamweaver that this is a page created in Fireworks:

```
<html>
<head>
<title>navigation_buttons.gif</title>
<meta http-equiv="Content-Type" content="text/html;">
<!-- Fireworks MX Dreamweaver MX target.  Created Sat Jul 27 21:04:42
GMT-0700 2002-->
</head>
```

2. To remove the table in this page, drag each button from its cell and drop it below the table. Now delete the empty table. Another fast way is to use the Clean Up HTML command to remove specific tags: `table`, `tr`, `td`. However you do it, you'll also have to remove spaces between the buttons. You can do so quickly using the arrow keys to move to the correct location and deleting the extra spaces.

3. Save the page as `navigation_buttons.htm` and close it.

4. Now, select the second, smaller spacer image located in the last cell of the top table in the homepage. Press left arrow to move the insertion point to in front of that image.

5. From the Common toolset in the Insert bar, click the Insert Fireworks HTML button, or choose Insert ➪ Interactive Images ➪ Fireworks HTML.

6. In the Insert dialog box, navigate to the `navigation_buttons.htm` page you edited just a few steps ago. Click OK. Save and test your page. Figure 34-17 shows the buttons in place. These buttons don't contain any rollover code, but if they did the code would also have been inserted into the Macromedia Dreamweaver page.

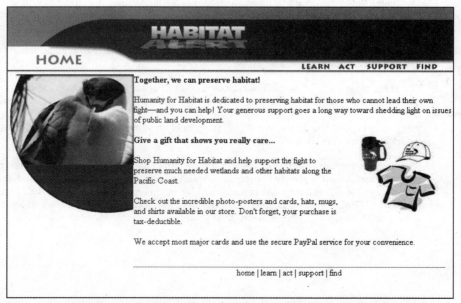

Figure 34-17: The buttons from the exported Fireworks HTML page are inserted into the layout.

You'll add interactivity to these buttons in Chapter 41.

This is an extremely useful way to work with Macromedia Fireworks and Macromedia Dreamweaver. A cropped component file is easier to edit, and you just saw how easy it was to modify and insert.

Using Great Table Tricks

You've probably seen table tricks in action — outlines that stretch to rounded corner tables. Have you ever wondered how it was done? Every designer/developer should build an arsenal of table tricks to use in their layouts to add a new level of sophistication to a page. Here are just a few of my favorites.

Creating great table borders

The problem with table borders is that they are kind of clunky. Of course, table borders can make content easier to read by helping the eye understand the relationship of a row or column of text. Although all browsers allow control over the presence and width of table borders, not all browsers render borders equally. Some browsers *bevel* the border, adding a 3-D effect with a light source from the top and left of the page. Others allow more control through the use of color and shading. No browser actually renders a single-pixel border. Borders are a table property; you cannot turn off the border for some cells and leave it for others.

Using cell padding and cell spacing

You can use cell padding and spacing to add white space to tables. Padding places space on all four sides of all the table cells in the table, so content placed in the cell doesn't touch the cell's edges. Where two cells meet, the space between them is doubled. Spacing adds room between the cells. The amount of space between cells is not doubled but rather is shared.

Here's a handy border trick to give you the control you want. This trick requires a nested table, so use it sparingly:

1. Create a new basic page. Add a one row, one column table set to 400px. Give the table zero border and spacing, but set the padding to 1px. You can use any width for your page, but work with this one for now.

2. Click the table cell and select it. Set the cell's background color to a color of your choice. Be sure you are setting the *cell's* color, not the *table's*.

3. With your cursor still in the cell, add a new table, setting the width to 400px, with three rows and three columns. Give your new table a zero border, 1px spacing, and 5px padding.

4. Select all the cells in the second and third rows by shift+clicking from the first cell in the second row to the last cell in the third row. Color these cells white.

5. Save and preview. As you can see in Figure 34-18, the spacing between the cells of the nested, inner table let the color of the outer table's cell show through. The white of the nested table's cells block the color, forming 1px outlines.

Figure 34-18: A one-pixel border showing around the nested table

6. Select all the cells in the top row. Merge them and set this cell to a table heading by checking the Header box in the Property inspector. Headings are automatically centered and bolded. Type a heading into the table; then save and preview.

Tip

You can merge cells and set different colors to control your border. You can even make the spacing wider to create a wider outline or change the color of the outlines. To make the outline wider, select the outer `<table>` tag and increase the cell pad (our border) value in the Property inspector. To change the color of the table borders, click the table and select the `<td>` that appears just before the second `<table>` tag.

Creating a rounded-corner table

This trick uses graphics to give a table a unique look by getting rid of the hard, boxy rectangular shape.

Fireworks MX

The next exercise uses files exported from Chapter 23, which is the Fireworks optimizing and exporting chapter.

A simple, fixed-width version

1. In Dreamweaver, use the Site panel to open `corners.htm` from the rounded_tables folder. This page was exported from Fireworks and contains *comments* — hidden notes in the code — to maintain a relationship between the Fireworks source file and the page.

2. Each cell contains a graphic. The gold graphics form the outlines and rounded corners for the table. Delete the center cell's image and type **put content here**. The side graphics keep this cell open. But they also make the table bigger than you want it.

3. You can set the center cell to Top align (Vert) and sample the corner graphics to set the center cell's background color. With the center cell colored (Figure 34-19), the text no longer appears to be against an edge.

4. Save and preview.

A relative-width (more complex) version

The simple fixed-width table was easy because Fireworks sets the width of each cell. Because the graphics in the cells match the width of the cells, all browsers render the table accurately. But making a relative table with rounded corners is like building a hybrid table; it's trickier to get all browsers to render it properly.

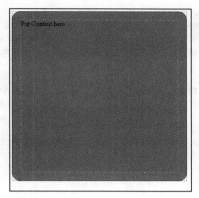

Figure 34-19: The center of the rounded table set to Top vertical alignment with the background color the same as the borders

1. Using the same `corners.htm` file, select the `<table>` tag and set the table's width to 50%, replacing the 400px width.

2. Save and preview your page in your target browsers. Open the browser to full window and don't be surprised to see the table fall apart — creating gaps beside all the corners — when you expand the browser window. Remember, this is a hybrid table.

3. To fix the table, set the top, center cell's width to 100%. (Press the right arrow to get into the cell or select the `<td>` tag and test again.) You should still see gaps, but only beside the right corners. The gaps are caused because the graphic in the top, and the bottom-center cells are too short to fill in the entire cell.

4. Click the top-center cell and select the `<td>` tag. Set the Bg image for this cell to the same graphic used in the foreground. Browse to locate the rounded_tables folder. Inside, you will find an images folder containing all the graphics for this page. Select `bg_top..gif`.

5. Save and preview.

6. Repeat the previous step for each of the outer cells, including the left and right side cells. Using these images:

    *   `bg_btm.gif` for the bottom row background
    *   `bg_left.gif` for the left side
    *   `bg_right.gif` for the right side

    As you add content to the center cell, you would experience the same gaps you saw when you expanded the table. By placing background images in all four cells, the outline seems to magically expand, whatever the size of the table!

7. Replace the foreground images in the four sides with spacer GIFs. Leave the spacers set to 1×1 to allow the table to shrink horizontally and vertically in response to sizing the browser window and reduced cell content.

Tip

Here's a fast way to add the spacers: Double-click the first image and select `spacer.gif`. Select the second foreground side image. Press Ctrl+Y (Command+Y) to repeat the last step. Because you are using the same image, Macromedia Dreamweaver sets this image source to `spacer.gif`.! (This may not work for Windows XP systems.) Repeat until all four images are replaced.

8. Set the center cell's height to a minimum of 100px. Save and test the page. As you add content to the center cell, it expands vertically. But it only expands horizontally as you widen the browser window.

Tip

Keep in mind that the 50 percent width of this table reacts to the browser window because that is its container; if the same table were nested in a fixed-width table cell, it would not expand horizontally at all.

Round-trip editing between Fireworks and Dreamweaver

There are several options for editing your corner graphics. You could simply go to Fireworks, reopen the source file, and re-export only the graphics into the image folder. That is a valid way to work. But the integration between Dreamweaver and Fireworks makes it possible to edit the table with a single click:

1. Select the table.

2. Click the Edit button. This launches Fireworks MX, opening the source file for the page. Because you moved this file into the Chapter 34 folder Dreamweaver may not be able to find the source file. Navigate to the rounded tables folder and select it.

    The code in the top of the table and the Macromedia Fireworks Src path in the Property inspector tell Macromedia Dreamweaver where to find the source file.

    ```
    <!-- fwtable fwsrc="corners.png" fwbase="corners.gif"
    fwstyle="Dreamweaver" fwdocid = "742308039" fwnested="0" -->
    ```

3. In the Fireworks toolbar, toggle the slice visibility by clicking the Hide Slices and Hotspots button; then click the Swap Strokes and Fill button below the Stroke and Fill color pickers. This changes the table to a blue table with gold outlines.

4. Click the Done button at the top of the Document to close Fireworks and return to Dreamweaver. To finish the alterations, you have to change the background cell color for the center cell.

Fireworks respects the changes made to the table in Macromedia Dreamweaver and does not try to return the table to its original state. The spacers in the sides are still in place as well. Although complex tables may not always be so easy to update, if you use Fireworks HTML, be sure to check out this handy integration feature.

Summary

Dreamweaver MX builds clean table code with very little effort. In this chapter, you learned about tables and Macromedia Dreamweaver table tools. You learned just how hard it can be when you use a single table for a layout when you edited a Fireworks HTML table. Using hybrid tables, you built the Habitat Alert page, tapping into the power of Studio MX integration to insert a Macromedia Fireworks component to add navigation buttons to the site. Finally, you tossed a few great table tricks into your developer's bag, learning to build fancy table borders and rounded corner tables.

Project Summary

Let's look at what you did that will be used in the Habitat Alert site.

Files Prepared for the Habitat Alert Web Site

Files	What Was Done	Where to Now?
index.htm	You added the tables and images for the homepage layout of the Habitat Alert site.	Links still need to be added in Dreamweaver You use similar pages in the rest of the site, learning to build a template to speed up the development process.
		Additionally, you add complex navigation scripting to the buttons you inserted with the Insert Macromedia Fireworks HTML tool.

Building Basic Navigation Links

Hypertext links are the mainstay of the Internet. In this chapter, you discover the different ways you can browse, point, or drag to build all kinds of links, using text and images.

Understanding URLs and Links

There are many ways to build links between one spot in your site and another: Some links move from page to page; others move you around *in* a page, but however they act or look, most links involve creating a path from one point to another. There are three different types of paths you can use to build a link:

✦ An absolute path (URL)

✦ Document-relative path

✦ Site root-relative path

Absolute URLs

A URL, or *Uniform Resource Locator*, is a method of accessing an Internet address that starts from a specific point. The starting point for most standard Web pages is the Internet or World Wide Web. Most URLs include the protocol (http://) plus the server's name (www.studiomxbible.com) plus the path to the page from the site's root (/index.htm).

HTTP stands for *HyperText Transfer Protocol*. Another protocol is *File Transfer Protocol (FTP)*. HTTPS is the protocol for secured servers. Between each portion of the URL, forward slashes indicate new directories. So, the example given in the previous paragraph would read www.studiomxbible.com/index.htm when used as a path in a link. Absolute URLs are used in Dreamweaver MX when the targeted page is outside of the defined site.

External link assets

When a link is created by typing in the absolute URL to a target that is outside of the defined site, an asset is created. The Assets panel (Figure 35-1) keeps track of all external links. To reuse the same URL, select the text or image to use as the link; then open the Assets panel (press F11) and click the Link icon. Select the correct URL and drag and drop it over the selected text or image.

Figure 35-1: Absolute URLs for the Habitat Alert site are stored as link assets.

Document-relative paths

Most of the time, links built within a site are document-relative, and the paths used are measured from the document that contains the link. Relative paths omit the part of the absolute URL that would be the same for all pages *within the site*. The path is written in the *href* (hypertext reference) as `href="path"`.

For example, the Habitat Alert site contains four major sections and each of the four sections' pages are contained within folders named for the sections. A link from the home page to the Learn section's starting page would read `learn/index.htm`, taking the user down into the learn folder to locate the starting page. A link from that page back to the home page would read `../index.htm`. Two dots and a forward slash indicate movement up out of a directory. These are all document-relative links and are easily configured using Dreamweaver. They are the most appropriate type of links to use when you are not sure where your site will be located on a server.

Root-relative paths

A root-relative link is a bit like an absolute URL in that it starts from a set point, but the set point is a folder (the site root) on a Web server. Paths that are root-relative start with a forward slash, measured from the root folder. The choice to use root-relative linking is made when selecting a file to link to. The Relative To menu, shown in Figure 35-2, defaults to Document; for root-relative links, select Site Root from the menu.

Root-relative links require a Web server for interpretation. Opening a page with root-relative links in a browser without using Preview in Browser doesn't work. Any images will display as broken links and linked pages will not be found because your local browser doesn't understand where the root folder is. Using Preview in Browser allows Dreamweaver to convert the links temporarily (image and page paths) to document-relative links. However, any page called *will not* have root-relative links converted and will therefore render improperly.

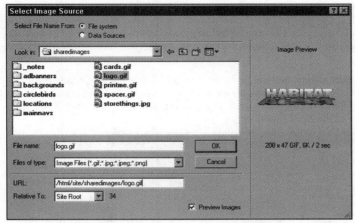

Figure 35-2: Choosing the site root from the Relative To menu

Windows users may preview root-relative pages via their local server using IIS (Internet Information Services) or PWS (Personal Web Server) if they set up a testing environment and choose Preview Using Local Server in the Preview in Browser category of their Preferences.

About HTML links

The HTML tag used to create a hypertext link is the *Anchor* tag, written as a pair of opening and closing `<a></a>` tags. When linking to other pages, the anchor tag includes an `href` attribute to contain the path to the target page, resulting in code that looks like the following:

```
<a href="learn/index.htm">link</a>
```

Other links can be made to link within a page or to send e-mail. Some links are *null* links, or placeholder links that indicate no path but do provide a way to apply JavaScript or other scripted behavior.

Building Text Links

Most Web pages contain hypertext links, sometimes as main or secondary navigation, inline in the body of text content, or as footer-style navigation at the bottoms of pages. By default, text links appear underlined, first as blue text. Later, after the target page has been visited, the visited text link appears purple. While clicking a text link (in the browser), the link might temporarily turn red or some other color. This is an active link. You can reset the default color of links through the use of HTML in the Page Properties settings. Alternatively, you can control the appearance of links, including the underline decoration, using Cascading Style Sheets.

Cross-Reference See Chapter 36 for information about using CSS style sheets to control link appearance.

The two main methods for building text links are Browse for File and Point to File.

Browse for File link method

To build a link using Browse for File, select the text or image that serves as the link. Click the folder icon found next to the Link field in the Property inspector. Navigate to the targeted file and select it.

The Select File dialog box provides the Document or Site Root-relative linking options. The path structure is given in full. Feedback about whether the select object (image or page) is within the currently defined site is shown at the bottom, as shown in Figure 35-3.

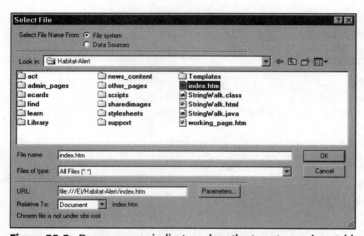

Figure 35-3: Dreamweaver indicates when the target page is outside of the site.

Point to File link method

To build a link using Point to File, select your text or image link; then press and drag away from the small, target-like icon to the right of the Link Field in the Property inspector. Drag to the desired file listed in the Site Files panel and release.

Alternatively, when working with text links only, you can access the Point to File icon directly from the page. After selecting the text, press Shift. Then click and drag away from the text selection (Figure 35-4). The same target icon on its tether appears, and you can release it over a page in the Site File.

Link History

As you build text links, a history is created, which you can access with the Link field pull-down menu in the Property inspector. Link History is built only with text-based links and remains only as long as the current Dreamweaver session lasts. Because Dreamweaver maintains the proper relationship of pages to one another, you can choose links from the menu, and the program adjusts paths, if needed.

Caution

Because Link History is session-based, it is possible to see history for more than one site if you work on more than one site while the program is open.

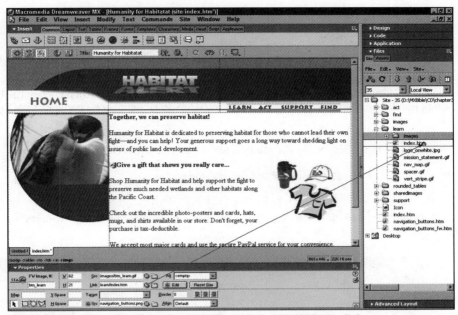

Figure 35-4: The contextual Point to File tool works only with text links.

Building Image Links

To make a link from an image, select the image and browse or point to the target file. Images cannot access Link History, nor do they build it. Image links appear outlined in blue rather than underlined unless the border attribute for the image is set to zero. Dreamweaver automatically sets the zero value for images used as links.

Cross-Reference

More complex uses of images as links are covered in Chapter 41.

Creating an image map

Generally, only one `href` may be added per image. When designing graphics to be used for a site, a layout is sliced into separate images that are exported from Fireworks. Sometimes it isn't practical or convenient to create separate images for each button or link needed, and an image map is used instead.

An *image map* uses one or more sets of coordinates called *hotspots* that are measured from the upper-left edge of the image. The coordinates are defined in `<area>` tags, and you can assign an `href` and/or other attributes. The `<area>` tags are listed between the opening and closing `<map></map>` tags. You make references to the specific map inside the `<img>` tag.

Map-drawing tools

You draw image map coordinates with the map tools located in the Property inspector. To access the tools, you must first select an image. Image maps require a reference name to the map, which determines which map coordinates are applied for the image.

Save the Habitat Alert34 folder from the chapter34_exercise folder to your hard drive. Define a new site. Hint: If you already have another Habitat Alert site defined, then choose the Edit Site option in the Site panel of the Site Definition drop-down menu and change the path to the Local Root folder.

Let's build an image map using the Mission Statement page from the Habitat Alert site.

1. Open `mission_statement.htm` from the find folder.

2. Select the graphic `navmap.gif` using the pointer tool.

3. Name your map in the field supplied in the bottom-left corner of the Property inspector, as shown in Figure 35-5.

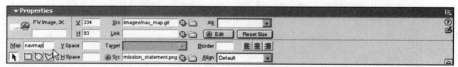

Figure 35-5: Name your map and build hotspots with the map drawing tools.

4. Use the rectangular drawing tool (blue rectangle below the Map name) to create a rectangle over the HOME button text. This map's shapes are easily created as rectangles. Other maps may require use of the ellipse or polygon tool to draw hotspots.

5. With the home hotspot selected, notice the change in the Property inspector. Leave the placeholder null link in the Link field and the target field blank. In the Alt Text field, type **Click to close this window and return to the home page**.

6. Draw a rectangle hotspot for each section, adding the Alt text from Table 35-1. Figure 35-6 shows the map.

Table 35-1: Image Map Settings

Text	Alt Text
HOME	Click to close this window and return to the home page.
LEARN	Click to close this window and Learn More.
ACT	Click to close this window and Act Now!
SUPPORT	Click to close this window and Support Habitat Alert.
FIND	Click to close this window and Find More Resources.

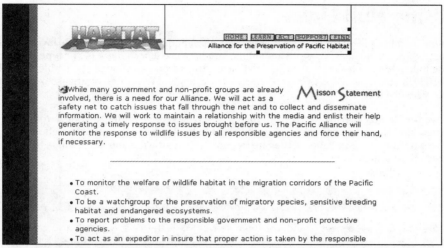

Figure 35-6: The hotspots added to make the image map and the Alt text added as well

The Polygon tool

The Polygon tool is a bit trickier than the rectangular or elliptical hotspot tools. The polygon tool works like a pen tool in drawing programs in a connect-the-dots fashion. Use it to create irregular hotspots. First, click to create a starting point. Move to the next logical point and click again. Don't try to put too many points in your hotspot because they generally are not necessary. The idea is to add enough points to roughly outline the desired shape.

As you begin to return to the starting point, a see-through bluish fill appears inside the hotspot you are drawing. Occasionally, the fill appears to be outside the shape, but this is only temporary; don't let it influence your outline as it will correct itself when you continue to close your finished hotspot. Take the outline all the way back to the starting point to finish the hotspot.

Note

To start a new polygon shape with the tool, deselect the current shape by switching to the Pointer tool and clicking the image outside of any hotspot shape. Then reselect the Polygon tool and begin your new polygon hotspot.

To adjust the points of your polygon hotspots, use the Pointer tool to select a point and move it. To adjust the location of any hotspot, use the Pointer tool to select the hotspot shape and drag the hotspot to a new location. Select a hotspot with the Pointer tool to update its link, target, or alt text.

Fireworks MX

You can build an image map in Fireworks, too, for use in pages exported from that program and opened in Dreamweaver MX. Or, crop it to the map slice, and export it using the new Quick Export feature in Fireworks. See Chapter 23 for more detail.

Using Null Links

A *null link* is a placeholder `href` that is most often added so you can attach JavaScript behaviors to a page element. To write a null link, you may use a *hash mark* (#) or type **javascript:;** in the link field for a text or image. In most cases, the second method is preferable but either works. In some Netscape browsers, the hash mark might trigger an hourglass or spinning cursor when clicked.

Save the Habitat Alert34 folder from the chapter34_exercise folder to your hard drive. Define a new site. Hint: If you already have another Habitat Alert site defined, then choose the Edit Site option in the Site panel of the Site Definition drop-down menu and change the path to the Local Root folder.

Building a Command from the History Panel

One of the many panels contained in Dreamweaver MX is the History panel. You can open the History panel by choosing Window ➪ Others ➪ History. The panel's main purpose is to represent visually the steps taken in an opened document. By default, the History panel can show up to 50 steps. To increase (or decrease) the number of steps recorded, use the programs preferences (Edit ➪ Preferences ➪ General category) to set an alternative value. Keep in mind that more steps increases the amount of memory used by the application. To erase all the history steps in the panel, use the panel Options ➪ Clear History.

The slider to the left of the recorded steps is used to move back and forth within the history of the document, as shown in the following figure. To restart earlier in the document's history, set the slider back to that point and begin working in the document.

The slider moves back and forth in the page history.

You can also select one or more steps and replay them in the current document or choose to copy the steps and play them in another document. Another powerful alternative is to select one or more steps and create a Command (History Options panel ➪ Save as a Command). A command is a powerful macro that can remember and run a series of saved steps. Not all the steps recorded by the History panel can be saved or replayed. As shown in the following figure, the listed steps that display red Xs may not be part of the command.

Continued

Continued

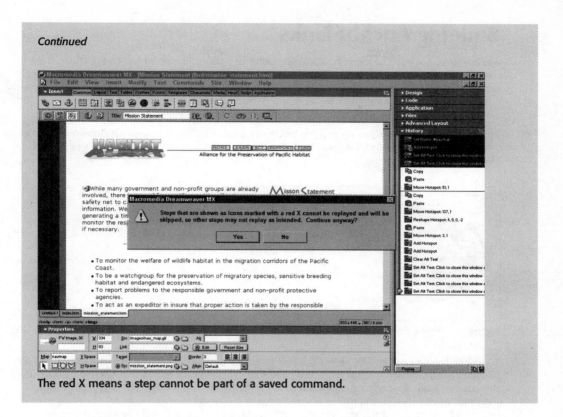

The red X means a step cannot be part of a saved command.

Let's build a null link in the Habitat Alert homepage and save it as a command. These steps presume you are working through the project exercises and have defined the project site. You can use the same in any page:

1. Open `index.htm` from the site folder. This should be your current project home page, which contains a set of text links along the bottom of the page.

2. Select Home from the footer text.

3. In the Link field, type **javascript:;**

4. Open the History panel by choosing Window ➪ Others ➪ History. Select the step that says Make Hyperlink: javascript:;.

5. From the panel Options menu, choose Save as Command.

6. Name the command Make Null Link, then click OK.

7. Select Learn from the footer text. Choose Commands ➪ Make Null Link. Repeat for each of the footer text selections; then save your page and close it.

Building Anchor Links

Anchor links are used to move to a specific point in a page. The point may be in the current page or any other page. The target point is first set up with a Named Anchor — an empty set of tags that add a reference name to a specific point. To set up the named anchor, place your cursor at the desired spot and choose Insert ➪ Named Anchor, or click the Anchor icon in the Insert bar's Common toolset.

To see a named anchor, you must have Invisibles enabled. Click the View Options menu in the Document bar and choose Visual Aids ➪ Invisibles. An anchor icon displays in Design view, as shown in Figure 35-7.

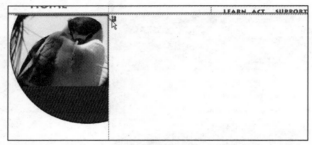

Figure 35-7: The Named Anchor icon

To link to the named anchor, select the text or image that serves as the link, drag the Point to File icon to the named anchor icon, and release it. This is fairly easy when both items are in the current page. If your named anchor is above or below the visible area of the page, drag the Point to File icon to the top or bottom edge of the document and wait for scrolling to begin and release the anchor. The Link field displays a hash mark and the anchor's name.

To link to a named anchor in another page, it may be faster to append a page link: With the text or image selected, drag the Point to File icon to the correct page in the Site panel and release it. When done, go to the Link field for the current link and type a hash mark plus the name of your anchor after the current page link, as shown in Figure 35-8.

Figure 35-8: A link to a named anchor in a different page places the hash mark and name of anchor after the page link's path.

Setting Up E-mail Links

You can use text or an image to set up an e-mail link. An e-mail link uses an `href` that begins with `mailto`:

```
<a href=mailto:info@studiomxbible.com>send email</a>
```

Keep in mind that using this method exposes you to unscrupulous users that search the Web to locate valid e-mail addresses for junk mail targeting (spam). Because your e-mail address is right there in the code, it is easy to find by setting up a spider — a robot or 'bot program — to look for and collect addresses with the @ symbol.

Tip

Check out `www.manastungare.com/asp/preventspam.asp`, at the site of Manas Tungare, a developer from India, living in Atlanta, Georgia. This nifty page encodes the letters in your e-mail address with special characters that are not so easily read by e-mail 'bots. An e-mail address like the one for studiomxbible becomes

```
<A HREF=
"mailto:%69%6E%66%6F%40%73%74%75%64%69%6F%6D%78%62%69%62%6C%65%2E%63%6F
%6D">Send Email</A>
```

Enter your e-mail address into the Email field and click the Obfuscate button. To use the newly encoded address, copy and paste it into your Link field in Dreamweaver.

You can also add an e-mail link using Insert⇨Email Link, as shown in Figure 35-9. A dialog box opens where you enter the text of the link and the e-mail address.

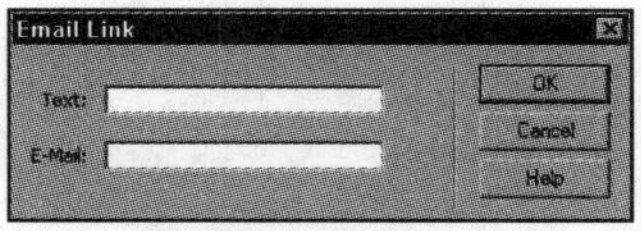

Figure 35-9: Insert Email Link window

Summary

In this chapter, you used text and images to build links to pages, name anchors, and to open and send e-mail messages. You learned how to show a hidden named anchor and how to make the document window scroll up or down with the Point to File icon. Using the History panel, you created a command for later use in your program.

Project Summary

Let's look at what you did that will be used in the Habitat Alert site.

Files Prepared for the Habitat Alert Web Site

Files	What Was Done	Where to Now?
mission_statement.htm	You built an image map.	This will be used to control a parent window with JavaScript.
index.htm	Null links were placed in the footer text.	

✦   ✦   ✦

Using Cascading Style Sheets

As a specification set forth by the W3C (World Wide Web Consortium), Cascading Style Sheets (CSS) is a standard designed to separate the visual presentation of content from the actual structural markup — a language used to render structured documents, such as HTML and XML, on screen, on paper, and verbally in speech.

What does this mean for you as a developer? It means that you no longer need to wrap a font tag around every block element to get the look you want. It means you can put the control of the way your page appears into a single location. It means that suddenly, your life just got easier!

Dreamweaver contains a revamped CSS Styles panel and an improved rendering of CSS within the Design view.

The Advantages of CSS

The most important argument for using CSS is that it removes all the extraneous markup that controls how the content *appears*, leaving the HTML structural markup as it was originally intended to be — a set of selectors that are applied so that any user agent (browser, reader, printer, and so on) can interpret the content structurally and present it as needed. After all, a printer has different needs than a Web browser has; the reader used by a sight-impaired user definitely doesn't need <font> information. Block element selectors in HTML have meaning. With CSS, the HTML can return to a purer form, uncluttered by unnecessary markup.

The biggest advantage of using CSS comes with how and where rules are defined. Instead of controlling the appearance of text (for example) at the block level, a single rule may be written in a separate page and applied to all pages within a site. When you want to change the information in a rule, only one edit is needed. That is a definite time-saver. It also means that pages tend to be more consistently styled, because all pages share the same rules, more or less.

Understanding CSS

Most modern browsers (version 4 and up) support the use of Cascading Style Sheets to control the appearance of content marked up with HTML or XML tags. The exception to this is Netscape 4x, whose support for inheritance and certain properties is quirky at best and downright buggy in practice. The way styles render in different browsers depends entirely on how that browser supports the CSS specification. Before you begin to use Cascading Style Sheets, you need an understanding about what CSS is and how it works.

Cascading Style Sheets is a specification that uses its own syntax to write *rules* that control the appearance of content in a Web page. These rules are called *styles*, which together are collectively known as a *style sheet*. Style rules are governed by *The Cascade*, which in turn uses the principles of *Inheritance*, *Specificity*, and *Importance* to determine which rule(s) apply where conflicting rules exist.

Selectors and declarations

Style rules are made up of two parts: *selectors* and *declarations*. A *selector* is most often an HTML tag. A *declaration* is a set of properties and values written in a specific syntax. Dreamweaver knows how to write declarations, so you don't have to learn the syntax at all, but you do need to understand the principles to help you decide how to use the CSS tools and features in the program.

Selectors

There are many kinds of selectors: The simplest selector is generally an HTML tag, but it might also be a custom tag defined in Extensible Markup Language (XML). For simple selectors, the tag itself is redefined to incorporate specific properties and values that will be used every time that tag appears in the page. If you redefine the `<p>` tag to use Verdana text, size 14-point in green, all paragraph text will be green, 14-point Verdana.

Classes and IDs

Class or *ID* selectors are tags that use the attribute of Class or ID. A *Class* rule is independent of any selector and can be applied to different selectors in a page. The way the selector appears when a class is applied depends upon the selector and the rule's properties. The name given to a class always starts with a period, and you may not use spaces or odd characters in the name.

IDs are like classes, except they are applied only once in the page. ID rules are always started with a hash mark (#) symbol. Both classes and IDs are applied, meaning that the page author picks selectors and sets them to use a class or ID:

```
<p class=".maincontent"> or  <p ID="#firstparagraph">
```

Pseudo-classes and Pseudo-elements

Rules written to govern the appearance of *pseudo-classes* and *pseudo-elements* are not controlled by the structure of the document but rather by a predictable state of the element or document.

The best example would be the anchor tag's predictable states: visited, hover, and active. None of these is a selector, but instead is a state. When a link appears in a page, it may display using a defined set of property values; when the state changes, as in the users move their cursors over it, click, or visit the target page, the values for those properties change. The rule written to govern how the properties change is not applied within the page but instead depends on the state of the page to change and automatically engage the new values.

Contextual selectors

Contextual selectors combine a class with one or more selectors to create a selective and powerful rule. Applying a basic class rule to a containing element creates context. Additional rules can be set up to declare property values that apply only when the specific selector occurs within the container of that class.

Inheritance

All HTML pages are governed by their structure, which is a key part of the basic markup. For example, you cannot put the body tag into the table tag; a paragraph can't contain a table, but table cells can contain paragraphs. These basic structural rules create parent–child relationships between the elements in the page. Almost every element is either a parent or child, or both. This parent–child or ancestor–descendent relationship governs the way CSS rules are applied to the page; it's not surprising that the major principle at play in these relationships is called inheritance. *Inheritance* is the mechanism for determining how style rules are applied — not only for the specific element, but for its descendents, too.

For example, if the body of a page is set to use a specific text color, all text in all elements should inherit that text color unless specifically set otherwise. This is the theory and should be the case, but there are exceptions: some due to special settings, and some due to the vagaries of inconsistent browser support. Additionally, not all properties are inherited. Text color and size is inherited; border and box margin and padding properties are not. Experience through practice and careful attention to reference resources will help you gain insight to this guiding principle of CSS.

Specificity and importance

Two more guiding principles of CSS are *specificity* and *importance*. Specificity describes the relative *weights* of style rules. IDs have a relative weight of 100. Classes weigh in at 10, and simple selectors have a specificity of 1. This is important because it is entirely possible, even likely, that you may have rules and apply them in ways that set up conflict. For example, say you define a rule for all paragraphs <p> that sets them to use red text. You also define a custom class called mainparagraph that uses green text. When you apply the custom class to a paragraph, you end up with the following:

```
<p class="mainparagraph"> text content here </p>
```

The text cannot be both red and green; which will it be? This is where specificity applies. Because classes have a greater specificity, it overrides the simple selector's rule and so this paragraph will sport green text. This is a simple example; specificity is almost always more complex than this. To further complicate matters, inherited values lose their specificity. Any explicit rule overrides an inherited rule. An example here would be:

```
body {color:blue}
p {color: red}
```

If you type words into the body of the page, they appear in blue text. Make those words a paragraph and their color changes to red. Why? *Specificity.* Although the blue is inherited, the text within the paragraph is controlled by the properties of the explicitly defined paragraph style.

!important

!important is a declaration that can be used to override specificity; adding this to the correct position in your declaration gives the value *precedence*. Dreamweaver doesn't really have a mechanism to add !important to your rules, but with easy access to the defined rules, you can add it by hand. !important must always be added just before the ending semicolon of a property declaration:

```
p {color: #003366 !important; background: #CCCC99;}
```

Each property that is important would have its own !important declaration.

The ever-useful cascade

Style rules may originate in an external page or be embedded within the head of a specific page; style rules may even be defined at the block level or inline, although this practically defeats the advantages of using CSS. External style sheet(s) are linked or imported in a page, but that page may also have embedded and inline rules. It can even have more than one externally linked or imported sheet.

The cascade also determines what happens when properties for a specific selector conflict; the general rule is that the "closest" rule's property value wins, although there can be exceptions. Given the same selector and property, an inline value overrides an embedded value, which in turn overrides an external value. If the declarations are in one or more linked or imported sheets, the style value in the last sheet read has precedence. This same principle means that the author's styles override default values provided by the browser (user-agent).

CSS versus HTML formatting

If the closest value wins, what happens if you use font tags (or set a table cell's bgcolor) in a page that also contains CSS styles? Many new users of CSS try to cover their bases by including both styles and HTML markup. This defeats the purpose of CSS because the same rules that apply to CSS styles also apply to font and other HTML formatting. Cascade applies and for the most part, the HTML formatting is always closer.

Tip

Use the Clean Up HTML Command (Commands ➪ Clean Up HTML) to remove existing font tags by enabling the Specific Tags option and typing in **font, b, i,** and any other possible HTML formatting markup.

When developing your page HTML, don't set properties using HTML methods. For example, if you plan to have all table structures use a header row with a background color, set that value using CSS. That way, if you decide to change the color later, you can simply edit the style.

CSS properties

Many properties are definable using CSS, including text, block, border, box, list, and more. Each category of property contains attributes, such as color, size, and other definable values. Many resources list which properties are acceptable for specific elements, from the W3C specification (www.w3c.org) to books and online development forums. Rather than list properties, we'll approach creating styles with properties using the tools in Dreamweaver.

CSS Style Tools and Features

With a bit of knowledge of how CSS works, you're ready to incorporate CSS into your site, using the powerful tools and features available in Dreamweaver. The most obvious place to start is the CSS Styles panel.

The CSS Styles panel is part of the Design panel group by default. If you changed your default panel groups, you can always open the panel by choosing Window ⇨ CSS Styles or by pressing Shift+F11. The panel displays style rules for the active open document only.

Apply versus Edit

The CSS Styles panel has two modes: Apply and Edit. You can build new styles in either mode, but the Edit mode enables you to see all the styles defined for a page, whether external or embedded. The advantage of separate modes is that you can click any style listed in Edit mode and directly access the dialog boxes used to define properties and values for style rules.

Although there are several different options for applying style rules to page elements, the Apply mode of the CSS Styles panel offers an easy, foolproof method of setting a rule to a specific element when needed. To apply a class to a selector, place your cursor into an element, and click the style in Apply mode. Other methods include right-clicking (Control+clicking) the active tag in the Tag selector (Figure 36-1) or right-clicking (Control+clicking) in the document in Design view to access the context menu, as shown in Figure 36-2.

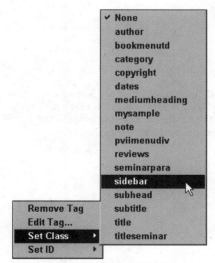

Figure 36-1: Applying a class via the Tag selector

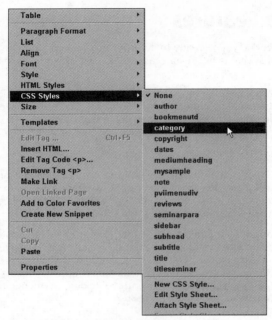

Figure 36-2: Applying a class via the context menu in the document in Design view

Defining Style Rules

Defining style rules for selectors, classes, IDs, and contextual selectors begins with options chosen in the New CSS Style dialog box shown in Figure 36-3. To open it, add a new style (click the plus button on the bottom of the CSS Styles panel). Choosing a type of style and selecting either an external or embedded origin is required for every new style.

Figure 36-3: The New CSS Style dialog box and options

Type of style

Earlier in this chapter, you learned about the different kinds or types of selectors for which style rules can be defined. You use the Type options to determine the nature of the rule you are creating:

✦ Use Make Custom Style (Class) to define classes.

✦ Choose Redefine HTML Tag to create style rules for simple selectors.

✦ Select Use CSS Selector when grouping simple selectors, defining ID styles, working with pseudo classes or elements, or building contextual selectors.

Style sheet origin

The second required step to creating a new style is setting the origin of the style rules. In this case, you are choosing whether the rules are saved in an external file or are written to the head of the current document.

✦ To create an external style sheet, choose Define In: New Style Sheet File.

✦ To embed a style rule, choose Define In: This Document Only.

Save the Habitat Alert36 folder from the chapter36_exercise folder to your hard drive. Define a new site. Hint: If you already have another Habitat Alert site defined, then choose the Edit Site option in the Site panel of the Site Definition drop-down menu and change the path to the Local Root folder.

In this section, you build a style by creating an external style sheet to redefine the `<body>` tag used in the project homepage layout. To do this, follow these steps:

1. Open the home page (`site/index.htm`) and choose Modify⊅Page Properties. Remove any reference to a background image by selecting and deleting the path used. Delete all text, link, visited link, and active link values; then click OK.

2. Add a New Style by clicking the Add (+) button at the bottom of the CSS Styles panel (in the Design panel group).

3. In the New CSS Style dialog box, select Redefine HTML Tag and type **body** into the top field or choose the body tag from the menu of selectors.

4. Select Define In: External Style Sheet File; then click OK (Figure 36-4).

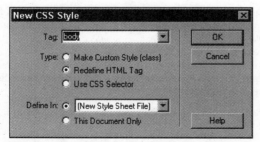

Figure 36-4: The CSS Style dialog box filled out for the new style

5. Dreamweaver prompts you to save the new external style sheet file to the site. Navigate into the stylesheet folder and save the file as **main.css.** You finish this style in the next section, so leave it open.

When you save an external style sheet, a document-relative path is created that must be maintained when the site is published. Later you see that code is placed in the head of the document that references the path to the page. This is what the code looks like:

```
<link href="stylesheets/main.css" rel="stylesheet" type="text/css">
```

Redefine HTML tag

A nice new feature in Dreamweaver is the title given to the Style Definition window when developing a style, shown in Figure 36-5. The labeled window makes it clear which style you are developing and where that rule is saved.

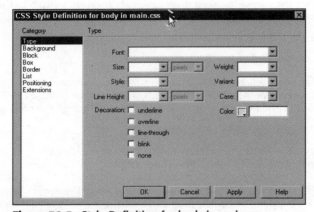

Figure 36-5: Style Definition for body in main.css

When defining properties for a selector, realize that not all properties need to be set. The goal when setting up your styles should be to let inheritance and specificity play as large a role as possible while still addressing the site's needs and any browser inconsistencies that might exist for your target browsers. Since the Habitat Alert site targets Netscape 4x browsers in addition to the newer Internet Explorer 5+ and Netscape 6+ browsers, this is a demanding task that you address as you develop styles for the site.

For the project site, all pages make use of the Verdana, Arial, Helvetica, sans-serif font list. Adding this information to the body declarations doesn't hurt and ensures that any text in the pages uses one of these font families:

1. In the Type category (the category list is on the left side), add the Verdana, Arial, Helvetica, sans-serif font-family list. CSS is powerful, but the users must still have a font in their machine for that font to be used.

2. Click to the Background category. The site's pages use a white background. Select #FFFFFF (white) using the Color picker for background color.

3. Each page also uses a background image that tiles along the top of the document to create the gold and blue textured area with the dark stripe along the bottom. Click the Browse button for the Background Image and navigate to the shared images and backgrounds folders, to locate `banner_bg.gif`. This adds a document-relative path (`../sharedimages/backgrounds/banner_bg.gif`) in the Background Image field. Note the `../` that indicates that the image will be found outside the stylesheets folder, in the sharedimages/backgrounds folders.

4. If you press the Apply button at this point, you see the properties in your page because the `<body>` tag *already exists* in the document. The page turns white and the background image tiles and repeats horizontally and vertically. To prevent the vertical tiling, set the Repeat menu to use repeat-x.

5. Click OK; then Save. Preview the page in all the target browsers.

Save the Habitat Alert36 folder from the chapter36_exercise folder to your hard drive. Define a new site. Hint: If you already have another Habitat Alert site defined, then choose the Edit Site option in the Site panel of the Site Definition drop-down menu and change the path to the Local Root folder.

To overcome this NN4*x* browser issue, define Background-Image (URL) in the document where the style will be used. The following steps show you how to adjust the project body style to address the problem in NN4*x*:

1. Double-click the body style listed in the Edit mode of the CSS Styles panel (click the Edit Styles radio button). When the Style Definition dialog box opens, click the Background category and remove the path in the Background Image field. Click OK to accept the change.

2. Now add a new style. Select Redefine HTML Tag, choose the body tag, and select Define In: This Document Only. Click OK.

3. Click to the Background category and Browse to locate the same background image file. Notice that the path created is different? No `../` is present. This style is measured from the current document and all browsers correctly interpret this URL.

4. Click OK. Notice in the CSS styles panel that there are now two styles. One is for the index page specifically and one is in the style sheet.

5. Save and preview the page in NN4x to be sure that the new URL works correctly. Test in the other target browsers, too, to be sure that no problems exist there, either.

As shown in Figure 36-6, the image tiles along the only x-axis, because the repeat-x value in the `main.css` external page still applies. It is not in conflict and therefore accumulates as one of the properties of the body style. The same is true of the white background page color.

About Background-Image (URL)

When defining styles that include Background-Image, a URL is needed to locate the required image. According to the W3C specification, this URL may be either absolute or *relative to where the style is defined*. All CSS-capable browsers, except Netscape 4x, get this path right. Netscape 4x browsers incorrectly interpret this type of URL, looking for the image *relative to where the style is used*. This is a big difference, resulting in the image failing to load.

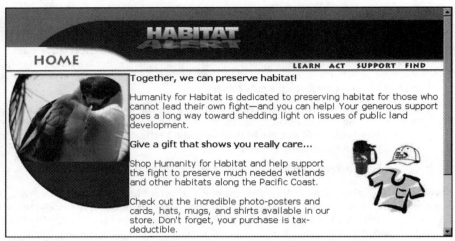

Figure 36-6: The page with its tiling background image and white page color

Grouping selectors

When one or more selectors share the same set of rules, it makes sense to define them by grouping the selectors. Defining styles for grouped selectors is the same as with any other style, except you must use the Use CSS Selector option in the New CSS Styles panel.

On the CD-ROM Save the Habitat Alert36 folder from the chapter36_exercise folder to your hard drive. Define a new site. Hint: If you already have another Habitat Alert site defined, then choose the Edit Site option in the Site panel of the Site Definition drop-down menu and change the path to the Local Root folder.

Using Color in CSS Styles

The standard HTML specification for colors exists in the CSS standards, too. You could choose a named color, selecting from the 16 cross-platform options listed in the following table, but Dreamweaver uses its standard Color picker. This results in a Hexadecimal value—the other HTML option. The same is true in Dreamweaver's CSS interface, but you can edit any style sheet rule by hand and use a named value. Other options include RGB (Red, Green, Blue) specified in percentage values, but again, Dreamweaver doesn't use this in the Style Definition interface. You may, however, opt to use it by hand-editing. Refer to the W3C.org specification to better understand how RGB is implemented.

White	Navy	Olive	Purple
Yellow	Gray	Green	Lime
Silver	Maroon	Black	Aqua
Teal	Blue	Fuchsia	Red

In the following steps, you add a pair of grouped selectors to the project site's external style sheet:

1. In Apply Styles mode, add a new style and choose Use CSS Selectors in the New CSS Styles dialog box. Be sure that the `main.css` style sheet file is selected in the Define In: menu.

2. Type in **p, td**. When text appears in paragraphs or table cells, you want it to use the same size and color text. Click OK.

3. Choose #333333 (dark gray) in the color picker; then type **11** into the Size field. Click OK.

Dreamweaver defaults the Size unit menu to select pixels as a unit of measurement for the font size. Many other options are available, however.

About length units

Many CSS properties, such as font size, margins, padding, and other box properties, depend on lengths. *Length* measurements can be expressed as positive or negative values followed by a length unit, such as pixels, points, and so on. Some properties, such as font size, accept only positive values. You can choose from two types of length units: absolute and relative. When you select a value (or type a value) in the field, you are opting to set lengths.

Absolute length units

Absolute units are probably the easiest units to understand as you use these units on a daily basis. There are five different absolute length units:

✦ **Inches (in)** — An American standard unit of measurement.

✦ **Centimeters (cm)** — There are 2.54 cm in an inch. One centimeter equals 0.394 inches.

✦ **Millimeters (mm)** — There are 10 mm to every cm. One millimeter equals 0.0394 inches.

✦ **Points (pt)** — This familiar unit is used by most word-processing applications. By definition, there are 72 points to an inch, but Windows-based machines and even some Macintosh browsers render points using a 96-dpi value.

✦ **Picas (pc)** — A basic typographical unit of measure, one pica is equal to 12 points, and there are 6 picas per inch.

Absolute lengths are the least attractive option in CSS, because they have no relationship to real values but instead are totally dependent upon the settings of the monitor or printer that displays or prints the page. It is not likely that you could hold a ruler up to your monitor and find that text set to use a 12-point size would be exactly one inch tall.

Relative lengths

Relative lengths are called so because their actual measurement change based on the user-agent (browser, printer, and so on) and user preferences. Additionally, some of these lengths are relative to their *containers* or ancestor/parent selectors. There are four relative lengths:

✦ **Pixels (px)** — A pixel is a dot or small box that makes up the visual or printed display as in points per inch (ppi) or dots per inch (dpi). Pixels are useful because images are consistently displayed on computer monitors at 72dpi. Because Macintosh and PC platforms use 72dpi when describing pixel measurements, it is generally assumed that choosing pixel values for font size (and other CSS properties) solves the inconsistencies of text sizing between platforms. Although this is not entirely true, there are advantages to using pixel lengths because text sized this way maintains a better relative relationship to images used in the page.

Caution

Netscape 4*x* browsers sometimes display pixels smaller than normal and printers may misinterpret the pixel values relative to their printing resolutions — equating pixels to ppi, resulting in very tiny text!

✦ **Em-Height (em)** — Generally used in Font measurements, the em-height is equivalent to the height of the character box for a font — typically a capital M (hence the association). In CSS, a setting of .5em depends on the default font and font size set by a browser and would be 50 percent of that value. Or, if font-family and font-size values exist for the container that holds the text styled with a .5em length, the value of .5em would be equivalent to 50 percent of whatever *those* measurements were. Although em-height seems complicated, it is a useful length.

✦ **X-Height (ex)** — The x-height for any font describes the height of any lowercase letter without ascenders or descenders, as in x, but not g or h. Most browsers assume that 1ex is 1/2 or 50 percent of 1em, but this is not true in all cases.

✦ **Percentage (%)** — Percentages are almost always computed relative to another value set for the containing element. For example, if the default size for text in a page is 12 points, a heading set to 150 percent would use 18-point text.

Larger, smaller, and XXS–XXL

Additional options for setting font size include larger, smaller, and XXS through XXL. Larger and smaller increase or decrease font size based on the containing element. XXS-XXL relates directly to sizes 1-7 in HTML font formatting, and these values depend upon the browser's default settings.

Adding a Custom Class

Sometimes it isn't practical to redefine a specific selector to set up a style. Remember, properties set for a selector apply every time that selector is used in the page. When you want to use a style selectively and independently of a selector, define a *custom class* and apply it as needed. To build a custom class in Dreamweaver, add a new style and choose the Make Custom Style (Class) option. Always begin the name of the class with a period. You cannot use spaces or special characters in the name, not even an underscore.

On the CD-ROM

Save the Habitat Alert36 folder from the chapter36_exercise folder to your hard drive. Define a new site. Hint: If you already have another Habitat Alert site defined, then choose the Edit Site option in the Site panel of the Site Definition drop-down menu and change the path to the Local Root folder.

In this section, you use the project site to build a custom class that sets the background element in the circle area of the page. Currently this page sets that element using the cell's background image property. The downfall of using HTML to set background image is that steps must be taken with the image to prevent unwanted tiling. In the case of the circle's background image, thousands of white pixels were added to the bottom of the image so that it would not repeat vertically. This results in a larger-than-necessary image. With CSS, you can avoid this trick and build the image without the extra white space at the bottom, and use no-repeat in the style. Follow these steps:

1. Still working in the home page (site/index.htm), place your cursor in the cell containing the circle image. Select the <td> using the Tag selector, and remove the value found in its Bg image field.

2. Add a new style and choose Make Custom Style (Class). Name this new style **.circlebg**. Be sure that you select Define In This Document Only. Remember, you are setting the URL for the background-image property.

   If the This Document Only isn't available, cancel and select index.htm in the CSS Styles panel, and add the new style.

3. Click the Background category and set the cell's background color to #FFFFFF (white). Then navigate to the sharedimages/backgrounds folder and locate circlebtm_plus.gif.

4. Choose no-repeat from the Repeat menu. Click OK.

5. You need to apply the circlebg style to the cell. Right-click the <td> tag and choose Set Class circlebg.

6. Save your page and preview it. Keep this page open for additional style exercises.

Building Link Styles

When you want to develop styles that control the appearance of your page links, you have several options. With HTML formatting, you can set the link, visited link, and active link values, adding the properties to the <body> tag in the page. With CSS, you get a fourth option (not in Netscape 4x) to set a value for *hover* — in effect, a mouse-over style.

You can set a single value to be used for all these properties by redefining the anchor <a> tag. To set one value for all, simply redefine the HTML tag <a> and choose your properties.

You can define separate values for one or more of the pseudo-selectors associated with the anchor <a> tag. *Pseudo-selectors* are equivalent to sub-sets of the tag. To use pseudo-selectors, you must select the Use CSS Selectors option in the New CSS Styles dialog box. Additionally, these styles must be set in a specific order:

a:link

a:visited

a:hover

a:active

Netscape 4x browsers do not support the hover property and ignore it. Although not supported by NN4x when set using HTML formatting, the Active state is broken when set via CSS. As usual, NN4x support for CSS is typically quirky.

Applying link styles

Links occur in your pages whenever the anchor tag is wrapped around text or images. When you opt to use link styles, you do not need to apply them; they are automatically applied when the page renders.

The Tao of Link

The familiar blue, underlined text we all know means something. In less than a decade, even the Web surfer realizes that blue, underlined text is clickable. Be careful when you choose to alter the default properties for your links; your visitor might not know to click it!

Setting Link Properties

HTML formatting of link properties allows only color selection. This is generally all you will use when creating your link styles via CSS, too. You may opt to set other options, but you do not know where links might appear. When setting colors, be aware that the color may need to be used over many different background colors or images. Using other properties, such as font weights (as in bolding) or font sizes (as in changing size), can cause a reflow of text that can be annoying to visitors to occur.

Text decoration

Text links are underlined because their Decoration is, by default, underlined. To remove the underline, set the Decoration property to None, or use one of several options available in the Type category of the Style Definition dialog box.

On the CD-ROM   Save the Habitat Alert36 folder from the chapter36_exercise folder to your hard drive. Define a new site. Hint: If you already have another Habitat Alert site defined, then choose the Edit Site option in the Site panel of the Site Definition drop-down menu and change the path to the Local Root folder.

Follow these steps to add basic link styles to the project site style sheet:

1. Add a new style in the external style sheet (main.css). Select Use CSS Selector and select a:link from the Use CSS Selectors menu. Click OK.

2. In the Style Definition dialog box, set the color value for all links to #666600, a dark olive green. Click OK.

3. For the project site, the link and visited link colors will be the same. Rather than build a new visited style, take advantage of the Duplicate feature in Dreamweaver to save time. In Edit mode, select the new a:link style and choose Duplicate from the panel Options menu.

4. When the Duplicate dialog box opens, be sure that your duplicated style is defined in the external main.css style sheet and select a:visited from the Use CSS Selectors menu. Click OK.

5. To define a hover style, select and duplicate the visited style, using the same process described in Step 4, but choose a:hover from the menu.

6. When you've closed the dialog box, double-click the hover style in Edit mode to open for editing. Because hover is a mouse-over effect, you want the property values to change. Choose #006699, a medium bright blue. Click OK.

7. Repeat the duplication process or add a new style to the external style sheet, selecting a:active from the menu and setting its color value to #999933, a light olive-gold green. Click OK. Save and test the page in your target browsers. Mouse over the text links at the bottom of the page. Keep the page open for additional CSS style exercises.

Using Contextual Styles

When used correctly, CSS offers incredible options for visual formatting just not possible with HTML. One of these options is the use of *contextual styles* — rules that apply only when a selector occurs in the context of a specific class of container. Using contextual styles requires a bit of forethought and planning to incorporate classes to create containers that serve as regions.

For example, the Habitat Alert site places the main content for each page into a large white area below the navigation buttons. Content added to this area is jammed up against the circle image to the left. You cannot add cell padding or spacing to the table, because it would affect the entire table. The only HTML solution is to alter the table structure to add a "spacer" or "gutter" column between the circle cell and the content cell. However, deciding to change the width of the gutter column would mean changing every page structurally.

Save the Habitat Alert36 folder from the chapter36_exercise folder to your hard drive. Define a new site. Hint: If you already have another Habitat Alert site defined, then choose the Edit Site option in the Site panel of the Site Definition drop-down menu and change the path to the Local Root folder.

Leaving the table structure as is, you can use the CSS to set white space around the main content in the table cell. By creating a class to apply to the cell, you can define a new style for the size 4 heading and paragraph tags, used only when size 4 headings or paragraphs occur within any cell set to use the `.maincontent` class. Follow these steps:

1. Open the index.htm page.

2. Add a new style to the `main.css` external style sheet. Choose Make Custom Style (Class) and name the new class **.maincontent**. Click OK.

3. In the Style Definition dialog box, click the Background category and set the background color to #FFFFFF (White). Click OK.

   Technically, you can create a class that contains no properties or values, which is useful when designing contextual classes. But Dreamweaver fails to write the new style if you do not choose at least one property with a value (which is why you added a white background). You can opt to edit your style after it is written to remove the property. Dreamweaver doesn't remove the style if you do this.

4. Click in the main content blank area (be sure your cursor is not in the text) and apply the new class. The easiest and most precise method of applying styles is to right-click (Control+click) the `<td>` tag in the Tag selector and choose Set Class ⇨ .maincontent. You won't see any changes.

5. Now add a new style, this time choosing the Use CSS Selectors option to create a new style in the external style sheet (`main.css`). Type **.maincontent h4** in the Selector field and click OK. Leave the Style Definition dialog box open and continue with the next section.

Setting box margins

In Dreamweaver, the margin property is located in the Box category. Of the several ways to add white space around page elements, the most supported method to use is a margin. Every element has a margin. With Cascading Style Sheets, you can control the top, right, bottom, and left margins separately. Netscape 4x browsers offer limited support for the margin property for some elements. To set the margins, follow these steps:

1. In the Style Definition dialog box, set the Type properties for `maincontent` size 4 headings to as follows:

    Size: 12px

    Weight: Bold

    Color: #999900, a light-golden green.

2. Click the Box category and uncheck the Use Same for All option over the Margin settings. Add the following margins; then click OK.

    Top: 0

    Right: 20px

    Bottom: 0

    Left: 20px

3. Click OK to close the dialog box. Figure 36-7 shows the settings used in the Box category. Your headings move away from the left edge of the table cell (Figure 36-8).

4. Use the same approach to control the margins of maincontent paragraphs. Add a new style, using the Use CSS Selector option. Type **.maincontent p** into the Selector field.

5. Set the font size to 11px; then click the Box category and set the margins as follows:

    Top: 0

    Right: 20px

    Bottom: 10px

    Left: 20px

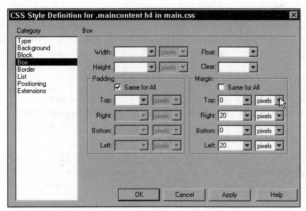

Figure 36-7: The settings used in the Box category

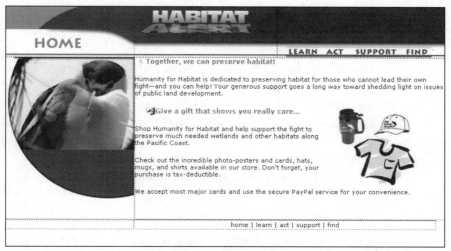

Figure 36-8: The properties for the head 4 titles applied to the maincontent style

6. Click OK and save your page. Preview it in your target browsers to see how the styles affect the presentation of the main content. With room around the content, it is much easier to read, as shown in Figure 36-9. And because you used CSS to control the margins, simple edits to these two contextual selectors reset values for every page using this style sheet.

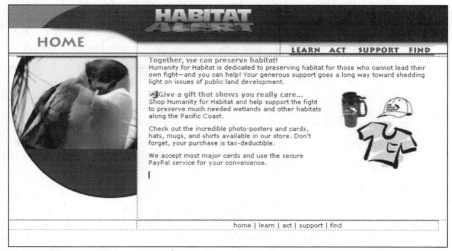

Figure 36-9: Margin around the content in the maincontent cell makes the page easier to read.

Contextual Link Styles

Use the same concept to add more than one set of link styles to your pages, something not possible using HTML formatting. Remember, the formula for a contextual style is .class plus a space plus the selector. For link styles, the selectors are pseudo-selectors, so your contextual link style would read `.class a:link` or `.class a:visited`, and so forth.

To define an additional, contextual set of link styles in a document, follow these steps:

1. Define a new site using the linkstyles folder inside of the chapter36_exercise folder as the root.

2. Open the page `more_link_styles.htm` from the linkstyles folder.

   This page has a set of default link styles that work well on the lighter-colored areas. If you click the different cells of the layout, you should notice that each cell is of a specific class; they all have a context. The default link colors don't work well in the footer cell because the color of the cell background and the color of the link are similar. Also, the main navigation links would be better if they were not underlined. In this exercise, you build two more sets of link styles specifically for each of these areas.

3. Add a new style to the external style sheet `linkstyles.css`. Choose Use CSS Selectors and type **.footer a:link**.

4. Set the font color to #FFFFFF (White). Click OK.

5. Select and duplicate the new style, adding **.footer a:visited** to the Selector field. You won't change any values, so click OK to close the Definition dialog box.

6. Select and duplicate the style again, naming this one **.footer a:hover**. Click OK. Then double-click the style in Edit mode of the CSS Styles panel to edit it. Change its font color to #000000 (Black).

7. Null footer links are set in the document. Save and preview in an IE browser to see the hover effects when you move your cursor over the links in the footer region.

8. Add another new style, again using the Use CSS Selectors option. Type **.navigation a:link** and click OK.

9. Set the color to #FFFFFF (White) and the text-decoration to None, Click OK.

10. Duplicate this style, typing **.navigation a:visited** in the Selectors field.

11. Duplicate again, typing **.navigation a:hover** in the Selectors field. Click OK. Now double-click the listed style in Edit mode to open it and change the text color to #000033 (Dark Blue). Click OK.

12. Save the page and test it in a browser.

The page now uses three sets of link styles, making it much easier to read links on the different backgrounds. Using contextual link styles also enables you to explore different decoration options without committing all your links to them.

CSS and Browser Issues/Solutions

Developing for the Netscape 4*x* browser is difficult at best; it isn't surprising that it is as difficult to deal with its quirky support for CSS. NN4*x* is, however, still a well-used browser, and as long as you are required to support it as a target browser, you need to know how to deal with its issues.

Create multiple style sheets when you simply cannot get your styles to work for both Netscape 4x and CSS-compliant browsers. Start by developing your initial style sheet using Netscape 4x supported styles. Don't worry about inconsistent margins and simple differences between platforms. When you have your styles completed, be sure to add comments to the style sheet to indicate each style's purpose.

Opening and commenting an external style sheet

Comments are notes that are written to explain or clarify the purpose of a block of code. They are hidden from the browser by special starting and ending symbols. An HTML comment is written as follows:

```
<!-- comment here -->
```

CSS comments use a different markup:

```
/* this is a comment */
```

Adding comments makes it easier for you (and those who come after you) to understand why certain methods or settings were used. When you plan to use multiple style sheets, add comments to clarify which styles use different settings or to indicate which styles are present in only one style sheet. To open an existing style sheet to add comments, locate the file in the Site panel (window) and double-click it. A .css file opens in Dreamweaver in Code view. To try this, open the style sheet used in the previous exercise, and follow these steps:

1. Navigate to the linkstyles folder and double-click linkstyles.css to open it.

2. Place your cursor in front of the body listing.

3. Add (a forward slash plus an asterisk) to form /*.

4. Type **These are the styles used in both style sheets**.

5. Type to form */ to close the comment.

6. Save the page.

Duplicating the style sheet

The easiest method to create a copy of the style sheet is to use Save As from the first style sheet. Don't forget that style sheets use the .css extension. To duplicate a style sheet, follow these steps:

1. With linkstyles.css (from the linkstyles defined site) open and saved, choose File ➪ Save As, Navigate to the linkstyles folder you copied to your hard drive, and save the second style sheet as **w3c_linkstyles.css**.

2. Close the open style sheet.

Attaching an external style sheet

When you have an existing style sheet and want to use it in another page of the site, you need to attach it to the new page. To attach a style sheet, open the page, and click the Attach Style Sheet button at the bottom of the CSS Styles panel. The same option is also available from the panel's Options menu.

In the dialog box that opens, navigate to select the desired style sheet. Figure 36-10 shows the two options — Link and Import — available for attaching a style sheet. Use Link unless you specifically want to exclude the Netscape 4x browser. Import uses the @Import directive — a method not understood by NN4I.

Figure 36-10: Attachment options in the Link External Style Sheet dialog box

Using @import with multiple style sheets

Use multiple style sheets when settings for a style's properties will not work in both NN4*x* and CSS-compliant browsers. You can use scripting to detect which browser is used and dynamically set the style sheet to use, which is not a simple process. Instead, use the @import directive to prevent NN4x browsers from reading alternate settings for your styles. Only the CSS-compliant browsers read and use the new (and last declared) settings.

To use two different browser-specific style sheets in the same document, import the second style sheet (this assumes you made one in an earlier exercise), as shown in this exercise:

1. With more_link_styles.htm open, go to Edit mode of the CSS panel, and click the listing of styles for the document. This ensures that any importing occurs in the HTML document and not in another style sheet.

2. Click the Attach Style Sheet button at the bottom of the CSS Styles panel and locate the second style sheet, and choose the Import option. Click OK. Save your HTML page.

3. Choose View ➪ Head Content. Figure 36-11 shows the style icon for embedded styles. Change to Split view and click the embedded styles icon to highlight these styles.

Figure 36-11: The Style icon pressed

Dreamweaver places the @import between style tags. If you have existing embedded styles defined, it adds @import at the beginning of the existing styles, which may cause problems in the way the browser determines specificity and cascade. To prevent this, place your cursor below the existing style tags and press Ctrl+T (Command+T) to access the Quick Tag editor. Type **style** and press the Enter key to exit the editor. Dreamweaver balances the tags by adding the ending </style> tag. Select the @import code and drag it to its new location between the new style tags.

You can see the newly imported style sheet listed in the CSS Styles panel when in Edit mode.

Using alternate style properties and settings

Trying to adjust style properties to work in all your target browsers is a tough job. Because Netscape 4x doesn't follow the W3C specification, settings that work in NN4x mess up the page in compliant browsers. For example, if you want to reduce the gap between headings and paragraphs, you have to use two style sheets.

To follow along continue using the more_link_styles.htm page used in the previous exercises. To resolve this issue, follow these steps:

1. Select the imported style sheet in Edit mode of the CSS Styles panel. Use the panel options or the icons to temporarily remove the attached style sheet.

2. Double-click the `<p>` tag style to edit it. Click the Box category and add a zero to the top margin field. Because Same for All may be checked, all margins use this zero value. Click OK.

3. Now edit `.maincontent p`. Its box margins use left, right, and bottom margins. Remove all the settings except the bottom margin, which is set to 10px.

4. Preview the page in a compliant browser. As shown in Figure 36-12, you should see space between the two adjacent paragraphs, but no extra space between the heading and the paragraph below it. The `.maincontent` h4 style has its top and bottom margins set to zero. Zero space occurs between the heading and paragraph. Ten pixels of space occur between the paragraphs.

5. Now preview the same page in Netscape 4x. Figure 36-13 shows how Netscape 4x renders lots of space below the heading but *none* between the two adjacent paragraphs.

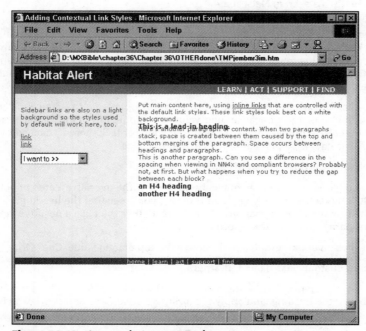

Figure 36-12: As seen in Internet Explorer 6

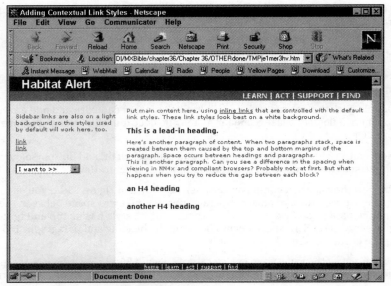

Figure 36-13: As seen in Netscape 4.4

The W3C specification says that vertical adjacent margins for block elements should "collapse" in favor of the largest value. Netscape is inconsistent (at best) in how it follows this rule. What you see in Dreamweaver is *definitely* not what you get. The `.maincontent` h4 style already has its top and bottom margins set to zero, so what else can you do? You might try a negative value for the paragraph as shown in these steps:

1. Double-click the .maincontent p style, and set the top margin to –.8em. Ems are especially useful for margins because their value is computed from the font size, so adjusting the font size automatically adjusts the spacing (or lack thereof) caused by the em value. .8ems equals 80 percent of the current font size.

2. Click OK and test this page in NN4*x*.

The heading and paragraph are spaced nicely, but look at the overlap created in between the paragraphs. If you preview in the compliant browser, you'll see that the heading and paragraph have the problem, but the paragraphs are fine. Rather than use a negative value that affects all your paragraphs, try this approach:

1. Double-click .mainparagraph p and remove the top margin value. Click OK.

2. Add a new custom class named **.firstpara**.

3. Add a –.8em margin and close the dialog box. Right-click (Control-click) the first paragraph below the heading, and apply the .firstpara style. Save and preview in NN4*x*.

4. Now that you've isolated the negative margin to the first paragraph, edit the <p> style. Uncheck the Same for All option, and add 1em to the top margin. Click OK.

   Looks great, doesn't it? Or better, at least. But what happens in the compliant browsers? Take a look. These browsers do exactly as asked and the result is a nasty overlap between the heading and first paragraph. Now you're ready to use a second style sheet.

5. Because you altered the first style sheet so much, duplicate the `.linkstyles.css` sheet again, overwriting the `w3c_linkstyles.css` sheet.

6. Attach the new version of the w3c_linkstyle sheet.

7. Locate the `.firstpara` style in the w3c style sheet and double-click to edit. Set the top margin to zero. The rest of the margin fields should be empty. Click OK and save the page. Test in both browsers.

The results should be fairly consistent between all browsers. What you've done is to create a conflict between the values used by the `.firstpara` style. The compliant browsers, which can read the imported style sheet, use zero instead of the negative −.8 em. Netscape 4*x* reads the negative value only.

To finish this section, delete any style in the second style sheet that isn't different from the first. Most browsers read both style sheets, and many style values from the first style sheet are the same in the second. This step can speed up the processing the user's computer must perform.

Summary

This chapter covered using Cascading Style Sheets to control the appearance of Web pages. You learned to use embedded and external styles to set properties and values for HTML tags, classes, links, and contextual classes. You encountered browser issues and learned solutions to overcome them; through the use of the `@import` directive, you learned how to use multiple style sheets to build more consistent styles.

Project Summary

Let's look at what you did that will be used in the Habitat Alert site.

Files Prepared for the Habitat Alert Web Site

Files	What Was Done	Where to Now?
site/index.htm	You added an external style sheet to the site and developed styles to add background images, control the appearance of the page's text. You also added default and contextual link styles to set different properties for links in specific areas.	This page will be made into a template.

✦　　✦　　✦

Working with Libraries and Templates

When developing or maintaining a Web site, it makes sense to work as efficiently and effortlessly as possible. In Dreamweaver, library items and Dreamweaver templates can lock down, modify, and update specific elements or entire pages in your site.

In this chapter, you see how to use library items to build page elements that are easily updated, allowing Dreamweaver to do all the grunt work of maintaining accurate paths to images and files. Build a library item by selecting page elements and clicking New Library Item. Drag library items from the Assets panel to your pages. When you need to modify an item, open, edit, and update. Dreamweaver does the rest of the work.

You also learn how to work with Dreamweaver templates to add more pages to a site, while maintaining a consistent, yet editable layout. Templates are like library items at the page level; you can use them to lock or modify multiple elements. New template features in Dreamweaver MX include editable Head regions, optional editable areas, editing of tag attributes, and even nested templates.

Using Library Items

Library items are useful whenever you have page elements that appear in many pages. It can be time-consuming task to locate, open, and edit every page with a specific element when changes are required; making a library item of the element(s) enables you to open a single, original source, make your edits, save, and update every occurrence of the item in all site pages. Any path structures, such as src paths to images or relative links to pages, are maintained and adjusted by Dreamweaver.

Library items are assets and as such are accessed via the Assets panel. Press F11 to open the Assets panel, which is found in the Site panel group. To view library assets, click the small book icon located in the stack of icons on the left side of the panel (Figure 37-1). Like all assets, library item functions can be triggered with the contextual icons found along the bottom of the Assets panel or through the panel's Options menu.

Figure 37-1: Library assets live in the Assets panel

How library items work

A library item is stored code. To build a library item, you first make a selection in a page. The code selected is copied to a new text file. The selection may contain any kind of code that exists in the *body* of a Web page, including graphics, text, and form objects. You are required to name each library item.

When you add a library item to a site, Dreamweaver creates a special folder named Library at the root level; Dreamweaver also creates a text file to hold the item code and stores it, using your chosen name, within the Library folder. Library item files use a .lbi extension. Special markup containing the name and path to the item file is placed around the library item code in the HTML page. The markup allows Dreamweaver to identify and update all instances of a specific library item in the site when changes are made to the original .lbi file. To push the changes to the published site, all updated pages must be uploaded to the Web server. However, all code for an item is contained in each page where the item is added; the Library folder need not be present on the server for the item to function. The code that Dreamweaver adds looks like this:

```
<!-- #BeginLibraryItem "/Library/bottom ads.lbi" --> elements here<!--
#EndLibraryItem -->
```

Library items are locked. Clicking to select an element within a library item selects the entire item, which is marked in the Tag selector as `<mm:libitem>`. To edit a library item, access the original .lbi file, make changes, and save. Dreamweaver asks whether you want to update any instances of the item. You are not required to update items. Options for updating later are available. If you choose to update, Dreamweaver looks through every page in the site to find markup for that item. The code between the items is replaced with the new code in the original file and Dreamweaver again adjusts and maintains proper paths. Any updated page that is not open is automatically saved. Open documents are modified but not saved; if you close an updated page, you will be asked to save it.

Building a new library item

To add a library item to the Assets panel, make a selection in your page in Design or Code view. The following exercise adds a library item to the basic page layout of the Habitat Alert site:

On the CD-ROM Save the Habitat Alert37 folder from the chapter37_exercise folder to your hard drive. Define a new site. Be sure you define it at the html level not in the site folder.

Using a library item for the bottom ad banners makes sense because many pages show the same ads. To change the ads, you need to change them only in the library item `.lbi` file and update the entire site. To make a library item, follow these steps:

1. Open `site/index.htm`.

2. This page contains three ad banners along the bottom of the page, as shown in Figure 37-2. Place your cursor in front of the text "Please support our sponsors:" and make a selection by clicking to the right of the last ad placeholder while pressing Shift.

Tip When you make your selection for the library item, be sure to include any HTML tags that provide alignment for the element such as `<p>`, `<div>`, and so on using Code view. In this example the beginning `<h4>` tag and the ending `</p>` weren't selected automatically.

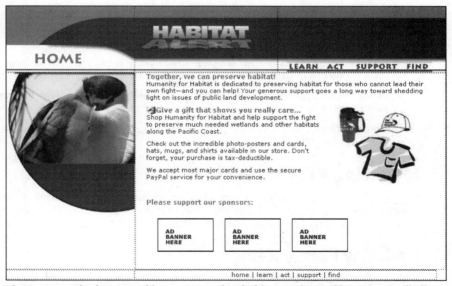

Figure 37-2: The bottom ad banners are placeholders. Making a library item will allow easy updating of the element when the site is completed.

3. Press F11 to activate the Assets panel and click the book icon to open the Library Assets panel. Click the Add button at the bottom of the panel.

Note

When saving a Library Item that uses a class style, Dreamweaver alerts you that the Item might not appear as designed when used. This is true if the destination page doesn't have the class defined as a style rule; in the example used in this chapter, the destination pages will be linked to the style sheet.

4. Always name your new library item before doing anything else. Name this item **bottom ads**. It is permissible to use spaces in item names.

The home page now contains an instance of the library item. If you try to select any part of the element, it is all selected. The Property inspector displays options for editing the items, as shown in Figure 37-3. You can also detach the item, which removes its link to the library item or Recreate which re-creates a missing or deleted library item.

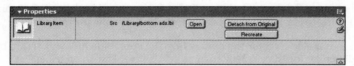

Figure 37-3: The Property inspector also provides access to the original item.

Adding an existing library item

You can use the following methods to add an existing library item to your pages:

✦ Insert your cursor in your HTML page where you want the item to be located and right-click (Control+click) on the desired item in the Assets panel, then select Insert.

✦ Insert your cursor into your HTML page, and select the library item. Press the Insert button at the bottom of the Assets panel to add the item.

✦ Drag the library item's icon from the Assets panel and drop it in your HTML page where you want the item added.

Modifying a library item

Making changes are what library items are all about. Simply open the original .lbi file (double-click its name in the Library panel) and make your changes; when you save, Dreamweaver prompts you to update pages that use the item.

Updating library items

When prompted to update all pages that use a modified library item, Dreamweaver looks through the entire site to find markup that matches the specific item. The page code is replaced with the new code from the .lbi file. You are not required to update pages that use an item; you can opt to delay an update by choosing Don't Update. When you are ready to update the pages, choose Update Site from the Library Assets panel options. The Update Site dialog box offers a couple of options.

Choose to look in the Entire Site if you have open documents that may contain library items. Changes made to all library items will be updated throughout the site. To initiate the update, click the Start button.

When updating you can choose the Files that Use (the item) option. This choice looks only for pages that use a specific library item — the one shown in the menu to the left of the Start button. This option doesn't update any currently opened, unsaved pages that use the item.

You may also choose to Update Current Page from the Library Assets panel options. No matter which method you choose, a useful log of all actions taken is displayed to tell you how many pages were examined, updated, or not updated.

Detaching a library item

The ability to push modifications is not the only useful function for library items. Dreamweaver manages the path structure of any link that occurs in a library item — and sometimes this alone is what makes the library item useful. At times you will want to be able to edit a portion of a library item. Because a library item is locked, you cannot individualize an instance of the item in one or more pages. To unlock the code of an item, select it and use the Detach button to remove the library markup. This leaves only the code of the item in the page, and you lose the option to update from the original library item.

Working with Dreamweaver Templates

When two or more pages in a site use a common layout, it makes sense to create a master document — or template — that contains the shared elements to use as the basis of pages you build for a site. Dreamweaver templates take this concept much further with features for managing path structures, and updating pages, plus a whole range of options for designating both locked and editable elements in pages based on the template.

How templates work

Dreamweaver builds a special folder to hold template assets, as it does with library items. Templates are saved as .dwt files into a Templates folder that the program adds at the root level of the site. Special markup in HTML pages based on a Dreamweaver template allows the program to locate and update parts of pages when modifications are made in the template file.

Dreamweaver templates are like library items on a page level. But, whereas a library item is completely locked down, a template contains both locked and editable regions. Locked template regions can't be edited in pages based on the template — only specially designated editable regions may be individualized on a page-to-page basis. Optional and repeating areas may also be specified, if needed, to accommodate data-driven, dynamic pages based on a template.

Locked and editable regions affect only the pages that are based on the template; everything in a template file is editable. However, only changes made in locked regions of the template are updated in the related pages. This makes perfect sense when you think about it: Editable regions are not updated by the template because each page's editable regions probably contain page-specific content. Like library items, the code for pages based on a template is contained solely in the HTML page; the original template and Templates folder are not required on the web server. When you update pages based on a template, all modified pages must be saved and uploaded to the Web server for your published site to reflect changes you made.

Building a template from scratch

To begin a template from scratch, click the New Template button at the bottom of the Template Assets panel, which you can get to by clicking the page icon above the Library Assets book icon. You can also choose New Template from the Template Assets panel options.

Like library items, the first thing to do when you start a template is to name it. When the .dwt file opens, you can work within it as you would any HTML page, adding representative content and using any structure desired. As you build the page, keep in mind that you will be selecting areas, called regions, that will be editable. Conversely, some regions will be locked. Ultimately, it is far easier to choose these regions when your page is designed modularly.

See Chapter 34 for more information about building modular layouts.

Building a template from an existing page

You may also create a template from an existing HTML document. To do this, open your document and choose File ➪ Save As Template in the dialog box that opens, and give the template a name.

With both methods, a templates folder is created at the root level of the site and the name of the template is used to name the .dwt file saved there.

Save the Habitat Alert37 folder from the chapter37_exercise folder to your hard drive. Define a new site. Hint: If you already have another Habitat Alert site defined, then choose the Edit Site option in the Site panel of the Site Definition drop-down menu and change the path to the Local Root folder. Just be sure that it's defined at the html level not the site level.

Most of the pages in the Habitat Alert site share the common interface found in the home page. The following steps show you how to build a template from it. As usual, be sure you have the site defined and are using the files from Chapter 37 before doing the exercise.

1. Open the site/index.htm home page.

2. Choose File ➪ Save As Template and name the Template **Basic Page** (see Figure 37-4). The site name will vary depending on how you have named your defined site.

3. Click OK to save the template.

The original page closes when the page is saved as a template. Be sure that you have saved the original page before this step, or changes made to the page will be lost.

Figure 37-4: The Save As Template dialog box

Defining Template Regions

Templates require editable regions — areas that may be modified in pages based on the template. This makes sense because your content will vary from page to page, even if the interface remains the same. By default, all portions of the template are locked; to add an editable region to your template, choose a containing element (table, cell, multiple cells) or make a selection; then choose Insert ⇨ Template Objects ⇨ Editable Region or press Control+Alt+V (Command+Option+V). You can also work with the Templates toolset in the Insert bar and create the new region by clicking the small button with the Pencil tool, as shown in Figure 37-5.

Figure 37-5: The Templates toolset in the Insert bar contains all the functions found in the Template Objects of the Insert menu.

There are four types of regions in templates:

✦ **Editable** — This is an unlocked area in the template and pages based on a template. All templates should contain at least one editable region to be useful. Changes made to the editable region in the template will not result in updates to these regions in pages based on the template. However, they affect any subsequent pages created from the template.

✦ **Repeating** — This is a portion of the page that is set to repeat to accommodate additional content, as needed. For example, many data-driven pages have content that varies based on the current state of a data source (database) where the content is added server-side. A repeating region isn't editable in the document unless you specifically add editable regions within the repeating region.

✦ **Optional** — An optional region is just that — optional. This is a portion of the page, such as a sidebar area, an image, or even a navigational element that is used on some pages but not others. Optional regions are controlled by conditional statements and may be set so that the region is editable or not.

✦ **Editable tag attributes** — Setting editable tag attributes allows certain properties of tags, such as alignment, background color, width, and so forth, to be editable even though the tag or element itself can't be removed. An example of this would be a table cell that contains an image. The cell itself can be locked (along with the image inside), but giving the cell editable attributes allows the properties of the cell to change in pages based on the template.

Adding an editable region

A successful template depends on careful and logical selection of editable regions. To add an editable region, select an HTML tag or make a selection in your content. Using a *container selector* allows additional selectors to be added in the container. Using *content selections* limits editing of the region to the replacement of the current content. For example, if you choose a table cell as the editable region, you can add additional HTML tags within the structure of the table; choosing the text within the cell allows only that text to be replaced.

On the CD-ROM Save the Habitat Alert37 folder from the chapter37_exercise folder to your hard drive. Define a new site.

In this section you, define regions in the Habitat Alert Basic Page template. You should still have the `Basic Page.dwt` template open; if you don't, open the template from Template Assets by double-clicking it, or locate and double-click the file in the Templates folder through the Site panel.

Because the page still needs scripting, much of it will be left locked so that later update of pages based on the Template is possible.

1. Place your cursor into the main content area. This area changes in every page, so it should be an editable region.

2. Select the `<td.maincontent>` tag for this area using the Tag selector. Activate the Templates toolset in Insert bar, and click the Editable Region button.

3. Name the new region **Main Content** and click OK, as shown in Figure 37-6.

4. Click the cell with the ad banners. This cell contains a library item. Regions containing library items should not be locked. Make this cell an editable region, too. Name the region **Bottom Ad**. Save but don't close the file yet, this exercise continues in the next section.

Setting editable tag attributes

Another awesome new feature of Dreamweaver templates is the option to set only the tag attributes for an element to be editable. For example, you may require that an image of a specific width and height be present in a set location but allow for different images to be used.

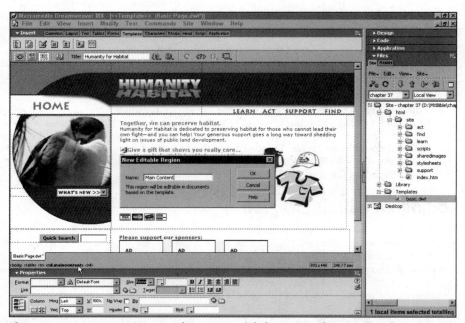

Figure 37-6: You may use spaces but not special characters when naming the new editable region.

The following steps set up some editable tag attributes for the image that displays the current section. In the Habitat Alert template, this image currently reads HOME.

1. Select the `location_home.gif` image. Choose Modify ➪ Templates ➪ Make Attribute Editable.

2. In the Editable Tag Attributes dialog box, choose SRC from the Attribute menu and enable the Make Attribute Editable option, as shown in Figure 37-7.

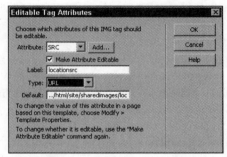

Figure 37-7: The Editable Tag Attribute dialog box

3. Label the attribute **locationsrc**. From the Type menu, choose URL. Click OK. The HOME image now shows as a broken image.

Attributes that are present in the current tag will be displayed in the Attribute menu; to add a new attribute, use the Add button and type any needed attribute. One amazing option would be to add a usemap# attribute so that you can use different image maps. To access the Attribute menu select Modify ➪ Templates ➪ Make Attribute Editable. To determine the attributes of any tag use the Tag inspector in the Code panel group. When you select a tag, its attributes display at the bottom of the panel.

Dreamweaver replaces the file source (SRC) for this image with @@(locationsrc)@@ to mark it as an editable attribute of an otherwise locked region. To modify an attribute in a page based on the template, use Modify ➪ Template Properties.

To remove an editable tag attribute from a template, reapply the attribute (Modify ➪ Templates ➪ Make Attribute Editable) and uncheck the Make Attribute Editable option. However, the code placed in the head of the page above the `<body>` tag is not removed; you must remove it by hand from Code view.

Adding an optional region

Optional regions allow the template developer to include elements (with or without scripting) in the template that might be needed in pages based on the template.

The circle area of the layout will be scripted as a slideshow that displays in many of the site's main pages, but not in all. DHTML scripting will be added later, so it makes sense to include it in the template so that you can update it in all pages later. But not all pages need the slideshow, so making this an optional region is the perfect solution. Follow these steps:

1. Select the heron image in the circle area (sidebar) and choose Insert ➪ Template Objects ➪ Optional Region or use the Optional Region button found in the Templates toolset of the Insert bar.

2. Name this new optional region **Sidebar Image.** Leave the Show by Default option checked.

   In Code view, special markup, as follows, is placed around the optional region:

   ```
   <!-- TemplateBeginIf cond="sidebarImage" --><!--
   TemplateBeginEditable name="EditRegion5" --><!-- TemplateEndEditable
   --><!-- TemplateEndIf -->
   ```

   In the head of the document this code is inserted:

   ```
   <!-- TemplateParam name="Sidebar Image" type="boolean" value="true" -
   ->
   ```

Editing to show or hide an optional region is done from Code view in a document based on the basic Template.

Adding editable optional regions

When an optional region is disabled or hidden in documents based on a template, other elements can replace it. The content may vary, so an editable region is needed. It's useful to develop potential content in the template so that any scripts needed are included in all pages based on the template. Setting an editable optional region is the best solution.

Tip

You can define an optional region and later insert an editable region between the optional region markup.

So you can use different jump menus (menu lists with an arrow to select options) as needed in pages built from the template, the following steps show you how to add an editable optional region to the circle area above the What's New jump menu:

1. Select the What's New jump menu in Design view and use the Tag selector to select the `<form>` tag. Press left arrow to move the cursor in front of the form code.

2. Choose Insert ➪ Template Objects ➪ Editable Optional Region. In the dialog box that opens, name the new region **Other Jump Menus.** Uncheck the Show by Default option. Click OK. The following code is placed into the page where the cursor is located:

   ```
   <!-- TemplateBeginIf cond="_document['Other Jump Menus']" --><!--
   TemplateBeginEditable name="EditRegion5" --><!-- TemplateEndEditable
   --><!-- TemplateEndIf -->
   ```

   In the head of the page just above the `<body>` tag, an additional reference to the optional area is added:

   ```
   <!-- TemplateParam name="Other Jump Menus" type="boolean"
   value="false" -->
   ```

3. To finalize this area, select the form for the What's New jump menu and make it an optional region named **Whats New.** Leave it showing by default. Figure 37-8 shows the labeled regions.

4. Save the template and close it.

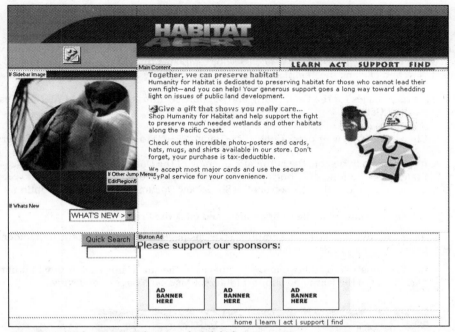

Figure 37-8: The regions showing their labels

Building Template-based Pages

With a template, you can easily add new pages to the site. Because key areas are left as locked regions, you can always go back to the template and add elements to push to all the pages. There are several ways to build new site pages from an existing template.

New From Template

To add a page based on your template, select the template in the Template Assets panel and right-click (Control+click) to choose New From Template. (You can also use the panel Options menu.)

To add the main page for the Act section of the site using the New From Template method, follow these steps:

1. Select the Basic Page template in the Template Assets panel (Template category).

2. Right-click (Control+click) and choose New From Template.

3. When the new page appears, it is important to *save* the document before you make changes to it. Save this document as **index.htm** in the act folder of your defined site. Close the page. You edit it later.

Document Gallery templates

When you create a template, it is added to the templates accessible from the Document Gallery. The Document Gallery is an assortment of different page types and layouts that you can use to build site pages. You can access your templates from the Gallery by choosing File ⇨ New and clicking the Templates tab, as shown in Figure 37-9.

Tip

Build the main pages for the Find, Learn, and Support sections of the Habitat Alert site using the Document Gallery:

1. Choose File ⇨ New or press Control+N (Command+N) to open the Document Gallery.

   It is possible to disable the automatic opening of the Document Gallery. Click the Preferences button at the bottom of the Template tab to access the application preferences and remove the check from the Show New Document on Control+N option.

2. Select the template in the right column, and click the Create button.

3. As usual, save the file before editing. Save this page as **index.htm** in the find folder. Close the page. You edit it later.

4. Repeat Steps 1–3 to add two more new pages to the site. Name each **index.htm** but place them in the learn and support folders. Close each page after saving.

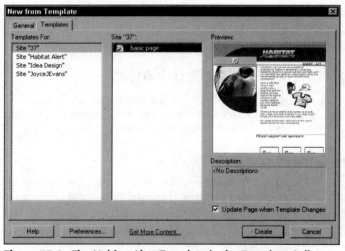

Figure 37-9: The Habitat Alert Template in the Template Gallery

Editing Pages Based on a Template

Editing pages that are template-based is straightforward. You will not be able to edit locked regions, and a red, circle-slash lets you know it. You can modify editable, as set up by the selectors you chose when you added the region in the template. Optional regions are controlled from Code view.

Follow these steps to edit the four new pages based on the Habitat Alert template.

1. In the Site panel, select each of the index pages in the act, find, learn, and support folders.

   Tip

   Shift+clicking non-contiguous files results in selecting unwanted files. Use Ctrl+click (Command+click) instead.

2. Right-click (Control+click) and choose Open or choose File ➪ Open. All four documents open.

   The way the documents are arranged depends on your workspace preferences. All open documents will be listed and are accessible in the Window menu. Because all the documents are named index.htm, it might seem hard to tell which page you are editing; you can tell which document you are working on by looking at the path structure at the top of the document.

3. Choose the `act/index.htm` page. The most obvious edit needed is the location image. Choose Modify ➪ Template Properties.

4. In the Template Properties dialog box, select the locationsrc attribute. You must hand-edit the path to display the proper image. Change the existing path to: ../sharedimages/locations/location_act.gif (change home to act); then click OK.

5. Save and preview the page. The new image is displayed. Close the page.

6. Repeat the process (Steps 3–5) for each of the section pages. The paths are the same for each except that the ending matches the sections, as shown in the following table.

Section/Page	locationsrc path
act/index.htm	../sharedimages/locations/location_act.gif
find/index.htm	../sharedimages/locations/location_find.gif
learn/index.htm	../sharedimages/locations/location_learn.gif
support/index.htm	../sharedimages/locations/location_support.gif

7. In the find/index.htm page, choose Modify ⇨ Template Properties, and select Sidebar Image. Uncheck Show Sidebar Image. Select Other Jump Menus and check the Show Other Jump Menus box.

8. Click the What's New listing and uncheck its Show box. Click OK.

9. The circle area in your page has probably collapsed in Dreamweaver view. Preview in a browser and you'll see that all is well. It will look like Figure 37-10 somewhat. Don't worry, you'll fix that now. If it is totally collapsed, place your cursor into the Main Content area and select its `<td>` tag. Switch to Code view. Click the `<td>` tag again. Now look above this cell's code to the cell that used to display the circle Sidebar image, which is no longer there!

Note

The need to click twice is a bug in the program that will likely be fixed for future releases. Meanwhile, clicking twice is a good workaround.

10. Scroll in Code view and place your cursor between the editable region tags to `<!-- InstanceBeginEditable name="EditRegion5" -->place cursor here<!-- InstanceEndEditable -->`. Then return to Design view.

11. Use the Image Assets to add a spacer image, setting its width to 231px. Leave the height at 1px. Press Enter to update and save the page. Figure 37-11 shows the new, empty blue circle area. Save this page. In the next chapter, you edit it to add more form content.

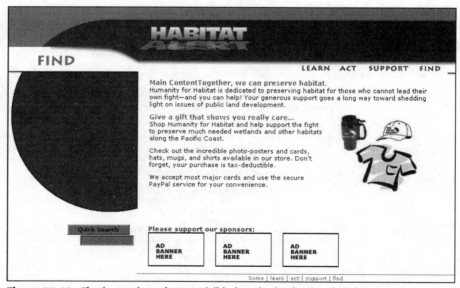

Figure 37-10: The image is no longer visible but the background of the circle is.

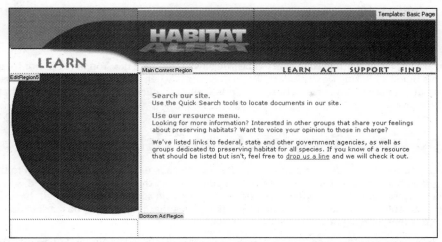

Figure 37-11: Look! No picture! The blue circle area is created by the background image for this cell.

Modifying the Template and Updating Pages

Using a template makes it possible to build all your pages without worrying about whether every element is complete. In fact, without having pages, it is extremely difficult to build navigation. Build your pages first, leaving incomplete areas locked; then revisit the template, add the navigation links, and update all your site pages.

All areas of your template are editable, but only the locked regions will be updated. To push changes to pages, save your template after modification. As with a library item, an Update Template Files dialog box opens to show all pages based on the template and to allow you to choose whether to update at this time; you may update later if desired.

Click Update to push the changes to the pages. A log that lists all activity displays the number of pages examined and updated. If changes to the template were only in editable regions, the log may indicate that no changes were made to the pages. In some cases, Dreamweaver may indicate that some pages could not be updated.

Follow these steps to link the main navigation buttons to the pages that have been built with the template:

1. Open the Basic Page template file either from the Template Assets panel (double-click) or from the Templates folder in the Site panel.

2. Select the LEARN navigation button. Use the Point to File icon in the Property inspector to link to the `learn/index.htm` page in the Site panel.

3. Repeat for the remaining buttons, each time selecting the appropriate index page in that button's folder.

4. Save the Template. When prompted to update, click the Update button.

You are not required to update every time you save a template file. You may opt not to update at this time by clicking Don't Update. To push changes when you are ready to update, use the Template panel's Options menu to select Update Site and click the Start button to begin the update process.

Applying a Template to an Existing Page

When you build a template from an existing page, the page used has no relationship to the template. Because you want this page to be updated when the template is modified, you must build a relationship between the page and the template. In some cases, you might have developed a template that must be applied to existing pages that may already be marked up with previous template regions. You have two options:

✦ You can create a page using any of the methods discussed earlier and overwrite the existing page. This may be your simplest option as long as you haven't spent a great deal of time adding specific content to the page after the template was created.

✦ You can apply the template to the page. In the open document, choose Modify ⇨ Templates ⇨ Apply Template to Page or use the Template Assets to select your template and right-click (Control+click) to choose Apply.

Dealing with Inconsistent Region Names

The difficulty of applying a template to a page lies in resolving inconsistent region names. The template contains region names; the page may not have any regions or may be based on earlier templates. In any case, inconsistencies exist, and Dreamweaver wants you to tell it what to do about them. Where should the current content go?

Figure 37-12 shows the dialog box that offers a means of placing the current content of the page within the structure of the regions created in the template. If the page is based on a different (perhaps earlier) template, Dreamweaver attempts to correlate the regions. Where it cannot, you have to select the content and choose a region from the Move Content to New Region menu.

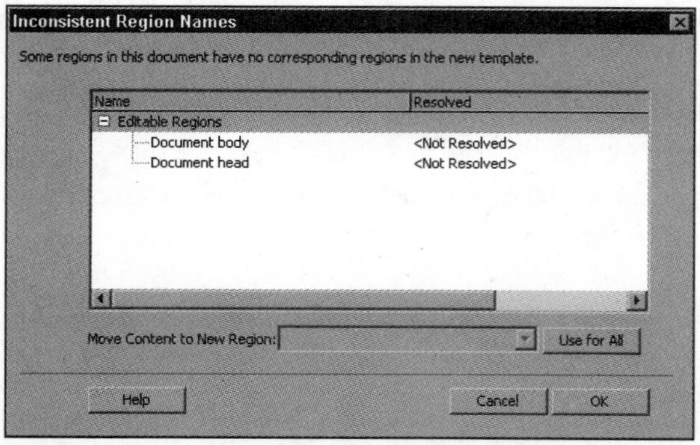

Figure 37-12: Resolving inconsistent regions

It is sometimes difficult to get this to work perfectly. It may be better to simply build a new template-based page and page in the proper content.

When the page is the document used to build the template and you opt to apply the template to the page, choose the first item listed, and choose Nowhere from the menu. Click the Use for All button to set the second item to use Nowhere (Figure 37-13), too. Save the page and you are good to go.

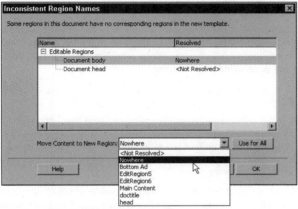

Figure 37-13: Selecting the Nowhere option

Use the easiest method to link the template to the homepage: Make a new page from the template and save as `index.htm` into the site folder. This overwrites the old version.

Converting Templates in Dreamweaver, by Brad Halstead and Murray R. Summers

So, you've purchased Macromedia Dreamweaver MX or Studio MX), installed it on your machine, and started to play with Dreamweaver MX templates. One of the first tasks on your mind is to enhance your Dreamweaver/UltraDev 4 (Dreamweaver 4) templates to incorporate some of the advanced new template features found in Dreamweaver MX. You may be thinking that Dreamweaver/UltraDev 4 template markup is different from Dreamweaver MX template markup. You may be wondering how those differences will impact you while you are modifying the template in Dreamweaver MX.

The official line says Dreamweaver MX can read and use Dreamweaver 4 template markup without issue. However, during testing, we found that Dreamweaver 4 template markup does not always play well with the improved Dreamweaver MX template engine. For example, Dreamweaver 4 doesn't enable you to position editable regions inside block-level elements of your page, such as <p>. Dreamweaver MX advises against this practice because you could end up with possible errors when using Dreamweaver MX to manage and modify your existing Dreamweaver 4 site. Your experience may differ depending on how your Dreamweaver 4 template markup wraps your HTML code. The only thing that we can say with certainty is that the new template engine in Dreamweaver MX is much stricter than its predecessor in Dreamweaver 4.

Note   Although Dreamweaver MX does enable you to place an editable region inside block-level elements (with a warning popping up), it is advisable to not do this for one very good reason. It may be that the person entering content into the editable region presses the Return key, thereby creating another block-level element. If that happens, Dreamweaver MX will complain.

For maximum performance and minimum difficulty with Dreamweaver MX, we recommend that you convert the document from Dreamweaver 4 template markup to Dreamweaver MX template markup, update your pages, upload the changes to the server, and enjoy Dreamweaver MX templates.

This tutorial details the manual conversion of Dreamweaver 4 templates to the new Dreamweaver MX template format. There is no automated tool currently available to do the job for you. We've listed the do's, the don'ts, and the process to follow in its entirety providing working source files, code listings, and screenshots for you to be able to follow along.

The code differences

As is the case with many development software packages, the code generated and recognized is typically different from version to version, and although backwards compatibility is almost always a concern for the software vendor, it typically is the case that the older version's code is recognized and used by the newer version of the software. However, the newer generation code is not backwards compatible with the older version of the software.

Dreamweaver MX is no different in this regard. It attempts optimal recognition of Dreamweaver 4 template markup but is not always 100 percent successful. Conversely, the code that Dreamweaver MX generates for template markup is not recognized at all by Dreamweaver 4 (including UltraDev 4 and previous versions). Dreamweaver MX introduces a whole new syntax and methodology for template markup and the template engine (the template markup interpreter) is much more advanced and strict with respect to the markup on the page.

As you may already know, Dreamweaver 4 allowed two template markup types: editable and noneditable regions. DMX allows the aforementioned regions as well as a host of new region types (Optional regions, MultipleIf Conditional regions, Repeating regions, Repeating Table regions, and Editable Tag attributes). It offers additional template markup (Parameters, Expressions) that enables some dynamic manipulation of these regions. Dreamweaver MX also introduces a much stricter and more robust template engine (template markup interpreter) as well as the power to create Nested Templates and it gives you the ability to lock dynamic server code that you position above/below the opening/closing <html>, </html> tag, respectively.

This tutorial deals with the differences between the common template markup of Dreamweaver 4 and Dreamweaver MX, specifically the base template markup as well as Editable region markup.

The following code shows the markup for a base Dreamweaver 4 generated template. This code is recognized and usable by Dreamweaver MX.

```
<html>
<head>
<!-- #BeginEditable "doctitle" -->
<title>Untitled Document</title>
<!-- #EndEditable -->
<meta http-equiv="Content-Type" content="text/html; charset=iso-
8859-1">
</head>
<body bgcolor="#FFFFFF" text="#000000">
```

```
</body>
</html>
Markup (Opening): <!-- #BeginEditable "doctitle" -->
Markup (Closing): <!-- #EndEditable -->
```

The following code shows the markup for a base Dreamweaver MX generated template. Dreamweaver 4 doesn't recognize any of the editable regions and considers them standard HTML comments.

```
<!DOCTYPE HTML PUBLIC "-//W3C//DTD HTML 4.01 Transitional//EN">
<html>
<head>
<!-- TemplateBeginEditable name="doctitle" -->
<title>Untitled Document</title>
<!-- TemplateEndEditable -->
<meta http-equiv="Content-Type" content="text/html; charset=iso-
8859-1">
<!-- TemplateBeginEditable name="head" -->
<!-- TemplateEndEditable -->
</head>
<body>
</body>
</html>
```

```
  Markup (Opening): <!-- TemplateBeginEditable name="doctitle" -->
  Markup (Closing): <!-- TemplateEndEditable -->
```

You might ask, "What's the differences between these two listings?"

You've already seen the opening and closing markup as related to each version of Dreamweaver, as shown in the first listing and and the second one.

For ease of explanation, look at the region ending code (Editable region closing tag).

✦ Dreamweaver 4 version: `<!-- #EndEditable -->`

✦ Dreamweaver MX version: `<!-- TemplateEndEditable -->`

The difference here is the syntax of the template markup (proprietary HTML comment). Simply stated, the # in the Dreamweaver 4 markup has been replaced with the word `Template` in the Dreamweaver MX markup (this replacement is more than cosmetic, as it enables you to easily determine whether the code is in a template or a child page).

The differences between the region opening code (Editable region opening tag) are more robust!

✦ Dreamweaver 4 version: `<!-- #BeginEditable "doctitle" -->`

✦ Dreamweaver MX version: `<!-- TemplateBeginEditable name="doctitle" -->`

As with the ending code (shown previously), the # has been replaced by `Template`. In addition, Dreamweaver MX gives the region a labeled and valued attribute (`name="regionname"`); whereas Dreamweaver 4 only uses the defined attribute value (`"regionname"`).

Unlike Dreamweaver 4, Dreamweaver MX automatically inserts a region named `head` on saving a page as a template. This region is useful, because when you have custom scripts in a child page, they are automatically added to the child page's `head` region and aren't updated when you update the template. Along with scripts, custom CSS and meta tags can be added to give each child page some unique quality. If you wanted this region in Dreamweaver 4, you had to add it manually.

Caution

After you modify a Dreamweaver 4 template by adding any new Dreamweaver MX region type, the template no longer functions properly in Dreamweaver 4. You can, however, freely insert Dreamweaver MX standard editable regions and the template will continue to function as expected in Dreamweaver 4 as long as you do not perform this conversion process. With this in mind, ensure that you and your coworkers are absolutely finished with this site in Dreamweaver 4 prior to performing the template conversion.

The conversion process

Now that you know what the differences in template markup are, it's time to start the conversion process from a Dreamweaver 4 template to a Dreamweaver MX template. The information from the "The code differences" section appears here in table format (see the following table) for easy reference. What you need to do is convert all the editable region's start and end code to the new format. You also want to add the default editable region named head into the Dreamweaver 4 template document during the conversion process.

Template Code Differences

Markup Type	DW4	DMX
Editable region start code	`#BeginEditable`	`TemplateBeginEditable name=`
Editable region end code	`#EndEditable`	`TemplateEndEditable`
New editable region		`<!-- TemplateBeginEditable name="head" -->`
		`<!-- TemplateEndEditable -->`

To make it easier on you, we have made three Dreamweaver MX find-and-replace (F/R) query files that you can find in the `chapter37_exercise` folder. This archive is named `ConvertQueries.zip` and contains three files (which, when extracted retaining folder information, will be housed in a folder named Queries). These files are associated with the three operations you need to perform (see the following table). Don't worry about how to reference them; that will be covered in the exercise 1.4. All you have to remember is where you have saved these three files on your hard drive (`C:\` so the extracted location would convert to C:\Queries).

F/R Queries

Script	Function
`ERStart.dwr`	Converts ALL Dreamweaver 4 editable region start code to Dreamweaver MX start code
`EREnd.dwr`	Converts ALL Dreamweaver 4 editable region end code to Dreamweaver MX end code
`ERHead.dwr`	Adds the head editable region into the template document, but doesn't check whether it already exists on the page

Caution

These queries must be run on only Dreamweaver 4 template files from within the Dreamweaver MX find and replace interface. Running them on child pages, Dreamweaver MX generated templates, or from within the Dreamweaver 4 find and replace interface may produce undesirable results.

Setting up the site

To begin, download the sample files and create a DMX site definition. Start by downloading the sample files from the `chapter37_exercise` folder. This archive is named `ConvertSource` and contains the sample site source files.

Exercise 1.1: Setting up your site definition

Before you can do anything to the Dreamweaver 4 generated template and site, you have to define the site in Dreamweaver MX. (This applies only if this was a site that did not exist any longer in Dreamweaver 4 or if when you installed Dreamweaver MX it did not pick up the site definitions from Dreamweaver 4 properly.)

1. Start Dreamweaver MX.

2. Select Site ⇨ New Site... in the dialog box that opens, select the Advanced tab.

3. Select Local Info Category, and in the textbox beside Site Name type **Convert Source**, in the textbox beside *Local Root Folder:* Click the Browse button to locate the folder `ConvertSource`. Your site definition should look similar to the following figure.

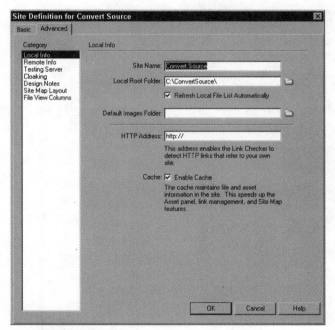

Completed Local Info category

4. Select Testing Server in the Category pane. Make sure to select None from the choices presented in the Server Model drop-down list, as shown in the following figure.

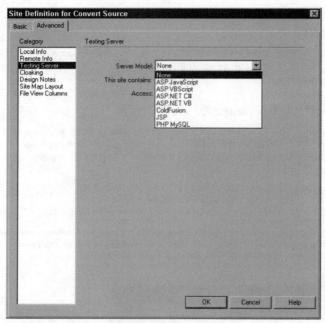

Completed Testing Server Category

5. Click OK to close the dialog box, create the site, and open the site in the Site panel.

6. If the site is collapsed, expand the site so that you see all folders expanded as shown in the following figure.

Expanded Site tab

7. Leave Dreamweaver MX open for the next exercise.

That's all there is to setting up the site definition. No additional items need to be configured for this demonstration. However, before you can actually complete the conversion, you must tackle a couple more preliminary steps.

Backing up

Before you start changing any code, you should perform a preventative maintenance backup. (This step could save your bacon and should be part of your normal routine prior to modifying any site.) You should perform two kinds of backups: first, make a duplicate copy of your site file and folder structure somewhere on your hard drive outside of the currently defined site structure; second, make a duplicate copy of your template file.

"What I do for my site backup is use my file manager software (Windows Explorer), navigate to my site root folder, select the folder, and make a zip of the entire tree (saving folder structure) using WinZip." – Brad Halstead

You may opt to perform your backup differently.

Perform the steps outlined in the Exercise 1.2 to make a pseudo-backup of the template file prior to any conversion processes.

Exercise 1.2: Backing up the template file

Performing these steps ensures that your template file is backed up in the same defined site so that it can be restored with ease:

1. Start Dreamweaver MX (if it isn't already running).

2. Open the defined site that you want to modify. In this case, open the site defined as Convert Source in Exercise 1.1 (if it isn't already selected).

3. Expand the Templates folder (if it isn't already).

4. Open the `DW4Base.dwt` template by double-clicking it.

5. Select File ➪ Save As...; in the dialog box that opens, type the same template name but add a **–bu** preceding the .dwt. Your name should look like this: `DW4Base-bu.dwt`.

6. Close the renamed template. Your Templates folder should have two templates now (see the following figure), and no documents should be open at this point.

7. Leave Dreamweaver MX open for the next exercise.

Because you have made this backup, the template, links, and image references all stay intact and if you accidently changed the original template. You can easily overwrite the changed one with your backed up copy by renaming the backup template to the original filename.

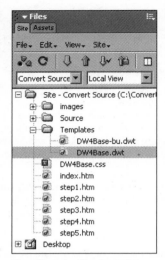

The Site tab after template
backup

Check template syntax

Dreamweaver 4 does not include any method of manually initiating a template syntax check. You
can happily go about editing your template in Dreamweaver 4 without having to worry about anything until you save the template. At that point, the template engine performs its duties by updating
the pages associated with it or tells you that there is an error and roughly where the error occurred.
You must find and clean up the problem manually.

Dreamweaver MX includes a handy tool for manually verifying that your template syntax is correct
prior to saving it or updating the associated files. Exercise 1.3 takes you through the steps required to
verify that your Dreamweaver 4 template syntax is correct. Although, as in Dreamweaver 4, you are
required to manually fix any errors that are encountered until the template passes the syntax check.

Exercise 1.3: Verify the DW4 template is syntactically correct

This step must not be skipped and should be performed on your Dreamweaver 4 created template
prior to performing any additional steps. If errors are detected, they must be repaired prior to performing the conversion or data loss might occur:

1. Start Dreamweaver MX (*if it isn't already running*).

2. Open the defined site you want to modify. In this case, open the site you defined as Convert
   Source in Exercise 1.1 (*if it isn't already selected*).

3. Expand the Templates folder (*if it isn't already*).

4. Open the DW4Base.dwt template by double-clicking it.

5. Select Modify ➪ Templates ➪ Check Template Syntax.

   One of two dialog boxes opens. the Template Syntax is Correct. dialog box or the Error dialog
   box, shown in the following figure.

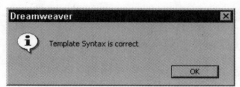

Syntax Check OK dialog box

Syntax Check showing an error dialog box

If you see the Template Syntax is Correct dialog box, move onto the next step. If you get an error message, it's time for some troubleshooting. You should see the Template Syntax is correct dialog box with this template.

6. Click OK to close the dialog box.

7. Leave the template and Dreamweaver MX open for the next exercise.

Perform the conversion

As you've seen so far, a lot of preliminary work that must be done to avoid poor results. If you work through this tutorial step by step, you will get reliable results each and every time with your template conversion.

Exercise 1.4: Running the F/R Queries to convert the template.

It's time to perform the base conversion of the Dreamweaver 4 template into a Dreamweaver MX template. The easiest way to do this is to use Dreamweaver MX's built in Find and Replace command. Thanks to the forward thinking of the Macromedia engineers, you can save find-and-replace queries to a file and recall them later using the Load option in the find and Replace dialog box:

1. Start Dreamweaver MX (if it isn't already running).

2. Open the defined site you want to modify. In this case, use the site you defined as Convert Source in Exercise 1.1 (if it isn't already selected).

3. Expand the Templates folder (if it isn't already).

4. Open the DW4Base.dwt template by double-clicking it (if it isn't open already).

5. Select Edit ➪ Find and Replace to open Find and Replace dialog box shown in the following figure.

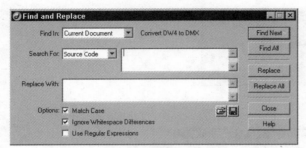

Blank Find and Replace dialog box

6. Click the *Load Query button* (the small folder icon near the Close button) and navigate to the chapter37_exersize\queries folder and select the saved query named ERStart.dwr. All the fields should populate as shown in the following figure.

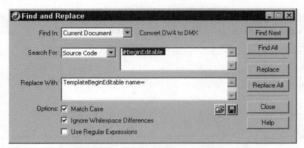

Competed Find and Replace Dialog box source code

7. Be sure the Find In field of the Find and Replace dialog box is set to Current Document. If it is not set to Current Document, change it using the drop-down list beside the field.

8. Click the Replace All button to perform the document find and replace. After the command performs its magic, a report dialog box should provide you with the results or the query as shown in the following figure.

Query Results for Start code F/R

9. Click OK to close the results.

10. Repeat Steps 5 through 9 twice more (prior to saving the changes made!), first selecting the saved query named EREnd.dwt and again selecting the saved query named ERHead.dwr. Be aware that what you see in the two previous figures will differ depending on the saved query you are accessing.

11. Choose File ⇨ Save. When prompted with the Update Template Files dialog box (see the following figure), click the Don't Update button.

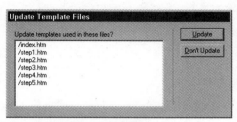

Update Template Files dialog box

You don't update the child pages, because the template code conversion doesn't affect child pages built from the Dreamweaver 4 version of the template unless you are adding/removing regions or updating uneditable content of the DMX converted template. The converted template will work as expected for all new pages created from it. With this in mind, make sure the existing child pages are updated to use the new template markup.

12. Select any uneditable area (position your cursor just before the closing `</body>` tag) and select Insert ⇨ Template Objects ⇨ Optional Region. In the dialog box that opens, click the Basic tab, leave the Name field at its default, and ensure that the Show by Default: check box is cleared (as seen in the following figure). Click OK to close the dialog box and add the region to your page.

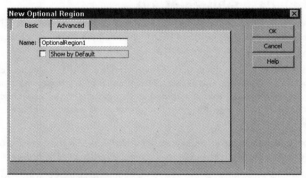

Optional Region dialog box

When you insert an optional region you force the child pages to update to the new template format.

13. Choose File ⇨ Save. When prompted to update the site by the Update Template Files dialog box, click the Update button.

The Update Pages dialog box shows a report of the files updated by the modified template. Click Close.

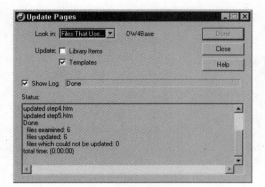

Update Pages dialog — completed

14. Open any of the .htm pages to verify that the changes discussed above indeed took effect.

15. Close all open files and close Dreamweaver. You're done with the conversion.

When you are satisfied that your local copy of the converted site is functioning as expected, the last thing you must do is upload the changed files to the server that hosts you site. You can do this using the Dreamweaver MX FTP engine or you can use your favorite FTP program. Remember to update the whole site, not only the root documents or you may run into problems.

Server language template considerations

The instructions provided previously apply to templates made for child pages based on static (HTML) or server-oriented languages (CFML, ASP, JSP, .NET, or PHP). However, if your pages are for server-oreinted language site, you must perfom one additional step.

Suppose that your template so it contains your Web site's login information so that a database can be accessed. This, in itself, is good coding practice and minimizes the number of keystrokes and mouse clicks required to build the site. Suppose also that you upload the template(s) to the server because you build the site collaboratively with a remote designer. Suppose someone accesses your site's Template folder and views your template file.

.DWT files can be opened by IE without issues in most cases. Because the file is not recognized by the server, it is not parsed and served to the browser, but instead it is delivered as is to the browser.

This means that anyone who knows how Dreamweaver templates work can hack your site, grab your database, or do a multitude of things that you won't even know about.

There is one very simple thing that you can do to protect your data: use Dreamweaver's Site Manager or Site panel to rename the template.

For example, say you have a template that contains all the ColdFusion database connection data and the filename is `cfsample.dwt`. If you rename this template, using the Site panel or Site Manager, to `cfsample.dwt.cfm` and update the child pages when prompted, in effect you have told the server that this template file must be processed and served to the browser, thereby hiding your connectivity information. The following table provides a complete breakdown of recognized template extensions that Dreamweaver MX can use.

Template Extension Listing

Language	Template Extension
CFML	.dwt.cfm
ASP	.dwt.asp
JSP	.dwt.jsp
.NET	.dwt.aspx
PHP	.dwt.php
HTML	.dwt

This security issue is present only if you are updating a dynamic template from Dreamweaver 4 or UltraDev 4. If you check your site definition and ensure that your server model is selected, future templates will not require this to be manually configured for this site definition. The Server Model can be configured through Site ⇨ Edit Sites. Select the desired site and click the Edit button. Choose the Advanced tab and then Testing Server category. Choose your Server Model by selecting it in the Server Model drop-down list.

The server model is a little strange: for Studio MX, ColdFusion is automatically used but for the stand-alone version of Dreamweaver MX, None is the default. Ensure that you set the desired Server Model at the same time that you originally define the site or you will have issues with server-side includes (if you use them).

Don't forget to delete the .dwt file from the server *Templates* folder.

Conclusion

Congratulations! You just completed your first Dreamweaver 4-to-Dreamweaver MX template conversion. Remember the steps, because they are important. To recap: Backup the site. Backup the template. Check your template syntax. Use the three provided find-and-replace queries. Add an optional region. Save the template and update the site. Along with the exercises, this chapter provided some common cautions and notes as they apply to the template conversion process.

Summary

In this chapter, you learned the basics of working with Dreamweaver productivity features, including library items and Dreamweaver templates. You built a library item so that you could modify its content later. You learned that library items are element-based locked code; whereas templates work at the page level. You added a template based on an existing page and defined regions for the template. You learned to set optional regions and to include editable tag attributes, which you edited in pages you built from the template. You also modified the template to include links between the pages and passed those changes to your pages.

Project Summary

In this chapter, you created a template for the Habitat Alert site and built the main pages for all four sections of the site.

Files Prepared for the Habitat Alert Web Site

Files	Techniques Used
site/index.htm	You added a library item for the bottom ad banners that may be present on pages of the site. When ad banners for this area need to change, you can update the library item and push those changes to any page that contains the item.
Templates/Basic Page.dwt	You built this template from the index.htm page.
act/index.htm find/index.htm learn/index.htm support/index.htm	You built these pages from your template and modified the editable tag attributes for their location graphics.
find/index.htm	You chose options to hide or display content in optional regions and added a spacer image to an editable optional region to keep the circle area table cell open.
site/index.htm	You applied the template to the home page to build a relationship between it and the template, so that later modifications of the template would be reflected in the home page.

✦   ✦   ✦

Tapping into the Power of Forms

HTML forms are powerful page elements that you can use to collect data or interact with site visitors. What you do with a form is based on its purpose and the type of technology available to you. Dreamweaver can help you build and power your forms to collect data, generate dynamic content, or store information gathered in a database.

This chapter covers the basics of how forms work and shows you how to use Dreamweaver's extensive form tools. In Chapter 46, you learn how to choose a technology and power your forms in conjunction with a database.

Understanding How Forms Work

Forms are created with HTML tags. The `<form></form>` pair surround other form object tags, such as `<input>`, `<select>`, and `<submit>`, to name a few. Form objects are used to collect, and sometimes to display, information. You give each form object a unique name when you use it in a form so that the combination of the form object's name and the information supplied by the user (value) results in a name-value pair.

Name-value pairs are useful. They can be delivered in an e-mail, stored as data for a field column (where name = field, value = column), or remembered as a scripted variable by the visitor's computer. The way name-value pairs are used depends upon the type of technology used to handle or process the form.

Form technologies

Dreamweaver contains easy-to-use tools for building forms, but a form by itself really has no power. A client or server technology is required to tap into the values of the form objects. The first step to using a form is to define its purpose, which you accomplish by choosing and using an appropriate technology.

Cross-Reference See Chapters 46 and 48, in which ASP and ColdFusion technologies power forms that collect, store, pass, and display data.

Mailto:

The simplest method of using form name-value pairs collected from a form is to e-mail them to an individual who then transfers the data to some type of paper or digital storage. All that's required is that you place the e-mail address in the form of `mailto:` in the action field of the form tag, as shown in Figure 38-1. This is generally not a secure method of transfer and most browsers inform you of this fact when you submit the form. This technology is appropriate for only the most casual of information, and data delivered this way isn't formatted for easy reading.

See Chapter 35 for more on creating mailto links.

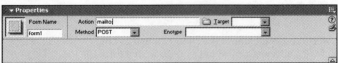

Figure 38-1: Simple but insecure form. Place the mailto:e-mail address in the action field of the form tag.

Cookies

Some form of data is collected for use on the Web and stored using client-side scripting as a "cookie" on the visitor's computer hard drive. *Client-side* means that processing is done on the visitor's computer. *Cookies* are tiny bits of information that are stored for a set time period in a special location on the visitor's computer, and JavaScript is generally the power behind this type of form handling. A typical example of cookie usage would be to collect a visitor's name and preferences. The information is stored and then accessed via additional scripting during the current or subsequent site visits. The down side of cookies is that many users block them from being written to their computer by changing their browser preferences.

Server-side processing

A more powerful use of forms taps into server-side solutions. *Server-side* means that processing occurs on a remote (Web or application) server, not the visitor's computer. Scripts that live on the Web server *parse* (process) the data and do one or any combination of three things with it:

✦ Send the information somewhere, usually by e-mail.

✦ Reuse the information in dynamically generated content.

✦ Store the information in a data source, either a database or text file on the Web server, for later use.

Server-side solutions are especially useful for retaining data. You cannot collect and store data from a form without some kind of server-side logic.

FormMail and other CGI scripts

Sometimes your form's purpose is to collect data and send it to someone. Most Web hosting companies have a standard CGI FormMail script that can e-mail form data to one or more recipients and even returns a thank you page after the form is submitted. This type of script uses *Common Gateway Interface* (CGI) protocol to control the way processed information is passed from the script or program back to the Web server and/or the user's browser. A CGI script enables a visitor to run or execute the script on the server. In the case of FormMail, an e-mail program on the Web server sends the collected and formatted data to the supplied recipient(s) address.

Most form data is collected via visible input fields or through menus, lists, radio buttons, or check boxes. Typically, a FormMail script includes one or more hidden fields that are contained in the source code but don't display in the browser. Visible form data values are most often supplied by the user; hidden field data is generally supplied by the Web page author.

To use a FormMail or any other CGI program, the script must be present on the Web server, generally in a cgi-bin folder, and specific permissions must be set to allow execution of the script. The path to a script is placed into the action field of the form tag. Generally, the type of path used is root-relative so that only Web pages on the same server may execute the script, which makes handling the URL easier for you as the developer. Some CGI scripts can also write data to a server, generally in the form of text files.

Web applications

Your form's purpose may be more complex than sending data via e-mail. The most powerful forms write and retrieve information to and from a data source that is stored on a remote server. In some cases, the information is reused as dynamic content in subsequent pages. This type of form requires handling by an *application server*—special software and drivers designed to interact and translate information to and from the database.

Typically, the form is placed into an HTML page that uses a **special extension** such as .asp, .cfm, .shtml, and so forth, to tell the Web server that the page must be processed before giving it to the visitor's browser. The scripting is processed as required, information is sent to the data source, and/or the HTML page is returned (minus the scripting) to the visitor. With Macromedia UltraDev now folded into Dreamweaver, you can select from several supported technologies to power your forms.

ColdFusion MX

You can use Dreamweaver to add server-side logic to your forms. See Chapter 46 and the entire ColdFusion section in Part VI for more information about how to set up and script the form examples, including the forms set up in this chapter.

Working with forms

After you have defined your purpose and the information you need from a form, it's time to build the form in an HTML page. If you choose to use application logic such as .asp or .cfm, with your forms, you need to use the correct extension for your HTML page. However, you can build the form in a normal HTML page and change the extension later.

Using Dreamweaver Form Tools

Dreamweaver makes adding form elements easy. You don't have to remember required properties, because Dreamweaver displays all available properties for a form element in the Property inspector. To add form elements (tags) to your page, use the Insert menu or bar. Figure 38-2 shows the Insert bar's Form tools. Click the Forms tab to open the correct panel in the bar.

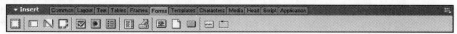

Figure 38-2: The Insert bar contains all the Form tools.

Following is a list of the form elements shown in Figure 38-2. These options are also available from the Insert menu using Insert ➪ Form or Insert ➪ Form Objects:

✦ **Form** — Places opening and closing `<form></form>` tags in the document.

✦ **Text Field** — Adds a text field. Text fields accept input in the form of letters or numbers. Different types of text fields include single line, multiple line, and password fields.

✦ **Hidden Field** — Places the input tag in the code that is invisible to users in their browsers, unless they view source code. Hidden fields provide a place for the developer to store values that you might use during processing.

✦ **Text Field** — A text field. You can set text wrapping (automatically wraps to the next line) here. Wrap Virtual hides unsightly horizontal scroll bars.

✦ **Check Box** — Inserts a check box in a form. Check boxes imply that more than one choice is acceptable in a single group of options.

✦ **Radio Button** — Inserts a radio button, generally as one in a group. The buttons are mutually exclusive. Selecting one button within a group deselects the others within a radio group.

✦ **Radio Group** — Contains one or more radio buttons that share the same form object name.

✦ **List/Menus** — Displays selection options. Lists display option values as a scrolling list; users may select multiple choices or options. Menus display choices on a pop-up (drop-down) menu; users can select only a single option.

✦ **Jump Menu** — Inserts a list or pop-up menu, used for navigation options, that is powered by a native Dreamweaver JavaScript behavior.

✦ **Image Field** — Inserts an image via the Browse function. Image fields are sometimes used as graphical replacements for submit buttons. Image fields require additional scripting to be effective.

✦ **File Field** — Allows selection of a file for upload to the Web server. It inserts a blank text field and a Browse button in a document.

✦ **Button** — Inserts a text button within a form. Buttons submit or reset form data, depending upon the properties set. The appearance of form buttons is controlled primarily by the browser on the user's computer. This is why you may want to use an image-field (your own button) instead of relying on the browser's default style.

Adding a Form

All form objects must be contained within form tags to display properly in all browsers. Add a form tag before adding your form objects. If you plan to use a table to format the layout of your form, place the table between the form tags.

To add a form tag, use the Insert bar Form tools or choose Insert ➪ Form. Because the form tag itself is not a visible object, enable View Options ➪ Visual Aids ➪ Invisible Elements to see the form tags visually represented as red lines. To modify properties of the form tag, place your cursor inside the form and use the Tag selector to select `<form>`.

Save the Habitat Alert38 folder from the chapter38_exercise folder to your hard drive. Define a new site. Hint: If you already have another Habitat Alert site defined, then choose the Edit Site option in the Site panel of the Site Definition drop-down menu and change the path to the Local Root folder.

In this section, you add a form for the options in the Find page. This exercise requires a defined site using the chapter38_ exercise folder and files.

1. Open `find/index.htm`. This page was created from the Basic Page template. The circle area has some optional regions settings. Sidebar Image is turned off; the What's New menu is off; but the Other jump menu's region is enabled. This is an editable region, and a spacer image set to 231px by 1px, formatted as a paragraph holds open the table cell containing the circle graphic.

2. Place your cursor into the blue circle cell. Select the `<p>` tag and press right arrow to move past this code.

3. Type **Quick Search**. Choose Insert ➪ Special Characters ➪ Other to open the Character Map dialog box. Click the tenth item from the top row, which should produce `&not;` as shown in Figure 38-3. Close the dialog box.

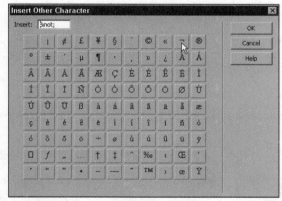

Figure 38-3: Use special characters for cross-platform consistency.

4. With your cursor in the new text, use the Format menu to set it to Heading 4. Select `<h4>` using the Tag selector, and press right arrow to move to the right of the closing tag.

5. Choose Insert ➪ Form.

   If your invisible elements are enabled, you see two red lines. You don't need to place a line break or paragraph return before adding the form, because forms (like tables) automatically form their own block.

6. Save your page and keep it open for the next exercise.

Adding Form Objects

To add form objects to your form, place your cursor in the form and click the desired form object button in the Form tools of the Insert bar. You can also use Insert ➪ Form Objects ➪ and choose the type of tag appropriate for the information you want to display or collect.

Tip   If you have a form object with specific values that you use often, consider building your own Form Object Tool button or saving the code as a snippet. Creating tools and snippets is covered in Chapter 43.

Choosing the correct form object

Certain form tags are conventionally used for specific tasks. For example, Radio buttons imply mutual exclusivity; if you want to offer a group of choices from which the visitor can select more than one option, use a check box. When space is an issue and you want the visitor to choose only one option from a group of options, use a pop-up or drop-down menu, instead of several radio buttons.

Labeling form objects

Provide a label or call to action for each form object. For example, clearly identify each text box or each radio button in a group. If a value is required for a form object, mark that label with an asterisk and explain the meaning of the asterisk in a paragraph above the form.

The first form added is a search function which could be powered by any server-side technology, such as ASP or ColdFusion. A label for the form function has been added already. A search function requires a text field and a form button at the minimum:

1. With your cursor in the form, choose Insert ➪ Form Objects ➪ Text Field.

2. Press right arrow and use the Insert bar Form tools to add a Button to the area (Figure 38-4).

3. Save the page and keep it open for the next exercise.

Figure 38-4: The text field and button added to the form field

Setting Form and Form Object Properties

All form tags require certain properties. Use the contextual Property inspector to select and add properties for your form tags. To access any existing form tag's properties, first select it in your page.

The Property inspector makes form-building a breeze because all the properties are right there — no digging around in a book looking up what properties are expected. If you prefer to hand-code, tag hints and code-balancing features in Dreamweaver speed up the process.

Naming form objects

Every form and form object is given a name by Dreamweaver. Naming the form or form object makes it possible to reference or control it through scripting. You can change the name using the Name field in the Property inspector. Some FormMail CGI scripts require specific names for specific tags to work properly. Logical names are easier to read when name-value pairs are sent via e-mail.

Form properties

Specify a path to the script or dynamic page (application) that will process the form data in the Action field. Use the Browse button to locate the script or page, but often these are not contained within your site and must be hand-written. Add a method for transmitting the data to the server, if needed. The following form methods are available:

✦ **POST** — Embeds the form data in the HTTP request.

✦ **GET** — Adds or appends the value(s) to the URL requesting a dynamic page. This method is limited to a total of 8,192 characters. If the amount of data sent using the GET method is too great, it will be truncated, resulting in errors. Because values are readily visible in URLs, it is unwise to send sensitive user data using the GET method.

✦ **DEFAULT** — Uses the browser's preferred or default method. Typically this is the GET method.

Choosing an Enctype sets a MIME type for the data you submit for processing. The default coding for all forms according the W3C standards is application/x-www-form-urlencode and is generally used with the POST method. For uploads of files, use the multipart/form data MIME type. Also, Dreamweaver now offers a target option to specify the destination window to be used by returned data.

More information about window targets is located in Chapters 39 and 42.

Form object properties

You use the Property inspector to set certain required and optional properties for form tags. Some form objects have more requirements than others:

✦ **Text Fields** — Choose single, multiple, or password. Specifying display size and the maximum number of characters the user can enter is optional. Text entered via the browser into a password text field displays as bullets, Xs, or asterisks, depending upon the user's system and browser.

✦ **Radio Buttons**—Radio Groups must share a common name. You specify a value for each button. When the user chooses a button, the result is name=value chosen. You may opt to have one button preselected.

✦ **Check Boxes**—These objects have unique names. You set a value for each box. Generally, the value implied is yes if chosen and no if not. For example: The label next to a check box might read, "Would you like a brochure?" The name of the check box might be send_brochure, and its value, if checked, should be set to Yes.

✦ **Menus and Lists**—This form object defaults to menu; to add a list, select that option. Menu and list options are added by clicking the List Values button. In the dialog box (Figure 38-5) the left column is what the user sees. The right column is the value passed via the form submission.

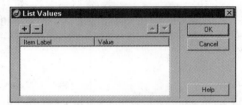

Figure 38-5: The List Values dialog box is where you add list or menu items.

In the following steps, you use the Property inspector to add some properties to the form elements:

1. Click the form. Use the Property inspector to name this form **quicksearch** in the Form Name field.

   Check to verify that you are really in the form by looking at the Tag selector. Do you see the <form> tag? If not, you are not really in the form. Go to Code view if necessary to place your cursor inside the form tags.

2. Select the forms text field. Set the object's name to **item** and set its Char Width value to 12. Select the <input> tag in the Tag selector and right-click (Right (Control)+click) to apply the .formbox style.

   At this point in the development cycle, additional style rules have been formulated and two style sheets are being used.

3. Select the form button and use the Property inspector to change the Label from Submit to Go (Figure 38-6).

4. Save your page and keep it open for the later exercise.

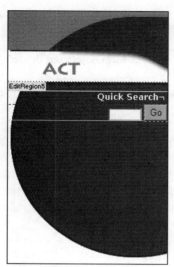

Figure 38-6: The text field with a value of 12 and a Go button

Using a Table to Format a Form

When your form requires many form objects, using a table helps you create a nicer looking layout through alignment and spacing options.

Remember to add the form tags first, then place your table inside them. A form can become dysfunctional if the opening and closing form tags are incorrectly placed.

In this exercise, you'll build a form to allow the site visitor to subscribe to the Habitat Alert newsletter from the Act section of the site.

1. Open act/register.htm from the Site panel.

2. Place your cursor into the main content area, just below the introductory text.

3. Choose Insert ➪ Form. Be sure to enable viewing of Invisible Elements in the View Options to see the red lines that indicate the beginning and ending form tags.

4. Add a table with 1 row, 2 columns at 90% width. Set padding and border to zero and spacing to 5px.

5. Click into the first cell and use the Tag selector to right-click (Control-click) the `<td>` tag and set its class to formheadings, which will set the cell's horizontal alignment to right and format the text you add. Now type **Last Name:** in this cell. Tab to move to the next cell.

6. Choose Insert ⇨ Form Objects ⇨ Text Field. Alternatively, you can click the Form tab in the Insert bar and use the Text Field object button.

7. With the text field selected, use the Property inspector to set its name to LastName. Set its Char Width to 20. Char Width controls the width of the form object but doesn't restrict the number of characters that can be added.

The width of form objects depends upon the browser and computer platform and system of the user. Typically, Netscape text fields are wider than those of Internet Explorer. Be sure to test if width is an issue in your design.

8. Tab to create a new row. Type First Name: and tab to the next cell. Add another text field, set its Char Width to 20, and name it FirstName.

By setting the CSS formatting for the first row's label cell, any subsequent rows added include the same formatting. That's why it's best to create only one row at first.

9. Tab to add a new row. Add the label Email:, then tab and add a text field named Email, set to 20 characters.

10. Tab to add a new row. Add the label Street Address:, then tab and add a text field named StreetAddress, set to 20 characters.

11. Tab to add a new row. Add the label State/Province:, then tab and add a list/menu form object named StateorProvince.

In this case, you can either build the required drop-down menu with all the states and provinces required, or you can use the Macromedia Dreamweaver Exchange to download and install an extension that adds this type of menu to the Insert menu. We recommend U.S. State Codes by Rabi Sunder Raj. You can find it at the exchange (`http://macromedia.com/exchange/dreamweaver`) by typing state into the search field. You must be a registered member to download from the exchange.

See Chapter 43 for more about using extensions in Dreamweaver MX.

12. Tab to add a new row. Add the label Zip/Postal Code:, then tab and add a text field named ZiporPostalCode, set to 11 characters.

13. Tab to add a new row. Add the label Country:, then tab and add a text field named Country, set to 20 characters.

Finally, it's time to add the all-important form submit button! A form needs a button to trigger the action field. A reset button is useful, too.

14. Tab to add a new row. In the first cell, add a form button and label it Register. Don't worry about naming this form object as it is not required.

15. Tab to the next cell and add another button. Click the Reset option, then re-label the button Clear Form.

16. Save your page and select the form tag using the Tag selector.

A form requires an action and method to work with a server-side technology. In this case, you'll set these in Chapter 48 to reference a ColdFusion template you'll build in that section.

Adding a Jump Menu

The jump menu in Dreamweaver is an easy-to-use form object that's often used for navigation; the menu lists different options, and a JavaScript behavior powers the options to switch pages on demand. Some jump menus use a Go button, but most visitors expect to have the page switch when they choose an item.

Jump menus are added in the same fashion as any other form object, but they have their own dialog box to allow easy development. To edit a jump menu, select the menu object and use the Behaviors panel to double-click the jump menu listing.

Here you'll build a Resource Menu to allow visitors to select from a dynamically generated list of resources, sorted by category. We are still using the find/index.htm page.

Cross-Reference

See the exercise dynamic_form_menus.pdf in Chapter 46's exercise files for more information about setting up dynamically generated form drop down menus. While the exercise uses ASP server technology, a similar process could be used with ColdFusion.

1. Click the form you just added (quicksearch) and select the `<form#quicksearch>` tag using the Tag selector. Press right arrow to move past the form code.

2. Type **Resource Menu** and add another `&not;` special character. Format this as Heading 4 and select the `<h4>` tag using the Tag selector.

3. Press the Right Arrow key to move past the heading and Insert ➪ Form Objects ➪ Jump Menu.

   You won't need to add a form first because the Jump Menu tool adds it for you if needed. You may opt to add the form first if you prefer .

4. In the Text field, type **Find a Resource**.

   Tip

   It is advisable to make the first item in a jump menu a call to action. Jump menus use a JavaScript function that works with the event onChange, meaning that the script is called only when an item is changed. Because the first item is already chosen, there's no way to choose it.

5. Add a new menu item by clicking the Add (+) button. In the Text field type **Gov't Agencies** for this item and place a hash mark (#) into the When Selected, Go to URL field. Figure 38-7 shows the Jump Menu dialog box.

6. Add these items, each time using a hash mark instead of a URL:

   • **State Agencies**

   • **Groups**

   • **Habitat Alert Links**

7. Click OK. Select the jump menu's `<form>` tag and name this form **resources**.

8. To finish this page, add some class to your form objects by setting style rules. Styles have already been created for this purpose. Select item (from the first form) and right-click (Control+click) to set its class to .formbox. Select the form button (input) and set it to .formbtn. Select the jump menu (select) and set its class to .formbox, too. Save your page and preview.

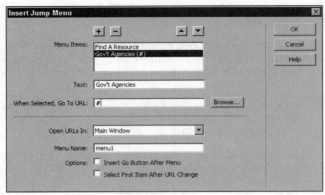

Figure 38-7: The Jump Menu dialog box

Note

Form styles are not well-supported in Netscape 4x and have no effect there, but they jazz up your form objects in W3C compliant browsers. Be careful about which properties you use if developing form styles, and always set these style rules in an imported style sheet to hide them from NN4x.

Figure 38-8 shows the page in Netscape 4x. Figure 38-9 shows Internet Explorer 6.0. The styles used to format this page are contained in two style sheets, with some adjustment to make NN4x happier.

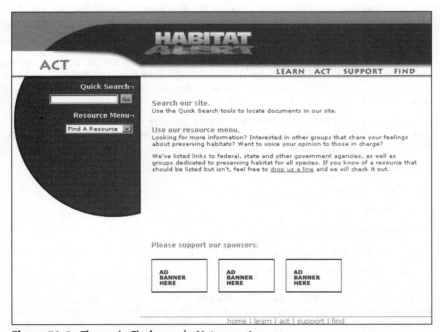

Figure 38-8: The main Find page in Netscape 4x

Figure 38-9: The main Find page as viewed in Internet Explorer 6.0

Summary

In this chapter, you learned to add form tags using the Insert menu and bar. You named and set properties for form tags using the Property inspector. When you needed a special character, you learned to add it via the Insert ➪ Special Characters ➪ Other menu option. You explored using a jump menu to build a section-specific navigation method. Finally, you styled your form objects using rules defined in an imported style sheet.

Project Summary

In this section, you created two forms for the main page in the Find section of the Habitat Alert site. This page can later be the basis of a nested template (if needed) to build more pages for the resources listed in the jump menu. The forms in this page will later be powered by ColdFusion. Pages that display search results or resources will be saved using the `.cfm` or `.cfml` extension.

Files Prepared for the Habitat Alert Web Site

Files	What Was Done	Where to Now?
find/index.htm act/register.htm	Basically, you developed forms that can later be powered by the server-side technology of your choice. You added a form to use as a search engine. You added a form to collect registration data for visitors that want to receive an e-mail version of the newsletter. You added another form as a Jump Menu that can be static or set up to be dynamically populated. Setting up forms ahead of time allows them to be approved and then later developed aspart of a web application to speed up workflow and site development.	A form requires an action and method to work with a server-side technology. In this case, you'll set these in Chapter 48 to reference a ColdFusion template.

✦   ✦   ✦

Building a Framed Site

Building a framed Web site is a complex and sometimes controversial issue. Although frames offer the advantage of displaying more than just one page at a time, the disadvantages of using frames are legendary. You wouldn't need to look far to find the Top Ten list of things not to do when building a site, which includes the use of frames. But, used appropriately, a framed site can provide a means to navigate and display content in a way that no other option provides.

Dreamweaver makes building a framed site fairly easy. When you want navigation that remains fixed and present at all times, using frames is the way to go. Despite issues with bookmarking and printing site pages, framed sites are still in demand. In this chapter, you learn to use Dreamweaver's frames features to build simple, complex framed layouts and explore how targeting is the key to successful navigation for framed sites.

Understanding How Frames Work

By default, a Web browser displays a single page at a time. To display more than one page in a single browser window, you need to tell the browser application how to divide the window into frames and then specify which HTML pages to display within each frame. The document that tells the browser how to divide the window is the frameset document. The `<frameset>` tag includes information about the number, size, and orientation of all frames, plus the options to enable or disable frame borders.

```
<frameset>
<frame>
<frame>
</frameset>
```

Each `<frame>` tag contains information about the page to display within the frame, margin settings, how scrolling will occur when the content of the page is greater than the size of the frame, and whether the user can resize the individual frame areas.

Building a framed site means that you will be working with three or more pages where previously you worked with only one. The most common use of frames is to isolate the navigation from the content.

Within each frame, standard HTML pages are displayed and work exactly as they would within a normal browser window, except that links target a specific frame. To target a frame means to tell the browser where to load the requested page. Generally, this means to tell the browser the name of the frame where the page should load.

The advantages of using frames

There are distinct advantages to using frames. When navigation is displayed in a separate frame, it can be accessible at all times, and users can scroll through the content without interacting with the navigation. This can also mean that the navigation doesn't reload when a new page is called.

Frames are popular for extremely large sites or intranet sites that have many groups, departments, or divisions, because frames allow compartmentalization of the page. One frame can hold the main navigation, which remains constant. Another frame might display different navigation, depending upon which group, department, or division is entered. A third frame might display content selected from the secondary navigation. With so much going on at one time, it's nice that the main and secondary navigation don't reload with every page call.

The disadvantages of using frames

The disadvantages of using frames are many and well-touted. Much of the dislike of frames comes from the frustration of visiting poorly designed sites that use frames improperly. Framed sites generally require more work since you are handling more pages; they also require specific linking methods. When done incorrectly, the pages don't work, which can make the user experience negative.

Perhaps the two most notorious drawbacks to frames are the bookmarking and printing of framed pages. When the user finds a desired page and tries to create a bookmark, it is the frameset document that is marked, not the specific page that appears in any frame. The browser remembers the only frameset document, not any page that was subsequently called into a specific frame.

Additionally, some search engines are not optimized to follow links across frames. However, each of these disadvantages may be overcome through scripting. When planning a framed site to meet stringent accessibility guidelines, it is imperative to use the built-in accessibility features provided to make it possible for aural readers to understand how to process and read the site.

Building a Simple Frameset

When building your framed site, you may start from scratch if you have no existing pages, or build a frameset to house existing pages. Dreamweaver enables you to work within the frameset so you can see how the pages will appear within the browser window. To work with framesets and frames, you use the Document window, Property inspector, and the Frames panel. To try the exercises given in this chapter, you need to define a new site. Name the site Chapter 39 and add the files from the chapter39_exercise folder.

Rows or columns?

The first thing to decide when building a framed site is the orientation of the frames used. A simple frameset can contain as many frames as you'd like, but all must share a common orientation of rows or columns. Rows divide the browser window horizontally; columns divide it vertically. Figure 39-1 shows the most common frameset options to use all rows, all columns, or a mix of both. When you opt to use rows and columns together, the frames are read by the browser from top to bottom, left to right. It's also possible to combine rows and columns in only one of the frames; this is called a nested frameset, which is covered later in the chapter.

To start a frameset document, follow these steps:

1. Choose File ➪ New and create a new basic page. Don't save the page yet.

2. Click View Options ➪ Visual Aids ➪ Frame Borders. Turn on the visibility of Frame Borders. Depending upon whether you want rows or columns, you click and drag to create a horizontal or vertical frame division. Drag from the top or bottom to create a row. Drag from the left or right to create a column.

3. If you want more than two frames, drag again from the appropriate side to create the new frame.

To undo adding a frame, use Edit ➪ Undo, Control+Z (Command+Z) shortcut for undo, or drag the frame border to the edge of the document until it disappears.

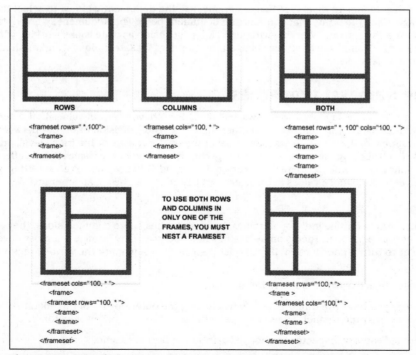

Figure 39-1: Simple framesets include rows only, columns only, or a shared row/column layout. Nested framesets are used when you want to vary the total rows and columns between frames.

Navigating the documents in a framed site

When building a framed site, you work with multiple documents in the Dreamweaver application window and need to access different documents to set up the properties of those pages. To work successfully and efficiently, it is critical to understand how to select the correct document. Open the Frames panel in your Panel Dock. By default, the Frames panel is grouped with Layers in the Advanced Layout group. You access it through the Window ➪ Others menu. The Frames panel shows a small version of your current frames layout.

To set frameset properties, you must first make the frameset tag active. To access the frameset, you can:

✦ Click the outer border in the document window.

✦ Click the outer border simulation in the Frames panel.

✦ Click a frame displayed in the Frames panel, and select the <frameset> tag shown in the Tag selector.

Dreamweaver provides a visual clue that the frameset is currently selected by outlining the entire frameset with a dotted line.

To work with a frame, click and select the desired frame in the Frames panel to make it active. A dotted line outlines the active frame to let you know which frame is selected. The Property inspector displays the properties of the active frame.

To work with a document displayed inside a frame, use the document window to select the desired page. Click the frame that contains the document page. The document's <body> tag displays in the Tag selector. Working with an HTML page inside a frame is like working with a page outside of a frame; you have access to all the standard tags, techniques, and methods you would normally use.

Setting frameset properties

When you've set up the layout of your rows, columns, or both, you can set values that determine the dimensions of the frames and whether there is a visible division or border between each frame. Some of these properties may be set at the frameset level or the frame level; others are strictly controlled by the frameset tag. Properties controlled at the frameset level affect all frames. If your frames will not share properties but have individual values for each setting, you may opt to determine those values at the frame level. Borders can be set at either level.

Borders

By default, borders outline individual frames; because frames share common sides, they also share border properties. Borders can be useful when you use many frames, but most developers prefer to turn off border visibility and let their page design mark the various regions of the site.

Follow these steps to turn off borders for all frames:

1. Be sure you have the frameset active by clicking the outer border of the document window or Frames panel. The <frameset> tag is bolded in the Tag selector.

2. Use the Property inspector to choose No from the Borders menu.

3. Add a zero in the Border Width field. This is required to explicitly remove all borders.

To set a shared border value for all frames, follow these steps:

1. Choose Yes from the Border menu.

2. Add the desired value to the Border Width field.

3. Choose a border color, if desired, by clicking the color box to access the standard Dreamweaver color palette. Click a color sample from other documents, or click the System Picker icon to access those options to choose a color.

Setting frame dimensions

One of the trickier tasks involved when building a frameset is determining the dimensions of each frame. The size of all frames is controlled at the frameset level, using the mini version of your frame layout shown in the Property inspector, as shown in Figure 39-2.

Figure 39-2: The mini-layout lets you select which frame to size.

Frames can use a specific pixel dimension, a percentage dimension, or be set to take up any available remaining space. This last option is called *relative*, although technically, a percentage dimension is also relative. The relative setting is similar to a wild card setting; it really means "whatever is left" after the set values are displayed.

Because the overall width of the user's browser window is not known, using only pixel values is impractical. Generally, you use a combination of set pixel values with at least one relative value or use percentage values exclusively. The layouts shown in Figure 39-2 use pixel values in combination with the relative (*) setting. This allows the frame or frames with specific values to be rendered first, then gives any remaining space in the browser window to the relative frame. The relative frame is "stretchy" and expands or collapses as the browser window is resized, leaving the fixed-pixel widths of the other frame(s) untouched.

When using percentage values for frame sizes, it is best to use them for all frames and to make the total settings add up to 100 percent.

Follow these steps to set frame sizes:

1. Select the frameset tag to bring up the frameset properties in the Property inspector.

2. Click one of the frames displayed in the mini-version of your current frames layout in the Property inspector.

3. Choose Pixels, Percentage, or Relative from the Units menu.

4. If choosing Pixels or Percentage, add a value in the Value field. If you choose Relative, a number is displayed in the Value field. You don't need to set it or change it, because the real value that will be added is the asterisk (*) sign to indicate that this frame is to use any available space.

5. Click into the next frame and set its values.

Saving a frameset

Saving your work as you build a framed site is tricky, and the way you do it depends upon whether you are starting from scratch (with no existing pages) or are using existing pages within your newly created frames. In all cases, you must first save the frameset.

To save a frameset, follow these steps:

1. Make the `frameset` tag active.

2. Choose File ➪ Save Frameset As. If the frameset is not active, you will not see this option.

3. Navigate to your site root folder and save the frameset page. Because the frameset document must load first, it is common to name this document using index or default so that it autoloads.

Dreamweaver must know where the frameset is saved to be able to build a relationship to the pages that display within the frameset's frames. With the frameset saved, you can work with framed pages without fear of losing any work.

Working with Frames

Now you are ready to develop your frames. The `<frame>` tag controls which page appears in the frame and whether the frame scrolls or resizes. You can also set border properties at this level or control the page margins for a page used within the frame. To work with a frame, click the frame in the Frames panel.

Naming your frames

When building a framed site, you must name the frames you create to be able to target them later when building links in the pages. Like any other HTML object, the reference name makes it possible to specifically address that object in the browser window.

To name a frame, select it in the Frames panel. Use the Property inspector to type a name for the frame, as shown in Figure 39-3. There are two schools of thought for naming your frames, both of which use descriptive naming. The first naming convention describes where the frame is, as in TopFrame or LeftFrame. The second convention is also descriptive but describes the function of the frame, as in NavFrame or MainContent. You can use any convention you desire but can't use spaces or special characters in the name.

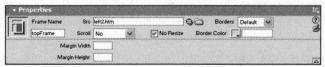

Figure 39-3: Add a name for each frame using the Property inspector.

Saving or setting the frame source

If you think of the framed site as a window (the browser window) you can think of each frame as a separate pane in the window. The view (page) for each pane can change on demand. However, when the frameset document opens, a set view (page) must load for each frame: this is the frame source (src). If you have existing pages you want to display in your frames, you may set a frame's source to use them.

Follow these steps to set the frame source if the page is within the root of the current site:

1. Click the frame for which you plan to set the page source.

2. Use the browse-for-folder or point-to-file methods to select the correct page from the Site panel (window) of the current site.

Follow these steps to set the src if the page is not local:

1. Select the correct frame.

2. In the Src field of the Property inspector, type the full (absolute) URL to the desired page.

If you don't have existing pages but plan to build them as you develop your site, you need only save the temporary pages that Dreamweaver supplied when you created your frames. To save the temporary page in a frame, click the frame in the document window, and choose File ➪ Save Frame As. Navigate to your root folder to name and save the HTML page. Repeat the process for each frame.

Note   You aren't really saving the frame; you are saving the unsaved, temporary document that Dreamweaver added to be able to display the frame in Design view.

Using Save All

The Save All option for saving a frameset and framed pages is useful but tricky. If your frameset and frames have never been saved, choosing File ➪ Save All triggers a dialog box for saving any *and all* opened, unsaved documents. The Save As dialog box automatically appears for each document to be saved, and it is up to you (the developer) to spot the visual clue (dotted line) to understand which document is being saved at the time.

If you have other unsaved documents open, the dialog box appears for those documents as well and you may not see any visual clue or misunderstand what document you are being asked to save. For that reason, it's easier to develop your framed site with no other documents open at the time.

Using Save All is common when you have made changes to a page, frame, or the frameset and is not quite so tricky after the initial saves have been made.

With frames, you have the option to provide scrollbars. You can also determine whether a user can resize the frame dimensions and set the margins of the pages a specific frame uses. Careful setting of these and other frame properties is important because you may not know exactly how your pages will display in a user's browser. Ideally, you want to give the user as much control as possible without compromising your design.

Setting scrolling

By default, your frames have scrollbars vertically and horizontally unless you opt to control the way they appear. Your options include Yes, No, and Auto. Unless you know that your content will never need a scrollbar regardless of what the user's browser preferences are, choose Auto. However, if a frame uses only images, which remain fixed whatever the user's preferences are, you may opt to not allow scrolling.

Resizing options

Frames may be resized by a user in their browser window unless you specifically set this option to No Resize. When borders are turned off, resizing a frame is much more difficult but still possible for the patient user.

Setting page margins

You already know how to change page margins for an HTML page by setting the page properties or using Cascading Style Sheets. You may control a page's margins at the frame level, too, for your convenience. To remove the default offsets for HTML pages, set the Margin Width and Margin Height fields to zero, just as you would at the page-property level.

Working with Framed Documents

To work with pages within a set of frames, click into the document you want to develop. At that point, you have access to Page Properties and any other developmental tools available in Dreamweaver. It's best to work on your individual pages in the frameset because the Design view gives you an idea of how your pages will look in the browser. Of course, you should still preview the pages because Design view doesn't show you how your pages appear in all browsers.

To preview a frameset and its framed pages, press F12 to access your primary browser, Ctrl+F12 (Command+F12) to access the secondary browser, or choose File ➪ Preview in Browser ➪ and choose the target browser to use. If your pages have unsaved changes, Dreamweaver prompts you to save the frameset and pages before viewing. If you set up your application preferences to view the actual document (not a temporary document), you may be required to save before continuing the preview process.

Setting a title for the framed page

Because only one title can be displayed by the browser, the title for your framed pages must be set in the frameset document. To set a title for display by the browser, select the frameset and enter the title in the Title field in the Document bar above the page.

It's useful to set titles for all your framed pages even though only the title for the frameset document displays in the browser, because search engines give a high level of importance to page titles when cataloging sites.

Setting page background colors and images

Setting page colors for pages within frames is the same as setting page color for any HTML document. The code is contained within the `<body>` tag and is accessed in Dreamweaver via Page Properties.

You can also set a background color for the frameset document. The `<body>` tag for the frameset document is contained inside the `<noframes></noframes>` region. The `<noframes>` region is used to display content for browsers that cannot understand frames. More about `<noframes>` is covered a bit later in this chapter.

Tip

Set a page color for your frameset document to match the color your pages use to avoid the flash-of-color changes as your framed documents load.

Setting a background image for your framed pages is a simple process, but you must take special care when planning to have images that line up across frames. This is most apparent when background images use curves that intersect frames and must line up. Netscape 4*x* and earlier browsers render frames with extra margins along the bottom and right edges, even when margin width and height are set to zero. Try to avoid using close fits between frames, and be sure to test in all target browsers on all computer platform targets. If you plan to allow 10 pixels of space between frames and avoid curved intersections, you shouldn't have problems.

Linking to Framed Documents

The most common mistake made when developing framed sites is improper links targeting. By default, any clicked link (whether text or graphic button) calls a new page, which replaces the page that holds the link. This is standard link behavior but not the ideal behavior for links in a framed site. If you have your navigation in one frame and want the pages to appear in a separate frame, you must target that frame.

About targets

The target attribute of a link specifies the frame or window in which the linked content opens. Dreamweaver generally offers four target options in the Target menu of the Property inspector: _blank, _top, _parent, and _self. The default target for all links is _self. A new window is launched with _blank. Both _parent and _top are often used with frames. When you are working within a frameset document, Dreamweaver adds your frame names to this list.

Setting link targets

Building a link in framed pages is the same as in non-framed HTML pages, but may require target changes. Here are some possible target scenarios:

✦ If the link you create should replace the current page that contains the link, you need not specify a target for the link. The default, _self, will be used.

✦ If your link needs to load a page in a different frame, use the Target menu to specify the desired frame. Your frame names should be listed in the menu.

✦ If you need a page to load and replace all the current frames, choose _top. Using _top overwrites all current frames and pages with the called page.

The _parent option is intended for replacing one frameset with another when the replaced frameset is the source page for an existing frame, as shown in Figure 39-4. If you are an experienced HTML coder, you may have used this target, but Dreamweaver doesn't generally build framesets in a way that accomodates its intended use. The proper setup of this kind of frameset is covered in the nested framesets section of this chapter.

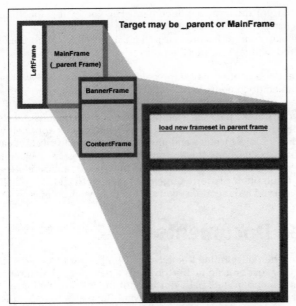

Figure 39-4: You may target the frame or use _parent when your configured framed site doesn't use the standard Dreamweaver nested frames approach.

Building Complex Framesets

When you decide to use mixed row and column layouts, Dreamweaver assumes that you want to build nested framesets. Figure 39-5 shows a standard nested layout.

To build this type of structure, follow these steps:

1. Create a new, unsaved page.

2. Turn on viewing of Frame Borders in the View Options ➪ Visual Aids.

3. Drag a horizontal division from the top frame border.

4. Click into the bottom frame and choose Modify ➪ Frameset ➪ Split Frame Left (or Split Frame Right).

Alternatively, you could complete these steps:

1. Create the new, unsaved page.

2. Turn on viewing of Frame Borders.

3. Drag a vertical division from the left frame border.

4. Press the Ctrl key (Command) and drag from the top frame border to force the two columns down in your page and create a row above both frames.

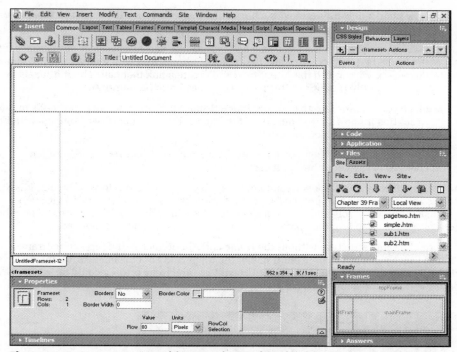

Figure 39-5: A common nested frameset layout that places two columns in the bottom frame of a two-row frameset

There are many options for complex nested framesets but keep in mind that the more frames and the more complex the structure, the more difficult it is to manage the site. Targeting links becomes more complex.

Parent/child framesets

Another way to accomplish the same sort of layout involves building a simple frameset and calling more framesets into one of the frames. To build the same kind of layout using an unnested method, follow these steps:

1. Create a new, unsaved page.

2. Enable Frame Borders.

3. Drag a vertical division out from the left or right frame borders.

4. Name the left frame **SubNavs** and the right frame **MainContent**. In the left page, type **home links here**. In the right page, type **home content here**.

5. Save the frameset as **home.htm**, the left page as **homesub.htm**, and the right page as **homecontent.htm**. Close the frameset.

6. Repeat the process to build another simple frameset with the same type of layout, this time naming the frameset **about.htm**, the left page **aboutsub.htm**, and the right page **aboutcontent.htm**. You should also change the text in these pages to read **about links here** and **about content here**. Save and close this frameset, too.

7. Now build a new frameset with a horizontal division. Name these frames **topFrame** and **btmFrame** and save the frameset as **index.htm**.

8. Place your cursor in the top frame and type **Home** and **About**. Place your cursor into the Home text. and create a link that points to home.htm with a target of btmFrame. Place your cursor into the About text, and create a link that calls about.htm, also with a target of btmFrame. Save this frame (page) as **homebanner.htm**.

9. Place your cursor into the bottom frame (btmFrame) and use the point-to-file method to set this frame's src to home.htm, the frameset that contains two columns with home page content and links.

10. Save and preview. When you click the About link, the frameset in the btmFrame changes to the about.htm frameset.

Although this may seem an overly complex way to get three frames in your layout, it isn't. This is actually a simple approach to creating columns-with-a-row layout and vice versa because it doesn't involve nesting of framesets. There are added advantages to this method because you can tap into the _parent target or use the frame name, as needed.

Imagine the same structure without the Home and About links in the top banner frame. Picture those same links in the left frame of the home and about framesets, as shown in Figure 39-6. In this case, the link targets can still be btmFrame or they could be set to _parent. Both the home and about framesets are child framesets inside a parent frame.

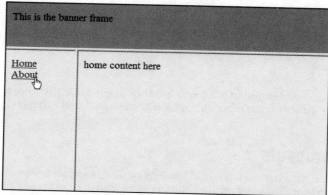

Figure 39-6: The Home and About framesets are child framesets in the btmFrame parent frame.

Using Go To URL

When you use nested framesets, you cannot call a new frameset in to replace only two frames as described in the previous example because there's no existing parent/child relationship. So how can you change two frames with a single click? The answer is through JavaScript and the Go To URL behavior included in Dreamweaver's Behavior panel.

To change two frames with a single click, follow these steps:

1. If you haven't defined a new site for the chapter39_exercise folder, do so now. Open the Go2 folder and open the index.htm page. This layout uses nested framesets to build a left MainNavs frame, a SectionBanner for each site section, and a MainContent frame for each section's content. The links in the MainNavs frame are the main navigation for the site with each section having its own banner and content.

2. To change the banner and content frame with a single link, place your cursor into the About link text. Notice in the Property inspector that there is a null link added. A null link is required here to apply a behavior.

3. Open your Behaviors panel and add Go To URL.

4. In the dialog box that opens, select the frame SectionBanner. Click the Browse button, and locate aboutbanner.htm in the Go2 folder. Don't close this dialog yet.

5. Now select the MainContent frame and use the Browse button to locate and select aboutcontent.htm from the Go2 folder. You should now have an asterisk by two of the frames, as shown in Figure 39-7.

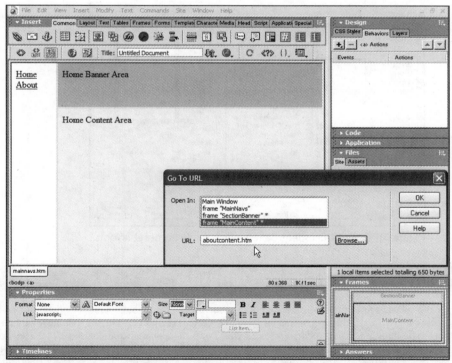

Figure 39-7: You can change multiple pages using the Go To URL method. Just select the frame and locate a page.

6. Click OK to close the dialog box. Save and test the page. Clicking the About link should swap out the banner and content frames.

7. Repeat the Go To URL method for the Home link, choosing the same frames but using the homebanner.htm and homecontent.htm pages.

The Document Gallery Framesets

The Dreamweaver Document Gallery contains many useful frameset configurations all pre-built and ready to roll. Their frames are sized and named, but you still have to save each page or use pre-existing pages for frame sources.

To use one of the framed layouts, choose File ➪ New or press Control+N (Command+N) to open the Document Gallery. As shown in Figure 39-8, clicking the Framesets category offers many different configurations of simple and nested framesets. To see an example and explanation of each, select a frameset. To choose a specific frameset, select it; then click the Create button.

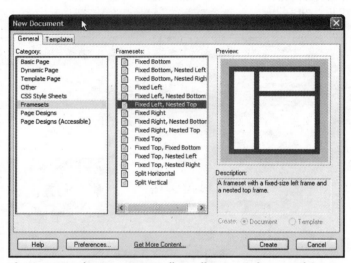

Figure 39-8: The Document Gallery offers many frameset layouts.

Why Add No Frames Content?

Dreamweaver MX lets you specify content for older graphical browsers and aural or text-based browsers through the use of the <noframes> tag. If your site is simple, you may be able to build a single large page that incorporates all your content. Use anchor links to move the visitor up and down the single page into each section of the site. If your site is quite large, you may need to provide an alternative site that is not frames-based. In both cases, avoid simply providing a link to update the visitor's browser; many users have good reason to use a browser that does not support frames.

To access the <noframes> tag, choose Modify ➪ Frameset ➪ Edit NoFrames Content. The Design view is cleared, and you can add text and other content as desired.

When you have a frameset chosen, you can save the frameset and then its pages or use the Save All method described earlier in the chapter.

Summary

This chapter showed you how to build and save a frameset. You learned several methods to save your framesets and pages and explored the target attribute of links in your framed pages. You also learned how to build more complex framed layouts through the use of nested frames and without nested frames. To set links that work in complex frames, you learned how to use the Go To URL behavior and how to set up a parent/child framed layout that uses the _parent target. Several options for providing content to browsers that do not support frames were discussed.

✦   ✦   ✦

Building Navigation with Behaviors

✦ ✦ ✦ ✦

In This Chapter

Working with rollover buttons

Building remote rollovers

Using navigation bars and pop-up menus

✦ ✦ ✦ ✦

To really make your site sizzle, why not add interactive navigation to your pages? Fireworks and Dreamweaver bring you a totally integrated solution for building rollovers, navigation bars, and pop-up menus with a few simple clicks.

Powered by JavaScript, *rollovers* are graphic buttons that change their visual imagery — to indicate that the button is a clickable link — when users move their cursor over the button. *Navigation bars* are rollovers with a third (and sometimes fourth) graphic to indicate a selected or down state. *Pop-up menus* are different from rollovers or navigation bars. They use DHTML or *Dynamic* HTML — JavaScript combined with Cascading Style Sheets — to generate submenus that appear on demand as visitors move their mouse over or click a text or graphic link. DHTML is covered in-depth in Chapter 44, but the Show Pop-Up Menu behavior is covered here because it is an easy-to-use navigational system applied with the Behaviors panel.

The JavaScript that powers rollovers, navigation bars, and pop-up menus are functions that are native to Fireworks and Dreamweaver. This tight integration means that you can build your graphic elements in Fireworks and export them in a variety of ways for use in Dreamweaver. Or, as many developers do, you can export graphics only from Fireworks and build your navigation in Dreamweaver. However you prefer to work, both applications are maximized to make your workflow smooth and efficient.

Understanding Dreamweaver Behaviors

Dreamweaver uses JavaScript to power the interactive operations of rollover buttons, navigation bars, and pop-up menus and all other Dreamweaver MX behaviors. A *behavior* is a combination of an *event* with an *action* triggered by that event. In the Behaviors panel, you add a behavior to a page by specifying an action and then, if needed, specifying an event that triggers that action. The action is a JavaScript *function* — an orderly declaration of specific variables and methods that allow the Web browser to track and manipulate various page objects. Dreamweaver behavior code is client-side JavaScript code; it is written to execute in the browser on the user's computer.

Behaviors can be attached to the document (the `<body>` tag) or to images, links, form objects, or other HTML elements.

About events

Events are messages that are generated by the browser when the Web visitor does something, such as click a link, load a Web page, or move the cursor over a rollover button. When the event for an object that has one or more behaviors attached occurs in the user's browser, the behavior's JavaScript function is called and the action is executed. Many possible events can be set to trigger Dreamweaver behaviors. Figure 40-1 shows the different browser options available from the Show Events For submenu accessed by pressing the Add (+) button in the Behaviors panel. The second option—4.0 and Later Browsers—is the most versatile and ensures that your page is viewable in a large range of browsers.

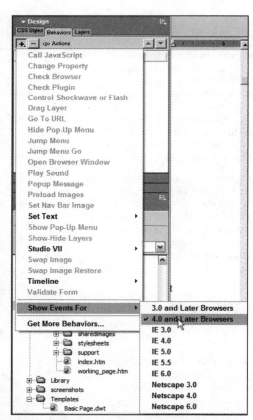

Figure 40-1: For greater browser compatibility, choose Show Events For ⇨ 4.0 and Later Browsers.

When you apply all behavior, a default event is chosen. The type of event depends on the nature of the behavior and the object selected in the page. For example, when an image is selected, the event will read (onMouseOver). The parenthesis surrounding the event lets you know that this behavior is attached to an image's anchor href. You can change the event associated with the behavior by selecting the behavior attached to the object. When the downward arrow appears, click it to select a new event from the menu that appears.

Dreamweaver behavior functions

Dreamweaver behavior functions are written in the head of the HTML document, surrounded by script tags and comments, as follows:

```
<script language="JavaScript">
<!--
(behavior functions here)
//-->
</script>
```

The script tag tells the browser to use JavaScript. The comments hide the JavaScript from browsers that do not support it.

Building Rollover Buttons

Rollover is the term used to describe the swapping of one image source (src) for another when the user moves (rolls) the cursor (mouse) over a graphic that has a JavaScript function attached to its link. The swapping occurs onMouseOver, and the second image is known as the Over state of the button. Rollovers are a great way to introduce additional information into a small space. You can even make one or both of your button states from animated GIFs.

See Chapter 22 for information about creating animated GIFs in Fireworks. Chapters 11 and 12 cover animation in FreeHand.

Inserting Fireworks rollovers

Fireworks MX

Use Insert Fireworks HTML (Insert ➪ Interactive Images ➪ Fireworks HTML) to place rollover buttons created in Fireworks into Dreamweaver pages. If you designed your rollover buttons within a complete page design, export only the navigational elements as a separate Web page with graphics for use in Dreamweaver.

Use the Export Area tool in Fireworks MX to build a secondary file with your navigation rollover buttons and export both HTML and Images into your defined Dreamweaver site. See Chapter 23 for details on how to use this method.

To insert the Fireworks HTML rollovers, follow these steps:

1. Place your cursor into your existing Dreamweaver page at the point where the buttons should be located.

2. Click the Insert Fireworks HTML button found in the Common tools of the Insert bar and use the Browse button to locate the exported Fireworks page.

3. Click OK.

Fireworks rollover buttons are written using native Dreamweaver behavior code. To edit the behaviors attached to the buttons in Fireworks, follow these steps:

1. Select the graphic to edit.

2. Open the Behaviors panel and double-click the attached behavior.

Using the Swap Image behavior

Although using the Insert Fireworks HTML button is useful, it is often easier and faster to simply export your graphics from Fireworks and build your rollovers in Dreamweaver using the Swap Image behavior.

Save the Habitat Alert40 folder from the chapter40_exercise folder to your hard drive. Define a new site. Hint: If you already have another Habitat Alert site defined, then choose the Edit Site option in the Site panel of the Site Definition drop-down menu and change the path to the Local Root folder.

In the following steps, you use the project site to see how to apply the Swap Image behavior in Dreamweaver.

1. Open the template (basic `page.dwt`) for the site pages from the Templates folder. This page contains graphics used as buttons, but they do not have any behavior attached.

2. Select the first of the buttons (LEARN). Use the Property inspector to give this graphic a "name" that is used to reference the object in the browser. Name this image `btn_learn`. Name each of your button graphics using the same convention, starting with `btn_` and using the text of the button. Names should be simple and contain no spaces or odd characters. You may use an underscore or hyphen. Names may not start with numbers.

   • btn_learn

   • btn_act

   • btn_support

   • btn_find

3. Reselect the LEARN button and open the Behaviors panel (in the Design panel group). Click Add (+) and select the Swap Image behavior.

   Naming your images is a smart thing to do. The Swap Image dialog box lists all images present in your page. If the images do not have names, they are listed as unnamed `<img>`, which makes them pretty hard to recognize!

   In the Swap Image dialog box, notice that the btn_learn image is preselected in the list of images. Dreamweaver assumes you are going to swap this image with another. In this case, Dreamweaver is correct.

4. Click the Browse button to locate the over state for the LEARN (btn_learn) button. Navigate to the `chapter40_exercise\Habitat Alert40` folder that you saved to your hard drive and to the `html\site\sharedimages\mainnavs` folder. Select `btn_learn_f2.gif` and click the OK button.

Fireworks MX

Fireworks uses two frames to create the two states of a rollover button. Unless you set it otherwise, Fireworks exports the second frame's graphics (the over state of the buttons) appending _f2 to the slice name, as explained in Chapter 23.

The autocheck Preload Images and Restore Images on MouseOut add two more functions that are almost always required for a typical rollover. The first (Preload Images) ensures that the over states of your buttons are downloaded and in browser cache, ready to be called by user events. The second (Restore Images on MouseOut) function keeps track of the original image and restores it when the user moves away from the button.

Tip

Uncheck the preload function when developing rollovers that use animated GIFs. If your animations preload in the background, the browser may start the animation on the frame that is currently loading rather than from the beginning.

5. Click OK to set the rollover. Repeat Steps 2–5 for each button, selecting the appropriate over state from the `mainnavs` folder.

6. Save your page. Because this is a template, you are asked to update all pages that use the template. Click Update. Preview the page in a browser to test the rollovers for each button.

Editing a Swap Image behavior

If you make a mistake and select the incorrect graphic or want to change the over state of your graphic, it's easy to edit the behavior and choose a different image. First, select the graphic to edit. In the Behaviors panel, double-click the Swap Image behavior listed for that graphic. Use the Browse button to select the correct graphic.

Rollover links

These buttons have links preset in the exercise files, but it is possible that when you build rollovers you may not have pages to link to. Because a link is required to attach a behavior to an image, Dreamweaver adds a null link to your image when a link is not present.

When you are ready to change the null link to a real path to a page, select the button and use the Point-to-File method to select the target page.

Removing the Swap Image behavior

To remove an attached behavior, first select the object to which the behavior is applied. In the Behaviors panel, highlight the selected behavior and click the Minus (-) button or press Delete to remove it.

Building Remote Rollovers

Remote rollovers — also known as disjoint rollovers or multiple-event rollovers — are graphics that use the Swap Image behavior to trigger an image swap for a graphic rather than the triggering button graphic. Remote rollovers are useful because they allow more than one image to display in a single location — triggered by users moving their cursors over different button graphics.

To incorporate remote rollovers into your pages, use the Swap Image behavior. You can set up a remote rollover to work in conjunction with existing rollover buttons or as a separate interactive element.

Adding remote rollovers to existing rollover buttons

The key to adding a remote rollover when you already have rollover buttons set up in your page is to add to the existing Swap Image behavior rather than add a new Swap Image function. To do this, you edit the existing attached behavior for each button.

In the following steps, you add remote rollovers to the Habitat Alert page provided for this exercise. This page contains existing rollover buttons as added in the previous rollover buttons exercise. In this exercise, you use the image in the circle as a region to add a remote rollover:

1. In your Chapter 40 defined site, using the Site panel, locate the folder and file html\site\remote_rollovers\remote_rollovers.htm.

2. Select the circle image (the bird) and name it **remoteinfo** using the Property inspector.

3. Now select the LEARN button (btn_learn) and go to the Behaviors panel to edit the attached Swap Image behavior. Double-click the Swap Image behavior to open it.

4. Click the image list to locate and select remoteinfo.

When you try to select a new image from the list of images in the Swap Image dialog box, a small bug in the program pops the list back up to the preselected button image. To work around this, click into the list anywhere, locate the desired image, and select it. While annoying, this bug is not serious, and it is likely that Macromedia will fix it with the next release.

5. Click the Browse button and navigate to remoteimages folder inside the remote_rollovers folder. Locate and select the learn.jpg image.

6. Notice that two of the images listed have asterisks beside them. The asterisks indicate that an image swap will occur for this image. Click OK.

7. Repeat Steps 3–6 for each button, each time opening the existing rollover's Swap Image behavior and selecting remoteinfo in the list before clicking the Browse button to choose the correct image from the remoteimages folder.

8. Save and test this page. Move your cursor over the buttons to view the remote rollovers. Figure 40-2 shows the image that swaps into the circle when you move the cursor over the LEARN button.

The more thought put into your remote rollovers during the design process, the more useful they'll be to your site visitor. If you chose an image that conveys what will be found in a site's section, your remote rollover provides clarity for the user. You can even incorporate graphic text into images to explicitly state what might be found in the section.

Every image increases the overall download time for your page. The clarity those graphics provide isn't useful if the user gets tired of waiting for the download to end.

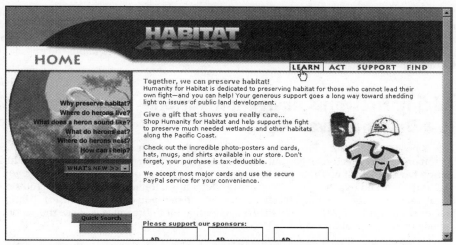

Figure 40-2: The circle image swaps as you move your cursor over the buttons.

Other remote rollover options

Existing rollover buttons are not required to set up a remote rollover. You can trigger an image swap for any image on your page by moving your cursor over any link, image, or text. Two things are required:

✦ An image, named and surrounded by an <anchor> tag, must already be present in the page.

✦ A remote link, text, or graphic must be selected to add the Swap Image behavior.

You cannot use the Swap Image behavior to make an image appear where no image already exists; this behavior swaps only the image src. But any link can be used to trigger the remote rollover.

To set up a remote rollover in this fashion, place your cursor into the triggering link, add the Swap Image behavior, and select the named image that should be swapped. Click the Browse button to locate the correct image and click OK.

Also, be sure that all the images used for the swap have the same dimensions as the original image. Only the src swaps; width, height, and all other attributes remain the same. This is true for rollover buttons as well.

Building Navigation Bars

A navigation bar differs from a set of rollover buttons because it keeps track of which button is clicked or selected. Navigation bar elements (buttons) can have more than two states. The common states are the *up* and the *over* states by you can add a third state of *down* and, sometimes, even a fourth state of *over while down*. Only the up state is required. Whether you opt to build the navigation bar in Fireworks or export the images and build the bar in Dreamweaver, the Set Nav Bar Image behavior powers the navigation bar's interactive elements.

Caution

The Navigation Bar Object and the Set Nav Bar Image behavior contain several wicked bugs at the time this book was written. Macromedia may have released an updated version that addresses these bugs. Check at www.macromedia.com/support/dreamweaver. If there isn't an update or it doesn't fix the bugs, be sure to look for Caution notes about the bugs in the following paragraphs.

Fireworks MX

Adding Fireworks navigation buttons to a Dreamweaver page

This is not referring to the Fireworks Nav Bar behavior, which shows the down state of each button on their respective pages but a row of buttons to form a navigation area. To add a navigation bar to an existing Dreamweaver page, place your cursor into the page where you want to add the bar and use the Insert Fireworks HTML button found on the Common toolset of the Insert bar to add the Fireworks HTML page. Alternatively, you can choose Insert ⇨ Interactive Images ⇨ Fireworks HTML. To add the Nav Bar behavior in Dreamweaver see the section coming up in this chapter called, "Using the Set Nav Bar Image behavior."

Cross-Reference

Chapter 20 shows how to build navigation buttons. You can find a tutorial for the Fireworks Nav Bar behavior at www.joycejevans.com/tutorials/Fireworks/FWMX/Nav%20Bar/nav_bar.htm.

Building a navigation bar in Dreamweaver

Most professional developers prefer to export only the images for the button states from Fireworks and build their navigation bars in Dreamweaver. There are two options for adding a navigation bar, the Set Nav Bar behavior or the Navigation Bar object. The Navigation Bar object, located in the Common toolset of the Insert bar, provides a simple, one-screen interface for adding the different button states for each button in the navigation bar.

The Set Nav Bar Image dialog box (Figure 40-3) provides fields for naming your bar elements and Browse buttons to locate the various states for each button. You can also add alternate text and a URL link and set a target frame for navigation bar buttons used in a framed site. Use the Show Down Image Initially option to display the down state of the button for the current page. For example, if you have a set of four buttons plus a home button, you would set the home button to be down initially on the home page only. Click the Add (+) button to move to the next element of your bar and repeat the process of naming the button and adding the buttons states, URL, and alternate text. When you build the navigation bar in a section page, set that section's button to be down initially, too.

At the bottom of the dialog box, you can indicate whether your navigation bar is to be inserted horizontally or vertically and can also choose to add it within a table structure. When you click OK, the navigation bar is inserted into the page.

Using navigation bars in framed sites

Navigation bars are especially useful in framed sites because a single page can be used to indicate where the user is within the site. JavaScript maintains the button states, eliminating the need for multiple pages to display down buttons when in a site section. In a framed site, be sure to choose the target frame when setting the When Clicked, Go To URL link. The menu to the right of this field should display your named frames.

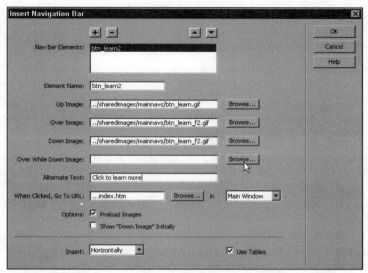

Figure 40-3: Name your button elements and select their buttons states. Add alternate text and locate the page for each button link. Click the Add (+) button to move to the next element of the navigation bar.

Tip If the frame you want to target doesn't appear in the menu to the right of the URL field, close the Insert Navigation Bar dialog box and name your frames.

Using the Set Nav Bar Image behavior

When your pages already contain the buttons you want to use for a navigation bar, use the Set Nav Bar Image behavior to add navigation bar functionality. Instead of adding the buttons as elements in a single dialog box, select a button and use the Behaviors panel to add the Set Nav Bar Image behavior. Any names, alternate text, or targets already existing for the selected button populate the appropriate field in the Set Nav Bar Image dialog box.

Caution If your buttons already contain links, adding the Set Nav Bar Image behavior may actually create a nested anchor tag upon adding the behavior. This is invalid HTML and should be fixed. To workaround this bug, remove your page links before adding the behaviors to the buttons.

To add navigation bar functionality using the Set Nav Bar Image behavior, follow these steps:

1. Select a button element.

2. Use the Behaviors panel to add the Set Nav Bar Image behavior.

3. In the Basic screen of the dialog box, use the Browse button to locate the various states for this button.

4. Add alternate text, a URL, and a target, as desired.

5. If working in the page that is the URL for this button, add a check in the box to set this button to Show Down Image Initially.

6. Click OK.

7. Repeat Steps 1–4 for each button. Perform Step 5 for a button only when building the navigation bar in the page that is the target of the button.

Tip

To avoid having to rebuild the navigation bar in all your pages, try building the bar as a Library Item; then add the item to the site pages. You won't be able to set the initially down state for buttons until you detach the Library Item, of course.

Navigation bars and templates

Using a navigation bar in a template (dwt) file is problematic; ideally, you want the region to remain locked until you have the pages for the site built from the template. But, if the region is locked, you cannot change the initial down state for the various buttons on their pages.

Although there may be complex, code-intensive methods to accomplish setting an initial down state for a navigation bar in a template, it is easier to fake the navigation bar appearance and not use the behavior at all.

Here's a work-around to mimic a navigation bar in the Habitat Alert site using editable attributes and building nested templates for each section:

1. In the Chapter 40 defined site, open basic `page.dwt` from the Templates folder.

2. Select the LEARN button (btn_learn) and choose Modify ⇨ Templates ⇨ Make Attribute Editable.

3. The SRC attribute should be selected but if not, choose it from the Attribute menu. Check the Make Attribute Editable box. Name this editable attribute **learn button src**.

4. From the Type menu, choose URL because an image src requires a path. The path given is correct, and you don't have to modify it. Click OK to close this dialog box and be prepared to see your button image become a placeholder image. This is as intended because the previous path is replaced by a parameter, written as `@@(_document['learnt button src'])@@`.

5. Repeat the process for the remaining three buttons, using the same naming convention with each button: **act button src**, **support button src**, and **find button src**.

6. Save the template and update the pages when prompted.

7. Open the instance pages and choose Modify ⇨ Template Properties. Select the appropriate Editable Attribute for the page and change the path by appending **_f2** just before the extension.

   Unfortunately, there's no Browse button to make this easier, but because Fireworks outputs the over state as _f2, you know that this is all you need to make the proper path to the image used for the over and down states. In Chapter 44, you want the selected button graphic to remain selected as a DHTML menu appears below it.

   The resulting pages use the second graphic when they load, letting the users know that they are in that section, while maintaining a locked set of navigation buttons in the template. Figure 40-4 shows the main page from the Learn section of the Habitat Alert site after setting up the Editable attribute.

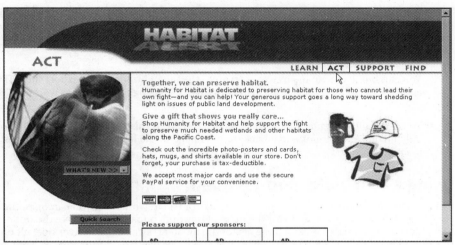

Figure 40-4: The Down state of the button reinforces the current location in the site.

The next step would be to build nested templates from the instance pages, as described in Chapter 37, so that all pages built for a specific section would have that section's navigation button in the down state.

Building Pop-Up Menus

A *pop-up menu* is a set of links created on the fly or on demand when the users moves their mouse over or clicks a link. The pop-up menu is stored as a JavaScript *array*—an ordered collection of one or more pieces of data—and is powered by a complex set of functions stored in an external JavaScript (.js) file. The external file is named mm_menu.js. You can use Fireworks and Dreamweaver can be used to build a pop-up menu, but Fireworks can build one that uses a graphic background image stored as a CSS style. Dreamweaver can build only text-based pop-up menus.

Pop-up menus have advantages. One major advantage is that the menus (and submenus) don't take up screen real estate until the user requests the menu by moving the mouse over or clicking a link. Another distinct advantage comes from the use of submenus; your navigation system can drill down into your site, giving users one-click navigation to the page of their choice, right from the home page of the site.

On the down side, pop-up menus use advanced JavaScript and Cascading Styles Sheets, so only version 4+ browsers may be used to view the menu. Not all browsers render CSS faithfully—as in the case of Netscape 4*x* (both Macintosh and Windows platforms) and Internet Explorer 5 (Macintosh platform).

If you decide to use a pop-up menu, take heart: Building these complex creatures is a lot easier in both applications and the JavaScript functions—Show and Hide Pop-Up Menu—are native to Dreamweaver, making editing your menu a snap.

There are three possible methods for creating a pop-up menu using the native Pop-Up Menu behaviors:

✦ You can build your pop-up menu entirely in Fireworks, export HTML and images, and use the page in a Dreamweaver site.

✦ You can build a menu in Fireworks, crop to the menu buttons, and export the HTML and images for later insertion in Dreamweaver MX using the Insert Fireworks HTML object.

✦ You can build the entire menu in Dreamweaver. With this option, you are limited to text-only menus and cannot add a background image to the buttons of the menus or sub-menus.

Fireworks MX

Using a Fireworks pop-up menu

If you design and export the entire pop-up menu from a Fireworks file, you can open the page in a Dreamweaver site and edit the menu. Fireworks pop-up menus have the option to use a background image for each table cell of the menu arrays. Dreamweaver doesn't offer this option because it cannot create images as Fireworks can: To edit the images used in a Fireworks pop-up menu, you have to edit in Fireworks. Fortunately, the integration between the two programs is tight and you can trigger the edit from Dreamweaver.

Fireworks MX

Editing the image-based pop-up menu

An image-based menu uses a background image in the CSS for the button arrays. This image can only be edited in Fireworks. You can choose to open Fireworks and change the menu images and re-export the page. However, you can trigger this same option from within Dreamweaver. Select the menu button graphic and click the Edit in Fireworks button in the Property inspector. You can edit other properties of the pop-up menu in Dreamweaver. These properties are covered in the following paragraphs. Figure 40-5 shows the four screens you use within Fireworks to edit your menu.

Caution

You must have Fireworks installed to edit a Fireworks-based pop-up menu.

Dreamweaver asks whether you want to edit the source file for the image or just modify the current .gif or .jpg file. Because you want to rework the images used in the menu, choose to open the entire file.

Cross-Reference

See Chapter 20 for details about creating, modifying, and exporting a Fireworks pop-up menu.

When you've located the source file, Dreamweaver launches the Fireworks application in Edit from Dreamweaver mode.

Note

You must have Fireworks selected as the primary editor for images in your Dreamweaver preferences for the editing process to work. To set this up, choose Edit ➪ Preferences and select the File Types/Editors category. The PNG, GIF, and JPG file types should all have Fireworks as the primary editor. If you installed all the programs from the Studio MX CD, this is probably already set up.

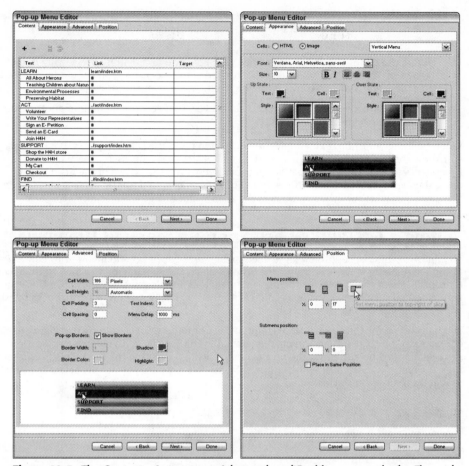

Figure 40-5: The Contents, Appearance, Advanced, and Position screens in the Fireworks Pop-Up Menu Editor are used to modify the menu items.

Inserting a Fireworks MX pop-up menu into an existing Dreamweaver page

Most developers will tell you that the main reason to build and export your pop-up menu from Fireworks is to be able to use the Images option, but you need not use the entire page. Like any other Fireworks-created elements, you can crop to only those elements and export as a separate page with graphics. Using the Insert Fireworks HTML object (button), you can insert the pop-up menu into your existing Dreamweaver pages.

In this section you add a pop-up menu to a sample Habitat Alert page to learn to add the Fireworks-based menu to your Dreamweaver page:

1. Open the page `popup_test.htm` from the `Habitat Alert40\html\site` folder.

2. Insert your cursor into the table cell where the navigation buttons are normally found in the site pages.

3. Click the Insert Fireworks HTML, or choose Insert ⇨ Interactive Images ⇨ Fireworks HTML; then click Browse in the dialog box that opens to locate `Chapter 40\html\site\popup_menus\popup_menu.htm`. Leave the Delete option unchecked.

   When the dialog box loses, check out your new pop-up menu by previewing it in a browser. This menu's links aren't set up and won't work, but you should be able to trigger the menu and submenus by rolling your cursor over the site menu button.

4. Close the browser and return to Dreamweaver. To insert the menu into another page, repeat the process.

Tip

When building your pop-up menu in Fireworks, don't add the URLs to pages. It isn't likely that you know the correct paths anyway, and it is far easier to select the proper pages in Dreamweaver. In any case, the paths are contained within the arrays in the head of each page using the menu. The path structures added in Fireworks would not be correct unless every Dreamweaver page using the menu is at the level within the site's directory structure.

Fireworks MX

Editing a Fireworks-based pop-up menu in Dreamweaver

To edit everything except the images used in an image-based pop-up menu or to edit a text-based menu made in Fireworks, use the Show Pop-Up Menu behavior attached to the menu's button(s). Select the button for the pop-up menu and double-click the Show Pop-Up Menu behavior. The resulting dialog box is similar to the Pop-Up Menu editor in Fireworks but does not contain the option to use images.

To edit the text for the menu choices, edit in the Contents screen, as shown in Figure 40-6. To edit an item, select the item, and change its text in the Text field. To change the location of an item, select the line and press the up/down/ arrows to reposition the item. This is different than the method used in Fireworks Pop-Up Menu editor where you simply select the item and drag it up or down in the menu.

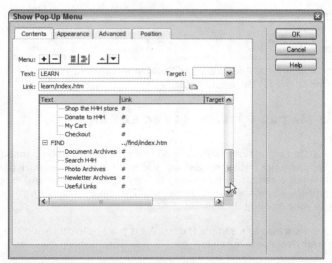

Figure 40-6: The Contents screen is where you edit menu items, including their URLs.

Changing the URL link

Another difference you'll see when editing a Fireworks pop-up menu in Dreamweaver comes when changing the URLs for your menu items. In Fireworks, you must hand-code the path structure or have a URL library available to select the path from the menu given. In Dreamweaver, you edit the URL by selecting the item in the Contents screen and clicking the small folder icon (Browse for Folder button) next to the Link field.

You can also hand-edit the code to change the link for any of your pop-up menu's items. The URLs are contained in the arrays used to generate the dynamic menus and are found in the head of the page containing the pop-up menu. Figure 40-7 shows where to look for the URLs for your main items; the URLs for the submenu items are easy to spot.

If your menu is used in pages that are at different levels in your site, you will have to edit each menu to have the correct path structures.

Using an inserted menu in a template

Because template operations rely on document-relative path structures, using a pop-up menu in a Dreamweaver template is a difficult and limited process. However, it is possible if you understand the restrictions:

✦ Fireworks pop-up menu elements (the HTML page, images, and external `mm_menu.js` file) should all be exported to the root level of your site.

✦ The template file in which you insert the pop-up menu using the Insert Fireworks HTML object does not display the pop-up menu properly. However, pages based on the template, which must all be saved in the same folder as the original exported Fireworks page and external `.js` file, should behave as expected.

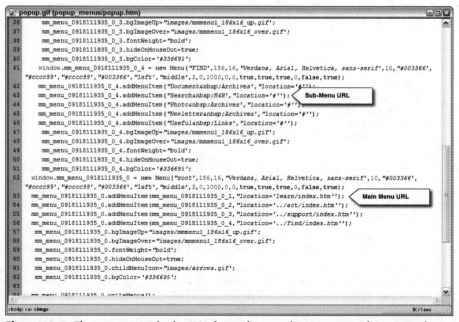

Figure 40-7: The arrays contain the URL for each menu item, among other properties.

Building a pop-up menu in Dreamweaver

If you don't plan to use an image as the background for your pop-up menu items, building the pop-up menu in Dreamweaver MX is easy. You use the Show Pop-Up Menu behavior. A text or graphic button is used to trigger the pop-up menu.

To build a pop-up menu, follow these steps:

1. Click the Trigger button.

2. Click Add (+) in the Behaviors panel to add the Show Pop-Up Menu behavior.

3. In the dialog box, add the items you need for your main menu and any submenus, as seen in Figure 40-8. To create a main menu item, type the item's text into the Text field. Add the next item by clicking the Add (+) button. To make an item part of a submenu for a main item, use the Indent button. To outdent an item, use the Outdent button.

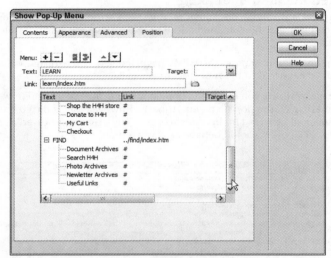

Figure 40-8: The Contents screen in the Show Pop-Up Menu dialog box lets you enter the text and format your main menu and submenu items.

4. To move an item's location, select it, and press the up/down arrows. Submenu items associated with a main menu item move when the main menu item is moved.

5. To select the page called when the user clicks a menu item, click the Browse for Folder icon located to the right of the Link field.

6. To change the text, link, or target of an item, select the item and make the changes. Tabbing or clicking another menu item forces the update in the list of menu items.

7. When your menu items are set, click the Appearance tab to enter the Appearance dialog box, where you set the formatting of your pop-up menu, choosing font, size, alignment, and color options. You also have the option to create a vertical or horizontal menu. An approximate preview helps you decide how to format the menu.

8. Click the Advanced tab when you are satisfied with the appearance of your pop-up menus. This dialog box offers a wide range of controls for your pop-up menu. You can let the size of your menus be automatically set (default) or set the width and height in pixel values. You can also determine cell padding or spacing, control the indent and timing of the menus, and set border properties.

9. Click the Position tab when you are finished setting the advanced menu properties. You set the menu positions by clicking one of the four position buttons. Although it's not entirely clear, the blue-green element in the examples displayed represents the pop-up menu, and the boxy element is the button. You can also position the menus by entering x,y values.

10. Click OK when the menu(s) are positioned.

11. Save and test your menu in a browser.

Summary

In this chapter, you learned to build and edit the most common types of navigation elements using Dreamweaver behaviors. You learned how to do basic rollover buttons as well as disjoint rollovers. How to insert navigation buttons that were exported from Fireworks was discussed. You also learned how to add the Nav Bar behavior to the Fireworks buttons. Not only did you see how to use Fireworks buttons, but you learned how to use the Nav Bar behavior in Dreamweaver. The chapter wrapped up with adding Fireworks and Dreamweaver pop-up menus.

Project Summary

The exercises in this chapter modified the navigation for the Habitat Alert Web site, adding rollovers to the original basic page template. You set editable attributes for the main navigation buttons. When the pages based on the template were updated, modifying the template properties let you set a down state for the button of the current page.

Files Prepared for the Habitat Alert Web Site

Files	*What Was Done*
Templates/basic page.dwt	Rollover buttons were added to the template and updating the template added them to the pages based on the template. Editable were set for the buttons to allow editing of the button graphic src.
index.htm	Rollovers added.
learn/index.htm act/index.htm support/index.htm find/index.htm	Rollovers added and each button's image src was set (in the page for that button) to the _f2 graphic to give the appearance of the button being selected.
Templates/act page.dwt Templates/learn page.dwt Templates/support page.dwt Templates/find page.dwt	Though not specifically done in this chapter, building nested templates from the updated index pages in the act, learn, find, and support folders is a logical next step.

✦   ✦   ✦

Inserting Media Elements

✦ ✦ ✦ ✦

In This Chapter

Working with Flash buttons and text

Using sound and video in your site

Adding Flash SWF media

Adding a Java applet

✦ ✦ ✦ ✦

Adding audio and video files, Flash buttons, and scrolling text are nice ways to spice up your Web sites. Add a Java applet to create scrolling text. While sound and movie files do add quite a bit to your page's download time, giving your site's visitors access to multimedia can enrich and enliven their experience. With careful design and by providing optional links, the user can choose to view (or hear) your files — or not.

Flash buttons and text can be added to your pages right in Dreamweaver. These scalable, easy-to-use Flash elements make button building without using a graphics program possible. Adding Flash movies that can contain sounds, interactivity, and even connect to a database increases the value of your site. Dreamweaver MX makes it easy to insert a Java applet into your site as well. Java applets can provide amazing functionality that just isn't an option any other way.

Media objects require a browser to use plug-ins or helper applications — programs that are recognized automatically by the browser. In this chapter, you look at inserting media objects that require the use of plug-ins — Flash and QuickTime — as well as media presented through ActiveX and Java.

Working with Flash Buttons and Text

Macromedia Flash MX delivers vector-based graphics and animation powered by complex client-side and server-side logic. But you don't need Flash MX to do this; you can tap into some Flash content right in Dreamweaver MX. There are three different types of Flash files:

✦ **Flash Authoring File** (FLA) — The source file for a Flash project and is created using Macromedia Flash. As a source file, it cannot be used by Dreamweaver and will not display in a browser.

✦ **Flash Movie File** (SWF) — The compressed output of the .FLA source file. Optimized for viewing online, an SWF file can be previewed in Dreamweaver and in a browser. This file cannot be edited in Flash, however, as the source information is removed when the SWF movie is created. Flash buttons and Flash text placed into HTML pages with Dreamweaver are SWF files.

✦ **Flash Template File** (SWT) — Flash5 (with Generator) output containing parameters modifiable via external input. Flash buttons and text are created from SWT files modified in Dreamweaver, resulting in SWF files added to the HTML page. The templates used to create Flash buttons and text objects are contained in the `Dreamweaver\Configuration\Flash` Objects folders. Flash templates may only be created in the Macromedia Flash 5 application. Flash MX does not support Generator.

Audio, video, Macromedia Flash, and Director movies are all assets and as such, are organized within the Assets panel. To open the panel, press F11 or choose Window ➪ Assets. The Asset panel is normally part of the Site panel group. Java applets are not visible as assets.

Inserting Flash buttons

The Flash button object is a customizable button that is based on a Flash 5 template (SWT) file. Through the insert bar's Media tab, you can chose, modify, and insert Flash buttons into your saved HTML page. Flash buttons are *scalable*. As vector graphics, changing the width and height of the button causes the output of the button to be re-rendered, without any resulting degradation of the graphic. You can insert a Flash button object in Design or Code views.

To insert a Flash button, you have three options:

✦ You can choose Insert ➪ Interactive Images ➪ Flash Button.

✦ You can use the Media toolset on the insert bar. Click the Flash Button object.

✦ You can drag the Flash Button object from the Media toolset in the insert bar to your document.

All three methods open the Insert Flash Button dialog box where you can review, select, modify, and insert a Flash button.

Flash button options

The Sample field displays the button options available to you by default in Dreamweaver MX. To review the available buttons, highlight a button style by selecting it in the Style list. After you click into the Styles list you can use your up and down arrow keys to move through the items. Move your cursor over and/or click the sample button display to see/hear any animation and/or sound associated with the button. Set a font choice, font size, and other options, as shown in Figure 41-1. Set the URL link and Target (if you are using frames or want your button to open a file in a new window) and choose a background color to match the color in the HTML document. You can opt to keep the default name automatically suggested by Dreamweaver or give the file a different name, but button SWFs must be saved in the same directory as the current file to maintain the document-relative links.

When your Flash button is selected and customized, click OK to close the dialog box and insert your button.

Tip

You may add more Flash button choices by clicking the Get More Styles button within the Insert Flash Button dialog box, which will take you to the Macromedia Exchange Site where more buttons styles are available for download.

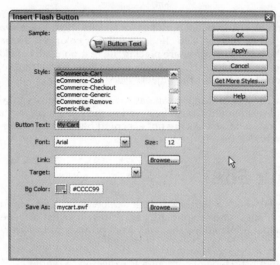

Figure 41-1: The Insert Flash Button dialog box options

Flash text

Flash text objects function like Flash buttons. They are created from SWTs (Flash templates) and are saved as SWFs. They, too, are scalable vector files and are quite versatile because, unlike a GIF or JPG graphic file with set dimensions, you can resize a Flash text object in the actual HTML file without destroying the quality of the graphic. The options for Flash text are shown in Figure 41-2.

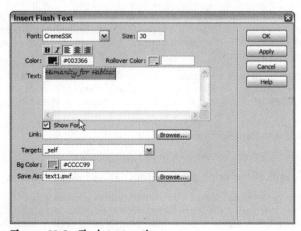

Figure 41-2: Flash text options

To create a Flash text object, choose Insert ⇨ Interactive Images ⇨ Flash Text. Choose a font, text size (in points), and set the text color. Additional options — Style and Align — are available for formatting your Flash text object. You can also choose a rollover color. Set the background color to match the area of the page where you are placing the text object by clicking the color swatch and sampling the open document. Click Apply to see your formatting selections in the document prior to clicking OK to insert the object.

Browse to set a link URL. Although a Browse button is available to locate a directory in which to save the object, Flash buttons and text should always be saved to the same directory as the file in which they are used. Site root-relative links are not accepted because browsers don't recognize them within Flash movies.

Using Sound in Your Site

If a picture is worth a thousand words, what's a sound worth? It can be worth a lot, enriching the visitor experience greatly. But adding sound to your site pages presents a list of issues related to file types, plug-ins, and helper applications that vary from browser to browser, and platform to platform.

A Web browser needs information about the type of content it is expected to render. Multipurpose Internet Mail Extension Types, or *MIME* types, form a standard way of classifying file types on the Internet. Web servers and browsers all have a list of MIME types, so that they can transfer files of the same type in the same way, no matter what operating system (platform) they are working from. A properly configured browser opens the file in the browser (for example, HTML), plug-in (such as QuickTime or Flash), or helper application (such as Adobe Acrobat or Windows Media Player).

The developer's reality is that different browsers support different media types and, unfortunately, no browser supports every type of media available. Therefore, browsers make use of plug-ins and helper applications. *Plug-ins* are software programs that extend the capabilities of browsers in a specific way, giving you, for example, the ability to play audio samples or view video movies from within your browser. Internet Explorer browsers also use Active X technology (controls) to support different media and file types. *Helper applications* are programs that are assigned to handle multimedia file formats (audio, video, images, and so on) that a Web browser itself does not understand.

Many plug-ins begin their existence as helper applications but evolve to the plug-in method to provide a more seamless Web experience. Helper applications and plug-ins enhance the functionality of a browser, but helper applications are separate programs; the disadvantages of helper applications are

✦ The user may need to wait for the application to load.

✦ The user might not have enough memory to run a helper program.

✦ In some browsers, helper applications or plug-ins may open in a separate window.

Additionally, sound files can be quite large and slow to download unless you use a specific compression format that optimizes the file for the Web. Compare, for example, an audio track (*Acoustic Alchemy*) created by Jason Leroy Finnern (SonicMint.com), found in the Chapter 41 CD files in the sound folder. The track is a folk style guitar loop with one file in the WAV format and the other, MP3. The WAV file is 1.37MB (1,442,988 bytes), far too large to expect the average Web visitor to download. By the time the file is completely downloaded, the user would have moved on to a different page. But the same loop in the MP3 format is surprisingly small—only 128KB (131,690 bytes)—and can be used quite easily as a background sound because the MP3 format streams. *Streaming* is when a file can begin to play before all its content is downloaded, a useful feature for Web content because connection speeds can vary so widely across a target audience. Finally, it may be even better to add your sound file to a Flash movie and to insert that into your pages. Flash media is handled exceptionally well by most browsers and the same WAV file inserted into Flash MX, then exported as an SWF file that compresses the sound using MP3 technology results in the file being only 16.6KB (17,027 bytes), small enough to be easily downloaded, even by site visitors with slow dialup connections.

Linking to an audio file

Linking to an audio file is the easiest way to incorporate a sound file into your Web page and has the added benefit of letting the user opt to listen to the sound. To link to an audio file, select a text or button link; then use the Property inspector to locate the file with the link's Browse for File button. It is generally considered good form to let the Web visitors know the file download size so that they may make an informed decision about clicking the link that plays the file.

Sound File Formats

WAV (Waveform Extension) is the default Windows system sound file format. WAV files are supported by most modern browsers but can be quite large, even with a short sound. They do not require a plug-in but are handled by a helper application.

AIF/AIFF (Audio Interchange File Format) is the default Macintosh system sound format. It has good quality and can be played by many browsers. AIFFs also are handled by a helper application and don't require the use of a plug-in. However, the relatively large file size of AIFF sound files limits their use in Web pages.

MID/MIDI (Musical Instrument Digital Interface) is a musical instrument file that is basically a set of instructions to your computer to use specific instruments to create digital music. MIDI files are surprisingly small for their relatively long sounds and do not require the use of a plug-in.

MP3 (Motion Picture Experts Group Audio or MPEG-Audio-Layer 3) is a specially compressed file format that was created specifically for Web use. The sound quality is superb for its super-small file size and MP3 files *stream*—playback of the sound can begin before the entire sound is downloaded. However, a helper application or plug-in, such as Windows Media Player, QuickTime, or Real Player, must be installed and used to play back the file in the browser.

RA/RAM/RPM (Real Audio) like MP3 files, are highly compressed and result in very small files sizes, but their quality is no where near that of an MP3 file. A helper application or plug-in is required for use in Web pages.

AU/SND (or Sun or Java format) is similar to WAV and AIFF formats, only au compression is more flexible. The au format is used primarily within Java applets and is popular with Sun/Unix platforms.

Embedding an audio file

To use a sound file as a background sound, you need to embed it. The `<embed>` tag references the audio file and a means of playing it, generally a plug-in or helper application. Commonly used plug-ins or helper applications are Windows Media Player, QuickTime Player, and the RealOne Player.

To embed an audio file, work in Design view and use one of these methods:

✦ Use the insert bar's Media toolset and click the Plug-in object button.

✦ Use the insert bar's Media tools and drag the Plug-in object button to your page.

✦ Choose Insert ⇨ Media ⇨ Plug-in; then navigate to locate your sound file.

Embedding the file includes setting certain properties the browser needs to control the appearance of the controller for the plug-in. For example, Width and Height, Align, Vspace and Hspace, and Border all affect the controller used by the plug-in. The Src field lists the path to the sound file. Add a URL to the Plg Url to set a location where the browser looks for the plug-in if the user does not have it installed. You can also click the Play button to view (listen to) the file in the Dreamweaver document.

Where to download sound-related plug-ins

Here's an exercise to embed a sound loop into your HTML page. Be sure to define a site and copy the Chapter 41 files from the CD into your root folder before attempting the exercise.

Note   PC users take note that when you define a site and copy a file from a CD to the root folder, those files will be locked and read-only. To enable editing of HTML files copied to your site, select the root folder and choose File ⇨ Turn Off Read Only from the File menu at the top of the Site panel.

This exercise uses the audio track "Acoustic Alchemy" created by Jason Leroy Finnern, at SonicMint.com:

1. Open the page `sound/index.htm` from the Site panel (window). Click the page.

2. Choose Insert ⇨ Media ⇨ Plug-in and in the dialog box that opens, navigate to the Sound folder and select `AcousticAlchemy.mp3`. The path structure should be set to document-relative. Click OK. You should see an icon that looks like a puzzle piece, which represents the embedded object.

3. With the object still selected, look at your Property inspector. In Figure 41-3, the values you see are modifiable; for example, the 32 × 32 W and H are the default settings for the width and height of the controller. If you want the controller fully visible, increase the settings to something like 144 × 60; then view your page in Internet Explorer and Netscape.

Figure 41-3: The sound file and plug-in properties

Most users like to be able to control the sound for a page, so giving them the controller is suggested, but if you don't want the user to have it, there are methods for hiding the controller. For example, you might try setting the W and H values to zero but be sure to test the page in your target browsers to be sure that they accept zero values.

4. If the visitor doesn't have a plug-in that can handle the embedded sound, the browser uses the URL you provide in the Plg Url field to download the appropriate plug-in.

Here are the URLs for some of the more popular plug-ins:

Shockwave: www.macromedia.com/software/shockwaveplayer/index.html

Flash Player: www.macromedia.com/software/flash/

QuickTime Player: www.apple.com/quicktime/

RealPlayer: www.real.com

Beatnik: www.headspace.com/beatnik/

VivoActive Player: www.vivo.com/products/playfree/vaplayer.html

5. Set the Border property to zero.

6. Now save this page and keep it open for the next exercise.

Setting parameters for embedded audio

Parameters are attribute settings passed to the browser. Width and Height are parameters, too, but Dreamweaver MX lets you edit those from the fields in the Property inspector. Other parameters are typed into the dialog box you can access by clicking the Parameters button. For example, to have your background sound file play over and over, you would add the paramether LOOP and set its value to true. Different plug-ins respond to different parameters. For example, the VOLUME=10% parameter is honored by Netscape 4x but not Internet Explorer 6x, because it uses the Windows Media Player to play the sound file.

Following are some commonly used parameters:

✦ AUTOSTART=TRUE — This starts the sound playing as soon as it loads. Most plug-ins have built-in keyboard shortcuts, and those could be explained to the site visitor, if needed, so that the user can still stop/start the sound file.

✦ LOOP=INFINITE **or** LOOP=TRUE — Add this parameter if you want the sound to repeat continuously as long as the visitor has the Web page open.

✦ HIDDEN=TRUE — When set to true, this hides the control panel for the audio file. It is generally a good idea to give your visitors the control panel so they can control the sounds on your Web page. If you want the control panel to appear onscreen, don't add the hidden attribute. The default setting is false.

✦ VOLUME=n — Use a value between 1 and 100.

Where to Find Sound Files

Like images, movies, and other online files, sound files are intellectual property and if not public domain, are likely to be owned by someone. But many sites online offer great sound files for your personal and even commercial use for free. Some good sites include the following:

✦ **FlashKit**—www.flashkit.com

✦ http://dmoz.org/Arts/Music/Sound_Files/Samples_and_Loops/

✦ **SonicMint**—www.sonicmint.com

Using Video in Your Site

The limited bandwidth of the Internet is the restraining hand when it comes to adding video files to your Web pages; video clips should be small in download size or visitors should be offered the option to choose to view a video file.

Tip

As you would with audio files, give your site visitors the total file size for a video clip so they can make an informed decision.

Video is a great way to entertain and educate your audience. You may add AVI or MOV files to your pages by linking to the file with a standard anchor tag using the Property inspector or by embedding the file just as you would an audio file.

Common Video Formats and Plug-in Options

Common Video Formats

AVI (Audio Video Interleave) is the current standard for Internet video and is supported by the Windows platform. AVI files don't require any special hardware, but cannot be used for full-screen motion pictures because of frame size limitations.

ASF (Advanced Streaming Format) may soon replace the AVI format and is also supported by newer versions of Windows. It uses streaming media technology to provide live video over low- and high-bandwidth connections.

MPEG (Moving Pictures Expert Group) requires an MPEG player to view the videos that have .mpg or .mpeg extensions.

MOV/QT (QuickTime) is supported by most browsers. The latest QuickTime formats use MPEG4 technology.

RA (RealVideo) uses streaming media technology to provide live video over low- and high-bandwidth connections.

Typical Browser Plug-in Implementations

QuickTime Player

The QuickTime Player plug-in is supported by all Macintosh and earlier Windows platforms and can play MPEG video on Windows. This powerful and well-designed plug-in supports MPEG video and audio, plus many other formats (MOV, QTVR, AVI, AIFF, WAV, AU, MIDI, and so on), and it fits seamlessly into the visitor's Web experience. You can download this software from www.apple.com/quicktime/download.

QuickTime pros:

✦ It supports most file formats.

✦ It offers a well-designed controller interface.

✦ It uses smart-streaming based on current downloading speed.

✦ It's powered by an efficient MPEG playback engine.

✦ The basic player is free.

QuickTime cons:

✦ It doesn't use the standard Windows user interface look and feel.

✦ It's not supported by newest Internet Explorer browsers on the Windows platform (IE5.5 and 6.0).

✦ It costs $30 U.S. to enable professional features for editing video files.

Windows Media Player

Streaming playback of embedded video and audio is directly integrated into recent versions of Internet Explorer on the Windows platform. Although older versions of Internet Explorer browsers try to use the installed-on-demand ActiveX control called ActiveMovie, newer browsers typically use Windows Media Player, which is also available for the Macintosh platform but is not generally preinstalled in browsers on that platform. Download the latest Windows Media Player plug-in at www.microsoft.com/windows/windowsmedia/players.asp.

Windows Media Player pros:

✦ It is a standard part of Windows.

✦ It supports many file formats.

✦ It has a simple user interface.

✦ It uses an efficient MPEG playback engine.

✦ It uses hardware acceleration, for example MMX, if available

✦ It's suitable for playing local files as well as files on Web sites.

Windows Media Player cons:

✦ It's not typically installed on Macintosh platform and must be downloaded.

✦ It might require manual configuration of a Web browser.

Continued

Continued

RealPlayer

Another plug-in used to play Web video is the *RealPlayer*—a free plug-in that is available for all platforms. With streaming audio/video support and handy subscription and channel features, RealPlayer is capable of handling most file types but is not installed by default. You may download the RealPlayer from `www.real.com/realoneplayer.html`.

RealPlayer pros:

+ It's cross-platform.

+ It includes a free player.

+ It can handle most media types.

RealPlayer cons:

+ It's not typically preinstalled.

+ It often plays media in a separate window instead of inline.

Adding video to your pages

To link to a video file, build a link in your page and use the Property inspector to select the video file. If the user's computer understands the file type and has a helper application or plug-in to handle the file, the browser plays the file. If not, a dialog box opens so users can select of a playback application or the file to their hard drive.

To embed a video into your page, you can use the `<embed>` or `<object>` methods. Using `<embed>` works only with plug-ins. Using `<object>` is designed to work with ActiveX components. ActiveX controls are reusable components (like miniature applications) that act like browser plug-ins. The ActiveX object in Dreamweaver lets you enter the appropriate classid, codebase, and parameters necessary for the user's browser to properly display the object. ActiveX is not supported on the Macintosh platform or in Netscape browsers. When using ActiveX components, you must supply a classid to identify the ActiveX control to be used. A classid supplies a long string of numbers and letters that indicate the registry status of the object. The codebase supplies a URL for downloading the control object if the user's computer doesn't have it available. To learn more about ActiveX technology, visit the Microsoft site (`www.microsoft.com`) and type active classid into the search field.

Internet Explorer and the QuickTime Player plug-in

Until recently, the plug-in installed as part of QuickTime worked for Netscape browsers and Microsoft Internet Explorer on Windows and Macintosh. Now Windows users who try to play a QuickTime movie in Internet Explorer version 5.5 (sp2 or later) or Internet 6.0 will encounter a broken plug-in icon until they install the new QuickTime ActiveX control from Apple *in addition to the QuickTime plug-in*. Users of other browsers on Windows or Macintosh are unaffected; they may use the plug-in installed with QuickTime and do not need to get the new QuickTime ActiveX control.

QuickTime uses a plug-in mechanism to display movies from your Web page in the user's browser. If you follow the Dreamweaver MX Help instructions for inserting video into your Web pages, you would use an `<embed>` element to display QuickTime content within the browser; however, to overcome the problem for newer IE browsers on the Windows platform, you should wrap the `<embed>` code within the `<object></object>` tags to make the new ActiveX control for QuickTime available to the browser, as in the following code example:

```
<object
classid="clsid:02BF25D5-8C17-4B23-BC80-D3488ABDDC6B"
codebase="http://www.apple.com/qtactivex/qtplug-in.cab"
width="360" height="228"
id="movie1">
<param name="SRC" value="Birdy_Flight.mov">
<embed
src="Birdy_Flight.mov"
plug-inspage="http://www.apple.com/quicktime/download/"
width="360" height="228"
name="movie1">
</embed>
</object>
```

When using this method for QuickTime movies (`.mov`) the classid must always equal `clsid:02BF25D5-8C17-4B23-BC80-D3488ABDDC6B`. The codebase must always equal `www.apple.com/qtactivex/qtplug-in.cab`, and the plug-ins page must always equal `www.apple.com/quicktime/download/`.

Let's use an MOV file from the Habitat Alert project site to set up the ActiveX and plug-in methods for viewing the movie in a Web page.

1. Open the file `quicktime_movie\index.htm` from the Site panel (window). This file is set up to accept a video file and has buttons that you use later to control the movie through JavaScript.

2. Place your cursor into the table cell `<td>` just above the Play and Stop buttons. Choose Insert ⇨ Media ⇨ ActiveX.

3. In the dialog box that opens, select the `Birdy_Flight.mov` file from the `quicktime` folder.

4. With the object selected in the document window, go to the Property inspector and set the following values, as shown in Figure 41-4:

   - W: **360**.

   - H: **228**.

   - ClassID: **clsid:02BF25D5-8C17-4B23-BC80-D3488ABDDC6B**.

   - Embed: Enable by checking the box.

   - Src: Birdy_Flight.mov. (You will have to click the Browse button, then show All Files in the Files of Type menu for the Select file dialog box.)

   - Base: **http://www.apple.com/qtactivex/qtplugin.cab**. (Dreamweaver actually codes this as `codebase=http://www.apple.com/qtactivex/qtplugin.cab`.)

   - ID: **movie1**. (Dreamweaver adds this to the object code only.)

Figure 41-4: Enter settings required using the Property inspector.

5. Save and try your page in an Internet Explorer browser. You won't see your movie yet because IE doesn't know the source for the movie file. If you look in your existing code, you should see that no `src` information appears in the `<object>` code, only in the `<embed>` code. To rectify this, you must add the parameter `SRC=`.

6. Click the Parameters button. Click the Add (+) button and type **SRC** into the Parameters field. Tab twice to get to the Value field (the first tab only selects the dynamic data icon) and enter the path to your movie. The path you would use is **Birdy_Flight.mov**.

Tip

You can copy the src path from the Property inspector's Src field before you click the Parameters button, which is a good idea when the path is more complicated than the one used in this example!

7. Tab twice to add a new parameter or click the Add (+) button again. This time you add a parameter that keeps the controller from showing, as you will be using JavaScript to control your movie. Add `CONTROLLER=FALSE`, putting `CONTROLLER` into the Parameters and `FALSE` into the Values, as you did with SRC.

8. Save and test your movie in IE and in NN4x. The movie should load but not play. You can press the spacebar to see the movie play; spacebar is the keyboard shortcut enabled in QuickTime to toggle start/stop movie. Keep this page open for the next exercise.

Tip

You can find a complete list of the parameters available for QuickTime movies at `www.apple.com/quicktime/authoring/embed.html`.

Using JavaScript to control a QuickTime movie

With the exception of Internet Explorer 5 for the Mac OS platform, you can use JavaScript to control the play of your QuickTime movie in most modern Netscape and Internet Explorer browsers. To allow the use of JavaScript to control the movie, you must pass a parameter to the plug-in that says that JavaScript is enabled.

1. Select the movie object in the file `quicktime_movies\index.htm` and click the Parameters button.

2. Click Add (+) to add a new parameter and type **ENABLEJAVASCRIPT** into the first field, tab twice, and type **TRUE** into the value field.

3. Click OK to close the dialog box. Save your file.

   At this point, only the `<object>` has a reference name for the movie file (movie1), which is written as `id="movie1"` in the tag. However, you also need a reference name in the `<embed>` tag so that JavaScript can control the file. Normally, you would add a name by typing it into the field at the top-left corner of the Property inspector when you have the object selected. However, at the time that this exercise was written, if you add a name there, it is written as `name="movie1"` (which is correct), but it is placed in the `<object>` and `<embed>` tags. Having `name=""` in the `<object>` tag causes JavaScript control of the QuickTime movie in Netscape 6*x* browsers to fail.

4. To work around the bug, add movie1 into the field, but then switch to Code view and delete `name= "movie1"` from the object tag.

5. Save your file and keep it open for the next exercise.

Scripting the movie control buttons

To control your movie using JavaScript, you enabled the use of JavaScript via a parameter. Now you need to use JavaScript to pass play, stop, and other functions to the QuickTime movie. To do this, you add some JavaScript to the `hrefs` of the buttons already in place in your file.

To control your movie, add JavaScript to the links for the buttons in the file. The script will reference the movie1 object.

1. Select the Play button in the `quicktime_movies\index.htm` file.

2. Type **javascript:document.movie1.Play();** and press Enter to be sure that the value is accepted.

3. Select the Stop button and type **javascript:document.movie1.Stop();** and press Enter.

4. Select the SoundOn button and type: **javascript:document.movie1.SetVolume(100);**.

5. Select the SoundOn button and type: **javascript:document.movie1.SetVolume(0);**.

6. Save your file and preview in IE6, NN4*x*, and NN6*x* browsers to be sure that the buttons work.

Setting Width and Height Values for Movies

Two very important settings required to properly display your movie are width and height. To determine the dimensions of your movie, press F11 to open the Assets panel and click the Movies icon. Select your movie listed in Movies Assets. If your movie is not displayed, try clicking the Refresh icon to update your movie assets. When you have the movie selected, right-click (Control+click) the movie and choose Edit. This should open the QuickTime Player. Under the Movie menu item, choose Get Movie Properties. The first menu in the dialog box that opens lets you choose the video (Movie) or audio track(s) and the second gives you the choices for different properties of the tracks. Choose Movie in the first menu and Size in the second. Note the width and height and use the values in Dreamweaver.

For the controller to appear properly, add 16 pixels to the height of a movie. Never set height or width to less than 2, even if the movie is hidden. To hide the movie controls, set the `HIDDEN` parameter equal to `true`.

The most common JavaScript functions include the following:

- **Play();** — Starts the movie.
- **Stop();** — Stops the movie.
- **Rewind();** — This causes your movie to rewind to the beginning.
- **Step(1);** — This steps the movie frame by frame in a forward direction.
- **Step(-1);** — This steps the movie frame by frame in a backwards direction.
- **SetVolume (n);** — Sets the volume of the audio track with n being a value between 1-100.

To read more about controlling movie and track properties of a QuickTime movie through JavaScript, see `http://developer.apple.com/techpubs/quicktime`.

Adding Flash SWF Movies to Your Pages

You can add a whole new world of interactivity to your pages through the addition of Macromedia Flash SWF movies. Whether simply entertaining your site visitors with a quick-to-load animation for visual interest, providing truly interactive content, or using Flash to provide sound to your site, Flash movies are easy to place in your pages by choosing Insert ⇨ Media ⇨ Flash. Dreamweaver uses the `<object>` and `<embed>` methods when inserting a Flash movie to get the best results in all browsers.

Your movie files will play using the Flash Player plug-in in Netscape browsers and with an ActiveX control in Microsoft Internet Explorer (on the PC). Flash Players are incorporated in the latest versions of Netscape Navigator, Microsoft Internet Explorer, and America Online.

Flash movies are assets and are viewable and playable from the Assets panel. To view your Flash assets, press F11 to open the Assets panel and click the Flash Assets icon. Select a SWF file. The Preview space above the list of assets can be expanded for better viewing. To play your Flash asset, click the arrow in the Preview space, as shown in Figure 41-5.

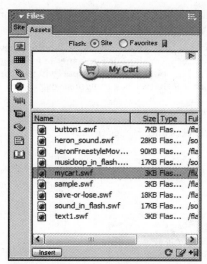

Figure 41-5: Flash Assets can be played in the Assets panel or in the document after a SWF is inserted.

In this section you add an interactive Flash movie (SWF) to a page in the Habitat Alert site. This movie features rollovers that provide information about the different kinds of herons that have endangered habitats:

1. Use the Site panel to locate the flash_movies folder and open index.htm form. Click to change to Design view.

2. Place your cursor into the page, and choose Insert ➪ Media ➪ Flash. In the dialog box, navigate to the flash_movies folder and select heronFreestyleMovie.swf. Click OK.

   You can also use the Media toolset in the insert bar by clicking the Media tab. Click the Flash button or drag it to your page and drop it in the desired location. In either case, the Insert Flash Movie dialog box opens to enable you to select the Flash movie.

   Another method for inserting a Flash file uses the Assets panel. Select a Flash asset in the Assets panel and click the Insert button located at the bottom of the panel or right-click (Control-+click) to place your movie in the document.

   Like audio and video files, a placeholder is put into the page. With Flash movies, the width and height are preset for you because Dreamweaver can get the information from the file; however because Flash is vector-based, you can scale the movie as you desire.

Tip

To maintain proportional width and height, hold down the Shift key and drag the bottom-right corner to scale your movie smaller or larger. A Reset Size button is available in the Property inspector if you want return the movie to its original dimensions.

3. Click below or beside the newly inserted movie. In this step, you add another Flash movie to provide a background sound in the page. This file contains only a sound and

is only 1 × 1. Add the movie Heron_sound.swf from the sounds folder. Set the W and H of the file equal to zero and turn off the Loop option using the Property inspector.

4. You can press F12 to preview your Flash content in a browser, but one fabulous new feature of Dreamweaver MX is the ability to interact with your Flash media in Design view. With the placeholder selected, click the Play button in the Property inspector. Move your cursor over the eggs to see the interactivity. Click the goose egg to see what happens. To stop movie, click the Stop button.

Tip

You can preview all Flash content in a page by pressing Control+Alt+Shift+P (Shift+Option+Command+P) to set ll Flash objects and movies to play.

5. Save your page and preview it in a browser.

As shown in Figure 41-6, some properties of your inserted Flash movie are preset by Dreamweaver.

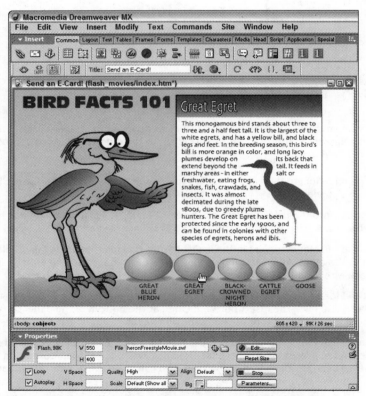

Figure 41-6: Use the Property inspector to modify Flash movie properties or to add parameters.

The properties in the Property inspector are as follows:

✦ **Name** — Provide a name to identify the movie for scripting in the unlabeled field at the top, left side of the Property inspector, just below where it says Flash and the file size.

✦ **W and H** — Specify the width and height of the movie in pixels. You may also use picas (pc), points (pt), inches (in), millimeters (mm), centimeters (cm), or percentage of parent container (%). The abbreviations must follow the value without a space (for example, 400px or 50%).

✦ **File** — The path to the Flash or Shockwave movie file. Click the Browse for Folder icon to locate a file, or type the correct path.

✦ **Src** — This displays only when Design Notes are being maintained and the SWF file was exported to the Dreamweaver site. The Src is the path to the original authoring file (FLA) for the Flash movie selected.

✦ **Edit** — This button lets you launch Macromedia Flash MX to update an FLA file, but it is disabled if you do not have Macromedia Flash MX installed on your computer.

✦ **Reset Size** — Returns the movie to its original size. To size a movie, enter new W and H values or drag the bottom-right corner of the movie. Hold the Shift key to maintain proportional W and H.

✦ **Loop** — Use to set a movie to play continuously. Uncheck it to have the movie play once and stop.

✦ **Autoplay** — Automatically plays the movie when the page loads when checked.

✦ **V Space** and **H Space** — Specifies the number of pixels of white space above and below and/or to the left and right of the movie. Use this to provide a margin around the movie when text or other content is contained in the same block.

✦ **Quality** — Controls anti-aliasing in playback of a movie. A movie looks better with a high setting but requires the user to have a faster processor to work well. Low emphasizes speed over appearance. High favors appearance over speed. Auto Low emphasizes speed at first, but improves appearance where and when it's possible. Auto High emphasizes speed and appearance, but favors speed over appearance if playback suffers.

✦ **Scale** — Determines how a movie fits into the dimensions set in the width and height fields.

  • Default displays the entire movie.

  • No Border fits the movie into the set dimensions so that no borders show and the original aspect ratio is maintained.

  • Exact Fit scales the movie to the set dimensions, regardless of the aspect ratio.

✦ **Align** — Floats the movie in the same way you might float or align an image relative to other content in the block.

✦ **Bg** — Sets a background color for the movie area, which also appears during loading and after playing, when the movie is not playing.

✦ **Parameters** — Opens a dialog box for entering parameters to pass to a movie. Your Flash movie must have been designed to receive additional parameters.

Editing a Flash movie

You can edit the original Flash file (FLA) from within Dreamweaver MX, just as you can edit the original source file for any Fireworks image. To initiate editing from Dreamweaver, select your Flash SWF file and click the Edit button in the Property inspector. You must have Flash MX installed on your computer. The Edit button isn't available if you do not. You must also have Design Notes enabled for the site so that when you export your movie (SWF) from the authoring file (FLA), a note is placed in the site.

When you click Edit, Dreamweaver launches Flash MX, and Flash MX attempts to locate the original source file from information stored in a Design Note (MNO). This information is present only if you exported your SWF from Flash into a Dreamweaver site and if Design Notes are enabled.

Note　Some SWF files may be created using Macromedia FreeHand 10. When this is the case, Dreamweaver displays the Edit button and launches Flash MX, but you will not be able to select the FreeHand file to open it because its extension is .fh.

Editing links for Flash SWF movies

You can update links used in your SWF files from Site Map view in your Dreamweaver site. To view a site map and edit your links, you must define a home page for the site and display dependent files. To switch to Site Map view in the Site panel (window), click the Expand button in the docked Site panel, as shown in Figure 41-7. For Mac OS, use the small white expander arrow located at the bottom of the Site window to view the Local and Remote sides of the Site window. Click the Site Files and Map icon to enter Map view.

Figure 41-7: Expand the Site panel (window) to enter Site Map View.

Select the link to update, which appears beneath the SWF file. You may opt to change the link for just one occurance or change it sitewide:

✦ To change the link for just this instance, right-click the link; then choose Change Link. Type the new URL (path) in the dialog box that opens.

✦ To update all instances of a link, choose Site ⇨ Change Link Sitewide. There are two steps to the process. First, browse to or type the path of the link you are changing in the Change All Links To field; then browse to or type the new URL in the Into Links To field.

When the paths are set, click OK and collapse the Site panel with the Expand/Collapse toggle button (Windows) or the white expander arrow (Mac).

Adding a Java Applet

Java is a programming language that is used to create executable applications that can run in a Web page. Unlike JavaScript, which is a client-side scripting language, Java must be compiled — made into a class file — and stored in the same directory or a subdirectory of the page that loads the class. Parameters can be used to pass specific information in the applet if it is designed to accept it.

Inserting an applet works the same as audio, video, or Flash. You have three options:

✦ You can choose Insert ⇨ Media ⇨ Applet.

✦ You can click the Applet icon from the Media tools found in the insert bar.

✦ You can drag the Applet icon from the insert bar to the document.

In all cases, a dialog box to locate the class file opens. After selecting the class file, you can use the Property inspector to size the applet, add a codebase where the appropriate files are located if the user needs them, and/or add parameters by clicking the Parameters button.

In this section you add a Java applet to the home page of the Habitat Alert site. The StringWalk applet (created by Bryan Harianto — www.geocities.com/bharianto/StringWalk/StringWalk.html) runs a scrolling news ticker that you can customize to include your own messages, complete with targeted links. It contains parameters where you may add as many messages as you like by using the parameter caption$n$. For example, caption0 may display the message "Visit our new Habitat Alert store..." Other parameters that this applet accepts are url$n$ and target$n$, as in url0 and target0, which would be set to www.habitat-alert.org/store/ and _self. The common number (caption0, url0, and target0) let the applet know that these things are associated and the caption text becomes a link when the user mouses over the text. When clicked, the page loads into the current browser window because the link target is _self.

To add a Java applet to the Habitat Alert home page, follow these steps:

1. Use the Site panel (window) to locate the java_applets folder and open the file index.htm. This is the Habitat Alert home page.

2. Place your cursor beside the "Give a gift that shows you care..." text and add a paragraph return.

3. Choose Insert ⇨ Media ⇨ Applet and navigate to the java_applets folder in the dialog box that opens. Locate StringWalk.class and select it. Click OK to insert.

   This applet already has the necessary parameters to contain several captions, URLs, and targets. You can modify how fast the text will move on the screen (right to left), set the color of the background, text, links, and more. A complete list of the parameters follows this exercise.

4. To set the speed of the scrolling text, select the applet, click the Parameters button, and select Delay. Press Tab twice to move to the Value field and add the value **25**. A lower number speeds up the scroll effect; whereas a higher number slows it down.

5. Add a new caption (caption3) by clicking the Add (+) button. Name the parameter **caption3**. Press Tab twice to reach the Value field, and type **Show your support!**

6. Add another parameter named **url3** and press Tab twice. Add the value **http://www.habitat-alert.org/store/**.

7. Press Tab twice to add another parameter. Name this `target3`. Press Tab twice for the value and type `_self`.

8. Click OK to close the Parameters dialog box, save your file, and preview by pressing F12.

As shown in Figure 41-8, your captions scroll across the page, and moving your cursor over the text displays the underline to let the site visitor know that this is a clickable link.

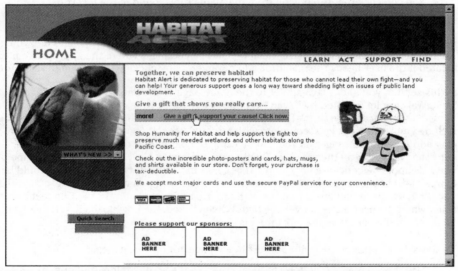

Figure 41-8: The parameter accolor sets the color for the link and makes the text look clickable.

StringWalk Parameters include the following:

✦ `delay` — Sets the speed of the scrolling text. Text scrolls from right to left.

✦ `fontface` — Sets the font family used to display the text.

✦ fontstyle—Lets you set plain, bold, or italic text styles.

✦ fontsize—Sets the size of the text.

✦ bgcolor—Sets the color used behind the text. Uses R, G, and B values.

✦ fgcolor—Sets the color used by the text captions.

✦ accolor—Sets the color of the link when users move their cursors over a caption.

✦ bdcolor—Sets the color of the border around the applet.

✦ captionn—Adds the text to scroll across the applet space. Change *n* to next sequential integer (for example, if caption3 already exists in the parameters, use caption4). The number must be placed directly after the word without spaces.

✦ urln—Adds the URL (absolute) to be used when the visitor clicks a caption. Set the number to match that of the caption for this URL.

✦ targetn—Adds a target for the called page. _self opens the file in the current document. _blank opens a new browser window for the file. _frame, _parent, and _top work with frame-based sites. The number used (*n*) should match the caption and URL for the page.

Summary

In this chapter, you explored the options for adding multimedia to your Web pages. You learned to use Flash buttons and text in Dreamweaver. Using the <object> and <embed> tags, you learned how to insert, modify, edit, and set parameters for each type of media, including audio, video, Flash, and Java. Additionally, you learned about browser issues related to displaying multimedia elements and discovered the need to accommodate the Windows and Macintosh platforms and browser versions.

Project Summary

In this chapter, you created a page to display an e-card created in Flash MX and added a Java Applet to scroll text across the home page for the Habitat Alert site.

Files Prepared for the Habitat Alert Web Site

Files	Where to Now?
java_applet/index.htm	You added the StringWalk scrolling text applet to the Habitat Alert site, setting properties and adding parameters to customize its use for this site.
	You could insert the same applet into different sections of the site, changing the parameters appropriately.
flash_movies/index.htm	You added an e-card to a page that could be configured to pop up from another location.

Working with Behaviors, Custom Scripts, and Snippets

Dreamweaver contains an array of JavaScript functions that add increased functionality to your site pages, including pop-up windows, form validation, and customized scripts. Dreamweaver also includes a snippets panel that enables you to store code for later use in all your sites. Snippets can either be complex functions or text bits you use on a regular basis.

Introducing Dreamweaver's Built-in Behaviors

Dreamweaver behaviors place JavaScript code in a document to let visitors interact with Web page elements through events. *Events* are user-actions, such as clicking (onClick), rolling the cursor over a page element (onMouseOver), or loading a page (onLoad) among many others. A behavior is a combination of an event with an action triggered by that event. *Actions* are Dreamweaver's name for JavaScript functions. *Functions* set up client-side logic that is called when a specified event occurs. In the Behaviors panel, you add a behavior to a page by selecting it from the Behaviors panel. You may then specify the event that triggers the selected action.

You've already explored some of the built-in behaviors found in Dreamweaver when you designed and scripted your navigation elements using Swap Image, Set Nav Bar image, and Show Pop-Up Menu. But there are many more behaviors that you can tap into to add increased functionality to your site, as seen in Figure 42-1. Some behaviors are grayed out depending upon the selected object in the current document. The list of events you may select from changes depending upon what your target browsers are. You may change the list of events available by choosing Show Events For. This doesn't change the list of behaviors — only the events that may trigger the actions, but events and the JavaScript functions (actions) may be affected by the user's browser. Browsers, like any other program, evolve and more modern browsers understand and use a richer, more complex version of JavaScript, which makes use of more events than earlier versions did.

Call JavaScript
Change Property
Check Browser
Check Plugin
Control Shockwave or Flash
Drag Layer
Go To URL
Hide Pop-Up Menu
Jump Menu
Jump Menu Go
Open Browser Window
Play Sound
Popup Message
Preload Images
Set Nav Bar Image
Set Text   ▶
Show Pop-Up Menu
Show-Hide Layers
Studio VII   ▶
Swap Image
Swap Image Restore
Timeline   ▶
Validate Form

Show Events For   ▶

Get More Behaviors...

Figure 42-1: Dreamweaver's behaviors. Which behaviors are available depends on what object or link is selected in the current document.

Cross-Reference

The entry for Studio VII shown in Figure 42-1 was added through extensions created by Project Seven. You'll read more about Extending Dreamweaver later in Chapter 43.

If all this talk of JavaScript functions and user events is overwhelming, don't worry. Using Dreamweaver doesn't require that you know which code to modify. You use the Behavior panel to select a new event and Dreamweaver makes the changes for you. With years of testing and much input from a vast team of engineers and beta testers, you can be sure that the code produced will work in your target browsers, too. That said, if you are a coder by nature, rejoice! DreamweaverMX, like the versions before it, provides easy access to the JavaScript behind the behaviors. Whether you prefer Design view or Code view, you will appreciate the time-saving, easy-to-apply functionality of Dreamweaver behaviors.

Using Dreamweaver's built-in behaviors

Dreamweaver MX contains many useful built-in behaviors, some of which have already been used in previous chapters. Here are some simple exercises designed to help you understand how some of the behaviors may be used. In some cases, the behavior has already been explained and used in another chapter — or will be used in a later chapter — so look for the cross-references.

Call JavaScript

Use Call JavaScript to call a custom function or line of JavaScript code that should be executed when an event occurs. When adding this behavior, type your own script or use code that is easily and freely available online.

On the CD-ROM

Save the chapter42_exercise folder to your hard drive. Define a new site.

Here's a simple example of a back button created using this behavior:

1. Locate and open _exercisechapter42\behaviors\showdate.htm. This page contains a custom dynamic date function (mydate) written in the head of the page.

2. Place your cursor into the write date link.

3. Click the Add (+) button to add Call JavaScript.

4. In the dialog box, type the following call to the mydate function: **mydate()**

5. Close the dialog box and set the Event to onClick, if it is not already set.

6. Save the page and preview it in a browser. Click the write date link to see the dynamic date.

Change Property

Use the Change Property behavior to change the value of an object's properties in the current document through the use of CSS. Which properties you may affect depends upon the user's browser — more properties may be changed in newer browsers (those with more support for dynamic CSS) and some browsers may not allow this method at all. Use this action only if you are familiar with HTML and your target browsers' capabilities. Here's an example exercise using the Change Property behavior to create a rollover effect in a layer with a text link inserted into a table cell:

1. From the chapter42_exercise defined site, open the file change_property.htm from the chapter42_exercise\behaviors folder in the Site panel.

2. Place your cursor anywhere in the text. The text is a single link that has a CSS style set to control the color and Text Decoration of the link. It is inside a table cell that is contained within a layer named popad. The layer has a background color property set to #CCCC99.

   Cross-Reference: For more about CSS links, see Chapter 36. For more about layers and DHTML (Dynamic HTML), see Chapter 44.

3. Use the Behaviors panel to Add (+) the Change Property behavior.

4. In the dialog box that opens (Figure 42-2) you must first choose the type of object to populate the Named Object field.

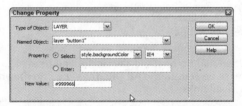

Figure 42-2: The Change Property dialog box

Note: You cannot "choose" LAYER if it is already the chosen type of object. First select a different type of object; then switch back to LAYER. This triggers the Named Object field to load the available layers. (There's only one named popad.)

5. Select the popad Named Object. Choose Select from the Property options and choose style.backgroundColor from the first menu and leave the second menu set to IE4. Internet Explorer 4+ and Netscape 6+ browsers recognize more properties. Other browsers simply ignore the attempt to change the properties.

6. Enter a New Value of **#999966**. Close the dialog box and set the Event to onMouseOver.

7. With your cursor still in the Button link, add the behavior again, repeating the same options but adding a New Value of **#CCCC99**. After closing the dialog box, set this event to onMouseOut, which restores the original background color to the color first used.

8. Save and test the page. When you move your cursor over the link, the layer background color should mimic the rollover effect normally possible only with images.

Check Browser/Check Plugin

The Check Browser is used to verify the user's browser brand and version and is especially useful when the site pages incorporate functionality that may otherwise be unavailable when the user's browser brand or version doesn't support it. This behavior is most often attached to the <body> tag to occur onLoad. You may also send the user to an alternate page that contains explanation and links to update their browser.

1. Open the page check_browser.htm from the behaviors folder in the Chapter 42 site.

2. Select the <body> tag and Add (+) the behavior Check Browser.

3. Browse to set the URL to index.htm in the behaviors folder.

4. Set the Alt URL to get_new.htm in the behaviors folder.

5. As shown in Figure 42-3, set the Netscape Navigation 4.0 options to Go to URL and otherwise, Go To Alt URL. Do the same for Internet Explorer 4.0 options. Set Other Browsers to Alt URL.

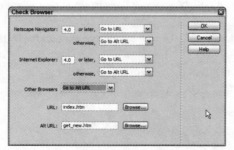

Figure 42-3: The Check Browser dialog box

If the browser is 4.0 or newer, it should understand JavaScript and be sent to the URL page (the homepage) or otherwise be sent to the Alt URL (get_new.htm), which provides details and possibly download links.

6. Save and test your page (check_browser.htm) to see what happens. Assuming you have a relatively new browser, you should be sent to the home page.

Caution   If the user's browser is set to disable the use of JavaScript, the detection of the browser will not occur since it uses JavaScript to do the detection!

7. In some browsers, it is possible to disable JavaScript. To see this in action, disable your scripting options by using a Netscape browser and choosing Edit ➪ Preferences, as shown in Figure 42-4 (NN 4*x*) or Figure 42-5 (NN6*x*).

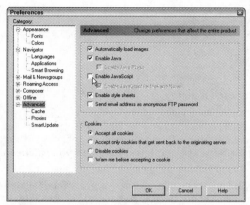

Figure 42-4: In Netscape 4*x*, turn off JavaScript by unchecking the option.

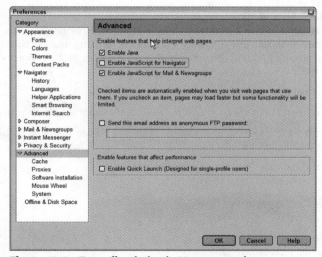

Figure 42-5: Turn off scripting in Netscape 6*x* here.

8. Now test the check_browser.htm page in Netscape. Because JavaScript is disabled, the Check Browser function never occurs.

To get around this problem, you must resort to a non-JavaScript method.

9. In check_browser.htm, choose View Head Content and click the Head Content bar that opens above the document.

10. Choose Insert ➪ Head Tags ➪ Refresh to add a meta refresh to this page as shown in Figure 42-6. Set the Delay to **5** seconds and browse to set the URL to get_new.htm. After a set time (5 seconds) the page takes the user to the get_new.htm (Alt URL) without the use of JavaScript.

Figure 42-6: A meta refresh doesn't require JavaScript to function.

11. Save and test the page in Netscape. You will find yourself at get_new.htm after 5 seconds. If you enable scripting for Netscape and retest the page, you will be taken to the home page.

You can use Check Plugin to verify the presence of a *plug-in*—a program designed to handle a specific file type that the browser itself may not be able to handle. You can't detect specific plug-ins in Internet Explorer using JavaScript. However, selecting Flash or Director adds the appropriate VBScript code to your page to detect those plug-ins in IE for the Windows platform. Plug-in detection is not possible in Internet Explorer for the Macintosh platform.

Control Shockwave or Flash

Use the Control Shockwave or Flash behavior to play, stop, rewind, or go to a frame in a Shockwave or Flash movie. To use this behavior, your movie must be named. You may add a movie name by selecting it and adding the name to the top-left field in the Property inspector. When done, follow these steps:

1. Select the object used to control the movie and add the behavior.

2. Select a Shockwave or Flash movie from the menu of those movies in the current page.

3. Choose Play, Stop, Rewind, or Go to Frame, as shown in Figure 42-7. If you choose go to frame, specify a frame number.

4. After you closed the dialog box, choose the desired event.

Figure 42-7: Select the type of action needed to control your named Shockwave or Flash movie.

Drag Layer

Drag Layer is a behavior designed to allow *layers*—page objects created through CSS positioning and the <div> tag—to be moved on the page. The layer(s) may be moved freely or be constrained. Because the objects associated with use of this behavior require CSS, this behavior is restricted to version 4+ browsers that support advanced JavaScript and style sheets.

See Chapter 44 for an exercise using this behavior.

Go To URL

The Go To URL behavior is a JavaScript method of sending the user to a new document, either within the site or external to the site. It is often used with framed sites to facilitate the loading of pages within two or more frames.

See Chapter 39 to find out more about this behavior.

Hide Pop-Up Menu/Show Pop-Up Menu

The Show/Hide Pop-Up Menu behaviors are used to build, show, and/or hide complex arrays of navigational elements. This behavior may also be used to modify/edit a pop-up menu created in Fireworks.

See Chapter 40 for example exercises using the Show Pop-Up Menu behavior.

Jump Menu/Jump Menu Go

Jump menus are forms-based menu objects that contain selectable items and URLs. The script is triggered by choosing (changing) the `<option>` item in the drop-down menu. Jump Menu Go is the same, except it provides a Go button that triggers the page change.

See Chapter 38 to read more about Jump Menus.

Open Browser Window

Use the Open Browser Window behavior to add a pop-up window to your site either when a page loads (`onLoad`) or when a user clicks a link (`onClick`).

To promote the option to send a Flash-based e-card relating to preserving wildlife habitat, a pop-up window will announce the e-card feature. The pop-up window will occur when the homepage loads, so its event will be onLoad:

1. Use the Site panel (window) to open the behaviors folder and open `index.htm`.

2. Select the `<body>` tag using the Property inspector and use the Behaviors panel to Add (+) the Open Browser Window behavior.

3. In the dialog box that opens (Figure 42-8) click the Browse button to locate `behaviors\change_property.htm`. This is a page with an announcement of the e-card site feature.

Figure 42-8: Use the Open Browser Window dialog box to set up your pop-up window.

4. Set the desired width and height for the new window. Keep in mind your target monitor resolutions when selecting the values used. This window is set to open at 350px by 150px.

5. Use the check boxes to provide browser window options — sometimes called "chrome." It is generally a good idea to allow scrollbars and resizing because the size of HTML text may vary so widely from user to user. You may also name the new window to be able to control it with JavaScript, but it is not required.

6. Click OK to close the dialog box. Save your page and preview in your target browsers.

Tip

Setting any attribute for the window automatically disables those not explicitly set. For example, setting scrollbars and resizing means only that your window will not have menu buttons, status bar, or any other options.

Play Sound

The Play Sound behavior lets you set a sound file to play when a specific user-event occurs. Because sound files are handled in so many different ways, this behavior may or may not work for all users because of the way their browsers are set to handle specific sound file types. The example given here uses a short .wav file.

1. Open the page `playsound.htm` from the `Chapter42\behaviors` folder.

2. Place your cursor in the Play link and use the Behaviors panel to add (+) the Play Sound behavior.

3. Browse to locate `heron.wav` in the `behaviors\sounds` folder. Select the sound and close the dialog box.

4. Set the event to onMouseOver. Save and test the page in both IE and NN browsers.

Cross-Reference

See Chapter 41 for more about the use of sound in your pages.

Popup Message

Provide information to the user with a JavaScript alert window created with the Popup Message behavior. You may embed a valid JavaScript function call, property, global variable, or other expression in the text by placing it inside curly braces {}. If, for some reason, you need to display curly braces in your message rather than use them in your script, place a backslash before the brace (\{).

1. Open `popmessage.htm` from the `Chapter42\behaviors` folder.

2. Place your cursor in the Play button link.

3. Use the Behaviors panel to add (+) the Popup Message behavior.

4. Add the following text: **This is the sound of the Black-Crowned Night Heron** and click OK.

5. Save the page and test it in several browsers to see how the alert is handled.

Preload Images, Set Nav Bar Image, Swap Image, and Swap Image Restore

These behaviors are most often used when creating rollovers, remote rollovers, and navigation bars that require the preloading, swapping, and restoring of images.

See Chapter 40 for exercises that use these behaviors.

Set Text (of Frame, of Layer, of Text Field, of Status Bar)

The Set Text behavior is used to change dynamically the content and formatting of frames, layers, and form text fields. Set Text ⇨ Set Text of Status bar is used to add a text message to the browser's status bar. For the first three options, you may use any valid HTML and/or embed JavaScript function calls, variables, properties, or expressions.

Any HTML content entered in the text box provided in the Set Text dialog box is coded using special characters. For example, adding the HTML `<br>` to create a line break results in `%3Cbr%3. %3C=<, br=br, and %3=>`. This can be daunting to users who seldom work in Code view.

See Chapter 44 for example exercises using the Set Text ⇨ Set Text of Layer and Set Text ⇨ Set Text of Status Bar behaviors.

Show-Hide Layers

Show-Hide Layers lets you set the visibility of CSS layers. This behavior is perfect for creating a slide show of images or complex navigation menus.

See Chapter 44 for an example of using Show-Hide Layers.

Timeline (Go To Frame, Play Timeline, Stop Timeline)

When using *timelines* — complex, scripted dynamic HTML elements — in your pages, you may control how the user interacts with the Timeline using the Timeline behaviors. Options include Play, Stop, and Go To Frame.

See Chapter 44 for exercises using the Timeline behaviors.

Validate Form

The Validate Form behavior may be used to verify that content is added to a form field and to ensure that the correct type of content is added. For example, you may use the behavior to require that an e-mail address is given. Figure 42-9 shows the options you have with the Validate Form behavior. For this example, check the Required box and select the Email Address option. The most likely events used with the Validate Form behavior are `onBlur` and `onSubmit`.

Figure 42-9: The Validate Form dialog box lets you choose a form element, specify whether content is required, and then check the type of data provided.

Cross-Reference

See Chapter 46 for an exercise that validates form content.

Show Events For

This behavior option lets you set what events are available in the Events menu. Earlier browsers understand fewer events. Newer browsers, particularly IE browsers, understand many different events. For greatest compatibility combined with a fairly large range of events, choose Show Events For ➪ 4.0 and Later Browsers.

Get More Behaviors

The Get More Behaviors option opens your primary browser and takes you to the Macromedia Exchange where you can download new behaviors for your application.

Cross-Reference

See Chapter 43 to learn more about extensions, including adding new behaviors to your Dreamweaver program.

Using Custom Scripts

Although Dreamweaver provides many built-in behaviors to add JavaScript functionality to your site, you are not limited to using only those scripts provided. You can use several methods to add your own scripts, either by linking to an external file or by embedding the script code into the document. How you choose to incorporate your scripts may depend upon how often your site's pages access the script.

For example, if you have a script that displays the current day, date, and year that you want to display on your home page, you may use the Insert menu to embed (place inline) the code into your document. However, if you plan to have the same date script on all of your site's pages, it makes sense to build an external JavaScript file (.js) and link all the site pages to that file. The external page is then requested from the Web server and its contents are placed in the browser's cache. This is an efficient method for reducing the overall download required by your site.

You can also build a script link to create a function call by typing into the link field in the Property inspector. However you choose to incorporate your custom scripts, Dreamweaver provides an easy-to-use interface.

Embedding a custom script

Use the Insert ➪ Script Object ➪ Script menu option to place custom JavaScript into your document. This opens the Insert Script dialog box. Alternatively, you can use the Insert bar's Script toolset and click the Script object button to open the Insert Script dialog box.

In the following steps, you add a dynamic date script to the Habitat Alert homepage by embedding the custom code into the HTML document:

1. Use the Site panel to open `index.htm` from the root level of the Chapter 42 site. Also locate and open `scripts\datescript.js`.

2. Select all of the content in `datescript.js` and copy. Close the file.

3. Place your cursor into the space just above the first paragraph in the homepage (`index.htm`) and choose Insert ➪ Script Object ➪ Script to open the Insert Script dialog box, shown in Figure 42-10.

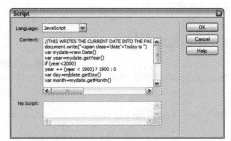

Figure 42-10: Paste a script or type it (if you're hand-coding) into the Content field.

4. Paste the copied code. This script doesn't contain the opening and closing `<script>` tags, but they will be added by the `Insert` function. Click OK to close the Insert window and save your page. Preview in a browser to see the dynamic date in action. As shown in Figure 42-11, the date is displayed as Today is Monday, 30 September, 2002.

An embedded script is not visible in Design view unless Invisible Elements are enabled, in which case a small yellow icon marks the script code. To remove the embedded script, select the icon and delete, or use Code view to locate and remove the code.

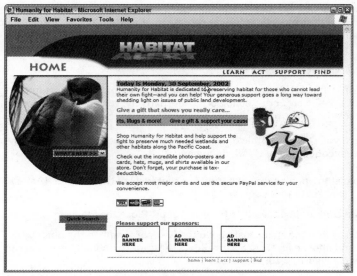

Figure 42-11: The dynamic date displays in the browser.

Linking to an external JavaScript file

If you plan to use a script in many of your site's pages, create an external file and link the pages to it using the Assets panel. External script files are saved with the .js extension and are recognized as assets.

In the following steps, you add the dynamic date script to the home page using an external file:

1. Reopen `index.htm` from the root level of the Chapter 42 site. Enable Invisible Elements and select the icon representing the embedded date script (if you added it in the previous exercise) and delete it. Save the page.

2. With your cursor inserted just above the first paragraph of copy, press F11 to open the Assets panel. Look for the Script icon (third icon from the bottom) and click it to bring up your script assets.

3. Select `datescript.js` and press the Insert button at the bottom of the panel. Alternatively, you could right-click (Control+click) and choose Insert.

4. Save your page and preview the dynamic date in a browser.

The `datescript.js` file uses a fairly standard method of calling Date functions. If you are even a bit familiar with JavaScript, you can easily modify the script to present the date in many different formats. (You can always get another copy of the `datescript.js` file from the CD.) The date is dynamically written using the `document.write` method.

The script also makes use of a class style (.date) that can be added to your site's style sheet to control the appearance of the date content. In the preceding example, no date class exists in the style sheet used by the page (`Chapter42\behaviors\stylesheets\main.css`) so it inherits the properties of the redefined .main content H4 style instead.

Working with Snippets

One of Dreamweavers' best new additions is the Snippets panel (Figure 42-12), located in the Code panel group. A *snippet* is a stored block of code saved via the Snippets panel into the Configuration\Snippets directory inside your Dreamweaver program files. Through the Snippets panel, you can create and insert codeblocks of HTML and JavaScript, as well as other scripting types (ASP, CFML, and so on). Your saved snippets are available to you in all your Dreamweaver sites because their code becomes part of the Dreamweaver program.

Figure 42-12: The Snippets panel comes with many predefined code snippets.

Inserting a code snippet

Dreamweaver ships with many built-in, predefined snippets that may be used in your site pages. These snippets are organized in folders (within the Configuration\Snippets directory in the Dreamweaver program files) that are arranged in the Snippets panel. To open the Snippets panel, press Shift+F9 or open the Code panel group and click the Snippets tab.

To review the available snippets:

1. Locate a folder that interests you and select a snippet.

2. Place the insertion point in the desired position in the document; to insert a code snippet around a selection, make the selection in the document.

3. In the Snippets panel (Window ➪ Snippets), double-click the snippet.

   You can also right-click (Windows) or Control + click (Macintosh) the snippet, and choose Insert from the pop-up menu.

Creating a code snippet

When creating a snippet, you can decide whether you want the code to wrap around a selection or to be inserted as a block of code. For example, you can take the datescript used in the example for the embedded JavaScript and build a snippet for use in any site. To make the snippet more user-friendly, be sure to add comments that explain the code. To create a code snippet from the script:

1. Open the `datescript.js` file from either the Assets (Scripts) panel or from the scripts folder found at the root level of the Chapter 42 site.

2. Choose Edit ➪ Select All or press Control+A (Command+A) and copy the code. Close the file.

3. Open the Snippets panel and open the JavaScript folder. Locate and open the date folder so that when you create the new snippet, it is saved into this folder. (You could also simply create your new snippet anywhere and later drag it to a folder so that it is easier to locate later.)

4. Click the New Snippet icon at the bottom of the panel. When the Snippet dialog box opens (Figure 42-13) name the snippet and provide a description so that others will understand what this code will do.

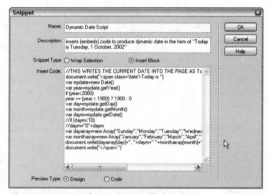

Figure 42-13: The Snippet dialog box

5. Choose Insert Block and paste the copied datescript code into the Insert Code field. You may choose between the Design or Code Preview Type, but in this case, it will not matter much because the rendering of the script can only be done in the browser.

   Normally, the preview type lets you set which view is triggered when inserting a snippet. If Design view is set as the preview type, the code is rendered there. Since the date script is processed client-side in the browser, you will not see the dynamic date in Design view.

6. Click OK to close the dialog box. Now when you need the date script, you can simply embed it via the Snippets panel.

If your snippet is code that should wrap around other content or tags, use the Wrap Selection option and place the first portion of the code in the Insert Before field. Place the last portion in the Insert After field.

Editing or deleting a code snippet

Snippets are easy to edit or delete. To edit, simply select the snippet and either right-click (Control + click) and choose Edit or select and use the Edit button at the bottom of the Snippets panel.

To delete a snippet, select it and use your Delete (Backspace) key or click the Delete icon at the bottom of the Snippets panel.

Sharing your snippets

One of the things that make snippets so useful is that you can share them with others who use Dreamweaver. Predefined snippets are stored as files in the Dreamweaver program but custom snippets (and snippet folders) are saved within user-specific configuration folders. To share a snippet, follow these steps:

1. Locate and copy the snippet file (or folder of files).

2. Give the file to other members of your team.

3. Let them know that they can place the file(s) or folder(s) inside their own user-specific configuration folder or within the **Program Files** (Applications)\Dreamweaver MX\Configuration\Snippets **folder.**

Where to Look for User-Specific Configuration Folders

Windows XP and Windows 2000

c:\Documents and Settings\username\Application Data\Macromedia\
Dreamweaver MX\Configuration

In Windows XP, this folder may be inside a hidden folder. To locate the folder, run a search that incorporates hidden files and folders and look for Application Data. When the Application Data folder (username) is found, right-click and choose Properties. Uncheck the Hidden option. Another dialog box will ask whether you want this to include sub-folders and files. Choose that option.

Windows NT

c:\WinNT\Profiles\username\Application Data\Macromedia\Dreamweaver MX\
Configuration\

Macintosh OS X

Hard disk:Users:username:Library:Application Support:Macromedia:
Dreamweaver MX:Configuration

Summary

In this chapter, you looked at ways to use predefined behaviors that ship with Dreamweaver. You learned to use the behaviors and how to use custom JavaScript by embedding the code or linking to an external file that contains the code. You also learn how valuable snippets can be by creating your own snippet to store a dynamic date script.

Project Summary

In this section, you added a dynamic date to the home page of the Habitat Alert site.

Files Prepared for the Habitat Alert Web Site

What Was Done	Where to Now?
behaviors/index.htm	Added a dynamic date script to display the current day of the week, date, month, and year.
behaviors/index.htm Habitat Alert site	Added a pop-up window to display a link to the new e-card feature for the This window can be used for puzzles or e-cards which are made in Flash. One of the puzzles is made in Dreamweaver.
change_property.htm	Set up a rollover effect for the e-card link without the use of images!

Extending Your Dreamweaver

✦ ✦ ✦ ✦

In This Chapter

Discovering the power of extensions

Building a command with the History panel

Modifying the Insert bar

✦ ✦ ✦ ✦

Dreamweaver is extensible, meaning it has the ability to add new features, functions, and capacity to your application through the use of *extensions*. An extension is an addition to the Dreamweaver program. It can be as simple as a command that builds a null link, an object button in the Insert bar that quickly builds a commonly used HTML table, a behavior added that helps show and hide layers, or as complex as a series of objects, behaviors, and commands all in one extension that builds a fantastic (and powerful) array of navigational elements.

For years, scripting gurus have been modifying their copies of Dreamweaver to include functionality not provided in the retail package and, quite often, giving away these modifications (with or without directions) to the general public for free. With Dreamweaver 4, Macromedia joined hands with these visionary coders and put together the Macromedia Exchange — an online repository of objects, behaviors, commands, and other assorted functions. In Dreamweaver MX, the legend continues, and the scope and power of extensions freely available on the Web is yours as a gift. Now there's no need to reinvent the wheel; chances are that someone has already packaged whatever you need as an extension, and all you need to do is find it, download it, and install it.

Discovering the Power of Extensions

Extensions are packages that install code files (most often HTML and JavaScript) into the Dreamweaver application to create new functionality by adding new objects, behaviors, and commands to the program's menus and panels. *Objects* insert a string of code into a user's document and appears in a tab in the Insert bar and in the Insert menu when its file is stored in a subfolder of the Configuration\ Objects directory. *Behaviors* add interactivity to a Web page by adding JavaScript in the form of functions (actions) that are called through an event. Behaviors are accessed via the Behaviors panel. *Commands* are used to edit a user's current document, other open documents, or HTML documents on a local drive. They insert, remove, or rearrange HTML tags and attributes, comments, and text, and are accessed via the Commands menu.

Where to find extensions

You can find extensions at many Web sites, but the main source is the Macromedia Exchange (http://macromedia.com/exchange/dreamweaver). The fastest way to get to the Exchange is from Dreamweaver:

✦ Choose Insert ➪ Get More Objects.

✦ Open the Behaviors panel and click Add (+) to choose Get More Behaviors.

✦ Choose Commands ➪ Get More Commands.

You may also go there via your browser. Once there, you can review the available extensions by category or keyword or do an advanced search to locate extensions by function, date, or author.

To download extensions, you must sign up as a member of Macromedia.com. Membership is free, comes with other benefits, and — assuming you pay attention when filling out forms — your privacy is respected. Use your membership ID and password to log in and download extensions.

When you locate an extension at the Exchange, click the appropriate download icon to begin the download. You have two options. You may run the installer from the site or download the package to your hard drive.

Downloading extensions means you already have them should you need to reinstall. For efficiency, create a folder called DW_Extensions somewhere on your computer and download extensions there.

Other locations to download great extensions are

✦ **Project Seven** — www.projectseven.com

✦ **MassimoCorner** — www.massimocorner.com

✦ **Yaromat** — www.yaromat.com

✦ **Web Assist** — www.webassist.com

✦ **Rabi** — www.dreamweaver-extensions.com

✦ **UDZone** — www.udzone.com

Installing extensions

To install an extension, use the Extension Manager, which is installed on your computer at the time you install the Studio or Dreamweaver program. You access the Manager by choosing Commands ➪ Manage Extensions or by locating the Extension Manager in your Macromedia program or application files.

There are two approaches to installing an extension:

✦ You double-click the .mxp package, which launches the Extension Manager if it is not already open.

✦ First, make sure that the Extension Manager's Program menu is set to the Dreamweaver MX program. Then, from the Extension Manager, choose File ➪ Install Extension.

The Extension Manager takes you through a series of disclaimers and agreements after which the extension's files are placed into Dreamweaver. In most cases, you will be prompted to restart the Dreamweaver application.

In the Extension Manager's interface, you can also review all your installed extensions, as seen in Figure 43-1. By selecting an extension, you may review any notes or directions associated with it. You can easily uninstall an extension as well by unchecking the On box.

Figure 43-1: Notes associated with an extension provide quick-start information about the extension.

Some Popular Extensions

Here are some really useful extensions you should check out. Where indicated, these extensions are used in chapter exercises.

The following extensions are from the Macromedia Exchange:

✦ **Set Permissions** — by Jay London. Use this extension to set file permissions on most Web servers. After installing, you can access this extension from the Remote portion of the Site panel by right-clicking (Control + clicking) a file. See Chapter 45 for more information about Set Permissions.

✦ **508 Accessibility Suite** — UsableNet.Inc. An extension to help you make your pages more accessible. Identify potential accessibility problems and repair them with FixWizard for tables and images and more. A must-have if your site must meet accessibility standards.

✦ **fiXMovie** — by Jonathan Krop. This extension makes inserting a QuickTime movie pretty easy by adding the proper class ID and Codebase information that allows newer IE browsers (PC) to download the ActiveX QuickTime control and plug-in. It also embeds the plug-in for browsers that use plug-in technology. Access this function from the Insert menu or bar. See Chapter 41 for more information about using QuickTime issues.

Continued

Continued

+ **What can we say?** Al Sparber and Gerry Jacobsen are the gurus of DHTML, and their extensions rock! Access these extensions from the Behaviors panel under the Studio VII ⇨ listing. See Chapter 44 for exercises using many of the PVII extensions listed here. The following extensions are from Project Seven.

+ **Snap Layers** — Used in conjunction with Auto Layers, this extension makes it possible to implement sophisticated cross-browser/cross-platform drop-down menus that can be relatively positioned. You can use this to build menus or even a ToolTip or two.

+ **Auto Layers** — No more Show-Hide Layers, thanks. Why waste time setting the visibility of each layer when you can let this little gem batch handle your layers? Use it with Snap Layers to build drop-down menus or with AniMagic to build slideshows.

+ **V Scroller and H Scroller** — With either of the scroller extensions you can build "frame-like" windows for your content without using frames.

+ **Layout Designer 2** — Wow. CSS-P without the headache. This extension helps you use layers that you can position relative to another layer or to the browser window.

+ **AniMagic** — An amazing extension that makes animating layers as easy as 1-2-3. Use this to create slideshows, build sliding menu systems, or just to animate a layer across your page.

+ **Style Sheet Loader** — Not a behavior, but a command. This extension helps you use multiple style sheets for CSS-compliant browsers and noncompliant browsers. Access the extension from the Commands menu.

The following extension is from Web Assist:

+ **PayPal E-Commerce Toolkit** — Pay Pal is an inexpensive e-commerce solution that is safe, secure, and free (well, cheap, anyway) and this extension makes it easy to implement Pay Pal for a single item or many. See Chapter 46 for more information about the PayPal E-Commerce Toolkit.

Building a Command with the History Panel

Dreamweaver uses commands to modify your documents, from cleaning up boggy Microsoft Word HTML to formatting and sorting tables. You can tap into the power of Dreamweaver's extensibility and build your own commands from steps recorded as you complete them in your document. To build a command this way, you need to use the History panel.

About the History panel

The History panel records steps you make in the current (active) document. By default, it can record up to 50 steps. History is kept only as long as the document is open. Once closed, the history is purged. The panel does not record history across frames.

Tip

To set a higher number of history steps, choose Edit ⇨ Preferences and click the General tab. Set the Maximum Number of History Steps to a new value. More history steps require more memory usage.

The History panel is a visual representation of the steps you take and can be used to step back and forth through the steps by sliding the small thumb up and down. This is a great alternative to using Control+Z (Command+Z) to undo and Control+Y (Command+Y) to redo, mainly because it is easier to see the steps and control how many steps (back or forward) you take. When you've made a step and want to proceed from that point, simply continue to work on the document and the "future" steps are overwritten. You can also clear the entire history by using the panel options.

You can also use the History steps to repeat tasks you perform often. There are three methods you can use:

✦ You can record steps as you take them. Recording limits you in what you can do, specifically preventing steps that may not be recorded, such as making a selection with the cursor. Recording is saved only as long as you do not make another recording and only for as long as the active document is open. While recording, Dreamweaver won't record steps taken if you switch from the active document to another.

✦ You can select steps listed in the History panel and make a new selection and replay the steps. In a similar vein, you can copy the steps and replay them in another document. Copied steps are saved only as long as the maximum number of steps are not surpassed and as long as you do not copy again.

✦ You can make a selection of steps in the History panel and save them as a Command. This is the most versatile method of reusing History steps because the command is saved to the program and is available in the current document, any other open document, and in later Dreamweaver sessions after the site and/or the program has been closed.

Some limitations to what steps can be replayed exist, be it by replaying or by making a Command. As you create steps in the History panel, you may see black lines separating some steps but not others — some mouse movements, such as making selections in the document window (by clicking or dragging) can't be played back or saved as part of a command. Try to avoid movements that can't be played back by using the arrow keys instead of the mouse to move the insertion point within the document window. If you need to make or extend a selection, hold down the Shift key while pressing an arrow key. You may find, too, that dragging an element from one location to another on the page causes a step with a red x to appear in the History list. Such steps are not repeatable in a replay or Command.

If this all sounds too complex to be useful, it isn't. Incredibly useful commands can be made from a single step. Give this a try:

1. Create a new Chapter 43 site, copying the chapter43_exercise files from the CD into the site folder.

2. Open the page `make_command.htm` from the Commands folder.

3. Select the words null link in the page.

4. In the link field of the Property inspector, type **javascript:;** then press the Enter key to be sure that the information is accepted.

Tip

Pressing Enter forces the Design view (and the History panel) to accept the entry.

5. Open your History panel by choosing Window ➪ Others ➪ History or by pressing Shift+F10.

6. In the History panel, select the entry made for creating a Hyperlink.

7. From the History panel's menu options, choose Save As Command (Figure 43-2).

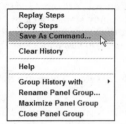

Figure 43-2: The History panel options include Save As Command.

8. As shown in Figure 43-3, name the Command make null link and click OK.

Figure 43-3: The Save As Command dialog box is where you name your command.

9. Now add some paragraph returns after the null link text and type a new word or two. Select the new words and choose Commands ➪ make null link.

Having a null link command is useful because it remains there for every site. While Link History can and will record javascript:; as you add it the first time to build a null link, the Link History is lost when you close the Dreamweaver application — but the null link command you just created remains, and the next time you open Dreamweaver and need a null link, you can use your null link command!

Creating Your Own Insert Bar Objects

You can work more efficiently in Dreamweaver by creating your own custom objects (tools) for Dreamweaver's Insert bar. Objects are designed to insert a specific string of code into a user's document. Objects appear in one of the tabbed panels of the Insert bar (and in the Insert menu) when the object's file is stored in a subfolder within the Configuration\Objects folder. In most cases, if you add a new object to the Insert bar, you must add a new subfolder for it within the Configuration\Objects folder and also edit the insertbar.xml file. With simple objects, you place the files associated with the object into any of the existing directories within the Objects folder.

About objects

All objects are HTML files. In more complex objects, the <body> of its file can contain an HTML form that accepts parameters for the object (the number of rows and columns to insert in a table). In many cases, the <head> of the object's file contains JavaScript functions that process form input from the <body> and control what is added to the user's document. In some cases, a link to an external JavaScript file also adds to how the parameters for an object are handled. As a result, complex objects that allow the user to modify object parameters may have three related components:

✦ The object file that defines what is inserted in your document

✦ An 18 × 18 pixel image that appears on the Insert bar

✦ The insertbar.xml file that defines where the object appears on the Insert bar

But the simplest objects contain only HTML to insert, without a `<body>` and `<head>` tag, and you really don't need to be a JavaScript whiz to build one for yourself.

Building the Table object

A simple object is an HTML file without `<head>` or `<body>` tags. To build a custom table object, you would first build a regular HTML page, add the table desired, and then remove the disallowed code or copy the desired code and create a new text page with it. In the exercise that follows, you use a table premade for you. Be sure that you've defined a Chapter 43 site and have added the CD exercise files for Chapter 43:

1. In the Site panel, open the Objects folder. Open `sidebar_table.htm`. Place your cursor into the table and select the `table` tag using the Tag selector. This 100 percent wide table has 1 row, 2 columns with a padding of 5 pixels, no spacing, and no border. The first column is set to 200 pixels wide and uses a background color in the cell. The second column is set to 100 percent wide because this is a hybrid table.

Cross-Reference

For more detail about hybrid tables, see Chapter 34.

Inside the table, there are two placeholder images. The first holds open the fixed-width column against the push of the 100 percent value of the second column. Regular spacer GIFs are not used because a relative path to the actual image cannot be made for Dreamweaver objects; therefore, a placeholder is used. Note that the Alt text for each placeholder gives the user directions to replace the image. When the sidebar_table

Where to Find Your User Data Files

When customizing your Dreamweaver application on a multi-user system, you'll need to know where to look for files that Dreamweaver created when it was installed. This is where you'll save any files you modify or add while extending — or customizing — your Dreamweaver.

In older operating systems like Windows 98, Windows ME, and Mac OS9x, a single set of Dreamweaver Configuration files is shared by all users, even if the operating system is configured to support multiple users. For newer systems, like Windows NT, 2000, XP, or Mac OSX, a separate set of user files is created as follows:

✦ **Windows NT:** `C:\WinNT\profiles\username\Application Data\Macromedia\ Dreamweaver MX\Configuration`

✦ **Windows 2000 and XP:** `C:\Documents and Settings\username\Application Data\Macromedia\Dreamweaver MX\Configuration`

✦ **Mac OS X:** `Hard Disk/Users/username/Library/Application Support/ Macromedia/Dreamweaver MX/Configuration`

In some instances (Windows XP) the files may be hidden. To change the hidden state of the user files, do a search on your system that includes hidden files and folders. Search for the appropriate Application Data (or Library) file and right-click the folder (in the search results) to choose Properties or select it and press Command+I to get info.

becomes a sidebar_table object and is used to insert this table into a page, the image could be selected and edited using the Fireworks Edit button.

2. In Design view, select all by either choosing Edit ➪ Select All or select the `<table>` tag.

3. Click to Code view. Your selection is still selected. Copy. Now select all again. You want all the head and HTML code to be gone, then press and delete.

4. Now paste the code back into the page. Switch back to Design view and choose File ➪ Save As.

   Now comes the tricky part — getting this file into the correct location.

5. Navigate to the Objects folder within your username Configuration folder (be sure to read the sidebar about multi-user systems) and create a new folder called **Custom_Tables**. Save `sidebar_tables.htm` into the new Custom_Tables folder.

6. From your desktop, locate your Chapter 43 site folder. Open it and Alt+drag (Option+drag) a copy of the `sidebar_table.gif` file to the desktop. Take that copy and place it into the same folder (Custom_Tables) as the `sidebar_table.htm` file you saved in the previous step.

The idea is to have the file and the gif in the same folder. Because both share the same name, they have an association, but that alone would be enough to make Dreamweaver pay attention to the new file — if you had placed both files into an existing folder in the main program (applications) Configuration folder of Dreamweaver MX. To use an example for Windows XP, if you had placed both files into `Program Files\Macromedia\Dreamweaver MX\Configuration\Objects\Tables`, Dreamweaver would add them to the existing Tables Insert bar panel.

Caution When adding custom objects to existing Objects folders, take extreme care not to overwrite existing files by using the same filenames.

But, because you added the files to a custom folder to create a new panel (tab) for the Insert bar, you must make one more modification to get Dreamweaver to pay attention and create the new Insert bar panel.

Modifying the Insert Bar XML file

To tell Dreamweaver about the Insert bar panel you want to create, you must modify the `insertbar.xml` file found in the username's Objects folder. A backup of the file exists (`insertbar.xbk`) but it is always safer to make a copy on your desktop before you begin any modifications to the main `insertbar.xml` file, because changes to the file may have been made by installing new extensions.

1. From your desktop, locate your username Configuration\Objects folder. In it, find `insertbar.xml`. Make a copy on your desktop. Alt+dragging (Option+dragging) is a great way to do this or Windows users can use the right-click copy/paste method.

2. In Dreamweaver MX, choose File ➪ Open and navigate to your username Objects folder and open `insertbar.xml`.

   The code (XML) contained within `insertbar.xml` controls how Dreamweaver builds the Insert bar. For each panel, there is a `<category></category>` pair of tags. Between the tags, information about the HTML file and associated GIF file is provided for Dreamweaver on start up. The code shown here builds the Script panel in the Insert bar.

```
<category folder="Script" id="DW_Insertbar_Script">
<button enabled="" file="Script\Script.htm" id="DW_Script_Script"
image="Script\Script.gif" name="Script" showIf="" />
<button codeOnly="TRUE" enabled="" id="DW_Script_Noscript"
image="Script\Noscript.gif" name="noscript" showIf="" tag="noscript"
/>
<button enabled="" file="Script\SSI.htm" id="DW_Script_SSI"
image="Script\SSI.gif" showIf="" />
</category>
```

Your goal is to build your own category for Custom_Tables. You won't need as much code as this, though.

3. Scroll to the ending `</insertbar>` tag. Place your cursor in front of it and type the following code, being sure to put all the code between brackets on one line, even though you won't see it like that here:

```
<category folder="Custom_Tables" id="DW_Insertbar_Custom_Tables">
<button file="sidebar_table.htm" id="customtable_sidebartable"
image="sidebar_table.gif" />
</category>
```

Because you are putting this last, your new panel would be last in the Insert bar. If you move the code to just after the existing Tables category code, then your new panel's tab would appear just after the Tables tab.

4. Save the page and close it. To see your new Insert bar panel, you must either reload extensions or restart Dreamweaver. In Figure 43-4, you can see the new Custom Tables tab just after the Tables tab.

Tip To reload extensions, press the Control key (Options key for Mac) and click the Insert bar's panel options and select Reload Extensions.

Figure 43-4: Your new set of table tools

To add more custom tables, simply build the HTML file with the table, modify it as shown in the exercise, and save it as described. Use Fireworks MX (or any other graphics program) to create an 18 × 18 GIF icon with a matching name and save it into Custom_Tables. Then modify the Custom_Tables category in the `insertbar.xml` file by copying the existing sidebar_table code, pasting, and changing the reference to sidebar table as needed.

Summary

In this chapter, you looked at ways to extend Dreamweaver through the use of prepackaged extensions you download from the Macromedia Exchange or from many different developer sites. You learned how to install an extension and how to use the History panel to build a command. You added new tools to your program by creating new objects and learned how to modify the Insert bar to include a new panel for the tool.

Project Summary

No Habitat Alert pages were created or modified in this chapter, but you will use many of the extensions in other chapters to create features for the site. You could also build object tools for items used repeatedly for the site.

✦   ✦   ✦

Building a Dynamic Site with DHTML

Dynamic HTML (DHTML) is a combination of HTML with a scripting language that enables you to change style or positioning properties of HTML elements. In this chapter, you learn about layers and explore many of Dreamweaver's built-in behaviors (and several extensions) that enable you to create some snazzy DHTML elements, such as drop-down and pop-up animated elements. You'll work through the exercises to create a draggable jigsaw puzzle, an image slideshow, several navigation menus, and even a scrollable "viewport" made with layers. All the elements in the exercise are cross-platform and work in most modern browsers, even Netscape 4x.

Understanding Layer Basics

To build DHTML elements, it's important to understand some key layer basics.

What's a layer?

Using layers doesn't mean you'll use a `<layer>` tag. The `<layer>` tag was a Netscape 4x tag that even Netscape doesn't support anymore. When working with layers in Dreamweaver, you will be working with a positioned `<div>` tag. A `<div>` is an empty HTML element. You can place it around other HTML elements. By itself, a `<div>` is pretty ordinary but when you use CSS to position it, it becomes magical — and, it becomes a layer. Lest you worry that you need to brush up on your CSS, relax; Dreamweaver contains a special Layers panel and Layer object that helps you build CSS-positioned `<div>`s without ever opening the CSS Styles panel. Working with the Layers panel, object, and the Property inspector (Figure 44-1), you can build layers by drawing or inserting them.

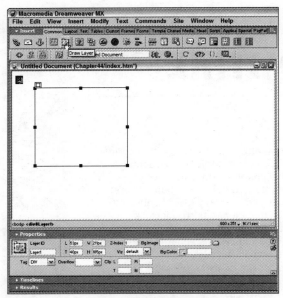

Figure 44-1: Layer tools include the Layers panel, the Draw Layer object, and the Property inspector.

Because layers are created with CSS, only version 4.0+ browsers recognize them. Like other CSS elements, a browser that doesn't understand CSS ignores it. But this doesn't mean your layer won't exist. It does, but only as a `<div>` with other HTML elements within it. The `<div>` is rendered inline where it occurs in the code rather than positioned with X, Y, and Z values.

Special layer properties

Layers have special properties that no other page elements have, and the Z-index is one of those properties. Besides the usual X, Y coordinates that all elements have (relative to the top-left corner of the current HTML document) layers have a third Z coordinate that indicates the layer's position in the Z-index or stack. Layers exist in the document and can overlap each other, much like stacking sheets of different-sized paper. To keep track of which layer is on top or below, the Z-index is used. The lower the value, the lower the layer is in the stack. The new document's default Z-index is zero.

Layers also have a visibility property. A layer may be visible, hidden, or can inherit either state from another layer. By default, layers are visible. There are many other special properties for layers that you will discover in the exercises given in this chapter. All layer properties may be edited with the Property inspector:

✦ **Layer ID** lets you specify a name to identify the layer in the Layers panel and in JavaScript code. Every layer must have a *unique* name—layer styles (CSS) are applied as IDs rather than classes. Names may use only standard alphanumeric characters. No special characters, such as spaces, hyphens, slashes, or periods, are allowed.

✦ **L** and **T** (left and top) specify the position of the layer's top-left corner relative to the top-left corner of the page, or of the parent layer if nested.

✦ **W** and **H** specify the width and height of the layer. Measurements (lengths) are pixels (px) by default but other units (mm, cm, in, pc, pt, and %) may be used. The unit must follow the value without any space between. Neither value is required and layers will "stretch" to accommodate content if the Overflow property is set to Visible. In many cases, it is best not to specify a height.

✦ **Z-Index** determines the z-index, or stacking order, of the layer. In a browser, higher-numbered layers appear in front of lower-numbered layers.

✦ **Vis** specifies whether the layer is initially visible. The default value is visible but may be set to Hidden or Inherit, which is derived from a Parent layer. Hidden hides the layer contents, regardless of the parent's value.

✦ **Bg Image** specifies a background image for the layer. Click the folder icon to browse to and select an image file.

✦ **Bg Color** specifies a background color for the layer. Leave this option blank to specify a transparent background.

✦ **Tag** specifies the HTML tag used to define the layer. Generally (for cross-platform, cross-browser compatibility) use `<div>`.

✦ **Overflow** controls the way layers (created with `<div>` and `<span>` only) appear in a browser when the content exceeds the layer's specified size.

• **Visible** — Extra content appears in the layer, and the layer stretches to accommodate.

• **Hidden** — Extra content is not displayed in the browser.

• **Scroll** — The browser should add scrollbars to the layer whether needed or not.

• **Auto** — The browser displays scrollbars for the layer only when content exceeds the layer's boundaries.

Caution

The Overflow option has uneven support across browsers.

✦ **Clip** defines the visible area of a layer. Left, top, right, and bottom coordinates define a rectangle in the containing layer (from the top, left corner of the layer). The layer is "clipped" so that only the specified rectangle is visible, like a view port.

✦ **Src** enables you to display another HTML document within the layer. Click the folder icon to browse to and select the document.

Note

Dreamweaver does not display the other document in the layer.

Draw versus Insert Layer

The two main methods of adding layers to a page are to draw them with the Draw Layer object in the Common toolset of the insert bar or to use the Insert menu to choose Insert ⇨ Layer. There are dramatic differences in the way your layers are rendered and behave in a browser based on how you created the layer.

Draw Layer places the `<div>` code above all other HTML content and below the `<body>` tag. Insert Layer places the `<div>` code in the document wherever your cursor is located. Where layer code is placed in the rest of the HTML code is important. For the most part, it should always be separate of the other (ordinary) HTML elements. After all, it's CSS that specifies where the layer appears in the page, not where the code is in the document. But the fact is, placing positioned <div> tags in other block elements (such as a table cell) can cause dramatic problems with your page. Different browsers render layers in different ways. Some browsers always measure from the top, left of the document; others look at the parent container, be it the document or a table cell.

Many developers believe that layer code should be placed below all other HTML elements, just above the closing </body> tag. Why? It's quite possible that a browser may have Styles disabled. Because positioned <div> tags require CSS, the positioning fails and the <div> renders inline. Would you rather have the mess be above your other content or below? It's up to you, but thankfully, you can easily move the <div></div> layers anywhere you want in Code view.

Tip You can select code in Code view and drag it to a new position.

Because layers and the tools used in Dreamweaver are so complex, this chapter will contain many exercises to show the finer points of DHTML in addition to explanations.

Building a Drag Layer Puzzle

Drag Layer is a Dreamweaver behavior that enables the dragging of layers in an HTML page. The function also includes options to constrain the drag direction and amount, snap the layer when within a specified distance to a target, and the option to add alerts if the user correctly positions the layer. You can use Drag Layer to build movable interface elements or, as shown in Figure 44-2, a jigsaw-style puzzle. Figure 44-2 shows the puzzle as it will appear when you finish the following exercise.

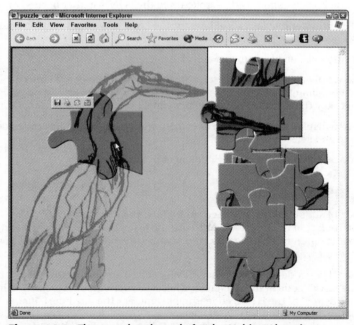

Figure 44-2: The completed puzzle for the Habitat Alert site

Save the Habitat Alert44 folder from the chapter44_exercise folder to your hard drive. Define a new site. Hint: If you already have another Habitat Alert site defined, then choose the Edit Site option in the Site panel of the Site Definition drop-down menu and change the path to the Local Root folder.

Let's use the Drag Layer behavior to build the Habitat Alert card puzzle. For this exercise, the layers necessary were created during export from Fireworks.

1. Use the Site panel to locate and select puzzle\puzzle_card_done.htm and press F12 to preview it in a browser. The puzzle pieces are stacked to one side. Drag pieces to put the puzzle back together. Some of the pieces pop up an alert when you successfully place them in the correct position.

2. Close the finished example and open puzzle\puzzle_card.htm. The Drag Layer behavior requires layers; in this case, the puzzle tray and all its pieces were created in Fireworks using masking and the CSS Layers export option. Click to select the first puzzle piece image (images are exported as rectangles) and delete its name in the Property inspector. Repeat for all puzzle piece images. See caution note for explanation. Save your page.

Export CSS Layers from Frames in Fireworks uses the frame names for the image files, as the image name, and for the layer names. Because layers must have unique IDs, the Drag Layer behavior will fail unless you either remove or rename the images.

For more information about masking in Fireworks, see Chapter 19.

3. The Drag Layer function must be called before the user can drag any layer so it is best to attach the behavior to the <body> tag using the onLoad event. Select the <body> tag using the Tag selector.

4. Use the Behaviors panel. Click Add (+) to add the Drag Layer behavior. The Layer menu lists all the layers in the active document. Select layer p1. Click the Get Current Position button. All of these layers are already in their final Drop Target positions because that's how they were created in Fireworks. The behavior uses the coordinates to know when the user moves the draggable layer to the correct location Before you finish the exercise, you move all the layers (except for the puzzle tray) to new positions so that the puzzle is ready to use. Set the Snap if Within field to 10px to make the puzzle a bit harder, as shown in Figure 44-3. Because the user may need to move the puzzle pieces in all directions, leave the movement of the pieces unconstrained.

Use Constrained (limited) movement when creating moveable interface elements, such as slider controls or a sliding menu.

Figure 44-3: The Drag Layer basic options

5. Click the Advanced tab of the Drag Layer dialog box and leave the default settings (Figure 44-4) but add **alert('way to go!');** in the When Dropped, Call JavaScript field. This creates a pop-up alert window with the text as indicated. The Call JavaScript field can also accept similar expressions or function calls but executes whether or not the user drops the layer successfully.

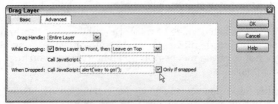

Figure 44-4: The Advanced Drag Layer options include adding JavaScript alerts.

6. Close the dialog box.

7. Repeat Step 5 for each layer except the puzzletray, each time selecting the correct layer, getting the current location, and setting the target zone.

8. After all pieces are draggable, randomly reopen the Drag Layer behaviors for some of the pieces and set an alert, as you did in Step 6, changing the message between the single quotes.

When done, save the page and preview in a browser to be sure that all pieces are draggable. It's easy to accidentally forget a layer or use the same layer twice, and you want to be sure that all layers are draggable before you move the layers from their original positions in Dreamweaver.

9. After you have tested and are sure that every piece is draggable in a browser, return to Dreamweaver and move all the layers to the right of the puzzle tray. Click an image and select its layer. When layers are at the top of the document, you can't grab the layer handle; use the Tag selector to select the `<div>` instead.

Grabbing the image to move the layer drags only the image out of the layer. Always grab the layer handle or select the <div> and use the arrow keys. Hold the Shift key down to move in 10-px increments.

Creating Simple Slideshows

Slideshows are a popular way to display images, and there are lots of methods to set them up. In Dreamweaver, you can use the Timelines panel to trigger Swap Image to switch slides or set up your images in layers and use Show-Hide Layers to do effectively the same thing.

About the Timelines panel

Timelines use DHTML to change the properties of layers and images over time. No plugin, ActiveX control, or Java is required, but JavaScript is used. Timelines involve frames that mark time as the Timeline is played. In the context of Timelines, a frame is a moment in time and you may set the number of frames that play (frames per second) in any timeline. Using a Timeline, you may change the position, size, visibility, and stacking order of a layer.

Behaviors may be added to a Timeline that triggers in a specific frame. For example, you could trigger a Swap Image in Frame 10, 20, 30, and so on, or have one of a series of layers show while the others hide by using the Show-Hide Layers behavior. A special channel of frames is reserved for adding behaviors, as shown in Figure 44-5.

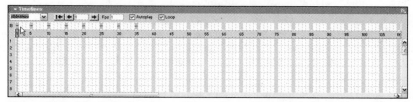

Figure 44-5: The Behavior channel is used to add JavaScript functions. They are triggered when the playback enters the frame, and use an onFrame event.

Swap Image slide show

Because a slide show is just a series of images that change one after the other, the Swap Image behavior is an obvious candidate for powering the show.

1. Use the Site panel to select slideshow\swap_image_done.htm and press F12 to preview. Watch as the slideshow plays through. Besides Swap Image, Set Text ➪ Set Text of Status Bar was also added to provide a caption for each slide, as shown in Figure 44-6.

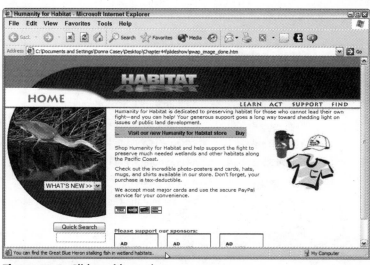

Figure 44-6: Slides with captions

2. When done, close the finished version and open `swap_image_slideshow.htm`. Choose Window ➪ Others ➪ Timelines to open the Timelines panel. Name the Timeline **slideshow**.

3. Select the bird image in the HTML document. Note that the image is named "slide" so that you can refer to and control it with JavaScript. Click in Frame 1 of the slideshow Timeline's behavior channel and click Add (+) to add the Swap Image behavior.

4. In the Swap Image dialog box, select the slide image from the Images list.

5. Browse to the `sharedimages\circlbirds` folder and select `circlepic0.jpg`. This is the same image that is already in place in the document. You add it to the Timeline so that when the Timeline loops, that image displays. The image inserted into the document will not reappear. Close the dialog box, leaving Preload Images checked.

6. To add the status bar caption, click Add (+) Set Text ➪ Set Text of Status Bar. In the field provided, type **An immature Black-Crowned Heron.** and close the dialog box by clicking OK.

Note that the event for both of the behaviors is `onFrame1`. When working with Timelines and adding behaviors, it is critical that you always click into Frame 1 of any animation channel prior to making any modifications to the HTML document, especially if you are adding behaviors not related to the Timeline itself. Failure to do this may result in non-Timeline behavior events being `onFrame#` rather than `onClick`, `onMouseOver` and the like.

7. Click into Frame 5 and repeat Steps 5 and 6, but this time choose `circlepic1.jpg` and set the status bar text to **A nesting Blue Heron gathers twigs for the nest.** Note now that the events for both behaviors are `onFrame 5`.

8. Repeat the steps for each slide using the information from Table 44-1 as you add images and status bar captions.

Table 44-1: Slide Show Images and Info

Frame Number	Image File Name	Status Bar Caption
1	circlepic0.jpg	An immature Black-Crowned Heron.
5	circlepic1.jpg	A nesting Blue Heron gathers twigs for the nest.
10	circlepic2.jpg	Patience is a virtue for the stalking Blue Heron.
15	circlepic3.jpg	A very young Night Heron.
20	circlepic4.jpg	A noise startles the young Black Heron.
25	circlepic5.jpg	You can find the Great Blue Heron stalking fish in wetland habitats.
30	circlepic6.jpg	The male brings nesting materials to the female Blue Heron.

9. After you added all the images and captions, set the frames per second to 1. This means that each slide will display for 5 seconds. For a longer interval, drag the behaviors to different frames; for example, move the behaviors to 1, 10, 20, 30, and so forth to get a 10-second interval.

10. Check the Autoplay option in the Timelines panel. A dialog box (Figure 44-7) lets you know that the behavior Timeline ➪ Go To Timeline Frame is being added. Check the Don't Show option to avoid seeing this dialog box again.

Figure 44-7: The Autoplay dialog box

11. Check the Loop option to cause your Timeline to repeat. The Loop dialog box (Figure 44-8) lets you know that the Timeline➪ Go To Frame action will be added to enable the loop. Because this action is added in the frame just after your last slide behaviors, grab the Loop behavior and drag it to a later frame. If each slide is five frames apart, move it five frames past your last slide.

Figure 44-8: The Loop dialog box

12. Save and preview to check out your slideshow.

Be sure you preview in all your target browsers because different browsers display status bar messages in different locations. Keep the message short.

Show-Hide Layers slide show

You can create a similar slide show by placing each image into its own layer and using the Show-Hide Layers behavior to show one of a group of layers. If you preview s-h_slideshow_done.htm (in the slideshow folder of the Chapter 44 site), you can see that this slide show works just like the one using the Swap Image feature, except no status bar caption was added. Layers were added over the circlepic image. Each layer contains one of the slide images. To create the layers, follow these steps:

1. Open show-hide_slideshow.htm from the slideshow folder.

2. In Design view, grab the Draw Layer tool from the Insert bar/Common panel and click and drag to draw the layer. When you let up, the layer appears and is named Layer 1 in the Property inspector and the Layers panel.

3. Rename the layer **pic0**. You may double-click the Layer1 name in the Layers panel or the Property inspector to change the name.

4. Select the layer by its small handle (top-left of layer). Move the layer over the circle picture area (the position should be Left 0 and Top 119). There are several ways to move a layer:

   - With its handle.

   - By selecting the layer, and using the Property inspector to change the L (left) and T (top) coordinates.

   - By selecting the layer and using the arrow keys to move 1px per key press. Holding the Shift key down changes the increment to 10px.

5. Click into the layer and add the image `sharedimages\circlebirds\circlepic0.jpg`.

6. Select the layer again. Because you already have the image inside the layer selected, you can use the Tag selector to select the layer container. Layers display in the Tag selector with the `<div>` tag and CSS ID, as in `<div#pic0>`. Copy the layer (Edit ➪ Copy) and paste it six times (Edit ➪ Paste). Be sure your cursor is outside the layer before you paste, otherwise you'll paste inside the layer.

7. In the Layers panel, you should see seven pic0 layers. Double-click the layer second from the bottom of the list and rename it **pic1**. Move up a layer and name that one **pic2**, and so on until you have **pic6**.

8. Clicking the Layer panel's eye icon sets layer visibility. Use the master icon at the top of the layer list to set all the layers to hidden (closed eye). There are three settings. Open-visible, closed-hidden, and no eye-inherit.

   All the layers should be hidden because you will show one layer at a time. If you click into the document (not on a layer) the layers all disappear. The visible bird image is the actual image in the HTML layout.

9. Use the Layers panel to select any layer except the bottom one. A hidden layer displays in the document if it is selected to facilitate working in the layer. Double-click the image in the layer and change it to `circlepic1.jpg`. Repeat selecting each layer and changing the copied image to one of the slides, working your way up the Layers list.

10. Add a Timeline (Windows➪Others➪Timelines), naming it **slideshow**.

11. Click add (+) to add the Show-Hide Layer behavior to Frame 1 of the Behavior channel. Use the buttons (Figure 44-9) to set all layers except pic0 to Hide. Set pic0 to Show. Close the dialog box. Allowing 5-10 frames between behaviors, add the Show-Hide Layers behavior, each time showing only the appropriate layer while hiding all the others.

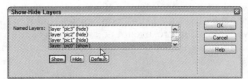

Figure 44-9: The Show-Hide behavior dialog box

12. When finished, enable Autoplay and Loop, and move the Loop behavior 5-10 frames to the right to allow the last "slide" layer to display.

13. Save and preview. You could easily add a Set Text of Status Bar caption to each behavior frame as you did in the Swap Image slideshow.

Tip

Add comments to your code when using layers (or any complex structures) so that the page code is easy to understand and edit. For example, `<!-- STARTS THE LAYERS FOR THE SLIDESHOW -->` enables any developer to know that the layers for all slides start below the comment. An ending comment can also be useful. `<!-- is placed before the text comment and -->` after to hide the text of the comment from the browser.

Using Set Text of Layer to Create Submenus

Set Text of Layer is a behavior that dynamically writes HTML to an existing layer. The existing layer is visible in the HTML document, but it is *empty* and therefore appears *hidden*, because layers are see-through unless a background color or image is set or other visible HTML content is placed within.

Caution

An empty layer whose `<div>` code is above other HTML structures may cause the HTML structures (tables, images, text, and so on) to displace in IE5 for Mac OS. To avoid this, place a nonbreaking space `< >` inside the "empty" layer.

You can use Set Text of Layer to create submenus for navigation buttons, as shown in Figure 44-10. A single layer is used and the Set Text of Layer behavior writes each submenu's links on demand—onMouseOver. The set text of layer behavior is used to both dynamically write the desired menu items into the layer (onMouseOver the button) and to dynamically write "nothing" (as in no text at all) into the layer (onMouseOut) It is hiding nothing; instead, it is writing back the nonbreaking space, which cannot be seen.

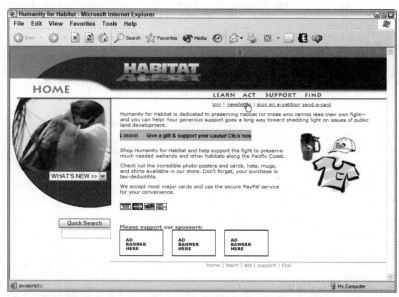

Figure 44-10: Submenus are written dynamically onMouseOver.

1. Select and preview `set_text_done.htm`. Move your mouse over each button to see its submenu. Move your mouse off a button and wait. After 10 seconds, the submenu disappears because the timer writes back the empty layer.

2. Open `index.htm` from the set_text folder and draw a layer that is 300 × 30 and is positioned at L=460 and T=125. Name the layer **submenu**.

3. Open `links.htm` from the `set_text` folder. Select all (Edit ➪ Select All) and copy. Close the file.

4. Select the first button (Learn) and click Add (+) to add the Set Text ➪ Set Text of Layer behavior. In the dialog box that opens (Figure 44-11), paste.

Figure 44-11: The Set Text of Layer dialog box

Tip

Always create your submenu content in another file and copy its code. Note that the file you copied from had no `<head>` or `<body>` tags and therefore was in Code view by default. Always copy the code from Code view when pasting into a Set Text of Layer window.

5. Change the text of the links (and even the null links) to make this button's submenu items. Organizing the links on separate lines makes the code easier to read. To add more links, paste more times. Delete unwanted links.

6. Repeat for each button, changing the link content and paths as needed.

7. Select the (empty) layer. Right-click (Control+click) over the `<div>` tag using the Tag selector and set its class to .subs. Because your submenus are in paragraphs, a CSS style sets properties to add margin, font-family, and more to style the submenu.

8. Save and preview to see the submenus.

When you need a behavior to occur after a set interval, a Timeline is the perfect answer; add the behavior you need to have occur in a Behavior channel. Which frame you add the behavior to sets the interval. To increase the amount of time, move the behavior to a later frame and vice versa.

1. In `index.htm` (set_text folder) (still open from the previous exercise) add a new Timeline and name it **hidesubs**.

2. Click into Frame 10 in the Behavior channel and click Add (+) Set Text ➪ Set Text of Layer. In the dialog box, type ** .**

3. Close the dialog box. Click into Frame 1 of any of the animation channels. (See previous caution about `onFrame` events.) Set the frames per second to 1fps. The layer "hides" after 10 seconds.

4. Select the first button (learn) and click Add (+) Timeline ⇨ Go To Timeline Frame. In the dialog box, choose the timer Timeline (hidesubs, leave the Go to Frame: box set at 1 and the Loop: box blank. Then click OK.). All Timelines would be available in the menu if more Timelines were present in the document. Multiple Timelines are allowed.

5. Set the event to onMouseOut.

6. Add the behavior Timeline ⇨ Play Timeline (hidesubs) and click OK. Set the event to onMouseOut.

7. Add the behavior Timeline ⇨ Stop Timelines and choose the hidesubs Timeline from the menu. Click OK and set the event to onMouseOver.

   Here's what you get: When the user mouses over a button, Set Text ⇨ Set Text of Layer writes the dynamic submenu. If the user moves to a new button, a new submenu is written. If the user moves off the Learn button but not to another button (onMouseOut), after 10 seconds the layer "hides" as the timer starts from Frame 1 and plays until it gets to Frame 10. But as long as the user remains over the Learn button, the timer does nothing because the time is stopped onMouseOver.

Tip

   Be sure to allow users enough time to find the link they want in the submenu. The timer is only needed here because it's a way to get back to the "hidden" submenu without using Show-Hide Layers.

8. Repeat the three Timelines behaviors for each button:

   - onMouseOut | Timeline⇨Go To Frame 1(hidesubs)

   - onMouseOut | Timeline⇨Play Timeline (hidesubs)

   - onMouseOver | Timeline⇨Stop Timeline (hidesubs)

9. Save the page and preview to test.

Animating a Sliding Menu Bar

Some very cool menus are easy to build when you use the AniMagic by PVII extension, freely available on the Project Seven Web site (www.projectseven.com). You need to install this extension to do the exercise in this section. To build a similar style menu (Figure 44-12) that uses layer animation would involve adding the layer (object) to a Timeline and setting up Keyframes. In the example menu, you'd need to set up two Timelines, one that moves the layer from L=-200 to L=0 and one that moves the same layer object from L=0 to L=-200. While not impossible, it is a rather complex process that involves adding the same layer object to two different Timelines and setting one behavior to occur onMouseOver and the other onClick.

Cross-Reference

Chapter 43 discussed how to download and install extensions.

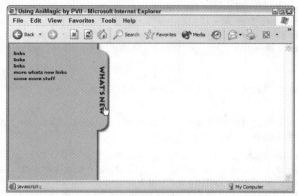

Figure 44-12: A sliding "What's New" menu

With AniMagic by PVII, getting the same results is far easier. You build the layer, add a table and the tab graphic, use a few CSS styles to control the appearance of the layer's and the menu's text links, and add the AniMagic action. We'll be using this menu system for the Habitat Alerts administration pages. Here's how it works:

1. You must have the AniMagic extension installed. Select and preview `slidemenu\` `index_done.htm` in the `chapter44` folder. When you mouse over the What's New tab, a layer animates and moves to the right 200 pixels to display What's New links. Click the What's New tab to close the menu.

2. Open `slidemenu\index.htm`. This page contains a layer that is ready to use. It contains a table, the tab graphic, and some applied styles. The menu's background element is created with a Y-repeat of a background image applied to the layer itself. The layer is already in the closed position and the goal is to animate it to open when the users move their cursor over the tab and animate it to close when users click the tab. Using two different events makes this a much easier task.

3. Select the tab graphic and use the Behaviors panel to click Add (+) StudioVII ⇨ AniMagic by PVII.

4. Select the layer to animate (whatsnewLayer) from the Layer Name menu (Figure 44-13). Set the Slide to Target Positions. The layer is currently at L=-200px and T=0px. The negative (-200) value means that the majority of the layer is off-screen to the left. When users move their cursor over the tab, you want the layer to open. Set L=0 (it should already be at zero anyway) and leave T=0. You don't need any vertical movement in this case. All Slide to Target Position settings are measured from the top-left corner of the document.

    FrameRate and *Delay* affect the animation of the layer. Lower FrameRates produce slower animations; higher results in faster animations. The FrameRate determines the number of pixels the layer moves per frame. The Delay time affects how many milliseconds elapse between frames. Another way to think about this is you are setting the *frames per second* for your animation.

5. Set the FrameRate to 5 and the Delay to 10. The remaining settings don't apply for this exercise. Click OK to close the dialog box and set the event to `onMouseOver`.

6. With the tab still selected, click add (+) to add the same AniMagic behavior again. Select your layer (whatsnewLayer) and this time, set L=-200 and leave Top at zero.

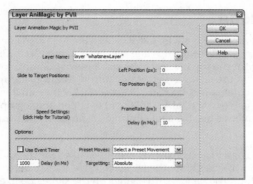

Figure 44-13: Add settings to open the menu in the AniMagic by PVII dialog box.

7. Set FrameRate to 5 and the Delay to 10. Click OK. Set the event to `onClick`.

8. Save your page and preview. Move your mouse over the tab to see the menu and click it to close.

Snapping Menus

A Snap menu is a thing of beauty. Using the Snap Layer and AutoLayers extensions — freely available from the Project Seven Web site (`www.projectseven.com`) — you can build menus that appear on demand and hide just as easily. In fact, the functionality of the example you'll see is triggered entirely `onMouseOver`. The menus use no Timeline and may be relatively positioned. And, you have a lot more control over the positioning of the submenus in each menu you add. Preview `chapter44_exercise\snapmenus\snaps_done.htm` and move your cursor over the rollover buttons. Figure 44-14 shows the Snap menus for the Learn button. Each button has its own submenu.

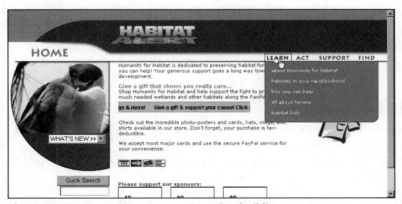

Figure 44-14: Snappy menus are a "snap" to build!

Understanding the menu

This menu system functions using the onMouseOver event. There are four menu layers (MenuLearn, MenuAct, MenuSupport, and MenuFind) and one layer named MenuCloser. The main menu layers contain an image at the top to create the small down-pointing arrow; each menu uses a different graphic so that the arrow is below the button. Below the graphic, a table is added. The table uses one column and is set to 266px wide. Each menu item has its own row. Below the table another single-celled table (at 266px) is added and a graphic to create the menu bottom is added. All menus use the same bottom graphic. All the menu layers are hidden.

Edit your Tag Library (Edit ⇨ Tag Library) and change the settings used for the <table> tag to Line breaks after tag only. The line break before the table tag causes a gap between the menu's top and the table, putting the <img> and <table> tags on the same line fixes the problem.

There are lots of ways to design your menus. This menu design has all the submenus set at the same width, and they all line up flush to the left edge of the Learn button. You can use a similar method to create menus that line up under different buttons; the design and logic is up to you.

The MenuCloser layer is larger than the largest of the menus. Its width is 300×200 and a spacer GIF has been inserted into the layer and its dimensions are also 300×200. The MenuCloser will be used to "hide" any open menu. The MenuCloser has a Z-index of 1 and all the menus have a higher Z-index value; this is critical because the MenuCloser must be below any menu. A behavior to hide all menu layers is applied to the spacer. The hide occurs onMouseOver.

The buttons have two behaviors applied to them: Snap Layers positions a menu relative to the Learn button's left and top edge, using offsets to give pixel-perfect placement. The same Snap event also moves the MenuCloser layer to nearly the same position, except the offsets place it just to the left of the button so that a portion of the MenuCloser layer and spacer GIF are exposed to the left, right, and bottom of the snapped menu. Both layers (Menu and MenuCloser) are made visible with the AutoLayers behavior (onMouseOver) applied to the button.

With the button's menu visible and the (invisible) MenuCloser below it, the user can select any item from the menu. But when the user moves to the left, right, or below the menu, the cursor encounters the MenuCloser's spacer with its AutoLayers functions set to hide any open menu (and the MenuCloser itself, as well). The same AutoLayers function is set to spacers that surround the buttons, too, just in case the user escapes the buttons to the left, right, or above.

Building the menu

The snapmenus\snaps.htm file contains all the necessary layers. Here's what you do:

1. Open snapmenus\snaps.htm from your Chapter44 site folder that you've defined. You must have the Snap Layer and AutoLayers extensions downloaded and installed.

2. Open the Layers panel to check the layers. All the layers are hidden but if you select a layer, you can temporarily see it in the document without making it visible. All the layers are in different locations. Use the Layers panel to Shift+click all the layers to select them. In the Property inspector (Figure 44-15) set the multiple-layers position to T=0 and L=0, then press the Enter key to update the document.

Figure 44-15: Use the Property inspector to position multiple layers.

Select a menu layer in the Layers panel. Note that the layers do not have a height setting; it's often better to avoid setting a height for layers unless you have a good reason to have one. The content of the layer expands the height; setting a height could result in problems if the overflow of content isn't set to be visible.

3. Select the MenuCloser using the Layers panel. When visible, click to select the spacer inside the layer. Click Add (+) to add the behavior StudioVII ⇨ AutoLayers (Figure 44-16). When the dialog box opens, choose Set Two from the Set menu. Don't select anything in the Layers list; it may look like something is selected, but it isn't. Click OK to close the dialog box. Those actions tell the browser that the list of layers is Set Two and to hide all these layers.

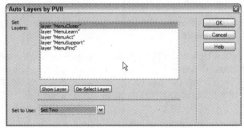

Figure 44-16: By not selecting any layer to show, all layers will be hidden. The Set to Use menu is useful when you have other layers that are not part of the menu.

Tip

Note the event for the behavior. Chances are that it isn't onMouseOver. Because all functions for this exercise use the onMouseOver event, you can simplify the steps by clicking the event to choose Show Events For ⇨ Version 3.0 and Later Browsers. This doesn't affect the actions but does limit the event to the one you need.

4. Select the Learn button. Click Add (+) to add the behavior StudioVII ⇨ Snap Layers. As shown in Figure 44-17, choose btn_learn from the Anchor Object menu. Choose MenuLearn from the Layer to Snap. Each of the menu buttons are 17px tall. Leave the Left offset at zero, but set the Top offset to 17 so that the menu won't be over the button.

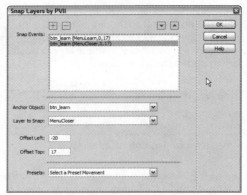

Figure 44-17: The Snap Layers dialog with two
Snap actions, one for the button's menu and
the other for the MenuCloser

5. Add a new snap action by clicking the (+) button at the top, left of the dialog box. Leave
   the Anchor Object set to btn_learn, but change the Layer to Snap to MenuCloser. Set
   the Left offset to -20. The menus are 266px wide. The MenuCloser layer is 300px wide.
   By setting the MenuCloser back about 20px from the left edge of the Learn button, the
   spacer extends beyond the area of the menu on all sides except the top. Leave the Top
   offset at 17.

Caution

Never offset the MenuCloser so that it covers the button or weird flickering occurs as
the button is covered by the MenuCloser.

6. Close the Snap Layers dialog box. Click add (+) to add the behavior AutoLayers
   (StudioVII ➪ AutoLayers) and show (Figure 44-18) both the MenuCloser and the
   MenuLearn layers. Choose Set Two from the Set to Use menu. Click OK. Because you
   have the Behavior events to use v3.0 events, the event is already set to onMouseOver.

Figure 44-18: Showing the MenuCloser and
MenuLearn layers in Set Two

7. Repeat Steps 5 and 6 for each button. Because of the design of the menus (aligning with
   the Learn button) the Anchor object is always btn_learn, although the Layer to Snap
   changes with each button. And don't forget: Every button snaps the MenuCloser. Use
   the values in Table 44-2 for each button.

Table 44-2: Snap Layers and AutoLayers Values

Button	First Apply Snap Layers	AutoLayers	Event
Learn	Action #1: Anchor Object=btn_learn Layer to Snap=MenuLearn Left=0 Top=17 Action #2: Anchor Object=btn_learn Layer to Snap=MenuCloser Left=-20 Top=17	Select Set Two Show MenuCloser Show MenuLearn	onMouseOver
Act	Action #1: Anchor Object=btn_learn Layer to Snap=MenuAct Left=0 Top=17 Action #2: Anchor Object=btn_learn Layer to Snap=MenuCloser Left=-20 Top=17	Select Set Two Show MenuCloser Show MenuAct	onMouseOver
Support	Action #1: Anchor Object=btn_learn Layer to Snap=MenuSupport Left=0 Top=17 Action #2: Anchor Object=btn_learn Layer to Snap=MenuCloser Left=-20 Top=17	Select Set Two Show MenuCloser Show MenuSupport	onMouseOver
Find	Action #1: Anchor Object=btn_learn Layer to Snap=MenuFind Left=0 Top=17 Action #2: Anchor Object=btn_learn Layer to Snap=MenuCloser Left=-20 Top=17	Select Set Two Show MenuCloser Show MenuFind	onMouseOver

8. Save and preview your page. Try every menu. Try moving away from a button by moving upward; this leaves the menu displayed and is a problem because there's no MenuCloser to trigger the hiding of the menu layers.

9. To the left of the Learn button, to the right of the Find button, and above all the buttons are spacer GIFs. Apply the AutoLayers behavior (onMouseOver) to each spacer, choosing Set Two and leaving all layers unselected to give these spacers the same functionality as the MenuCloser. Save and preview again to see how this fixes the problem of capturing the user's mouse exits from the buttons.

Summary

In this chapter, you created animated DHTML elements using layers and Timelines. Taking advantage of several must-have extensions, you tapped into Dreamweavers extensibility to make your tasks easier. You learned to use Dreamweaver's Drag Layer, Show-Hide Layers, Set Text ➪ Set Text of Status Bar, and Set Text of Layer, functions as well as the Timelines behaviors. Using the Project Seven extensions AniMagic by PVII, Snap Layers and AutoLayers, you explored how you might use DHTML to build different menu systems.

Project Summary

In this section, you added several menu options to the project site and built a slideshow that appears inside the site's graphic circle element. You also added a draggable jigsaw puzzle.

Files Prepared for the Habitat Alert Web Site

Files	What Was Done	Where to Now?
puzzle/puzzle_card.htm	You added an interactive puzzle. The source files and development concepts were used to create online puzzles for the habitat kids section of the project site.	Will be added to the site design.
slideshow/swap_image_slideshow.htm or slideshow/show-hide_slideshow.htm	Behaviors were used to swap images. The second option of hiding and showing layers was used.	Either method of creating the circle slideshow could be added to the template page for the project. If you want the slideshow on the homepage only, explore setting an optional region.
snapmenus/snaps.htm	Used an extension to snap the menus.	The snap menus you built in the example page could be added to the project site by building them in the template. By keeping the template region locked, you can push the menus to all the site's pages and update the menus after the site is complete to make the menu links active.

✦   ✦   ✦

Publishing Your Site

You're finally ready to get that page or site online—you've developed the site, added navigation, the images are in place, and you've even put a little zip in the pages with some interactive media or DHTML elements. So now what? Getting your site published—generally through file transfer (FTP) to a Web server—involves moving the site files from your local computer to a remote location on a Web server. In Dreamweaver MX, this is done with the Site panel, a Web server solution, and connecting through your ISP.

But where do you publish? Many Internet Service Providers (ISPs) offer free Web server space with an account. You may also "rent" Web server space through hosting companies. Some ISPs also offer hosting, sometimes called virtual servers, at reasonable prices. But how do you know whom to choose? And, once you have Web server access, how do you get the files from your computer to theirs?

Macromedia Dreamweaver includes software that lets you connect your computer to a remote Web server through FTP or a Local Area Network (LAN). Options for secure connections and versioning control are also available. However you connect, Dreamweaver's publishing client makes it easy to upload your site, download from any existing site, and/or manage your site's pages in both locations.

Getting Ready to Publish

Before you move your site to a Web server, there are some useful features in Dreamweaver that you should use to ensure that the site is really ready to publish. These features include spell checking, link verification, and testing for target browsers. Of course, there's no reason to wait until the last moment to use any of these features, but definitely use them before you publish. Additionally, adding meta tag information to your site ensures that potential visitors can find your site easily.

Check spelling

Choose Text ⇨ Check Spelling to check the spelling in the current (active) document. The Check Spelling command ignores HTML tags and attribute values. The spell checker uses an English (U.S.) spelling dictionary by default. To change the dictionary, choose Edit ⇨ Preferences ⇨ General or Dreamweaver ⇨ Preferences ⇨ General (Mac OS X) and select the dictionary you want to use from the menu of dictionary options. You can download more dictionaries from the Dreamweaver Support Center (www.macromedia.com/support/dreamweaver).

To check and correct spelling, choose Text ⇨ Check Spelling or press Shift+F7. The Check Spelling dialog box opens when an unrecognized word is found. In the Check Spelling dialog box (Figure 45-1), choose from the following options:

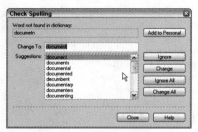

Figure 45-1: Check Spelling suggests changes for mispelled or unrecognized words.

- ✦ **Add to Personal** — Adds the unrecognized word to your personal dictionary
- ✦ **Ignore** — Ignores this instance of the unrecognized word
- ✦ **Ignore All** — Ignores all instances of the unrecognized word
- ✦ **Change** — Replaces this instance of the unrecognized word with text that you type in the Change To text box or with the selection in the Suggestions list
- ✦ **Change All** — Replaces all instances of the unrecognized word in the same manner.

Unfortunately, there's no sitewide spell check option, so every document must be opened, checked, and saved. A Check Spelling on Save extension (by Public Domain, Ltd.) is available at the Macromedia Exchange. To enable it, choose Edit ⇨ Check Spelling on Save. The Check Spelling on Save function will be invoked for every saved document, and the dialog box used is the standard Check Spelling dialog box.

Checking links

Before you publish, it is critical to check the validity of every link in your site. Broken links (pages that produce 404 error messages in the browser) and orphaned pages (unreferenced pages in the site file, not accessible from any site page) are a problem. Broken links frustrate your site visitors, and orphaned files may cause missing content and otherwise waste server space. When a site may contain hundreds (or even thousands) of pages, checking link validity can be a time-consuming process.

The Check Links feature can search for broken links and unreferenced files in a single (open) file, a folder (portion) of a local site, or an entire local site. Dreamweaver can validate internal links within the current site; a list of external links that appear in the selected document or documents is compiled but not verified. The Link Checker panel (Figure 45-2) is opened after Dreamweaver checks the links to display the results. The Link Checker is located in the Results panel group. You can use the following methods to check links:

Figure 45-2: The Results panel houses the Link Checker.

✦ To check links for the current file, open a file from the root folder. Choose File ➪ Check Page ➪ Check Links. A Results report appears in the Link Checker panel. Save the report by clicking the Save Report button.

✦ To check links for files or folders in a local site, select the files or folders to check in the Site panel. Start the check by right-clicking (Control+clicking) a file and choosing Check Links ➪ Selected Files/Folders from the context menu. Again, a results report appears in the Link Checker panel. In the Link Checker panel, select a specific link report from the Show pop-up menu to view another report. Your choices are Broken Links and External Links. You can save the report.

✦ To check links in an entire site, use the Site panel to choose a site; then choose Site ➪ Check Links Sitewide. A report appears in the Link Checker panel. View the Broken Links, External Links, or Orphaned Files reports by clicking any of these options in the Link Checker panel. Orphaned files may be deleted directly from the report list.

Fixing broken links

You can fix broken links and image references in the Link Checker panel or you may open files from the list and fix links using the Property inspector:

✦ To fix links in the Link Checker panel, first run a link check report. Select a broken link. Click the folder icon that appears next to the link to browse to the target file or type the correct path and filename. Press Tab or Enter to accept the URL change. A dialog box may appear to prompt you to fix the references in other files with the same link. Click Yes to have Dreamweaver update all the documents on the list that reference this file. Click No to have Dreamweaver update the current reference only.

✦ To fix links in the Property inspector, double-click an entry in the File column of the Link Checker. Dreamweaver opens the document. Select the broken image or link, and highlight the path and filename in the Property inspector. Use standard methods (Browse for File or Point to File) to fix the link or type in a new URL.

Checking target browsers

Technically, it is best to perform browser checks long before you are ready to publish for efficiency's sake. Dreamweaver can test your page code against specific browsers and report on whether your tags and elements are supported by the browser chosen. Check Target Browser does not change the page in any way. Text files called browser profiles are used to determine which tags are supported. You may update browser profiles at www.macromedia.com/support/dreamweaver. The following browser profiles are included:

✦ Netscape Navigator versions 2x–4x, and 6x

✦ Microsoft Internet Explorer versions 2.x-6x

✦ Opera versions 2.1x-6x

You can run a target browser check on a document, on a directory, or on an entire site by clicking the green arrow in the Check Target Browser panel, as shown in Figure 45-3.

Figure 45-3: Check target browsers for a page, files or folders, or the entire site.

✦ For the current document, first save. Dreamweaver performs checks on the last saved version of the file and does not include unsaved changes.

✦ For a folder or site, use the Site panel to select a site. Dreamweaver performs the target browser check on all HTML files in this folder and any subfolders. Target browser checks may be performed on local files only.

Save the results by clicking the Save Report icon at the left side of the panel. If you don't save it, the report is lost.

Script files are not checked.

Adding meta tags

A *meta* tag is a `<head>` element that supplies information about the current document. Some meta tags include character encoding, author, copyright, keywords, and descriptions. You can use other meta tags to supply information to the server, such as an expiration date or refresh interval and URL. The following meta tags are available:

✦ **Attribute** — Specifies whether the `<meta>` tag contains descriptive information about the page or HTTP header information.

✦ **Value** — Specifies the type of information for the tag. For example, `type="description"` or `type="keywords"`.

✦ **Content** — The actual information for the tag. An example is Meta Keywords, where the content is a list of keywords separated by commas.

Meta keywords and descriptions

Keywords and descriptions provide valuable information about your site to "*spiders*" and "*robots*" (software programs specifically designed to "harvest" site information on the Internet) that use them to categorize sites. When you do a search at a portal, such as Yahoo or Google, the information returned by the query displays meta information gleaned from keyword lists and descriptions, among other items.

To add keywords to your current document, follow these steps:

1. Choose Insert ⇨ Head Tags ⇨ Keywords.

2. In the dialog box that opens, list your words, separating them by commas. Close the dialog box.

3. To re-access the list of keywords for editing, choose View ➪ Head Content. Click the key icon and look in the Property inspector.

4. To add a page description, choose Insert ➪ Head Tags ➪ Description and type your descriptive sentence into the dialog box and close it. Access description meta tags from the Head Content bar (View ➪ Head Content) and modify them using the Property inspector.

Tip

You may copy meta tags from one document to another by selecting the meta tag icon and copying. Switch to a new document, view its head content, and paste.

Cross-Reference

See Chapter 42 for more about Meta Refresh.

Setting Up Web Server Access

A Web server is a special computer connected to the Internet that contains software to serve — send — Web pages upon request. A Web server is required to publish or "make public" your site's pages. Where your site is located depends upon how you aquire Web server access. Whether you use space at an ISP, have hosted space, or run your own Web server, moving your files to the Web server requires server access. You provide the access method and information to Dreamweaver using the Site Setup options:

✦ You may use the Site Definition Wizard (Basic site setup) and provide the information in the screen "" as shown in Figure 45-4. Choose Site ➪ Edit Site and click the Edit button for an existing defined site or choose Site ➪ New Site when starting from scratch.

✦ You may click the Advanced tab and choose the Remote Info category and enter the information there, as shown in Figure 45-5.

Figure 45-4: Questions in the Site Definition Wizard are designed to elicit the proper information about how you connect to your Web server and where the server is located.

Figure 45-5: The Remote Info category is accessed in the Site Definition's Advanced screens.

In both cases, after you select the proper Server Access method and provide the information about the server, you can test the connection with the Web server by clicking the Test Connection button. A successful connection message occurs if Dreamweaver can connect using the information, as shown in Figure 45-6.

Figure 45-6: A successful connection test

Server access options

No matter how you choose to set up your remote server access — using Basic or Advanced site setup — certain information is required. You must choose from the following methods of accessing the Web server:

   ✦ **(LAN) Local Access Network** — To access a Web server that is part of a local network or Internet Information Services (IIS) or Personal Web Server (PWS) folders on a computer in the network.

   ✦ **(FTP) File Transfer Protocol** — To move files to a remote Web server using specific protocols for handling the various files as binary or text files.

   ✦ **(RDS) Remote Development Services** — Remote HTTP-based access to files and databases for Web servers that support ColdFusion.

✦ **(VSS) SourceSafe Database** — Connect to your Web server using a SourceSafe Database. SourceSafe Database support is only available for the Windows platform when Microsoft Visual SourceSafe Client version 6 is installed.

✦ **(WebDAV) Web-based Distributed Authoring and Versioning** — Connect to a Web server using WebDAV protocol. For this access method, you must have a server that supports the protocol, such as Microsoft Internet Information Server (IIS) 5.0 or Apache Web server.

The vast majority of sites are uploaded via FTP. Besides the FTP server access option, you must provide a minimum of information in your site definition, as shown in Figure 45-7.

✦ **FTP Host** — This varies depending upon how you aquire Web server access. For a domain, it might be www.mydomain.com or simply mydomain.com. It may be the actual IP numbers (as in 121.23.983.4) or, as most ISPs require, may start with ftp://

✦ **Host Directory** — This is the top-level folder to which you have access if nothing is added to the field. To specify a subfolder, add its path here.

✦ **Login** — Your username or ID to access the Web server.

✦ **Password** — The password used to verify your username. Adding the password in the Site Definition saves it. If you choose not to add it here, you will be prompted for it when connecting to the Web server.

Figure 45-7: The Remote Info panel using FTP server access

Optional information

Other information is optional or required only for specific servers that are protected by a *firewall* — hardware and/or software that prevents unauthorized access to the server. Add firewall information by enabling the Firewall option and clicking the Firewall Settings button. Passive FTP and SSH — encrypted secure logon — are server-specific options.

Domains and Server Solutions

If you are using space provided by your ISP, chances are that your site lives in your account's directory, and the URL to get to your site may start with the ISP's *domain name*. A *domain* is an "alias" for a set of Internet Protocol (IP) numbers that represent a computer on the Internet. Anyone may purchase a domain name, and many online companies provide a service that lets you do this. The alias must be unique and is actually "rented" for a year or more at various prices. Common domains are.com, .org, and .net among others. Some domains are reserved for government or educational institutions. A bevy of newer domain types relate to countries other than the United States.

A virtual Web server — generally a "hosted" solution where a company specializing in Web server access rents you server space for your domain — contains many sites. The actual location of your site's folder (its physical path on the computer) is different from the URL for your domain. For example, the site `www.n2dreamweaver.com` lives buried in the folder structure of a hosting company at `www.cravis.com`. Similarly, the site for Habitat Alert has a URL of `www.habitat-alert.org`, but it lives on a server at Nexpoint (`www.nexpoint.com`).

Uploading design notes

Design notes are files saved into a special _notes folder in the site. Information about source files (as in Fireworks or Flash design files) or added status files that contain information about the state of a site file are saved as `.mno` files. By default, design notes are uploaded with the rest of the site. To disable uploading or to disable the keeping of design notes, click the Design Notes category of the Advanced Site Definition. Use the check boxes to disable or enable.

Using FTP

When you've added your Web server information to your site definition, you may connect to your Web server and transfer files from your local root folder on your computer to a remote root folder on the Web server. The Host Directory field provides the path to the remote root folder.

A *mirrored* structure between the local and remote folders is ideal and makes the most of Dreamweaver's FTP features. *Mirroring* means setting up a structure that compares folder to folder. For example, let's say that your Web files must live in a folder named wwwroot on your Web server. An index page placed in that folder would be your homepage. To mirror the local and remote folders, your local root folder would be equal to wwwroot. If you have more than one site, you can place different sites in different folders. In that case, the host directory path provided in a site's definition would reflect the matching root folder to be found on your Web server, as shown in Figure 45-8.

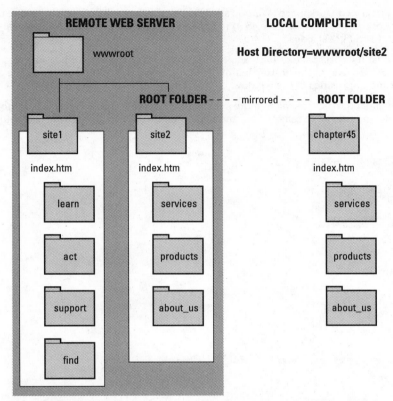

Figure 45-8: The host directory indicates the remote root folder, which ideally should mirror the structure of the local root folder.

Tip You cannot specify a folder in the host cirectory path that doesn't exist on the Web server. This often perplexes new FTP users; how do you connect, if you cannot specify the folder? The trick is to build a site that you will use to administer your Web server access at the top or root level. Connect and use the same right-click (Control+click) method used to add new folders to your local site to add new folders to your remote directory. Then change the host directory path for your site definition to include the new folders.

Connecting to the Web server

Because Windows and Macintosh versions of Dreamweaver's Site panel (window) are different, using the FTP client varies a bit, too. There are several ways to work with the Site panel when uploading or downloading files:

✦ For the integrated workspace (Windows only) click the Expand/Collapse button at the top right of the Site panel (Figure 45-9) to expand the docked panel so that it reveals the Remote and Local sides.

✦ For the floating workspace or for Macintosh systems, click the small white arrow (Figure 45-10) found at the bottom left of the Site window to expand and reveal the Remote and Local sides of the window.

Click the Connect icon to access the Remote server for OS or workspace. Figure 45-11 shows a connected site and the list of remote files and folders on the Web server. These root folders are mirrored.

Figure 45-9: Expand the Site panel.

Figure 45-10: Click the arrow to expand the Site window.

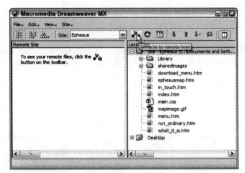

Figure 45-11: Connecting to the Web server reveals the mirrored Web files and folders.

Put and get files or folders

When you move a file or folder from the local root to the remote Web server, you are putting the file or folder. When the direction is the opposite, you are getting files or folders. There are several ways to put or get files:

✦ You may use the Put and Get arrow icons from the expanded or collapsed Site panel (window). First select a file, folder, or the entire site (root folder); then click Put to move the files to the Web server.

✦ You may put or get the current document by clicking the File Management icon in the document bar to access menu options, as shown in Figure 45-12.

✦ You may choose Site ➪ Put (or Get) to upload the current active document, as shown in Figure 45-13.

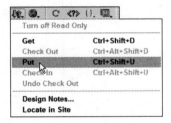

Figure 45-12: File Management Put and Get options

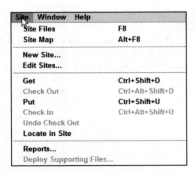

Figure 45-13: Put or get the current document using the Site menu.

When you put a file that is contained within a subfolder of the local root folder, Dreamweaver builds the matching structure to maintain the *relative location* of the file within the site.

Tip

You can also drag a file, a folder, or a selection of files and/or folders to any folder accessible to you on the Web server. A small + icon appears next to the cursor when you drag your selection to a remote folder.

Synchronizing site files

A Sychronize option is available in the Site menu that you can use to move newer files in either direction (put and get). It works by comparing the modification dates for files on the Web (remote) server and the local computer. Your options (Figure 45-14) are

✦ **Synchronize** — Selected Local Files or Entire Site

✦ **Direction** — Put Newer Files to Remote; Get Newer Files From Remote; or Get and Put Newer Files (both directions)

Figure 45-14: Synchronize dialog box

When you click Preview to start the synchronization process, you a log of files (Figure 45-15) that Dreamweaver will put or get, depending on the choices you made. You may uncheck any file and click OK to start the put or get or both.

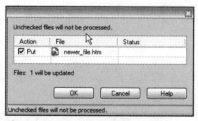

Figure 45-15: A preview of the proposed synchronization

Caution

Some Web server software prevents Dreamweaver from getting the actual time, in which case Dreamweaver may either disable the Synchronization feature (grayed out in the Site menu options) or actually give false information about the status of a file. Servers using Serve U FTP software will not work with Dreamweaver's synchronization unless the host disables the option to use all lowercase for files and directories in the setup.

Summary

In this chapter, you learned how to check spelling and links, and to test your code against browser profiles. You also learned how to provide information to Dreamweaver about the Web server to which you will publish your site, by modifying the site definition to include FTP settings. Finally, you learned the basics of moving your files and folders from your computer to a Web server and back, by putting, getting, and synchronizing a site.

✦   ✦   ✦

Building a Web Application

One of the key advantages to Macromedia Dreamweaver as a Web-development tool is the inclusion of visual tools to build data-driven, *dynamic* Web pages — without extensive knowledge of complex, server-side programming languages needed to create a Web application. A *Web application* is a collection of static and dynamic Web pages that is accessed via a Web browser or other HTTP user agents, generally working in conjunction with a database. Using a database to store the information you want to display enables you to separate a site's HTML design from its content, and building a Web application makes it possible to rapidly obtain, store, retrieve, display, and otherwise modify content on demand.

Dreamweaver works with all the major server technologies — Macromedia ColdFusion (CFM), Microsoft Active Server Pages (ASP) and ASP.NET, Sun JavaServer Pages (JSP), PHP Hypertext PreProcessor pages (PHP) and PERL to process your site's data. You can take advantage of Dreamweaver's predefined server behaviors or write your own.

The exercises used in this chapter are on the CD in the chapter46_ exercise folder rather than in the text of this chapter. Look for the "On the CD-ROM" icons to see where exercises are optionally available in the exercise files. A text file with all steps will be listed.

Understanding Database-Driven Sites

Until now, your site pages have been *static* — the content in them is hard-coded into each page's HTML structure. You may have used *client-side* logic (JavaScript) to add some interactivity, such as rollovers and DHTML elements, but for the most part, what the site visitor sees is the same as what you put into each page. The visitor types in the URL or clicks a link to request the page from a Web server. The Web server receives the request and sends the HTML to the visitor's browser, where it is processed and displayed. This sort of page generally uses an .htm or .html extension because that is what it consists of — HTML.

A *dynamic* page is different; its content is partially undefined and is either drawn from a data source after the Web server receives the request for the page or is generated through stored variables or procedures. Content sources can include a column in a *recordset*, a value submitted by an *HTML form*, the value contained in a *server object*, or even data stored in a *session variable*. In all cases, special instructions for generating or processing the required content are included in the page along with the HTML. Dynamic pages use different extensions (`.cfm`, `.asp`, `.shtml`, and so on) to let the server know that processing is required. That processing is done by an *application server*—special software that handles the server logic included in tags inserted into the HTML of the page. The Web server passes the page to the application server that is designed to scan the page for the instructions, which are carried out. The application server then returns the page as HTML with the added content.

Often the required content is drawn from a database. A *database* is a collection of tables that use columns and rows to build relational data sets or records. The instruction to extract data from a database is a *query* and the language that is used in a query is Structured Query Language (SQL). Application servers and databases cannot communicate with each other directly; software (a database *driver*) is necessary to act as an interpreter. Through a connection made with the driver, a subset of the information stored in the database (a *recordset, resultset,* or *dataset* depending upon the technology used) is extracted via the query for use in the requested page. The recordset, resultset, or dataset is returned to the application server and the data is merged into the HTML page, which is returned to the Web browser as HTML only, as shown in Figure 46-1.

Note　For examples (and CD exercises) in this chapter, a recordset is used because the technology chosen is ASP/VBScript.

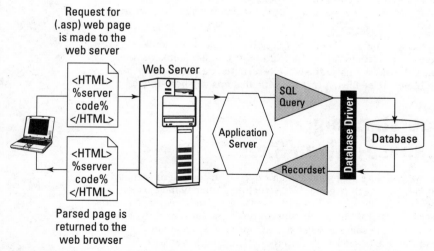

Figure 46-1: Dynamic, data-driven pages must be processed by the application server and a recordset extracted against a database via a query passed back and forth through a database driver.

Choosing a dynamic content source

There are many sources of dynamic content. In Dreamweaver, a data source can be *request*, *form* or *server variables*, *stored procedures*, a *database*, or a combination of these. The data source you use depends on what you need to accomplish. For example, a database is practically a requirement if you want to store collected data on a permanent basis. All other data sources are temporarily stored in the memory of the server, or on the user's computer as a *cookie* — a small set of data stored in the user preferences of the Web browser. Cookies are generally given an expiration date and because there are limits to the total number of cookies maintained by the browser, a cookie can be displaced by other cookies, thus destroying the stored data.

Understanding databases

A *database* is one or more groups of information (tables) that contain entry records (rows) that store a specific type of information (columns). For each table, it's likely that the columns are related. For example, a "contacts" table's columns might include names, addresses, phone numbers, e-mail addresses and the like — bits of separate data that together provide the information needed to reach that person. Generally, one column is set to be a *primary key* — a unique identifier — that may be used when inserting or editing records. In the case of a contacts database, trying to use only one column, like a last name, to identify a user is problematic; it's possible that there is more than one person listed with the same last name. In this type of case, the database developer would have the database autogenerate a number to identify each person and that would serve as the primary key. On the other hand, if the data is such that one column is unique — say a social security number or driver's license number — the database developer may opt to use that unique number as the primary key.

Primary keys may be used to compare data across tables. Special relationships between a column of one table may be made with column(s) in other tables (one-to-one or one-to-many). For example, a social security number might be the primary key for one table and could be equated to the customer ID of another table, which in turn might be equal to the account number in yet another table. Such relationships may be defined in the database itself, or created when certain columns are requested where specific operators (such as if, when, where, and, or) are used to compare the columns (as in =, <, >, etc.). Dreamweaver provides tools to locate data where one column compares to another by building queries to generate recordsets.

Where does the database come from?

The data management choice you make depends on your computer platform and/or a combination of Web server support, server technology, resources, and budget. Getting a database set up is often the hardest hurdle to overcome for new developers, from deciding what type of database to use to building the database tables.

Tip

Dreamweaver has nothing to do with building a database, but a useful resource for users new to database logic can be found in the help files for Dreamweaver. To access the help files, choose Help ➪ Using Dreamweaver and in the Contents category, click open the Appendixes section to locate the "Beginner's Guide to Databases."

Databases come in many forms and some solutions are more robust than others. For example, a commonly used solution is a Microsoft Access database. Easy to install and use on most Windows computers, Access provides a solution that is affordable, simple and adequate for most sites, but it does have some limitations in overall size and number of concurrent users (2GB/255 users). More robust solutions include Microsoft SQL Server, DB2 (IBM) or Oracle9i, but these solutions are also quite expensive. Many Unix, Linux, and Mac OSX users opt for MySQL (a popular open-source database system).

Tip

Whether your database and development is locally or remotely tested, the proper permissions and access to the database folder must be set up. Users accessing the database via your pages must be able to read, write, and execute the functions set up by the logic of each page. Typically, Windows-based solutions allow permissions and network access for folders via the Properties dialog box, as shown in Figure 46-2.

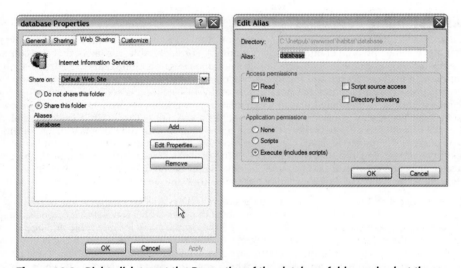

Figure 46-2: Right-click to get the Properties of the database folder and select the Web Sharing tab to share the folder. Create an alias for the folder. Use the Edit Properties button to set up READ and EXECTUTE permissions.

On the CD-ROM

The database used in the exercise files (admin.mdb) is an Access 2000 database. It is located in the Chapter 46\Admin_Site\database folder.

Setting Up a Web Application

Both static and dynamic pages are served to a browser from a Web server such as IIS, iPlanet Web Server, Netscape Enterprise Server, or Apache HTTP Server, that handles HTTP requests. To develop and test dynamic Web pages, Dreamweaver must have access to a Web server running the appropriate *application server software*. The Web server and application software may be

✦ **Local** — Running on the same computer as the Dreamweaver application. This may be a complete solution or used only temporarily during the development process, after which, a remote solution is used.

✦ **Remote** — Where the Web server and application software are set up on a computer that is accessed via FTP or through Local/Network (LAN). This is the most common solution for final publishing of dynamic content, where sites are either remotely hosted on *virtual* servers (one big computer that is subdivided into many separate domains or accounts) or on a Web server set up as part of a network of computers, most often the case in intranets, where all connected computers are behind a firewall.

With dynamic content, you must decide what *type* of server-side logic will be used to generate the undefined content. The Web page extension (`.asp`, `.cfm`, `.jsp`, and so on) is often the site visitor's only clue of a page's dynamic nature — it's the extension that tells the server to process the page via application server software. Different server technologies use specific programming or scripting languages to write the structured queries that make requests of the data source.

Dreamweaver supports five different technologies, which have their own requirements in servers and programming languages (see Table 46-1).

Table 46-1: Technologies Supported by Dreamweaver

Server Technology	Web Server Options	Programming Languages
Macromedia ColdFusion (.CFM)	Macromedia ColdFusion MX	ColdFusion Markup Language (CFML)
Microsoft Active Server Pages (.ASP)	Microsoft IIS or PWS Sun Chili!Soft ASP	JavaScript or VBScript
Microsoft .NET (ASP.NET)	Microsoft IIS5 with .NET Framework	Visual Basic or C#
Sun Java Data Base Connectivity (JDBC)	Macromedia JRun IBM WebSphere Apache Tomcat BEA WebLogic	Java
PHP Hypertext Preprocessor (PHP)	PHP server	PHP

Each technology has specific server requirements. Consult your computer's documentation to determine whether a specific technology is supported.

Defining a dynamic site

Of course, to work with Dreamweaver, a site must be defined, as you've seen throughout the Dreamweaver section of this book. To build dynamic pages using any data source, Dreamweaver must know what the server-side logic will be. You set this up in the Testing Server category of the Site Definition. To build dynamic pages that use content from a database, Dreamweaver must additionally know what type and where the database and its driver are.

Typically, a single server technology solution is used throughout a site. You enter information about the location of the Web and application server into the Site Definition. A Connection string is created that contains the type and location of the database and its driver based on the information you entered. Set up for your dynamic site is basically the same regardless of the technology, except that you might use a different driver, database, or server type and the syntax for connecting to the data source may vary. The concept is, however, the same.

The examples and exercises used in this chapter use a Microsoft Access 2000 database developed and deployed locally. A DSN-less connection string uses a Microsoft Access Driver, and the database is stored within the root\database folder with permissions to share the database folder given to all.

Using a local solution

Using Microsoft IIS or PWS on your local computer is a common solution when developing a dynamic site. You can set this up easily using either the Site Definition Wizard or in the Advanced tab's categories when defining a new site or editing an existing site. Although this is useful for development, it is seldom a final solution, because it is unlikely that your personal computer will double as a Web server. The Web server is often purposefully isolated (with software) from the rest of the network. By keeping it separate from the network, the data on other computers are protected from public access.

The Site Definition Wizard does not provide a means to define a local testing server and a remote application server. This configuration must be set up using the Advanced mode.

To define a dynamic site, you must set up the following:

✦ A local folder where your working files are stored. This can be anywhere on your local computer, even using the same folder defined as the testing server root folder in the Inetpub\wwwroot directory, if you decide to use a local server solution, such as IIS or PWS. Otherwise, this would be the same folder you might use for the local root folder of a static site.

✦ A remote folder in your Web server where your site will ultimately be published. This can be remotely hosted by another computer accessed via FTP, LAN, or could be your local computer if it serves also as a Web server connected to the internet (IIS or PWS). If you use your local computer, the folder will be in the Inetpub\wwwroot folder. Otherwise, this would be the remote root folder as you might set up for a static site.

✦ The location of the application software used in testing and for final publication of the site. Generally, this is the same URL as the remote root folder, but it is not a requirement that it be so. The Web server and application server can be located on different computers. Dreamweaver also needs to know the URL prefix that is appended before page names during testing.

Using the site definition wizard (basic)

To set up a new site definition, follow these steps:

1. Create a root folder for your Web application on the computer running the Web server. For example, on a computer running PWS or IIS, any file in the Inetpub\wwwroot folder or in any of its subfolders can be served to a Web browser.

2. Choose Site ➪ New Sites (for new site definitions) or Site ➪ Edit Site (for existing site definitions).

3. Click the Basic tab. In the Editing screens, you provide information regarding the local root folder for your site. First name your site; then click Next.

4. Choose to use a server technology. Selecting this option adds a menu where you would choose your technology. For the examples used in this chapter, you would choose ASP/VBScript. Click Next.

5. Choose how you will work with your files. For most users, you have four options, as shown in Figure 46-3. If using IIS or PWS on your local computer (to do exercises or for development only) the first option is most likely. For a practical approach and if you have the resources, the second option is realistic; you can develop locally and then move everything to a host Web server, which may entail building a different connection string. For Macintosh, you would likely use the same remote solution for development and publication. This screen is different on the Mac platform because you do not have the same local options as Windows users. You would choose to access a Web and application server connected to a network via LAN or use a remote hosted solution for both. Click the Next. Some options for Mac OSX exist locally but are not well-supported by Dreamweaver.

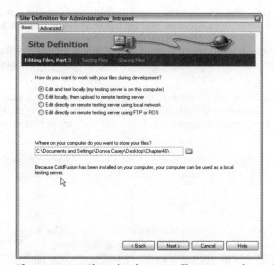

Figure 46-3: Choosing how you'll test your dynamic pages

Tip

Besides using the built-in Dreamweaver help pages, the Macromedia Dreamweaver support pages offer detailed tech notes that can help you troubleshoot all aspects of building a Web application, including site setup. Visit www.macromedia.com/support/dreamweaver to read the latest tech notes. Tips and tutorials for all aspects of using Studio MX products can also be found in the Designer/Developer section of the Macromedia site www.macromedia.com/desdev.

6. Choose the way you'll access the testing server. Choose FTP if using remote or LAN for a network server. If you chose to edit and test locally in the previous screen, you see a field where you enter the URL to the root folder in IIS or PWS. Typically, this would be something like: http://localhost/rootfolder.

If you chose to test locally and publish remotely *and* you access your testing server via FTP, you need to provide the information necessary to access that server. This information is the same as what you might provide in the Remote Info category of a static site, except that the location should point to a Web server with application server software. If you access the application server via a LAN, you would browse to a folder in a Web server (with application software installed) on the network where you plan to store the files. Mac users typically choose a remote, hosted Web and application server option will provide FTP information for the host server.

7. If a Test Connection button is visible, you must be connected (online) to get a successful result for the test. Test the URL to be sure that Dreamweaver can connect to the application server. Click Next.

8. Provide a URL where you would browse to see your site pages. Generally, Dreamweaver pulls the appropriate information from previous entries, but the URL may not be accurate for your server. For example, Dreamweaver combines the host server information (n2dreamweaver.com) with the Host Directory information (wwwroot/siteroot folder) to produce the URL of www.n2dreamweaver.com/wwwroot/siterootfolder but this would not work correctly in some cases. Removing the wwwroot/ portion provides the appropriate URL. You can use the Test URL button to see whether Dreamweaver can connect using the URL provided by Dreamweaver, but if it fails, consider whether any of the directories in the path structure should be removed. In the previous example, wwwroot equals the public site of the domain www.n2dreamweaver.com. Although the wwwroot portion is necessary for FTP, it isn't part of the actual HTTP path to the public site.

The remaining screens offer options to use Check In/Out features and provide a summary of the choices you made in the Site Definition Wizard. Check In/Out is an option typically used in teams and provides a feature to identify and lock pages on the Web server when in use by a team member.

Tip

Be sure to compare your Basic screens with the information in the corresponding Advanced screen to familiarize yourself with where each bit of information goes when using the Advanced setup.

Caution

With your dynamic site defined, you can begin to build your site pages. The server model you've chosen defines the default type of page used for new pages. If using ASP/VBScript, using the right-click method to add a new file to your root folder in the Site panel results in an ASP page with the file extension .asp. Even if you give the file an .htm or .html extension during naming, code for ASP pages is automatically added to the page, which can result in errors during page previews. To build a basic HTML page in a dynamic site, be sure to use File Í New to access the New Document Gallery and choose a basic page.

On the CD-ROM

See define_site.pdf in the chapter46_exercise files on the CD for directions to define the dynamic site "Administrative Intranet" using IIS or PWS. Mac users need to have a remote solution and follow steps in remote_hosted.pdf instead. PC users with a remotely hosted testing server can use remote_hosted.pdf, too.

Using the advanced site setup

Defining a dynamic site using the Advanced mode assumes you understand what the requested information is used for. You must complete three required categories:

✦ **Local Info** — As with any Dreamweaver site definition, you must supply the site name and select a local root folder.

✦ **Remote Info** — Select your Web server access using the Access menu options. This may be the same location as the testing server folder (next category) or a different folder on a remote server. A local testing option uses Local/Network access. A remote solution probably uses FTP, unless a company has set up special version control access. Consult your provider for details about the host server, host directory, login name, and password required to access your remote Web server.

✦ **Testing Server** — Select a server model and choose your access method. Locate the testing server folder and supply the URL prefix. The testing folder may be local or remote. The URL prefix is the absolute path you would type to access your site whether local (IIS or PWS) or remote (a Web server accessed through the internet). Generally, a local testing URL prefix would be `http://localhost/rootfolder`. A remote URL prefix would be something like `www.mydomain.com/` or if the root folder is not equal to the domain, `www.mydomain.com/path/rootfolder`.

Building a Connection to a Database

When you use a database to store collected data, you must provide parameters about the database to Dreamweaver (and the browser, via the Web and application servers). That information minimally includes the *type* and *location* of the database. The type specifies the *database driver* used (for application server — database communication) and the *location* is the specific path to the database. The information is stored as a connection script. Dreamweaver builds a special Connections folder and saves the information in a page with the appropriate extension, for example. The server technology you choose affects the type of connection you build.

✦ **DSN connection** (Data Source Name) — A DSN is a single-word identifier or name containing all the parameters for connecting and communicating with a database. Parameters can include server name, path to the database, ODBC (Open Database Connectivity) Driver, and possibly, a user name and password. A DSN is an alias that requires a registry "lookup" to recover the information for the connection string.

✦ A **Custom Connection String** (DSN-less) **Connection** — Used to create an ODBC or OLE DB connection between the application server and the database. Provides the same information as might be given in a DSN but doesn't require lookup and is often considered more server "friendly" using fewer resources. Dreamweaver includes a reference to the connection page. When the page is processed, the include is processed first, before the rest of the logic for the current page. You must use a connection string when using an OLE DB provider or when an ODBC driver is not installed on a Windows system.

The database drivers you use may depend upon the database. For an ASP site, you would likely use the database types listed in Table 46-2.

Table 46-2: ASP Database Options

Database	Database Driver
Microsoft Access	Microsoft Access Driver (ODBC)
Microsoft SQL Server	Microsoft SQL Server Driver (ODBC)
Microsoft SQL SErver Provider (OLE DB)	
Oracle	Microsoft Oracle Driver (ODBC)
Oracle Provider for OLE DB	

Consult your ISP or hosting company for information about the required type of connection you'll need to make if you use a remote hosting solution. Many companies will create a DSN for a database that you upload to your virtual server based on the name you request and the path you provide to the database. Some companies may require a DSN-less connection and provide a specific driver and path to use when building a custom connection string. Of course, your hosting solution must allow using a database and support the server technology you choose. For example, you might not be able to use ASP if your site is hosted on a Unix-based server.

If you are using a local application server, you should first ensure that your system has the proper driver for your database. Consult your computer's help files for installing a database driver. To access a list of ODBC drivers, use one of the following methods:

✦ **Windows 95/98/NT** — Choose Start ⇨ Settings ⇨ Control Panel. Double-click the ODBC Data Sources icon, which could also be called ODBC or 32bit ODBC. Click the Drivers tab to see a list of drivers installed on the system.

✦ **Windows 2000** — Choose Start ⇨ Settings ⇨ Control Panel ⇨ Administrative Tools ⇨ Data Sources. Click the Drivers tab.

✦ **Windows XP** — Choose Start ⇨ Control Panel ⇨ Performance and Maintenance ⇨ Administrative Tools ⇨ Data Sources [ODBC]. Click the Drivers tab.

Note

If the required driver is not installed, you may need to download and install the Microsoft Data Access Components (MDAC) 2.5 and 2.6 packages. Download them for free from Microsoft's Web site. You'll need to install MDAC 2.5 before installing MDAC 2.6. If MDAC does not have an ODBC driver for your database, see your database vendor.

Adding a DSN connection in Dreamweaver

A DSN connection requires the creation of the registry lookup and varies depending upon your system. Consult your system's help files for creating a system DSN for local testing. Consult with your host provider to have your DSN set up. If developing locally and publishing to a remote location, be sure that the DSN setup in both locations uses the same name.

To add a DSN Connection in Dreamweaver, follow these steps:

1. Open a dynamic page in your site.

2. Open the Application panel group and click the Databases tab.

3. Click the Add (+) button and select Data Source Name (DSN).

4. In the Data Source Name dialog box (Figure 46-4) type the DSN name or choose from DSNs listed in the menu below the name field. Dreamweaver lists all system DSNs on your local computer or network (Figure 46-4). If you are online and using a remote testing server, any DSN setup on that system lists in this menu.

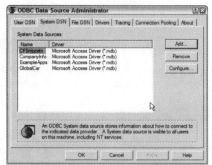

Figure 46-4: System DSNs are available to all users on the local computer or network.

5. Add a user name and password if required and select whether the DSN is for a local or remote testing server.

Adding a custom connection string in Dreamweaver

Your connection string will vary based on the type and location of your database and Web server. In the following steps, an Access 2000 database and a local testing server are assumed:

1. Create a blank or open an existing asp page in your site.

2. Open the Applications panel group and click the Databases tab.

3. Click the Add (+) button and choose the Custom Connection String option.

4. Name your connection.

Typically, developers start connection string names with `conn`, as in `connHabitats` or `connSitename`. That way, when you see `connSitename` anywhere in your code, you may be sure that it refers to the connection string.

5. Add the proper driver and database path to the Connection String field, as shown in Figure 46-5. For this example you would add (all on one line):

```
Driver={Microsoft Access Driver (*.mdb)};Dbq=c:\Inetpub\wwwroot\
siteroot\database\dbname.mdb
```

Figure 46-5: The Connection String dialog box

6. Use Driver on this Machine because this example assumes a local testing server.

   A remote testing server setup could use a similar string, except that the path could be quite different. For example, a virtual remote server path might look something like:

```
Driver={Microsoft Access Driver
(*.mdb)};Dbq=d:\n2dreamweaver.com\wwwroot\siteroot\database\
dbname.mdb
```

7. Test the connection by clicking the Test button. A local testing server does not require being online but a remote one would. If you receive an error message, copy or write down the message before you close the pop-up window. Check your string carefully because the syntax used is critical. If that still doesn't help, consult the Dreamweaver Application Search Help feature (Help ⇨ Using Dreamweaver) or the Dreamweaver support section of the Macromedia Web site, using the error number as a keyword in the search.

8. If the test is successful, click OK.

Dreamweaver builds a Connections folder at the root level and stores the string information in an ASP page within, using the Connection name as the filename. In each page where you need access to your database, you will query the database via the connection, using a record-set to "bind" data to your page. Figure 46-6 shows the newly created Connections folder at the root level in the Site panel and displays the now available subscribers table from the admin.mdb database that is accessed via the new connection.

On the CD-ROM

See the exercise add_connection.pdf in the chapter46_exercise files on the CD to create a custom connection string in the Administrative Intranet project site. A complete list of connection strings used for the most popular configurations of databases and drivers may be seen in connection_strings.pdf.

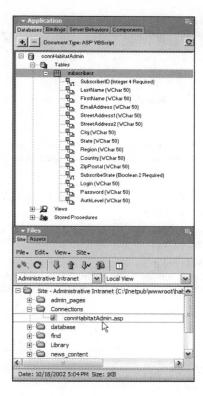

Figure 46-6: With your connection in place, you can view fields for the tables available in your database.

Binding Data

The purpose of your dynamic page is to allow partially undefined content to be defined on the fly by pulling selected content from a data source. In the case of a database, you must first create a recordset that includes any columns you need access to via the Applications panel group Bindings panel. The examples and exercises provided in the text files on the CD use a database but also make use of variables and form parameters.

Adding a recordset

Ideally, the logic required for your dynamic page has been carefully considered and planned. Recordsets are the result of queries, which can be simple or advanced. Dreamweaver makes either type of query easy to build, but you must know what you want to accomplish and what data columns you will need. For advanced queries, you must also plan whether data will need selective comparison. The type of query you build determines what data you'll have available in your page.

There are many methods to adding a recordset (resultset or dataset, as well) but the extensive scope of this book and the limited number of pages make examination of all an impossibility. Consult the program help files (Using Dreamweaver) for in-depth details and instructions. However, a typical *simple* scenario would be as follows:

1. Open your dynamic page.

2. In the Application panel group's Bindings panel click Add (+) to add a recordset.

3. Name the recordset.

Tip   Typically, developers use the convention `rsRecordName` for easier code troubleshooting . You may use any name, but many developers use a name that reflects the function of the page, as in `rsAddUser` or `rsViewMembers`.

4. Select a connection from the Connection menu, or if you haven't already defined a connection string or DSN, click the Define button and do so.

5. Select a table from the Table menu, which is populated by all the tables in your database. (Remember that the connection string points to this database.)

6. Choose whether you need access to all the table columns, or just a selected set. If you choose a selected set, remove the unwanted columns by highlighting them and deleting. Figure 46-7 shows the Recordset dialog box with all data columns to be available.

Figure 46-7: Making all data columns available to the page

Tip   You may select multiple contiguous columns by shift+clicking or noncontiguous columns by Control+clicking (Command-clicking).

7. If needed, you may filter or sort records; then click OK to close the dialog box.

On the CD-ROM   See the exercise `view_users.pdf` in the chapter46_exercise files on the CD for steps to add a recordset to the `view_users.asp` page in the Administrative Intranet project site.

Filtering chooses records based on a specific column that is compared to another column from a URL parameter, form, session, or application variable or an entered value. A typical example might be filtering the data for records that match a ZIP code entered by the user, as you might to display only records that contain that specific ZIP code, or show only prices for a region that includes that ZIP code.

Sorting allows the data to be selectively displayed by one specific column in a chosen order, as in LastName, Ascending.

Advanced queries

More complex, advanced queries can be built in the Advanced screen of the Recordset dialog box. When the dialog box opens, click the Advanced button and add a name and select a connection. If you are familiar with using SQL to build queries, the SELECT, WHERE, and ORDER BY buttons can be used to build complex data sets. Figure 46-8 shows an advanced query that requests only records where the data field "AuthLevel" is equal to the value Admin. Advanced queries cannot be created in the Simple panel and after created, you cannot view the recordset in the Simple panel.

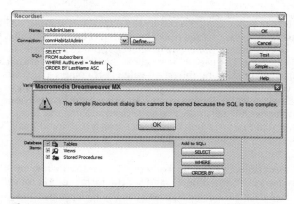

Figure 46-8: Complex queries built in the Advanced panel cannot be displayed with the Simple panel.

After you close the Recordset dialog box, you may view your data columns in the Bindings panel by clicking the Expand button next to the listed recordset. To copy a recordset from one page to another, first select the recordset in the Bindings panel or in the Server Behaviors panel. Right-click (Control+click) the recordset and choose Copy. In the destination page, open either the Binding or Server Behaviors panel, right-click (Control+click) and choose Paste. To remove a recordset, select it in the Bindings panel and use the Minus (-) button.

Form and URL parameters

Forms play a huge role in dynamic pages, enabling you to interact with or gather information from a site visitor. You can gather information from users and store it in the server's memory by submitting the form using either the POST or GET methods. A form sends the information either as *form parameters* or as *URL parameters*. If you set the form's method to POST, the browser includes the form's values *in the body of the message* sent to the server. If you set the form's method attribute to GET, the browser *appends the form values to the URL* specified in the action attribute and sends the information to the server when requesting the page.

See Chapter 38 if you are unfamiliar with building a form.

You can also send data to be stored in the server's memory by clicking a hypertext link. This creates a URL parameter.

How form and URL parameters work

Because each form object is named, form parameters pass data as `objectname=entered-value`. When a precise value is required, it is best to use a form object that does not allow the user to "decide" how to write the value. For example, if you need to have the two-letter "official" state postal abbreviation, don't let your visitor type it; provide a drop-down form menu object with a list of values that pass the exact (correct) value.

A URL parameter works by appending the name-value pair(s) to the URL of a requested page, taking the form of name=value. The parameter begins with a question mark (?) and each parameter is separated by an ampersand (&). Thus, a typical URL parameter might appear as follows:

```
http://server/path/document?firstname=firstvalue&secondname=secondvalue
```

You can use URL or form parameters in processing the requested page. For example, a cellular phone company might have users that want to see new plans offered on the Web site. If the company is national, it might offer different plans (with different phones and rates) depending upon where the user is located. The user's location can be determined with a ZIP code. The zip code parameter is passed containing the name-value (`zipcode=value`) which is stored (temporarily) in the server's memory. Processing of the requested "plans" page uses the URL parameter to choose and dynamically display plans (with the appropriate phones and rates) for the region which includes that ZIP code. A similar scenario can use form parameters to store a login name and password when a user accesses a restricted page.

Creating URL parameters

A URL parameter is created from form object values by using the GET method when submitting the form. Create your form, name your form objects, and set the form method to GET. In the Action field of the form, add the URL for the page that will use the URL parameters.

A URL parameter can be created from hypertext links by using the `href` attribute of the `anchor` tag. Add the URL parameters using the method given earlier, appending the URL with a question mark followed by a name=value parameter, as follows:

```
<a href="http://server/page.asp?name1=value1">choice1</a>
<a href="http://server/page.asp?name2=value2">choice2</a>
<a href="http://server/page.asp?name3=value3">choice3</a>
```

You can build the URL parameters in Code view or use the Property inspector to type the parameters.

See `url_param.pdf` for steps to create pages that first obtain a value as a URL parameter then use that variable to set the background color of an HTML page.

Retrieving parameters

When you've stored the parameter(s) you can retrieve it on demand by defining variables. You must be sure that you have submitted the name-value pairs via the parameter.

To define a parameter for use in your page, open the Bindings panel:

1. Click the Add (+) button and choose one of the options available in the menu. For an ASP page, you would choose Request Variable ⇨ Request.Form. For ColdFusion or PHP pages, Form Variable is used. A JSP page uses Request Variable.

2. The Form Variable box opens. Enter the name of the form variable and click OK. This is generally the name of the form object (field, and so on) used in the form that passed the parameter.

3. The Form Parameter appears in the Bindings panel, much as a recordset does. Use the Form Parameter as you would a database column to build dynamic content.

Session variables

In fact, you can store information from parameters as a session variable that is "remembered" as long as the user remains in the site or until the session is explicitly destroyed. Session variables make the stored parameters available to all the site's pages throughout the user's session and persist as the user moves from page to page. Session variables may be used to insert values into HTML page code, to assign a value to a *local* variable, or to provide a value to evaluate a conditional expression.

Before creating a session variable, you must first collect the data, as in creating a form or URL parameter and request a page. The server-side logic and the Web server you use affect the code you'll need to create to store and access the data as a session variable. For ASP and ASP.Net, you would use `<% Session("variable_name") = value %>` but for a ColdFusion site, you would use `<CFSET session.variable_name = value>` where the value expression is generally a server expression, such as `Request.form("FormObjectName")` or `Request.QueryString("FormObjectName")`. Actually, there are many other expressions you might use depending upon the server type and server logic used.

When you've stored a value in a session variable, you can use Dreamweaver to retrieve the value and use it in your Web application or insert it (as a value) into an HTML page. For the example of a session variable that stores the user's login name and password, you could prevent or enable access to restricted site pages by checking the user against a list of authorized users and/or insert the user's login name into text written dynamically in the page.

See `validate_user.pdf` for an exercise that uses a session variable to maintain the login name and password of the user throughout the user's visit to the Administrative Intranet site.

Application variables

When using ASP or ColdFusion, you may use application variables for data storage and display. Application variables are maintained for the life of the application or until the Web server is stopped. Because of this longer-term persistence, they are ideal for maintaining information for all users, such as a date, a currency exchange rate, or other non-user specific information.

To define an application variable when using ASP, follow these steps:

1. Open your asp page.

2. Open the Bindings panel in the Applications panel group.

3. Click the Add (+) button and select Application Variable from the menu.

4. Type the name of the variable as defined in the application's source code.

5. Click OK. The variable appears in the Bindings panel.

To remove an application variable, expand the application variable in the Bindings panel, select the named variable and click the minus (-) button.

Server variables

Server variables are useful for storing information gathered from a variety of sources, from form and URL parameters, session and application variables, cookies, browser states and more. Server variable syntax varies depending upon your choice of server technology.

For ASP, you may use the following server variables as a source of dynamic content:

- ✦ `Request.Cookie`
- ✦ `Request.QueryString`
- ✦ `Request.Form`
- ✦ `Request.ServerVariables`
- ✦ `Request.ClientCertificates`

To define a server variable for an ASP page, follow these steps:

1. Open the Bindings panel from the Applications panel group and click the Add (+) button.

2. Choose Request Variable from the menu.

3. Select one of the request collections available.

4. Click OK.

Request Collections in ASP

For ASP sites, the request collection you choose depends upon the nature of the data you need. For example, if you want to find and store the type of browser the visitor is using, use `Request.ServerVariables ("HTTP_USER_AGENT")`. If you're looking to access data from a form, use `Request.FormVariables ("FormObjectName")` instead.

- ✦ **QueryString Collection** — Retrieves information appended to the sending page's URL using the `GET` method with a form or through values appended to the `href` attribute of a hypertext link.

- ✦ **Form Collection** — Retrieves Form parameters created by passing name-value pairs via the `POST` method to the page listed in the Action field of a form.

- ✦ **Server Variables Collection** — Retrieves values of predefined environment variables. For a complete list of ASP server environment variables, see your IIS or PWS documentation.

- ✦ **Cookies Collection** — Retrieves values stored in cookies sent in an HTTP request. For example, a cookie called `thissite_prefs` is stored on the user's computer. On the server, the values of the cookie are stored in the variable `Request.Cookies("thissite_prefs")`.

- ✦ **ClientCertificate Collection** — Retrieves certification fields from an HTTP request sent by the browser. The certification fields are specified in the X.509 standard.

Binding data to the page

After you add a recordset by building a query or through passing a form or URL parameter, you can "bind" data in several ways by replacing static content, attributes, or form elements with one or more recordset columns or variables. Dreamweaver offers several methods to accomplish this, through the use of the Bindings panel. Typically, each involves selecting a content source and setting a dynamic attribute:

✦ You may drag the data from the Bindings panel and drop it either in the page or onto a selected bit of text, form object (Design view), or into specific areas in the HTML code (Code view).

✦ You may place your cursor where you want dynamic data to appear and select the data from the Bindings panel. Click the Insert button to add the dynamic data to the page.

✦ You may select a page element, such as an image or form object, and highlight (by selecting) the data field in the Bindings panel. Use the Bind To menu of attributes to select which part of the tag will use the dynamic data. Click the Bind button to add the dynamic data attribute.

On the CD-ROM

See the exercise `dynamic_attribute.pdf` in the chapter46_exercise files on the CD. The exercise shows binding the e-mail address data column to the mailto: href for users listed in the `view_users.asp` page in the Administrative Intranet project site.

Dynamic text

You can replace regular text in your pages or insert a data source reference where you want the dynamic text to appear. Dynamic text can be formatted with HTML or CSS typographic styles.

Dynamic images

In Design view, place your cursor into the page where you want an image to appear. Choose Insert ➪ Image. Click the Data Sources option (PC) or Data Source button (Mac) and select a content source from the list that appears. The source should be a path to the image you want. The path may be absolute, root relative, or document relative.

Note

Dreamweaver does not support binary images stored in a database.

Another method for adding dynamic images is to insert a placeholder image into the page. Select the image; then use the Bindings panel to select the data column of a recordset (or form or URL parameter) and use the Bind To menu to choose img.src. Click the Bind button.

HTML page attributes

You can use the Bindings panel to set dynamic sources for your HTML page elements, too. For example, let's say you want to allow users to set the page background color for the duration of their site visit. In a Start page, you might ask the user to select the page color by offering a form menu with the color choices. When the user selects a color and clicks the Choose Color button, that information is passed as a URL parameter that is stored in temporary server memory.

In the page requested, a variable is set up that takes the parameter. You can then select the `<body>` tag using the Tag inspector and locate its bgcolor attribute and use the Dynamic Data button (the lightening bolt) to choose the request variable. When the user's browser loads the new page, it uses the bgcolor passed by the prior page.

On the CD-ROM

To try this exercise, follow the steps in the file `url_param.pdf` to set the background color for a site page based on a choice the user makes.

The Tag inspector

There are several methods for binding data to page elements but the Tag inspector is probably the easiest to use. This great new feature of Dreamweaver makes it possible to access every attribute of any element in your page. Simply open the Code panel group and click the Tag inspector tab. Scroll through the various page elements; the panel displays `<head>` and `<body>` tags. When you select a tag, use the bottom window of the panel to view the tag's attributes. If you cannot see the attributes, be sure to expand the panel by dragging on its borders, as shown in Figure 46-9.

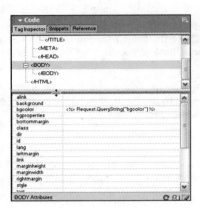

Figure 46-9: The Tag inspector is a valuable tool when working with dynamic page attributes. Be sure to expand the panel fully to view the attributes.

Application Objects and Server Behaviors

What makes Dreamweaver so attractive as a Web development tool is that it ships with most of the functionality you'll ever need to display, add, delete, and modify data sources. It contains complex server-side logic (server behaviors) that helps control page access, authenticate users, show content when specific conditions are met or not — in short, you need not ever write a line of code to build complex page functionality. Dreamweaver also ships with Application Objects — HTML elements that incorporate server behaviors — to save you time and effort when developing page functions.

Access Application Objects via the Insert ⇨ Application Objects menu, as shown in Figure 46-10.

Add server behavior logic to an existing HTML element or page via the Server Behavior panel's menu, as shown in Figure 46-11.

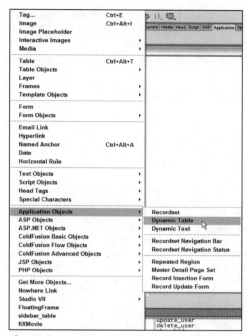

Figure 46-10: Insert application objects that build HTML elements with server behaviors already incorporated.

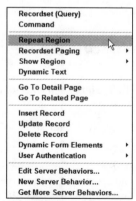

Figure 46-11: The Server Behavior menu options

Here is just some of the functionality that can be incorporated into your page through the use of the Server Behaviors panel or through the Insert ⇨ Application Objects bar or menu options:

✦ **Recordset** — Defines a recordset from an existing database. The recordset you define is stored in the Bindings panel.

See exercise `add_recordset.pdf` in the chapter46_exercise folder on the CD for steps to add a recordset to a page.

✦ **Repeat Region** — Repeats a selected region (as in table row) to display multiple records on a single page. You select an entire table or individual cells or rows that contain dynamic content, and specify the number of records to display on each page view.

See exercise `repeat_region.pdf` in the chapter46_exercise folder on the CD for steps to repeat a table row for displaying database records in your page.

✦ **Dynamic Table** — Used to create and insert a dynamic table into a page to show database table records. Useful for quickly building a table that contains the exact number of columns contained in the database table. Options include limiting the number of records displayed or displaying all records. Limited table formatting is included but you may change the format of the table through the Property inspector or by applying CSS to the table elements. When you choose to limit the number of records displayed, you must also add recordset navigation behavior.

✦ **Dynamic Text** — Used to insert a dynamic text object from a datasource into a page.

See exercise `say_hello_user.pdf` in the chapter46_exercise folder on the CD for steps to use dynamic text and a data source to personalize a page.

✦ **Recordset Navigation** — Used to insert a record navigation bar for navigating through database records. Creates links that enable a user to view previous and next records from a database record.

See exercise `next_user.pdf` in the chapter46_exercise folder on the CD for steps to add navigational elements that allow movement through database records.

✦ **Recordset Navigation Status** — Adds a record counter to help users keep track of how many records where returned, and where they are in the returned result.

See exercise `which_record.pdf` in the chapter46_exercise folder on the CD for steps to add element to identify database record(s).

✦ **Master Detail Page Set** — A combination of behaviors that selects a number of records to display in a page and adds functionality to enable one field to link to a detail page that displays a specified set of data for that record. Dreamweaver inserts records, a recordset navigation bar, and a recordset navigation status bar into the current page and adds a table into the destination page to display specified fields for the selected record.

See exercise `user_details.pdf` in the chapte 46_exercise folder on the CD for steps to set up the selection of a specific user to display complete details for the user's record.

   ✦ **Insert Record** — Builds a form based on the fields available in the recordset that allows modification of the database by inserting a new record.

See exercise `add_user.pdf` in the chapter46_exercise folder on the CD for steps to add a new user to the database records.

   ✦ **Record Update Form** — Adds a form for the selected recordset and displays a single record from the database. A user can modify the data displayed and change the database record. Adds navigation objects for selecting specific records.

See exercise `update_user.pdf` in the chapter46_exercise folder on the CD for steps to update an existing user's database record.

   ✦ **Delete Record** — Removes an existing record from a database.

See exercise `remove_user.pdf` in the chapter46_exercise folder on the CD for steps to remove an existing user from the database.

   ✦ **Show/Hide Regions** — Displays or hides an HTML element and its content when specific conditions are met.

See exercise `show_hide.pdf` in the chapter46_exercise folder on the CD for steps to display content based on specific conditions.

   ✦ **User Authentication** — A set of behaviors that compares user information against a data source to allow or restrict access to pages in the site.

See exercise `login_user.pdf`, `create_variables.pdf`, restrict_access.pdf, and `validate_user.pdf` in the chapter46_exercise folder on the CD for steps to build a login form, create form parameters, restrict access to site pages based on the authorization level of the user, and to create a session variable that maintains the user's login state throughout the site pages.

Adding server behaviors to a page

Depending upon your level of expertise with the server-side technology of your choice, you have several methods available to incorporate server behaviors into your pages:

   ✦ If you are new to dynamic pages, use the Insert ➪ Application Objects menu to insert the appropriate HTML element and server behavior functions into your page.

   ✦ If you're an experienced developer, build your own HTML elements and use the Server Behaviors panel to apply specific functionality.

Removing server behaviors from a page

The best method of removing server behaviors from a page is to select the behavior in the Server Behaviors panel and use the Minus (-) button to remove it. If you simply select the element on your page that has the behavior attached, you may be prompted by Dreamweaver to undo the step and use the panel instead. Deleting the page element doesn't remove all the associated server behavior code.

Summary

In this chapter, you explored the tools, features, and methods for building a dynamic or data-driven site — a Web application — to define content dynamically from a data source. You learned the steps necessary to set up and test your server-side logic, from providing URLs to an application server to setting up a custom connection string that you used to communicate between application server and a database. Using the exercises presented on the CD that accompanies this book, you worked through most of Dreamweaver's server behaviors to build pages that restrict user access to the administrative intranet site and built pages to add, edit, and delete subscribers for both the administrative intranet and the public internet sites.

Project Summary

Working through the exercises for this chapter, you added ASP (Active Server Pages) VBscript server-side logic to the administrative intranet site that supports the public internet site for the project. You defined the site (using a local testing server), added a connection string, and built recordsets through queries that allow the modification of the admin.mdb database. You built pages that control access to the database to users (subscribers) with Admin authorization level only.

Each of these tasks might be used with any database and are standard practice when functions for a site include transient users. An administrative site is typically required for "good housekeeping" and restricting access to the functions is sensible. The more critical the information, the more important such a restriction is. In most cases, the intranet site would be protected further by situating it on a secure server that might itself contain logic requiring additional verification of identity and authorization.

Files Prepared for the Habitat Alert Web Site

Files	What Was Done	Where to Now?
view_users.asp	Used to view all users/subscribers in the database. You could use the same methods to view only users with a specified AuthLevel or view a list of users from a specific zip code by filtering the results of your recordset.	Ready for upload to a server.
default.asp	As the entry point to the intranet site, you set up a login form to gather LoginName and password for the user, which is passed to a validation page.	Ready for upload to a server.

Files	What Was Done	Where to Now?
validate_login.asp	You set up this page to verify the login and password of the user, checking their AuthLevel against the database of subscribers. You used server behaviors to control content presented to the user based on their authorization level. To prevent users from accessing this page directly, you added code that restricts access to the page and built a session variable in the page to store the users info for the entire site.	Ready for upload to a server.
add_users.asp new_user_success.htm username_inuse.htm	Using a server behavior to insert a record, you set up a form to allow creation of any level user and used Dreamweaver's built-in Form Validation behavior to ensure that all fields contained entries. You set up a redirect page where the user is sent if the task is successfully completed. You set up a check against the list of login names to prevent duplication of such and created a page where the user is sent if the entry is duplicated. You also restricted access to this page, preventing any user from typing in its URL to bypass the login page, by sending the non-logged-in user back to the login page.	Ready for upload to a server.
delete_user.asp	Using a server behavior, you set up this page to remove a record from the subscribers table in the admin.mdb database and added another redirect page used when the task is completed successfully. You also restricted access to this page.	Ready for upload to a server.
modify_users.asp	You set up this page to allow changes to be made to existing user records in the database. You used server behaviors to display a single record and created both a navigation object and a status object for moving through and identifying which record is displayed. Access to this page was also restricted.	Ready for upload to a server.
not_authorized.htm	You set up a redirect page (not_authorized.htm) to which users are sent when menu links are clicked and the user is not logged in.	Ready for upload to a server.

✦   ✦   ✦

Creating Dynamic Content with Macromedia ColdFusion MX

The Role of ColdFusion in Your Web Sites

When Macromedia merged with the Allaire Corporation in 2001, it added an extremely powerful tool to its arsenal of design applications: ColdFusion. ColdFusion gives Flash developers and Dreamweaver designers the ability to create technically sophisticated Web and Intranet applications, and — unlike many programming languages — makes it easier and more intuitive for nonprogrammers to do so.

In fact, the relationship between ColdFusion and other Macromedia Studio products is now so closely integrated that it's possible that you may have already been using ColdFusion features in your Flash movies or Dreamweaver sites without realizing it. Dreamweaver, in particular, makes it easy to create basic ColdFusion applications without having to know much about ColdFusion Markup Language (CFML) or how ColdFusion Server works.

All of the chapters in Part VI are designed to take you beyond the basics — to help you understand what goes on in a ColdFusion application, how it works with other Macromedia tools, and how you can use it to add functionality to the Web sites you build. Some of the examples will be shown in the context of the Dreamweaver interface, but most will be displayed as plain text to help you understand how ColdFusion's programming language works behind the scenes in your application.

If you've come to ColdFusion by way of a design background, don't worry. Although ColdFusion is a different tool from Dreamweaver, Flash, or Fireworks, it has still been designed with simplicity and ease of use in mind. Let's begin by looking at some of the basic concepts you'll need to understand before you move into the hands-on examples in the following chapters.

ColdFusion MX and the Client–Server Relationship

If you installed the special development edition of ColdFusion along with the other Macromedia Studio products, you probably noted that unlike Flash or Dreamweaver, ColdFusion doesn't have its own dedicated graphic interface. That is, ColdFusion isn't a traditional development application in which you open a GUI and start creating pages. Instead, it's a program that runs in conjunction with your Web server (or a Web server on a remote host). When ColdFusion is present on a Web server, it gives designers and developers the ability to create *applications* — Web sites that do much more than look nice.

Note

If you didn't install ColdFusion with the other Studio products, don't worry. You learn more about installation and configuration in the next chapter.

To understand how ColdFusion works as a server, start by considering a typical Web page. When a user types a URL into his or her browser (the *client*) and clicks the Go button, the browser sends a request for a page to a Web server somewhere on the Internet (the *server*). The server accepts the request and returns the requested HTML page.

However, if you've ever worked with a basic CGI program, such as a "mailto" form processor, you know that URLs don't always have to call plain HTML pages. They can also call programs, such as CGI applications or applets written in Perl, C, or Java. These programs are designed to perform a series of actions and then, typically, return the results of those actions to the user as HTML that's visible in a browser.

For example, consider that basic mailto CGI program: It takes the user's input from a form, formats it into an e-mail and then sends the mail off to a predesignated address. Now imagine you're working for a client who asks you to expand the basic mailto function so that a registrant's name and e-mail address are archived in a system database at the time the form is submitted. It's likely that the original mailto program is written in Perl or C, both of which are powerful languages, but which make it difficult to customize even a basic program like mailto unless you happen to have programming knowledge to match your designer's skills.

Enter ColdFusion, which is designed to give nonprogrammers the ability to build basic programs like mailto, as well as more sophisticated programs that can drive entire Web sites — all without the developer having to learn a complex programming language. ColdFusion accomplishes this by installing itself as a companion program to your Web server software. When your server receives a request for a plain HTML page, ColdFusion does nothing. However, when it gets a request for a page ending with the extension .CFM (known as a *template* in ColdFusion jargon), it processes the program instructions on the page and returns the results to the user, usually as HTML visible in his or her browser.

Understanding the Different ColdFusion Versions

The version of ColdFusion that ships with Macromedia Studio is a special developers' edition designed to let you preview your ColdFusion pages and applications on a local server. In most cases, this is all you need to get started working with the program, because it's likely you'll be developing and testing your pages locally and then transferring them to a live environment that also supports ColdFusion. But it's also important to understand that there are two different versions of ColdFusion Server, and many different options available among them.

Version 1: Macromedia ColdFusion Server

This is the most common version of ColdFusion Server, and the one you're most likely to find deployed in hosted environments. It includes all the infrastructure needed to run ColdFusion applications, and an embedded Java server based on Macromedia's JRun. It comes in two varieties: Professional, which is the standard, and Enterprise, which includes additional security and performance features designed for large-scale Web applications.

Version 2: Macromedia ColdFusion for J2EE application servers

This special version of the program is designed to Java 2 Platform, Enterprise Edition, or as its more commonly known, J2EE. With this version, ColdFusion MX runs on top of an existing J2EE application server, such as IBM's WebSphere. This version is most often found in environments where ColdFusion pages will be used in conjunction with J2EE applications.

Introducing ColdFusion Markup Language

When you open the source of a CGI program, such as mailto, in a text editor, you see a lot of programming code that's likely to be unfamiliar. Even diehard Perl programmers admit that their language is one of the least intuitive for nontechies to understand. In contrast, when you open the source of a ColdFusion template in a text editor (or Dreamweaver's code view), you see code that looks like a standard HTML page containing familiar elements, such as HTML tags, and additional elements similar to those shown in the sample page Listing 47-1.

Listing 47-1: A Sample ColdFusion Template Containing HTML and CFML Tags

```
<cfmail from="admin@somedomain.com" to="jim@anotherdomain.com"
subject="User Info Request">
     Hi Jim;

     A user has requested information from the Web site:

     Name: #form.firstname# #form.lastname#
     Email: #form.email#
</cfmail>

<html>
<head>
     <title>Your Form Has Been Submitted</title>
</head>

<body>
<h1>Your Form Has Been Submitted</h1>

<cfoutput>
     <p>Thanks, #form.firstname# #form.lastname# for requesting more
information. Mail has been sent to our site administrator announcing
your interest. You will be contacted shortly at the e-mail address you
supplied, #form.email#.</p>
</cfoutput>

<cfif form.registerdrawing is 'yes'>
     <p>In addition, you have been entered in our site drawing.</p>
<cfelse>
```

Continued

Listing 47-1 *(continued)*

```
     <p>You have chosen not to register for our drawing. Thanks for
visiting our site.</p>
</cfif>

</body>
</html>
```

CFML is a tag-based language, which is why even nonprogrammers usually take to it quickly. Like HTML tags, most CFML tags have an opening tag, such as `<cfoutput>`, and a closing tag, such as `</cfoutput>`. Text or other elements appearing within a set of tags inherit properties assigned to the tag. Even without prior knowledge of programming or ColdFusion, you can open a template like Listing 47-1 and quickly get an idea of what's going on. That's one of the main attractions of ColdFusion, and one of the features nonprogramming designers find most endearing.

Understanding Dynamic Page Content

ColdFusion enables you to add *dynamic* content to your Web pages and Flash MX movies. In this case, "dynamic" isn't a measure of quality, but rather denotes that some or all of a page's content may be inserted into the page at the time a user's browser requests it.

Note

The opposite of dynamic content is static content: plain HTML pages or Flash movies in which images, text, and so on are fixed and can't be changed without editing the files.

Consider a basic shopping-cart application. As you move through the store selecting products, the contents of your cart change with each item you select for purchase. Obviously, there's no designer sitting at the store's headquarters frantically creating new HTML pages or Flash movies each time you select a product; the store application is generating dynamic content behind the scenes.

One of the reasons ColdFusion is an ideal tool for producing dynamic content is that it enables developers to quickly and easily connect their Web pages to databases. As the contents of your databases change, so do your Web pages — in real time and without any additional design on your part.

How ColdFusion Works with Databases

ColdFusion can connect to a variety of common database formats, including Microsoft Access and MS SQL Server, Oracle, MySQL, and more. It does so via software called Java Database Connectivity and ODBC (Object Database Connectivity (JDBC), which provide a relatively common ground so that the program code you build to access the contents of one brand of database is portable to another database product with a minimum of modifications.

When you begin building templates in ColdFusion, you'll set up *datasources* (DSNs), which are essentially JDBC pipelines to your database files or server. Datasources enable you to bring information in and out of your databases using the Web as a gateway. For example, a Microsoft Access database of products and customers can be displayed as a Web page or series of Web pages with only a few minutes' work in a ColdFusion template. In addition, developers can quickly create simple Web forms allowing the same database to be used as a repository for user data.

Understanding the ColdFusion Administrator

ColdFusion is unique among the Macromedia Studio tools in that it doesn't have a formal inter-face. Rather, it is administered from a special Web URL, and *only* through a Web browser. Macromedia recommends Microsoft's Internet Explorer, because some of the administrator's fea-tures may not be supported in other browsers.

If you installed the program in the default folder, point your browser to `http://localhost/cfide/administrator` to access the ColdFusion Administrator.

If you're using the Web server that comes with ColdFusion rather than your own stand-alone server, you need to append port 8500 to the server name: `http://localhost:8500/cfide/administrator`

You'll be asked to log in using the password you supplied when you installed ColdFusion. After you're in, you'll see settings allowing you to change the way ColdFusion runs, displays error mes-sages, connects to databases, and much more. If it seems like unfamiliar territory, don't worry. The examples in this section introduce you to the administrator's features you need to know.

How ColdFusion Works with Other Macromedia Studio Products

With the release of Studio, Macromedia has created new systems of integration among its products. ColdFusion's closest allies are Dreamweaver and Flash.

Integration with Dreamweaver

Because ColdFusion doesn't have a design interface of its own, most developers turn to Dreamweaver as the tool of choice. Within the Dreamweaver GUI, Macromedia has added sev-eral wizard-like functions that automate otherwise tedious ColdFusion tasks. For example, with the click of a Dreamweaver button or two, you can generate ColdFusion SQL queries, insert code to send e-mail from a template page, display the contents of a database, or build a basic form to input data into a table.

Because Dreamweaver supports both design and code views, it's ideal as a ColdFusion development tool. Those who come to ColdFusion from a designer's background can take advantage of Dreamweaver's timesaving functions within a graphic interface; veteran ColdFusion developers will find all the features to which may have grown accustomed in ColdFusion Studio.

Integration with Flash

Savvy Web developers have been using Flash and ColdFusion together for several years. The combination of Flash's ability to create sophisticated Web interfaces and ColdFusion's ability to handle complex programmatic tasks make it possible for individuals and small teams to quickly design sites that would take months or years with other tools. With the introduction of Studio, developers have a new set of tools that allow Flash and ColdFusion to talk to each other and exchange data. For example, using Flash Remoting Services, the contents of a complex ColdFusion query can easily be sent to a Flash movie, where they can be displayed dynamically. Variables generated by a ColdFusion template can be passed off to Flash ActionScript for processing in real time.

In addition, Studio has introduced the concept of the ColdFusion *Component*, essentially a chunk of program code in which both input and output can be shared between ColdFusion templates and Flash movies.

Summary

In this chapter you learned about the basic concepts that make ColdFusion work, as well as how it is often employed in Web applications. You learned that ColdFusion is a server-side application that works in conjunction with your existing Web server, and that when it's present on a server you can quickly build template pages that your site's users can access in the same way they view a standard HTML file. You also learned about ColdFusion Markup Language (CFML) and the concept of dynamic data, which may be used to build truly interactive sites. Finally, you learned how ColdFusion MX works closely with all major brands of database software, and other products in the Macromedia Studio collection.

✦   ✦   ✦

Creating a ColdFusion Application in Dreamweaver

◆ ◆ ◆ ◆

In This Chapter

Setting up a datasource and a testing server

Using basic CFML tags

Using Structured Query Language (SQL)

Creating a page to display the contents of a database

Creating a page to process the results of a form

Using Dreamweavers timesaving ColdFusion features

◆ ◆ ◆ ◆

Now that you've learned about the basic concepts behind ColdFusion, it's time to take your knowledge into a hands-on environment and begin constructing some basic templates. In this chapter you return to the Habitat Alert Web site to create a couple of templates that perform two common Web tasks: displaying the contents of a database containing names and addresses, and inserting form data into a database. When you complete the chapter, you'll know enough about basic ColdFusion tags to adapt the templates for your own projects. With a little tinkering, the two templates you build in the following examples can be customized to become a simple guestbook, a user registration system, or a technical support request interface.

Note The tutorials in this and subsequent chapters require that you have ColdFusion installed and running. If you don't, please see Chapter 1 for instructions.

Creating a Page to Display Newsletter Subscribers

You begin by building a simple template that displays the names and addresses of users who've subscribed to the Habitat Alert newsletter. This template uses ColdFusion to pull dynamically the subscriber information from a Microsoft Access database and display it to the user as an HTML page. This type of page might be used by the Habitat Alert Site administrator to monitor the list of current subscribers.

Because you don't yet have any subscribers, you need to start with a sample database populated with some usernames, located on the CD-ROM accompanying this book. The Microsoft Access database `ha.mdb` contains a table called subscribers, which in turn contains several fields, or columns, all defined as the text datatype, except for SubscriberID, which is a numeric, "long integer" datatype as shown in Figure 48-1.

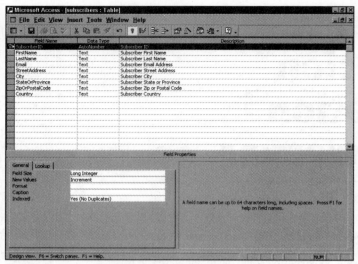

Figure 48-1: The subscriber database table shown in Microsoft Access' design view

When you change Microsoft Access to show the Datasheet view (View ➪ Datasheet View), you see the sample users currently stored in the table, as shown in Figure 48-2. Each row in the view is called a *record* and contains the information for a unique subscriber.

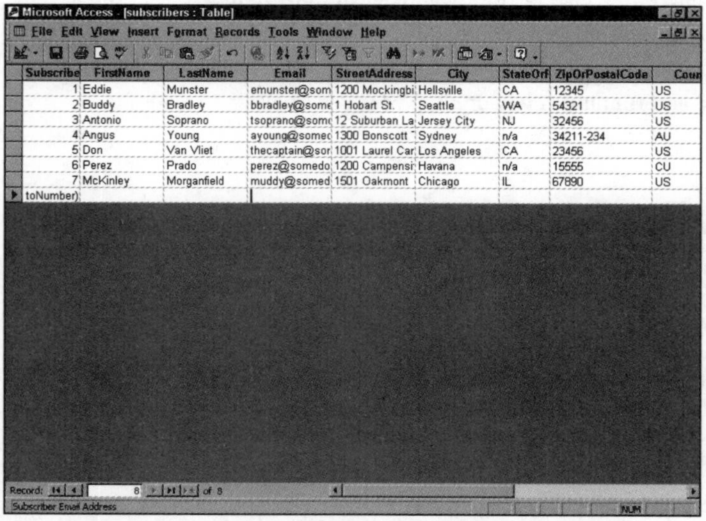

Figure 48-2: The subscriber database table shown in Microsoft Access' Datasheet view

Inside the habitat_alert folder is a database folder. Copy the ha.mdb database file from the CD-ROM (Chapter 48\database folder) and paste into the database folder of habitat_alert. Next, start Dreamweaver and open your Habitat Alert site.

Tip

It's a good security measure to keep databases that will be used as ColdFusion datasources out of the publicly available folders on your Web site. That's why you placed ha.mdb in a folder at the same level as "html" (a publicly readable folder) rather than within it.

Setting up a testing server and datasource

Before beginning the ColdFusion template, you need to give Dreamweaver a few details about your site:

Note

1. With the Habitat Alert site open in Dreamweaver, create a new file. When prompted for a file type, choose the category "Dynamic Page" and the document type "ColdFusion." Using the Page Properties dialog box, title the page **Subscribers** and save it as `show_subscribers.cfm`.

   To preview ColdFusion templates, they must reside within a folder available to your stand-alone Web server or the built-in Web server that comes with ColdFusion (usually `c:\cfusionmx\wwwroot`).

2. Open the Application panel at the right of the screen. Click the Database tab. The first two items should already be highlighted, assuming you've opened the Habitat Alert site and have specified a new ColdFusion document. Click on the third, Set up the site's testing server.

3. Follow the Setup Wizard, and supply it with your server details. If you installed ColdFusion on your local machine, your home URL is usually `http://localhost/`. If you're using ColdFusion's built-in Web server rather than a stand-alone server (such as Microsoft IIs), your URL needs to include port 8500, or `http://localhost:8500/`. If you're unsure about your home URL, use the Test URL button to verify it.

4. When your testing server is set up and verified, return to the Database tab under the Applications panel and choose Specify RDS Login Information. Supply the password you entered for Remote Development Services (RDS) when you installed ColdFusion.

5. Create a ColdFusion datasource by clicking on the "Modify Data Sources" button. Dreamweaver attempts to open your default Web browser and load the ColdFusion datasource setup panel. Remember that if you're using the built-in Web server that comes with ColdFusion, you need to modify the URL to include `:8500` after `localhost`.

6. Log in to the ColdFusion administrator using the password you supplied when you installed ColdFusion. This opens the ColdFusion Administrator's Datasource panel, as shown in Figure 48-3.

7. In the Datasource Name box enter **"ha"**; then choose the Microsoft Access driver to signify that you're setting up an Access Database. Click Add to see an expanded dialog box. Click the Browse Server button next to the Database File form box. A selection box opens, allowing you to navigate to the location of your sample database, `ha.mdb`. When the database has been selected, click Apply, and then Submit. You should see your database in the list of datasources, with an "ok" in the right column.

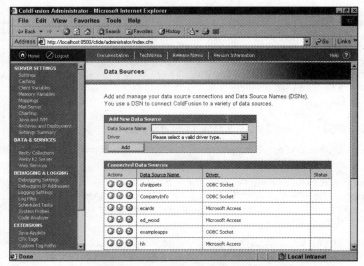

Figure 48-3: ColdFusion MX Administrator's Datasource panel

Note

If you're working with Windows 98 or ME, the process of setting up a datasource is slightly different. You'll need to first set up a Windows ODBC datasource using the "ODBC Datasources" icon in your Windows control panel. Then return to ColdFusion Administrator's datasource page, supply a datasource name and choose "ODBC Socket" as the driver type. When you submit this information, you'll see a list of all your Windows ODBC datasources, from which you can pick the one you set up in the previous step.

Creating a database query

You set up your database as a ColdFusion datasource and are ready to begin creating a template that draws information from the database in real time and displays it to your users as a Web page. Your template will begin with a query section, which uses Structured Query Language (SQL) to access your datasource and retrieve the names and addresses of newsletter subscribers stored in the database. SQL is a powerful language used by many programs to communicate with databases and select one or more records.

Follow these steps to create a database query:

1. Click the Bindings tab in the Applications panel.

2. Click the plus sign in the upper left and choose Recordset (Query) to add a new recordset.

3. Title your recordset **GetSubscribers**, select your datasource (ha), and leave all parameters at the default settings. Your completed dialog box should look like the one in Figure 48-4.

Figure 48-4: Defining a Recordset query in Dreamweaver

A look behind the scenes can give you a better idea of how ColdFusion and Dreamweaver work together. Click OK to add the new recordset; then choose View ➪ Code and Design to see the code Dreamweaver MX has inserted. At the top of the standard HTML `<head>` and `<body>` tags, you should see something like this:

```
<cfquery name="GetSubscribers" datasource="ha">
SELECT * FROM subscribers
</cfquery>
```

Dreamweaver autogenerated a ColdFusion query tag, `<cfquery>`. The opening tag includes two *tag attributes*: `name` and `datasource`. In many cases these are the only attributes your queries require. The name is thus far unimportant; you could use any name as long as it's intuitive and you use the same name later in your `<cfoutput>` code. The datasource is "ha," the name you used when you set up your database as a ColdFusion datasource in the previous section.

The code within the `<cfquery>` tags is a SQL statement. In this case, you're using a basic query that says "retrieve the contents of all the fields in all the records in the subscribers table." In SQL, an asterisk (*) denotes "everything" or "all fields." You learn more about SQL as you progress through this and later chapters.

Creating dynamic output

After you've added a query to your page, you need to add some code to display the results of the query, or the actual names and addresses that reside in the database. Dreamweaver offers a couple of timesaving, wizard-based solutions for doing so, but start by inserting some code manually to further your understanding of how ColdFusion works.

1. Type the following code snippet between the `<body>` and `</body>` tags in the code pane of your template; then choose File ➪ Preview In Browser to see the results as they'll appear to your users.

```
<cfoutput query="GetSubscribers">
     <p>#FirstName# #LastName#</p>
</cfoutput>
```

2. Save your work as `show_subscribers.cfm` in the main Habitat Alert Web folder.

You added a `<cfoutput>` tag to your code. Like `<cfquery>`, `<cfoutput>` has many attributes that you can use with it, although you're using only one, "query." In this case, query is defined as "GetSubscribers," the name you gave your query in the previous section.

The code between the `<cfoutput>` tags consists of a pair of standard HTML tags (`<p>` and `</p>`) along with two variables. In ColdFusion, variables are denoted by hash marks (#) on either side of their names. These variable names correspond to field names in your Microsoft Access database.

Tip   Because ColdFusion variables are denoted by hash marks, any hash mark appearing within a `<cfoutput>` section on your page is interpreted as the beginning of a variable name. However, if you need to use a hash mark literally — such as when defining a font color — you can escape it by typing two hash marks in succession, `<font color = "##ffffff">`

To get a better idea of how variables work, amend your `<cfoutput>` section to match the following snippet and then preview the results:

```
<cfoutput query="GetSubscribers">
    <p><a href="mailto:#Email#">#FirstName# #LastName#</a></p>
</cfoutput>
```

You added some more standard HTML tags to your code — mailto link that gets populated with the contents of the Email field in each database record.

Tip   Standard HTML tags can be used anywhere within `<cfoutput>` tags to format the results of a query.

Even though you only have one line of code containing FirstName, LastName, and so on, when you preview the page, you see the names of all subscribers in the database, because when `<cfoutput>` is used with the query attribute, everything within its tagset repeats until all the query results are exhausted. To get an idea of how this works, open up the Access database `ha.mdb` and manually add a few subscriber names by typing them into the Access Datasheet view. Reload the preview page in your Web browser to see how ColdFusion dynamically displays your data.

Formatting dynamic output

Now that you have a better understanding of the inner workings of `<cfquery>` and `<cfoutput>` work together, take a look at one of Dreamweaver's timesaving features for formatting the output of a query:

1. Start by deleting the entire `<cfoutput>` section you added in the previous section. Your page should retain the `<cfquery>` section, but should have an empty `<body>` section.

2. In your page's code view, place your cursor anywhere within the `<body>` tags and then select Insert ➪ Application Objects ➪ Dynamic Table. Select the Get Subscribers recordset; then choose All Records. After clicking OK, preview the page in your browser. You'll see something like Figure 48-5.

Testing Your ColdFusion Templates

As you build ColdFusion templates in Dreamweaver, you'll most likely test them by selecting File ➪ Preview In Browser, or by pressing F12. This is by far the easiest way to preview your work during development, but what happens if you click a .CFM file from outside Dreamweaver, say from Windows Explorer?

You may have already found that you don't get the response you'd expect. That's because .CFM files can't stand alone as can HTML documents or Flash movies. They require that you view them through your Web browser *and a Web server*, using the full URL path to the file, usually `http://localhost/SomeFolder/SomeFile.cfm`.

Error messages

As you work the examples in this section, it's inevitable that you'll encounter some errors as the result of a typo, a misplaced tag, and so on. Fortunately ColdFusion displays a detailed error report in your browser window, showing which tag failed, on which line the error occurred, and where applicable, it provides a suggestion about how to correct the problem.

Debugging

When the standard error messages don't give you enough information to fix a problem, you can turn to ColdFusion's debugging option. Access the Debugging Settings page in ColdFusion Administrator and check Enable Debugging. This causes some additional information to display at the bottom of every ColdFusion page you load. Remember that in a live environment, debugging options should be restricted to your local computer's IP address so that your site's users don't see the extra data.

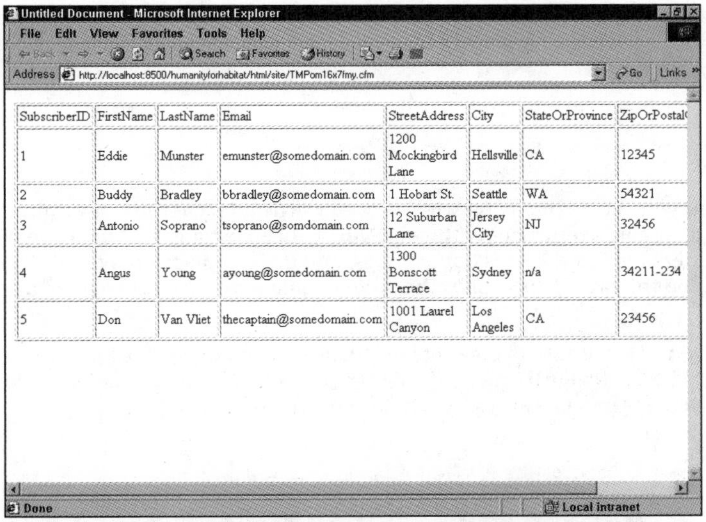

SubscriberID	FirstName	LastName	Email	StreetAddress	City	StateOrProvince	ZipOrPostal(
1	Eddie	Munster	emunster@somedomain.com	1200 Mockingbird Lane	Hellsville	CA	12345
2	Buddy	Bradley	bbradley@somedomain.com	1 Hobart St.	Seattle	WA	54321
3	Antonio	Soprano	tsoprano@somdomain.com	12 Suburban Lane	Jersey City	NJ	32456
4	Angus	Young	ayoung@somedomain.com	1300 Bonscott Terrace	Sydney	n/a	34211-234
5	Don	Van Vliet	thecaptain@somedomain.com	1001 Laurel Canyon	Los Angeles	CA	23456

Figure 48-5: The output of Dreamweaver's dynamic table function

Now take a closer look at the code the Dynamic Table function inserted into your page, shown in Listing 48-1.

Listing 48-1: A Table Produced by Dreamweaver's Dynamic Table Function

```
<table border="1" cellpadding="2" cellspacing="2">
  <tr>
    <td>SubscriberID</td>
    <td>FirstName</td>
    <td>LastName</td>
    <td>Email</td>
    <td>StreetAddress</td>
    <td>City</td>
    <td>StateOrProvince</td>
    <td>ZipOrPostalCode</td>
    <td>Country</td>
  </tr>
  <cfoutput query="GetSubscribers">
    <tr>
      <td>#GetSubscribers.SubscriberID#</td>
      <td>#GetSubscribers.FirstName#</td>
      <td>#GetSubscribers.LastName#</td>
      <td>#GetSubscribers.Email#</td>
      <td>#GetSubscribers.StreetAddress#</td>
      <td>#GetSubscribers.City#</td>
      <td>#GetSubscribers.StateOrProvince#</td>
      <td>#GetSubscribers.ZipOrPostalCode#</td>
      <td>#GetSubscribers.Country#</td>
    </tr>
  </cfoutput>
</table>
```

Remember that when you use <cfoutput> with its query attribute, everything within the tagset repeats until all records returned by the query have been exhausted. Dreamweaver has placed the table headers *outside* the <cfoutput> tags, and instead places only the second table row (<tr>) within the tags. This causes the table to gain a row each time a record is processed.

You can manually edit the table and its contents in Dreamweavers Design or Code views. You can move things anywhere, change the table header titles, cell padding, and so on, as long as the variable names remain the same and stay within the <cfoutput> tags.

A Word About Variable Scopes

Note that the query variables Dreamweaver inserted in Listing 48-1 are slightly different than those you manually typed in the previous section. They use a prefix or *scope*, separated from the variable name by a period. The `GetSubscribers.` scope identifies that the variables come from the query "GetSubscribers."

For the purposes of this basic sample template, the variable names `#LastName#` and `#GetSubscribers.LastName#` are interchangeable as long as they're used within `<cfoutput>` tags that identify the "GetSubscribers" query. However, as your templates become more complex, providing scopes with your variable names becomes more important. For example, if a variable comes from a form submission, your template might refer to it as `#form.FirstName#`, which differentiates from other `#FirstName#` variables, such as those that may have been returned by a query.

Scopes are also important in more complex templates because they can reduce the time it takes ColdFusion to process a page. For example, in a page that has several variables called `#FirstName#` in play, a scope helps ColdFusion quickly identify which particular instance you mean.

Using SQL to select more-specific recordsets

Now that your template has query and output sections, try experimenting with a few alterations. Remember that the actual SQL statement your template uses to fetch records from the subscribers is currently a basic one that was autogenerated with Dreamweaver's Recordset (Query) function:

```
SELECT * FROM subscribers
```

This type of query is used when you simply want to get all the records in a table. If you want to be more selective, you can limit your selection by using SQL's `WHERE` operator. Alter your query to the following and then preview the template in your browser:

```
SELECT * FROM subscribers WHERE Country = 'US'
```

The output section shows only the subscribers who have *exactly* the letters "US" in their Country field. The phrase after `WHERE` adds a qualification to your statement. You're still using the asterisk to select of the fields, but you're narrowing your query to only U.S.-based subscribers.

Try another, this time using the value of SubscriberID to limit your query. Continue to preview your work in your browser as you make each of the following query alterations:

```
SELECT * FROM subscribers WHERE SubscriberID > 3
```

This query omits subscribers 1-3 by using the *greater than* operator. When you supply a numeric value, you don't enclose it in single quotes as you do with a text string.

Caution   Whether SQL considers a field numeric or text is determined by the datatype you gave the field when you created your database. For example, the SubscriberID field in subscribers is set to the numeric datatype Long *integer* (refer to Figure 48-1), while the ZipOrPostalCode field was set to a *text* datatype, even though it often contains only numbers. (The reason for this is that many ZIP and postal codes contain dashes, which aren't allowed in fields of the integer datatype.) So if you write a query filtered by zipcode, you still have to enclose the string in single quotes, for example, `SELECT * FROM subscribers WHERE ZipOrPostalCode = '12348'`.

Using wildcards to perform partial matches

The preceding queries select records only when something *exactly matches* the string or number supplied in the `WHERE` clause. But you can also use SQL to select records based on wildcards. For example, a query like the following selects only subscribers whose last names begins with a "B":

```
SELECT * FROM subscribers WHERE LastName LIKE 'B%'
```

`LIKE` signifies that you want a partial, rather than exact, match. It's used with one or more percent signs (%) to denote characters that don't have to match. In the preceding example, the percent sign follows the B, to signify that you want last names that begin with B, followed by any other characters. You can also use percent signs on either side of a matched letter:

```
SELECT * FROM subscribers WHERE LastName LIKE '%V%'
```

This selects only records in which the subscriber's last name contains a V, anywhere in the name. However, note that in real-world applications you would almost never use a `LIKE` clause with two percent signs, as it would be extremely taxing on your server.

Caution   Because the subscribers table contains only nine fields, it's okay to use the asterisk to denote that you want to select all of them in your queries. However, when you're working with more complex tables, or in an actual production environment, you should always specify only those you want, separated by commas. For example, if your `<cfoutput>` section were designed to display only names and e-mail addresses, you could limit your field selection like this: `SELECT FirstName, Lastname, Email FROM SUBSCRIBERS`. This is good programming practice because it reduces the amount of time and memory required by ColdFusion when your queries execute. It also makes your code self-documenting so that other developers can see what you're up to.

Using compound SQL statements

SQL also enables you to use the *Boolean operators* `AND` an `OR` to perform more complex record selections. For example, you might want to select only U.S. residents whose last names start with a B:

```
SELECT * FROM subscribers WHERE Country = 'US' AND LastName LIKE 'B%'
```

Or just residents of the United States and Australia:

```
SELECT * FROM subscribers WHERE Country = 'US' OR Country = 'AU'
```

Sorting the results of an SQL query

So far, all your SQL queries have returned records in the order they were found in the database table. You can customize this behavior by adding an `ORDER BY` clause and specifying a field on which to sort. For example, to display the U.S.-based subscribers alphabetically by last name, you'd use this query:

```
SELECT * FROM subscribers WHERE Country = 'US' ORDER BY LastName
```

You might also want to display the subscribers in reverse order, so that the most recent display at the top of the page. Because the database uses Access' autonumber feature to generate SubscriberID, more recent subscribers have a higher ID.

```
SELECT * FROM subscribers ORDER BY SubscriberID DESC
```

`DESC` specifies that the records should be sorted in descending order, from highest to lowest. It's the opposite of `ASC`, which is the default sort method.

Note   When using `ORDER BY`, numeric fields are sorted numerically, text fields alphabetically, and date fields chronologically. Note that memo fields can't be sorted with `ORDER BY`.

You can also sort on more than one field, which is useful if you want to group the subscribers by country and then alphabetize them by last name within each country group:

```
SELECT * FROM subscribers ORDER BY Country, LastName
```

Creating a Page to Process Data Sent by a Form

The previous example creates a page to display subscribers before you have created the mechanism to get subscriber data *into* the database. That's because the previous section introduced you to some concepts you need to know before moving on. You set things right in this section by creating a ColdFusion template that accepts subscriber data from a form, inputs it into a database, sends the subscriber data to a Habitat Alert administrator, and returns a confirmation to the user.

Recall that in Chapter XX you created a basic form page in Dreamweaver MX, saved as the filename XXXXXXXXX. If you take a closer look at the form's source, you'll see that the variable names you used to collect data correspond exactly to the field names used in the subscribers table. This isn't absolutely necessary, but it's good programming practice and it saves lots of time, particularly on larger projects.

When a user fills out and submits this form, it sends the data to an action page, in this case, the ColdFusion template you're about to create.

Inserting a new record into a database table

The ColdFusion tag used to insert database records is `<cfinsert>`. Follow these steps:

1. Start by creating a new ColdFusion template (File ➪ New and then choose Dynamic Page and ColdFusion).

2. Using Page Properties, title your page **"Subscription Succeeded"** and save it as `subscribe_action.cfm`, the same name you used in the action attribute of your form.

3. To use Dreamweaver's code generator, select Insert ➪ ColdFusion Basic Objects ➪ CFINSERT. Your dialog box like the one in Figure 48-6 opens.

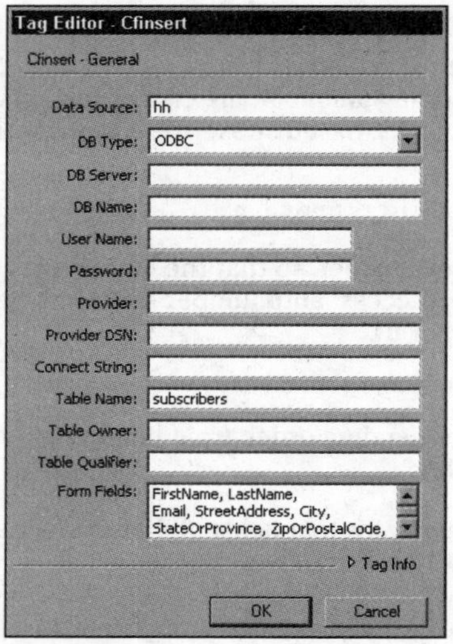

Figure 48-6: Using Dreamweaver
MX to Generate a <cfinsert> Block

The <cfinsert> tag offers lots of attributes, but you only need a few of them for a basic form insert. Note in Figure 48-6 I've supplied only the following:

✦ A datasource name.

✦ The name of the table in which the user information will be inserted.

✦ A comma-delimited list of the variables that will be passed by the form. These should correspond exactly to the fieldnames in the database. (If they don't, see the sidebar "Using SQL To Insert and Update Database Information")

When you press OK, Dreamweaver adds the following code to your new template:

```
<cfinsert datasource="ha" dbtype="ODBC" tablename="subscribers"
formfields="FirstName,LastName,Email,StreetAddress,City,StateOrProvince
,ZipOrPostalCode,Country">
```

Caution   When you use Dreamweaver's code generator to place a <cfinsert>, it will automatically add the code dbtype="odbc" if you use the default settings in the dialog box. The dbtype attribute is a holdover from previous versions of ColdFusion and isn't used in ColdFusion MX, so you should manually delete that attribute from your <cfinsert> line.

Note that the <cfinsert> tag is one of many in ColdFusion that doesn't require a closing tag.

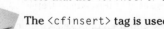

Note   The <cfinsert> tag is used only when you want to insert a new record into a database. If you need to change the data for an existing record, use <cfupdate>, which accepts the same parameters as <cfinsert> with the exception that at least one of the fieldnames supplied must be your table's primary key, a unique identifying field that lets ColdFusion know exactly which record to update. In the subscribers table, the primary key is SubscriberID.

Before you test your action page, add the other elements.

Sending mail from a ColdFusion template

The second requirement of your action page is that it send an e-mail to a Habitat Alert administrator, advising that someone has subscribed to the newsletter and passing along the subscriber's contact information. ColdFusion makes this a simple task. The tag you use to accomplish the task is `<cfmail>`

Before you can use `<cfmail>` in a template, you need to know some things about how mail will be sent from your Web site:

✦ The name of a mail server that will accept mail sent from your Web server

✦ A valid "from" address on that server

✦ The "to" address of the person who should receive the mail

To insert a `<cfmail>` block into your page, follow these steps:

1. Choose Insert⇨ColdFusion Advanced Objects⇨CMAIL. This tag has many possible attributes, but you need to only supply a few.

Note

In hosted Web environments, system administrators often choose to define the name of the system mail server in ColdFusion Administrator, which means you don't need to supply it as an attribute of the `<cfmail>` tag. However, it's also common for such mail servers to be picky about the address that appears in the "from" line of your mail, so check with your host's support staff to see whether they have any special requirements.

The General tab

Under General, you'll need a To address, which is the person who should receive the notification. In this case, it's a Habitat Alert employee using the address subscriptions@ habitatalert.com. The From address *must* be one belonging to a valid sender on your mail server. It would be nice if you could make the mail appear that it came from the user who's subscribing, but most mail servers won't allow this due to the potential for spam.

Finally, enter a subject line. In this case, "A User Has Subscribed to the Newsletter." See Figure 48-7 for a completed General tab.

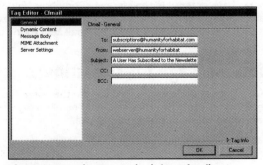

Figure 48-7: The General tab in `<cfmail>`

The Message Body tab

The body of the message contains the actual text to be sent. You can use ColdFusion variables within the body; just remember to denote them with hash marks. In this case, the user data (FirstName, LastName, and so on) will be sent from the form that calls your action page, so you can use this data in the body of the e-mail. See Figure 48-8 for an example of how the body might be formatted.

Figure 48-8: The Message Body tab in <cfmail>

The Server Settings tab

The only other tab you need to worry about for this basic mail example is Server Settings, and even that may be optional if you or your system administrator has already supplied the name of a mail server in ColdFusion Administrator.

Tip

When you're testing ColdFusion templates in a local setting, you can usually use your ISP's mail server to test mail functions (see the "outgoing" or "smtp server" settings in your e-mail program). In this case you can also use your own e-mail address in your mail's from line.

When you click OK, Dreamweaver inserts the <cfmail> tag into your document.

Dreamweaver MX

When Dreamweaver inserts the body of your mail between the opening and closing <cfmail> tags, it omits any carriage returns you may have entered in the Message Body box. You can manually edit the tag in Code view to add returns as required. Except for variables, all text within the tags is treated literally, so a tab in the code equals a tab in the mail sent to the user.

Generating a confirmation message for subscribers

Your template now contains two actions: it inserts the subscriber data into the database, and sends a notification to a Habitat Alert employee. The only other element you need is a confirmation message to show users that their subscription has been successful.

You can add this by inserting some code between your template's <body> tags:

```
<body>
<p>You have been subscribed to the Habitat Alert Newsletter.</p>
<p>Your user information has been saved in our database, and your
contact information has been forwarded to our newsletter editor.</p>
<p>Here's the user data you supplied:</p>
<cfoutput>
```

```
          #form.FirstName# #form.LastName#<br>
          #form.StreetAddress#<br>
          #form.City#, #form.StateOrProvince#
#form.ZipOrPostalCode#<br>
          #form.Country#<br>
          #form.Email#
</cfoutput>
</body>
```

The confirmation is HTML-formatted text, along with a short <cfoutput> section to display the data entered by the user. In this case, <cfoutput> is used without a query attribute, because you need to display only the values of the form variables, rather than those being returned by a query. Remember that your variables always need to be within a <cfoutput> tagset, otherwise they'll display as literal text. Try removing them from the preceding snippet to see what happens.

The entire code for the subscription_action.cfm template is shown in Listing 48-2. Remember that the end user doesn't see the <cfmail> or <cfinsert> blocks. Those items execute behind the scenes, and only the confirmation message is displayed.

Listing 48-2: **subscription_action.cfm**

```
<cfinsert datasource="ha" tablename="subscribers"
formfields="FirstName,LastName,Email,StreetAddress,City,StateOrProvince
,ZipOrPostalCode,Country">

<cfmail to="subscriptions@habitatalert.com"
from="website@habitatalert.com" subject="A User Has Subscribed to the
Newsletter">
   The following user has subscribed to the newsletter:
   Name: #form.FirstName# #form.LastName#
   Address: #form.StreetAddress# #form.City#, #form.StateOrProvince#
#form.ZipOrPostalCode#
   E-Mail: #form.Email#
</cfmail>

<html>
<head>
<title>Subscription Successful</title>
<meta http-equiv="Content-Type" content="text/html; charset=iso-
8859-1">
</head>

<body>
<p>You have been subscribed to the Habitat Alert Newsletter.</p>
<p>Your user information has been saved in our database, and your
contact information has been forwarded to our newsletter editor.</p>
<p>Here's the user data you supplied:</p>
```

Continued

Listing 48-2 *(continued)*

```
<cfoutput>
    #form.FirstName# #form.LastName#<br>
    #form.StreetAddress#<br>
    #form.City#, #form.StateOrProvince#
#form.ZipOrPostalCode#<br>
    #form.Country#<br>
    #form.Email#
</cfoutput>
</body>
```

Summary

In this chapter you constructed your first templates using two of the most powerful tags in ColdFusion's arsenal: `<cfquery>` and `<cfoutput>`. You learned how to set up a ColdFusion testing server and datasource, and how to use ColdFusion's debugging data to troubleshoot your work. You learned how to display the contents of a database table as a Web page, and how to construct a basic form-processing page that might serve as a replacement for many popular CGI scripts that would otherwise defy customization. You learned how to use Dreamweaver's tag interfaces to assemble your pages quickly, but you also ventured a step further and learned about the workings of the actual ColdFusion tags that are inserted behind the scenes.

Project Summary

The following table outlines what you've done in this chapter that will be used in the Habitat Alert Web site.

Files Prepared for Habitat Alert Web Site

Files	Where to Now?
show_subscribers.cfm	Ready for deployment in Dreamweaver
subscription_action.cfm	Ready for deployment in Dreamweaver

✦   ✦   ✦

Using Program Flow in ColdFusion MX

So far the ColdFusion templates you've built have been designed to handle only one set of circumstances. That is, you built them to perform a set of actions one after another, in a linear fashion, without having to make any decisions along the way. But because CFML is a programming language, you may have guessed that it has additional tools that enable you to handle multiple conditions.

In this chapter, you learn how to use a powerful family of tags called `<cfif>`, first to display a custom greeting based on your user's referring URL, and later, to build a simple, form-based poll allowing users to record their opinions on an issue.

Understanding Program Flow

When you create pages that can actually make decisions, you're using a programming technique called *program flow*. If you were to describe a program's flow in a plain English sentence and from the program's point of view, you might use a phrase like this one:

> If a user selects "no" from the pull-down box, record the response in a database and display a confirmation that no action has occurred. If the user selects "yes," open the main registration form.

Program flow describes a series of conditions and what happens as a result of each condition, much like a flowchart illustrates a business process. ColdFusion MX templates handle this type of decision-making with a trio of tags called `<cfif>`, `<cfelse>`, and `<cfelseif>`. By using these tags in conjunction with one or more *condition* statements, you can create templates to handle a variety of conditions. In the following examples, you learn more about how program flow works and when to use it.

Displaying a Custom Greeting Based on a User's Referring URL

When users visit your site via a link somewhere else on the Web, it's often useful to know where they came from (their *referring URL*). For example, your online store might offer a discount to users who came from a certain advertiser's site; or it may simply display a custom greeting acknowledging where the user came from. To build actions like this into a ColdFusion MX template, your code needs to be able to make a decision. It needs to first determine where the user came from and then perform one or more actions based on that determination.

First, you need to know a little about a special CGI environment variable called `http_referer`. Although it's not generated by ColdFusion MX itself, it *is* available within any ColdFusion template.

Tip

CGI environment variables are not a function of ColdFusion MX — rather, they're present any time a communication occurs between a browser and a Web server. They're used in a variety of Web programming languages to get information including the user's browser type (`http_user_agent`), the user's IP address (`remote_addr`), or the name of the Web server on which a page resides (`server_name`). For a complete list of such variables, do a Web search for the term "CGI environment variable."

Start by creating a new Dreamweaver site called "Examples." Then start a new dynamic ColdFusion page within it, naming your template `check_referral.cfm`. Add the following code within your template's body tags:

```
<cfoutput>#http_referer#</cfoutput>
```

Note

The spelling of `referer` in `http_referer` is incorrect in the English language, but it remains so as a holdover from the early days of the Web.

Now create a second page, this time just a standard HTML document. Save the page as `links1.htm`, in the same folder as `check_referral.cfm`. Place the following code within the body tags:

```
<a href="check_referral.cfm">Click here to view check_referral.cfm</a>
```

Now preview `links1.htm` in your browser and click the link you created. Your template `check_referral.cfm` displays the URL of the referring page, as seen in Figure 49-1.

You might see a slightly different URL depending on where your pages are stored. In this case, the referring URL is a local page that resides on your server, but `http_referer` also works if the referring page is at a remote location, say someone else's Web site. In this example, you're using `links1.htm` to test your work because it's much easier than calling up a friend with a Web site and asking her to post a link to `check_referral.cfm`.

Next you need to click File⇨Save As in Dreamweaver to make two copies of `links1.htm`, named `links2.htm` and `links3.htm`. Load each in your browser, click the link, and your ColdFusion template displays the URL corresponding to `links1.htm`, `links.htm`, or `links3.htm`, depending on which page you were viewing when you clicked the link.

Tip

As a CGI variable, `http_referer` may also be named using the CGI scope: `cgi.http_referer`. For more on variable scopes, see Chapter 48.

You're now able to track and display where your users have come from. The next step is to provide a custom greeting based on the page from which the user arrived. You use `<cfif>` and its companion tags to do this by adding some new code to `check_referral.cfm`, as shown in Listing 49-1.

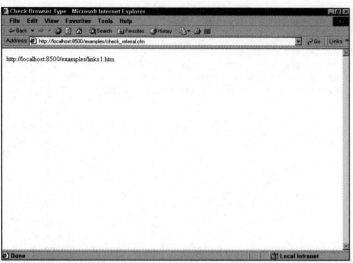

Figure 49-1: The output of the http_refer variable in a ColdFusion MX template

Listing 49-1: **check_referral.cfm**

```
<html>
<head>
<title>Check Referral</title>
<meta http-equiv="Content-Type" content="text/html; charset=iso-
8859-1">
</head>

<body>
<h2>Welcome To Our Site</h2>

<cfif http_referer contains 'links1'>
    <p>We notice you're visiting us via a link on links1, which is one
of our most valued advertisers. We appreciate you taking the time to
look around and hope you have a valuable experience while you're
here.</p>

<cfelseif http_referer contains 'links2'>
    <p>We notice you're visiting us via a link on links2, a site run
by our good friend Jim Smith. Please be sure to tell Jim what you
thought of our site.</p>
```

Continued

Listing 49-1 *(continued)*

```
<cfelseif http_referer contains 'links3'>
    <p>We notice you're visiting us via a link on links3, a site we no
longer wish to be associated with. If you speak to your friends about
our site, please don't do it in the same breath with links3.</p>

<cfelse>
    <p>Thanks for visiting. Please look around and mail us if you have
any questions.</p>

</cfif>

</body>
</html>
```

After you add this code, `check_referral.cfm` *acts* on the contents of `http_referer` rather than simply displaying it literally. It includes a `<cfif>` block, the section of code beginning with `<cfif>` and ending with `</cfif>`. Within the block are four conditions: one for each of the links pages, and one default condition for instances when the user has arrived at your site via a link unknown to you.

Note When you use a variable name as part of a `<cfif>` tag, you don't have to enclose it within hash marks. For example, `#http_referer#` becomes `http_referer`. This is the case with most CFML tags, although a few exceptions are covered in later chapters.

Let's take a closer look at the code in Listing 49-1. The template's body section begins with a header, `Welcome To Our Site`, which is placed outside the `<cfif>` block because the header remains the same regardless of how the user has arrived. Next is the opening `<cfif>` tag, along with the first condition. The condition states that the environment variable `http_referer` must contain the string `links1`. If the condition is satisfied, all text within the first `<cfif>` and the first `<cfelseif>` is displayed to the user. If the condition isn't satisfied, the text doesn't display, and ColdFusion MX's processor moves on to the next condition, and so on.

In the condition `http_referer contains 'links1'`, `contains` is just one of several tests you may use to create a condition. The others are shown in Table 49-1.

Table 49-1: Tests Used in <cfif> Conditions

Test	Description	Examples
is or eq	Determines whether two strings or numbers are identical	`<cfif name is 'John'>`
`<cfif count eq 12>` is not or neq	Determines whether two strings or numbers are not identical	`<cfif name is not 'John'>`

Test	Description	Examples
`<cfif count neq 12>`		
contains	Tests for a substring within a string; used with non-numeric data	`<cfif address contains 'Ave'>`
does not contain	Determines whether a substring does not occur within a string; used with non-numeric data	`<cfif address does not contain 'Ave'>`
lt	Less than	`<cfif age lt 21>`
lte	Less than or equal to	`<cfif age lte 21>`
gt	Greater than	`<cfif days gt 30>`
gte	Greater than or equal to	`<cfif days gte 30>`

Tip

It's good programming practice to indent any code or HTML text that appears within a `<cfif>` block to make it easier for you or other developers to identify your template's program flow from its source code. Also, as your templates grow in complexity and you begin to use nested `<cfif>` blocks, indented code is essential in identifying parent and child blocks.

The second CFML element within the `<cfif>` in Listing 49-1 is a `<cfelseif>` tag. This tag essentially states, "if the previous condition wasn't satisfied, then try this one." It differs from `<cfelse>` because it is always used with a condition; whereas `<cfelse>` simply says, "if none of the above conditions were satisfied, do this."

Listing 49-1 uses `<cfelse>` as the last item in the `<cfif>` block because you want to create a default condition that occurs if none of the others are satisfied. Users who visit the page from a link other than those matched in the conditions see a generic "Thanks for visiting" message rather than a custom one.

When you enter code like Listing 49-1 into Dreamweaver's code box, the design box displays the text for *all* the conditions, but it uses a ColdFusion element icon to denote the entire `<cfif>` block, and another to show where each condition occurs, as shown in Figure 49-2.

Now try loading each of the three links pages and clicking through to `check_referral.cfm`. You'll see how `<cfif>` causes your template's behavior to change depending on the referring URL. One example is shown in Figure 49-3, which appears when you click through from the page `links3.htm`.

Caution

Versions of ColdFusion prior to MX display an error if your template refers to `http_referer` and the variable is not defined. This situation occurs when users type your page's address in their browser's URL window or use a bookmark — both cases in which there is no referring URL. If you're using an older version of ColdFusion, you can guard against this problem by testing for the presence of `http_referer` with a function called `IsDefined()`. You'll learn more about functions in the next chapter.

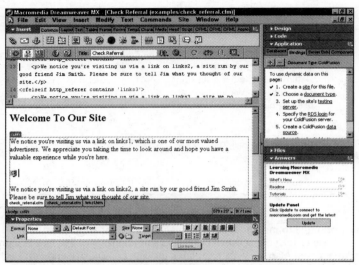

Figure 49-2: Viewing a <cfif> block in Dreamweaver's Design View

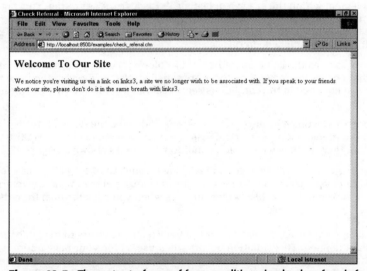

Figure 49-3: The output of one of four conditions in check_referral.cfm

Using Program Flow Techniques to Create a User Poll

In this section, you learn more about <cfif> as you use it to create a simple user poll. The goal is to create a form that collects a user's answer to a multiple-choice question. When the form is submitted, your template records the answer in a database and displays the current poll results back to the user. Finally, and here's the trick, both the form and action page will be included in the same ColdFusion MX template.

Creating the datasource

First, you need to create a ColdFusion MX datasource to house user responses to your poll.

1. Start by creating a new Microsoft Access database, called **polldata.mdb**. Save it in a folder called "poll" in your Web root. Within the database, create a new table with just one field, **response**.

2. In Design view, set the field to the **text datatype** and set the field size to **100**. Save the table as **question1** and allow Microsoft Access to add a Primary Key column. In Design view, your table should look like the one in Figure 49-4.

3. Set up the table as a ColdFusion MX datasource called **polldata**. See Chapter 48 for a step-by-step description of setting up a datasource.

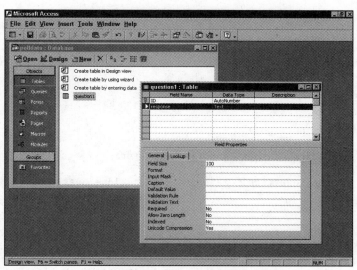

Figure 49-4: Creating polldata.mdb in Microsoft Access

Creating the template

Your form will contain a question, followed by three multiple-choice answers using radio buttons for selection.

1. Since this example isn't part of the Habitat Alert site, you'll need to create a new site in Dreamweaver. Title it **Polls** and assign it to the **polls** folder you created in the previous section.

2. Set up the site's testing server and supply an RDS login, as detailed in Chapter 48. Remember, if you're using ColdFusion MX's built-in Web server, the host name you specify in the testing server URL requires the 8500 port designation, as in `http://localhost:8500/polls`.

3. Create a new ColdFusion dynamic page within your site and save it as `question1.cfm`. Using Dreamweaver's Page Properties, title the page **Question One**.

4. Study the code in Listing 49-2 and the description that follows it; then add similar code to your template `question1.cfm`. Note that you can have any questions and answers, as long as they are consistent between the template's form and action sections.

Listing 49-2: **polldata.cfm**

```
<cfparam name="action" default="">

<html>
<head>
<title>Question One</title>
<meta http-equiv="Content-Type" content="text/html; charset=iso-
8859-1">
</head>

<body>

<cfif action is not 'go'>

    <!---if action is not 'go', show the form--->

    <form name="question1" method="post" action="question1.cfm">

    <h2>Question One:</h2>

    <p>For whom will you vote in the next Senatorial election?</p>

    <blockquote>
    <input type="radio" name="response" value="Barney Fife"> Barney
Fife<br>
    <input type="radio" name="response" value="Mickey Dolenz"> Mickey
Dolenz<br>
    <input type="radio" name="response" value="Bobby Hill"> Bobby
Hill<br>
    </blockquote>
```

```
        <input type="hidden" name="action" value="go">
        <input type="submit" value="Vote!">

    </form>

<cfelse>

    <!---if action is 'go' user must be submitting the form, so
process the data and show results--->

    <!--- insert user's answer into question1 table--->
    <cfinsert datasource="polldata" tablename="question1"
formfields="response">

    <!---get current totals for each response type, using the SQL
aggregate function 'count'--->

    <cfquery name="get_barney" datasource="polldata">
        select count(response) as total
        from question1
        where response = 'Barney Fife'
    </cfquery>

    <cfquery name="get_mickey" datasource="polldata">
        select count(response) as total
        from question1
        where response = 'Mickey Dolenz'
    </cfquery>

    <cfquery name="get_bobby" datasource="polldata">
        select count(response) as total
        from question1
        where response = 'Bobby Hill'
    </cfquery>

    <!---display the results--->

    <h2>Question One Results</h2>
    <cfoutput>
        <h3>Your Vote:</h3>
        #form.response#

        <h3>Current Rankings:</h3>
        Barney Fife: #get_barney.total#<br>
        Mickey Dolenz: #get_mickey.total#<br>
        Bobby Hill: #get_bobby.total#<br>
    </cfoutput>

</cfif>
</body>
</html>
```

Listing 49-2 includes several items that will be new to you. So the following sections examine each one in more detail.

The <cfparam> Tag

The opening tag in Listing 49-2, `<cfparam>`, is used to set a default value for a variable, that is, it only comes into play if a variable is undefined. In this case, it's also the key element, which enables you to include a form and its own action page in a single template. Note that the action defined in the `<form>` tag is `question1.cfm`, which causes this same page to reload when the user submits data.

By creating a default value for `action`, you're setting up your template to handle two conditions. When a user visits the page the first time, `action` won't be defined, so the `<cfparam>` tag kicks in and defines it as a blank value. Now take a closer look at the condition in the first `<cfif>`. It says that if `action` isn't "go," show the form. Otherwise (meaning if `action` *is* "go"), assume that the user is submitting the form and process the results.

Note In ColdFusion MX, as with most programming languages, there is a marked difference between a variable that hasn't yet been defined and one that is defined but contains an empty string (""). For example, if your code calls upon a variable that hasn't been defined, ColdFusion will return an error, but it won't do so if the variable has been defined as an empty string.

How does `action` get set to "go"? Take a look at the end of the form section. Just before the Submit button, `action` is defined as a hidden field and set to a value of `go`. When a user submits this form, this value gets passed as the page is reloaded, triggering the actions in the second half of the page.

Code commentary

Like any good programming or markup language, ColdFusion MX includes a method for commenting your code. In Listing 49-2, the phrases bracketed with `<!---` and `--->` are comments meant to aid you and/or other developers in understanding what's happening in a template.

Note Although ColdFusion MX comment markers are similar to those used in HTML, note that they include an extra dash. The difference between the two is users can view HTML comments by choosing View Source in their browser. Users can't view ColdFusion comments.

It's good programming practice to comment your pages liberally. Although your methods may be clear to you, they may not be to other developers who have to revise your templates later.

SQL's Aggregate Functions

The SQL statements you use in ColdFusion MX queries can go beyond just selecting the contents of database fields. You can also generate summarized information about your data by using SQL's *aggregate functions*.

These functions enable you to generate a variety of statistics about data stored in your tables. For example, consider a table that stores customer information along with the dollar totals each customer has spent at your client's store. To see the collective dollar amount spent by all of your client's Utah customers, you could use a SQL aggregate function called sum(). Assuming the database field containing the customers' spending totals was named "total_spent," your ColdFusion MX query might look like this:

```
<cfquery name="get_utah_totals" datasource="some_datasource">
    select sum(total_spent) as total
    from customers
    where customer_state = 'Utah'
</cfquery>
```

Note that in ColdFusion MX, you almost always use SQL's aggregate functions with an alias. In the preceding query, the alias total gives a name to the results generated by sum(total_spent). This situation enables you to refer to the figure later as #get_utah_totals.total# within <cfoutput> tags.

The sum() function is just one of many available in SQL. Other commonly used functions are shown in the following table. Each uses the format *function(fieldname)*.

Aggregate Function	What It Does
Avg()	Finds the numeric average of items in the specified field
Count()	Counts the values found in a field
Min()	Finds the lowest number in numeric fields, or the lowest alphabetic value in text fields
Max()	Finds the highest number in numeric fields, or the highest alphabetic value in text fields
Sum()	Adds the total of all numeric values in a field

It's important to note that SQL's aggregate functions are not the same as CFML functions, about which you learn more in the next chapter.

SQL's count function and aliases

Take a look at the three queries in the latter half of the page. Each is designed to count the database entries for a candidate. They use a SQL *aggregate function* called count to see how many records include a response field containing a given candidate's name. You always use count with parentheses containing the name of the table field you want to count. You'll find more information on SQL's aggregate functions in the sidebar accompanying this chapter.

Following count(response) are the words as total, which is a SQL *alias*. An alias is simply a way of giving something a temporary name that's often more convenient than its actual name. For example, if your table includes an extremely long field name, you would use a query similar to the following to save a lot of text farther down the page:

```
<cfquery name="get_employee" datasource="some_datasource">
select people_in_the_accounting_department_first_and_last_name as name
from employees
</cfquery>
```

Although the actual database field is named people_in_the_accounting_department_first_and_last_name, the query shown in the preceding example creates an alias called name. If you were to use the results of this query in a <cfoutput> section later, you would use the alias rather than the long name, as the following example demonstrates:

```
<cfoutput query="get_employee">
#name#
</cfoutput>
```

The poll example uses the alias name total so that you can later refer to a candidate's vote count by using the format *[query_name].total*:

```
#get_mickey.total#
```

Reviewing program flow

Now that you're more familiar with the new elements in Listing 49-2, you are ready to review the program flow. When a user visits the page the first time, no action variable is present, so <cfparam> creates one and sets it to an empty, dummy value. The first <cfif> condition states that if action is anything other than go, display the form, as shown in Figure 49-5.

The form is a fairly standard one except that its action attribute points back to this same page, question1.cfm. It also includes a hidden field, action, which is set to go. When a user chooses a candidate and submits a form, action=go is passed along with the candidate information. This triggers the second half of the <cfif> statement, rather than the first.

In the <cfelse> section, the page first inserts the user's candidate selection into the response table. Then it performs three queries to count the number of votes currently recorded for each candidate. Finally, it displays the user's selection and the current standings for each candidate, as shown in Figure 49-6.

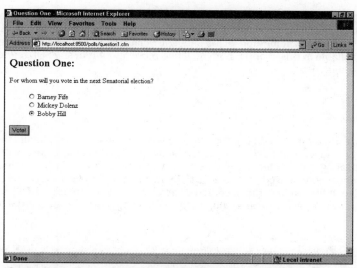

Figure 49-5: The output of question1.cfm when no action is passed

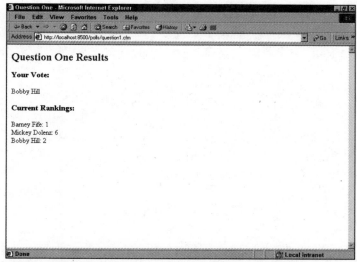

Figure 49-6: The output of question1.cfm when action is "Go"

Tip

The action page `question1.cfm` uses three distinct queries to count the number of votes for each candidate. This method was used to illustrate the use of program flow. However, know that there's a much more efficient method–SQL's `GROUP BY` clause. Use of this clause goes beyond the space available in this chapter, but you'll find more about it in any SQL reference or Microsoft Access' help files.

Summary

In this chapter, you learned how to add program flow to your templates by employing the `<cfif>` family of tags. You learned how `<cfif>` code blocks are used in conjunction with a condition statement, allowing your templates to handle a variety of situations. To further understand these concepts, you used `<cfif>` tags to build a page that sends a customized greeting to a user, depending on how the user arrived at your site. You also created a simple poll template, using `<cfif>` tags to create a single page containing both a form and the form's action.

✦   ✦   ✦

Using ColdFusion MX Functions

◆ ◆ ◆ ◆

In This Chapter

Understanding functions

Using functions to perform client- and server-side form validation

Working with times and dates

◆ ◆ ◆ ◆

I f you're new to programming languages, it may be helpful to think of functions as mini-programs designed to undertake a variety of common tasks. ColdFusion MX supports literally hundreds of functions, and with each release of the software the list grows longer. As you learn in this chapter, ColdFusion includes functions that enable you to manipulate text strings or the contents of variables, to provide you with data about your variables, and to work with dynamic dates and times in your Web pages.

Note that the examples in this chapter are designed to get you comfortable with using functions. This chapter covers only 10 functions out of a library of over 200, so after you get your feet wet you'll want to turn to your ColdFusion MX documentation for a complete list of other functions and what they do.

Understanding Functions

To understand what functions do and how they're useful in your templates, this section starts by looking at one of the most commonly used functions in the ColdFusion MX arsenal, Left(). The Left() function is used to display a specified number of characters beginning at the left of a string, so you often use it when you have a long string but only want to display the first few words or letters.

For example, assume that you've used <cfquery> to retrieve titles of developer seminars from a database. You want to display these titles on a page, but they're so long that they cause problems with your page design. One solution is to use Left() to truncate the seminar titles to a specific number of characters, say 50. The following code example assumes that the seminar titles have been previously retrieved by a query named get_seminar_titles and that they're found in a field called title:

```
<cfoutput query="get_seminar_titles">
    #Left(title, 50)#[...]<br>
</cfoutput>
```

Note that the ellipse in the brackets is not a special ColdFusion element. It's a literal ellipse in brackets that shows the reader that the titles have been truncated. Depending on the contents of your database, the preceding code might create output like the page shown in Figure 50-1.

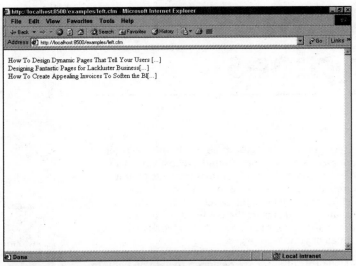

Figure 50-1: Using Left() to truncate text strings

Like most ColdFusion MX functions, Left() accepts one or more items as *input*, and then it generates something as *output*. In the preceding example, the input consists of the two items within the parentheses: the variable title, which tells Left() the variable you want to truncate, and the number 50, which tells Left() how many characters to display, starting from the left side of the string.

Note

When you're displaying the output of a function within a <cfoutput> section, you use hash marks around the entire function, not around the variable name itself:

```
<cfoutput>
#Left(name, 3)#
</cfoutput>
```

When you use a function within a CFML tag the hash marks usually aren't required:

```
<cfif Left(name, 3) is 'Mr.'>
```

Not all ColdFusion MX functions accept or require the same parameters, however. To illustrate, consider another commonly used function, DollarFormat(), which you use when you have a numeric variable you want displayed as a monetary value. For example, say that you're building an auction site in which users can enter a bid into a form box, hit Submit, and see the results of their bid. Some users may enter just the numeral 3; another may enter 9.5 (showing one decimal place) or 12.00 (showing two decimal places). To maintain consistency in the way these values are displayed, you could use DollarFormat() on the form's action page to standardize the way the user's input is displayed:

```
<cfoutput>
Your Bid: #DollarFormat(form.user_bid)#
</cfoutput>
```

This would cause any number the user typed into the form to display as currency, with a dollar sign and two decimal places:

```
$3.00
$9.50
$12.00
```

Note that unlike `Left()`, the `DollarFormat()` function accepts only one element—either a number or a variable containing a number.

The remainder of this chapter introduces you to several of the most commonly used functions and gives examples you can use in your templates. There obviously isn't space to cover all of ColdFusion MX's 200-plus functions here, so you should refer to the Macromedia product documentation for a complete list.

Tip ColdFusion MX also enables you to design your own functions to handle custom tasks not covered by its existing tag library. For more information, check your ColdFusion MX documentation for details on *user-defined functions*.

Using Functions to Validate Form Data

As you grow in your usage of ColdFusion MX and begin to develop larger and more complex sites, its likely you'll wish you had more control over the data your users supply in your sites' Web forms. For example, if you create a user registration form in which the users must supply their first and last names, how can you be sure they actually supplied that information when they submitted the form?

The solution to this and similar problems is to use ColdFusion MX to validate form data before it gets inserted into a database table. In this way, you can be sure that you're getting a complete name, address, phone number, or whatever other data you require of your users. Form validation techniques also help ensure that you're building a solid database, and that ColdFusion MX templates that "read" that user data later will remain error free because they're getting names, phone numbers, and addresses in the format they expect. This type of form validation is known as *server-side validation* because the actual checks are done by the server, as opposed to the client (the user's browser).

Tip ColdFusion MX offers a client-side tool to perform basic form validation: `<cfform>` (which is discussed in more detail later in this chapter). However, `<cfform>` requires the user's browser to be JavaScript enabled, so for flexibility's sake it's important to be familiar with both `<cfform>` and server-side validation principles like those described in this section.

To understand form validation, take a look at the basic HTML form shown in Listing 50-1. You'll also find the form's source code on the CD that accompanies this book.

Listing 50-1: registration.htm

```
<html>
<head>
<title>Registration Form</title>
<meta http-equiv="Content-Type" content="text/html; charset=iso-
8859-1">
</head>

<body>
<h2>User Registration Form</h2>

<form action="registration_action.cfm" method="post">
    <p>First Name:<br>
    <input type="text" name="firstname"></p>
    <p>Last Name:<br>
    <input type="text" name="lastname"></p>
        <p>Your Email:<br>
        <input type="text" name="email"></p>
    <p>Your Age:<br>
    <input type="text" name="age"></p>
    <p>Your Five-Digit Zip Code<br>
    <input type="text" name="zipcode"></p>
    <input type="submit" name="Register">
</form>
</body>
</html>
```

In Chapter 48 you created an action page similar to the one that would be required by the form in Listing 50-1. But that page didn't include any measures for checking that the users supplied information in all of the boxes, whether they supplied the correct type of information for each form field, and so on. It's time to take things a step further and learn how you can use ColdFusion MX functions to handle this type of validation.

To work through the following examples, you'll need to set up a datasource titled "registration":

1. Start by copying the sample database registration.mdb from the CD-ROM to your hard drive. If you're using ColdFusion's built-in Web server, a good place to store the database is c:\cfusionmx\db.

2. Open ColdFusion administrator using either its Start Menu icon, or by entering its URL in your browser: http://localhost:8500/cfide/administrator (remember that if you're not using ColdFusion's included Web server, the "8500" port is usually not required in the URL).

3. Navigate to the Data Sources page, and enter "registration" as the new Data Source Name; "Microsoft Access" as the driver. Click "Add".

4. On the next screen, click "Browser Server" next to the Database File box. Navigate to where you stored the `registration.mdb` database and select it. When you return to the main data source dialog, click "Submit."

> **Note**
>
> Remember that If you're working with Windows 98 or ME, the process of setting up a datasource is slightly different. You'll need to first set up a Windows ODBC datasource using the "ODBC Datasources" icon in your Windows control panel. Then return to ColdFusion Administrator's datasource page, supply a datasource name and choose "ODBC Socket" as the driver type. When you submit this information, you'll see a list of all your Windows ODBC datasources, from which you can pick the one you set up in the previous step.

Once your datasource is set up, you can use the registration database to test the following examples.

Start by considering a basic `<cfinsert>` action. The action page for the form in Listing 50-1 might contain a `<cfinsert>` tag to insert the form data into a database table, as follows:

```
<cfinsert datasource="registration" tablename="users"
formfields="firstname, lastname, age, email, zipcode">
```

But what happens if a user types in only a first name and leaves the other fields blank? If your datasource is a Microsoft Access database with the default design parameters, ColdFusion MX simply inserts the contents supplied in the `firstname` form field and allows the rest to remain empty. That doesn't create a very useful user record.

One method of ensuring you get a complete user record is to change your database table design to `Required=Yes` for critical fields like `firstname` and `lastname`. A user who types in only a first name sees a ColdFusion MX error message like Figure 50-2.

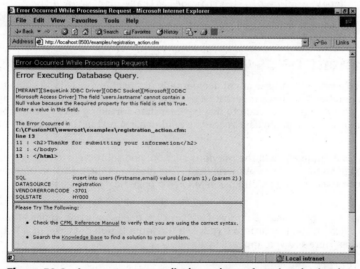

Figure 50-2: An error message displays when a form is submitted without required data.

Checking data length with Len()

The trick is to use a ColdFusion function called `Len()` in conjunction with a `<cfif>` statement to make sure the user supplied data in all of the required fields. If a user skips one or more fields, your action page displays a prompt for the user to return to the form, rather than try to insert the incomplete data as-is.

`Len()` is short for "length." It takes a variable name or a string as input and returns as output the number of characters present. That makes it a great way to check for fields that may be empty, because if a user doesn't supply a value for `firstname`, its length will be 0. Here's an example of `Len()` in action:

```
<cfif Len(form.firstname) gt 0 and Len(form.lastname) gt 0>
     <cfinsert datasource="registration" tablename="users"
formfields="firstname, lastname, age, email, zipcode">
<cfelse>
     You haven't supplied a full first and last name. Please use your
browser's "back" button to return to the form and try again.
</cfif>
```

The preceding code uses `Len()` to determine whether either the `firstname` or `lastname` fields have been left empty. If not, the `<cfinsert>` is performed. If so, the user sees a prompt.

Because the form in Listing 50-1 requests a five-digit ZIP code, you could also use `Len()` to ensure that the user supplied five digits:

```
<cfif Len(form.zipcode) eq 5>
     <!---perform database insert--->
<cfelse>
     You must supply a five-digit zip code. Please use your browser's
back button and try again.
</cfif>
```

Checking numeric fields with IsNumeric()

Now consider the age form field. A user might accidentally or mischievously type some text there, rather than a number, which would create a user record that might cause problems. For example, if you later design a template to display user data sorted by age, your template might fail with an error because some user records would contain text in the age field rather than a number.

As with the first and last name fields in the previous section, one solution is to change your database table's design so that age is a numeric field. This disallows the insertion of text data, but it also causes your users to see a ColdFusion MX error page rather than a friendly prompt.

The function `IsNumeric()` provides a solution. Like `Len()` it needs only one item as input: either a variable or a text string. It returns a 0 (false) if the input is non-numeric, or a 1 (true) if the input is a number. Here's how it appears in action:

```
<cfif IsNumeric(form.age)>
     <cfinsert datasource="registration" tablename="users"
formfields="firstname, lastname, age, email, zipcode">
<cfelse>
```

```
        You must supply a numeric age. Please use your browser's back
     button and try again.
     </cfif>
```

Tip

ColdFusion MX functions like `IsNumeric()` that return a true or false can stand alone in a `<cfif>` condition. For example, the condition `<cfif IsNumeric(form.age)>` is satisfied if age is a numeric value. To check for a negative value, use `<cfif not IsNumeric(form.age)>`.

Using <CFFORM> to create client-side form validation

The server-side validation methods described thus far in this chapter offer a lot of flexibility for verifying your users' data, but you can imagine how it might be tedious to write such code to validate forms with 20 or more fields. Fortunately ColdFusion MX includes an alternative option that's a little more convenient. It's called `<cfform>`, and it enables you to create a form page that's validated on the *client side* — that is, the validation is built into the form rather than the action page. If users don't provide the correct type of data specified by a `<cfform>` element, they get a pop-up notification when they try to submit the form.

The only drawback to `<cfform>` is that your users must have a JavaScript enabled browser, and — with some of the more sophisticated tags in the `<cfform>` family — the latest version of Java Runtime Edition installed on their computers. This isn't as much of an issue as it would have been say, three or four years ago, but it's worth considering if your intended users may have JavaScript disable.

The `<cfform>` tag functions as a replacement for a standard HTML form. To use it, your form page must be a ColdFusion template (a .cfm file) rather than an HTML document. You open and close a `<cfform>` block the same way you do a standard form:

```
<cfform action="some_action.cfm" method="post">
    <!--- cfform or standard html form elements go here--->
</cfform>
```

Within the block, you can use the companion tags of `<cfform>` to create input elements. The most common of these is `<cfinput>`, which essentially duplicates a standard HTML form input except that it enables you to specify whether it's a "required" field. As you'll learn later, `<cfinput>` has other benefits as well.

Each element is validated separately and can have a unique error message appear when the a user leaves a field blank:

```
<cfform action="some_action.cfm" method="post">
    First Name: <cfinput type="text" name="firstname" required="yes"
message="You must enter a first name"><br>
    Last Name: <cfinput type="text" name="lastname" required="yes"
message="You must enter a first name"><br>
    <input type="submit" value="Submit Registration">
</cfform>
```

Users who fail to provide data in any `<cfinput>` box that has been designated as "required" see a pop-up alert containing the text specified in "message," as in Figure 50-3.

Figure 50-3: An error message occurs when a <cfform> element is required but is left empty.

You can also use <cfform> to do more sophisticated checks on data than whether it exists or not. For example, you can verify whether a user has entered a phone number by using the validate attribute with a <cfinput> box:

```
Telephone Number: <cfinput type="text" name="phone" required="yes"
validate="telephone" message="You must enter a phone number in the
format xxx-xxx-xxxx">
```

The "telephone" validate attribute is just one of several supported by <cfform>. You can also validate dates, European dates, times, integers, ZIP codes, credit-card numbers, and social security numbers. Check your ColdFusion MX documentation for more information on <cfinput> validation types, as well as other input tags in the <cfform> family.

This client-side method obviously makes for less code on a form's action page, because the form itself already verified the existence of all required fields.

Combining validation elements

Now that you've gained some understanding of how you can use functions to validate data, take a look at the complete action page in Listing 50-2 to see how functions can be combined with a <cfif> statement to check for several conditions.

> **Listing 50-2: registration_action.cfm**
>
> ```
> <html>
> <head>
> <title>Registration Status</title>
> </head>
> ```

```
<body>
<cfif Len(form.firstname) eq 0 or Len(form.lastname) eq 0>
    <p>You must supply a complete first and last name</p>
<cfelseif not IsNumeric(form.age)>
    <p>You must supply your age as a numeric value</p>
<cfelseif Len(form.zipcode) neq 5>
    <p>You must supply a five-digit zip code</p>
<cfelse>
    <cfinsert datasource="registration" tablename="users"
formfields="firstname, lastname, age, email, zipcode">
    <h2>Thanks for submitting your information</h2>
    <p>Your information has been saved in our database. Thanks!</p>
</cfif>
</body>
</html>
```

Using Functions to Work with Dates

Another commonly used function in the ColdFusion MX toolbox is Now(), a unique function that requires no input. It simply generates a ColdFusion *date/time object* containing the current date and time on your server. However, Now() is almost always used in conjunction with other functions. By itself, it's not that useful as you'll see if you place it in one of your templates as is:

```
<cfoutput>#Now()#</cfoutput>
```

If you load the page in your browser, you see the current date and time on your server, but in a format that isn't exactly ready to plug into your site design:

```
{ts '2004-08-16 18:04:24'}
```

The reason is that ColdFusion date/time objects are designed to work in conjunction with other functions. For example, if you simply want to display a date at the top of your ColdFusion MX templates, you use Now() as the input for another common function, DateFormat():

```
<cfoutput>#DateFormat(Now())#</cfoutput>
```

Note the syntax: Now() is enclosed within the parentheses of DateFormat().

Note Almost all ColdFusion MX functions can be nested within one another. Although there's no limit to the number you can nest, keep in mind that functions nested more than five or six levels begin to cut into the loading time of your templates.

Viewed in a browser, this combination produces something like this:

```
16-Aug-02
```

It's beginning to look more like a date you'd expect to see in a Web page, but it still needs a little work. Fortunately, DateFormat() enables you to include an optional mask as input. A *mask* is a representation of the way you want the date to display, using identifying strings like "mmmm" to signify that you want the month to display as a long name (as opposed to a number, and so on). You enclose the mask in quotes and set it off with a comma:

```
<cfoutput>#DateFormat(Now(), "mmmm dd, yyyy")#</cfoutput>
```

The preceding line produces output that's much more useful in the average Web page:

```
August 16, 2002
```

Using a different mask, you could also use Now() to display only the current month:

```
<cfoutput>#DateFormat(Now(), "mmmm")#</cfoutput>
```

The preceding line would simply display August assuming that's the current month on your server.

To display the current time, you can use another function called TimeFormat(), again using Now() as input (remember that Now() holds both the current date and the current time). TimeFormat() also accepts a mask as input:

```
<cfoutput>
    #DateFormat(Now(), "mmmm dd, yyyy")#<br>
    #TimeFormat(Now(), "h:mm tt")#
</cfoutput>
```

The previous code produces output like this:

```
August 16, 2002
6:29 PM
```

Tip   You'll find a complete list of mask characters and details on how to use them in your ColdFusion MX documentation, under the sections covering the DateFormat() and TimeFormat() functions.

Tip   For international sites that need to display dates and times in non-U.S. standard format you can use the LSDateFormat() and LSTimeFormat() functions. Refer to the ColdFusion MX documentation for more information on these functions

Summary

In this chapter, you gained understanding of ColdFusion MX functions and how they're used like mini-programs to accomplish common tasks, such as truncating a text string or changing the way a date displays, quickly. You learned that functions are valuable tools in validating user form data, and that ColdFusion MX offers both server-side and client-side options for doing so. Finally, you learned about the date/time object Now() and how it's used to display dates and times in a variety of formats. At this point, you have a working knowledge of functions, how they accept *input* and generate *output*. You can turn to your ColdFusion MX documentation for its complete list of over 200 functions, and begin to use them in your own work.

✦   ✦   ✦

Working with ColdFusion MX Variables

The templates you've created so far have used only two types of variables: the *form variable*, in which a user types information into a form box, and the *query variable* in which `<cfquery>` is used to fetch records from a database and make the results available as variables within your template. But as you begin to envision ways to use ColdFusion in your own projects, it's likely you've realized that you'll need other ways to get variable data in and out of your templates.

In this chapter you'll be introduced to several other types of ColdFusion variables, and you'll get a close look at two of the most common ones: the *URL variable*, a variable used to pass information from one template to another via URLs; and the *list variable*, a special type of "complex" variable capable of holding more than one data element. You'll also learn about some tools ColdFusion offers for working with the various variable types and how to use them to create common applications, such as "drill-down" displays and basic keyword search engines.

Understanding Drill-Down Applications and URL Variables

To begin your exploration of URL variables, start with a common set of pages you'll find used all over the Web — the "drill-down" or "summary-detail" application. Take a look at Figures 51-1 and 51-2, which show the two elements of a basic drill-down application.

The template pictured in Figure 51-1 is designed to show the user only the title of films stored in my database. When users click a title, they see something like Figure 51-2, which shows more complete details about the film they selected.

Figure 51-1: The "summary" page of a sample drill-down application, showing only film titles

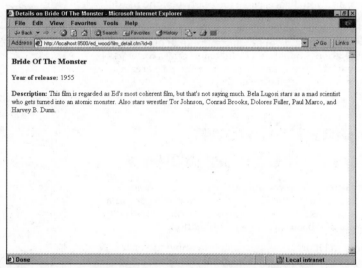

Figure 51-2: The "detail" page of a drill-down application, showing details on a single film

Again, this display method is used often on the Web in shopping carts, catalogs, discographies, genealogy sites, and so on. ColdFusion makes it easy to construct such an application. As you may have guessed, the sample application is displaying film data that has been stored in a database. Because it generates the summary and detail pages dynamically, any new film titles added to the database automatically appear in the summary and are ready to serve up as detail pages.

Setting up the sample files

To get a closer look at the sample drill-down application, you need to define datasource and copy the relevant files to your Web directory. On the CD-ROM that accompanies this book, you'll find a Microsoft Access database named `ed_wood.mdb`. Copy it to your hard drive (the `db` folder in `cfusionmx` is a good spot for sample datasources), then access the ColdFusion MX Administrator and set up your database as a new Microsoft Access datasource called `ed_wood`. Remember that if you're using Windows 98 or ME, the process is slightly different–see Chapter 48 for details.

Also on the CD-ROM are two templates named `film_summary.cfm` and `film_detail.cfm`. Create a new folder called `ed_wood` in your Web root (usually `cfusion\wwwroot`) and copy the two files there.

To test the application, start by accessing the film summary page, the one pictured in Figure 51-1. Your URL should be similar to this one:

```
http://localhost:8500/ed_wood/film_summary.cfm
```

Now place your mouse over any of the film title links and note the URL displayed in your browser's status bar:

```
http://localhost:8500/ed_wood/film_detail.cfm?id=8
```

This URL links to `film_detail.cfm`, the page pictured in Figure 51-2, but it also passes some additional information. Everything after the `.cfm` file extension is called a *query string*. In this case, the query string contains one variable, `id`, which is set to a value of 8.

In URLs, query strings are always separated from the name of a page by a question mark. If more than one variable is used in a query string, each variable is delimited by an ampersand (&), for example:

```
some_page.cfm?firstname=John&lastname=Smith&age=21
```

Query strings can't contain spaces, control characters, or punctuation marks, other than those used to identify variables and a handful of special characters such as a dash (-). Many Web technologies other than ColdFusion, including CGI scripts, Active Server Pages, PHP3 pages, and so on, use query strings.

Variables passed in a query string are called *URL variables*. These variables are available for use in the called page (in this case, `film_detail.cfm`) like variables that have been passed by a form, or those that result from a `<cfquery>`. As you learn in the next section, when you refer to a URL variable in a ColdFusion template you enclose it in hash marks as you would any other ColdFusion variable. It's also good practice to add a scope to the variable, using the prefix `URL`, such as `#URL.id#` or `#URL.firstname#`.

Examining a detail page

Before you look at the code that produces the summary page, work backwards and first take a look at code that produced the detail page shown in Figure 51-2. You can open `film_detail.cfm` in Dreamweaver, or view its source in Listing 51-1.

Listing 51-1: **film_detail.cfm**

```
<!---query the database for a specific film, based on the ID sent in
the URL--->

<cfquery name="get_film" datasource="ed_wood">
    select *
    from films
    where id = #URL.id#
</cfquery>

<html>
<head>

<!---display the film's title in the browser title bar--->

<title>
    Details on <cfoutput>#get_film.title#</cfoutput>
</title>

<meta http-equiv="Content-Type" content="text/html; charset=iso-
8859-1">
</head>

<body>

<!---display the details on this film--->

<cfoutput query="get_film">
    <h3>#title#</h3>
    <p><b>Year of release:</b> #year#</p>
    <p><b>Description:</b> #description#</p>
</cfoutput>

</body>
</html>
```

Note the `<cfquery>` section in the file. It's designed to retrieve only one record: the one in which the `id` is equal to the ID value passed in the query string. In the page displayed in Figure 51-2, the query string specifies `id=8`, so the display page shows the details for the film *Bride Of The Monster*. To see why, take a look at your copy of the `ed_wood.mdb` database, or Figure 51-3, which shows the films table in Datasheet view.

When I created this table in Microsoft Access, I allowed Access to automatically create an ID field. This gives each film a unique numeric identifier and makes it easy to query for a specific record.

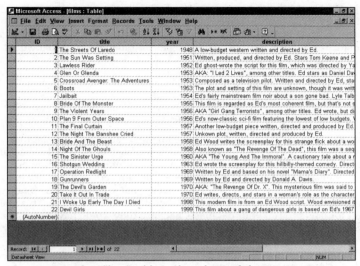

Figure 51-3: The "films" table in the ed_wood datasource

What happens if you specify a different ID value in the URL? Try it and see. Manually edit the URL in your browser to look like this one:

```
http://localhost:8500/ed_wood/film_detail.cfm?id=14
```

You see the detail page, but this time populated with information on the film with the ID of 14, as shown in Figure 51-4.

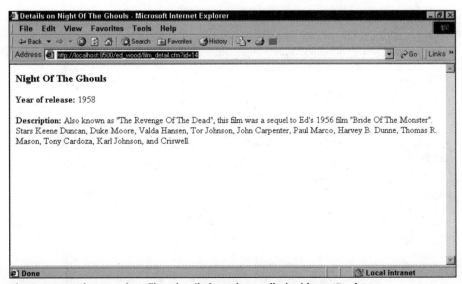

Figure 51-4: The template film_detail.cfm, when called with an ID of 14

When the value of the URL variable `id` changes, so does the content of the page.

When you use ID values as the identifiers for a drill-down application, there's a danger that a tech-minded user could "run" your database by creating an automated script that would fetch your pages in numeric order, as follows:

```
http://some_site/show_member.cfm?member_id=1
http://some_site/show_member.cfm?member_id=2
http://some_site/show_member.cfm?member_id=3
```

This would allow the user's script to fetch a detail page for each record in your database sequentially and save it for the user's own purposes. For a database of Ed Wood films, this isn't a problem, but it would be if your database contained proprietary information on your site's users. To guard against this, one quick solution is to use non-sequential, random ID values. Microsoft Access, for example, enables you to specify that your id field be made up of randomly generated, nine-digit numbers that may be either positive or negative. This makes it much more difficult for users to run your database, because they would have to write a program to fetch every ID between -999999999 and 999999999, one page at a time.

Examining the summary page

Now take a closer look at the summary page that displays film titles, `film_summary.cfm` (see Figure 51-1). In addition to simply retrieving and displaying the film titles stored in the database, the summary page also creates links to pass the correct ID to the detail page. Take a look at the source code in your copy of the file, or in Listing 51-2.

Listing 51-2: **film_summary.cfm**

```
<!---get the id and title for all films in the database--->

<cfquery name="get_films" datasource="ed_wood">
    select id, title
    from films
</cfquery>

<html>
<head>
<title>The Films of Ed Wood</title>
<meta http-equiv="Content-Type" content="text/html; charset=iso-
8859-1">
</head>

<body>
```

```
<h3>The Films of Ed Wood</h3>

<!---display the query results as an unordered list, wrapping each
title in an <a href> tag pair to create a link to the detail page. each
link will pass the film's database ID in its URL--->

<ul>
<cfoutput query="get_films">
    <li><a href="film_detail.cfm?id=#id#">#title#</a></li>
</cfoutput>
</ul>

</body>
</html>
```

The query section of the template should be familiar by now. It simply gets the title and ID for each film record in the database. Further down the page, the `<cfoutput>` section uses that data to display the title and link for each film:

```
<a href="film_detail.cfm?id=#id#">#title#</a>
```

This URL links to the detail page and uses a query string to pass an ID corresponding to the film's title. Recall from the discussion in the previous section that the detail page uses the passed ID to determine which film to display.

Note Why use ID values as the identifier for a record? Why not use something more intuitive like the film's title? The answer is that while you could use film titles as identifiers, it would create some problems. For example, the URL used to access the detail page would look like this:

```
http://localhost:8500/ed_wood/film_detail.cfm?title=Plan 9 From Outer
Space
```

Because query strings can't include spaces, this would cause an error in the user's browser. There are ways around this problem — notably the `URLEncodedFormat()` function–but in general it's much more foolproof to use a numeric field such as an ID.

Using ordering and groups to sort query output

When the `<cfquery>` in Listing 51-2 retrieves film titles, it fetches the records in the order it finds them in the database. If you wanted to display the film titles in alphabetic order, you could use SQL's `ORDER BY` clause to sort the query results by title, as covered in Chapter 48.

But what if you wanted to display the films grouped year of release? Take a look at Figure 51-5.

The list is grouped so that films with a common field — year, in this case — are shown together. Creating a page like this requires two modifications to the original summary page:

✦ Your query must be sorted on the field on which you want to group your output.

✦ You must use the `"group"` attribute in your opening `<cfoutput>` tag to specify the field on which to group.

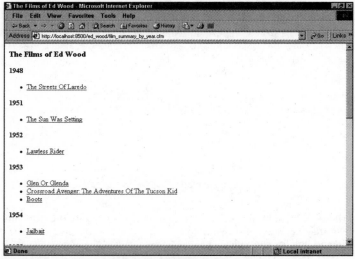

Figure 51-5: Grouping query results by year

Take a look at the following source code (you'll also find this file on your CD as film_
summary_by_year.cfm).

```
<!---get the id and title for all films in the database. order them by
the "year" field to allow for grouping--->

<cfquery name="get_films" datasource="ed_wood">
    select id, title, year
    from films
    order by year
</cfquery>

<html>
<head>
<title>The Films of Ed Wood</title>
<meta http-equiv="Content-Type" content="text/html; charset=iso-8859-1">
</head>

<body>
<h3>The Films of Ed Wood</h3>

<!---display the query results grouped by year--->

<cfoutput query="get_films" group="year">
    <b>#year#</b>
    <ul>
    <!---display the sub-elements of the "year" group--->
    <cfoutput>
```

```
        <li><a href="film_detail.cfm?id=#id#">#title#</a></li>
    </cfoutput>
    </ul>
</cfoutput>

</body>
</html>
```

Note that the `<cfquery>` section is similar to the one in original summary page, except that it includes `"year"` as one of the fields to retrieve, and it uses `ORDER BY` to sort the query results by year.

The `<cfoutput>` section is also modified. It includes `group="year"` to specify a grouping, and it also includes an extra set of `<cfoutput>` tags within the main `<cfoutput>` section. When you use the `"group"` attribute, ColdFusion ignores duplicate items in the grouped field, meaning that the main `<cfoutput>` section displays its contents only once for each *unique* year it finds. To display subelements of a group (the films released in a given year), you use a second set of `<cfoutput>` tags.

To better understand how the two `<cfoutput>` sections work together, open the source code for `film_summary_by_year.cfm`, experiment by placing some text within the outer set of `<cfoutput>` tags, and then preview the page. Next try placing something within the inner set and notice how that affects output.

You can group on any field, as long as your `<cfquery>` orders your query results by that field. In the films database, however, `"year"` is the only field that would provide a meaningful group, because none of the other fields contain any duplicate entries.

Note   The "group" attribute used with <cfoutput> is not related to the GROUP BY clause used in SQL statements. Don't confuse the two.

Using List Variables

Until now, all the variables you've used in your ColdFusion templates have held simple values — either a string or a number, such as `id=25` or `fullname="Don Van Vliet"` or, in the case of query variables, they've held the results of SQL queries. But like most programming languages, ColdFusion supports variables capable of holding complex data. One of these is the *list* variable type, which can hold a list of values — either strings or numbers. To understand how a list variable might be used, consider a Web form that contains several check boxes. The check box section of the form might look like this:

```
<h3>Select Your Hobbies</h3>
<input type="checkbox" name="hobbies" value="sports"> Sports<br>
<input type="checkbox" name="hobbies" value="loafing"> Loafing<br>
<input type="checkbox" name="hobbies" value="reading"> Reading<br>
<input type="checkbox" name="hobbies" value="eating"> Eating<br>
```

All the check boxes use the same variable name, but each has a different value associated with it. This is a common technique in Web forms designed to record user preferences. If a user checked the first three boxes and then submitted the form, `hobbies` would be sent to the form's action page containing the following:

```
sports,loafing,reading
```

So rather than containing a simple value, hobbies actually contains three values, separated by commas. This type of variable is called a *list variable*.

Note   List variables are one of several types of complex variables supported by ColdFusion. The others include structure variables, which store data indexed by key names, such as firstname="Charles" lastname="Mohnike" and array variables, which store data in multiple dimension, indexed by position. ColdFusion MX also supports components, objects, and XML documents as complex variables. While these variable types are beyond the scope of this chapter, you touch on some of them in future chapters. You'll also find a more complete reference to both variable types in your ColdFusion documentation.

ColdFusion includes several tools for working with list variables, notably a set of functions that enable you to find and retrieve individual items in a list, as well as a tag called <cfloop> that enables you to perform an action for each item in a list.

Note   Commas are the default delimiters for list variables, but they're by no means the only ones. In fact, ColdFusion enables you to use just about any character as a delimiter in a list as long as you specify that character when you use list functions or <cfloop>. You learn how to do so in the following sections.

Using <cfset> to Define a Variable Manually

You've already learned how variables can be defined by the output of a SQL query, from form input, or from a URL. ColdFusion also provides a tag enabling you to manually create and define variables within your templates manually: <cfset>.

Using <cfset> is straightforward:

```
<cfset firstname = "Charles">
<cfset visit = 0>
```

String values are enclosed in quotes, as in the first example; numeric variables don't require the quotes, as in the second.

You can also use numeric operators, ColdFusion functions, and existing variables in the process of defining a new variable with <cfset>:

```
<cfset visit = visit + 1>
<cfset initial = Left(last_name, 1)>
```

You may also manually define list variables with <cfset>:

```
<cfset interests = "skating,eating,loafing">
```

After you define a variable with <cfset>, you can call it anywhere in that template using the same hash-mark method as other ColdFusion variables:

```
<cfoutput>#firstname#</cfoutput>
<cfoutput>#visit#</cfoutput>
```

Using ColdFusions list functions

To explore the use of ColdFusion's list functions and understand how to use them in common tasks, start by copying the form `personal_data_form.htm` on the accompanying CD-ROM to a folder in your Web root. If you still have it, the `polls` folder from the examples in Chapter 49, that makes a great place to store the form.

Note

You can design your own form and use it with the following examples as long as it uses multiple check boxes with the same `name` attribute.

For reference, the form's source is shown in Listing 51-3.

Listing 51-3: personal_data_form.htm

```
<html>
<head>
<title>Personal Data Form</title>
<meta http-equiv="Content-Type" content="text/html; charset=iso-
8859-1">
</head>

<body>
<h2>Personal Data</h2>
<form action="personal_data_action.cfm" method="post">
    <h3>Select Your Hobbies</h3>
    <p>
    <input type="checkbox" name="hobbies" value="sports"> Sports<br>
    <input type="checkbox" name="hobbies" value="loafing"> Loafing<br>
    <input type="checkbox" name="hobbies" value="reading"> Reading<br>
    <input type="checkbox" name="hobbies" value="eating"> Eating<br>
    </p>

    <h3>Select Your Interests</h3>
    <p>
    <input type="checkbox" name="interests" value="current events">
Current Events<br>
    <input type="checkbox" name="interests" value="religion">
Religion<br>
    <input type="checkbox" name="interests" value="politics">
Politics<br>
    <input type="checkbox" name="interests" value="travel"> Travel<br>
    </p>
  <input type="submit">
</form>
</body>
</html>
```

To test the functions in the following sections, you also need to create an action page for the form. Create a new ColdFusion template called `personal_data_action.cfm` and save it in the same folder as your form.

Finding a list item with ListFind()

You might want your action page to display a custom message to users who express an interest in politics. One way to achieve this is with the function `ListFind()`, which accepts two items as input: the name of a list variable in which to search, and string to search for. It returns the *index number* of the list where the string was found, or `"0"` if the item isn't found.

Insert the following snippet of code into your action page:

```
<cfif ListFind(form.interests, "sports")>
    <p>You specified an interest in sports. May we suggest you visit
Wild Wally's Sports Haven for a variety of sports memorabilia and
sporting goods?</p>
<cfelse>
    <p>You aren't interested in sports? That's too bad.</p>
</cfif>
```

Take a closer look at the first line of code. The `ListFind()` function includes the `form` scope with the `interests` variable — not absolutely necessary in a page this basic, but good practice. The string you want to search for is enclosed in quotes.

The code also uses `<cfif>` with its `"not equal"` operator to determine whether `ListFind()` finds the word `"sports"` in the list variable `interests`. For example, if `"sports"` is the first (or only) item in the `interests` list, the function returns a value of `"1"`; if it were the second item in the list, the function would return, and so on. In this case you don't need to be concerned about *where* sports occurs in the list, only that it *does* occur, hence the `neq 0`.

Note   You may be wondering why to use `ListFind()` to check for the occurrence of a string in a list variable. Why not just use the `<cfif>` operator `contains` as detailed in Chapter 49.

```
<cfif form.interests contains 'politics'>
```

You'd be correct that `contains` would also work in the current example. However, consider a situation in which there were two check boxes, `"politics"` and `"politics: international"`. Using `contains` to search for `"politics"` would return a match even if the only item in the list was `"politics: international"`. `ListFind()` provides a more exact match because it returns a positive result only if the specified string is *exactly equal* to an entire list element.

Note   The `ListFind()` function is case-sensitive. When you want to match a string without case sensitivity, use `ListFindNoCase()`.

Adding a list item with ListAppend()

As users submit the form, you might want to add a default interest to the list variable automatically. You can do so with the function `ListAppend()`, which takes as input the name of a list and the string you want to append. Try adding the following snippet to your action page:

```
<cfset form.interests = ListAppend(form.interests, "filling out Web
forms")>

<p>Thanks for completing our survey. You've shown an interest in the
following areas:</p>
<p><cfoutput>#form.interests#</cfoutput></p>
```

This example uses `<cfset>` (see the sidebar in this chapter) to change the value of `form.interests`, the list variable sent by the user's form submission. The phrase `"filling out Web forms"` is added to the variable as a new list element, so if the user checked only the first Interests box on the form, the value of `interests` after the `ListAppend()` action would be as follows:

```
current events, filling out Web forms
```

You can also use `ListAppend()` to append the contents of a variable to an existing list. For example, if you want to combine the contents of the `hobbies` and `interests` variables into one, you could use code like this:

```
<cfset interests_and_hobbies = ListAppend(form.interests,
form.hobbies)>
```

This would create a new list variable, `interests_and_hobbies`, containing the contents of both `hobbies` and `interests`.

Tip   Another ColdFusion function, `ListPrepend()`, enables you to add a value to the beginning of the list rather than the end.

Counting list elements with ListLen()

If you want to show your users a count of the items they checked, you can use `ListLen()`. This function accepts only one parameter — the name of a list variable — and returns the number of elements in the list:

```
<cfoutput>Thanks for completing our form. You selected
#ListLen(form.hobbies)# hobbies and #ListLen(form.interests)#
interests.</cfoutput>
```

Tip   All of ColdFusion's list functions support an optional extra parameter specifying the delimiter to use when evaluating a given list variable. For example, consider a list like this one:

```
<cfset pasttimes = "Travel, Eating Exotic Food, Reading">
```

If you use a function such as `ListLen()` to evaluate the length of `pasttimes` but don't use the optional delimiter parameter, `ListLen()` assumes you want to use the default list delimiter, the comma. In this case, the length of `pasttimes` would be 3. However, if you used `ListLen()` with a different delimiter, such as a space as follows:

```
<cfoutput>#ListLen(pasttimes, " ")#</cfoutput>
```

`ListLen()` would return a value of 5, because there are five elements in `pasttimes` when you use a space, rather than a comma, as a delimiter. The elements are

```
Travel,
Eating
Exotic
Food,
Reading
```

By using different delimiters you can nest one list inside another. For example, the following:

```
<cfset nestedList = "Sam,Neff,Contributor|Joyce,Evans,Author">
```

Is a pike (|) delimited list of comma (,) delimited lists.

Creating a keyword search with <cfloop>

List variables enable you to perform an action for each element in a list. For example, you could build a form allowing users to enter one or more keywords, and then query a database for each of those keywords, one by one. This section starts with a sample form and action page, after which you can customize the code to work with one of your own databases.

Use the ed_wood datasource you set up earlier in this chapter. You start with a form to collect users' keywords. You can build your own using the code in Listing 51-4, or find a file titled film_search_form.htm on the CD-ROM accompanying this book.

Listing 51-4: **film_search_form.htm**

```
<!DOCTYPE HTML PUBLIC "-//W3C//DTD HTML 4.01 Transitional//EN">
<html>
<head>
<title>Search the Ed Wood film database</title>
<meta http-equiv="Content-Type" content="text/html; charset=iso-
8859-1">
</head>

<body>
<h3>Search the database of Ed Wood films</h3>

<form action="film_search_action.cfm" method="post">
    <p>Enter some keywords for which to search:</p>
    <p><input type="text" name="keywords"></p>
    <input type="submit">
</form>

</body>
</html>
```

A user who completes this form may supply just a word, such as "monster," or a list of words, such as "monster ghoul ghost." It doesn't matter how many items the user chooses because your action page treats the passed keywords variable as a list. This list may have only one element, or it may have 10; the code won't care either way.

The action page for this form uses a powerful ColdFusion tag, called <cfloop>, to process the list and perform a search for each element found within. Because <cfloop> is a new tag in your arsenal, take a closer look at it before you move on. Here's a stripped-down example of <cfloop> in action:

```
<cfloop list="#form.interests#" index="interest">
    Thanks for selecting <cfoutput>#interest#</cfoutput><br>
</cfloop>
```

<cfloop> processes lists in much the same way <cfoutput> processes the results of a query. When used in "list" mode, all the code or text contained within the <cfloop> tag set repeats for each element in a list. For example, if a user checked three interests on a form, the preceding snippet would display the following output to the user:

```
Thanks for selecting current events
Thanks for selecting religion
Thanks for selecting politics
```

Take a look at the opening <cfloop> tag. It specifies a list variable, including the hash marks, and creates a name for the list's *index*. The index is an arbitrary variable name you use within the <cfloop> to denote the list item currently being processed. The preceding snippet could have used index="blahblah" as long as it also used "Thanks for selecting #blahblah#" within the loop tags.

Note

Processing the contents of a list is only one of <cfloop>'s capabilities. See the sidebar in this chapter for some other uses.

Now move on to the keyword search function. Listing 51-5 shows one way to use <cfloop> in your search form's action page.

Listing 51-5: **film_search_action.cfm**

```
<html>
<head>
<title>Search Results</title>
<meta http-equiv="Content-Type" content="text/html; charset=iso-
8859-1">
</head>

<body>
<h2>Search Results</h2>
```

Continued

Listing 51-5 *(continued)*

```coldfusion
<cfloop list="#keywords#" index="keyword" delimiters=" ">

  <cfquery name="search" datasource="ed_wood">
          select id, title
          from films
          where title like '%#keyword#%' or description like
'%#keyword#%'
  </cfquery>

  <h3>Results for Keyword <i><cfoutput>#keyword#</cfoutput></i></h3>
  <ul>
  <cfif search.recordcount eq 0>
    <li>No items were found for this keyword</li>
  <cfelse>
      <cfoutput query="search">
        <li><a href="film_detail.cfm?id=#id#">#title#</a></li>
      </cfoutput>
  </cfif>
  </ul>
</cfloop>

</body>
</html>
```

Like ColdFusion's list functions, `<cfloop>` enables you to specify a list delimiter other than the default comma. The `<cfloop>` tag on the form's action page specifies a space as the delimiter, so if the user enters "monster bride plan," each word is treated as a unique list element.

For each element, it finds in the `keywords` list, `<cfloop>` performs a query looking for either a film title or description containing that word. If the user entered only one word, this process completes only once, and so on. Figure 51-6 shows sample output when the user inputs "monster bride plan."

Tip

The sample action page in this section omits form validation for the sake of clarity. For example, a user who clicks Submit without entering any keywords won't see a message prompt requesting at least one keyword. In a real-world environment, you could improve on this basic action page by adding form validation, as described in the previous chapter.

Listing 51-4 also contains another new tool, the `recordcount` variable. After a `<cfquery>` completes, you can get a count of the records it selected by referencing a special variable:

```coldfusion
#[query name].recordcount#
```

In the context of a search, `recordcount` is particularly valuable because you can use it in conjunction with `<cfif>` to display a "no records found" if the query doesn't return any results.

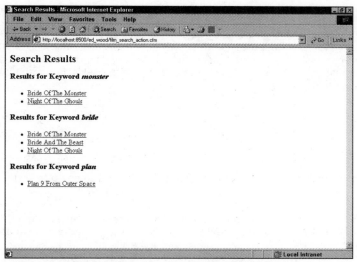

Figure 51-6: Displaying search results using <cfloop>

The text appearing within a <cfloop> tag set behaves much the same way as text within <cfoutput> tags. In Listing 51-5, the action page takes advantage of this by displaying the current keyword to the user, then lists the films in which that keyword was matched in the film title or description (if any).

Tip

For best performance, it's a good idea to only use lists with small groups of data, say up to a dozen elements. Larger groups should use other methods such as an array.

More about <cfloop>

When you use the <cfloop> tag with the "list" attribute, the tag automatically goes into list mode, in which it loops through each element in a specified list. But that's just one use of <cfloop>. It can also be used as a powerful flow-control tag to give you more control over the processes in your templates. Following are two other types of loops used with <cfloop>. For details on either, check your ColdFusion documentation.

The For loop

This type of loop is used when you need an action to occur for a specified number of times. For example, to populate a form select box with the months 1 through 12, you would write the following code:

```
<select name="month">
<cfloop from="1" to="12" index="month">
    <option value="#month#">
</cfloop>
</select>
```

Continued

Continued

For loops include `"from"` and `"to"` attributes, which specify how many times the loop should run. They also accept an optional `"step"` attribute, which causes the `"from"` value to increment by a number other than the default of 1. For example, to populate a select box with multiples of 5, you would write the following code:

```
<select name="players">
<cfloop from="1" to="100" index="players" step="5">
    <option value="#players#">
</cfloop>
</select>
```

This code produces a select box populated with the numbers 1, 5, 10, and so on up to 100.

The While loop

While or conditional loops run continually as long as a specified expression remains `true`. For example, to display a count from 1 to 10, you could use a loop like the following. (`lte` means "less than or equal to.")

```
<cfset count = 0>
<cfloop condition = "count lte 10">
    <cfset count = count + 1>
    The current count is <cfoutput>#count#</cfoutput><br>
</cfloop>
```

Summary

In this chapter you expanded your knowledge of ColdFusion variables. You learned how to pass variables in a URL and how that technique makes it easy to build the drill-down display pages common in many product catalogs, shopping carts, and general information sites. You also learned to use the `<cfset>` tag, which enables you to define variables within the context of your ColdFusion templates manually.

You also learned about one of ColdFusion's complex variable types, the list variable. Unlike standard variables, list variables can hold more than one chunk of data, and you learned how to use this capability to handle form data. You also learned how list variables are often used in conjunction with the `<cfloop>` to peform one or more tasks for each element in a list. To illustrate this concept, you constructed a keyword search engine that searches a database for one or more user keywords, one at a time.

✦   ✦   ✦

Using Client, Session, and Application Variables

The applications you've built in the previous chapters have all consisted of only a page or two. But as you venture further into ColdFusion, you'll begin to develop more complex applications that span multiple pages. In these cases, it's helpful to consider your applications as a whole rather than a collection of individual templates. When you formally define a group of templates as an application, you gain access to a powerful set of tools allowing you to easily share variable data from one page to another—without having to pass variables in a URL or form. These tools also enable you to create variables that persist for a fixed duration, from one user session to another, or for as long as your application remains running on your server.

Using Application.cfm Pages

The key to grouping your templates together as applications is a unique file called Application.cfm. You create this file yourself, usually before you begin developing other templates in an application. The file functions in much the same way as .ini files, which may be familiar to Windows and Unix users: It defines parameters that are used throughout an application.

Application.cfm files are always stored in the uppermost folder of your site. When they're present, their contents are automatically included in every ColdFusion template that lies within their folder. The same applies for files stored in folders below the one containing Application.cfm, as long as those folders don't contain Application.cfm files of their own. Take a look at Listing 52-1 to see a sample Application.cfm file.

Listing 52-1: A simple Application.cfm file

```
<cfapplication name="my_web_store">

<cfset dsn = "store_datasource">
<cfset store_name = "My Web Store">
```

The file in Listing 52-1 is a simple one. It defines the application with the `<cfapplication>` tag; then it defines a couple of variables that will be used throughout every template in the application. Since the contents of this page will automatically be inserted into every template residing in this file's folder and those below it, you could then use code like this to define a query:

```
<cfquery name="some_query" datasource="#dsn#">
select * from users
</cfquery>
```

Instead of supplying the actual name of a datasource in your `<cfquery>` tag, you can use the variable value #dsn#, which is defined in `Application.cfm`. Why is this valuable? Let's say that a few months after you've developed your application you decide to move it to another server, one that requires a different name for your datasource. Rather than go through all of your templates that include `<cfquery>` to change the name of the datasource, you can simply change the value of the variable in `Application.cfm` once and be finished.

The same applies for store_name in this example. By defining it in `Application.cfm` and then using the variable #store_name# in your templates, rather than the actual name of the store, you make it easy to change the name at a later date.

Using <cfinclude>

Another way of inserting code from an external file is the `<cfinclude>` tag. It takes one parameter—template—which contains the path name or filename containing the code to be inserted. For example, to create a header section that is consistent throughout your site, you could save the HTML and/or CFML code in an external file named header.cfm and then add some code like this to all of the pages in your site, wherever you want the header code to display:

```
<cfinclude template="header.cfm">
```

If the header template is stored in a folder other than the one using the `<cfinclude>`, you need to specify the file path:

```
<cfinclude template="../../header.cfm">
```

Code that's inserted by a `<cfinclude>` tag is processed exactly as if it had been typed into the file. `<cfinclude>` can be an enormous timesaver for headers, footers, or other code that repeats frequently throughout your site.

Note

The variables `dsn` and `store_name` are just examples of how variables defined in `Application.cfm` are available to any template within the application (with the exception of custom tags and ColdFusion components, as you'll learn later in this section). You can use any variable names you'd like: In fact many complex applications define scores of variables in their `Application.cfm` files.

The value of `Application.cfm` files goes far beyond their ability to insert code into templates, however. In the next sections you'll learn how using `Application.cfm` to formally define your applications.

Understanding the Web's "Statelessness"

There's a problem inherent in building programs that use HTML as an interface—*statelessness*. To better understand statelessness, consider the way users views Web pages. Typically, they either type an address, select a bookmark, or click a link. This causes their browser to contact a specific server and request a page. When the page and its contents are returned to the user, the connection between user and server no longer exists. The server has no way of sending or retrieving data from the user unless the user requests another page. Neither can the server know whether the user is still looking at the page, whether they've moved on to another Web site, or whether they've closed their browser and left their computer chair.

That presents a problem for many programming languages, because there are lots of common programming tasks that require variables to persist for long periods of time, or throughout various aspects of a program. A shopping cart, for example, needs to store data on products a user has selected in a store. This data may need to persist for as long as a user is browsing the store, or in some cases, for weeks or months in case the user leaves the site, returns later, and wants to recall the products selected in the previous session.

Another example is a login system, whereby a program may need to periodically check whether a user has successfully logged in before showing the user a protected page. The Web's standard request-and-serve system has no way to handle these persistent variables. A Web server isn't capable of storing program variable data once its connection with a user has terminated. This is called statelessness.

ColdFusion provides several solutions to combat the Web's statelessness in the form of client variables, session variables, and application variables. These are collectively called *client-state management* tools. All are capable of storing variable values that may be associated with a specific user or user session, persist over time, and can be recalled by any template within an application—without having to pass the variables via a URL or a form.

Understanding How ColdFusion Manages Client States

When you build applications, you can enable ColdFusion's client-state management tools with a line of code in your application's `Application.cfm` file, as you'll learn in the next sections. When these tools are enabled, ColdFusion automatically creates a couple of variables the first time a user visits any page in your application. It internally assigns a `cfid` and a `cftoken` to specifically identify that user.

Think of a user's cfid/cftoken identifier a "drawer" in which information may be stored and later recalled. After a user has a drawer, you can place standard variables within it, allowing your templates to recall them at any time, and from any template within your application. The contents of a user's drawer can persist for as long or as short a period as you specify.

Using Client Variables to Preserve Data Through Multiple User Visits

Consider an application in which you allow the user to customize some of the display patterns to his or her liking. For example, a user can build his or her own custom portal page by defining a background color, font color, and font style; then each time that user returns to your site, the information is preserved. ColdFusion's' client variables make this possible. By using client variables, you can allow the user to custom-define background and font parameters that exist every time a user visits your site.

The first time he or she visits, ColdFusion automatically sets a cookie on the user's machine containing the cfid/cftoken autogenerated for that particular user. This creates a drawer for the user, into which you can place any variables you'd like. These variables will until the user deletes the cookie.

Enabling client variables in Application.cfm

To use client variables, you need to "turn them on" by including some text in your Application.cfm file. Take a look at Listing 52-2.

Listing 52-2: **Application.cfm**

```
<cfapplication name="portal_site" clientmanagement="yes">

<!---define default values for colors and font face. These will be used
throughout the site until the user defines his or her preferences--->
<cfparam name="client.bgcolor" default="##FFFFFF">
<cfparam name="client.fontface" default="Arial">
<cfparam name="client.fontcolor" default="##000000">
```

The listing adds clientmanagment="yes" to the <cfapplication> tag, which is all that's required to enable client variables.

Note Remember that this Application.cfm page applies to all templates in the current directory, and all folders within it that don't contain their own Application.cfm page.

The listing next uses <cfparam> to define three default values for background color, font face, and font color. These variables use the special scope client to signify that they will be persistent client variables that "live" indefinitely and are associated with a specific user. You use any variable names you like, as long as they use the client scope. At this point you're just defining default values—in a moment you'll learn how to allow the user to change these values. Note that an extra hash mark is used before the hex color values to let ColdFusion know that the hash mark should be interpreted as a literal rather than part of a variable name.

Note

Client variables are designed to hold string values rather than complex variables like structures and arrays. You'll learn more about the latter in Chapter 54.

Creating a preference selection form

After the variables are defined, you can use them the same way you would any ColdFusion variable. In this example, you'll need to plug them into your templates' `<body>` and `<font>` tags, as shown in Listing 52-3. Figure 52-1 shows the form as it appears in the user's browser.

Listing 52-3: customize_form.cfm

```
<html>
<head>
<title>Customize Your Page</title>
<meta http-equiv="Content-Type" content="text/html; charset=iso-
8859-1">
</head>

<cfoutput>
<body bgcolor="#client.bgcolor#">

<h2><font face="#client.fontface#" color="#client.fontcolor#">Customize
Your Page</font></h2>

<p><font face="#client.fontface#" color="#client.fontcolor#">Choose
from the values below to customize your viewing experience on our
site.</font></p>

<form action="customize_action.cfm" method="post">
    <p><font face="#client.fontface#"
color="#client.fontcolor#">Choose a Background Color:</font>
    <select name="bgcolor">
        <option value="##FFFFFF">white</option>
        <option value="##FFFF00">yellow</option>
        <option value="##00FFFF">cyan</option>
    </select></p>

    <p><font face="#client.fontface#"
color="#client.fontcolor#">Choose a Font Face</font>
    <select name="fontface">
        <option>Arial</option>
        <option>Times New Roman</option>
        <option>Courier</option>
    </select></p>

    <p><font face="#client.fontface#"
color="#client.fontcolor#">Choose a Font Color:</font>
```

Continued

Listing 52-3 *(continued)*

```
        <select name="fontcolor">
            <option value="##000000">black</option>
            <option value="##FF0000">red</option>
            <option value="##008080">teal</option>
        </select></p>

        <input type="submit">

    </form>

    </body>
    </cfoutput>

    </html>
```

This listing is a form that allows the user to choose custom values for page parameters. We'll discuss the form itself for a moment, but let's first concentrate on the `<body>` and `<font>` tags used throughout the page. Note that the entire body section is enclosed in a pair of `<cfoutput>` tags, allowing you to display the contents of ColdFusion variables throughout the body of the page. The variable `#client.bgcolor#` is inserted into the `<body>` tag where you'd usually supply a hex value, `#client.fontface#` goes in the `<font>` tag where you'd usually supply a font face, and so on.

Now, take a look at the form elements in Listing 52-3. This form allows the users to select a background color, font face, and font color to customize their experience. As you've probably guessed, the action page you'll create next uses the user's selections to redefine the values of `client.bgcolor`, `client.fontface`, and `client.fontcolor`.

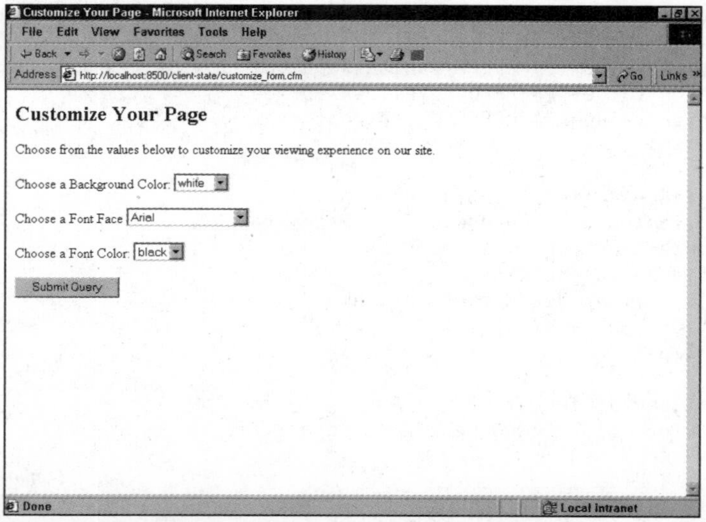

Figure 52-1: Collecting user preferences with a form

Note Notice that the color values in the form in Listing 52-3 use an extra hash mark (#). Remember that all literal hash marks used within `<cfoutput>` tags need to be preceded by an extra hash mark so that ColdFusion doesn't attempt to interpret the surrounding text as a variable name. A user who makes a selection and submits the form is taken to the action page shown in Listing 52-4.

Setting client variables on an action page

Listing 52-4 shows the action page for the form created in the previous section. It uses `<cfset>` to assign the user's color and font face selections to the three client variables. When this template is executed, the new variable values overwrite the default values supplied in `Application.cfm`, and the variables remain in that state until the user either changes them again, or deletes the cookies from his or her system.

Listing 52-4: customize_action.cfm

```
<!---set client variables based on user preferences passed by form--->
<cfset client.bgcolor = form.bgcolor>
<cfset client.fontface = form.fontface>
<cfset client.fontcolor = form.fontcolor>

<html>
<head>
<title>Customization Complete</title>
<meta http-equiv="Content-Type" content="text/html; charset=iso-
8859-1">
</head>

<!---show results to user, using user's specified font face and color
preferences--->
<cfoutput>
<body bgcolor="#client.bgcolor#">
<h2><font face="#client.fontface#"
color="#client.fontcolor#">Customization Complete</font></h2>

<p><font face="#client.fontface#" color="#client.fontcolor#">Your
settings have been saved and will be preserved when you next visit our
site.</font></p>

</body>
</cfoutput>
</html>
```

These variables persist the next time the user visits your site. Note that you could extend the user's preferences throughout an application by inserting the `client.bgcolor`, `client.fontface`, and `client.fontcolor` variables anywhere you'd normally use a static bgcolor, font face, or font color value. One possible result of this action page is shown in Figure 52-2.

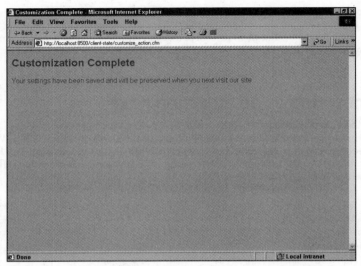

Figure 52-2: The result of a preference change; note that a user's preferences are saved between visits.

Tip

When you use client variables, ColdFusion saves the user's `cfide/cftoken` identifier as a cookie on the user's system. But the contents of the users "drawer" — the client variables created by your templates — are stored in the ColdFusion server's registry by default. ColdFusion also enables you to store this information in a database, which is the preferable method if your application makes extensive use of client variables. See your ColdFusion documentation for more on this subject.

Using Session Variables to Preserve Data During One Browsing Session

Unlike client variables, which persist each time a user visits your application, session variables are designed to persist for only a limited amount of time. Consider an application that requires a user to log in via a standard user/password form. After a user logs in, he or she should be able to view protected pages without having to perform the login action each time he or she views a page. However, once a user leaves the site for a length of time, the "logged in" status should be reset so that the user is required to log in again upon the next visit. In cases like these, you don't want variables to persist between multiple user sessions, but just for the current one. Session variables provide the solution.

You enable session variables much the same way you do client variables — by adding a line in `Application.cfm`. When you do so, you can either supply a custom *timeout* value, or use ColdFusion's default value of 20 minutes. The timeout value specifies how long a user's session may remain inactive before the session is considered complete and the session variables disappear. For example, the default timeout value of 20 minutes will allow a user to walk away from his or her computer in the middle of a browsing session, return 15 minutes later, and continue browsing with all session variables intact. However, if that user were to return 25 minutes later, the session variables would no longer exist, and in the case of a login function, he or she would have to log in again to continue viewing protected pages.

Note The maximum value allowed for timeouts is set in ColdFusion MX Administrator. Once this is done, the value can't be overridden by a greater value in your `<cfapplication>` tag.

After session variables are defined, any template within an application can access them. This presents a significant savings in development time over having to pass variables only from a URL or a form. For example, using URL variables exclusively would require that all necessary variables are included in the URL of every link on your site–not a very practical method for passing data.

Enabling session variables in Application.cfm

To create a simple login application, you begin with an `Application.cfm` page. Listing 52-5 shows one that enables session variables and defines a session length of 30 minutes.

Listing 52-5: **Application.cfm**

```
<cfapplication name="protected_site" sessionmanagement="yes"
sessiontimeout="#CreateTimeSpan(0,0,30,0)#">

<!---define a default value for session.logged_in, which will later be
used to check whether the user has successfully logged in--->
<cfparam name="session.logged_in" default="no">
```

This `Application.cfm` file also defines a default value for a session variable, `session.logged_in`, which you'll use in the next sections. Note that like client variables, session variables can be defined just by using the `session` scope.

Tip Session timeout values are defined using the `CreateTimeSpan()` function. This function accepts four input parameters: days, hours, minutes, and seconds. For example, a session timeout value of two days would be written as `#CreateTimeSpan(2,0,0,0)#`; a value of 10 minutes would be written as `#CreateTimeSpan(0,0,10,0)#`.

Creating a login form

Creating a login page for an application driven by session variables is straightforward; you only need to collect a username and password, and pass it on to an action page, as shown in Listing 52-6.

Listing 52-6: **login_form.cfm**

```
<html>
<head>
<title>Login Page</title>
<meta http-equiv="Content-Type" content="text/html; charset=iso-
8859-1">
</head>

<body>
<h2>Login Page</h2>

<p>Please log in using the user name and password provided by your
system administrator.</p>

<form action="login_action.cfm" method="post">
     <p>Username: <input type="text" name="username"></p>
     <p>Password: <input type="password" name="password"></p>
     <input type="submit" value="Log In">
</form>
</body>
</html>
```

Setting a user's login status on an action page

After a user submits a login form, the action page can use a `<cfif>` statement to check the supplied username and password against the correct values. If the login information is incorrect, the user is notified and directed back to the login form. If the information *is* correct, a session variable, `session.logged_in` is redefined to `yes`, acknowledging that the user has successfully logged in. This session variable persists for the timeout value specified in `Application.cfm`—in this case, 30 minutes. Listing 52-7 shows an example of the checking process as well as the session variable definition.

Listing 52-7: **login_action.cfm**

```
<html>
<head>
<title>Login Results</title>
<meta http-equiv="Content-Type" content="text/html; charset=iso-
8859-1">
</head>

<body>

<!---if supplied username and password match newuser/coldfusion, set a
session variable acknowledging a successful login--->
```

```
<cfif form.username is 'newuser' and form.password is 'coldfusion'>

     <cfset session.logged_in = "yes">

     <h2>Login Successful</h2>
     <p>Thanks for logging in. You may now proceed to the <a
href="index.cfm">protected material.</a></p>

<!---if login incorrect, show error and direct user back to form--->

<cfelse>

     <h2>Login Unsuccessful</h2>
     <p>The username and/or password values you supplied are incorrect.
If you believe this to be in error, please try the <a
href="login_form.cfm">login form</a> again.</p>

</cfif>

</body>
</html>
```

Using a session variable to check login status

After a user submits correct login data, `session.logged_in` contains the value `yes`. You can then use a snippet like the following one on any page in your application that may require protection:

```
<cfif session.logged_in is 'no'>
     <!---redirect user to login form--->
     <cflocation url="login_form.cfm">
<cfelse>
     <!---display protected page contents here--->
</cfif>
```

This code uses a `<cfif>` block to check the contents of `session.logged_in`. Remember that this variable by default is set to `no` by the `Application.cfm` page. In this case, the user is redirected back to the login form with a handy ColdFusion tag called `<cflocation>`. The tag takes one attribute—a URL to which the user should be directed.

If a user has successfully logged in at some point during the current session, the value of `session.logged_in` will be `yes`, and thus the user will be shown whatever text or code lies within the `<cfelse>` block. Most often this would be the body of a protected page.

After a user logs in, the preceding snippet allows him or her to view protected material for the duration of the session. After the session has timed out, the user is redirected to the login page as if the initial login had never occurred.

Using Application Variables to Preserve Data Throughout an Application

The third item in ColdFusion's client-state management toolbox is the *application variable*. While they're not used as client and session variables, application variables still serve a vital purpose. They enable you to define variables that persist as long as the application is running, or usually from the time the application is first accessed by any user until the server is shut down or restarted.

The unique thing about application variables is that unlike session and client variables, they aren't associated with any particular user. This means that their values are the same for every user of your application.

Note   Unlike session and client variables, application variables are enabled by default any time you use an `Application.cfm` file.

For example, you could use an application variable to create a simple page counter that would show how many times a page has been loaded since the application has been running:

```
<cfparam name="application.counter" default = "0">
<cfset application.counter = application.counter + 1>

<cfoutput>This page has been viewed #application.counter# times since
the server was last restarted</cfoutput>
```

Each time any user loads a page containing that snippet, the global value of `application.counter` is increased by 1 and the current count is displayed to the user. Again, note that application variables are not relative to any user. For example, the 301st user would see a count of "301," not "1" as he would with a session or client variable. Application variables are good places to store data that will be accessed by many pages in your application but does not need to be user-specific.

Using <cflock> to Ensure Data Integrity on Busy Sites

When you use session or application variables, there's a danger that two or more users may access a page at the same time. This would cause ColdFusion to simultaneously read or write two chunks of data to one memory space on your server, which could result in inaccurate data being recorded or displayed to users.

The solution is to use the `<cflock>` tag wherever session or application variables are used. Using `<cflock>` ensures that ColdFusion places simultaneous read or write requests in a queue and processes them one by one. When a section of code enclosed in `<cflock>` tags is encountered, ColdFusion gives exclusive priority to that session until the code is complete.

For example, to ensure the integrity of an application variable, you use `<cflock>` like this:

```
<cflock scope="application" type="exclusive">
    <cfset application.counter = application.counter + 1>
    <cfoutput>This page has been viewed #application.counter# times
since the server was last restarted</cfoutput>
```

This code would prevent an incorrect value of `application.counter` from being displayed if a second user somewhere on the system happened to access this page in the split second between the time the first user's `application.counter` was incremented and the time it was displayed in his or her browser.

The `scope` attribute used with `<cflock>` specifies whether the variable you're locking should be locked at the *application, session,* or *server* level. In most cases you'll use the *application* scope for application variables, or the *session* scope when locking session variables. The third scope, *server*, is rarely used in typical ColdFusion applications since it's designed to work with variables that apply server-wide, i.e., for all applications running under an installation of ColdFusion MX.

The `type` attribute tells `<cflock>` whether the variable should be locked for exclusive access, as in the example above, or whether the variable will only be read rather than written to, in which case you would use the type "read-only."

Summary

This chapter introduced you to the concept of the ColdFusion application, in which a series of templates are grouped together. You learned about the special file `Application.cfm`, and that when it is stored in the uppermost folder of a site, its contents are automatically inserted into every ColdFusion template lying within that folder structure. You also learned how to formally define an application within an `Application.cfm` file, and how doing so allows you to begin using session, client, and application variables. These unique variables allow your applications to share data from one template to another, to preserve variables for a specific length of time, or even to store variable data for use every time a specific user visits your application.

✦   ✦   ✦

Creating ColdFusion MX Custom Tags

◆ ◆ ◆ ◆

In This Chapter

Using custom tags in
your applications

Using Macromedia's
Developer Exchange

◆ ◆ ◆ ◆

Like all good programming languages, ColdFusion is extensible,
meaning that if it doesn't have the tools you need to complete a
job at hand, you can create your own. One of the easiest ways to do
so is through the use of *custom tags*, or snippets of CFML code that
can be custom-written once, then used many times throughout one
or more applications. As with many ColdFusion features, building
custom tags is easy; in fact it's just like creating a standard template.
In this chapter you'll learn about the concepts behind custom tags,
build a simple tag to compute sales tax, and learn more about
Macromedia's Developers' Exchange, where you'll find hundreds of
custom tags written by others and available for use in your own
applications.

Understanding Custom Tags

To understand how custom tags work and why you'd want to use
them, start by considering an online store. Users navigate through a
catalog selecting products and arrive at a checkout area where they
view their product total — sales tax included. After confirming their
order and providing their user information, users choose a shipping
method and see a new total including shipping charges and, again,
tax. Finally, they provide their credit card data and their card is
charged for the total, once again including tax.

This type of application is ideal for ColdFusion MX, and in fact
there are several ready-made shopping cart applications available
in the Macromedia Developers' Forum. However, for the purposes
of this chapter let's focus on just one element of the application —
computing sales tax. Note from the previous description that there
are no less than three pages upon which tax must be computed and
displayed to the user. One solution would be to simply include identical tax-computation code in each of the three pages, but as you might
have guessed, that's inefficient programming.

A wiser solution is to use a ColdFusion custom tag. You could write the tax computation code once, save it in a separate file as a custom tag, and then *call* it from each of your three store pages.

Note   "Calling" a custom tag simply means referring to its filename using a special naming convention, about which you'll learn more in the next section.

By breaking the tax computation code out into a separate file, you'd be ensuring two things:

✦ That your store pages' source would be easier to understand and troubleshoot, because the more complex tax computation code isn't included

✦ That you could reuse the tax computation code elsewhere on your site — or even in a another application — simply by calling the tag.

These are the two primary reasons for using custom tags, although you'll learn a few more later in this chapter.

Note   Custom tags are similar to the concept of *subroutines*, which are found in many programming languages. Both allow developers to break out blocks of code either to simplify a program's source, or to re-use it with other programs.

Saving custom tags

Once you've broken some code out into a custom tag, you have to be careful where you save it: ColdFusion needs to know where it resides. There are three options:

✦ You can simply save the custom tag in the same folder as the pages that call it. This method is the easiest, but it isn't always practical in cases where the calling templates may reside in different folders on your site.

✦ You can save the tag in ColdFusion MX' default tag directory, usually `c:\CFusionMX\CustomTags`. Doing so makes the tag accessible by any template on your site(s).

✦ You can use ColdFusion Administrator to define a new path or paths where custom tags will be saved. You do so by accessing the Custom Tag Paths link in Administrator's Extensions section, as shown in Figure 53-1.

Calling custom tags

You'll learn more about creating custom tags in later sections, but first let's examine how they're called. After you've created a custom tag, you use it much the same way as any CFML tag, with the exception that most custom tags don't use a closing tag. Listing 53-1 shows how the tax computation tag described previously might be called in a template.

Listing 53-1: total_purchase.cfm

```
<html>
<head>
<title>Your Total Purchase</title>
<meta http-equiv="Content-Type" content="text/html; charset=iso-
8859-1">
</head>
```

```
<body>
<!---set values for product total and state (in a complete application,
these would probably come from totaling the user's purchases and the
user's form input, respectively)--->
<cfset product_total = 3.25>
<cfset state = "CA">

<!---call a custom tag to compute tax--->
<cf_tax_compute product_total="#product_total#" state="#state#">

<!---compute grand total based on "tax" variable returned by custom
tag--->
<cfset grand_total = 3.25 + tax>

<!---display output to user--->
<cfoutput>
    Your total purchase, including tax, comes to
#DollarFormat(grand_total)#.
</cfoutput>

</body>
</html>
```

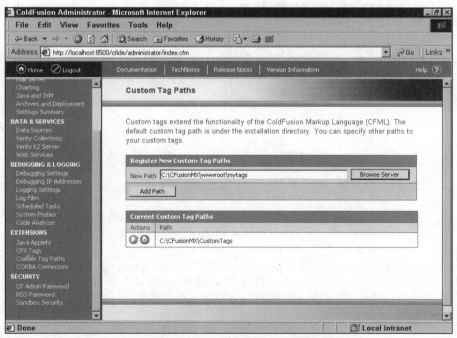

Figure 53-1: Defining custom tag paths in ColdFusion Administrator

The first line in Listing 53-1 calls the custom tag and supplies two attributes, `product_total` and `state`. As you'll learn when you later build this tag, it is written to accept these two attributes and then return a variable called `tax`, which will contain the total tax for the user's purchase, based on the user's state. This variable is used on the second line of the snippet to compute the user's grand total.

The tag reference begins with the prefix `cf` (the letters `cf` followed by an underscore). This tells ColdFusion that the tag you're referring to is a custom one, rather than a standard tag in the CFML library. The actual filename of the tag is `tax_compute.cfm`, but by calling it with the `cf_` prefix and no `.cfm` extension, you specify that it is a custom tag.

Tip

Another extensibility feature offered by ColdFusion is the use of ColdFusion Extensions (CFXs). Like custom tags, CFX tags are designed to perform tasks not possible with standard CFML. Unlike custom tags, which are written in CFML, CFX tags are written in C++, Java, or Delphi. For more information, see your ColdFusion documentation.

Creating the Tax Computation Tag

Now it's time to create the actual tag, a process that's similar to creating a standard ColdFusion template. For the sake of simplicity, assume that your custom tag needs to compute tax for only three states, California, Oregon, and Arizona. Any other state will be taxed at a rate of 0. Also assume that all cities and counties in a given state share one tax rate.

As you might guess, the tag needs to use `<cfif>` to determine whether the state supplied by the caller page is one of those that requires tax. Start by creating a new ColdFusion document in Dreamweaver. Save it in the folder `c:\CfusionMX\CustomTags\` and enter the code you see in Listing 53-2.

Listing 53-2: **tax_compute.cfm**

```
<cfif attributes.state is 'CA'>
     <cfset tax_rate = .0725>
<cfelseif attributes.state is 'AZ'>
     <cfset tax_rate = .083>
<cfelseif attributes.state is 'OR'>
     <cfset tax_rate = 0>
<cfelse>
     <cfset tax_rate = 0>
</cfif>

<cfset caller.tax = attributes.product_total * tax_rate>
```

Caution

Don't forget that the filenames you use for your custom tags should not include the `cf_` prefix. The prefix is used only when calling the tag from a template.

As Listing 53-2 illustrates, the syntax used in a custom tag is standard CFML, with a couple of exceptions:

✦ When you want to refer to a value that was passed as a tag's attribute (see the line that calls this tag in Listing 51-1), you refer to it using the special scope attributes before the attribute name.

✦ When you want a variable to be available to the page that called the custom tag, you create it using the special scope caller before the variable name.

Recall from the discussion of the caller page (Listing 53-1) that the tag will be sent two attribute values, state and product_total. It uses these with the attributes scope to determine a tax rate for the user's state, and multiplies that value by the product_total. Finally, a new variable, tax, is defined, using the caller scope so that the variable will be available to the calling page.

Listing 53-2 uses <cfif> and <cfelse> to check the contents of the state variable. An alternate method that uses less code is to use the <cfswitch> and <cfcase> tags, which are ideal for these type of checks. See your ColdFusion MX documentation for details.

Now that you've created the tag and stored it in ColdFusion's custom tags folder, you can use it with any page in any one of your sites by referencing it like any other ColdFusion tag:

```
<cf_tax_compute state="some state" product_total="some product total">
```

If you plan to use a tag like cf_tax_compute in an actual production environment, with more complex tax schemes, you could use a simple database table to store the tax rate for each locale, and then use a <cfquery> to look up the relevant rate. That way when tax rates change, you need to update only the database rather than rewrite your custom tag.

Understanding the Difference Between Custom Tags and <cfinclude>

In a sidebar accompanying the previous chapter, you learned about <cfinclude> and how it can be used to include the contents of one template in another. At this point you may be wondering how this process differs from using a custom tag.

The answer is that <cfinclude> causes the included page's code in to be executed in-line with the calling page just as if it had been hard-coded into the calling template. In this way, any variables present on the calling page are automatically shared with the included page. In contrast, custom tags are used more like separate programs, whereby you must specifically pass attributes to the custom tag, and in turn the custom tag must specifically define variables to be returned to the calling page.

The advantage to custom tags is that because their variables are isolated from the calling page, they are much more portable and can be used in a variety of settings without modification.

Using <cfmodule> to Call a Custom Tag

Usually, the best way to use a custom tag is to save it in an "approved" directory (see "Saving custom tags" earlier in this chapter) and then call it using the standard syntax:

```
<cf_some_tag_name some_attribute>
```

However, in some rare cases this method doesn't suffice. For example, if you have a custom tag named `get_user_info.cfm` designed for one application, and you or another developer on your system has a tag also named `get_user_info.cfm`, a conflict will result. By calling the tag with `<cfmodule>`, you can specify a specific path to a specific tag's file to avoid confusion. Instead of

```
<cf_get_user_info>
```

you could use

```
<cfmodule template="../../get_user_info.cfm">
```

ColdFusion then processes the file as if it had been called as a custom tag.

You can also pass along attributes accepted by the tag by supplying them in the `<cfmodule>` call:

```
<cfmodule template="../../get_user_info.cfm" user_id = 12
user_state="CA">
```

When you do so, `<cfmodule>` passes the attributes along, as-is, to the custom tag you called.

The `<cfmodule>` method is also handy when you need to supply the name of a tag dynamically, because you can't do so with standard tag syntax. For example, if a form gave the user a choice of shipping methods, you could use a special custom tag for each shipping service and then call the correct one dynamically. The following snippet assumes that the variable `shipping_method` contains a name like "fedex," "ups," and so on, and that you have tags named `compute_fedex.cfm`, `compute_ups.cfm`, and so on.

```
<cfmodule template="compute_#shipping_method#.cfm" zipcode="#zipcode#">
```

Finally, `<cfmodule>` is also useful for calling tags that for one reason or another may not be saved in one of the "approved" locations. Because you can supply a complete file path with `<cfmodule>`, you can use it to call any file anywhere on your Web server as a custom tag, providing the file itself is suitable for use as a custom tag.

When to Use Custom Tags

Now that you better understand how custom tags work, consider some situations in which you should consider using them. As you progress to more advanced levels of ColdFusion development, knowing where and when to use custom tags becomes an increasingly important skill. Custom tags can make complex applications much easier to work on and offer significant time savings when building and maintaining a site. Following are some situations that call for custom tags.

Complex code

Liberal use of custom tags can make complex applications much easier to view and troubleshoot. By breaking complex sections into tags, you create modular applications that are easier to maintain. Well-named custom tags don't usually require any extra explanation, meaning that if another developer replaces you at a later date, he or she can easily understand your code without your help.

Multi-developer environments

When one or more developers will work on an application, custom tags are critical. They allow developers to view a template's source and quickly get the big picture of what's happening in template, without having to wade through the specifics of actions, such as computing tax values, and so on.

Custom tags also allow different developers to focus on tasks suited to their skill level. For instance, in a two-person team consisting of one beginning ColdFusion developer and one advanced, the advanced user might focus on the more complex computations by breaking them out into custom tags. This would allow the beginning developer to work on basic display elements without having to know what's going on within the custom tags themselves. For example, a beginning developer could insert tags, such as `<cf_todays_weather>` or `<cf_banner_manager>`, without knowing how the tags work.

Similar functionality in one or more applications

As mentioned briefly in the first section of this chapter, custom tags are ideal for situations in which you need to reuse functionality throughout your site or sites. In addition, if you develop applications for more than one client, custom tags can be enormous timesavers because they enable you to write code once and use it many times.

Implementing common tasks

Custom tags also provide developers with an easy way to share code that has been designed for tasks that are common to many types of Web sites. For example, if the tax computation tag in this chapter were fleshed out to include tax rates for all locales in the United States, it would be valuable not only to you, but to many other developers. You could then share your work with others, either for free or for a fee. Many developers do so, as you'll learn in the next section.

Tip

New with the release of ColdFusion are ColdFusion Components (CFCs), which are similar in concept to custom tags. However, unlike custom tags, CFCs can be called by a variety of interfaces—not just ColdFusion templates. They can be used to pass information to and from Flash movies, Web pages, and Web services. In addition, CFCs can be called *remotely*, for example, by clients outside of your local server. You learn more about CFCs and Flash in the sidebar accompanying the final chapter of this section.

Exploring Macromedia's Developer Exchange

You can take advantage of other developers' work by visiting Macromedia's Developer Exchange at `http://devex.macromedia.com/developer/gallery/`. There you'll find hundreds of custom tags created to handle common Web tasks, such as managing banner ads, creating Web stores, and building online knowledge bases. Many tags are free of charge; others may offer a trial download but require a fee for registration.

You can often save hours, days, or weeks of development work by making use of a prewritten custom tag. For this reason, it's important to familiarize yourself with the contents of the Developer Exchange and check it regularly for updates.

Not all custom tags are written by experienced developers who take care in their work. It's always important to test all downloaded tags thoroughly before using them in a live environment. It's also a good idea to look for tags written by established developers, and those that have a good track record with other users.

Web Services: Revolutionizing Application Integration, *by Samuel Neff*

Web services are the latest technology that allow one application to remotely call and utilize the functionality and data of another application. The development of SOAP-based Web services enables more than simply integrating functionality but provides the ability to describe that functionality and the programmatic interfaces. In this tutorial, I describe how to use ColdFusion MX to create and consume Web services.

Creating a Web service

To create a Web service in ColdFusion MX, start by creating a component. If you're not familiar with ColdFusion Components, refer to the components tutorial in Chapter 54. With a completed component, change the access level for the function you want to expose to remote consumption. For example, review the following code, which demonstrates a weather forecasting service:

```
<cfcomponent>

  <cffunction
    name="getWeatherForecast"
    returnType="string"
    access="remote">

    <cfargument name="zip" type="string">
```

```
<cfscript>
  switch (RandRange(1,5)) {
    case 1:
      forecast="Sunny";
      break;
    case 2:
      forecast="Partly cloudy";
      break;
    case 3:
      forecast="Rain";
      break;
    case 4:
      forecast="Hail";
      break;
    case 5:
      forecast="Thunderstorm";
      break;
  }
</cfscript>

<cfreturn forecast>

</cffunction>

</cfcomponent>
```

Simply by adding `access="remote"` to your component function, you can expose it to the world as a Web service. This function can be called from ColdFusion applications on another server as well as Java, ASP, VB, Perl, and any other client that supports SOAP or WDDX.

Web service descriptions

There are many standards for creating Web services. The most popular standard is Simple Object Access Protocol (SOAP), and all major companies in the field have current or planned support for SOAP-based Web services. One of the major advantages that SOAP has over other standards is its related technologies. Web Services Description Languages (WSDL) is one of these technologies. WSDL provides a standardized way to describe the programmatic interface to a Web service.

ColdFusion MX automatically generates WSDL files for Web services by appending `?wsdl` to the end of a URL. The following URL generates the WSDL for a weather-forecasting service: `http://127.0.0.1/StudioMXBible/WebServices/Listing01.cfc?wsdl`.

When entered into a browser, this displays the WSDL file in the following figure.

```xml
<?xml version="1.0" encoding="UTF-8" ?>
- <wsdl:definitions targetNamespace="http://webservices.Studiomxbible"
    xmlns:wsdl="http://schemas.xmlsoap.org/wsdl/"
    xmlns:xsd="http://www.w3.org/2001/XMLSchema"
    xmlns:wsdlsoap="http://schemas.xmlsoap.org/wsdl/soap/"
    xmlns:intf="http://webservices.Studiomxbible" xmlns:impl="http://webservices.Studiomxbible-
    impl" xmlns:SOAP-ENC="http://schemas.xmlsoap.org/soap/encoding/"
    xmlns="http://schemas.xmlsoap.org/wsdl/">
  - <wsdl:message name="getWeatherForecastResponse">
      <wsdl:part name="return" type="SOAP-ENC:string" />
    </wsdl:message>
    <wsdl:message name="CFCInvocationException" />
  - <wsdl:message name="getWeatherForecastRequest">
      <wsdl:part name="zip" type="SOAP-ENC:string" />
    </wsdl:message>
  - <wsdl:portType name="listing01">
    - <wsdl:operation name="getWeatherForecast" parameterOrder="zip">
        <wsdl:input message="intf:getWeatherForecastRequest" />
        <wsdl:output message="intf:getWeatherForecastResponse" />
        <wsdl:fault name="CFCInvocationException" message="intf:CFCInvocationException" />
      </wsdl:operation>
    </wsdl:portType>
  - <wsdl:binding name="listing01.cfcSoapBinding" type="intf:listing01">
      <wsdlsoap:binding style="rpc" transport="http://schemas.xmlsoap.org/soap/http" />
    - <wsdl:operation name="getWeatherForecast">
        <wsdlsoap:operation soapAction="" />
      - <wsdl:input>
          <wsdlsoap:body use="encoded"
            encodingStyle="http://schemas.xmlsoap.org/soap/encoding/"
            namespace="http://webservices.Studiomxbible" />
        </wsdl:input>
      - <wsdl:output>
          <wsdlsoap:body use="encoded"
            encodingStyle="http://schemas.xmlsoap.org/soap/encoding/"
            namespace="http://webservices.Studiomxbible" />
        </wsdl:output>
      </wsdl:operation>
    </wsdl:binding>
  - <wsdl:service name="listing01Service">
    - <wsdl:port name="listing01.cfc" binding="intf:listing01.cfcSoapBinding">
        <wsdlsoap:address
          location="http://sam.blinex.com:8052/studiomxbible/webservices/listing01.cfc" />
      </wsdl:port>
    </wsdl:service>
  </wsdl:definitions>
```

WSDL file for the weather forecast service

Luckily, the WSDL file is not meant to be read by a person. As you'll see later, the WSDL file allows for simplified consumption of Web services.

Complex Web services

The weather forecast service is a simple Web service. It accepts a single argument, the ZIP code, and returns a description of the weather in that area. Two options can expand the Web service to return more information.

The first option is to return a structure from the function. Review the following code, which returns a more detailed weather forecast in a structure:

```
<cffunction
  name="getWeatherForecastDetailed"
  returnType="struct"
  access="remote">
```

```
<cfargument name="zip" type="string">

<cfscript>
  detail=StructNew();
  detail.temperature=86;
  detail.sunrise=CreateTime(6,48,0);
  detail.sunset=CreateTime(7,46,0);
  detail.description=This.getWeatherForecast(Arguments.zip);
</cfscript>

<cfreturn detail>
</cffunction>
```

If you look at the WSDL file for this service, you'll see the following description for the returned value shown in the following code:

```
<complexType name="Map">
  <sequence>
    <element name="item" minOccurs="0" maxOccurs="unbounded">
      <complexType>
        <all>
          <element name="key" type="xsd:anyType" />
          <element name="value" type="xsd:anyType" />
        </all>
      </complexType>
    </element>
  </sequence>
</complexType>
```

The preceding fragment of the WSDL describes the data returned from our Web service. This tells the calling application that our service is providing a set of key/value pairs. Both the keys and the values can be of any type. The problem with this is twofold. First, the calling application has no way to know what the expected keys are and the types of values being returned. Second, this key/value pair definition is specific to ColdFusion MX and is not usable from all Web service clients, including .NET and MSSOAP.

To provide greater information to the calling application, ColdFusion MX allows a function to return another component. By using the `cfproperty` tag within the component being returned (as seen in the following code), you are telling ColdFusion what type of data to expect and this information can then be relayed to clients through the WSDL.

```
<cfcomponent>
  <cfproperty name="temperature" type="numeric" />
  <cfproperty name="sunrise" type="date" />
  <cfproperty name="sunset" type="date" />
  <cfproperty name="description" type="string" />
</cfcomponent>
```

The component is simple. It's sole purpose is to define the structure for your new detailed weather forecasting service, shown in the following code:

```
<cffunction
  name="getWeatherForecastDetailed"
  returnType="WeatherForecastDetail"
  access="remote">

  <cfargument name="zip" type="string">

  <cfscript>
    detail=CreateObject("component","WeatherForecastDetail");
    detail.temperature=86;
    detail.sunrise=CreateTime(6,48,0);
    detail.sunset=CreateTime(7,46,0);
    detail.description=This.getWeatherForecast(Arguments.zip);
  </cfscript>

  <cfreturn detail>
</cffunction>
```

Only two lines have been changed. Instead of returning a structure, you have specified `returnType="WeatherForecastDetail"`, which indicates you're returning an instance of the component `WeatherForecastDetail`. Next, you have changed the `StructNew()` function call with a call to `CreateObject()`, which instantiates your return component. Otherwise, the functions are identical.

The WSDL for your new function closely matches the return component, as shown in the following code. This detailed WSDL file enables non–ColdFusion clients to consume your Web service and also gives all consumers greater detail about the information you're returning:

```
<complexType name="weatherforecastdetail">
  <sequence>
    <element name="Description" nillable="true" type="xsd:string" />
    <element name="Sunrise" nillable="true" type="xsd:dateTime" />
    <element name="Sunset" nillable="true" type="xsd:dateTime" />
    <element name="Temperature" nillable="true" type="SOAP-ENC:double"
/>
  </sequence>
</complexType>
```

Now that you know how to create both simple and complex Web services and the corresponding WSDL descriptors, the next section discusses how to consume Web services within ColdFusion.

Using Dreamweaver MX to consume Web services

Dreamweaver MX greatly simplifies the process of consuming Web services within ColdFusion MX. To list the functions provided by a Web service within Dreamweaver MX, follow these steps, as demonstrated in the following figure.

1. Expand the Application panel.

2. Click the Components tab.

3. Choose Web Services from the drop-down list.

4. Click the plus (+) sign.

5. Enter the URL to the WSDL file.

6. Choose ColdFusion MX as the proxy generator.

7. Click OK.

**Using Dreamweaver MX to parse a WSDL file
for a Web service**

After you specify a Web service, Dreamweaver MX provides a list of the functions provided including the return type and arguments, as shown in the following figure. The Web service shown here is a currency converter provided by xmethods.net:

```
http://www.xmethods.net/sd/2001/CurrencyExchangeService.wsdl
```

**Dreamweaver MX displays a
list of functions provided by
the Web service.**

To generate the ColdFusion MX code to consume the Web service, drag the function name to the code window. Doing this generates the following code:

```
<cfinvoke

webservice="http://www.xmethods.net/sd/2001/CurrencyExchangeService.wsd
l"
 method="getRate"
 returnvariable="aRate">
  <cfinvokeargument name="country1" value="enter_value_here"/>
  <cfinvokeargument name="country2" value="enter_value_here"/>
</cfinvoke>
```

As you can see, Dreamweaver MX leaves identifiers for the argument values. Change the values to **usa** and **uk** to return the exchange rate between the U.S. dollar and British pound.

Consuming a Web service

As you can see from the earlier example, ColdFusion MX uses two new tags to consume Web services. Use cfinvoke identifies the Web service being consumed, the method to call, and the variable name for the returned value. Use cfinvokeargument to specify the value for all arguments to the Web service method. An alternative to cfinvokeargument is to use the argumentcollection attribute of cfinvoke to specify a structure that has key/value pairs corresponding to the method's arguments.

ColdFusion MX also provides a second method for consuming a Web service. You can create a Web service proxy object through the CreateObject() function by specifying the object type as webservice and the URL to the Web service. Then, calls to the Web service are made by calling the methods as functions of the proxy object, as shown in the following code.

```
<cfscript>

currencyExchange=CreateObject("webservice","http://www.xmethods.net/sd/
2001/CurrencyExchangeService.wsdl");
  aRate=currencyExchange.getRate("usa","uk");
</cfscript>
```

This code has the same effect as that in the preceding code listing. The advantage of using CreateObject() over cfinvoke becomes obvious when calling multiple methods of the same Web service. Although performance is the same for both methods, programming multiple calls to a Web service is simpler with CreateObject().

Both publishing and consuming Web Services is very simple in ColdFusion MX. Including Web Services in your application allows you to expand the possible uses beyond the HTML forms you create to any client application with which you want to integrate. By consuming Web Services within your application, you can provide your users with greater functionality that otherwise would not be possible.

Summary

In this chapter you learned about ColdFusion custom tags and how they're used to break out related blocks of code from a main template. You learned that by doing so your source code becomes easier to read, by you and other developers who may work on your projects. You also learned how custom tags enable you to write a chunk of code once, and reuse it many times within one or more applications. You created a sample custom tag to compute tax values and learned how to store it and how to call it from a standard ColdFusion template. Finally, you learned about the many situations in which custom tags should be employed, and how to use Macromedia's Developer Exchange to find tags written for a variety of common Web tasks.

✦   ✦   ✦

Using ColdFusion MX with Flash Remoting

While Flash has traditionally been considered a designers' tool and ColdFusion a programmers' tool, the release of Macromedia Studio MX has done much to bring the two worlds together. Using a series of tools collectively called *Flash Remoting*, developers who are used to working in either program can now create integrated applications that share data between a Flash MX interface and ColdFusion MX programming logic. In this chapter, you learn how the two programs communicate, and you construct a basic ecard application to illustrate the basic concepts of Flash Remoting.

Note To follow along with the Flash Remoting application presented later in this chapter, please install the Flash Remoting components that you can download from: Macromedia's Web site at this URL: `http://www.macromedia.com/software/flashremoting/downloads/components/`.

Understanding the Link Between Flash MX and ColdFusion MX

Prior to the merger of Macromedia and the Allaire Corporation (the creators of ColdFusion), there was no easy means of exchanging data between a Flash movie and a ColdFusion application. Still, developers recognized the inherent power in using the two programs together and came up with their own methods for doing so. These included elaborate ActionScript procedures, using XML documents as "translators," and other techniques that, while functional, were time-consuming to create and maintain.

But starting with the release of Macromedia Studio MX, the two programs communicate with one another with a series of tools collectively called *Flash Remoting*. Using Flash Remoting, Flash MX movies can display the output of a ColdFusion MX query, for example, and they can also send complex data back to a ColdFusion MX application for processing. This union gives Flash designers the ability to work with dynamic data and ColdFusion MX developers the ability to create user interfaces that go far beyond the capabilities of standard HTML.

In general, applications that employ both Flash MX and ColdFusion MX are often considered in terms of *display* elements and *logic* elements. Display elements are those that display information to a user and are usually constructed in Flash MX. Logic elements are the parts of the application that perform computations, retrieve data from a database, and so on, and these are usually constructed in ColdFusion MX. Although there are no hard-and-fast definitions for either, it's good practice to design your integrated applications with a clear understanding of which program handles each of your application's various functions.

If you've worked with variables in previous versions of Flash, you know that it has the capability of reading a text file containing simple variable values:

```
first_name=Matt&last_name=Hogan
```

A Flash movie can then use those variables as part of its display, for example, to show a "detail" page for a single user. But what about a list of users that changes daily? In this case, there is more than one defined pair of `first_name` and `last_name` variables, and the Flash movie must be prepared to display anywhere from one to possibly thousands of first name/last name combinations.

The solution lies in complex-variable types. Remember that some special types of variables can hold more than a simple numeric or string value. In Chapter 51 you learned about list variables and how a single list variable is used to store multiple values. Flash Remoting can use even more powerful variable types to pass complex data between ColdFusion and Flash. These may include structures, arrays, queries, scalars, and components. You learn more about some of these types as you proceed through this chapter.

In ColdFusion, the variable types most often used when communicating with Flash are *stuctures* and *arrays*. When a ColdFusion structure is passed to Flash, Flash treats it as an *object* or an *associative array*.

ColdFusion's structure variables can hold more than one value, but they go a step further by giving each value a *key* to identify it. Array variables are even more powerful, because they allow for multiple dimensions, meaning that there can be more than one value for say, `first_name` or `last_name` within a single array variable. You find more information on structures and arrays in the two sidebars accompanying this chapter.

Understanding ColdFusion MX Structures

Structures are special ColdFusion variables that can hold multiple values. They employ a *key* to refer to an item by a name. The following code defines a structure called `user` within a ColdFusion template:

```
<!---create a new structure called "user"--->
<cfset user=StructNew()>

<!---define some keys and values--->
<cfset user.first_name="Don">
<cfset user.last_name="VanVliet">
<cfset user.street_address="12 Mojo Lane">
<cfset user.city="Los Angeles">
<cfset user.state="CA">
```

After the structure is defined, you can create any name/value pairs you like, as long as you use the structure's name as a scope when you define each variable. In the preceding example, the key names are `first_name`, `last_name`, `street_address`, `city`, and `state`.

To display the value of an item, you call it by its structure name and key:

```
<cfoutput>#user.last_name#</cfoutput>
```

The preceding snippet displays the value `VanVliet`.

An alternative way to display the same value is to use *associative array syntax*, which accepts the name of a structure and the name of key:

```
<cfoutput>#user[last_name]#</cfoutput>
```

That may seem like a more complicated way of displaying a simple value, but it's a useful tool when you want to display the complete contents of a structure as part of a loop. For example, to display all of the elements of the `user` structure defined above, you could use `<cfloop>` in "collection" mode, like this:

```
<cfloop collection=#user# item="key">
    <cfoutput>
        #key#: #StructFind(user,key)#<br>
    </cfoutput>
</cfloop>
```

This special kind of loop enables you to quickly "unpack" the contents of a structure without having to refer to each key by its specific name. It displays output like the following:

```
first_name: Don
last_name: VanVliet
street_address: 12 Mojo Lane
city: Los Angeles
state: CA
```

Note that you don't have to include the value of the key in your output. It's only used here to show you how `<cfloop>` loops through the collection, one key at a time. Later in this chapter, you learn how to use a similar `<cfloop>` to unpack the contents of a special structure called `flash`, which contains the information sent from a Flash MX movie to a ColdFusion MX template.

Understanding How ColdFusion MX and Flash MX Communicate

Before you begin to build your first Flash Remoting application, take a quick look at the steps that make integration possible.

First, any Flash movie that will communicate with a ColdFusion template must include the special class `NetServices.as`. After it's included in a movie's ActionScript, that movie can call upon a ColdFusion template as an ActionScript function.

The called ColdFusion template can perform any number of queries, computations, and so on, as long as it saves the desired result as an object named flash.result. The Flash movie can then use that special object variable as input. The flash.result data may contain a simple variable, such as a name, or it may contain a more complex group of data, such as a set of records returned by a ColdFusion query.

Conversely, for a Flash movie to pass data to a ColdFusion MX template, the movie's ActionScript must call the ColdFusion template as a function and pass any necessary data as function arguments. When a ColdFusion template is called this way, the data passed by Flash is available as a special variable called flash.params, which may be used as input for further operations in the ColdFusion template. You gain a greater understanding of this process as you build a sample Flash Remoting application in the next section.

Creating an Ecard Application with Flash Remoting

To get a feel for Flash Remoting, you start by constructing an ecard application for the Habitat Alert site. This basic application shares some qualities with the "drill down" application you constructed in Chapter 51, but the entire card selection and viewing interface will be built in Flash MX, rather than in standard HTML.

Flash Remoting requires that your users have Flash Player 6 or greater.

The application uses a Flash interface, enabling a user to select from a thumbnail images of picture "postcards." After selecting a card, the user sees a full-sized version of the card as an animated Flash movie. The movie displays for a few seconds and then a Next button appears. After the user clicks the button, the movie advances to the next frame that has a form that allows the user to specify a greeting and the e-mail address of another user to whom the card will be mailed. The recipient will get an e-mail announcing the card and containing a link to view the card and custom greeting.

As you may have guessed, this application draws much of its information from a database. The titles, thumbnail paths, and Flash movie names for each postcard are stored in a table named cards. The users' custom greetings and e-mail addresses are inserted into a table named greetings. You'll find the Microsoft Access database titled ha.mdb on the CD-ROM accompanying this book. Note that if you've worked the examples for the Habitat Alert site in the previous chapters, you'll already have the database installed as a datasource and may skip the next section.

Why store the card information in a database? Why not just hard-code the titles and thumbnail images into the Flash movie? The reason is that you're creating an ecard application that will be *scalable*, so that if Habitat Alert wants to add new cards or modify data on existing cards, they can do so simply by editing text information in the ecards database, rather than having to redesign a Flash movie.

Setting up the datasource

If you completed the newsletter application in Chapter 48, you should already have the datasource ha defined in ColdFusion administrator, and you can move on to the next section. If you didn't, start by copying the database ha.mdb from the CD-ROM to a folder within your ColdFusion MX Web root. If you're using ColdFusion's built-in Web server, a good path is c:\cfusionmx\db.

Next, open the Habitat Alert site in Dreamweaver and define a new datasource. In ColdFusion administrator's datasource panel, name the datasource ha; then navigate to the location of the database.

Creating the ColdFusion summary function

When users visit the ecard section of Habitat Alert, the first page they'll see is a Flash MX interface showing the current list of card titles and thumbnail images stored in the database. We'll call this the "summary" page. You'll use ColdFusion to retrieve this list with a <cfquery> and then pass the results to Flash for display.

Note

When using Flash Remoting, it's important to pay close attention to the folder and filenames you use for your ColdFusion MX templates, because when you call a ColdFusion template from Flash, the folder in which the template is stored becomes the name of the ActionScript *service*, and the template filename becomes the ActionScript *function*. You learn more about this in the next section.

Using Dreamweaver's Files pane, create a new folder within the Habitat Alert site titled ecards. Within it, create a new ColdFusion document titled get_all_cards.cfm. Listing 54-1 shows the entire contents of the page. Note that because Flash MX will be handling the display of data, this ColdFusion page doesn't need the standard HTML headers automatically inserted by Dreamweaver when a new page is created. You can simply delete them.

Listing 54-1: get_all_cards.cfm

```
<cfquery name="flash.result" datasource="ha">
    select id, card_title, card_thumbnail, card_movie from cards
</cfquery>
```

Listing 54-1 contains a basic ColdFusion MX query that retrieves the ID, title, and thumbnail columns for all records found in the cards table. There is one unique element though: notice that the query name is flash.result. This is the special variable name used to pass information between ColdFusion and Flash. In the next section, you learn how this query object becomes available to your Flash display page.

Using Flash Remoting to link ColdFusion with Flash

A Flash movie is the logical choice as a user interface for choosing the ecard and entering the ecard greeting and other data. Flash Remoting makes it possible for a Flash movie to interact with ColdFusion files and retrieve information from a database. You could hard code the

Understanding ColdFusion Arrays

The structure in the previous section contains information about only one user. What if you want a single variable object that contains similar data about several users? Enter the *array* variable, which—among many uses—may be used to store data for more than one user.

To illustrate this concept, consider a ColdFusion query that returns just one user record from a database. That's similar to a structure, because it contains only one `first_name` column, one `last_name` column, and so on. However, if the same query returned information for several users, there would be more than one value for `first_name`, `last_name`, and so on. That's more like an array. To put it another way, a structure contains data much like a single database record, whereas an array is capable of containing multiple records and thus can be used more like an entire database table.

In fact, it's helpful to think of arrays like database tables that are stored in memory—as a variable—rather than in a file. Though you never work with arrays in a graphic interface, they store information much the same way as a table.

Unlike structures, arrays are typically used with numbers rather than key names. For example, to define a two-dimensional array (you learn more about dimensions in a moment) called `users` that holds data on three users, you use code like this:

```
<!---create a new, two-dimensional array called "user"--->
<cfset users=ArrayNew(2)>

<!---define the first user as array row "1"--->
<cfset users[1][1]="McKinley">
<cfset users[1][2]="Morganfield">
<cfset users[1][3]="15 Park Place">
<cfset users[1][4]="Clarksdale">
<cfset users[1][5]="MS">

<!---define the second user as array row "2"--->
<cfset users[2][1]="Ellas">
<cfset users[2][2]="McDaniel">
<cfset users[2][3]="1241 Gretsch Drive">
<cfset users[2][4]="McComb">
<cfset users[2][5]="MS">

<!---define the third user as array row "3"--->
<cfset users[3][1]="Eugene">
<cfset users[3][2]="Klein">
<cfset users[3][3]="12 Witz Avenue">
<cfset users[3][4]="Newark">
<cfset users[3][5]="NJ">
```

In a two-dimensional array, each array element is referenced by a pair of numbers, each in brackets. To use the database-table analogy, the first number refers to a row, while the second refers to a column.

> To display a specific element of an array, you use the same syntax, referring to it by its "row" and "column:"
>
> ```
> <cfoutput>#users[3][2]#</cfoutput>
> ```
>
> This snippet returns the value Klein, or the second column in the third row of the array users.

Flash movie with the names of the ecards and their titles, and load the thumbnail images from the document library. However, this method requires you to update the Flash movie every time the client adds or deletes an ecard from the queue, or modifies an existing ecard. Updating the database is the easier and more elegant solution.

The Flash Remoting service is standard with ColdFusion MX. However, you have to add the necessary components to create remoting applications with Flash MX. You can download these components from Macromedia's Web site at this URL: http://www.macromedia.com/software/flashremoting/downloads/components/. If you purchased Macromedia Flash Remoting MX, you already have the components installed. Figure 54-1 shows the Remoting objects that are added to the Flash MX Actions panel after you download the remoting components from Macromedia's Web site. Note that the Actions Panel has been enlarged in this screenshot so that all of the Remoting additions are visible.

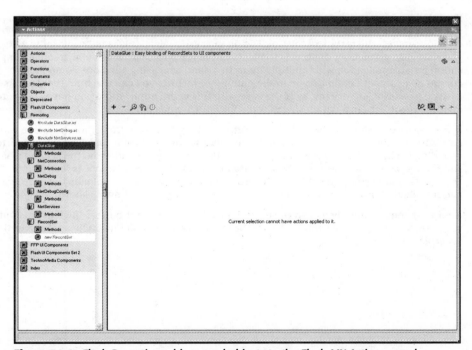

Figure 54-1: Flash Remoting adds several objects to the Flash MX Actions panel.

The Flash Remoting objects, as with other ActionScript objects, are organized in their own book. The objects in the Remoting book have their own methods and make it possible for you to create a connection with the gateway to Netservices.

About the Ecard Flash movie

The source file for the Flash movie (eCard.fla) for this exercise can be found on the CD ROM that accompanies this book. The movie is comprised of three frames. In the first frame, ActionScript calls the ColdFusion file to retrieve the information from the database. The information is stored in four arrays. After the arrays are populated, the loadMovie action is used to load a thumbnail image into a target window. Users can preview available ecards by clicking the forward and back arrows shown in Figure 54-2. The images could have been loaded into smaller windows, much like a table in an HTML image gallery. However this would limit the number of ecards that could be displayed in the interface. Loading individual images into the window allows for future expansion should Habitat Alert decide to increase the number of ecards they make available to users.

After the viewer chooses an ecard, the ecard is loaded into Level1 of the ecard movie. Frame 2 of the movie uses a timer component to pause the movie for a few seconds allowing the viewer to look at the Ecard. Then the movie advances to Frame 3. The ActionScript on Frame 3 loads a Next button, that when clicked unloads the ecard movie. After the movie unloads, the viewer sees the form that can be filled in and submitted to send the Ecard and a personalized greeting to a friend or colleague.

Flash MX has several components that can be used for applications of this sort; for example you can use the list box, or combo box components, and use a function to populate either component with the results of the ColdFusion query. However, this is only advisable when you have a small number of objects to display from the database. When you create an application for an application with multiple items in a database, using a list box component or combo box component limits you to the number of records you can use from the database. By using an associative array, as is the case with this ecard application, you have access to multiple records from a database and room for future expansion.

Users can select an ecard by clicking the button below the text to the left of the image window. After clicking the button, the movie advances to the next frame and the SWF file corresponding to the image is loaded into Level 1. A timer pauses the movie on the second frame and then advances the movie to the third frame. An additional SWF movie is loaded into Level 2. This movie has one object, a Next button, that when clicked unloads the ecard movie and reveals the form used to input the recipient's data and a greeting, as shown in Figure 54-3.

After users enter data, they send the ecard by clicking the Submit button. Clicking this button sends the greeting information to the database. At this point, ColdFusion files take over the process.

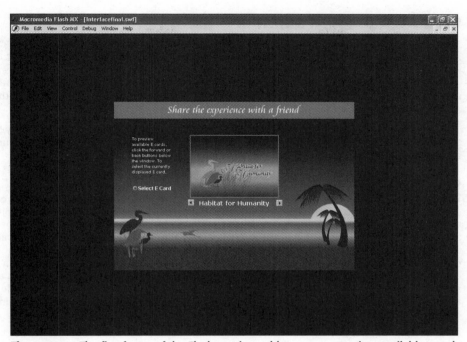

Figure 54-2: The first frame of the Flash movie enables users to preview available ecards.

Figure 54-3: The third frame of the movie provides users with a form for entering data.

Creating the Flash summary frame

For an ecard application, you can create a Flash movie with animation and sound. You can also create a more elegant user interface than is possible with standard HTML. For this tutorial, an interface has been created and populated with a target window, plus there is an animation of a bird to keep viewers entertained while selecting an ecard. To follow along with upcoming sections, copy the eCard.fla file from the Chapter 54 folder on the CD ROM that accompanies this book, launch Flash MX, and open the file.

The ActionScript in the first frame of this application connects the Flash movie remotely to NetServices. After the remote connection is made, the ColdFusion file in Listing 54-1 is summoned as a service. The results of the file are loaded into arrays.

Creating the remote connection

When you create your own Flash Remoting applications, the first order of business is to create the ActionScript to remotely connect the Flash movie with Net Services. You accomplish this by including the NetServices.as object to your script. You'll find this object by opening the Actions panel and navigating to the Remoting book that was added when you downloaded the Remoting components from Macromedia's Web site. You can add the NetServices.as object to your script in Normal mode by double-clicking its title, or by selecting and then dragging and dropping it into the Script pane. If you add the object in this manner, Flash automatically adds a semi-colon to signify the end of a line of code. Switch from Normal mode to Expert mode and delete the semi-colon, otherwise you get an error message. The following code shows the proper format for adding this object to your script.

```
#include "NetServices.as"
```

Creating a gateway connection

After enabling net services, you must supply the URL where the NetServices can be accessed by the Flash movie. You need to create a gateway connection as well. You achieve both of these tasks by adding methods of the NetServices object. When you are initially creating your Flash application the URL for the gateway to flashservices will be your local host, which ColdFusion MX defines as: http://localhost:8500/flashservices/gateway.

Next you create the code that sets the gateway connection. This involves adding setDefaultGatewayURL to the script and defining the default gateway. The default gateway you set when testing the application with the ColdFusion MX is the local host on your system. The URL to the default host on your local computer is: http://localhost:8500/flashservices/gateway. You have to change the URL to the directory where flashservices reside on your Web hosting service before uploading the application. The next step is to add the createGatewayConnection method of the Net Services object to your script, which connects your application to the Flash Remoting service on your application's server. In the case of the ecard application, you'll be connecting to a ColdFusion server; hence it makes sense to give the object the name of CFServer. You can do this by creating a named variable and setting it equal to the createGatewayConnection method of the NetServices object, or by entering the code in Expert mode. When you create your own Flash Remoting applications after you define the URL for Flash services and create the gateway connection, your code should be similar to Listing 54-2.

Listing 54-2: **Creating a Gateway Connection**

```
#include "NetServices.as"
NetServices.setDefaultGatewayURL("http://localhost:8500/flashservices/g
ateway");
CFServer = NetServices.createGatewayConnection();
```

Accessing NetServices

For a Flash application to communicate with ColdFusion files, you use the `getService` method of the `NetConnection` object, which is located in the Remoting book in the Actions panel. For the ecard application, you need to unpack the information from the database as defined by the query in the ColdFusion file: `get_all_cards.cfm`. When you call a NetService, the service is defined by the server directory where the function is located. In the case of the ecard application, the ColdFusion file is located in the server's ecard directory; hence the service is ecard. You need to name the service object. You can do this by creating a new variable, or by hard coding the script in Expert mode. For the ecard application, you'll be getting the information about each ecard from the database. One of the items you'll be using will be the title of each ecard; therefore you can name the service object, *svcTitles*. After you define the service, you add the ColdFusion function to your ActionScript. The ColdFusion file `get_all_cards.cfm` queries the database for the information needed in your Flash movie. You add that information to the service as a function. To add the service to your script, insert the ActionScript code shown in Listing 54-3.

Listing 54-3: **Accessing a Remote Service**

```
svcTitles = CFServer.getService("habitat_alert.ecards", this);
svcTitles.get_all_cards();
```

Creating the function

After you call the remote service, you create ActionScript that interprets the results into a format that you can utilize in your application. For the ecard application, you'll need the following fields from the cards table of ecard database: ID, card_title, card_thumbnail, and card_movie. After your application remotely calls the NetService, the data from the `get_all_cards.cfm` file is returned as a result. The result of the remote service contains the items from the database queried by the ColdFusion function.

To create the function that interpolates the data, you begin by creating a new array for each item queried. You populate the arrays with items from each database field using a `for` loop. The number of items in the database fluctuates; therefore your loop executes until the number of items (`length`) of the database is exhausted. The final duty your function performs is to load the first ecard thumbnail into a target window instance, which has been labeled, `eCardTarget` and resides on the root timeline. To finalize the code for the first frame of the e card application, enter the code shown in Listing 54-4.

Listing 54-4: Creating the Result Function

```
function get_all_cards_Result(result) {
    card_id = new Array();
    titles = new Array();
    thumbnails = new Array();
    movies = new Array();
    for (var i = 0; i<result.items.length; ++i) {
        card_id[i] = result.items[i].ID;
        titles[i] = result.items[i].card_title;
        thumbnails[i] = result.items[i].card_thumbnail;
        movies[i] = result.items[i].card_movie;
    }
    loadMovie("images/" + thumbnails[0], "_root.EcardTarget");
    _root.eCardTitle.text = titles[0];
    k = 0;
}
```

No doubt you noticed the addition of a new variable, k, as the final line of code. This initializes a counter for the buttons that load the ecard images. Your code for the first frame of the ecard application should read as shown in Listing 54-5, which includes a stop() action at the start of the script. This action prevents the movie from going to the second frame until the user selects an ecard.

Listing 54-5: ActionScript for the Application's First Frame

```
stop();
#include "NetServices.as"
#include "NetDebug.as"
NetServices.setDefaultGatewayURL("http://localhost:8500/flashservices/g
ateway");
CFServer = NetServices.createGatewayConnection();
svcTitles = CFServer.getService("habitat_alert.html.site.ecards",
this);
svcTitles.get_all_cards();
function get_all_cards_Result(result) {
    titles = new Array();
    card_id = new Array();
    thumbnails = new Array();
    movies = new Array();
    for (var i = 0; i<result.items.length; ++i) {
        titles[i] = result.items[i].card_title;
        thumbnails[i] = result.items[i].card_thumbnail;
        movies[i] = result.items[i].card_movie;
        card_id[i] = result.items[i].ID;
        NetDebug.trace(card_id[i]);
```

```
        NetDebug.trace(titles[i]);
        NetDebug.trace(thumbnails[i]);
        NetDebug.trace(movies[i]);
    }
    loadMovie("images/" + thumbnails[0], "_root.EcardTarget");
    root.eCardTitle.text = titles[0];
    k = 0;
```

Coding the buttons

Users click the buttons at the bottom of the target window to view images of the ecards. When the user clicks a button clicked, a new image loads and the title of the image updates as well. As previously mentioned, the image loads into a target window with the instance name of `EcardTarget`. A dynamic text box below the target window with the instance name of `EcardTitle`, displays the name of each ecard. The counter you initialized in the `get all cards Result` function increments by 1 when the user clicks the Forward button and decrements by 1 when the user clicks the Back button. The Forward button's code has a conditional statement that prevents the variable from exceeding the number of elements in the array, and the Back button's code has a conditional statement that prevents the variable from having a value less than 0. Listing 54-6 shows the code for the Forward button. Listing 54-7 shows the code for the Back button.

Listing 54-6: **ActionScript for the Forward Button**

```
on (release) {
    ++k;
    if (k>titles.length-1) {
        k = titles.length-1;
    }
    loadMovie("images/" + thumbnails[k], "_root.EcardTarget");
    root.eCardTitle.text = titles[k];
}
```

Listing 54-7: **ActionScript for the Back Button**

```
on (release) {
--k;
    if (k<0) {
        k = 0;
    }
    loadMovie("images/" + thumbnails[k], "_root.EcardTarget");
    root.eCardTitle.text = titles[k];
}
```

After viewers decide which ecard to send, they can select it by clicking the Select E Card button. The ActionScript for this button, shown in Listing 54-8 is fairly straightforward. It advances the movie to the next frame and loads the ecard SWF file into Level 1 of the movie.

Listing 54-8: **Coding the Select Ecard Button**

```
on (release) {
    gotoAndStop(2);
    loadMovieNum("site/ecards/" + movies[k], 1);
}
```

Notice that the code that loads the movie is an expression. It concatenates the directory (ecards) where the ecards reside on the server with an element from the array movies. The element corresponds to the counter variable.

Coding the second and third keyframes

The ActionScript for the second and third keyframes of the movie are fairly simple. In the second frame of the movie, add a stop() action. If you examine the second frame of the movie closely, you'll notice a registration point outside the boundaries of the Stage. This is a timer component, which pauses the movie for a period of four seconds before advances to the third frame.

Tip

The timer component pauses a movie on a frame for the time period you specify in the Parameters tab of the Property inspector. To use the timer in another movie, choose File ⇨ Open as Library. Navigate to the directory where the FLA file for this exercise is stored. Drag the timer component into the current document library, and add it to the movie keyframe where you want to pause the production.

The third keyframe loads another movie into Level 2. The movie has one object, a Next button, that when clicked unloads the ecard movie, as well as the Next button movie. The code for the third keyframe is shown in Listing 54-9.

Listing 54-9: **ActionScript for the Third Keyframe**

```
loadMovieNum("next.swf", 2);
stop();
```

Creating the Flash detail frame and form

The third frame of the ecard movie contains input text boxes where users enter their names and e-mail addresses, as well as the recipient's name and e-mail address. There is also an input text box in which the user can compose a greeting, as shown in Figure 54-4. The Submit button at the bottom of the Stage compiles the information and forwards it the ColdFusion page detailed in the next section.

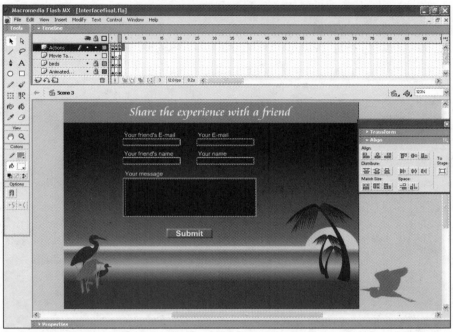

Figure 54-4: Users enter information and send the ecard from frame 3 of the movie.

Each input text box has been given a unique instance name. When users click the Submit button, the data is compiled and forwarded to the `send_card.cfm` page. To finalize the code for the project, select the Submit button and then open the Actions panel. Create a variable for each field in the greeting table of the ecards database and set its value equal to the text data in each input text box. You use the `getUrl` action to send the information to the `send_card.cfm` page. The `POST` method is used to send the variables to the ColdFusion page. The complete code for the Submit button in the ecard application is shown in Listing 54-10.

Listing 54-10: **ActionScript for the Submit Button**

```
on (release) {card_id = card_id[k];
    sender_email = _root.senderemail.email3.text;
    sender_name = _root.sendername.email4.text;
    recipient_email = _root.friendsemail.email1.text;
    recipient_name = _root.friendsname.email2.text;
    greeting = _root.yourMessage.message.text;
getURL("http://localhost:8500/habitat_alert/html/site/ecards/send_card.
cfm", "_self",
    }
```

Using the NetConnection Debugger

When you're creating an application that uses Flash Remoting, it's difficult to tell whether you've received the queried information from the remote service. You can enable the NetConnection Debugger by adding one line of code to your ActionScript: `#include "NetDebug.as"`. After you add this line of code to your script, you can then use the `trace` method of the `NetDebug` object in the same manner as you'd use a trace in a nonremote Flash application. The following is the code for frame one of the ecard application with the `trace` method being used to check array contents.

```
stop();
#include "NetServices.as"
#include "NetDebug.as"
NetServices.setDefaultGatewayURL("http://localhost:8500/flashservices/gat
eway");
CFServer = NetServices.createGatewayConnection();
svcTitles = CFServer.getService("habitat_alert.html.site.ecards", this);
svcTitles.get_all_cards();
function get_all_cards_Result(result) {
    titles = new Array();
    card_id = new Array();
    thumbnails = new Array();
    movies = new Array();
    for (var i = 0; i<result.items.length; ++i) {
        titles[i] = result.items[i].card_title;
        thumbnails[i] = result.items[i].card_thumbnail;
        movies[i] = result.items[i].card_movie;
        card_id[i] = result.items[i].ID;
        NetDebug.trace(card_id[i]);
        NetDebug.trace(titles[i]);
        NetDebug.trace(thumbnails[i]);
        NetDebug.trace(movies[i]);
    }
    loadMovie("images/" + thumbnails[0], "_root.EcardTarget");
    root.eCardTitle.text = titles[0];
    k = 0;
}
```

You open the NetConnection Debugger by choosing Window ➪ NetConnection Debugger prior to testing your movie. The NetConnection Debugger is shown in the following figure.

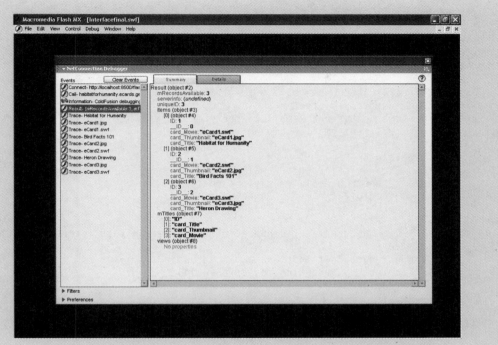

You can debug your Flash MX remote applications using the NetConnection Debugger.

Creating the ColdFusion action page

After the user has selected a card and supplied details, such as the recipient name, e-mail address, and so on, the Flash movie sends the form data to ColdFusion MX for processing. In this final step, the user leaves the Flash interface and is taken to a ColdFusion template that performs three actions:

1. Saves the data entered by the user in the "greetings" table

2. Sends an e-mail to the recipient announcing the ecard

3. Displays a confirmation to the user that the announcement has been sent

The action page uses neither `flash.params` or `flash.result`, because the Flash movie will simply be passing along standard form data.

Create a new ColdFusion MX document in the `ecards` folder titled `send_card.cfm`. Listing 54-11 contains the basic code, although you can customize the e-mail announcement and sender confirmation text to your liking.

Listing 54-11: **send_card.cfm**

```
<!---insert the greeting data into the database--->

<cftransaction>

    <cfquery datasource="ha">
        insert into greetings
        (card_id,sender_email,sender_name,
        recipient_email,recipient_name,
        greeting)
        values
        (#card_id#,'#sender_email#',
        '#sender_name#','#recipient_email#',
        '#recipient_name#','#greeting#')
    </cfquery>

    <!---get the greeting_id number of the greeting just inserted--->

    <cfquery name="get_last" datasource="ha">
        select max(greeting_id) as [new_id]
        from greetings
    </cfquery>

</cftransaction>


<!---send mail to the card recipient--->

<cfmail to="#recipient_email#" from="webmaster@habitatalert.com"
subject="Someone Has Sent You an E-Card">
  Dear User;

  A member of our Website has sent you an e-card. To retrieve it,
please visit this URL:


http://localhost:8500/habitat_alert/html/site/ecards/view_card.cfm?gree
ting_id=#get_last.new_id#
</cfmail>

<!---display a confirmation to the sender--->

<html>
<head>
<title>Card Sent</title>
<meta http-equiv="Content-Type" content="text/html; charset=iso-
8859-1">
</head>
```

```
<body>

<h2>Card Sent</h2>

Your card information has been stored, and an announcement has been
sent to <cfoutput>#recipient_name# at #recipient_email#</cfoutput>.
</body>
</html>
```

In Listing 54-11, the first `<cfquery>` tag inputs the sender's greeting data into the greetings table using SQL's INSERT command. Next, the second `<cfquery>` section uses the SQL aggregate function `max()` to retrieve the greatest ID number present in the greetings table. In this case, this number will be the one Microsoft Access autogenerated when `<cfinsert>` inserted the sender's data. This number is important, because it uniquely identifies the current greeting.

Notice that the two queries are enclosed in a pair of `<cftransaction>` tags. The function of this tag is to group multiple queries so that ColdFusion treats them as one event. In this case, it performs the insert and retrieves the maximum `greeting_id` in one step. Why? Consider a very busy Web site in which two unique users submit the ecard form at the same time. If ColdFusion processed the queries separately, it's possible that it might insert one user's data first and then report the wrong maximum `greeting id` to the other user's page. By using `<cftransaction>`, you can ensure that the maximum `greeting_id` returned to the user is the one created by the insert of that person's distinct information.

Next, an e-mail is sent to the card recipient via the `<cfmail>` tag. The body of the mail includes the full URL path to a page called `view_card.cfm` and a query string containing the greeting ID of the new greeting inserted by this template.

Caution

Remember that the "from" value in any `<cfmail>` tag needs to be an address that's acceptable to the SMTP server through which the mail will be sent.

Finally, a confirmation is displayed to the sender, showing that mail has been sent. For verification, the recipient's name and e-mail address are also displayed.

Creating the ColdFusion view page

When a recipient receives an e-mail announcement, it contains some text like this:

```
From: website@habitatalert.com
To: someuser@somedomain.com
Subject: Someone Has Sent You an E-Card

Dear User;

A member of our Website has sent you an e-card. To retrieve it, please
visit this URL:

http://localhost:8500/habitat_alert/html/site/ecards/view_card.cfm?gree
ting_id=5
```

You now need to construct `view_card.cfm`, the page that displays the card and greeting to the recipient. In essence, this page functions much like the detail pages described in Chapter 51, where an item ID is passed in the URL, a query is performed using the passed ID as input, and the resulting item details are displayed to the user.

The `greeting_id` passed in the recipient's URL enables you to query for the greeting details, but you also need a second query to get the details on the card itself — the title and the flash movie, for example. Take a look at Listing 54-12.

Listing 54-12: **view_card.cfm**

```
<!---get greeting details based on greeting_id passed in URL--->
<cfquery name="get_greeting" datasource="ha">
    select recipient_name, sender_name,
    sender_email, greeting, card_id
    from greetings
    where greeting_id = #URL.greeting_id#
</cfquery>

<!---get card details based on the card_id retrieved by the previous
query--->
<cfquery name="get_card" datasource="ha">
    select card_title, card_movie
    from cards
    where id = #get_greeting.card_id#
</cfquery>

<html>

<head>

<!---begin cfoutput section--->
<cfoutput>

<!---show recipient name in page title--->
<title>A Greeting Card for #get_greeting.recipient_name#</title>

<meta http-equiv="Content-Type" content="text/html; charset=iso-
8859-1">
</head>

<body>

<!---show recipient name in header--->
    <h2>A Greeting Card for #get_greeting.recipient_name#</h2>
    <!---embed flash movie based on the card_movie value retrieved in
the "get_card" query--->
<div align="center"><object classid="clsid:D27CDB6E-AE6D-11cf-
96B8-444553540000"
```

```
codebase="http://download.macromedia.com/pub/shockwave/cabs/flash/swfla
sh.cab##version=6,0,0,0"
 WIDTH="550" HEIGHT="400" id="Interface" ALIGN="">
 <param NAME=movie VALUE="#get_card.card_movie#"> <param NAME=quality
VALUE=high> <param NAME=bgcolor VALUE=##000033> <embed
src="#get_card.card_movie#" quality=high bgcolor=##000033  WIDTH="550"
HEIGHT="400" NAME="#get_card.card_movie#" ALIGN=""
 TYPE="application/x-shockwave-flash"
PLUGINSPAGE="http://www.macromedia.com/go/getflashplayer">
</embed>
</object></div>
     <p align="center">#get_greeting.greeting#</p>
     <p align="center">This card has been sent to you by
<ahref="mailto:#get_greeting.sender_email#">#get_greeting.sender_name#<
/a>, courtesy of Habitat Alert</p>
<p align="center">To send your own greeting card, click
<a href="http://localhost:8500/habitat_alert/html/ecard.html">
here</a></p>
<!---end cfoutput section--->
</cfoutput>

</body>
</html>
```

The first query retrieves the greeting details; the second gets the card details based on the card_id retrieved by the first query.

Listing 54-12 also uses `<cfoutput>` a little differently than previous examples. Usually when `<cfoutput>` is used to display the results of a query, it's used in conjunction with a query attribute, such as the following:

```
<cfoutput query="some_query_name">
```

But in this case, your template contains two queries and your display needs to draw information from both of them. The solution is to use a generic `<cfoutput>` and then supply the name of a query as a qualifier, each time you reference a variable, as in the following snippet, which references the title returned by the get_card query and the greeting returned by the get_greeting query:

```
<cfoutput>
#get_card.title#<br>
#get_greeting.greeting#<br>
</cfoutput>
```

Listing 54-12 also embeds the relevant Flash MX movie, based on the filename stored in the card_movie field. Finally, it displays the sender's greeting and name, and provides a link to the main ecard page to enable the recipient to send his or her own ecard.

ColdFusion Components, *by Samuel Neff*

Components are as notable an enhancement to ColdFusion MX as user defined functions were to ColdFusion 5. With ColdFusion components developers not only have a new mechanism for code reuse, but they are introduced to a programming concept long held as the cornerstone of advanced software design. Components bring the power of object-oriented programming but keep the tradition of simplicity that has made ColdFusion the ideal development platform for the Web.

A ColdFusion component (CFC) is a collection of properties and functions used to encapsulate related functionality. To demonstrate, look at an example from a survey question application. The following skeleton code outlines a component for a list of survey questions.

```
<cfcomponent>

  <cffunction
    name="getQuestionIdList"
    returnType="string"
    access="remote">

  </cffunction>

  <cffunction
    name="getQuestionText"
    returnType="string"
    access="remote">

    <cfargument
      name="questionId"
      type="numeric"
      required="true">

  </cffunction>


  <cffunction
    name="setAnswerText"
    access="remote">

    <cfargument
      name="questionId"
      type="numeric"
      required="true">

    <cfargument
      name="answerText"
      type="string"
      required="true">

  </cffunction>

</cfcomponent>
```

Creating a Component

All code within the CFC must be contained within `cfcomponent` tags. Only comments can be placed outside these tags. Within the component you're defining three functions with the `cffunction` tags. The only required attribute is name. The `returnType` attribute defines the type of value being returned from the function. `String` indicates any text value and `void` indicates the function does not return anything.

Two of the functions require arguments. To define a function's arguments use the `cfargument` tag. This tag accepts a name and type and validates on each call that the value passed matches the type specified. You can also optionally specify that the argument is required, and in cases where it is not, you can specify a default value.

Dreamweaver MX can be helpful in creating CFCs; it provides a graphical user interface for creating the component structure. To create the above component using Dreamweaver MX's interface, follow these steps.

1. If the Application panel is not visible, click on Window and then Components.

2. If the Application panel is already visible but collapsed, click the arrow next to Application to expand it.

3. Click on the Components tab inside the Application panel.

4. If you haven't already defined a site, click on the "site" hyperlink to define a site. See Chapter 48 for information on defining a site.

5. If you haven't already identified the document type for the site, click on the "document type" hyperlink to specify the server model as ColdFusion.

6. If you haven't already specified the testing server information, click on the "Testing Server" hyperlink to specific the testing server details.

7. If you haven't already specified the RDS login, click on the "RDS" hyperlink to enter the RDS password.

8. If CF Component is not selected in the drop down box, select it.

9. Click on the Plus sign next to the drop down box to display the Create Component interface.

10. Under Name enter **questionAnswer**.

11. Under Component Directory specify a directory under your wwwroot to store the component.

12. In the Sections list box, click on Functions.

13. Click the Plus sign to add a new function.

14. Under Name enter **getQuestionIdList**.

15. Under Access enter **remote**.

16. Under Return Type enter **string**.

17. Repeat steps 13 through 16 for each of the functions in the above listing.

18. In the Sections list box, click on Arguments.

19. Select getQuestionText from the drop-down list box.

20. Click on the plus sign to add an argument.

21. Enter **questionId** for the name.

22. Enter **numeric** for the type.

23. Click the Required check box to specify the argument as required.

24. Repeat steps 18 through 22 to add the arguments for setAnswerText.

25. Click OK.

26. Dreamweaver MX displays a new CFC with the functions and arguments you specified.

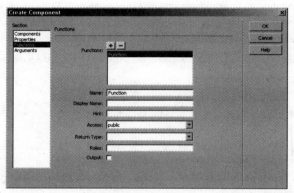

Using Dreamweaver MX to create a component outline

In the questionnaire example, you run database queries within each of the functions to provide the desired functionality:

```
<cffunction
  name="getQuestionIdList"
  returnType="string"
  access="remote">

  <cfquery name="questionIdQuery" datasource="StudioMXBible">
    SELECT QuestionID
    FROM Questions
  </cfquery>


  <cfset idList=ValueList(questionIdQuery.QuestionID)>
  <cfreturn idList>

</cffunction>

<cffunction
```

```
      name="getQuestionText"
      returnType="string"
      access="remote">

      <cfargument
        name="questionId"
        type="numeric"
        required="true">

      <cfquery name="questionQuery" datasource="StudioMXBible">
        SELECT QuestionText
        FROM Questions
        WHERE QuestionID=#Arguments.questionId#
      </cfquery>

      <cfreturn questionQuery.QuestionText>

  </cffunction>


  <cffunction
      name="setAnswerText"
      access="remote">

      <cfargument
        name="questionId"
        type="numeric"
        required="true">

      <cfargument
        name="answerText"
        type="string"
        required="true">

      <cfquery name="questionQuery" datasource="StudioMXBible">
        UPDATE Answers
        SET AnswerText=
          <cfqueryparam
            cfsqltype="cf_sql_varchar"
            value="#Arguments.answerText#">
        WHERE QuestionID=#Arguments.questionId#
      </cfquery>

  </cffunction>
```

Notice that the functions, `getQuestionIdList` and `getQuestionText`, which return a value do so through the `cfreturn` tag. This tag accepts an expression and returns the expression to the caller as the function result. With your component completed, you're ready to begin using it in your application.

Save this file to a new folder within your wwwroot and call it questionAnswer.cfc.

Using a Component from a ColdFusion Template

To begin with, you to create a simple HTMLform that displays the questions and an input block for users to provide an answer. Enter the following code into a blank ColdFusion template and save it as survey.cfm in the same directory as questionAnswer.cfc.

```
<cfoutput>
  <form action="action.cfm" method="post">
    <cfset qaCFC=CreateObject("component","questionAnswer")>
    <cfloop index="questionId" list="#qaCFC.getQuestionIdList()#">
      <h3>#qaCFC.getQuestionText(questionId)#</h3>
      <textarea name="Answer_#questionId#" cols="60"
rows="5"></textarea>
    </cfloop>
    <br/>
    <input type="Submit" value="Submit">
  </form>
</cfoutput>
```

ColdFusion MX includes three mechanisms to create a CFC from local CFML code, cfobject, cfinvoke, and CreateObject. Besides structure, the primary difference between these methods is component life. When used independently, cfinvoke creates the component, calls the method, and then releases the component. With cfobject and CreateObject the programmer is in complete control of the component life, which is important when calling multiple functions of the same component within a request.

Because your component simply encapsulates functionality and does not store any of its own data, you can store the component in the default Variables scope and allow it to be released at the end of the request. When components are used to store data and encapsulate functionality, they can be stored in the Server, Application, Session, and Request scopes. For more information on scopes refer to the "A Word About Variable Scopes" sidebar in Chapter 48.

With you form page created, you can move on to the action page and use the same component for storing data back to the database:

```
<cfset qaCFC=CreateObject("component","questionAnswer")>

<cfloop index="varName" list="#Form.fieldNames#">
  <cfif ListGetAt(varName,1,"_") IS "Answer">
    <cfset questionId=ListGetAt(varName,2,"_")>
    <cfif Len(Form[varName])>
      <cfset qaCFC.setAnswerText(questionId,Form[varName])>
    </cfif>
  </cfif>
</cfloop>

<h3>Answers updated</h3>
```

When you review the code in the ColdFusion templates and ColdFusion component, compare them with the equivalent code using traditional methods. Traditionally a form template would include a query to retrieve the data and populate the form from the query results. The action template reads the form data and creates queries to update the database. This traditional development style intertwines the database access and form display code which hampers maintenance. With the survey questionnaire example all code regarding the database interaction is entirely encapsulated within the component. The form templates concentrate on form display and leave all database interaction to the component. The result is a clear separation between business logic and display code. This simplifies development and maintenance.

Save this last file as action.cfm and test it by starting with the surven.cfm form, answering the questions, and clicking submit.

Using a Component from Flash MX

To understand upon why this separation is beneficial, take your example to the next step. The HTML form is functional, but you want the application to be more appealing. To accomplish this, you move the client code to Flash MX. From within Flash you build a form and then call your component through Flash Remoting.

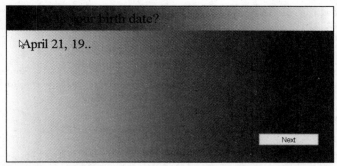

Flash MX application that provides the question-and-answer form for your component

To begin working with the Flash MX example, download and install the Flash Remoting components from Macromedia's Web site, as explained earlier in this chapter. Then create a new movie with two dynamic text fields named question_txt and answer_txt and a push-button named next_pbtn. The push-button should be labeled Next and should have a click handler of nextQuestion. With this layout complete, add the following ActionScript to the first frame:

```
#include "NetServices.as"

if (inited==null) {
  inited=true;

NetServices.setDefaultGatewayURL("http://127.0.0.1/flashservices/gateway");
  var gate = NetServices.createGatewayConnection();
  var qaCFC =
gate.getService("StudioMXBible.Components.questionAnswer",this);
  qaCFC.getQuestionIdList();
}
```

This code sets up a connection to the Flash gateway on the local host. Then it retrieves the `questionAnswer` component. The fully qualified component name is a modified version of the component's path. In this case, the component is stored as `/StudioMXBible/Components/questionAnswer.cfc`. Change the path to the component to reference the component you createed earlier in this tutorial, relative to the wwwroot and using dots instead of slashes.

After you have a connection to your component, you can call the `getQuestionIdList` method to retrieve a list of question IDs. Notice that even though the function returns a value, you do not set variable equal to the returned value, because all calls to CFCs are asynchronous. Flash initiates the call and immediately returns execution to your Flash application. When the CFC is done processing and returns the value, it calls a function within your Flash application that has a name identical to the component method with the suffix `_Result`.

```
var idArray=new Array();
var questCounter=-1;

function getQuestionIdList_Result(idList) {
  idArray=idList.split(",");
  nextQuestion();
}
```

As you can see the value returned from the component method is passed to the `Result` function as an argument. Because it is a list, use the String object's `split()` method to create an array for easier manipulation:

```
function nextQuestion() {

  if (questCounter>-1) {
    qaCFC.setAnswerText(idArray[questCounter],answer_txt.text);
  }

  questCounter++;
  if (questCounter < idArray.length) {
    qaCFC.getQuestionText(idArray[questCounter]);
    question_txt.text="Retrieving next question..."
    answer_txt.text="";
  } else {
    question_txt.text="The survey is complete. Thank you.";
    answer_txt.text="";
    next_pbtn.setLabel("Close");
  }
}

function getQuestionText_Result(questionText) {
  question_txt.text=questionText;
  answer_txt.text='';
}
```

Because you've initialized the question counter to negative one, you use that to determine whether you have an answer to save. If you do, call the component function to save the current answer. Then increment the counter. If there are still questions remaining, call the component to retrieve the next question. Then update the application user interface to inform the user that you're retrieving the next question. If you're already on the last question, tell the user that the questionnaire is complete.

The listing also includes another result function for retrieving question text. Upon receipt you update the two text fields. Notice, however, that there is no result function for the `setAnswerText` function, because this function does not return a value.

That small bit of ActionScript is all that is required to create a database-driven Flash application. Compare this to using `LoadVariables` and XML in previous versions of Flash and you'll see that using CFCs is not only simpler but provides for code that is easier to understand and maintain.

Components can and should revolutionize the way you program in ColdFusion. They add structure and facilitate the encapsulation of data and business logic. Using components leads you to developing applications in a multitiered approach, which improves maintainability and flexibility. While there may be a small adjustment in programming style to use components, you will find the change beneficial.

ColdFusion MX XML Support, *by Samuel Neff*

Extensible Markup Language (XML) is a structured data format ideal for serialization and data exchange. Converting data to an XML format encapsulates the data itself and descriptors about the data, referred to as meta-data. This encapsulation greatly simplifies automated communications and collaboration.

ColdFusion developers have long had the ability to convert any data to XML through Web Distributed Data Exchange (WDDX), an XML grammar developed by Allaire for this specific purpose. With ColdFusion MX, developers now have the ability to work with any XML data using native ColdFusion tags and functions.

Creating an XML Document Object

ColdFusion MX provides three mechanisms for creating an XML document object including one new tag and two new functions. The `cfxml` tag enables you to embed XML text within your ColdFusion template and create an XML document object from that text, as in the following code.

```
<cfxml variable="MyXML" caseSensitive="">
  <classroom roomNumber="210">
    <teacher>
      <firstName>John</firstName>
      <lastName>Smith</lastName>
    </teacher>
    <students>
      <student>
        <firstName>Jim</firstName>
        <lastName>Johnson</lastName>
      </student>
      <student>
```

```
        <firstName>Jane</firstName>
        <lastName>Davis</lastName>
      </student>
    </students>
  </classroom>
</cfxml>
```

As you can see you wrap the XML content inside the `cfxml` tag, which takes two attributes. `variable` is required and provides a name for the new XML document object. `caseSensitive` is optional and specifies whether ColdFusion should enforce the case of the elements and attributes during lookups. Even with `caseSensitive` set to no, the default, ColdFusion preserves the case of XML elements and attributes, and leaving it at no enables you to use the simpler structure dot notation, discussed later in this tutorial.

To examine how ColdFusion MX stores an XML document object internally, the `cfdump` tag introduced in ColdFusion 5:

```
<cfdump var="#MyXML#" label="MyXML">
```

XML Document Object Explained

At the very top, `MyXML` is an XML document object (see the following figure) which contains one immediate child, `classroom`, also referred to as the root element. `classroom` is an XML element node that is treated internally much like a structure. The `XmlText` key provides the text contained within the element but not in any child elements, which in this case is none. The `XmlAttributes` key provides a substructure with key-value pairs associated with each attribute. In this case it contains the `roomNumber` attribute and the value `210`.

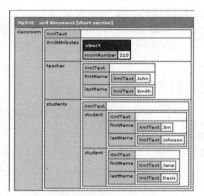

ColdFusion MX's internal
representation of your XML
document object

In addition to these two built in keys, classroom also has two child elements, `teacher` and `students`, as structure keys. Each of these is also an XML element node with keys for `XmlText` and the child elements. This implementation of using structure type objects internally makes using XML within ColdFusion much simpler when compared to DOM-compliant object models. For example, if you want the classroom teacher's first name, you simply reference it as follows.

```
<cfoutput>#MyXML.classroom.teacher.firstName.XmlText#</cfoutput>
```

The first variation arises when you look at the `students` element and its child elements, `student`. Because there are two student elements within `students`, `student` is stored as an array. To reference any of the student values, use array notation after the student element reference. For example, if you want the first student's first name, reference it as follows.

```
<cfoutput>
#MyXML.classroom.students.student[1].firstName.XmlText#
</cfoutput>
```

Modifying an XML Document Object

This structure and array based implementation also means you can use all of ColdFusion MX's structure and array functions to modify an XML document object. You combine these functions with the new `XmlElemNew` function to add new students to your classroom.

To add another student, need to create a new student element and then add the student as a child of the students element. However, you can't directly add the student to the student array; you have to use the special XML element key `XmlChildren`, which lists all child elements of a parent element:

```
<cfscript>
  newStudent=XmlElemNew(MyXML,"student");
  ArrayAppend(MyXML.classroom.students.XmlChildren, newStudent);
</cfscript>
```

With the new student added, you can specify the student's information via the `firstName` and `lastName` elements using the same functions:

```
<cfscript>
  firstName=XmlElemNew(MyXML,"firstName");
  firstName.XmlText="Jill";

  lastName=XmlElemNew(MyXML,"lastName");
  lastName.XmlText="Jones";


ArrayAppend(MyXML.classroom.students.student[3].XmlChildren,firstName);

ArrayAppend(MyXML.classroom.students.student[3].XmlChildren,lastName);
</cfscript>
```

Searching an XML Document Object

ColdFusion MX also supports complex searches on an XML document object using the W3C standard language called XPath. XPath is used to specify a set of XML nodes based on certain criteria. To fully understand the power of XPath, you enlarge the classroom example to include a small school.

```
<cfxml variable="MyXML">
  <school>
    <classroom roomNumber="210">
      <teacher>
        <firstName>John</firstName>
        <lastName>Smith</lastName>
      </teacher>
      <students>
        <student>
          <firstName>Jim</firstName>
          <lastName>Johnson</lastName>
        </student>
        <student>
          <firstName>Jane</firstName>
          <lastName>Davis</lastName>
        </student>
      </students>
    </classroom>
    <classroom roomNumber="305">
      <teacher>
        <firstName>Julie</firstName>
        <lastName>Robbins</lastName>
      </teacher>
      <students>
        <student>
          <firstName>Jodi</firstName>
          <lastName>Katz</lastName>
        </student>
        <student>
          <firstName>Kelly</firstName>
          <lastName>Davis</lastName>
        </student>
      </students>
    </classroom>
  </school>
</cfxml>
```

An XPath expression is a path structure to a specified XML element node. You start all your XPath examples with the document root, '/', and drill down from there. The following example returns all students in the school:

```
<cfset studentNodes=XmlSearch(MyXML,
"/school/classroom/students/student")>

<cfdump var="#studentNodes#"
label="/school/classroom/students/student">
```

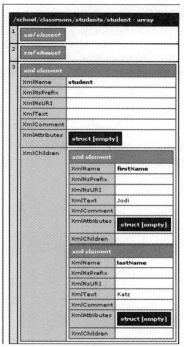

The elements returned by a call
to XmlSearch()

By using XPath you listed all students in the school, regardless of which classroom they are in. XPath also provides for filtering the returned list using square brackets. For example, the following XPath expression returns all students with the last name Davis:

```
<cfset studentNodes=XmlSearch(MyXML,
"/school/classroom/students/student[lastName='Davis']")>
```

The filtering expression can even use any valid XPath selector. For a more complicated example, use the following XPath expression to return all students whose teacher's last name is Smith.

```
<cfset studentNodes=XmlSearch(MyXml,
"/school/classroom/students/student[../../teacher/lastName='Smith']")>
```

As you can see, XmlSearch is a powerful tool for finding and listing XML elements within a ColdFusion MX XML document object. Another equally powerful function new to ColdFusion MX is XmlTransform, which performs XSLT transformations on an XML document object.

Transforming an XML Document Object

XSLT is a stylesheet language for transforming one XML document into a different XML document. This is commonly used when sharing data between programs that use a different XML grammar or for creating a standard compliant document out of custom XML. Although XSLT is far beyond the scope of this book or tutorial, you review a couple of simple examples.

For your first XSLT demonstration, create a new ColdFusion template that includes the code from Listing 1, the simple classroom example. Then add the following code.

```
<cfsavecontent variable="classroomToSchoolXSLT">
  <xsl:stylesheet
    version="1.0"
    xmlns:xsl="http://www.w3.org/1999/XSL/Transform">

    <xsl:output
       method="xml"
       indent="yes"/>

    <xsl:template match="/">

      <school>
        <xsl:apply-templates/>
      </school>
    </xsl:template>

    <xsl:template match="node()|@*">
      <xsl:copy>
        <xsl:apply-templates select="node()|@*"/>
      </xsl:copy>
    </xsl:template>

  </xsl:stylesheet>
</cfsavecontent>


<cfset school=XmlTransform(MyXML, classroomToSchoolXSLT)>
```

First notice that you used the `cfsavecontent` tag instead of the `cfxml` tag. ColdFusion MX always uses a plain string for the XSLT and not an XML document object. After you have your XSLT stored as a string in a variable, use the `XmlTransform` function to create a new XML document object by applying the XSLT transformation to the classroom example.

Let's examine the components of your XSLT. It starts with a stylesheet element within the XSLT 1.0 namespace, `http://www.w3.org/1999/XSL/Transform` and specifies that this is a version 1.0 stylesheet. Then you specify what type of output you want to return from the transformation with the `output` element. Options are xml, html, or text. `output` also has an `indent` attribute, which enables creation of pretty printed XML documents.

Next you have two template elements, which provide a match pattern and replacement content. The `match` attribute is an XPath expression that returns a set of nodes in the source document. ColdFusion MX replaces each of the nodes returned by the expression with the content within the template element.

The first match pattern returns the root of the document. This is not the root element, but the root of the document itself. The content of this match indiciates that you want to enclose the entire document inside a `school` element. Then you use the `apply-templates` element to continue matching source elements against patterns in the XSLT.

The second match pattern is actually two patterns. The pike character (`|`) is a union operator that matches both sets of expressions. The `node` function returns any node other than the document node and attributes. The `@*` expression matches all attributes. For each node you find, you use the `copy` element to copy the source node forward.

Because all this transformation does is wrap the source inside a `school` element, it is not a useful example but is simply a demonstration of the technology. For a more practical example, use XSLT to create an XHTML document out of your school example, as follows:

```
<cfsavecontent variable="schoolToXHTML">
  <xsl:stylesheet
    version="1.0"
    xmlns:xsl="http://www.w3.org/1999/XSL/Transform">

    <xsl:output method="html"/>

    <xsl:template match="school">

      <html xmlns="http://www.w3.org/1999/xhtml">
        <head>
          <title>Our School</title>
        </head>

        <body>
          <xsl:apply-templates/>
        </body>
      </html>

    </xsl:template>

    <xsl:template match="classroom">
      <table
        border="1"
        bgcolor="blue"
        bordercolor="blue"
        cellpadding="3"
        cellspacing="2">

        <tr>
          <td colspan="2" style="color:white;font-weight:bold">
            Classroom
            <xsl:value-of select="@roomNumber" />
          </td>
        </tr>
        <xsl:apply-templates/>
      </table>
      <br/>
```

```
    </xsl:template>

    <xsl:template match="teacher">
      <tr>
        <td bgcolor="lightblue">Teacher</td>
        <td bgcolor="white">
          <xsl:value-of select="firstName"/>
          <xsl:text> </xsl:text>
          <xsl:value-of select="lastName"/>
        </td>
      </tr>
    </xsl:template>

    <xsl:template match="students">
      <tr>
        <td valign="top" bgcolor="lightblue">Students</td>
        <td bgcolor="white">
          <xsl:apply-templates/>
        </td>
      </tr>
    </xsl:template>

    <xsl:template match="student">
      <xsl:value-of select="firstName"/>
      <xsl:text> </xsl:text>
      <xsl:value-of select="lastName"/>
      <br/>
    </xsl:template>

  </xsl:stylesheet>
</cfsavecontent>

<cfset xhtml=XmlTransform(MyXML,schoolToXHTML)>

<cfoutput>#xhtml#</cfoutput>
```

This longer example matches each of the XML elements in the source document and replaces them with snippets of XHTML resulting in a complete XHTML document to display each classroom within a separate table.

Classroom 210

Teacher	John Smith
Students	Jim Johnson Jane Davis

Classroom 305

Teacher	Julie Robbins
Students	Jodi Katz Kelly Davis

An XHTML representation of
our school data after applying
an XSLT transformation

As you can see, ColdFusion MX has gone far beyond basic support of XML. It includes a simple- to-use object model for creating, modifying, and reading XML document objects as well as functions for advanced searches and transformations of XML. These tools will greatly simplifyy the implementation of XML technologies in your applications and automated communications.

Summary

In this chapter you learned about Flash Remoting, and how by including the NetServices as a class in your Flash movie's ActionScript, you transfer variable data between Flash movies and ColdFusion templates. You learned about structures and arrays, two complex variable types that are used by Flash Remoting to package data. To illustrate these concepts, you constructed a scalable ecard application that benefits from the sophistication of a Flash MX interface, but which relies on ColdFusion MX to handle the more programming-oriented tasks, such as retrieving information from a database and automatically sending e-mail.

✦   ✦   ✦

What's on the CD-ROM

This appendix provides you with information on the contents of the CD that accompanies this book. For the latest and greatest information, refer to the ReadMe file located at the root of the CD. Here is what you will find:

✦ System requirements

✦ Using the CD with Windows and Macintosh

✦ CD-ROM contents

✦ Troubleshooting

System Requirements for the CD

Make sure that your computer meets the minimum system requirements listed in this section. If your computer doesn't match up to most of these requirements, you may have a problem using the contents of the CD.

For Windows 9x, Windows 2000, Windows NT4 (with SP 4 or later), Windows Me, or Windows XP:

✦ PC with a Pentium processor running at 120 Mhz or faster

✦ At least 32 MB of total RAM installed on your computer; for best performance, we recommend at least 64 MB

✦ Ethernet network interface card (NIC) or modem with a speed of at least 28,800 bps

✦ A CD-ROM drive

For Macintosh:

✦ Mac OS computer with a 68040 or faster processor running OS 7.6 or later

✦ At least 32 MB of total RAM installed on your computer; for best performance, we recommend at least 64 MB

Using the CD with Windows

To install the items from the CD to your hard drive, follow these steps:

1. Insert the CD into your computer's CD-ROM drive.

2. A window opens with the following options:

   - **Install** — Gives you the option to install the supplied software and/or the author-created samples on the CD-ROM

   - **Explore** — Enables you to view the contents of the CD-ROM in its directory structure

   - **Links** — Opens a hyperlinked page of Web sites

   - **Exit** — Closes the Autorun window

Note Copy the exercise files and the `habitat_alert` files and folders to your hard drive. The files will be locked, so you'll need to Shift+select them all. Right-click and choose Properties. Remove the check from Read-Only (you won't have to do this if you used the install button). You can also unlock files from within Dreamweaver in the Site panel.

If you do not have autorun enabled or if the Autorun window does not appear, follow these steps to access the CD:

1. Click Start ⇨ Run.

2. In the dialog box that opens, type **d:\setup.exe**, where *d* is the letter of your CD-ROM drive. This opens the Autorun window.

3. Choose the Install, Explore, Links, or Exit option from the menu. (See Step 2 in the preceding list for a description of these options.)

Using the CD with the Mac OS

To install the items from the CD to your hard drive, follow these steps:

1. Insert the CD into your CD-ROM drive.

2. Double-click the icon for the CD after it appears on the desktop.

3. Most programs come with installers; for those, open the program's folder on the CD and double-click the Install or Installer icon. (To install some programs, drag the program's folder from the CD window and drop it on your hard drive icon.)

CD-ROM Contents

The following sections provide a summary of the software and other materials you'll find on the CD.

Author-created materials

All author-created material from the book, including code listings, and exercise files, are on the CD in folder names that match the corresponding chapter number. The Bonus Tutorial folder has additional Fireworks and Flash projects files to enhance your learning. The Movies folder has movies for FreeHand and Fireworks to help you master some of the more complex tasks.

Applications

The following applications are on the CD:

Acrobat Reader 5.0

A Freeware version of the Acrobat reader is included to view PDF files with.

Eye Candy 4000, from Alien Skin Software

A demo version of Eye Candy 4000 ROM for PC and Mac platforms is in the Alien Skin folder on the CD-ROM. In this demo version of Eye Candy, all of the filters are fully functional for 30 days from installation. After 30 days, Eye Candy previews only the filters' effects.

Eye Candy 4000 is a collection of 23 time-saving filters. The filters combine effects such as shadows, bevels, and glows with stunning effects such as chrome, fire, smoke, and wood.

For more information, go to www.alienskin.com/.

Flix (Pro and Lite) 2.5, from Wildform inc.

A demo version of Flix 2.5 for PC and Mac platforms is in the Wildform folder on the CD-ROM. These are fully functioning demos of Wildform Flix. However, the output video contains a "Wildform" watermark, and the audio output contains a "Flix demo" audio mark.

Pro: Flash video encoding and design tool helps you easily create professional caliber video. Edit, crop, encode, and post your video in your own custom branded player in minutes.

Lite: Put your video on the Web in three clicks with Flix Lite! Flix Lite encodes virtually every type of video, audio, and image file into Flash.net.

For more information, go to www.wildform.com.

Image Doctor, by Alien Skin Software

A demo version of Image Doctor for PC and Mac platforms is in the Alien Skin folder on the CD-ROM. In this demo version of Image Doctor, all the filters will be fully functional for 30 days from installation. After 30 days, Image Doctor previews only filters' effects.

Image Doctor has image-correction filters for performing tasks such as removing blemishes, repairing over-compressed JPEGs, and replacing unwanted details and objects. It's compatible with Photoshop, Fireworks, and paint Shop Pro as well as other editors.

For more information, go to www.alienskin.com/.

Splat! 1.0, by Alien Skin Software

A demo version of Splat! 1.0 for PC and Mac platforms is in the Alien Skin folder on the CD-ROM. In this demo version of Image Doctor, all the filters will be fully functional for 30 days from installation.

Splat! contains a set of filters that combines frames, textures, edges, borders, mosaics, and more.

For more information, go to www.alienskin.com/.

Toon Boom Studio, by Toon Boom Technologies Inc.

An evaluation of Toon Boon Studio in PC and Mac platforms is in the Toon Boom folder included on the CD-ROM.

Toon Boom Studio revolutionizes animation production for the Web. Just a few of the things you can do are: automatically map mouth drawings to the lip chart, use sound scrubbing to synchronize sound to the image precisely, and lay out elements visually in the 3-D scene space. Toon Boom Studio automatically interpolates size changes for the content of each layer.

Go to www.toonbommstudio.com/main to learn more about this product.

TopStyle Pro 3.0, by Bradbury Software LLC

A trial version of TopStyle Pro 3.0 for Windows is in the TopStyle folder included on the CD-ROM.

TopStyle is a stand-alone CSS editor or works in conjunction with editors such as Dreamweaver. You can edit your HTML, XHTML, and CSS, check your CSS syntax against multiple browsers, upgrade outdated HTML, including font tags to CSS, convert HTML to XHTML with TopStyle's HTML integration. Plus, you can find CSS class usage throughout your site. You can also see a side-by-side preview using Interenet Explorer and Netscape Gecko.

For more details and instructions on how to use this software with Dreamweaver MX, go to www.bradburysoftware.com.

Shareware programs are fully functional, trial versions of copyrighted programs. If you like particular programs, register with their authors for a nominal fee, and receive licenses, enhanced versions, and technical support. *Freeware programs* are copyrighted games, applications, and utilities that are free for personal use. Unlike shareware, these programs do not require a fee or provide technical support. *GNU software* is governed by its own license, which is included inside the folder of the GNU product. See the GNU license for more details.

Trial, demo, or evaluation versions are usually limited either by time or functionality (such as being unable to save projects). Some trial versions are sensitive to system date changes. If you alter your computer's date, the programs will time out and no longer be functional.

Troubleshooting

If you have difficulty installing or using any of the materials on the companion CD, try the following solutions:

✦ **Turn off any antivirus software that you may have running** — Installers sometimes mimic virus activity and can make your computer incorrectly believe that it is being infected by a virus. (Be sure to turn the antivirus software back on later.)

✦ **Close all running programs** — The more programs you're running, the less memory is available to other programs. Installers also typically update files and programs; if you keep other programs running, installation may not work properly.

✦ **Reference the ReadMe** — Refer to the ReadMe file located at the root of the CD-ROM for the latest product information at the time of publication.

If you still have trouble with the CD, call the Wiley Customer Care phone number: (800) 762-2974. Outside the United States, call 1 (317) 572-3994. You can also contact Wiley Customer Service by e-mail at techsupdum@wiley.com. Wiley will provide technical support only for installation and other general quality-control items; for technical support on the applications themselves, consult the program's vendor or author.

✦   ✦   ✦

About the Guest Experts

Doug Sahlin is an author, graphic designer, and Web-site designer living in Central Florida. He is the author of ten books on graphic design, including: *How To Do Everything with Adobe 5.0, Flash MX ActionScript for Designers, Flash MX ActionScript for Dummies,* and *Fireworks MX Complete Reference*. Doug created an online Flash 4 course for DigitalThink. His articles and product reviews have appeared in national publications, such as 3D, Computer Graphics World, Video Systems, and Corel Magazine. His tutorials have been featured at numerous Web sites devoted to graphic design.

Japi Honoo resides in Venice, Italy, and designs Web sites and organizes the Italian Fireworks Web site www.escogitando.it. Before taking the plunge into Web design, Japi worked as a bookkeeper. A job in a software house, however, allowed Japi to free her creativity and turn her energies toward digital art. She has since dedicated her life to encouraging the appreciation of Fireworks (that's a slight exaggeration — but not much!). Her diversions include intense music, oriental culture, films, and a love of emoticons.

Kim Cavanaugh is the author of *Fireworks MX: A Beginner's Guide* and *Dreamweaver 4/Fireworks 4 Studio: A Beginner's Guide*. Kim began his adventures in the world of Web and graphic design in 1997, when he began developing a curriculum for a course in Web design for students at Congress Middle School of Math, Science, and Technology in Boynton Beach, Florida, where he teaches Dreamweaver, Fireworks, Flash, and Freehand and is the school technology coordinator. Kim is currently a Team Macromedia volunteer for Fireworks. Additional tutorials for Dreamweaver and Fireworks can be found at Kim's site: www.dw-fw-beginners.com.

Steven Grosvenor is cofounder of www.phireworx.com, a Fireworks resource site, contributing author of *Fireworks MX Magic, Special Edition Using Fireworks MX*, and *Fireworks MX Fundamentals*. Grosvenor is senior systems architect for a managed Internet security company in the United Kingdom. His background is in cross-platform systems integration, interface design, and interaction and architecture design. Demand from users for a customized, interactive experience led him to develop and create many timesaving and creative commands and behaviors for Dreamweaver and Fireworks, vastly reducing deployment time for corporate sites and increasing their portability and scalability. His drive to increase team productivity led him to develop extensibility add-ons for other products in the Macromedia Web suite, including Dreamweaver MX, Fireworks MX, and Flash MX. One of the new breeds of commands for Fireworks MX, "Twist and Fade 3.0," created by Grosvenor, had the accolade of shipping with Fireworks MX. His other publications include several Fireworks MX and Dreamweaver MX tutorials, which you can find at www.macromedia.com.

David C. Nicholls is a Web developer, physicist, writer, photographer, and a recognized authority on graphics-compression software, antique golf clubs, and regional fern species. He is co-author of the book *Playing with Fire — Tapping the Power of Macromedia Firework 4* with Linda Rathgeber. He has contributed articles to numerous publications, including PC magazines, hi-fi magazines and amateur radio journals, computer instruction manuals, book reviews in newspaper literary columns, scientific journals, and government reports. David lives in Canberra, Australia with his wife, Trish, and assorted computers named Grunter, Xerxes, Darius, Perseus, and Wally. He can be reached at www.dcnicholls.com and www.home.aone.net.au/byzantium/.

Charles E Brown transferred his creative skills from music (he has a doctorate in music and studied with Igor Stravinsky) to computers in 1981. Charles does Web designs for major corporations, is a busy trainer conducting nearly 100 workshops per year, and is a frequent speaker at conferences.

Brad Halstead (www.prettylady2.net) is a computer software engineering technologist by training, but deviated from that dream to join the Canadian military as an air weapons systems technician. In that role, he learned all about various computerized aircraft weapons systems as well as loading the munitions. Brad has dabbled in the Web in various capacities since 1989 and left the military to become a full-time computer technician. He tries to play an active roll in the support forums for Dreamweaver and Project Seven as time permits him to. He is HTML 4.01 certified and has contributed to *Dreamweaver MX Magic* and *Inside Dreamweaver MX*, in addition to being a technical editor for both publications. Recently, Brad and Murray Summers have written *Dreamweaver MX Templates*. He lives in London, Ontario, with his cherished partner Brenda and their 8-year-old daughter Megan, 13-year-old daughter Amanda, 12-year-old son Aaron, 2 Yorkshire Terriers, and a cat.

Murray Summers is a biochemist by training, but has spent the last 20 years working in the computer industry. In 1998, Murray started his own Web site production company, Great Web Sights (www.great-web-sites.com). As a Team Macromedia Volunteer, he also participates in the sponsored newsgroups for Dreamweaver and other Macromedia products. He lives in rural Philadelphia with Suzanne, his lovely wife, their teenage daughter Carly, a Golden Retriever, an Eskipoo, and some goldfish. Murray is a Macromedia certified Web site developer and Dreamweaver developer and has contributed chapters to *Dreamweaver 4 Magic* by Al Sparber and *Dreamweaver 4: The Missing Manual*, by David Sawyer McFarland, in addition to serving as technical editor on the latter publication. He has managed to embarrass himself several times as an invited speaker at TODCON and will most likely do so again at TODCON II.

Samuel Neff is a senior software engineer with B-Line Express in the Washington, D.C. metro area. Sam is Advanced ColdFusion 5.0 Certified and a Team Macromedia volunteer for ColdFusion. He contributes to professional journals on programming topics, including ColdFusion and Visual Basic and speaks at ColdFusion user group meetings. He can be contacted at sam@blinex.com.

Mary Rich (technical editor). Once upon a time, when dinosaurs still roamed the earth, Mary Rich was working claims for an insurance agency. One day, she saw an ad in the newspaper for programmer trainees, so she made the switch, found out what programmers did, and fell in love. The affair continued through mainframes and mid-range systems and peaked when the first IBM-PCs arrived: a real computer, with 64K memory, two 320K floppy disk drives, a CPM emulation card, and a monitor — all of this on a desk at home! More toys followed, and she finally got involved with various graphics programs, then Web sites. A believer in Macromedia products, she found Dreamweaver and Fireworks to be an answer to a prayer for productivity. Mary provides consulting and training in many different areas to organizations in the Los Angeles, CA, and, via the Internet, to the world. She has a B.A. from Brown University and is pursuing a certificate in Computer Graphics from University of California, Los Angeles. Mary's cat, Friday, allows her to live with him in El Segundo, CA.

CD Photo Credits

These individuals and companies donated images for use in a couple of the Bonus Tutorials on the CD.

Todd McPhetridge (www.CobaltGraphics.com). Todd has been a photographer for more than 11 years and has more than 5 years' experience in search engine placement, Web design, and the graphic arts. Todd is a consultant for major corporations as well as small, family-owned businesses. Todd's photographs and designs have appeared in numerous publications, including *Integrating Flash, Fireworks & FreeHand f/x & Design*, authored by Joyce J. Evans and the periodicals "Manufacturing Engineering," "Purchasing Today," "Design News," "Desktop Engineering," and "MacWorld." You can reach him by phone at 770-684-2688 or send e-mail to todd@cobaltgraphics.com.

Habitat Alert, **Trevor Smith**, **Calvin Woods** (Co-Directors, Habitat Alert) and **Rod Watkins** donated the photographs used in the Web site.

Eyeland Studio. Photoshop Foundry is a membership area that contains a large variety of Web interfaces and buttons that you are free to customize for use in your own Web projects. These Web interfaces are stylized navigation systems for your Web site, with buttons, graphical widgets, space for your logo, an area reserved for a banner ad, etc.

Olaf Starorypinski was born in London, England, in 1964, the son of Polish immigrants. Olaf has always been fascinated with light, and he developed an interest in photography and lighting during his high school years. He has been involved in both photography and lighting design for nearly 20 years, including design companies both in the UK and the USA. Olaf moved to the Lehigh Valley, Pennsylvania, in 1990.

Olaf's experience and knowledge of light is the primary influence in his photographic work. Using light to sculpt subjects, he creates images from a unique perspective. Critics have described his photographs as "dynamic and sculptural," "works of subtlety and power," and "visual intrigue."

Olaf resides in Emmaus, Pennsylvania, with his wife and daughter.

Sounds and Applet

Jason Leroy contributed the audio track "Acoustic Alchemy" at SonicMint.com.

Bryan Harianto contributed the StringWalk applet www.geocities.com/bharianto/StringWalk/StringWalk.html.

Yvonne Rockwell began playing the piano at age eight. She has been writing and recording music for several years; she has composed background music for self-help audio programs and the musical score for a children's book that contains a spoken version of the story on a CD-ROM. It was an honor for Yvonne to contribute to *Macromedia Studio MX Bible* in the production of music for the Habitat Alert Web site. You can hear more of her music at www.nidus-corp.com/music.html.

◆   ◆   ◆

Installing Macromedia Studio MX

The Macromedia Studio MX disc contains an integrated suite of development tools for building professional Web sites and Rich Internet applications. The suite also supports emerging standards and web technologies. The applications included in the Macromedia Studio MX suite include FreeHand 10 (or MX), Fireworks MX, Flash MX, Dreamweaver MX, and, optionally, ColdFusion MX Developer Edition. All the applications have a common interface, cutting the learning curve considerably.

System Requirements

Before installing the Macromedia Studio MX, ensure that you have all the system requirements as listed in Table C-1.

Table C-1: The Windows and Macintosh System Requirements

Windows	Macintosh
300 MHz Intel® Pentium® II processor or better	Power Mac G3 processor or better
Windows 98 SE, Windows Me, Windows NT 4 (Service Pack 6), Windows 2000, or Windows XP	Mac OS 9.1 and higher, or OSX 10.1 and higher
96 MB of free available system RAM to open one application (128 MB recommended)	96 MB of free available system RAM to open one application (128 MB recommended)
Additional RAM required to open multiple applications simultaneously	Additional RAM required to open multiple applications simultaneously

Continued

Table C-1 *(continued)*

Windows	*Macintosh*
1024 × 768, 16-bit color monitor resolution (thousands of colors) or better	1024 × 768, 16-bit color monitor resolution (thousands of colors) or better
510 MB of available hard-disk space to install all applications	510 MB of available hard-disk space to install all applications
Adobe Type Manager Version 4 or later for use with Type 1 fonts	Adobe Type Manager Version 4 or later for use with Type 1 fonts (OS 9.x)
CD-ROM drive	CD-ROM drive
For Adobe PostScript printing: PostScript Level 2 or PostScript 3	For Adobe PostScript printing: PostScript Level 2 or PostScript 3
Netscape Navigator 4.0 or Internet Explorer 4.0 or greater	Netscape Navigator 4.0 or Internet Explorer 4.0 or greater
	CarbonLib version 1.3 or later required on Mac OS 9
	Dreamweaver MX requires Mac OS Runtime for Java (MRJ) 2.2 or above on Mac OS 9

Installing Studio MX

The installation process is quite simple. If you don't yet own Macromedia Studio MX, you may download trial versions from www.macromedia.com/downloads/. The following instructions are for the Macromedia Studio MX application disc. The following screenshots are for a Windows XP installation. To install, follow these steps:

1. Insert the Macromedia Studio MX disc into your CD-ROM. The install interface opens automatically, as shown in Figure C-1.

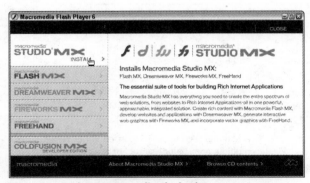

Figure C-1: The Macromedia Flash Player 6 opens to display the install screen.

2. Click Macromedia Studio MX Install.

3. The InstallShield Wizard opens. Click Next.

4. Click Yes to accept the License Agreement after you've read it.

5. Fill in your name, organization (optional), and serial number found on the CD wrapper.

6. You'll see a green check mark if you've entered the numbers properly. Click Next.

7. Click the Browse button if you want to select a new location for the install, and click Next.

8. Sit back while your applications install. Fireworks installs first, then FreeHand, Dreamweaver, and finally Flash.

9. The Flash Player is checked by default; click Next to install the Macromedia Flash Player for Internet Explorer (Figure C-2).

10. Click Finish (Figure C-3) when you see the Setup has finished installing window.

11. The Readme file automatically opens.

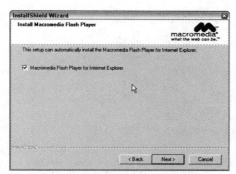

Figure C-2: The dialog box to install the Flash Player

Figure C-3: The Finish dialog box

Installing ColdFusion MX

ColdFusion MX Developers Edition does not automatically install with the rest of the studio. You'll need Windows to install on. To install, follow these steps:

1. If the Macromedia Studio MX CD is not in your CD drive then insert it now. Click the Macromedia ColdFusion MX Developer Edition button in the install window.

2. Click Next to install ColdFusion.

3. Click I accept the terms in the license agreement after you've read it; then click the Next button. (Figure C-4)

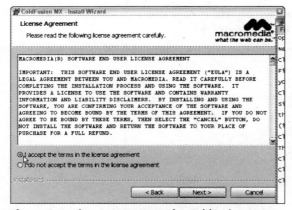

Figure C-4: License agreement for ColdFusion MX

4. Fill in the customer information (Figure C-5). If you've purchased the full version of ColdFusion, enter the serial number. If not, leave it blank, and it will operate as the free developer edition.

5. Click Next.

6. In the Web Server dialog box, click Next.

7. In the Custom Setup dialog box, you can choose to customize what is installed on your hard drive (Figure C-7). Click Next when you are done.

8. The Webroot Folder dialog box opens (Figure C-6). Change it if you want and click Next.

9. Enter a password for the ColdFusion MX administrator and for RDS users (Figure C-8), and click Next.

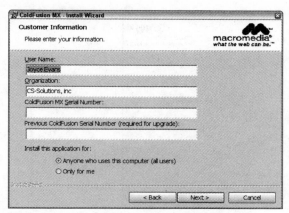

Figure C-5: The Customer Information dialog box

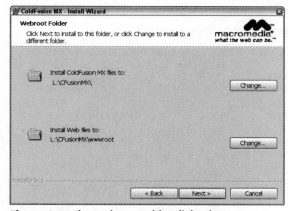

Figure C-6: The Webroot Folder dialog box

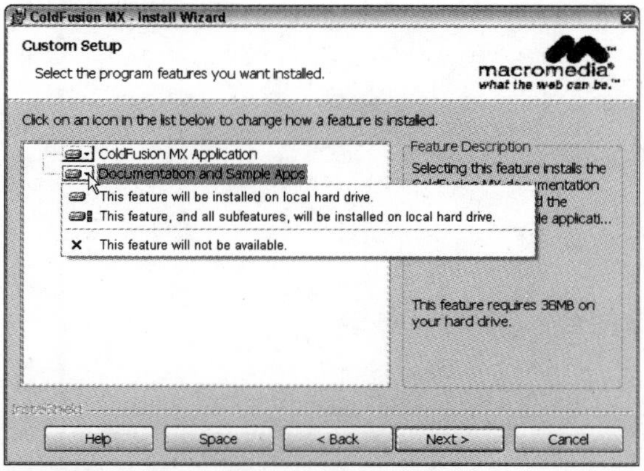

Figure C-7: The Custom Setup dialog box

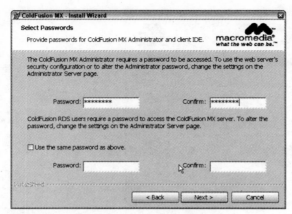

Figure C-8: The Select Passwords dialog box

10. Click the Install button.

11. The Install Wizard Completed dialog box opens; click Finish.

12. Click the red x in the upper-right corner to close the install interface.

✦   ✦   ✦

Index

Continued

Continued

continued

Continued

Continued

Continued

Continued

Continued

Continued

Continued

Continued

Continued

Continued

Continued

Wiley Publishing, Inc.
End-User License Agreement

READ THIS. You should carefully read these terms and conditions before opening the software packet(s) included with this book "Book". This is a license agreement "Agreement" between you and Wiley Publishing, Inc."WPI". By opening the accompanying software packet(s), you acknowledge that you have read and accept the following terms and conditions. If you do not agree and do not want to be bound by such terms and conditions, promptly return the Book and the unopened software packet(s) to the place you obtained them for a full refund.

1. **License Grant.** WPI grants to you (either an individual or entity) a nonexclusive license to use one copy of the enclosed software program(s) (collectively, the "Software" solely for your own personal or non-commercial purposes on a single computer (whether a standard computer or a workstation component of a multi-user network). The Software is in use on a computer when it is loaded into temporary memory (RAM) or installed into permanent memory (hard disk, CD-ROM, or other storage device). WPI reserves all rights not expressly granted herein.

2. **Ownership.** WPI is the owner of all right, title, and interest, including copyright, in and to the compilation of the Software recorded on the disk(s) or CD-ROM "Software Media". Copyright to the individual programs recorded on the Software Media is owned by the author or other authorized copyright ownerof each program. Ownership of the Software and all proprietary rights relatingthereto remain with WPI and its licensers.

3. **Restrictions On Use and Transfer.** (a) You may only (i) make one copy of the Software for backup or archival purposes, or (ii) transfer the Software to a single hard disk, provided that you keep the original for backup or archival purposes. You may not (i) rent or lease the Software, (ii) copy or reproduce the Software through a LAN or other network system or through any computer subscriber system or bulletin- board system, or (iii) modify, adapt, or create derivative works based on the Software. (b) You may not reverse engineer, decompile, or disassemble the Software. You may transfer the Software and user documentation on a permanent basis, provided that the transferee agrees to accept the terms and conditions of this Agreement and you retain no copies. If the Software is an update or has been updated, any transfer must include the most recent update and all prior versions.

4. **Restrictions on Use of Individual Programs**. You must follow the individual requirements and restrictions detailed for each individual program in the About the CD-ROM appendix of this Book. These limitations are also contained in the individual license agreements recorded on the Software Media. These limitations may include a requirement that after using the program for a specified period of time, the user must pay a registration fee or discontinue use. By opening the Software packet(s), you will be agreeing to abide by the licenses and restrictions for these individual programs that are detailed in the About the CD-ROM appendix and on the Software Media. None of the material on this Software Media or listed in this Book may ever be redistributed, in original or modified form, for commercial purposes.

5. **Limited Warranty.** (a) WPI warrants that the Software and Software Media are free from defects in materials and workmanship under normal use for a period of sixty (60) days from the date of purchase of this Book. If WPI receives notification within the warranty period of defects in materials or workmanship, WPI will replace the defective Software Media. (b) WPI AND THE AUTHOR OF THE BOOK DISCLAIM ALL OTHER WARRANTIES, EXPRESS OR IMPLIED, INCLUDING WITHOUT LIMITATION IMPLIED WARRANTIES OF MERCHANTABILITY AND FITNESS FOR A PARTICULAR PURPOSE, WITH RESPECT TO THE SOFTWARE, THE PROGRAMS, THE SOURCE CODE CONTAINED THEREIN, AND/OR THE TECHNIQUES DESCRIBED IN THIS BOOK. WPI DOES NOT WARRANT THAT THE FUNCTIONS CONTAINED IN THE SOFTWARE WILL MEET YOUR REQUIREMENTS OR THAT THE OPERATION OF THE SOFTWARE WILL BE ERROR FREE. (c) This limited warranty gives you specific legal rights, andyou may have other rights that vary from jurisdiction to jurisdiction.

6. **Remedies.** (a) WPI's entire liability and your exclusive remedy for defects in materials and workmanship shall be limited to replacement of the Software Media, which may be returned to WPI with a copy of your receipt at the following address: Software Media Fulfillment Department, Attn.: Macromedia Studio MX Bible, Wiley Publishing, Inc., 10475 Crosspoint Blvd., Indianapolis, IN 46256, or call 1-800-762-2974. Please allow four to six weeks for delivery. This Limited Warranty is void if failure of the Software Media has resulted from accident, abuse, or misapplication. Any replacement Software Media will be warranted for the remainder of the original warranty period or thirty (30) days, whichever is longer. (b) In no event shall WPI or the author be liable for any damages whatsoever (including without limitation damages for loss of business profits, business interruption, loss of business information, or any other pecuniary loss) arising from the use of or inability to use the Book or the Software, even if WPI has been advised of the possibility of such damages. (c) Because some jurisdictions do not allow the exclusion or limitation of liability for consequential or incidental damages, the above limitation or exclusion may not apply to you.

7. **U.S. Government Restricted Rights.** Use, duplication, or disclosure of the Software for or on behalf of the United States of America, its agencies and/or instrumentalities "U.S. Government" is subject to restrictions as stated in paragraph (c)(1)(ii) of the Rights in Technical Data and Computer Software clause of DFARS 252.227-7013, or subparagraphs (c) (1) and (2) of the Commercial Computer Software - Restricted Rights clause at FAR 52.227-19, and in similar clauses in the NASA FAR supplement, as applicable.

8. **General.** This Agreement constitutes the entire understanding of the parties and revokes and supersedes all prior agreements, oral or written, between them and may not be modified or amended except in a writing signed by both parties hereto that specifically refers to this Agreement. This Agreement shall take precedence over any other documents that may be in conflict herewith. If any one or more provisions contained in this Agreement are held by any court or tribunal to be invalid, illegal, or otherwise unenforceable, each and every other provision shall remain in full force and effect.